More Praise

✳ RAILRO

"[A] powerful book, crowded with telling details and shrewd observations about nearly every aspect of the world the railroad bosses made."
—Michael Kazin, *New York Times Book Review*

"Welcome to a scathing and wonderful new book about American business and its crimes more than one hundred years ago. Richard White, one of our country's greatest historians, has written a book that will entertain and outrage readers with scenes of corporate greed and mismanagement and the federal bailouts that enabled them. Think of *Railroaded* as Michael Lewis's *Liar's Poker*, set in a Gilded Age just as fantastically sick as the bond-trading offices of Salomon Brothers in the freshly-deregulated 1980s."
—Buzzy Jackson, *Boston Globe*

"Richard White is a Thorstein Veblen for our times. Dripping with venom, this book is nonetheless a model of the historian's use of primary sources, narrative skill, and insightful reinterpretation of the Gilded Age. It is easily the best business history I have read, and it carries a weight of argument and evidence that cannot be denied."
—Donald Worster, *Slate*

"*Railroaded* will be required reading for anyone interested in the history of American railroading and the astonishingly swift economic development of the American West that the transcontinentals made possible. This is an exciting story and well told."
—John Steele Gordon, *Wall Street Journal*

"A different and provocative view of the role of the transcontinentals in developing the American West. *Railroaded* will no doubt spark lively debate and become required reading for those seeking an insightful and recast history of the transcontinental railroad saga."
—Walter R. Borneman, *San Francisco Chronicle*

"A fresh and welcome agglomeration of wide-ranging historical detail, including eviscerations of some of the key figures—from Jay Gould to Leland Stanford—and an acute analysis that in failure came success and in many ways the map of the nation." —Scott Martelle, *Washington Post*

"White is brilliant in documenting and reconstructing the precise ways in which the Associates and others feasted on the opening the government gave them. [White's] book is imaginative, iconoclastic, immensely informative and mordantly funny. . . . [I]t will—and should—change our views of the role of railroads in transforming America." —Glenn C. Altschuler,
Pittsburgh Post-Gazette

"Richard White's . . . deeply researched, brilliantly rendered, and irreverent new book . . . offers a withering critique of how the transcontinentals were built: of their economic proclivities, their financial mismanagement, their political corruption, and their cost to the United States and its people. . . . The care and the patience with which he has mined the vast record collections, the critical eye and the questions that he has brought into the archives, his refusal to be seduced by the bravado of his main subjects together with the serious attention he accords them, enable White to find and trace the lifeblood of the transcontinentals. . . . White does a remarkably good job of . . . helping us understand company organization (more accurately, disorganization), from the financial and managerial operations to the workplaces. White paints very deft portraits of railroad workers at various levels of skill and influence, and of the tensions that emerged among them as well as between them and their bosses. He reminds us, too, of the breathtaking changes the roads demanded in how Americans conceived of time and space—of what it meant to calculate journeys not in feet and miles, but in hours and minutes or dollars and cents." —Steven Hahn, *New Republic*

"*Railroaded*, Richard White's trenchant history of the political economy of the first Gilded Age, told through a close examination of the transcontinental railroad corporations, could not be more timely. Parts of the book read like a Matt Taibbi exposé of fraudulent high finance and venal politics, but the bulk of it resembles a *Vanity Fair* article that gasps even as it sympathizes with insiders divulging the details of how things went terribly wrong. White chronicles the many instances of greed, hubris, incompetence and, in some cases, outright stupidity of the railroad tycoons that culminated in colossal business failures and bloody social clashes. Though there is no shortage of stealing at the top and suffering at the bottom, the story White tells is not about omnipotent robber barons. Instead of recycling Frank Norris's iconic image of a corporate octopus slowly and purposefully strangling states and even whole regions, White describes 'a group of fat men in an Octopus suit fighting over the controls' of a runaway train. . . . While White tells many horrifying and entertaining stories about corruption and incompetence, his overarching argument is primarily about the fundamental characteristics of capitalism and modernity."   —Robin Einhorn, *The Nation*

"White's portrait of an American government overwhelmed by corruption is breathtaking to behold and devastating to ponder. It alone is reason to read this book. . . . [White] provides us with the best account I have read of popular efforts in the 1880s and 1890s to free the republic from railroad and corporate rule. White's recounting of the confrontation between the American Railway Union and the federal government in the Pullman Strike of 1894 is particularly moving. [A] remarkable attempt to resurrect the spirit of the First Gilded Age."   —Gary Gerstle, *Dissent*

"In this exhaustively researched and splendidly written book, Richard White takes a thoroughly fresh and strikingly critical new look at the Union Pacific, Central Pacific, and the other steel links laid down after the Civil War."
                    —Elliott West, History Book Club

"White is a sharp writer, and he doesn't mince words in judging historical figures."   —*The Daily*

"Excellent big-picture, popularly written history of the Howard Zinn mold, backed by a mountain of research and statistics."
                    —*Kirkus Reviews*, starred review

"White reminds us that the railroads didn't just rearrange our sense of space and time but also introduced the idea of large-scale corporate culture—and the attendant greed. American history fans who don't mind some myth busting should enjoy."   —*Library Journal.com*

"[An] important and deeply researched history. . . . White delivers an opinionated, delightfully witty but astute account of sleazy Gilded Age politics, business, and journalism, as well as the complex (but uncomfortably familiar) financial maneuvers men used to enrich themselves."   —*Publishers Weekly*

"The research and scholarship are first rate. . . . Mr. White has given us an excellent reference work for the origins of the railroads."
                    —Wes Vernon, *Washington Times*

"Provides a fine, recast history of the transcontinental railroads and their impact on the West, documenting their many massive failures over the usual myths of innovative capitalism and achievement popularized elsewhere."
                    —*Midwest Book Review*

"[This] ambitious book is important reading for all those who care about the major themes at work in the history of the American West."
                    —Jon Lauck, *Mitchell Daily Republic*

"Contending that the transcontinentals were overbuilt money-losers and nodes of labor conflict, White crafts a readable, authoritative study."
                    —Gilbert Taylor, *Booklist*

"There is not a historian in America with a steadier gaze than Richard White's: with him, no assumption goes unchallenged, no wisdom is ever merely received. *Railroaded* is a wonderful book: fresh, provocative, witty, filled with foreshadowing of our world but always true to its time, and told with the narrative force of a locomotive roaring across the empty plains."
                    —Geoffrey C. Ward, author of
          A First Class Temperament: The Emergence of Franklin Roosevelt

"When it comes to the American West, there is no other writer like Richard White, a serious scholar with a highly original take on familiar subjects and wit and elegant prose besides. His subject, the making of the transcontinental railroads, is perhaps the pivotal story of the American West, but it's not the one most of us know from movies and mythologies. It's about the birth of all those things that most trouble us nowadays, a genesis story in which the serpent in Eden is the railroad itself writhing across the continent. A story of corporate power, industrialization, and political corruption, White tells it as it needs to be told." —Rebecca Solnit, author of *River of Shadows: Eadweard Muybridge and the Technological Wild West*

"Richard White is one of those rare historians with an unfailing ability to transform any topic he writes about, no matter how familiar that topic might seem. In *Railroaded*, he tells the story of the western transcontinentals as it has never been told before, with insights that speak as much to our own time as to the nineteenth-century era he explores with such wit and intelligence." —William Cronon, author of *Nature's Metropolis: Chicago and the Great West*

"Combining a robust wit with a dedication to endless labor in archives, Richard White delivers a sharp-edged new understanding of industrialization in the Gilded Age. *Railroaded* offers flabbergasting views of the human talent for self-justification and contradiction, provides a valuable—if unsettling— comparison to the financial troubles of our times, and shows why the best historians are compared to detectives. To readers intimidated by the topic of railroad finance: master your fears and stay on board for a very wild ride." —Patty Limerick, Center of the American West, University of Colorado

"This brilliant book will forever change the ways in which the great railroad projects of nineteenth-century America are understood. Stripping away easy assumptions of technological triumph and financial wizardry, *Railroaded* tells a richer and darker story of post–Civil War America. Smashingly researched, cleverly written, and shrewdly argued all the way through, this is a powerful, smart, even angry book about politics, greed, corruption, money, and corporate arrogance, and the America formed out of them after the Civil War."　　　　　　　　　　　　　　　—William Deverell, director, Huntington–USC Institute on California and the West

"This is history as dark comedy, brilliant and unsettling, puncturing facile economics and bland history alike. With ingenious research and iconoclastic perspective, Richard White recasts our understanding of a major chapter in American history. Mark Twain would be bitterly amused to learn just how gilded the Gilded Age really was."　　　　　—Edward L. Ayers, president, University of Richmond

"*Railroaded* is a leviathan, a provocative challenge to a major myth about the American West: that transcontinentals were a triumph of American entrepreneurship and ingenuity, and a godsend to those who invested in, worked on, rode, lived near, or encountered them. Far from it, Richard West argues in a strongly written narrative that barrels along the track as it draws on intimate vignettes of players great and small, these railroads often proved to be a disaster for all but the handful that dreamed them up and, abetted by cronyism and complacent governmental regulation, enriched themselves as they impoverished the rest. This tale of havoc is an unsettling allegory of today's financial collapse and essential reading for all unnerved by the thought that we seem doomed to repeat history whether we are aware of it or not."　　　　　　　　　　　—Shepard Krech III, author of *The Ecological Indian* and professor emeritus, Brown University

☀ RAILROADED ☀

RAILROADED

THE TRANSCONTINENTALS
AND THE MAKING
OF MODERN AMERICA

RICHARD WHITE

W. W. NORTON & COMPANY   NEW YORK • LONDON

Copyright © 2011 by Richard White

For information about permission to reproduce selections from this book,
write to Permissions, W. W. Norton & Company, Inc.,
500 Fifth Avenue, New York, NY 10110

For information about special discounts for bulk purchases, please contact
W. W. Norton Special Sales at specialsales@wwnorton.com or 800-233-4830

Manufacturing by LSC Harrisonburg
Book design by Dana Sloan
Production manager: Anna Oler

Library of Congress Cataloging-in-Publication Data

White, Richard, 1947–
Railroaded : the transcontinentals and the making
of modern America / Richard White. — 1st ed.
p. cm.
Includes bibliographical references and index.
ISBN 978-0-393-06126-0 (hardcover)
1. Railroads—United States—History—19th century.
2. Land settlement—United States—History—19th century.
3. National characteristics, American. I. Title.
HE2751W55 2011
385.0973'09034—dc22

2010054054

ISBN 978-0-393-34237-6 pbk.

W. W. Norton & Company, Inc.
500 Fifth Avenue, New York, N.Y. 10110
www.wwnorton.com

W. W. Norton & Company Ltd.
15 Carlisle Street, London W1D 3BS

6 7 8 9 0

To my graduate students, past and present

CONTENTS

LIST OF ILLUSTRATIONS

LIST OF MAPS AND CHARTS

Maps

Charts

ACKNOWLEDGMENTS

❧❦❧

FOR ANY WRITER at the end of a long project, the final book is really a ledger of debts. Like the railroads, I have accumulated more than I can repay. I am grateful to those who read all or parts of this manuscript over the dozen years it took to research and write it, particularly my patient editor, Steve Forman, and my valued colleague David Kennedy. Gordon Chang, Elliott West, Virginia Scharff, William Deverell, Eric Rauchway, Gavin Wright, and Anne Spirn also all read sections of various chapters for me. Colleagues at the Center for Advanced Study in the Behavioral Sciences, the University of California, Davis, the University of Pennsylvania, Harvard, MIT, the University of New Mexico, and Princeton organized forums that allowed me to present the work in progress and harvest valuable criticisms. Not all of them agree with my conclusions, but they have all helped make this a better book than it otherwise would have been. Richard Orsi and I are not as far apart on our evaluations of the railroads as casual readers might think, and Dick was unfailingly generous in helping me on this project. Georges Borchardt, my agent, is a wonder. He has been a reliable island of calm and good sense. Walter Johnson never read a word of this manuscript, but he did suggest its eventual title.

A great part of the pleasure of writing this book has been the time it allowed me to spend in archives. The paradox of archives is that there, among the relicts of the dead, the past seems most vital and alive. At Stanford, the legendary Margaret Kimball helped me go through the holdings and find what I needed. Jim Kent, who runs the media and microfilm room at Green

Library, and his staff helped me in ways probably best kept between us, while he tried to convince the Stanford administration that all necessary historical records will not be available on the Internet. At the Baker Library at Harvard, a rare accessible jewel in a library system usually heavily guarded against outsiders, Laura Linard and her staff were always kind and remarkably helpful. The Baker is a treasure that deserves wider use by historians. George Miles at the Beinecke Library at Yale helped me find sources that I would otherwise never have seen. I have been working at the Huntington Library for my whole career, and although my attempt to use a generous offer of a fellowship there fell apart in a comedy of errors through no fault of the Huntington, I still used that library extensively for this book, and I am grateful. I have written on many subjects, but what all of them seem to have in common is the Newberry Library in Chicago. It, like the Huntington, is one of the few remaining independent research libraries. The Newberry and its collections are invaluable. The Minnesota Historical Society collections were also critical to this book. Thriving state historical societies have become rare, and Minnesota's is a remarkable institution. William Dobak, whom I have known for years, was essential in helping me research sources at the Library of Congress and the National Archives, and Kelly Sisson-Lessens, who will have completed her own Ph.D. by the time this is published, helped me gather sources at the National Archives branch in San Bruno, California, when she was an undergraduate at Stanford. A group of graduate students at the University of Nebraska—Tonia Compton, Nathan Sanderson, Matthew Deepe, Leslie Working, Rob Voss, and Sean Kammer—immensely aided my research on the Union Pacific. They saved me much time and labor.

I would also like to thank the New York Public Library, the Baker Library, Stanford Library, and the National Portrait Gallery for permission to use the pictures in this book.

Since this book has taken such a long time, I want particularly to thank the MacArthur Foundation and the Andrew Mellon Foundation; each, in different ways, aided me while I was writing. I also want to thank the Center for Advanced Study in the Behavioral Sciences, which probably offers the single best fellowship in the entire world. I enjoyed my year there immensely. It allowed me to see how much more I needed to do for this book.

The Andrew Mellon Foundation funded the Spatial History Project at

Stanford long after this book was underway, and in doing so it provided me with the best collaborative research experience, and the best teaching experience, that I have ever had. In the notes I refer to sources developed by the Spatial History Project; the work on them was done by an amazing staff, outside visitors, and, to a great extent, Stanford undergraduates. Erik Steiner, Kathy Harris, Mithu Datta, Whitney Berry, and Killeen Hanson formed the core staff of the lab. Eleanor Wilking, Otto Murphy, and Toral Patel came from Harvard and Middlebury, and all three were critical to the project. Just as critical has been the work done by Stanford undergraduates. The things these students accomplished astonished me at first; eventually I just came to expect it. I want to thank Evgenia Shnayder, Peter Shannon, Jess Peterson, Kevin Fischer, Naveen Agrawal, Samantha Azure, Emily Brodman, Stephanie Chan, John Watson, Jordan Wappler, Lucas Manfield, Bea Gordon, Rebecca Jacobs, Cameron Ormsby, and Natalie Chadlek. Jeremy Zallen took charge of the Spatial History work when the lab was barely getting started and then went on to Harvard. He deserves special thanks. And Killeen Hanson, who took Jeremy's place and has steered this project past many shoals, deserves much of the credit for the visuals in the book and on the website. Her work has been invaluable.

Finally, I want to thank my graduate students, most of whom, I know, find my passion for railroads a bit odd and my interest in corporations suspicious. They indulge me in this and other things. My thanks to them goes beyond any single book. I am grateful because they have enabled me to remain as interested in and passionate about American history as I was thirty years ago. As I grow older, I realize the blessing American research universities bestow on their faculties when they allow them to teach graduate students. I admit I have not always felt this way while editing and reviewing the fourth draft of a graduate student's dissertation chapter, but I cannot imagine writing and researching without them. I have lived beside a stream of smart, curious, demanding, challenging, and fresh minds. I have been informed by my students at Michigan State University, the University of Utah, the University of Washington, and Stanford in ways they cannot know. I remain prouder of their work than of my own, and I dedicate this book to them.

INTRODUCTION

HE IDEA THAT railroads remade North America and in doing so created the modern corporate world is hardly new. Modern scholars have proclaimed it repeatedly, and in this they only follow the nineteenth-century intellectuals and promoters whom they cite.[1] All of the possibilities that arose with railroads seemed magnified in the transcontinentals, which came to epitomize progress, nationalism, and civilization itself not just in the United States but in Canada and Mexico as well. I have my doubts about civilization, but I will accept the rest. All I would change is that they created modernity as much by their failure as their success.

The very term "transcontinental" communicated the hubris and power of a new technology that wrapped the continent in iron and steel bands, but the term also communicated the illusory and deceptive qualities of these corporations, which were never quite what they seemed. For the transcontinentals did not really span the continent. In the United States they had their initial eastern termini in cities and towns along the Missouri River. For connections to Chicago they depended on what were often far more powerful and better-run roads—the Burlington system, the Chicago and Northwestern, the Rock Island, and others—that sometimes dallied with the idea of becoming transcontinentals themselves but settled for competing with the lines that reached the Pacific in their richest territories.

Only later would the American transcontinentals directly connect to major population centers in the Midwest, and they never stretched to the Atlantic Coast. The Canadian Pacific eventually patched together a line to

St. John, New Brunswick, but originally it terminated at Montreal with a connecting line to Quebec. It, together with the roughly 130-mile railroad across the Isthmus of Tehuantepec in Oaxaca that joined the Pacific to the Gulf of Mexico, were the only true nineteenth-century transcontinentals north of Panama, although numerous railroads terminating on the Pacific Coast took the name. When I write about transcontinentals and other western railroads, I am not necessarily talking about railroads in general— I don't have the evidence to do so. But I am still talking about some of the largest corporations in North America. In the late nineteenth century large corporations mainly meant railroad corporations and a few other powerful organizations—Standard Oil, Western Union, and Carnegie Steel—that were intimately associated with them. Although Americans still celebrate the West as a bastion of individualism, corporations, along with the federal government, were central to its creation.

Nineteenth-century North Americans became quite aware of what transcontinental railroads failed to do, but initially they embraced them, as they embraced all railroads, as the epitome of modernity. They were in love with railroads because railroads defined the age. The claims made for railroads by men who wrote about them were always extravagant. The kind of hyperbole recently lavished on the Internet was once the mark of railroad talk. "Here," wrote Charles Francis Adams, the railroad reformer who eventually became president of the Union Pacific, "is an enormous, an incalculable force practically let loose suddenly upon mankind; exercising all sorts of influences, social, moral, and political; precipitating upon us novel problems which demand immediate solution; banishing the old before the new is half matured to replace it; bringing the nations into close contact before yet the antipathies of race have begun to be eradicated; giving us a history full of changing fortunes and rich in dramatic episodes."[2] Joseph Nimmo, who wrote prolifically about railways, thought "the railroad with its vast possibilities for the advancement of the commercial, industrial, and social interests of the world ran directly counter to the pre-existing order of things."[3] Theodophilus French, a federal auditor of railroad accounts whose honesty was more suspect than his expertise, thought them "the great civilizer of modern times."[4]

I am far more interested in the operation of the transcontinentals and other western railroads in the United States, Canada, and northern Mexico than in the initial construction of these roads, on which there is already a vast literature.[5] What concerns me above all are the entrepreneurs who created them, the men who worked for them, and the large numbers of citizens who came to oppose them as dangerous, corrupt, and threatening. I group the trunk lines of western Canada and northern Mexico with the American transcontinentals because the American roads were so tightly linked to the Canadian Pacific and the railroads of northern Mexico that they cannot be unhooked. Taken together, the American, Canadian, and Mexican railroads were sources of great national pride and great national discontent, but in many ways their most striking quality was that they formed an international network linking the three countries. At one point I had illusions that this would be a comparative book, but I found that I was dealing with one large interconnected railroad system financed from the same sources and controlled by a relatively small set of interests.

The transcontinentals, more obviously than other railroads, were entwined with the state. Governments subsidized them, secured their rights of way, regulated them, and protected them. The first transcontinentals began as hybrid public/private enterprises and ended up as private corporations, but their public roots remained. By the end of the century, with the transcontinentals under political attack virtually everywhere, the government suppressed their workers and protected the rights—and enforced the obligations—of their owners and managers in the name of public good and public order.[6]

The railroads, in turn, were agents of the expansion of these states. What these railroads allowed the governments of the United States, Canada, and Mexico to accomplish in the late nineteenth century was remarkable. In the United States they took credit for conquering the Indians. As Charles Francis Adams put it, "the Pacific railroads have settled the Indian question."[7] The railroads also took credit for settling the West. They took credit, indeed, for all of the development between the center of the continent and the Pacific. Non-Indian settlement had taken two and a half centuries to reach just beyond the Mississippi River in the United States and had crept only along the eastern Great Lakes in Canada. Neither Spain nor Mexico, despite centuries of struggle, had managed to control the northern reaches of Mexico.

Together these railroads formed a lever that in less than a generation turned western North America on its axis so that what had largely moved north–south now moved east–west. Railroads poured non-indigenous settlers into a vast region that nation-states had earlier merely claimed. They did not do this in response to a popular demand for development of these lands; instead, they created the demand through vast promotions unlike anything seen until that time. Having promoted new settlement, they helped integrate these settlers into an expanding world economy so that wheat, silver, gold, timber, coal, corn, and livestock poured out of it.

It may seem both churlish and mad to question the railroads' accomplishments. No one, after all, claimed that they came without a cost, particularly to Indian peoples, or that mistakes were not made and a certain amount of corruption generated, but these admissions tend to be of the "say what you will" variety: say what you will, the result was worth the price, and the lives of tens of millions of people were the better for it. But questioning these accomplishments is what this book does. The issue is not whether transcontinentals eventually proved to be a good idea; it is whether they were a good idea in the mid and late nineteenth century. The idea of a transcontinental railroad was not in and of itself bad, but why were so many of these railroads built at a time when there was so little need of them? The nineteenth-century critics of the railroads were often right: these western railroads very often should not have been built when and how they were. Their costs over the long term, and the short term, exceeded their benefits.

In all three countries the railroad corporations either failed—ending up in receivership—or were rescued by nation-states, which forgave loans, renegotiated terms of payment, or nationalized the roads. Their failures as businesses were only the beginning. The railroads were also political failures. Having helped both to corrupt and to transform the political system by creating the modern corporate lobby, which they used to compete against each other, they then found it an expensive and sometimes nearly impossible burden to bear. Their political activities in the western United States and Canada were by the end of the century increasingly counterproductive. Politically, as well as financially, they often became wards of the courts. Finally, they were, in large part, social failures. They lured settlers into places where they produced crops, cattle, and minerals beyond what markets could profitably absorb and where their production yielded great environmental and social harm. It was no wonder that railroad corporations came to be hated, and that opposition to them as monopolies—one of the key words necessary in order to understand late nineteenth-century American and Canadian politics—fueled the reform movements of three countries. These railroad failures are essential to understanding the complicated development of modernity and the historical role of corporations in it.[8]

This book owes much to the great economist Joseph Schumpeter, although many readers will find such a claim astonishing. It is about the utter uprooting of older ways of life and older ways of communication and travel by a new technology in the hands of new men with a new form of corporate organization. It is, at first glance at least, about Schumpeter's "creative destruction"—the necessity of capitalism always to uproot the old in order to institute the new. It is a book whose central figures are entrepreneurs—and it was Schumpeter who made the entrepreneur the central and heroic figure of American capitalism. Railroads were, in the words of Schumpeter's biographer Thomas McCraw, "Schumpeters's favorite example of innovation by new men and new firms."[9]

Like Schumpeter, *Railroaded* emphasizes finance capitalism—the use of credit and the financial markets—as the central engine of corporate growth and expansion in late nineteenth-century North America. It was not "capital" that built the railroads but credit, and the capital that was ultimately at risk in the railroads did not belong to the men who controlled them. Thomas Scott, Jay Gould, Collis P. Huntington, Henry Villard, and others were entrepreneurs; the capitalists were the far more anonymous and numerous figures who bought the bonds that allowed the railroads to proceed.

The markets these entrepreneurs used and exploited were historical; they comprised particular practices, most with active state involvement: subsidies, regulations, military protection, and so on. In this book there is no such thing as a market set apart from particular state policies, institutions, and social and cultural practices. The question is not whether governments shape markets; it is how they shape markets. The transcontinentals were, as the economic historian Robert Fogel has written, "hothouse capitalism," but the distinctions between hothouse capitalism, garden-variety capitalism, and, to extend the metaphor, natural capitalism were ones of degree. A wild capitalism is as much an oxymoron as wild agriculture. Markets are cultivated. They can be cultivated in many different ways with many different possible results.

Although the transcontinental railroads emerged in markets shaped by large public subsidies and particular legal privileges, neither subsidies nor privileges were new in and of themselves. American states had subsidized and granted special privileges to canals, banks, and railroads in the 1820s and 1830s. These proliferating and often financially disastrous subsidies had brought about a constitutional reaction in the 1840s that dramatically curtailed the ability of the states to subsidize development and lend their credit.[10] It left the ground open for the federal government.

Railroad entrepreneurs were innovators. They sought advantage by adopting new techniques. But whereas the celebrations of entrepreneurs usually make their success synonymous with the firm, the men I examine usually succeeded at the expense of the firm.[11] The paradox at the heart of this book is that such individual success as there is usually comes at the price of corporate failure. Personal wealth often brings with it social failure. The innovations entrepreneurs brought to the railroads—financial mechanisms, pricing innovations, and political techniques—were as harmful to the public, to the republic, and even to the corporation as they were profitable to many of the innovators.

Many of my entrepreneurs obtained great fortunes, but they created inefficient, costly, dysfunctional corporations. These corporations did spur innovations in production, but that was the problem. They built railroads that would have been better left unbuilt, and flooded markets with wheat, silver, cattle, and coal for which there was little or no need. They set in motion a train of catastrophes for which society paid the price. They often squandered large amounts of capital and labor for no good end. Many of the investments would have been better made in other sectors of the economy.

There is a great truth in the idea of creative destruction, but when applied indiscriminately it begins to look much like a kind of trust in the ultimate benevolence of markets and entrepreneurs that is little different from the older trust in God's plan that Voltaire skewered in *Candide*. No matter what happens *tout est mieux*—all is for the best. The late nineteenth-century West was more Voltaire's country than Schumpeter's. All was not for the best.

A basic problem of the transcontinentals was that they were built ahead of demand. That a transcontinental railroad might be a good idea in 1900 does not explain building it in the 1860s, 1870s, and 1880s, particularly when the results contributed to two depressions in the 1870s and 1890s and a sharp, if short, economic downturn in the 1880s. The North American West needed railroads in the late nineteenth century. What it needed was what turned out to be the functional—if still often mismanaged—part of the system: feeder roads into Chicago, St. Louis, and San Francisco. It did not need transcontinentals, at least not the multiple roads that ran from the 100th meridian to the Pacific. These were the roads that never paid for themselves in the late nineteenth century and left disaster in their wake. They came too early, in too great an abundance, and at too great a cost.

The interesting issue is how this happened. To examine these railroad corporations is to see half a continent—the western United States, western Canada, and northern Mexico—in a new light. This is the story of the opening up of a continent that could easily have been opened up more slowly, more gingerly, and more humbly. This is a book about corporate failure and corporate mistakes that were by almost every measure—economic, social, political, and environmental—transformative mistakes. The railroads were like bad art; they were not accidents. People planned these things; they were purposeful. And insofar as their repeated failures and collapses were part of larger failures and collapses, the railroads also seeded the financial clouds that produced the storms that overwhelmed them.

This history of the transcontinentals begins with the genesis of these railroads in the Civil War and ends with the last and largest of their nineteenth-century failures in the depression of the 1890s. It runs against the grain of what is still a powerful, if long criticized, triumphal narrative of the opening of the West, particularly the western United States. In this traditional view, the West is about promise, progress, and success. It is the homeland of the American future. It is where people go to succeed, not to fail. It is the realm of individualism, not of the state and corporations.

This history also cuts against another powerful narrative, again much criticized, about the evolution of corporations and economic development in the United States.[12] The simplest explanation of the emergence of railroad corporations is that they are an expression of a universal economic rationality and that basic market factors—the costs of producing transportation and the revenues from selling it—determined the form of corporate organization.[13] But if this is the case then similar technologies and similar economies should produce similar corporations. Great Britain, France, and Prussia, however, did not replicate the American form of railroad organization, although each was a capitalist nation and each employed similar technologies.[14]

The best way to understand the transcontinentals' simultaneous failure as businesses and success as sources of individual fortunes for insiders is to regard them not as new businesses devoted to the efficient sale of transportation but rather as corporate containers for financial manipulation and political networking.[15] They employed rational managers, but they were led by financiers. The financiers made money through subsidies, the sale of securities, insider companies for the construction of the railroads themselves, and land speculation. Each funneled corporate resources into private pockets. To do this, they needed considerable political aid and protection.

In the paradox of transcontinental railroads as transformative failures lies their historical importance and interest. The transcontinentals were monuments to arrogance, ignorance, and greed, but this was not all they were. They shaped modern North America, and saying this involves five claims.

My first claim goes to their relationship with central governments—the state. In the United States the transcontinentals were children of the Civil War and the powerful federal government that Richard Bensel, the American political scientist, has called the Yankee Leviathan.[16] In Mexico they were the offspring of Porfirio Díaz, the Mexican dictator and centralizer. In Canada the Canadian Pacific was a product of Confederation. In the United States the state did briefly weaken after Reconstruction, but it retained far more strength in the West than elsewhere. When we look closely at the U.S., Canadian, and Mexican government relationships with the western railroads, we find an interlocking network of what I, using the language of nineteenth-century corporate officials and politicians, call friends. The railroads smudged the line between corporate competition and federal regulation. Corporations used the federal government to punish rival corporations while gaining advantages for themselves. They made politics a realm of private competition.

My second claim goes to how railroads reshaped the sense of time and, more significantly, space. Railroads, so the cliché goes, annihilated space and time, and they obviously did cut the time and cost of travel. They made the far near. But they did so unevenly and chaotically. Nineteenth-century shippers measured distance less by time of travel than by cost, but railroad costs, as we will see, were an ever-changing realm of mystery. When shippers tried to calculate and compare costs, the map of the West became a crazy quilt whose pieces seemed utterly incommensurate and unstable. Calculating distance by cost meant that places slid across the map in a wild and arbitrary manner. In Washington State, Spokane was geographically closer to Chicago and Seattle geographically more distant when measured by miles, but when measured by cost of shipping goods by rail Spokane sometimes slid out into the Pacific while Seattle moved seemingly effortlessly east across the Cascades. The railroads made their customers acutely aware of space, but they also rendered that space radically unstable and seemingly subject to the whims of distant corporations.

Virtually all of the bitter political and economic conflicts that followed the construction of railroads in the vast region stretching from the Canadian Pacific south nearly to Mexico City and from the Pacific to the eastern termini of the American transcontinentals were in some sense quarrels over the organization and production of space. People quarreled over where tracks would run, where people would get access to the trains, and whether there would be competing tracks. People argued bitterly and endlessly over the rates charged to move people and goods along those tracks. They argued about who should own those tracks and trains and who should control the terms of transportation.

The third claim of this book goes to the nature of these corporations. They were not the harbingers of order, rationality, and effective large-scale organization. In both Robert Wiebe's *The Search for Order* and Alfred Chandler's *The Visible Hand*, perhaps the two most brilliant and persistently influential books in shaping our ideas of the late nineteenth century, corporations became the architects of what the political scientist James Scott would later call high modernism. Scott identified high modernism as primarily a state project and made its hallmarks radical simplification and legibility. By legibility, he meant the ability of distant bureaucrats and managers to view, measure, and ostensibly control distant places. The census, the cadastral survey, the standardization of weights and measures, freehold property, and much more were aspects of high modernism.[17]

Wiebe and Chandler similarly identified the corporation with managerial capitalism and managerial capitalism with rationalization, order, simplification, and legibility. The markers of corporate simplification and legibility were as diverse as the timetable, the tables of tariffs for freight, the organization chart, time zones, and new methods of cost accounting. In Wiebe's formulation, the corporations became a kind of vanguard of American Progressivism, bureaucratizing, rationalizing, and seeking the services of experts ahead of the state itself. And in both Wiebe's and Chandler's view the corporation emerged as the realm of salaried managers, experts who displaced financiers, entrepreneurs, families, and even stockholders in the control of business enterprises. They were, for better or worse, a force for order.[18]

The railroad corporations in this book are not those of Wiebe and Chandler. On the level of aspiration—what the managers of corporations, as distinct from their owners and financiers, aspired to create—I have little quarrel with Wiebe and Chandler. The achievement is something else again. Managers blamed their failures on accidents and contingent events, but they also used them to cover their mistakes and claim quite fortuitous results as the fruits of their planning.[19]

In his work on the railroads Chandler relied on the records of boards of directors and the kinds of materials found in annual stockholders' reports, but mine is not a view from the boardroom, or at least not from the boardroom alone. I don't trust annual reports. I try to descend into the bowels of the organization. Move to the presidents' offices or, better yet, to middle management and the workers on and around the trains, and the actual practices of corporations become far more ambiguous and complicated. The corporation was often at war with itself.

Both Wiebe and Chandler were children of Max Weber. Modernity was synonymous with order imposed by impersonal large-scale organizations. The local yielded to the national, the premodern to the modern, individualism gave way to bureaucracy, and temporary disorder gave way to a more lasting order.[20] I do not discern a similar pattern. The organizations I describe here not only failed to institute the order they desired; they also just plain failed and repeatedly needed rescuing by the state and the courts. Railroad bureaucracy was rife with individualism. We shall see that those who took to their sickbeds or European tours, those who obsessed about manhood, those who were overwhelmed by a sense of failure, were not outsiders—victims caught, so to speak, on the tracks and in the path of an onrushing modernity symbolized by the railroads. They were driving the trains. The local was no less modern than the national. Throughout the book I try to draw a large-scale history down to ground level through stories of individuals whose lives were transformed by the railroads. Through their eyes we see a world that was closer to *Dilbert* than to Chandler. The dysfunctions of railroad corporations and their expression in individuals were not a mark of the persistence of old practices within new forms but rather a mark of their modernity.

My fourth claim goes to rehabilitating movements—particularly antimonopolism—that opposed corporations and are now consigned to the scrap heap of history. When late nineteenth-century North Americans tried to identify the centers of power that were transforming their worlds, they identified not the state but corporations, or monopolies, as they termed them. For all its failings, antimonopoly opposition to the corporation was significant. Wiebe interpreted resistance to both corporations and corruption—the basis of antimonopolism—as the rearguard and reactionary resistance of local societies at war with modernity. But the merchants, farmers, and workers battling corporations were as modern as the corporations themselves.[21] As state-subsidized railroads emerged as fully private property, they revealed all too clearly in the West the inequality of the new social relations of property. And opposition to this was at the core of antimonopolism.[22]

My final contention is somewhat defensive and an attempt to preempt what I anticipate will be the most common misinterpretation of this book: this is not a resurrection of the old Robber Baron literature that Wiebe and Chandler helped to kill. All of these western lines do lead back to a relatively small group of promoters and financiers. These men—Jay Cooke, Jay Gould, Thomas Scott, Collis P. Huntington, Leland Stanford, James J. Hill, John Murray Forbes, Henry Villard, and others—are hardly historical strangers, and they have usually been portrayed as bigger than life. Such tycoons were, in David Bain's recent words, "the heedless royalty of the developing republic, crushing enemies, exploiting the powerless, building empires."[23] I wish, if only for simplicity, that I could say, for better or worse, that these tycoons dreamed modernity, built empires, and gave us the world we know. They were, however, not that smart. Many were clever enough at soliciting money and not repaying debts. The shrewdest of them were masters at controlling and manipulating information. We have their equivalents today. They were more likely to feel abused and threatened than imperious. The power they achieved traveled porous channels. It leaked away and had unexpected outcomes. These were men whose failures often mattered as much as their successes. Their inability to turn the transcontinentals into profitable businesses led them into halls of power they otherwise would never have frequented. With perhaps the exception of Gould, there is a Sorcerer's Apprentice quality to them. They laid hands on a technology they did not fully understand, initiated sweeping changes, and saw these changes often take on purposes they did not intend.

This Sorcerer's Apprentice quality is why I find them so interesting, and so important. They at least gesture toward one of the mysteries of modernity. How, when powerful people can on close examination seem so ignorant and inept; how, when so much work is done stupidly, shoddily, haphazardly, and selfishly; how, then, does the modern world function at all? It is no wonder that religious people see the hand of God and economists invent the invisible hand. The transcontinental railroads are sometimes fetishized as the ultimate manifestation of modern rationality, but, when seen from within, these astonishingly mismanaged railroads are the anteroom to mystery.

Histories take a long time to be written. This one took about a dozen years. I spent those years teaching in two places, the University of Washington in Seattle and Stanford University in Palo Alto. The Seattle area is the home of Microsoft. Stanford sits in the Silicon Valley. These centers of the new technology proved to be fortuitous places to be thinking about corporations dependent on what was once a new technology and is now the very symbol of old technology: steam.

Writing where and when I did influenced this book a great deal. It is a historian's duty to be true to the past and try to re-create a world that those who lived in it would recognize. It is a mistake to make the past a place where people just like us think about things as we think about them now and do things just as we do them now. Historians, however, are also historically situated; they write from their own time and place, and this influences what they write. They are prone to notice parallels and similarities. History is always a negotiation between past and present, and being in Seattle and Palo Alto in the late 1990s and early twenty-first century made me notice how much railroad talk in the late nineteenth century was similar to Internet talk a century later; how both shared the certainty that they had obliterated time and space and with it all the old rules. There was, and is, a kind of wisdom and a kind of innocence in this talk, and sorting out the wisdom from the innocence is part of the task of this book.

At Stanford, itself a monument to a railroad fortune, I noticed something else. I came to the Silicon Valley in the midst of the dot.com boom at a time when very many people were becoming very rich by creating companies, or owning the securities of companies, that lost vast amounts of money. Having naïvely believed that owners of corporations made money from the profits earned by their corporations, I thought that this situation was peculiar. Eventually, I came to think of these new millionaires as descendants of men like Leland Stanford and his Associates. They had garnered large fortunes from heavily indebted corporations in ways that would not bear much looking into. Like the dot.coms, most of my railroad corporations went bankrupt or into receivership. The corporations failed, but very often the people behind them succeeded. The celebrated creative destruction of capitalism is, it seems, gentle with the rich. I began to see the larger theme of this book: failure and success are not always binaries. Certain kinds of failures impose more public than private costs. In failure as much as in success, the modern world takes shape.

Although historians have tried to diminish the corruption of the Gilded Age, it is hard to study the period without being aware of how corrupt the normal procedures of business and governance became in the late nineteenth century. The Gilded Age forced me to take corruption seriously, but it was writing about the Gilded Age and living in the early twenty-first century that made what I was studying seem more than just a phase, the unruly youth of corporate capitalism. There was Enron, the dot.com bust, followed by the credit crisis and the banking scandals of 2008 and 2009, and the government intervention to rescue corporations that in their own failure had brought the country to its knees. As in the nineteenth century, highly leveraged corporations, marketing dubious securities that were more inventive than comprehensible even to their creators, precipitated massive losses, receivership, government rescues, and severe economic downturns. The present seems so nineteenth century. The parallels, of course, are not exact—they never are—but they are startling.

By the time this book is published, the current downturn may be over, and there will be the perennial temptation to listen again to those who proved themselves so wrong before. Even now, as I write, some of them are saying that the combination of circumstances leading to the 2007–08 collapse—the contingencies, as historians say—were so extraordinary that they could neither be anticipated nor prevented nor, presumably, repeated. But if the late nineteenth-century situation and the current one are even roughly parallel, then the present seems less extraordinary. And if railroad corporations failed not once but many times, with dire effects over the course of the late nineteenth century, then so can their twenty-first-century equivalents.

In the nineteenth century there was a movement not only to control abuses and injustices but to rethink the relationship of the republic, and its citizens, to its economy. The larger rethinking failed, but over the next half century some reforms achieved significant success. Antimonopolism was the root of this reform. It was a flawed movement. In the West it was racist to its core, but its proponents created a politics that forced politicians to confront larger economic and social issues. Although not all readers will think so, this is a hopeful book. In paths forged and blocked, abandoned and resumed, history shows us that things need not be the way they are.

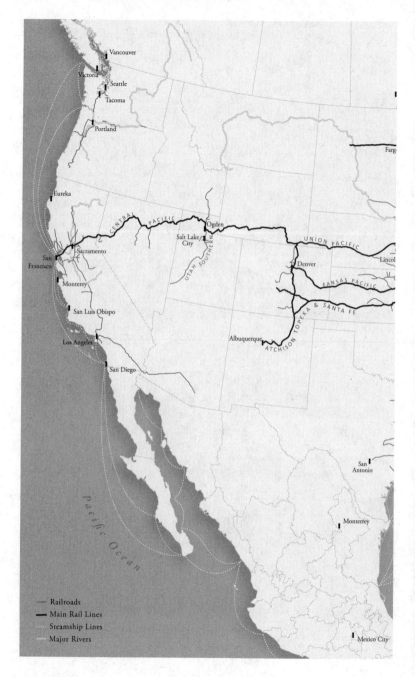

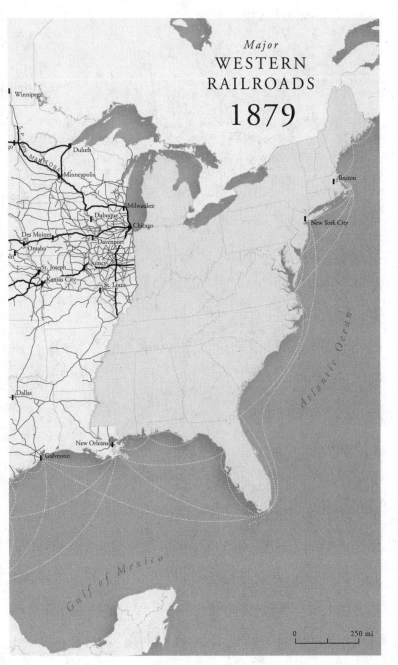

Major
WESTERN
RAILROADS
1879

Winnipeg

Duluth

Minneapolis

Milwaukee

Dubuque

Chicago

Des Moines

Davenport

Omaha

Quincy

St. Joseph

Kansas City

St. Louis

Dallas

New Orleans

Galveston

Boston

New York City

Atlantic Ocean

Gulf of Mexico

0   250 mi

Toral Patel

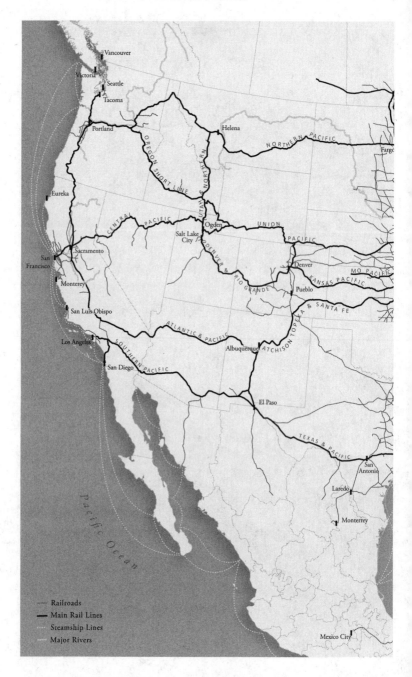

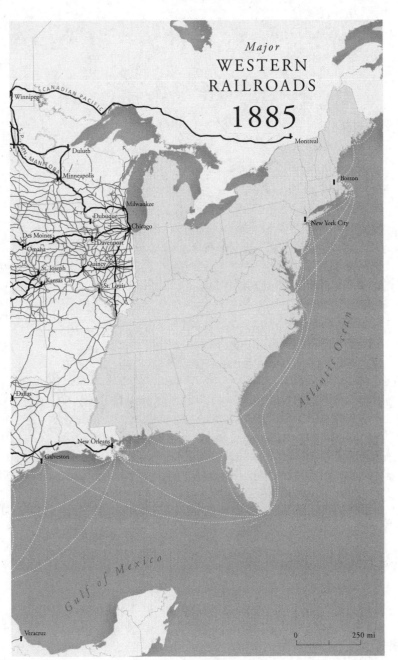

Major
WESTERN
RAILROADS
1885

Toral Patel

✦ RAILROADED ✦

CHAPTER 1

∽∾⊙∾∽

GENESIS

*It is easier, more delightful, and more profitable to build
with other peoples' money than our own.*

—NEWTON BOOTH[1]

IN 1860, THE year he won the Republican nomination for the presidency, Abraham Lincoln traveled from his home in Springfield, Illinois, to New York, a journey of about 825 miles as the crow flies, to give his famous Cooper Union speech. Lincoln, however, traveled considerably farther than the crow. Departing on Wednesday, February 22, it took Lincoln six hours to go by rail from Springfield to State Line, on the Indiana border, where he arrived at 4:30 P.M. and transferred to the Toledo, Wabash, and Western. The second leg of his trip took him from State Line to Fort Wayne, Indiana, where he arrived just in time to board another train, the Pittsburgh, Fort Wayne, and Chicago. It was now 1:12 A.M. on Thursday, February 23. The third leg, from Fort Wayne to Pittsburgh, took a little over twenty-four hours. He arrived in Pittsburgh at 2:20 A.M. on Friday, February 24. The fourth leg of the trip advanced him from Pittsburgh to Philadelphia and through yet another day. That train, fourteen hours late, reached Philadelphia early on Saturday morning, February 25. The final leg of his trip carried him from Philadelphia to New York. He waited several hours for the Pennsylvania Railroad train to New York, about as long as that train took to go between Philadelphia and Jersey City, from which he had to take the Paulus Street Ferry for New York. Reduced to numbers, the trip of twelve hundred miles involved five trains, two ferries, four days, and three nights. The numbers do not capture the discomfort imposed by schedules that shuttled passengers between trains in the middle of the night. They do not record the adrenaline rushes involved in making some transfers and the drowsy tedium of waiting to make others. This was train travel before the Civil War: at once technologically impressive and nearly incoherent. It was exhausting, aggravating, uncomfortable, yet, withal, far better than any existing alternative. Americans were prepared to love trains, hate trains, and be unable to live without them.[2]

Like the Union itself, American railroads did not quite cohere. The railroads had grown as fast, and were as disarticulated, as the nation that contained them. The 31,286 miles of tracks united the country only on a map. Impressive in the aggregate, these lines could hardly be thought of as a system or even a collection of systems. A major reason was that there was no single standard gauge for tracks. It was as if hobbyists were trying to connect Lionel with HO tracks. They would not fit together.

The standard gauge in North America today is 4 feet 8½ inches. It is an utterly arbitrary number that spread because the builders of a small English coal road had early success in building larger roads in England by using that gauge and because others conformed to it. By 1860 it was the dominant gauge in much of the eastern United States. It accounted for roughly one-half the total mileage, but it was only one of the more than twenty gauges in use. Five feet was the standard gauge in the South, and 5 feet 6 inches became the standard gauge in Canada.[3]

An individual railroad stopped where its track stopped, but, as long as the gauges were the same, a railroad's rolling stock could happily roll on along some other railroad's track, even if few roads at the time allowed such a thing. Different gauges were akin to dams in the thin streams of iron flowing through the continent. When gauges changed, traffic stopped. Passengers had to walk to a new train; freight had to be off-loaded at considerable expense or cars had to be jacked up and their wheels adjusted before the train could continue its transit. The lines that flowed so cleanly on a map ruptured in reality because of a small difference in space between the rails. Sometimes the different lines coming into a city never actually met. Freight coming into Philadelphia had to be off-loaded and carted across the city to get out of Philadelphia. In Ohio the usual mishmash of gauges and opposition to bridging the Ohio River forced the ferrying of cars. Railroads often did not share terminals, and tracks did not connect their different terminals. A railroad system was "articulated," the way the bones of a skeleton might connect, but the muscles and tendons were wagons, ferries, and human bodies. Take them away, and the railroad skeleton fell into unconnected pieces.[4]

The Civil War probably destroyed more railroads than it built, but it contributed a great deal to the organization of railroads and even more to the creation of financial and governmental institutions that would in the years following the war breed railroads like rabbits. The war gave free rein to men willing to take command, to imagine great things, to innovate, to experiment, and to lose all hold on reality. The abilities to organize, imagine, squander, and wreck unfortunately did not come in separate containers. They were part of a single package that when opened in the 1860s would create the first transcontinental railroads.

I. FIRST PRINCIPLES

Among the men whose lives would be entangled with the transcontinental railroads and whose reputations would have been far greater if they had, like Lincoln, died with the Civil War, were Tom Scott and Jay Cooke. Tom Scott may have been the quintessential railroad man of his generation. Scott is nearly forgotten now, but men whose names are well remembered once feared and admired him. Andrew Carnegie was his protégé. Jay Gould was his rival. Edgar Thomson recruited him to the Pennsylvania Railroad, and, by the outbreak of the Civil War, Scott had become its public face. He was a close friend of Simon Cameron, another railroad man, iron manufacturer, Republican senator from Pennsylvania, and, for a brief and disastrous period, secretary of war. Tom Scott had many friends.

At the outbreak of the Civil War, Tom Scott was vice-president of the Pennsylvania Railroad, a large industrial corporation. These may seem commonplaces today, but only a short time earlier there were neither vice-presidents nor large industrial corporations. Both were products of the rise of railroads. Railroads dwarfed textile mills and iron foundries, the other large enterprises of the United States, both in the capital they required and in the complexity of their management. In North America the word "corporation" would, until relatively late in the century, remain virtually synonymous with transportation companies—particularly railroads. And in the number of people they employed and in the elaborateness of their bureaucracies, these corporations had more in common with governments than with other business enterprises.[5]

Tom Scott's aptitude for organizing railroads made him an ideal candidate for government service, and he served his country well in the days following Fort Sumter when Confederate troops and Baltimore mobs threatened to cut off Washington from the North by severing the Baltimore and Ohio Railroad. In the dangerous and fearful early days of the war Scott, acting first as an adviser to the government and later as an official in the War Department, reorganized and rerouted the railroads serving Washington, forging the competing northern lines that served the capital into a coherent system. He put them on a war footing, and he created the framework for a set of standard and uniform rates to extend across the North.[6]

Scott's ability and energy did not surprise those who knew him, nor did his corruption. Scott was not so much tainted by corruption as impregnated with it. He was the seventh of a family of eleven children, and the death of his father when he was still a child caused him to be passed hand to hand from his widowed mother to an older sister, and then to a brother. Through his early jobs as a clerk, he became familiar with bookkeeping and money-making. Railroad fortunes would be a matter of bookkeeping. Scott was less adept at actually making things. His early ventures—a sawmill and an icehouse—failed. But he remained a striver who was also dependent on family and friends. It was not until Herman Haupt, the superintendent of transportation for the Pennsylvania Railroad, hired him on the recommendation of friends that he began his rise. Early poverty and failure impressed on Scott the importance of having friends. His experience formed a kiln that so fired

Scott's mortal clay that corruption became part of his very makeup. He had, just before the war, supervised the systematic bribery of the Pennsylvania legislature and manipulation of the press to remove the tax on freight passing over the Pennsylvania Railroad and substitute a flat annual payment. The taxes that remained unpaid—for the Pennsylvania had ceased paying— would not go to the state but be retained by the Pennsylvania Railroad and tributary roads for the construction of new lines. His reputation would only grow.[7]

Rates, not taxes, brought him trouble in the early years of the war. The federal government did not nationalize the railroads; instead, it made it worthwhile for the railroads to cooperate. A basic, unsettled question was how much the railroads were going to charge the government for the enormous amount of war traffic it would deliver. In 1861, at the request of Governor Curtin of Pennsylvania, the railroads met to set standard rates for government traffic. Scott used these rates as the basis for a circular on government freight rates issued the same year.[8] He created a standard rate that made no distinction between long hauls and short hauls.

Controversies over rates would resonate throughout the history of western railroads, as yet unborn, for years to come, and near the heart of them was the issue of local versus "through" rates. Railroads charged more per mile for short local shipments than for long hauls. Since much of the expense of hauling freight came in the labeling, directing, loading, and unloading of cargo, and since these costs were the same no matter how far a car traveled, in railroad economics all miles were not equal. Cost per mile was largely a matter of a numerator remaining constant while the denominator grew. The first mile that a loaded train traveled was the most expensive, and each mile that followed was progressively less expensive. Whether a railroad car was traveling a thousand miles or ten miles, it cost nearly the same to load it and switch it—that is, move it around a yard and attach it to a train. Such costs were substantial if divided by ten, but minimal if divided by a thousand. Furthermore, when a car sat idle, either loading or unloading—as it did repeatedly after short hauls—it was not making money. This justified higher local rates.[9] The longer the freight traveled, the less the charge per mile. By publishing a circular that gave the railroads the right to charge *all* government shipments as if they were local shipments, Scott gave the roads a huge bonus. Particularly in the western theater, railroads saw the opportunity to charge the government far more than they did private shippers.[10]

Charges of profiteering by railroads and kickbacks to quartermasters—particularly in the Military Department of the West, commanded by John C. Frémont—put Scott on the defensive early in the war. He countered that he had intended his circular to set maximum, not minimum, rates. Since Scott was an expert at making himself clearly understood, this story was not particularly convincing. The charges against Scott were politically motivated and reeked of self-interest because the managers of the Baltimore and Ohio, which Cameron accused of overcharging, were clearly interested in retaliating against Scott and the Pennsylvania Railroad, which they said Secretary of War Cameron corruptly favored. But Scott was a political actor, so this should not be surprising and that the charges were self-interested doesn't mean they were untrue. As in many quarrels of this kind, everyone was right. All the parties were corrupt.[11]

To have Simon Cameron complaining about corruption was like having Jefferson Davis complain about slavery. Without it, he would not have been where he was. A story, revealing but apocryphal, since it was applied to so many people, later circulated that Thaddeus Stevens, the Radical Republican congressman from Pennsylvania, had warned Lincoln against appointing Cameron secretary of war, intimating that he was dishonest. When Lincoln asked him directly whether he thought Cameron would steal, Stevens replied, "I do not think he would steal a hot stove." When Cameron heard of the exchange, he confronted Stevens, who promised a retraction. Stevens called on Lincoln and told him, "I have come up to take back what I said about Cameron. I am inclined to think that I am wrong in saying he would not steal a hot stove."[12]

The only trait Scott shared with Cameron was corruption; Scott was neither incompetent nor careless. Cameron's carelessness and incompetence spotlighted his corruption and forced Lincoln to exile him as ambassador to the czar of Russia. Scott, as Cameron's friend and a known corruptionist, survived, but only for the moment. The new secretary of war, Edwin Stanton, recognized that Scott's liabilities were canceling out his ability. With the Pennsylvania legislature trying to subpoena Scott in its investigations of bribery in the tonnage tax repeal, he was an embarrassment. Scott eventually, and inevitably, resigned from the War Department.[13]

The local rates and the corruption scandals were, however, the frosting rather than the cake in the government-railroad relationship, and if Tom Scott's great flaw was that he never could resist the frosting, he never mistook the frosting for the cake. Since railroads lived on high-volume cargoes, the cake was the tremendous traffic in men and material that the Union war effort demanded. When Secretary of War Stanton negotiated standard rates with the railroads in 1862, the railroads agreed to carry federal freight at a 10 percent discount from their usual rates. This was a savory deal for the railroads because it guaranteed them a high volume of traffic that would cover their fixed costs.[14]

The need to cover fixed costs obsessed Albert Fink, a German immigrant and engineer who became the general superintendent of the Louisville and Nashville, a railroad critical to the advance of Union armies in the western theater.[15] Railroads bought their stations, tracks, cars, and bridges on borrowed money. They paid interest on that money, and they had to pay more money to keep this infrastructure from rotting, rusting, and decaying as much from natural causes as from use. These costs were fixed; they had to be paid whether the railroad ran a hundred trains or no trains, and so it was essential for railroads to distribute these costs over the maximum amount of traffic. The more tons of freight that a railroad carried, the smaller the share of the fixed cost that each ton had to bear. High-volume railroads could charge lower rates.[16] But to obtain the highest possible profitable traffic, a railroad had to discriminate. To fill a train a railroad might accept traffic at the lower cost a shipper could afford to pay while prior purchasers were charged the higher going rate.[17]

The Union didn't need more railroads; it needed to use those it had more efficiently. Josiah Quincy, a New Englander and one of the most trenchant critics of the railroads, argued that an average train represented a colossal waste of energy and money. A locomotive could usually pull far more cars than it did on a given run, and indeed often pulled empty cars, which having brought freight to one location had no freight to haul on their return. Given such wasted capacity, it made sense to fill up cars that would otherwise have to be hauled back to another station empty and attach additional cars even if substantial discounts were needed to attract the freight to fill them. Every loaded car added to a train, up to the capacity of its motive power, cost less to haul than the previous one. Even if such freight yielded no profit, it could meet part of the road's fixed cost.[18] If a shipper such as the government could promise astonishing amounts of freight at fixed rates, then the railroads might as well be running to heaven.

Giving the government preferential rates removed the frosting of higher local rates, but the cake remained. The trains ran to capacity. The railroads met their fixed costs, upgraded and rebuilt their lines, and raked in record profits while avoiding the costly rate wars that plagued them under competitive conditions. For the roads most critical to the war effort, these were halcyon days.[19]

When Albert Fink later imagined a practical system of railroad governance and the legalization of pools that set rates and distributed traffic, he imagined something that roughly resembled the structure of northern railroads during the Civil War. The railroads constituting the system were in competition, but they had a common interest in "the proper management of the transportation business of the country so as to secure the best possible results to the people, with due regard to the rights of the proprietors of the roads." This could be secured only by the cooperation of the railroads under "some sort of government, with sufficient power to regulate and restrain the action of individual companies so far as necessary for the welfare of the whole." The federal government would not assume ownership or management but "merely [prescribe] regulations and the method in which the owners of the property shall control it in a legal manner without interfering with the just right of others."[20] The government should not impose tariffs, but rates should be made uniform "by the joint action of the roads interested."[21]

The pressure the war created for coordinating railroads was not the primary impetus for standardizing gauges, but it quickened the pace of change. The need to transport men and supplies rapidly without unnecessary breaks gave urgency to the complaints of merchants, who had long resented the added costs of transshipments. Lincoln's decision in 1863 to make the Pacific

Railway, the first transcontinental, standard gauge (4 feet 8½ inches) ratified a consensus that had already emerged, but the ratification was nonetheless important. It compelled the Pacific Coast, where the early gauge was 5 feet, to change and provided an incentive to all lines connecting with the Pacific Railway to adopt standard gauge. It was a major step toward continental uniformity. And although the South would continue to fight the standard gauge even after the Civil War, it lost that fight as thoroughly as it lost the war. It was always safest to bet against the South. When the American railroads in the 1880s extended subsidiaries into Mexico, the distance between the rails on most of them was 4 feet 8½ inches. When the Grand Trunk Railway, then the leading Canadian line, converted from broad gauge to standard gauge in 1874, the die was cast. Canadian railroads, including the Canadian Pacific, were largely on the same standard gauge as their American connections.[22]

II. PATRIOTISM AND PROFIT

Tom Scott worked directly with the railroads during the Civil War. He managed, coordinated, and centralized them into functioning systems. Jay Cooke, on the surface, had little to do with railroads. He was a banker and financier, but he created a way of financing the war that he, and others, could easily transfer to financing transcontinental railroads after the war.

Jay Cooke was an Ohio farm boy who started as a clerk with the banking firm of Enoch W. Clark in Philadelphia and made good. On January 1, 1861, as the Civil War loomed just over the horizon, he opened his bank on the ground floor of a brownstone building at 114 South Third Street in Philadelphia. His partner and brother-in-law, William Moorhead, a successful railroad promoter, provided most of the liquid capital of the bank, which totaled perhaps $5,000 or $10,000. New York had long before eclipsed Philadelphia as the country's financial center, but even in Philadelphia the House of Cooke was Lilliputian. Philadelphia's Gargantua, Girard Bank, with capital of $1,250,000, was down the block. Cooke's brownstone at 114 South Third Street seemed an unlikely source of finance for the Union war effort.[23]

Jay Cooke had real ability, and he had friends. His most important friends were politicians, and they came through his brother Harry, who had published the most prominent Republican paper in Ohio. It had lost money, but Jay Cooke covered the losses because the paper's value was in the connections it had made for Harry and, through him, for Jay. It was the major organ for Salmon Chase, a Republican senator from Ohio and by 1861 secretary of the Treasury in the Lincoln administration. Harry had followed Chase to Washington.[24] The secretary became Jay Cooke's friend.[25]

Friendships between wealthy men and politicians whose salaries did not meet their expenses would become common during the war and in the years that followed. Such friendship merged public business and private business in ways that enticed and alarmed both parties. The relations of Jay Cooke and Salmon Chase were a kind of Victorian financial seduction full of high-minded declarations of principles, real patriotism and sacrifice, mutual reassurances of rectitude, and dubious dealings.

There is no doubt that Salmon Chase and Jay Cooke rendered essential services to their country and helped save the Union. Chase came to trust Cooke's advice and acumen as he struggled to meet the enormous demands of financing the war. New York bankers and large investors proved unwilling to purchase government bonds except at large discounts from par. The government resorted to issuing paper currency, and with it came inflation. Each Union defeat early in the war further weakened the country's financial standing. The banks would not, and could not, finance the government's debt. The government, in turn, was unwilling to sell bonds below par or tax heavily enough to finance the war without borrowing. The only bright spot by 1862 was that inflation had made the sale of bonds at par easier. A purchaser could pay inflated greenbacks and get interest in gold, thus raising the real rate of return. Inflation, unfortunately, also reduced each bond's yield to the government in men it could pay and material it could buy.[26]

In October of 1862 Jay Cooke became sole agent for an existing but so far unsuccessful bond issue of $500 million. The bonds were called five-twenties because they were twenty-year bonds paying 6 percent interest that could be called in by the government after five years. By law they had to be sold at par.[27]

It was Cooke's genius to imagine a different way of selling bonds. He would appeal not to bankers or to the market's sense of what the bonds were worth but to the people's sense of what the Union was worth. He would appeal not to the calculations of economic men but to the emotions of patriotic men and women. Cooke would sell the bonds retail—to small investors in denominations as low as $50—but the market would be national. Cooke's subagents could be insurance men, real estate agents, or businessmen as well as bankers: anyone who had cultivated some degree of community trust and knew how to sell. Cooke advertised widely, paid generously, and ensured good press coverage by "kind and liberal treatment." Cooke organized, supervised, and tracked his agents as if they were a small army. He wanted frequent reports of progress and used the telegraph to get them. And Cooke's agents responded as if they were an army; as one wrote, "it is glorious work and stirs our blood."[28] Cooke sold U.S. government bonds with such creativity and zeal that he came to see himself as God's agent in saving the Union. The paradoxical mark of Cooke's triumph was a rise in the national debt from $65 million in 1860 to $2.75 billion by 1866.[29]

Cooke and his agents liked to portray their marketing of federal bonds as a species of patriotism, and it certainly was, but their patriotism paid. Cooke and Chase would eventually quarrel over the terms, but the payments on the first $10 million of bonds would allow Cooke one-half of 1 percent commission, with another one-eighth of 1 percent going to the subagents. Cooke would in return pay all the costs of publicizing the bonds. The costs of the publicity were substantial, but Cooke was after more than commissions. His status as sole agent of the bond issue led to denunciations of monopoly and favoritism, but it also made his name widely known and brought him other business. And from the beginning of the war, he had sought to have his bank act as a government transfer agent, holding federal funds until the government drew on them. This gave him temporary but lucrative use of federal money. The bonds, similarly, gave him additional capital as inefficiencies in engraving, printing, and selling the bonds, and delays in the transfer of the funds received for them, allowed him temporary use of the proceeds that piled up in his bank. The Civil War and federal business turned a minor banking house without access to significant liquid capital into a house to be reckoned with. Cooke and his agents had not only reaped considerable financial profit but also accrued dividends of patriotic regard and trust.[30]

In rendering essential services to the republic, Jay Cooke and Salmon Chase also rendered essential services to each other. During the war a ritual played out between them that would become familiar during the Gilded Age. Their efforts to save the Union gradually encompassed things of small moment, personal things, the stuff of daily life. In 1861 the secretary requested a favor—the purchase of a coupé or light carriage. In Philadelphia, Cooke personally selected the carriage and sent it as a gift. The secretary thanked him and refused it; as a public official he could not accept it, but, as it turned out, his daughter could. That would not violate his scruples. The issue became moot when the carriage proved unsuitable.[31]

In the midst of a war framed as a national moral crusade, Chase, an ardent abolitionist with ambitions for the presidency, had scruples, but he also had needs and desires. The scruples had to do not only with realities but with appearances as well. He did not want scandals that opponents could use against him, but he needed money for himself and friends. The secretary sought financial favors for the widow of Dr. Gamaliel Bailey, an old political ally. Then the secretary himself needed a loan. Jay Cooke provided it. Now the secretary had money to invest. Jay Cooke invested it, guaranteeing no risk, and promising amazing returns. He returned a $1,000 profit on a $13,000 investment within sixty days. Better yet, the secretary could deposit his money with the Cookes and draw on it as needed, even while Jay Cooke drew on the same account for Chase's investments. All this would be above board, of course. Jay Cooke would charge him interest on any deficit in the account, but interest made little difference when investments bought on borrowed money were guaranteed to pay. Chase insisted that they keep their private and public relations separate in their correspondence, even as he mixed them in the letter that made the request. Both men sporadically continued to mix them later; they were, after all, hard to separate. They assured each other that they were honest men and that, of course, Cooke's private favors had nothing to do with the public benefits he garnered.[32]

There were inevitably complications. There always were when American politics demanded both money and the appearance of rectitude. In 1862 the ghosts of the old republic, who feared that corruption would be the death of the American experiment in self-government, returned to haunt Salmon Chase. Someone brought to Chase's attention a 1798 law limiting the Treasury secretary's private investments in public securities and other outside business activities. Chase told Cooke that his private investments must conform to the law. Cooke expressed his surprise at such a law, praised Chase's honesty, and directed Chase's investments into private securities that were largely unimagined in 1798. The profits continued to roll in as certain as the tide.[33]

The tensions between moral scruples and financial desires reached a dual culmination in early June of 1863. It was a lovers' quarrel, both public and private. With subscriptions for the Union's bonds having yielded $12 million a week in May and with Cooke's "monopoly" under attack by the *New York World*, Chase, worried about his own political vulnerability, telegrammed Cooke on June 1 that for the remaining bonds he was reducing Cooke's compensation for the five-twenties from the ⅜ percent that Cooke demanded to ⅛ percent plus expenses for advertising. Cooke responded angrily; Chase soothed him and made some concessions, and the relationship continued. Chase needed Cooke; Cooke needed Chase.[34]

But on June 2 Chase sent a second letter regarding private rather than public affairs, or rather private affairs that he was afraid might become public. On June 1, the very day that Chase had lowered Cooke's public compensation, Cooke sent him word of a private profit of $4,200 made in a matter of weeks on the rapid turnover of a stock investment in a railroad, the Philadelphia and Erie. Chase had provided no money, and Cooke had not charged him any interest on the investment made in his behalf. Chase sent back the check. He was in an awkward position. He had not objected to the original investment, but he objected that the sale of the stock took advantage of market fluctuations that Chase as secretary of the Treasury could have influenced. He told Cooke of his determination "to avoid every act which could give occasion to suspicion that [he] would use the power conferred on [him] to affect markets unnecessarily." Cooke registered his astonishment, appreciated Chase's "noble sentiments," and told him that he was laying aside the money since it was Chase's and not his own. Chase's scruples did not stop him a week later from asking Cooke to give another thousand dollars to Mrs. Bailey, whose house Cooke had earlier purchased at Chase's request.[35]

Jay Cooke and, more particularly, Salmon Chase carried scruples that made their commingling of public and private affairs awkward, circuitous, and painful. They took the high road to the Gilded Age and arrived burdened with guilt and prone to windy self-justification. Salmon Chase represented the networks Jay Cooke created in Washington; Fisk and Hatch represented equally critical New York networks.[36] Cooke opened a branch of his own bank in New York, but he also recruited subagents, among whom was the firm of Fisk and Hatch, a partnership made in March of 1862 by Harvey Fisk and Alfrederick Smith Hatch. Both were from Vermont, and both had long experience in banking before opening their bank at 38 Wall Street in New York. Their working capital was $15,000.[37]

Harvey Fisk was a man much like Jay Cooke: self-made, familial, religious, and slightly sanctimonious. "Keep your own counsels," Fisk advised his sons. "Tell no one of your affairs."[38] Because they were dealing with small investors who had little experience in financial markets or securities and a deep suspicion of exchanging their money for paper rather than things, Fisk and Hatch had to educate their customers. It was an education in the arcane world of Wall Street, which had its own vocabulary as well as practices. They published a pamphlet entitled *Memoranda concerning Government Bonds for the Information of Investors*. By 1881 it was in its eighth edition and had grown to include a description of how the bond and stock markets worked.[39]

There were, the *Memoranda* explained, "two main classes of securities . . . bonds and stocks." A bond was "the obligation of a Corporation, City, County, State or Government to pay [the purchaser or holder] a certain sum of money at a certain time [usually twenty or thirty years from the date of issue], with a fixed rate of interest payable at certain periods, or, as in the case of income bonds, upon certain conditions." Bonds of business corporations were secured by the mortgage of all or specified portions of their property. Government bonds were secured by the faith of the government. One type of bond came with attached coupons, each dated according to the time when interest was due. An investor cut the coupons and exchanged them for the interest. A coupon or bearer bond was the property of the holder and was much more liable to theft but much easier to sell. A registered bond could be negotiated only by the person in whose name it was registered, and interest was paid by check to the owner or the owner's agent. There appeared, as time went on, a profusion of different kinds of bonds. Initially there were First Mortgage Bonds, which had first claim on assets, and Second Mortgage Bonds, which had a second claim after the first mortgage was satisfied. Then came other bonds: Debentures, Consols, Convertible, Land Grant, Sinking Fund, Adjustment, Income, and more—each having a different claim on the property and different conditions of payment. The riskier bonds usually yielded higher interest.

Stocks were "the share capital of a company" representing "an interest in its property over and above its liabilities, and in profits of its business after the expenses and interest on its bonds have been paid. This profit is known as a dividend." Interest on a bond represented "consideration received for the use of money loaned, while that derived from an investment in stock is called 'dividend,' because it is money divided to the stockholders from the profit of carrying on the business, after the fixed charges have all been paid." Bonds were a safer investment and better for assured income. Stocks, while potentially profitable, demanded a close scrutiny of the "company's standing and the success of its business." To own bonds was to lend money; to own stocks was to own part of a company.

But this was only the beginning of it, for there were so many ways of buying and selling these securities that Fisk and Hatch included a glossary to explain the negotiations in paper that went on in Wall Street. These negotiations made ordinary investors deeply suspicious. Pieces of paper took on a life of their own, and their exchange and manipulation produced profit without yielding any material value. Arbitragers, "bankers buying and selling stock and bonds in foreign markets, in order to benefit by the difference in price between the home and foreign markets," made money simply by moving paper from one site to another.

If paper stood for real things, then the connections between things and paper should be clear and their respective value honestly presented. Financial paper should be transparent and reveal the thing that gave it value. An investor should be able to examine a company the way a farmer examined a horse or cow. But small investors often relied only on published accounts—descriptions of the financial livestock—that were so ambiguous and deceptive as to render the securities opaque. Stocks and bonds were open to ballooning, or working up a stock "far beyond its intrinsic worth by favorable stories, fictitious sales or other means of deceptive inflation." It was hard to tell what paper stood for, and what real things stood behind it to give it worth.

Even harder to grasp were the various manipulations of paper that could yield profit. An investor could pay for the mere opportunity to buy paper—a "call" on stocks or bonds at a specified price at a given time, or buy the privilege of delivering a stock at an agreed-upon price in a certain number of days"—a "put." If an investor thought a stock's price was going to rise, it made sense to purchase the privilege of buying it later at its current price. But it was harder for novices to see how people could profit off of a "bear," or falling, market by "selling short." Stocks were sold short when sellers sold stock that they did not own. To make the sale, the seller borrowed stock for a fee promising to return the same number of shares on demand or at a fixed time. If the market fell, the borrower could replace the shares he had borrowed for a much lower price (called covering his shorts), returning to the lender the now lower-priced shares and pocketing the difference between his purchase and his sale as profit. To do this on a large scale and to try to force a decline in values was to "bear the market," a favorite tactic of speculators. The great fear of bears was that bulls, or those betting on a rising market, would drive prices higher, or even corner the market by locking up available stock, and ruin them since they would be unable to cover their shorts.[40]

In the 1860s this deep, murky sea of finance was beyond the range of small investors who were only sailing offshore in what seemed the sturdier and safer ships of government bonds. They were investing in their country. Patriotism and profit, Jay Cooke promised, would work in tandem. For the five-twenties this proved spectacularly true. But there were more promises to come, and these would be about railroads.

III. THE ACTS OF THE FOUNDERS

During the Civil War, Americans dreamed western railroads, but they could not build them. The United States had more pressing concerns than building new railroads in the lightly populated West. American railroad mileage had grown by less than 4,000 miles, to 35,085 miles, by the end of the war. Of these, 214 miles spidered through California, 19 were in Oregon, 162 in Kansas and Nebraska, and 465 in Texas.[41] In western Canada and northern Mexico no railroads ran at all.

Congress could, however, legislate transcontinental dreams. A transcontinental railroad was, as reckoning went in as young a country as the United States, an old idea in 1862. In the 1850s the government had sent expeditions to select routes and Congress had debated the routes, but further progress had fallen victim to the stalemate between the North and the South and the unwillingness of private capital to build the road. There was no commercial reason for a transcontinental railroad and no set of investors willing to fund, as F. A. Pike of Maine said in Congress, "1800 miles of railroad through an uninhabited country." Pike was of course wrong. The country was inhabited, just not by white people whom congressmen thought of as suitable customers for a railroad. Timothy Phelps of California succinctly gave the answer to critics like Pike. The immediate necessity was not commercial; it was "military necessity." And if there was no commercial demand for a railroad now, well, that made a railroad all the more necessary. It "was absolutely essential to our internal development." The question was how to build it. And the answer, according to Senator Henry Wilson of Massachusetts, was "the liberality of this government, either by money or land," to induce capitalists to invest. The result would be the "hothouse capitalism" in which the government created the conditions for private investment.[42]

The Pacific Railway Act of 1862 was justified on the grounds of military necessity. It was designed to preserve California and the West for the Union, but only a few dozen miles of rail would be laid before the war was over. Although the act did create the structure of loan guarantees and land grants to companies that would build the road, the inducements in the original act were insufficient bait for the capitalists Congress sought to attract. The lions and tigers and bears of capitalism stayed at a distance, but a collection of much smaller, if less timid, beasts came sniffing around the bait.

Two corporations secured the right to build with government aid, and Congress initially required each to have fifty miles of track laid by November of 1864. The Central Pacific, a California corporation, had, in the words of Theodore Judah, "drawn the elephant"—the right to build from the west—but it remained to be seen "if we can harness him up." Judah was then the chief engineer of the Central Pacific. He also became clerk of the House subcommittee responsible for reporting out the Pacific railway bill, and then secretary of the Senate Committee on the Pacific Railroad. Judah used these positions to distribute Central Pacific stock, with a par or face value of $66,000, where he thought it could do the most good.[43]

Backing Judah was a collection of Sacramento storekeepers who called themselves the Associates and whose net worth was probably no more than $350,000.[44] Collis P. Huntington had organized them late in 1860 to build a railroad east from Sacramento to the state boundary. They would also build a toll wagon road so that if the railroad failed, they would still have the Dutch Flat Road across the Sierras to the Comstock Lode. The core group eventually numbered five: Huntington, Leland Stanford, Mark Hopkins, and the Crocker brothers, Charles and Edwin. A stroke would later cripple Edwin, reducing the five to four and leaving the far less able brother the only Crocker involved. Except for Edwin Crocker, a lawyer, they were all hardware dealers, grocers, or dry goods merchants.

Collis P. Huntington was their driving force. Poorly educated, abstemious, and narrow as the upstate New York world that produced him, he was also undeniably clever, self-assured, and authoritarian; he always had an eye for the main chance. He combined bulldog tenacity, which he demonstrated when necessary, with a shrewd sense that few fights were worth fighting to the finish. Few men wanted to finish a fight with Collis P. Huntington. Tom Scott fought him longer than anyone, and Tom Scott would lose.[45]

His interest, Huntington grasped quickly, involved not putting much of his own money into the Central Pacific. The Associates' initial investment was small: $1,500 apiece for all of them except Edwin Crocker, and an additional $1,500 invested by James Bailey, a Sacramento merchant dealing in watches, clocks, and jewelry.[48] This $7,500 represented 10 percent down on 750 shares of stock whose par value was $100. A drive to sell stock in San Francisco failed utterly. Each of the Associates later bought an additional 345 shares with a total par value of $138,000, and other investors bought smaller amounts. Assuming they paid 10 percent down, that would have added another $13,800 to their total investment.[47] These two purchases by the Associates gave them a combined investment of $19,800. This was a considerable sum for storekeepers, but a pittance for a California railroad the estimates of whose costs averaged $100,000 a mile. Putting only a fraction of the stock price down left investors with the potential future demand for assessments to pay the remainder. In 1862 Huntington threatened assessments to force out Bailey and Judah, who had been given 150 shares.[48]

The Central Pacific existed prior to the Pacific Railway Act of 1862, but the act itself established the Union Pacific. It was the first corporation chartered by the federal government since the Bank of the United States, and initially it was a mere shell. The Union Pacific would not take on a real existence until commissioners appointed by Congress opened its subscription books and sold two thousand shares. Only then could the purchasers organize the railroad. As numerous cities, or would-be cities, competed for the eastern terminus on the Missouri River, Congress chartered both a trunk line—the Union Pacific that would build west from the 100th meridian in Pawnee country—and five branches that would connect it to various points on the Missouri. Only in 1863 did Abraham Lincoln, under the powers granted him in the Pacific Railway Act, make Omaha the eastern terminus. Congress prohibited the trunk line from discriminating against the branches, but Congress did not consider how difficult it would be to enforce that provision if the Union Pacific owned the Omaha branch.[49]

When the company opened its subscription books in September of 1862, it sold only twenty shares of stock, and the Union Pacific remained moribund until 1863 when Thomas Clark Durant took hold of it. Scheming, manipulative, at once calculating and volatile, Durant bridged antebellum America and the Gilded Age like some strange hybrid character from Herman Melville and Mark Twain. The only high roads Durant preferred were those on his railroad. He never took an ethical high road. He betrayed partners, and he betrayed strangers. When there was no low road, he blazed one. While calculating and shrewd, Durant was also extravagant. His extravagance paled beside his collaborator in the enterprise, the aptly named George Francis Train, whom the *Louisville Courier-Journal* compared to "a locomotive that has run off the track, turned upside down with its cow-catcher buried in a stump and the wheels making a thousand revolutions a minute." Train had moments of brilliance, but he was also a buffoon, and his trademark became brilliant buffoonery.[50]

With no one else investing, Durant and Train could take control with little investment of their own. They purchased shares, paid for in part from speculations in contraband cotton, and lent the 10 percent initial subscription price to others. This, too, was a speculation and a relatively small one. Durant's fifty shares had a par price of $50,000, but his 10 percent down represented an investment of only $5,000, and since only $500, or $10 per share, had to appear in the corporate treasury in cash, it is unclear how much actual money was ever involved. By 1863 Durant had gotten enough stock subscriptions to organize the Union Pacific.[51]

Storekeepers and speculators had secured the charters for the Pacific Railroad because it seemed such an unlikely enterprise to experienced railroad men. John Murray Forbes was a Boston capitalist who had started as a China trader and then funneled the profits of sailing ships, opium, silks, and tea into investments in Michigan and Illinois railroads. He even persuaded Hoqua, a prominent Chinese merchant, to invest in western railroads. At the outbreak of the Civil War his Burlington system was just taking shape; it contained only a little over two hundred miles of track.[52] Forbes had no interest in turning the Burlington into a transcontinental. He was a hard man: able and determined, but also opinionated, self-righteous, and narrow-minded. His circle of trust was limited largely to his own kind, but he knew railroads. The more men knew about running railroads for profit, the less likely they were to become involved in the Pacific Railroad.[53]

The transcontinentals were not like other railroads. In the early days of North American railroading, local investors built local railroads with considerable state aid to serve existing commerce. By the 1850s some capitalists were beginning to combine local roads into systems such as the New York

Central, which ran from New York City to Buffalo. But the transcontinentals were developmental roads that were supposed to create the traffic they would carry. Asking states or local investors at one end of the line to build a railroad that extended off into what seemed to them a vast emptiness was like bringing an elephant to a horse fair. It was a different beast, and they weren't buying.[54]

The transcontinentals were the mirror image of the Civil War that was wracking the nation. Building the transcontinentals and fighting the Civil War both involved great risk, immense expenditures of money, a sense of national purpose, and the organizational efforts of a newly powerful national state. Yet, as in a mirror, the resemblance was reversed. The Civil War demanded personal sacrifice for concrete collective goals; the railroads promised personal gain for projected public purposes. Having expended so much blood and treasure to restore the South to the nation, Congress hoped to connect the West without expending either.

The desire of Congress to build a railroad without taxing the public and the wish of promoters to build a railroad without investing their own money were at loggerheads. The Associates of the Central Pacific had by the winter of 1863–64 built eleven miles of railroad, and they were out of money. That spring they secured further aid from the California legislature, but that aid got tied up in court. The Union Pacific had built virtually nothing.[55] By 1864 it was apparent to both Huntington and Durant that Washington and New York loomed larger than the Rocky Mountains or the Sierra Nevada for the Union Pacific and the Central Pacific. Unless more concessions could be wrung from Congress and skepticism overcome in the financial markets, the Pacific Railway was going nowhere.

Huntington came east to lobby Congress and to try to sell bonds in the winter of 1863–64. He settled his family in New York's Metropolitan hotel and went to work. Durant was his rival and instructor. Huntington's first office, at 54 William Street, was on the same block as Durant's. Like Durant, Huntington shuttled between Washington and New York.[56] They rode railroads to build railroads. In Washington they did much of their work at the Willard Hotel, at Fourteenth Street and Pennsylvania Avenue. The Willard was, fittingly, the initial terminus of the Washington Street and Georgetown Street Railroad built by the Cookes and invested in by Salmon Chase. A collection of linked town houses, it grew like the country by adding adjacent real estate. Nathaniel Hawthorne had spent a rainy day there in 1862 and thought its hall and parlors "more justly called the centre of Washington and the Union than either the Capitol, the White House, or the State Department. Everybody may be seen there." Among the politicians "wirepullers, inventors . . . long-winded talkers" and more were "railway directors." There in the cigar smoke haze and calls for "mint-julep, a whisky-skin, a gin-cocktail, a brandy-smash, or a glass of pure Old Rye," men sought advantage.[57]

Seeking to modify the Pacific Railway Act of 1862, Huntington and Durant offered congressmen and others private favors to secure a public bounty. Durant and his allies distributed $250,000 in bonds to those who could help them.[58] This was almost certainly the occasion upon which the Central Pacific gave some of its convertible bonds—bonds that would be later exchangeable for federal bonds—to the men Mark Hopkins called "our friends of influence."[59] Such bonds would have value only if the act passed. For the country as a whole, the Pacific Railway Act of 1864 was the worst act money could buy.

The act would spread loaves and fishes across a continent, and all would multiply. It was taxless finance at its most grandiose. Like its 1862 predecessor, the 1864 act lent the companies $50 million worth of government bonds for thirty years, but it increased the speed with which they would flow to the railroads. The government guaranteed both the interest and the principal on the bonds. In making this promise, the majority of congressmen did not anticipate that it would cost the government any actual money. They assumed that the railroads would earn enough from land sales, government traffic, and freight to pay the semiannual interest on the bonds and that, as traffic increased, the railroads would establish sinking funds to pay off the principal at their maturity in the 1890s. Congress was so confident, or so reckless, that it reduced its own claim on railroad property to a second mortgage and allowed the two railroads to issue, between them, $50 million first mortgage bonds, thus doubling the debt of the roads. In case of default, the government could recover its investment only after the first mortgage bondholders had been satisfied.[60]

Congress combined this recklessness with ineptitude. Congressmen thought they were just lending the railroads $50 million worth of U.S. bonds. But the law was so sloppily drawn and the section on interest payments so ambiguous that the courts later decided that although the interest on the bonds was due semiannually, the railroads did not have to pay the interest as it accrued. They had to pay the government only the total amount of simple interest owed when the bonds matured. So for thirty years the government, not the railroads, would pay the interest on the $50 million worth of bonds.[61]

The courts' interpretation proved an incredible gift to the railroads. Looking at the benefits to the Union Pacific, whose share of the government bonds came to $27,236,512, we can see why. The United States was paying 6 percent interest on these bonds semiannually. At the end of the thirty-year period the Union Pacific would reimburse the government for this simple (not compound) interest and the face value of the bonds. This simple interest would amount to roughly $49 million, which, with principal, amounted to a total debt of $77,000,000. The difference between the $49 million that the railroads owed the United States but retained for thirty years and the amount of money that $49 million could earn as an investment during that time amounted to a tremendous windfall. The United States made semiannual payments of $810,000 in interest on the bonds, and this represented money the Union Pacific did not have to pay but could invest elsewhere. Invested at simple interest of 6 percent, the first payment would have earned $1,433,700 in interest over 29½ years; the last payment would have earned $24,300 for six months. In total the commercial value of the court decision came to $43,000,000 over thirty years. This was a donation to the railroads in addition to the loan of $77,000,000.[62] No other American railroad reaped such a bonanza of guaranteed bonds and interest payments, although the Canadian Pacific later obtained a similar guarantee from its government.[63]

The other piece of government largess—the land grants—followed the same free-lunch logic as the bonds. The Pacific Railway Act of 1864 doubled the land subsidy so that for every mile of road built, the companies would receive 12,800 acres and any coal or iron they contained.[64] The land would not be of much immediate help in building the railroad, although it could serve as security for bonds. As the railroads sold the land to settlers, however, they would receive money to pay off their mortgage bonds and other debts while simultaneously creating new customers and thus revenue.

Donating this land to the railroads would supposedly cost the government nothing. In the United States, and later Canada, the railroads received only the odd-numbered sections within a given township. Imagine a checkerboard that folds down the middle. The railroad right of way is the crease in the board; the red squares are railroad land; the black squares are public land.[65] Because the railroads acted as a magnet pulling people into its checkerboard, the U.S. government could recoup its loss in giving away half the checkerboard by doubling the price of the remaining public land within it from $1.25—the base rate—to $2.50 per acre and cutting the amount given as a homestead from 160 acres to 80 acres. The railroad created increased value; the government, in turn, through the land grant, gave a share of that increased value back to the railroads to reimburse the cost of construction. The doubling of land prices compensated the government for giving half the checkerboard to the railroads. The scheme seemed ingenious and foolproof. Even the greatest critic of railroad land grants, Henry George, regarded the grants as "plausible and ably urged." This same logic led to even more lavish land grants to subsequent transcontinentals.[66]

Railroads received the land equivalent of small countries or, in North American terms, the equivalent of an American state or a Canadian province. The federal grant to the Union Pacific roughly equaled the square mileage of New Hampshire and New Jersey combined. The main line of the Central Pacific got slightly more than the landmass of Maryland. The Kansas Pacific, one of the branches connecting with the Union Pacific trunk, had to settle for Vermont and Rhode Island. A later transcontinental, the Northern Pacific, which brought Cooke and then Henry Villard down, received a total land grant that was the equivalent of converting all of New England into a strip twenty miles wide in the states and forty miles wide in the territories stretching from Lake Superior to Puget Sound. In all, the land grant railroads east and west of the Mississippi received 131,230,358 acres from the United States. If all these federal land grants had been concentrated into a single state, call it Railroadiana, it would now rank third, behind Alaska and Texas, in size. The United States was hardly alone in this. The Canadian Pacific eventually received the equivalent of New Brunswick and Prince Edward Island plus change. This translated to slightly less than Kentucky or slightly more than Indiana.[67] This largess was the main course, but there were other grants that served as a kind of dessert. The Canadian Pacific received additional grants, 1,609,024 acres, for branches. And the American railroads received state land grants totaling 44,224,175 acres, or an area roughly the size of Missouri, with 33 million acres alone coming from Texas, which contained no federal lands.[68] Finally, cities and towns gave the railroads valuable lands for depots and yards, and simply as inducements to create connections.[69]

The government did not actually own much of this land; it belonged to Indians. But Indian ownership had never proved much of an obstacle to congressional schemes. Indeed, the very fact that it belonged to Indians initially seemed an asset in financing western railroads. Instead of land grants from the public domain complicated by competing claims from settlers, land might pass directly from Indians to the railroads. In 1862, the year of the first Pacific Railway Act, Senator Samuel Pomeroy of Kansas had written a railroad purchase clause into the Kickapoo Treaty. It provided for the sale at $1.25 an acre of surplus Kickapoo lands (those left after allotments to tribal members) to the Atchison and Pike's Peak Railroad, which, as it happened, was controlled by Pomeroy. Senator Pomeroy then steered the treaty through the ratification process in the U.S. Senate. The Kickapoos protested that the tribal agent and interpreter had been bribed, that the treaty clauses had not been properly interpreted, and that tribal leaders who objected to the treaty had been removed by the agent. Only one recognized tribal leader had signed the document. There were embarrassing investigations but no action. The treaty stood as a model of how treaties could deliver land directly to corporations, which could then sell the land at a markup to finance railroads. Mark Twain used Pomeroy as the model for his fictional Senator Dilworthy ("the golden-tongued statesman") in *The Gilded Age*, the 1873 novel that gave the era its name. Pomeroy became a man who ever after was less famous than his own parody.[70]

On paper land grants seemed to be foolproof; in operation they seemed the work of fools. The federal government protected its revenue at the expense of states and localities. Taxless finance—subsidizing railroads without direct public taxes—had ironic and unintended consequences: states and localities found that because of delays in issuing patents that conveyed title they could not easily tax railroad lands for the revenue needed to build roads, schools, and the basic infrastructure of local life.[71] The effects would reverberate throughout the rest of the century.

The crowning miscalculation of the 1864 act was its haziness about where the two roads were to meet. By failing to specify a meeting place, the act turned construction into a race for subsidies. The railroads were not racing for the land at the end of their routes—Utah and Nevada lands would be a burden to them—they wanted the bond subsidies. The more miles they built, particularly across the relatively flat desert, the more bonds they got. Whenever Congress couldn't decide on a policy in the American West, its default mode seems to have been to conduct a race. Pitting the Central Pacific against the Union Pacific ensured that what might have been done relatively methodically, efficiently, and cheaply would be done badly, expensively, but quickly. Much of it would have to be redone.

IV. BUILDING WITH OTHER PEOPLE'S MONEY

Getting Congress to increase its subsidies helped Durant and Huntington accomplish the other part of their task: borrowing the rest of the money they needed to build the railroad. The promoters of the Union Pacific and the Central Pacific later claimed that they had risked their honor and fortune on these roads, yet in most cases they possessed relatively little of either. And what they risked, they risked on the construction companies—the Crédit Mobilier, Charles Crocker and Company, and the Contract and Finance Company—that built the Pacific Railroad. To understand what they did, it is best to follow the money, which involves tracing the small amount they put into the railroads and the large amount they eventually took out.

Compared with the act of 1862, the Pacific Railway Act of 1864 reduced the obstacles between the promoters and the government bonds they needed, but obstacles still remained. Both roads now had to build twenty miles of railroad instead of fifty miles before the government would release its first allotment of bonds. And the new act lowered the price per share of the initial $2 million Union Pacific stock issue to $100 from $1,000, while removing restrictions on how much stock any one person could own. It also, however, tightened the requirements for actual investment by requiring that the board of directors make assessments of 5 percent of the par value of the stock every six months until the subscriber had paid its par price.[72] Taken together, these requirements were meant to guarantee substantial private investment and the construction of two railroads of at least twenty miles before the government committed its resources.

The law proved laughably easy to evade. Faced with the twenty-mile requirement, the companies returned to a compliant Congress. In March of 1865 Congress amended the Pacific Railway Act to allow each road to issue 100 miles worth of bonds—at $20,000 per mile—in advance of actual construction.[73] Bonds issued on track yet to be built, however, did not attract investors, and so to strip these bonds of some of their risk and make them negotiable, the Central Pacific made some of them convertible: they could be exchanged for federal bonds when those were released. The Central Pacific and the Union Pacific could now borrow and build with other people's money. As for the requirement that stockholders actually pay the par value of their stock, the United States never enforced it.

The Central Pacific was not federally chartered; it fell under the General Railroad Law of California, which, as amended in 1862, also took steps to ensure that the owners of railroads put their own money at risk. It required that a thousand dollars of stock be subscribed for every mile of railroad, and that 10 percent of the subscription price be paid before the railroad could legally organize. And, in what seemed a strong check on corporate malfeasance, the law made the stockholders personally liable for any debts that the company accrued while they were stockholders. The law sought to limit the amount of money the railroad could borrow to the amount of its capital stock; in practice this clause achieved the reverse. The Central Pacific never sold much stock, and so as it borrowed more and more money, it issued more and more shares to stay in compliance with the law. No cash was paid for this stock, which went to the construction companies owned by the same men who controlled the Central Pacific. The best estimates are that at most $100,000 was paid for shares of the Central Pacific. The company's annual report to the secretary of state of California that claimed $40 million in paid stock subscriptions in 1869 was fraudulent.[74]

By 1865 the promoters of the Pacific Railroad had successfully observed rule number one of building transcontinentals—put little or no money down—and were ready to move on to rule number two: negotiate among yourselves. The device for doing this was the insider construction company that made money by charging far more to build the railroad than the road actually cost. There was little new or original about the device, and this was very likely Durant's plan from the beginning. By receiving its pay partially in cash and partially in railroad securities, including stock, the construction company both profited from building the railroad and owned it. Both Congress and, in the case of the Central Pacific, the state of California had seemingly created a formidable obstacle to insider construction companies by putting personal liability clauses for stockholders in corporate charters and state law. If the railroad failed to pay the debts that its construction created, the debtors could sue the stockholders. That was not good.

There was, however, a way around this. In 1864 George Francis Train, acting for Durant, purchased an investment company named the Pennsylvania Fiscal Agency originally designed to build a southern transcontinental. Its only real asset was its very broad and flexible charter. Train renamed the company the Crédit Mobilier, after a similar French company. First and foremost, the Crédit Mobilier was a limited liability venture, which meant that it could serve to launder any Union Pacific stock that it might acquire. By the terms of its charter, neither the Crédit Mobilier nor its stockholders were responsible for the failure of any firms whose stocks it acquired. Second, the Crédit Mobilier not only was a finance company but it could also be a construction company that would build the railroads.[75]

The Associates, as was their fashion, appear to have blundered into a similar arrangement as a result of circumstance and then refined it by imitating the Crédit Mobilier. Collis P. Huntington and Mark Hopkins were often more opportunistic than calculating. Their greatest gift was recognizing the opportunities that their failures and miscalculations created. The Central Pacific initially employed several independent contractors, but soon decided to let only a single large contract to Charles Crocker and Company, which, as everyone suspected, represented the other Associates. Crocker and Company served as their primitive Crédit Mobilier. As the recipient of stock in partial payment for construction, it became the means for transferring Central Pacific stock into the Associates' pockets, but it did not remove the personal liability clause. Their initial preference was to sell stock, but in February of 1866 Mark Hopkins came to a fine realization. "[H]aving reached the present position [with] so little [stock] in outside hands, I think now it will pay us best to issue as little as possible & calculate to work it into the contractor & make it bring par or over within three years when the annual earnings of the road will be very large." This became their plan.[76]

The final refinements came from Edwin Crocker. By March of 1867 the Crockers had decided that they would "prefer a new construction contract directly to [them]selves and made by the present board." The board issued the contract to a new company, the Contract and Finance Company. The Associates later claimed that they incorporated the Contract and Finance Company in an attempt to attract outside capital, but there is no evidence for this. Its nominal incorporators actually held stock for the five Associates, who never paid anything for it. Instead, they gave their notes for the stock. The Central Pacific paid the Contract and Finance Company inflated prices for constructing the line. The Pacific Railway Commission later estimated that the Central Pacific paid roughly twice the actual cost of construction per mile. In 1868 the Contract and Finance Company received half of its $16,512,000 payment in gold and half in stock in the Central Pacific. This meant that the gold covered the cost of the line and the stock was a bonus. Other transfers in which the Contract and Finance Company received bonds as well as stock were more lucrative still. It was, as Collis P. Huntington wrote years later, "as rotten a corporation as ever lived."[77]

With the subsidies and financial mechanisms in place, there remained only the troublesome requirement of actually constructing railroads. The Central Pacific had already found its man to build railroads. James Harvey Strobridge was a taciturn misanthrope. He was both racist and brutal, but he could drive men and had fallen in with the right crowd when Charles Crocker hired him to head construction on the Central Pacific.[78] Strobridge hated the Chinese, and Leland Stanford, the president of the Central Pacific, had tried to exclude Chinese—the "dregs of Asia"—from California while governor. Both, however, came to see the advantage of good workers who could be employed at wages below those of white labor. Chinese labor proved to be the Central Pacific's salvation.[79]

In the East the end of the war freed up a pool of men experienced in building railroads quickly and under difficult conditions. General Jack Casement had learned railroad construction before the war and how to organize and lead men during it. He took charge of construction crews on the Union Pacific that would eventually build railroads and fight Indians who opposed their passage.

The chief engineer for the project was the corrupt and largely incompetent Silas Seymour, but the man responsible for much of the building was the more complicated Grenville Dodge. Dodge was from New England. He had moved to Iowa and, when the Civil War broke out, had fought in Missouri. Unlike many of the men who became active in the transcontinentals, he was no abolitionist. He hated abolitionists and he hated black people; he hated immigrants and Catholics with impartiality. He was an eclectic hater who hated people who often hated one another. He hated loudly and demonstratively. In a Boston restaurant, irritated by a black man who kept his eyes "on the brass buttons" of Dodge's coat, Dodge shoved a dish of stewed oysters in the man's face and then ordered another. He thought himself "highly eulogized by the crowd for giving the Niggar so just a punishment for his audacity."[80]

After moving West, Dodge got a job under Peter Dey on the Rock Island line. Dey was a skilled engineer who would later resign from the Union Pacific out of disgust with its insider construction contracts. Dodge was, like Dey, competent and, like so many men Dodge joined on the Union Pacific, corrupt. He was a man who would always exaggerate his talents, but he was not without talent. Often nasty, occasionally ridiculous, he was also sporadically and surprisingly able. He served in the Union army, and early in his military service he accidentally shot himself with a revolver he forgot he had in his pocket. He would describe it as a war wound. In battle at Pea Ridge, he behaved credibly and bravely, and yet his best moments could still become Grenville Dodge moments. A Confederate shell hit a branch, and the branch fell, hitting Dodge and knocking him from his horse. In Dodge's telling, the fallen branch became a wound that left him lying on the battle-field for ten days before he could be hauled 250 miles over rough roads to doctors who said he would not live. The original Confederate artillery shell was real, and Dodge did suffer a contusion from the falling branch that earned him a furlough; the rest was all fiction. Dodge's ability to build rail-roads was, however, not fictional. In 1864, using his troops and freedmen, he had in forty days restored 102 miles of railroad between Nashville and Decatur destroyed by the retreating Confederates. With only hand tools—axes, picks, and spades—they had rebuilt 182 bridges, albeit with temporary spans, laid rails, and repaired cars.[81]

With competent engineers in their employ and federal bonds flowing into their treasuries, the year 1865 began auspiciously for both the Union Pacific and the Central Pacific. By the summer the Central Pacific had made it as far as Clipper Gap, forty-two miles from Sacramento. The normally cautious Mark Hopkins saw profit in California, but his optimism bred more caution. Why not just stop at the California line? From there they could tap the Comstock Lode traffic, monopolize California, and let some-one else have Nevada and Utah, where there was little of promise.[82]

They would not stop, because they could not stop; they needed the bonds that building in Nevada would provide. The Central Pacific did not reach the summit of the Sierras until July of 1867. Building so slowly turned the flow of federal bonds into a trickle and hurt their ability to sell their own first mortgage bonds. They had to borrow more and more heavily. By February of 1867 their load of debt, secured in large part by personal notes, made E. B. Crocker "tremble for the future." A financial panic and the call-ing in of debts could destroy them. To get more federal bonds quickly, they jumped ahead of the stalled construction in the Sierras and began building into Nevada.[83] Only in June of 1868 did Crocker finally wire Huntington that they had crossed the mountains and linked their Nevada and California construction.[84]

The Union Pacific faced a different set of difficulties. Durant had origi-nally issued construction contracts to a dummy company headed by Her-bert Hoxie. This was the contract that led the Union Pacific's chief engineer, Peter Dey, to resign in disgust before the railroad laid any track. Once Congress allowed the company to issue bonds in advance of building, Hoxie assigned his contract to the Crédit Mobilier.[85] These first Union Pacific securities lacked federal guarantees, and so they were hypothecated at killing interest. "Hypothecate" is a wonderful old verb that in the nineteenth century most often meant to offer stocks or bonds as security for a loan. In this case the loans carried interest rates of nearly 20 percent. In need of cash, Durant turned to Boston capitalists to invest not in the Union Pacific but in the Crédit Mobilier. Chief among them were Oliver and Oakes Ames, the "Kings of Spades," who had made a fortune in New England manufacturing shovels. They had been active in western railroads before the Civil War, and Oakes Ames was also a member of the House Select Committee on Pacific Railroads. Along with them came Sidney Dillon, a Connecticut railroad contractor, who would be intimately involved with the Union Pacific for much of the rest of the century.[86]

Like the Associates of the Central Pacific, the Ameses and Dillons were part of an interlocking network of particular people centered on a particular place who invested in western railroads. The Associates were outliers, located as they were in Sacramento, and they would gradually be sucked into the orbit of New York, where they raised and borrowed their money. Other early railroad networks arose in Philadelphia, particularly around Jay Cooke and then Tom Scott, but they gradually declined as the fortunes of these two men declined. Networks centered on Boston and New York were far more lasting. They outlived the rise and fall of particular individuals. They were the real centers of control of western railroads. They dominated boards of directors with interlocking combinations of kin and men with longtime business relationships such as those growing out of the China trade.[87]

Over the years as things went sour, the various parties in the Union Pacific told different stories about why they went in, but in all the stories there is a Yankee shrewdness that was, in practice, almost too shrewd by half. The shrewdness recognized that if the Union Pacific paid a construction company inflated prices to build a railroad, then the construction company could profit no matter what happened to the road. The Bostonians also knew, however, that if everything had been going smoothly,

Durant would not have needed them. They had cash; Durant needed cash. The pump had to be primed, and the priming was the investment by the Ameses and the Bostonians. For the scheme to work, Durant and the Ames faction had to retain control of both the Crédit Mobilier and the Union Pacific. And so an elaborate charade took place. When construction contracts were assigned to the Crédit Mobilier, the Union Pacific wrote a check to the Crédit Mobilier in partial payment for construction. The Crédit Mobilier then returned the check in exchange for Union Pacific stock. The fiction allowed them to meet the requirement that the stock be sold at par, although no cash really changed hands. The Crédit Mobilier became the Union Pacific's largest stockholder. It later distributed the stock among its own stockholders as a dividend. The rest of the construction contract involved a payment in other Union Pacific securities. The men receiving the stock and other securities were the men who controlled both the Union Pacific and the Crédit Mobilier. Very few of them lived anywhere near where the line did business. Federal loans had created a railroad under the control of New York and Boston businessmen most of whom had invested little or no money of their own in the Union Pacific.[88] (See Appendix, Map A.)

The Ames brothers did not trust Durant; no one in his right mind would trust Durant, and the railroad and the Crédit Mobilier soon endured a war of faction. Durant's double-dealing and the widespread distrust he inspired had made him a burden to the whole enterprise, and the Ames faction forced its way onto both the Union Pacific and the Crédit Mobilier boards. True to his peculiar genius, Durant tried to destroy the Bostonians by employing a tactic no one expected from him: honesty. In 1867 Durant, on his own initiative, took the construction contract for the next section of the Union Pacific away from the Crédit Mobilier and gave it to another party, the aptly named L. B. Boomer, who would act as Durant's agent. The new contract allowed only a modest profit above the real cost of construction. The Crédit Mobilier was bleeding, and Durant was, in effect, denying the Bostonians the transfusion of bonds and cash that provided the Crédit Mobilier's only chance to live. Durant would watch it die; he would survive it. The result was a coup that displaced Durant from the Crédit Mobilier, and a long and tangled struggle within the Union Pacific. In the end the furious Bostonians canceled the Boomer contract and secured an extravagant construction contract for Oakes Ames, who then assigned it to the Crédit Mobilier. In the end they outmaneuvered Durant.[89]

The Bostonians defeated Durant, yet ironically what saved the Union Pacific was the success of a Durant ally, Cornelius Bushnell, in imitating Jay Cooke. Following the techniques that Jay Cooke had pioneered, Bushnell advertised Union Pacific bonds aggressively and sent agents to leading cities.[90] He created a market for Union Pacific securities, and the Crédit Mobilier turned them into cash. The lucrative Ames contract multiplied the original investment of the Bostonians many times over.[91] In the late 1860s Union Pacific bonds rose above par, and the stock even reached 30 in 1868. The risk seemed to have paid off.[92]

The Central Pacific also ultimately found salvation through techniques pioneered by Jay Cooke. Following the war, Fisk and Hatch, part of Cooke's Civil War consortium, made the regard and trust that they had reaped from the war available to the railroads.[93] They marketed railroad bonds on commission and also sold them to syndicates of bankers and large investors, in Europe and the United States, who bought them at a discount and resold them. The Central Pacific and other transcontinental railroads, their bankers, and the syndicates together lured investors, who had first ventured into the financial markets during the Civil War, along the financial gangplank one small step at a time. Investors proceeded from government bonds to government-secured railroad bonds, to convertible bonds, to mortgage bonds vouched for by the same people who sold the government bonds, to a whole array of financial instruments, and from there, potentially, into the drink. Fisk and Hatch were working with Huntington by 1865 and eventually offered the Central Pacific bond issues in all their profusion and variety.[94] There were first mortgage bonds and second mortgage bonds; there were mortgages on the trunk line and mortgages on the branches. There were land grant bonds and income bonds. There were bonds on anything and everything that investors might accept as collateral. The bankers as well as the railroads they represented trumpeted the security of these investments, but they were in effect so many carnival barkers. There was no real monitoring of the figures railroads offered in their annual reports or bankers in their prospectuses.[95]

By 1868 the crisis had passed for the Crédit Mobilier and the Contract and Finance Company, but how much profit flowed into the pockets of their organizers is difficult to establish. By the late 1860s the Crédit Mobilier was granting dividends to stockholders, including prominent politicians, of 50 percent and 100 percent a year. Charles Francis Adams made an early estimate of the total profit on investment at 750 percent.[96] In dollar terms reasonable nineteenth- and early twentieth-century estimates have run from $11 million to $20 million.[97] Forty years ago Robert Fogel put the profit of the Crédit Mobilier at an upper limit of $16.5 million, and estimated the promoters' profit for the period between 1864 and 1869 at from 480 percent to 610 percent.[98] By all calculations, the insiders accrued millions, and the Union Pacific compiled an immense debt.

The financial returns of Crocker and Company and the Contract and Finance Company are even harder to determine, for the simple reason that, when threatened with a congressional investigation, the books disappeared, never to resurface.[99] By the calculations of the Pacific Railway Commission, established by Congress to investigate the transcontinentals in 1887, the bond issues, federal and corporate, paid to Crocker and Company and the Contract and Finance Company roughly matched the cost of the road. Certainly when local and state bonds and revenue from the road up until 1870 are added, there appears to have been more than enough to build the road without any substantial investment from the Associates.

As Governor Newton Booth of California drily observed in a San Francisco speech in 1874, "It is easier, more delightful, and more profitable to build with other peoples' money than our own." The economic historian Heywood Fleisig estimated that the Associates of the Central Pacific Railroad took an actual investment, not all of it theirs, of about $275,000 and leveraged it into a corporation capitalized at $135,346,964 in 1873, a figure higher than the $116,658,824 capitalization of what was widely regarded as the best railroad in the United States, Tom Scott's Pennsylvania Railroad. A good deal of that $135 million was water—bloated securities with a face value much higher than what the Associates of the Central Pacific who owned them had paid for them (or could sell them). Real money came from taxpayers through federal, state, and local subsidies, and it came through bonds.[100] Investors paid cash for some part of the $52.5 million in bonds outstanding in 1873. An indeterminate part of that went into the railroads, as distinct from the pockets of their owners.[101]

By the later calculations of the Pacific Railway Commission, the Associates derived a profit of more than $10 million from paying themselves to build the road. The ultimate profit, however, came largely from the sale of securities. To realize that profit the Associates had to create a market for their heavily watered stock. Mark Hopkins was too sanguine in 1865 when he thought the rise in stock would come within two or three years. And above all, Mark Hopkins did not count on Sam Brannan.

In 1870 Leland Stanford made one of his many expensive mistakes when Sam Brannan tried to sell back his 200 shares of Central Pacific stock at par: $100 a share. Brannan, once a leader of the Mormon colony in California, was a buffoon, but a calculating and shrewd one. He had sparked the Gold Rush by walking through San Francisco waving his hat, holding a vial of gold, and shouting, "Gold! Gold! Gold from the American River." He left the church, became wealthy selling supplies to the miners, briefly ran a railroad, and used his wealth to become a legendary philanderer and drunk.[102] Drunk or sober, he was no man to brush off, and when Stanford brushed him off, Brannan sued, demanding a full financial accounting of the Central Pacific. Anticipation of what the Brannan suit might reveal terrified the Associates, who hurried to suppress the suit while buying up as much original stock as they could to prevent other suits. They were saved by Mrs. Brannan, who divorced Sam and received his stock as part of the divorce settlement. The Associates bought it from her at $850 a share, effectively squashing the suit.[103]

Brannan's suit and the books the Associates wanted no one to see halted the Associates' immediate attempts to sell the stock. Silas Sanderson, the company's lawyer, cautioned against selling any Central Pacific stock acquired through the Contract and Finance Company because the purchasers would acquire the right "to call the directors to account." Since the directors did not want to be called to account, they could not sell until they found a way to reorganize the railroad and have new stock issued.[104]

V. GOLDEN SPIKE

None of the history that led up to the transcontinentals and none of the ambivalence of the men whose lives came to revolve around them is revealed in the famous photographs of the trains meeting at Promontory Summit. There are only the trains, the workers, the dignitaries, the bystanders, and the Utah desert. Promontory Summit quickly became less a place than a metaphor, and as a metaphor, Promontory Summit was almost too perfect. Leland Stanford—ex-grocer, ex–Civil War governor of California, and on May 10, 1869, the current president of the Central Pacific Railroad Company—tapped a silver hammer on an iron spike. Rigged to telegraph wire, the spike sent a signal across the nation, triggering bursts of cannon fire in New York and San Francisco and of celebration and speech making across the country. The Union Pacific now ran 1,032 miles from Omaha to Ogden. The Central Pacific ran 881 miles from Ogden to Sacramento. The connections forged by the railroad were like that burst of energy transmitted across North America.[105]

The golden spikes Stanford brought to Promontory Summit to commemorate the event were inscribed with conventional purposes of nationalism and commerce. One, contributed by David Hewes, a San Francisco contractor, memorialized the brighter vision that Americans imagined the Pacific Railroad would achieve.

> *May God continue the unity of our country*
> *as this Railroad unites the two great oceans of the world.*
> *Presented by David Hewes, San Francisco*

The railroad was no longer necessary for the assertion of federal authority; the Civil War had settled that. And connection of the seas would never come to pass in the way that Hewes and other Americans imagined. Asian trade would by and large soon flow through the Indian Ocean to the new Suez Canal rather than across the Pacific and North America. Taken literally, the sentiments on the spike, like the date inscribed on it—May 8, not May 10—were hopeful, plausible, and mistaken. In that, the engraved spike was true to the Pacific Railroad's origins.

A country whose politics and whose waterways from the Atlantic to the Mississippi had, despite the Erie Canal, always oriented it largely north–south now also ran east–west. The railroads, like that signal across the wires, caused millions to imagine events and possibilities they could neither see nor hear. The transcontinentals were from their beginning always running ahead of schedule, always approaching places that did not quite exist. The transcontinentals were the means to something beyond themselves even if there was a certain lack of clarity about what those things might be. They were more than business propositions. They were, like the Civil War, exercises in nation building, but whereas the Civil War settled the question of the national authority of the central state and sutured together the North and the South, the transcontinentals opened the question of a national market and the relation of the East and the West.

A RAILROAD LIFE

H. K. THOMAS

Fittingly enough for a stationmaster on the Union Pacific Railroad in Wyoming Territory in 1870, H. K. Thomas's diary is bound in rawhide with his name and his town's name—Laramie—branded on the cover. Equally fitting for the place, there was snow on the day the diary opens, September 23, 1870. There was no sign of the pay car, and the number 4 train was nine hours late out of Ogden because of an accident on the Central Pacific. When the pay car arrived a week later, the weather felt like midsummer, at least during the day.[1] In Laramie the only constant was the wind. "Whole gale" meant that not only sand but also gravel was moving.[2]

Rawhide was easy enough to come by in Laramie in 1870. The railroad replaced domesticated animals as the engine for long-distance travel, but it multiplied their numbers for most everything else.[3] Mules, horses, and cattle—going both east and west—filled the trains.[4] The cattlemen were already shifting from their earlier year-round reliance on valley lands to transhumance—driving the herds into the surrounding mountains in the summer and wintering them in the valley.[5] The cattle moved into mountains whose forests still burned in the summer, covering the valley in a thick, smoky haze.[6] Long drives moved stock north from Texas, but after that the animals traveled by train. On July 19, 1871, Thomas recorded his trouble in "loading a large herd of wild Texas cattle . . . the worst lot to handle that [he] ever saw." Try as he and his men might, they could not load any more than 400 per day, and that meant four days' work to take care of 1,500 head. Even at this pace there were losses among the recalcitrant cattle. The station crew had killed one and injured several others that clear, warm July day.[7]

The pay car—whose absence meant a scarcity of cash in Laramie—and the cattle were just two signs of how virtually all lives in Laramie in 1870 were becoming railroad lives.[8] Nearby there were mines to produce the coal that fueled the railroads. And then there were the gold and silver mines. Thomas invested in syndicates that financed a miner or two to try their luck in new strikes in Utah and Wyoming. News of a strike sped the trains, carrying men as close to the mines as they could get before heading off into the mountains.[9] The railroad brought the bread of Wyoming Territory, and it brought the circuses.

The railroad instantly created the new without eradicating—at least not immediately—the old. Buffalo herds grazed along the tracks in 1870, and Thomas rode the train to Como to hunt elk. Those that he killed too far from the tracks he left for the wolves.[10] But game was declining as cattle were increasing, and the Laramie hunters in anticipation of new game laws killed all the antelope and elk they could find as 1870 approached 1871.[11]

There were still Indians around Laramie in 1870, Lakotas apparently, but Thomas did not always specify. He apparently did not know and apparently did not much care. One day he recorded that forty Indians came into nearby Fort Sanders, entering under a flag of truce. The commander ignored the flag and detained them—or threatened to—until horses stolen in the neighborhood were returned.[12] That he noted forty Indians was typical of Thomas. He was a man of numbers. He recorded the first execution at Cheyenne, the date and the time, Friday, April 21, 1871, at 12:30 P.M., and the blood quantum of the victim: a "half-breed known by the name of Boyer." Some feared that the Sioux would attempt to rescue him, "but nothing of the kind took place. The execution passed off quietly."[13]

The only Indian Thomas actually met was John Richau, "the outlaw, half breed of Red Cloud's tribe."[14] Richau came to Laramie on business, railroad business. He had "about 100 mules for sale and expects to sell them to a Montana freighter who arrived from the West today." On a cold, blustery day, Thomas passed the time with Richau and "found him to be on the square." The freighter, Kirkendall, would ship seventy-one of Richau's mules to Ogden; he drove the rest to Fort Fetterman.[15]

There were horse thieves. Sheriff Boswell promptly captured some inept ones in Hallville and brought them back to Laramie on the train—train number 4, as Thomas noted, but Laramie was less Wild West than industrial

West.[16] It was from the beginning a workingman's town, and its violence largely workingmen's violence. Men got paid and men drank. When the "soldiers have been paid off at the Fort," they had "a glorious time in town," Thomas, a temperance man, wrote sarcastically. "Many of them have recd. Broken heads, besides losing all their money."[17]

There were two "scrapes," as Thomas called them, on December 8. One involved guns, but no one was hurt. The other, at Sherman, was a quarrel between miners that was terminated by a blow of a shovel to the head of a man named Wood. Wood died. His assailant, Shipman, was later convicted of manslaughter by a jury of "three or four Dutchmen, a couple of Irishmen, one 'nigger' and the balance women."[18]

Men were armed, and when they drank, they were careless with their weapons. On December 12, 1870, Thomas "returned from the saloon opposite to our office, the general headquarters of all negroes in town. Walls, the pastry cook of the Laramie Hotel, was stretched out there dead having been shot by a waiter belonging to the same hotel named Lawrence. The bullet must have passed right through the poor old man's heart. He was a very quiet old fellow, have known him for a long time and I never saw the least thing out of the way in him. Those who saw the affair seem to say that it was accidental."[19] Lawrence, too, would be convicted of manslaughter.[20]

Far more dangerous than drink or the quarrels of men was the work itself. Just before Christmas an explosion in the coal mines at Carbon injured five men and set the mines on fire. They burned for weeks.[21] In January a brakeman "got his hand badly smashed coupling cars."[22] A bridge watchman, run over by a train, died a few days later.[23] The danger brought solidarity of a sort to workingmen against the men who employed them. But the solidarity was often shaky among transient workers, and it sometimes had to be enforced at the barrel of a gun. When five miners broke ranks and returned to work during the strike at the coal mines in Carbon, thirty miners armed themselves and waited for them to come out of the mines. When the government intervened, it was not on the side of the strikers. Orders had "been issued for a Co. of U.S. troops to be sent to the scene of the trouble from Ft. Steele."[24] The troops arrived quickly by railroad, ending the confrontation. Management fired the leaders of the strike and began importing Scandinavians to work the mine.[25]

The station at Laramie and scores like it were points where the relentless moving and the passing to and fro essential to the new industrial order were concentrated, recorded, and taxed. It was all traffic to H. K. Thomas, and he records it as heavy and light in his diary and much more specifically in the fortnightly reports that he dreaded writing and that took up considerable time. Thomas can judge the pace of business by how heavily laden were the freight and passenger cars that passed. When they grew too light, crews were laid off.[26] In the fall of 1870 the passenger traffic was mostly through passengers—190 on the number 3, as Thomas noted—heading toward the West Coast.[27] But such traffic could, and did, fall off in a matter of days. By October the traffic was light, and number 4 from the coast was carrying only thirty-five passengers.[28] In late January of 1871 "No. 6 was a heavy train of Tea, silk, Ore and four cars of fat cattle from Catton and Co."[29] In May of 1871 the traffic was heavy with coal—forty cars in one day.[30]

The mines spurred most of the local traffic. In April of 1871 there was a "great rush of passengers to the newly discovered mines in Utah, very heavy trains going west."[31] Two days after the miners passed, "a large number of Medical men are going west for the purpose of attending some convention in California."[32]

All of this was the commerce for which the railroads were built. Cattle, coal, medical men, and miners all reduced down to money. All these railroad lives could be calculated as revenue and expenses. The "ticket business very dull," Thomas wrote on January 8, 1871, "my quarter monthly report reached only $108.20 being lower by large odds than I have ever seen it here."[33]

The scheduled passage of trains intensified the odd ambience of the nineteenth-century West: in the place where Americans imagined lives to be lived most intensely and immediately, most of the people were emotionally displaced. They had left part of themselves somewhere else, the place they called home. In the year his diary covers, H. K. Thomas never referred to Laramie as home. Massachusetts was home. The railroad connected him with home. "Nearly every day I receive one and sometimes two papers from home," he recorded in March 1871, "more than I can find time to read."[34]

Home was where letters came from, particularly letters from Nellie, each numbered consecutively and each answered, and numbered, in turn. Each time Thomas visited home, which he could do in less than a week over the railroad, the old sequence of numbering stopped and a new one began. It was 127 letters since he had visited Nellie on September 25.[35] He visited home and Nellie in November for three glorious weeks. The tension between the still great distance and the new ability to bridge it quickly showed up in small things. Thomas returned to Laramie so quickly—in five days—that he had no time to adjust and was "very blue" on his return. Massachusetts was in one sense so close that when he forgot his toothbrush, his family sent it to him as if he had merely gone over to the next town.[36] It was so close that when, in May, R. Robinson, an old neighbor, passed through with his family on the way to California, he brought a picture of Nellie. Thomas was disappointed. He did "not think it looks quite natural enough." But home was also so far away that these tokens brought by train only tantalized. The numbers on the letters toted up the distance. Letter 27 arrived from Nellie that evening.[37]

Home was someplace else, but even poor men were so close to that someplace else now that when the worst happened, they could return. When Walls the pastry cook died of Lawrence's careless bullet, "the colored men around town . . . subscribed enough money to get a very fine casket and to send the body . . . home to his family in Alton Ill."[38]

The black men Walls and Lawrence, the white New Englander Thomas: the trains made the town seem diverse and promiscuous, but there were lines clearly drawn. Thomas sympathized with the freedmen in the town, but there were lines that neither blacks nor whites were supposed to cross. Sympathy with black men was one thing; socializing together was another. When they did, people noticed. On a smoky Friday in August 1871, as fires burned in the mountains, Thomas recorded "a great sensation here last night" in the shape of a "Fifteenth Amendment ball. Several of our boys attended and they have been the subject of comment ever since and probably will be for some time to come."[39] The trains themselves, however, were not segregated. Thomas could not control the people who rode the trains, but he could judge them. Two days before the Fifteenth Amendment ball, a train of Mormon immigrants had passed through on their way to Utah: "a low looking set taken as a whole, ugly and dirty."[40]

The railroad was Thomas's job, his link with home, and the courier in his romance with Nellie. Stationmaster in love, he recorded the letters the way he recorded freight, by their size and their frequency. He worried when the letters were late and light.[41] Even his dalliances on the side took place over the roads. In late February 1871 he was "much surprised to receive a letter from Lizzie Holbrook today (Somerville Mass.)." He replied, but only a short letter. A second set of correspondence ensued.[42]

H. K. Thomas was attentive to work, to Nellie, and to his possibilities. He lived at the Laramie Hotel, paying Mrs. Harper a dollar a day for board.[43] He was, it appeared, an active Mason and regularly attended lodge meetings.[44] He turned down an opportunity to run as a Republican for the Territorial Legislature.[45] He recorded rumors about who was rising in the ranks—"Mr. Sickles, our Chief engineer is to succeed Mr. Hammond as General Superintendent"—and the corporate politics of the road.[46] The railroad magnates Fisher Ames, Tom Scott, and Leland Stanford all entered into his diary, even as they were utterly unaware of his existence.

Thomas always remained alert to advantage. He introduced himself to passenger agents of other roads as they passed through so that he could get passes over their roads when he traveled east.[47] It was a privilege of his job, like shortchanging customers and passing counterfeit bills.[48] This casual dishonesty was apparently common. When railroad employees quit and left town, they "step[ped] out" on their unpaid board bills.[49] Offered the "Wahsatch [sic]" station, Thomas refused it, holding out instead for Evanston, due to open in the fall.[50]

Thomas had a presentiment of trouble, a stationmaster's presentiment. Letters were late and light sporadically during the summer of 1871.[51] The trouble came in August.

Monday Aug. 7, 1871: Weather quite pleasant. Recd. a letter from Nellie dated at Brewster, Aug. 2, probably the last but one that I shall ever receive from her. A sociable was held this evening at the hotel, the event being the departure of Revd. Jon. Cowell to Santa Fe, New Mexico. The Laramie Band discoursed some choice music so says the Laramie Sentinel.[52]

He wrote a reply on August 8. "Frailty, thy name is woman," he noted in the diary. After that his diary entries grew more sporadic. Nellie's last letter—announcing an engagement, perhaps—arrived on August 28, 1871.[53]

The hurt Nellie had inflicted moved all too easily into a more general misogyny that took the form of ridiculing Wyoming women in politics. Wyoming had enfranchised women, and in the fall of 1871 women were in full political activity. Thomas thought it amusing to see women "in different conveyances electioneering, they are running around in every direction carting up voters." But he seemed more angry than amused. The women were "as a general thing making complete asses of themselves."[54]

Amid shipments of tea and engines slowed because they were forced to burn wood, the diary drifted to a close in September of 1871, a year after it had started. A well-known lawyer was found dead in his bed, presumably from an overdose of morphine that he had picked up the habit of using. Fires still burned in the mountains, driving game into the valley. A bear was seen just outside town. Halfway down, the last page is ripped off, perhaps to remove an entry, perhaps only for a scrap of paper to write a note. Most of the rest of the diary is empty except for two pages.[55] Both contain poems. The longer reads,

> *Love thee?*
> *Oh yes, so well, so tenderly*
> *Thou art loved, adored by me*
> *Fame, fortune, wealth and liberty*
> *Were worthless without thee*
> *Though brimmed with blessings pure and rare*
> *Life's cup before me lay*

Unless thy love were mingled there
I'd spurn the draught away
Love thee? So well, so tenderly
Thou art loved, adored by me
Fame fortune, wealth and liberty
Are worthless without thee[56]

The poem was the last remnant of a railroad romance, love projected across a thousand miles. The railroads projected love, and they did so alongside imperial power. The forty Indians threatened by the military, the lone Indian dead at the end of a rope—an alien justice and a terrible violence delivered by rail. The railroads reconstructed space into empire. Railroads were tools of dispossession and possession alike. In Nellie's and Thomas's love letters they linked Wyoming and Massachusetts in an imaginative whole as necessary to American empire as the guns the soldiers carried.

CHAPTER 2

❧

ANNUS HORRIBILIS: 1873

I stay in my office not knowing just what to do.

—COLLIS P. HUNTINGTON, SEPTEMBER 1873[1]

ITERALLY AND FIGURATIVELY, railroads were creatures of the seasons. The railroads had supposedly conquered nature. When lakes, rivers, and canals froze, halting water transportation, they could, at least potentially, run on. When wagons sank into the mud following spring thaws, the railroads rattled forward across seemingly insurmountable barriers no matter what the weather. Or so it seemed. But not only could weather halt the railroads; it turned out that the very capital that sustained them was seasonal, ebbing and flowing with agricultural cycles of planting and harvest. Only in politics could the railroads manufacture their own weather, but that weather grew stormier and stormier until their blithe forecasts of perpetual spring vanished into a long winter of political and financial discontent.

Other aspiring transcontinentals found hope and inspiration with the completion of the Pacific Railroad; they found even more hope in the winter of 1869 when the Pacific Railroad faced its first great challenge and failed, miserably and nearly completely. Failures were the lifeblood of the transcontinentals. The failure of the Union had secured the subsidizing of the Pacific Railroad and in quick succession a host of other routes to other destinations on the Pacific Coast. The actual completion of the Pacific Railroad had proved that transcontinentals could be built, but it did not present any convincing argument for why more should be built. The country had its transcontinental railroad. Why build another one, let alone two or three or more? Why not wait until it was clear they were needed? That, after all, was how Americans usually built railroads. The answer that rival promoters offered was winter.

The claim that technology had conquered nature, time, and space turned out to be premature in regard to snow and ice. The cuts dug at such labor and expense through rises in the land to keep the line level filled with snow that buried the tracks and halted trains on the Union Pacific for more than a month. There were lessons in this about the complicated relation of railroads and nature, but engineers treated the snow and ice as technical problems to be solved by snow sheds in the mountains, snow fences on the plains, and plows on engines to dig through packed snow in the cuts.

There was a respite for the railroad in the winter of 1870–71, but when winter storms hit in 1871–72 traffic ceased to flow on both the Central Pacific and the Union Pacific for weeks at a time. By early December of 1871 the major passenger depots east of the Sierras resembled small cities under siege. Nothing entered and nothing left.[2] In mid-December, San Francisco's Christmas was stranded someplace out in the mountains and plains. San Francisco's merchants were short 150 cars of holiday goods and "threatening to ship by Panama hereafter."[3] Then, on December 19, a heavy storm hit California, taking out bridges, blowing down telegraph lines, and forcing the Central Pacific desperately to reroute traffic within California.[4] By December 21 the storm had been raging for sixty hours, and the barometer had fallen to the lowest point recorded up to that time in the state. The Central Pacific's workers kept the main line open, but the branch line from Sacramento to San Francisco Bay failed them. It, like other Central Pacific connecting lines, went down in a jumble of lost bridges, mud slides, flooded track, and collapsed embankments. The railroad reached San Francisco only by sending goods from Sacramento by river.[5]

The winter became a far worse nightmare for the Union Pacific. The storms that had begun in October created a snow blockade that shut the line entirely for nearly a month starting in mid-December. The blizzards defeated the initial deployment of snow fences and snowplows. The snow in the cuts was so dense and packed that the locomotives pushing the plows broke down. Passengers languished in stranded trains in places they could not even name. Goods did not move.[6] The only benefit to come out of it was the Union Pacific's adoption of rotary plows—giant blades turning on the front of steam engines—to clear the cuts. These helped, but they hardly solved the problem.

Bad winters plagued the Pacific Railroad throughout the 1870s, but even when the tracks were clear the steep grades proved a curse. In 1876 it took two engines to haul fifteen passenger cars, five of them empty, over the Sierras. The same engines could haul a slower freight train of nineteen cars, providing the tracks were good. This was the practical limit of a Central Pacific train leaving or entering California.[7]

With bad winters stopping transcontinental traffic and steep grades limiting it, there had to be a better route. Cyrus K. Holliday had launched the Atchison, Topeka, and Santa Fe Railroad from under the cottonwood trees of Wakarusa Creek in Kansas in the spring of 1869. The railroad ran five miles, but Holliday foresaw the track touching Galveston, Mexico City, San Francisco, and Santa Fe.[8] Its more southerly route would avoid the Pacific Railroad's disastrous encounters with winter.

The Atlantic and Pacific confidently claimed a route along the 35th parallel to San Francisco preferable for "its shortness, for its temperate climate, for the abundance of wood, water, and game." The route, in fact, crossed Indian Territory and plunged into the Great Plains before taking on hundreds of miles of deserts and mountains.[9] No matter. L. U. Reavis, a promoter and railroad publicist, informed the readers of the *Inland Monthly* of the "important fact" that the railroad had "for its axis the January isothermal line of forty-one degrees." All the great men of Europe and Asia had supposedly appeared within a few degrees of this line, which was the "path of empire." The Atlantic and Pacific was thus "in harmony with nature herself" in accomplishing the "destiny or mission of our people on the North American continent."[10]

Reavis became something of an expert in discerning the congruence between railway lines, nature, and American destiny. He later performed the same service for the Mexican International: "Let our second coming into the Mexican nation be like unto a divine mission, to regulate and reinvigorate old customs, old ideas and old institutions, and herald the progress and prosperity, the faith and mental illuminations of our race now dawning upon the western hemisphere which is destined to wrap the world in the new liberty given to mankind by this nation."[11]

Routes had multiplied like rabbits during and immediately after the Civil War, and in the early 1870s promoters saw the opportunity to make them real. The U.S. Congress had chartered the Northern Pacific to go from Duluth to somewhere on Puget Sound. A road north of the troubled Pacific Railroad seemed an odd answer to the problems with western winters, but promoters of the road made such claims for the mildness of the climate on the northern plains that skeptics dubbed it the banana belt.[12] The Kansas Pacific—designed to be a branch of the Union Pacific—threatened to become a transcontinental in its own right. Promoters pushed for a Canada Pacific Railroad to go, somehow, across the continent from the St. Lawrence to British Columbia.

The railroad network expanded rapidly following the war, more than doubling in the United States, from 35,085 miles in 1865 to 70,784 in 1873, with peak building between 1870 and 1872. In 1871 alone the United States added 7,670 miles of railroad. The greatest amount of building centered on Chicago and took place in what now is the Midwest, but railroads west of the Missouri, including Texas, formed a substantial tail of nearly 7,515 miles.[13]

The actual railroad network of tracks, bridges, stations, and trains had a doppelgänger—a network of promoters and investors who linked together separate lines. Some of these links were obvious: all the big transcontinentals relied on overlapping boards of directors to unite the various lines in their system. Less obvious were the networks that linked together seemingly separate lines. These networks revealed themselves in common members—largely from New York and Boston—of the boards of directors.

Eventually, membership on railroad boards overlapped with membership on the boards of banks and trust companies, which became a kind of headquarters for organizing these linked investments. So extensive and overlapping were these New York and Boston networks that it is hard to understand how Gilded Age Americans ever thought business was about individualism instead of the social links created by family through kinship and intermarriage or friendship through longtime associations. The railroads drew directors from all over the country, but, again with the exception of the Associates, directors drawn from west of the Missouri and even from Chicago were loosely networked, usually serving on a single road.[14]

Key Boston directors, however, were tightly networked. They formed three major groups. The one around John Murray Forbes served largely to link together the various Burlington roads, but through Jefferson Coolidge and Charles Paine it linked to a much denser network centered on Thomas Nickerson. The Nickerson network joined together at various times, the Atchison, the Mexican Central, the Atlantic and Pacific. The final group was the Ames family, centered on the Union Pacific. Benjamin Cheney, Charles Paine, Jefferson Coolidge, and Frederick Ames at various moments linked together all three Boston groups and railroads, and roads not so directly connected with Boston capital, such as the Chicago and North Western, the Missouri Pacific, and the Northern Pacific. The Boston network of the Ames family eventually became linked with a New York network centered on Jay Gould and his associates. In addition, there was a Vanderbilt network that reached west through the Chicago and North Western.[15]

While the makeup of a single railroad's board of directors changed from year to year, powerful families moved from board to board, sat on multiple boards at once, or had multiple family members sit on the same board at the same time. Certain families maintained influence on railroad boards of directors for decades. They used the boards less to direct the railroads than to manage their investments, culling inside information, and picking the ripest and lowest speculative fruits and insider contracts that the railroads had to offer. Key directors could link railroads and coordinate policy between them.

I. SPRINGTIME IN MEXICO

In Canada and Mexico many politicians reasonably feared that the expansion of the transcontinentals was paving the way for the expansion of the

United States. Money, railroads, nation building, and empire were not easily separated. As W. Milnor Roberts, eventually chief engineer of the Northern Pacific, wrote in regard to that road, it "will forever settle the question of white supremacy over an area of country covering at least 450,000 square miles."[16] Not all of those 450,000 square miles were necessarily, at least for the moment, within the United States. Thomas Canfield, the engineer who headed the preliminary survey that the Northern Pacific conducted along the Pacific coast in 1870, sought information on a route from Bute Inlet to Vancouver Island "in the event of Vancouver's Island ever belonging to the United States."[17] Such an event did not seem unlikely.

The only cure for Canadian and Mexican fears of American railroads appeared to be railroads of their own. Railroads could be both routes of invasion, literally and figuratively, and keys to national defense. No matter which, railroads in the North American West needed to suck the teats of some state in their infancy, because only this would give them the strength to garner the private capital they also needed. Like that of the United States, the governments of Canada and Mexico offered subsidies for new roads, hoping to reassure investors that what might seem risky enterprises involved no risk at all. To get these subsidies, men gathered in Ottawa and Mexico City just as they gathered in Washington, D.C. Very often they were the same men, which meant they were the very Americans whom Canadians and Mexicans feared. What superficially seemed three national systems of railroads would become one.

In Mexico in the 1860s charters and proposals for railroads were everywhere. Railroads would give Mexico as glorious a future as the United States, if only the Mexican government would subsidize them so that promoters could build them.[18] The Mexicans were correct in fearing the intentions of many of the Americans behind these proposals. Edward Plumb, who had served as the first secretary of the American legation in Mexico City, worked with leading figures in the Pacific Mail Steamship Service to secure a concession for the Mexican Pacific that was to run from Guaymas on the Gulf of California to El Paso, making it the shortest transcontinental of all.[19] George Church, one of Plumb's correspondents, mocked Mexican fears of building railroads that might aid American expansion. "They do not understand the problem of the age—the United States does not want them nor their territory, but civilization more powerful than the United States will sooner or later force upon them its inexorable Dictatorship—they will bend to it and perhaps break under it."[20] Plumb agreed, but he also thought that once railroads secured American control over Mexican trade and development, "we need not hasten the greater event," by which he meant annexation.[21]

There were Mexicans who thought they could ride this tiger. The most prominent among them was Matías Romero, who had been the Juárez government's ambassador to the United States during the dark days of the French invasion of Mexico from 1861 to 1867. He served in President Juárez's cabinet in the late 1860s and early 1870s.[22]

William Rosecrans came to Mexico as an ambassador appointed by Andrew Johnson in 1868, but also as an agent for American railroad interests. Johnson's successor, Ulysses S. Grant, had hated his fellow general Rosecrans during the Civil War, and he hated him still. He dismissed him, but Rosecrans stayed in Mexico, lobbying for railroads as a private citizen. He first worked as agent for Tom Scott and J. Edgar Thompson of the Pennsylvania Railroad seeking aid for a Mexican National Railroad anchored on Mexico City that would link El Paso, Tuxpan, on the Gulf of Mexico, and Acapulco on the Pacific. It would connect with Tom Scott's as yet uncompleted Texas and Pacific. Rosecrans, in the usual manner, invested heavily in Mexican land, hoping for his private speculative return when the railroads were built. He sought Mexican wealth, but he was willing to leave its sovereignty intact. Romero became his ally within the Juárez government.[23]

With the Texas and Pacific floundering, Rosecrans secured a second potential connecting road in the United States: William Jackson Palmer's Denver and Rio Grande. Palmer had served under Rosecrans at Chickamauga and been the private secretary to Edgar Thomson of the Pennsylvania Railroad before the war. At a time when virtually every railroad promoter in the United States thought east–west, Palmer dreamed north–south. He began building a narrow gauge south from Denver in 1870 and sought to go through El Paso and on to Mexico City. To do so, he sold bonds in Holland on a road "with nothing earthly for a basis except the right of way" with a success that astonished other promoters.[24]

By 1870, however, there was competition from a second group of American investors, some of them formerly associated with the Rosecrans group and centered on the National City Bank of New York. They proposed a line—the International Railroad—running from Laredo through Monterrey and on to Mexico City. Edward Plumb became their man in Mexico City and thus Rosecrans's rival.[25]

Mexicans remained torn between the hopes that railroads were the cure to their own weakness and the fear that railroad expansion was only American expansion in a different form and under another name.[26] Juárez died in 1872 and was succeeded by Lerdo, who was as deeply conflicted as Juárez had been. Speaking of the United States and Mexico, Lerdo supposedly said, "Between strength and weakness let us preserve the desert," but as president he "expressed himself very strongly" regarding the value of the railroad in securing control of his borders. Plumb wrote that revolts thrived in remote parts of the country such as "the Rio Grande frontier, to which for want of means of communication the power of the government reaches with great difficulty."[27]

In 1872, as the concessions hung fire, Palmer and Rosecrans rode the Pacific Railroad west to San Francisco, and then sailed south to the Mexican port of Manzanillo, in the state of Colima. From there they explored a route to Mexico City that would connect with Rosecrans's projected route to Tuxpan. A second party explored and surveyed the route from El Paso to Mexico City. The two routes formed an inverted T and would connect Mexico City to both oceans and the American border.[28]

Traveling with Rosecrans and Palmer was Rose Kingsley. She was one of those scribbling British travelers whose books multiplied across the West like ties across the rails.[29] Yet Palmer's search for a railroad route was more the occasion than the subject of Kingsley's book. Palmer, "General R"— Rosecrans—and Kingsley's brother, who was Palmer's associate, faded into the background. In Mexico they could not compete with the mountains and countryside and what to Kingsley seemed the exotic qualities of the Mexican people. These Anglo men, and the Mexican gentlemen who aided them, never quite vanished behind the fruit, flowers, birds, Indians, haciendas, churches, and bandits, but neither could they force themselves into the foreground. They were never sure what they were seeing or whom they could trust. They were even accompanied partway, as they later claimed, by Porfiro Díaz, whose rebellion against President Juárez had recently been suppressed and who was traveling incognito. The railroad men armed themselves, but then meekly surrendered their rifles to revolutionaries—the *pronunciados*—in the person of a major and his drunken soldiers. The major breakfasted with them, seeming so "embarrassed" that Rose Kingsley felt sorry for him even as she desired to do something "unspeakable" to him for taking the weapons.[30]

Rose Kingsley refused, or even more tellingly just neglected, to give the men in her book the mastery that railroad men gave themselves. Despite their failures and disappointments, railroad men always identified themselves with progress and civilization in their own published accounts. But only at the end of her journey, when she reached Mexico City and encountered an "ugly American engine, with its wide smoke stack," did Kingsley dutifully identify it as a "harbinger of law order and civilization" and a "joyful sight." It was left to her father, Charles Kingsley, the canon of Westminster, to supply the necessary platitudes and flesh out the moral of the journey in his preface to her book. In a couple of long paragraphs he offered the railroad as the key to making Mexico "the entrepot of a vast traffic, not only between California and New York, but even—so some think—between China and Europe." The combination of foreign capital and "that most potent of civilizers, the railroad," would in Mexico and the United States bring a "perpetual reinforcement of the good, to drive the bad further and further into the yet more desolate wilderness."[31] Everything that appalled, charmed, and interested his daughter would disappear.

II. SPRINGTIME IN CANADA

American promoters in Canada inspired similar fears and hopes. The British North America Act of 1867 had created the Canadian Confederation, and clause 141 of the act obligated Canada to build a road to British Columbia as part of the terms by which that province joined the confederation. A railroad running parallel to the Northern Pacific understandably aroused the interest of the directors of that road. It also interested Jay Cooke.

If there was a ringmaster in the early Gilded Age circus of hope and greed that the railroads organized in the wake of the Civil War, it would have to be Jay Cooke. Self-made, patriotic, well connected, and deeply religious, he was a man whose word was trusted because of his success in marketing the U.S. government bonds that financed the Civil War. Cooke recognized that his business in government securities was diminishing and that he had a national network of agents with time on their hands. American investors, the source of most of his business, were already moving into railroad bonds, lured by men who imitated his techniques. With the government about to retire and refund its debt at lower interest rates, even more investors would be looking for new opportunities. He needed a railroad, and the Northern Pacific needed him. Its only substantial asset was its immense land grant stretching from Minnesota to Washington Territory across an expanse still largely under Indian control.[32]

Jay Cooke's task was to secure the money to build the road. He became the Northern Pacific's banker and purchasing agent. He agreed to try to sell $100 million worth of railroad bonds paying 7.3 percent interest, but he guaranteed the sale of only $5 million. He promised to advance the road this $5 million to begin construction from Duluth within thirty days of signing the contract. Cooke was to receive twelve cents on the dollar for every bond sold at par; the railroad was to bear the cost of advertising. He promised further advances of up to $500,000. Cooke gained access to a total of 60 percent of the company's stock, but his contract specified that Jay Cooke and Company could name only two of the thirteen Northern Pacific directors and only a quarter of the members of the executive committee.[33] He did not control the actual operation of the railroad, and this would turn out to be his Achilles' heel.

On signing his contract with the Northern Pacific in 1870, Cooke had immediately turned around and tried to divide the risk by forming a pool of his twelve ownership shares, with each share costing $466,667. A share represented an obligation to buy one-twelfth of the $5 million in bonds at par. With each share the purchaser received one-twelfth of the stock issued to Cooke and Company. The investors were buying bonds; the stock, which had no market value, was an inducement.[34] Cooke sought to attract big investors, but it was a hard sell, as his partner Harris Fahnestock warned it would be. Why take Northern Pacific bonds at par when roads with revenue were selling at below par? Why, in other words, pay 100 for a Northern Pacific, when a Central Pacific went for 94, a Union Pacific for 84, and a Missouri Pacific for between 88 and 90? Some of these roads had federal guarantees, and all had tracks and trains, which were among the many things the Northern Pacific largely lacked.[35]

Cooke did not consider the Canadians' desire for a railroad paralleling his own an obstacle to his plans.[36] Canada's hold on its West was weak. The confederation's annexation of the old Hudson's Bay Company territory of Rupert's Land sparked the first Red River Rebellion of 1869–70. Led by Louis Riel, the Métis, the descendants of Indians (largely Cree) and Europeans (largely French), negotiated the creation of a new province of Manitoba. In its wake Americans conspired with the Fenians, Irish nationalists who were willing to carry the war against Britain to its colonial possessions, in order to weaken the Canadian hold on its West.[37]

Cooke fished in these troubled waters. He wrote that "the annexation of British North America, Northwest of Duluth to our country . . . could be done without any violation of treaties and brought about as the result of quiet emigration over the border of trustworthy men with families and with a tacit not legal understanding with Riley and others there." It should be done without violence or bloodshed.[38] The mysterious Mr. Riley was Louis Riel. Cooke, apparently confusing him with the Fenians, bestowed upon him an appropriately Irish name. When the Fenians did launch a raid, Cooke was unwilling to support it; neither were the Métis, whose goal was not annexation to the United States.[39]

Cooke's imperial daydreams, forgotten in the United States, have become part of the Canadian nationalist mythology that has made the Canadian Pacific Railroad, the successor to the Canada Pacific, the railroad that saved Canada. The iron backbone of a nation, it was a technological triumph that defeated both nature and a powerful and arrogant southern neighbor. The railroad stiffened Canada and held up its western mass, which would otherwise have sagged south into the waiting arms of the United States.

The Canadian story makes Canada's Prime Minister John Macdonald— sometimes drunk, sometimes sober, but always eloquent and resolute—the hero and Jay Cooke the villain. But in the early 1870s Cooke and Mac-donald worked together. Jay Cooke, it turned out, wanted Canadian busi-ness and British capital for his Northern Pacific Railroad far more than he wanted an expanded United States. Cooke realized that supporting filibus-ters and scheming to annex Canadian territory was not the most promising route to British capital.[40] He did not want to "prejudice" English capital "in any way." And he thought that "[t]here will be no road built in Canada that will not end at the Sault St. Marie in connection with the Northern Pacific Road," which would then convey traffic west to Pembina on the Minnesota–Manitoba border. As for the Canadian railroad that would proceed west from Pembina toward the Pacific, Cooke referred to it as the "Canadian Pacific tributary" in letters to his agents. It would give traffic to the Northern Pacific, not take it.[41]

Cooke was counting on the realities of Canadian geography and the dismal track record of British investments in Canadian railroads.[42] Canadian geography was friendly to American railroads. An all-Canadian route would have to run roughly seven hundred miles through the Canadian Shield along the northern shore of the Great Lakes from Georgian Bay to Thunder Bay. The Canadian Shield was as desolate as it was beautiful. The granite bedrock stunted the forests and beaded water into countless small lakes, and the lakes aged into innumerable muskeg bogs. The population was small and scattered and promised to stay small and scattered, railroad or no railroad. Traversing it would be expensive, and the expense would pay no dividends in increased traffic. How could such a road compete with American railroads running along the southern shore of the Great Lakes through fat lands, arable and productive and already dotted with great cities and full of traffic? A route across the Canadian Shield seemed, in the words of Alexander Mackenzie, the Liberal politician who opposed it, "one of the most foolish things that can be imagined." A businessman's railroad would, as Jay Cooke thought, drop south of the Great Lakes to Chicago and then move back north, west of Lake Michigan, to reach the border and the Red River valley and the vast prairies and plains stretching west toward the mountains.[43] John Macdonald was a practical man, and he was ready to accept a partial American route, one that avoided the Canadian Shield.[44]

The Grand Trunk Railroad was nearly as great an obstacle as the Canadian Shield. Financed by British capital, it already linked Ontario and Quebec with the eastern United States. Deeply in debt, often failing to meet the interest on its bonds, in chronic danger of bankruptcy, constantly in need of subsidy, plagued by inefficiency and dubious accounting, it seemingly provided a compelling argument for no further British investment in Canadian railroads. It proved all too successful, however, in attracting British capital. British investors continued to pour money into the Grand Trunk even as the Grand Trunk issued new bonds to pay the interest on old bonds. By 1872 its ratio of debts to equity was "an almost unbelievable 25–1." The ideal ratio was 1–1 with each dollar of debt paired with a dollar of equity securing the debt. The British continued to invest because they thought the Canadian government would bail them out. A new, subsidized Canada Pacific paralleling the actual, and anticipated, route of the Grand Trunk threatened the older road's investors and made it difficult to raise British capital.[45]

It was probably only a matter of time before Jay Cooke and Hugh Allan found each other. Allan was a Montreal shipping magnate who felt overcharged and underserved by the Grand Trunk. He feared that his ships would be shut out by a new steamship line being developed by the Grand Trunk.[46] Francis Hincks, Macdonald's minister of finance and a longtime advocate of Canadian-American free trade, brought Allan and Cooke together. Macdonald gave the union his tacit approval.[47] In 1871 Allan reached an agreement with the leading figures of the Northern Pacific. The Canada Pacific, all of whose incorporators were Canadian, gave the Americans a contract to build the Canada Pacific and "to form the Canada Land and Improvement Company to develop the expected land grant." They kept this agreement secret.[48]

III. THE INDIANS' PERPETUAL WINTER

The Northern Pacific's huge land grant involved Jay Cooke with the Indians. The Indians of most immediate concern to Cooke were the Wahpeton-Sisseton Dakotas.[49] In 1871 the Wahpeton and Sisseton discovered Northern Pacific surveyors marking a route through unceded land. This upset them, and they stopped the survey. There was nothing Cooke could do about this directly, since only the federal government had constitutional authority to acquire land from Indians. By 1871, however, the transcontinentals and the federal government were intertwined on such a variety of levels that it was sometimes hard to distinguish whether particular people were acting in their capacity of government officials or because of their connections to the railroads.

William Windom of Minnesota was both a U.S. senator and a member of the Northern Pacific board of directors. Gilded Age congressmen routinely suffered crises of conscience in going on railroad payrolls. It would be easier to take these crises seriously if their outcome were not so predictable. It was a ritual of sorts. Moral concerns were raised; the relationship was clarified; the moral rectitude of the official was validated by the very people who had tempted him, and the official became a friend of the railroad. Windom worried about the appearance of conflicts of interest in his dual role, but Cooke, who was not a man predisposed to irony, assured him there was no impropriety in Windom's serving as a director of the road, investing in it, and borrowing the money for that investment from Cooke. "[W]e take it for granted," Cooke wrote Windom, "that you are an honest man, and will do nothing that is not right strictly, especially when the subject of the Northern Pacific comes before Congress, which is the only possible complication."[50]

One of the things that came before Congress in 1871 was the matter of the Wahpeton-Sisseton. The device invented by Senator Pomeroy of using treaties to give Indian lands directly to railroads at bargain prices had flourished in the wake of the Civil War. The railroad man most adept at elbowing his way to the table was James Joy, then president of the Chicago, Burlington, and Quincy, who managed to obtain the Neutral Tract of the Cherokee Nation in Kansas for $1 an acre. The Supreme Court would validate the sale in 1872, and settlers would pay average prices that ranged from $9.15 an acre for the best land in the mid-1870s to $5.45 for the remainder at the end.[51] "King Joy," meanwhile, had an even bigger transaction with the Osage, who unlike the Cherokee were native to the region: a sale of over eight million acres for twenty cents an acre, nothing down. It was this treaty that came before Congress amid huge public uproar in 1871.

The uproar was on behalf not of the Indians but rather of white settlers who wanted those lands without having to pay the railroads a premium for them. The settlers had a case; they had played a crucial role in obtaining such cessions. By treaty and American law, the Indians should have been safe in their occupancy.[52] The squatters had settled the lands illegally, but the United States had refused to evict them and used the invasion as a lever for further cessions. The squatters assumed that the lands would pass in the usual manner from the Indians to the government to the public domain to the squatters, who were now legal preemptors; they had not counted on the railroads. Settlers failed to defeat the Cherokee Treaty, but they not only defeated the Osage Treaty; they brought down the whole treaty system with it by uniting popular grievance with congressional rivalries.[53] The Constitution reserved to the Senate the power to advise and consent on treaties, and the House had long resented being shut out of the treaty system. Since the House had to appropriate money for Indian Affairs and land purchases, it used its power of the purse to tack an amendment onto an appropriations bill in 1871, declaring that there would be no new treaties, although tribes would retain their status as semisovereign nations and existing treaties would be honored.[54]

Unable to use the treaty system in 1871 to get Wahpeton-Sisseton land in North Dakota for the Northern Pacific, Cooke and Windom argued that if the treaty system was dead, then Congress should abrogate Indian title unilaterally. Cooke had a bill introduced to strip the Wahpeton-Sisseton of their land, with Congress determining the price. The bill failed.[55]

The treaty system was less dead than in hiding. The House didn't end negotiations; it merely demanded a say in them. The agreements enacted after 1871 looked like treaties, walked like treaties, and even quacked like treaties, but they weren't treaties. They were agreements approved by Indians, the Senate, and the House. The Wahpeton-Sisseton negotiations showed how they worked. To get negotiations moving, Cooke authorized payments to Assistant Secretary of the Interior B. R. Cowen. Congress authorized a three-man commission to negotiate with the Wahpeton-Sisseton. One of the commissioners was James Smith Jr., an official of a subsidiary of the Northern Pacific. He, in turn, recommended to Cooke that the ex-Indian agent Benjamin Thompson be put on retainer by the railroad to secure Indian approval. Thompson would get $5,000 when the Indians signed and

$5,000 more when the agreement was ratified. Cooke, Smith, and Thompson were acting, or so Cooke persuaded himself, not just for the good of the railroad and the good of the nation but also for the good of the Indians.[56]

The Northern Pacific was never a road lucky in its employees. Thompson didn't do the railroad much good, but once hired he was retained for fear he could do it harm if angered. Still the Indians, under enormous pressure, agreed to a cession. The agreement was submitted to Congress, which substantially altered it. It went back to the Indians for approval, but in 1873 it was caught up in two quarrels. The first was among two Republican factions, the Mugwumps and the Stalwarts, and involved hard feelings left by the 1872 presidential election. Cooke mediated it. The second quarrel arose when the Indian agent Moses Adams, also one of the commissioners, refused to give Gabriel Renville and other polygamous tribal leaders annual payments due them under treaties until they banished their extra wives. They, in turn, refused to sign the revised agreement. In nineteenth-century American politics monogamy beat polygamy hands down, but it did not necessarily beat the railroads. Cooke wrote his brother Harry that the "Secy. Of the Interior should order this gentleman, whoever he may be, to treat all the Indians alike (no matter how many wives they have.)"[57] Harry talked to Windom; Windom talked to Secretary Delano, and Secretary Delano wrote Agent Adams. Adams rearranged his priorities. With the ratification of the altered agreement, the Northern Pacific obtained, Cooke claimed, "at once over 5 million acres between the Red River and the Missouri intact, not an acre of it lost. This of itself is worth a good deal more than the cost of the road on both coasts all the expenditures up to this date to say nothing of our other larger grant on the Pacific and in Minnesota & the completed railroad." It may have been the only good thing that happened to the Northern Pacific in 1873. It was only one on a long list of bad things that happened to Indians.[58]

IV. POLITICAL STORMS BREWING

Henry Dawes was a Massachusetts congressman who eventually produced legislation and reports that deprived the Indians of land on a scale even greater than losses to the railroads.[59] In the 1870s Dawes was not yet an

Indian reformer, but he was entangled in a web of friendships that linked Massachusetts business and politics. His relations with textile manufacturers eased his entry into similar relations with railroad men. In 1866 Dawes consulted, took payments, facilitated legislation, and then succumbed to the usual moral alarm. He had to insist that his "kind friends" recognize that their generous payments to him were in no way "inconsistent with official integrity and would be received without the slightest reference to official conduct."[60] Friendship was lucrative, and his friends had no desire to upset his sensibilities. Dawes had given Oakes Ames $1,035 for ten shares of stock in the Crédit Mobilier. Dawes received over the next six months $800 in Union Pacific bonds, $1,000 in Union Pacific stock, and $600 in cash as dividends on his Crédit Mobilier stock.[61] He also received other payments, which may or may not have been related to the Crédit Mobilier, since Ames also invested in Iowa railroads for Dawes.[62]

In the midst of the presidential campaign of 1872, Charles Dana's *New York Sun* proclaimed the Crédit Mobilier "The King of Frauds." The princes and princesses of frauds during the Grant administration were no slackers, and there were dukes and counts galore. The reason the Crédit Mobilier was the king lay a little farther down in the *Sun*'s layered headline: "Congressmen who have robbed the people and now support the national robber."[63] Among those supporting the "national robber"—the Crédit Mobilier—was Henry Dawes. The *Springfield Republican* picked up the attack, and Dawes lost his bid to become senator from Massachusetts, returning instead to Congress. Ames consoled him, joking that Dawes's new status as "the best abused man in the Country, except Grant, Cameron, Gr.ey [*sic*], and a few others," hurt Ames's pride of place, but he wrote as if Dawes still held stock. "What an awful thing it is to own stock in the U.P.R.R. Co. or Credit Mobilier."[64]

To the dismay of the accused, the scandal would not die. Senator J. W. Patterson, in rising to his own defense and the defense of the Crédit Mobilier, complained that Congress had "been occupied during the entire session with the investigation, agitation, and discussion on the subject of these trivial investments." The press never did get the financial details straight, but it did not have to: congressional attempts to quiet the scandal perversely kept it alive. Congress appointed two committees, named after their chairs to investigate the Crédit Mobilier: the Poland Committee in the Senate, which tried to keep the hearings secret, and the Wilson Committee in the House.[65]

The Wilson Committee investigation of 1873 is as good a marker as any for the beginning of the annus horribilis of the North American transcontinental railroads. The Crédit Mobilier scandal implicated not only the leadership of the Union Pacific Railroad but also Schuyler Colfax, the vice-president of the United States; James A. Garfield, a congressman who would be a future president of the United States; James G. Blaine, a Speaker of the House who desperately wanted to be president; and a covey of leading senators and representatives who scattered like so many quail for shelter. It was fitting that the members of the Wilson Committee never really understood the details of the railroad financing that they were investigating and that they allowed most of those implicated to go scot-free. Ignorance was the common currency of the transcontinentals: the promoters of railroads knew little about building them, investors in the railroads had only the shakiest grasp on what they were investing in, and the politicians who subsidized them and were supposed to oversee them were often a little unclear on specifics. The essence of the Crédit Mobilier, however, was clear. In order to curry congressional favor, the men running the Union Pacific had sold stock in the Crédit Mobilier to leading representatives, senators, and the vice-president of the United States below market prices.[66]

Oakes Ames, curt, belligerent, and often obtuse, was abandoned by his friends. Most implicated congressmen ducked and ran, but they ducked too low, ran too fast, and denied too much. The accused lied so voluminously and so ineptly that simply cataloging and refuting the lies became a full-time occupation for the press. Ames fought back. He opened his memoranda book. It contained names and numbers.

Ames had two lines of defense. First, he did not consider his sale of stock to a fellow congressman a bribe. He declared, "There is no law and no reason legal or moral why a member of Congress should not own stock in a road any more than why he should not own a sheep when the price of wool is to be affected by tariff."[67] In nineteenth-century politics, as much as now, the side with the best metaphors often wins. Ames had a bad metaphor. There were pretty transparent legal and moral reasons why a member of Congress should not accept an offer to buy a flock of sheep at discount before voting to impose a tariff on wool. Congressmen were acquiring stock through the Crédit Mobilier in a corporation they had chartered, one they had to supervise, and which repeatedly came before them for legislation. The elaborate ritual dances of moral probity engaged in by men like Dawes and Windom were eloquent signs of their own ethical uncertainty.

Ames had a stronger second position. He claimed that the stock was not a bribe, because a bribe was a quid pro quo. The distribution of the stock in the Crédit Mobilier was about friendship and reciprocity. Ames wanted congressional friends for his enterprises. He was drawing a distinction essential to railroad politics. The railroads distinguished between their friends and those they had to bribe, but the argument advanced by some congressmen that the stock could not have been a bribe because it did not meet the going price for a congressional vote was not helpful in restoring public faith in their representatives.[68] Except for the censure of Ames, a Republican, and James Brooks, the Democratic floor leader, no one was punished and no money was recovered. This made the scandal all the more lethal and long lasting. How, Ames wondered and critics continued to wonder afterwards, could Ames be punished for giving bribes when no one but Brooks was punished for taking them?[69]

Jay Cooke watched the Crédit Mobilier unfold with genuine consternation. Aid to transcontinental railroads had become politically toxic. The scandal removed any immediate possibility that Congress would guarantee Northern Pacific bonds, and it badly hurt Northern Pacific bond sales. The spectacle of a transcontinental looted by insiders did not inspire outsiders to invest in other transcontinentals.[70] And when the Justice Department threatened to recover Union Pacific bonds that had fraudulently passed to the Crédit Mobilier, Cooke feared that the remedy might be worse than the disease. Such an action, Cooke contended, would destroy confidence in railroad bonds since future buyers could never be sure whether the original sale of bonds had been legitimate. The courts ended that threat by ruling that the United States had no standing for a suit, since the damage had been done to the firm's stockholders and not to the United States. The only remedy available to Congress was revoking the Union Pacific charter.[71] Congress found other ways to punish the Union Pacific. An 1874 amendment to the general appropriation bill forbade the Union Pacific from issuing new stock "or mortgages or pledges made on the property . . . without leave of Congress." The act left the company at a competitive disadvantage.[72]

But it was not just the threat to his immediate interests that bothered Cooke: it was the public behavior of railroad men and their friends. Like Dawes and Windom, Cooke wanted the appearance of moral probity. Privately this was ensured by the mutual agreement of all involved that what they were doing was honest and upright, but the Crédit Mobilier had pushed railroad men and congressmen on a public stage and cracked their consensus. Schuyler Colfax, who insisted that he had received no dividends, and Oakes Ames, who claimed that he had paid such dividends to Colfax, could not both be right. The public believed that Colfax had told a "whopper."[73] The issue for Cooke was not whether Colfax had received dividends from the Crédit Mobilier. Colfax had, after all, also invested in the Northern Pacific, which was, Cooke assured him, "as fine and innocent [an investment] as ever was made by mortal man." Cooke reasoned that "if a member of Congress is anybody at all," he would be materially interested in some enterprise that came before Congress.[74] The issue was that Colfax and Ames were accusing each other of wrongdoing. It did not matter who was right and who was wrong. Such a public failure to acknowledge their mutual virtue and the compatibility of private profit with public duty would fracture the structure of mutual reassurance and friendship perhaps beyond repair.

V. INFORMATION AND TRUST

Cooke knew that his fate rode on the public's perception of his probity and on its trust in his competence and honesty. He wrote the president of the Northern Pacific, "You must remember, that my responsibility is greater than that of all the rest put together, as the money thus to be expended comes in 90 cases out of a hundred from those who purchase simply on my word, not on the word of Jay Cooke and Company in this case so much as my personal reputation."[75] Cooke had entered into a contract with his investors. They promised not only to buy Northern Pacific securities but also not to resell them; they would hold them as a "permanent" investment.[76]

Cooke depended on small investors. None of the transcontinentals attracted large outside investors in their formative stages. And, by and large, Cooke could not attract European investors. The Northern Pacific initially considered Europe the "great market for their bonds," but Europe was "flooded with bonds offered by every little Dutch house." The Northern Pacific needed a status and credibility these small Dutch and German banking houses could not give them; it required "a great house whose recommendation would give them preference."[77] The Northern Pacific never secured the great house it needed. First the Franco-Prussian War disrupted what looked like successful European negotiations. Then, when negotiations over reparations due the United States for British complicity in the activities of the Confederate raider *Alabama* threatened war with Great Britain, a second negotiation fell apart.[78] And so Cooke turned to his old sales force to sell to the same small investors who had bought Civil War bonds: prosperous merchants and farmers, the clergy, Union war veterans, and successful artisans.

Herman Melville had imagined the quintessential Gilded Age investment transaction, as he had imagined so much of the nineteenth century, before it became the norm. "All I have to do with you is to receive your confidence, and all you have to do with me is, in due time, to receive it back, thrice paid in trebling profits," Melville's confidence man had told the old miser, and in a sentence Melville captured the capitalist dilemma of trust: the exchange of cash for a promise.[79] Imagine the old miser as a banker who knows all too much about the confidence man, and there is one outcome. Imagine an investor who knows little and is beguiled, and there is another outcome.

The ultimate buyers of most railroad bonds lived at a distance from the railroad that they invested in, and they had no independent knowledge of the seller or the veracity of his claims. An investor encountered a virtual world of financial statements, prospectuses, newspaper accounts, and market values that at once stood in for and was inseparable from the actual railroads of a developing nation. The investor had to trust someone. The problem of trusting strangers was as old as long-distance trade. When a German banker, whose client was heir to a note signed by Huntington, Crocker, Stanford, and Hopkins, tried to ascertain "the responsibility and financial ability of said parties" through American intermediaries, he was a part of this older world.[80]

The new virtual world was, then as now, temptingly easy to manipulate. Numbers and words that were supposed to stand in for things could be changed and still maintain their influence; news could be altered or withheld; reports could claim assets that didn't exist and deny trouble that did exist. Altering the numbers and changing the words of this virtual world could prompt actions in the parallel universe where people paid money for bonds. Buying a bond was different from negotiating a promissory note, for several reasons. The first was the distance separating buyer and seller. A bond is essentially a corporate promissory note: a claim on the revenue and property of the firm. Unlike a note, however, it is replicated thousands of times over and issued to thousands of people. This replication was one difference between a bond and an IOU and its nineteenth-century banking equivalent, an accommodation loan. Another was that bonds ran for fixed period of time, whereas a short-term note was subject to call at any time. Finally, an accommodation loan not only was endorsed by a borrower but was guaranteed by other endorsers. The guarantee of a railroad bond was usually only the revenue and property put in trust to secure the bond, but at times a parent company would guarantee the bonds of its subsidiaries. In terms of personal relations, a bond was to an accommodation loan what a commercial greeting card was to a personal letter. A person drawing up an IOU, like someone sending a personal letter, usually has an existing relationship with a specific recipient; but those who issue bonds or produce greeting cards do not know the purchasers and usually have no specific recipient in mind. In the 1860s and 1870s the bond market overwhelmed this world of individual promissory notes with millions of pieces of printed paper. The bonded debt of American railroads rose from $416 million in 1867 to $2,230 million in 1874 and then, pausing after the Panic of 1873, to $5,055 million in 1890. The majority of these funds came from within the United States, but there was significant investment from Great Britain, the Netherlands, and Germany.[81]

The railroads needed banking houses to sell their bonds because, on the whole, there was little reason for investors to trust railroad promoters. Investors knew, although they might not have been able to articulate it, that information was asymmetric and that the men who ran the transcontinentals knew more about their condition and prospects than they were willing to tell. Banking houses had more ability to get information; that is why they became the intermediaries. The most trusted bankers, however, were not willing to get involved with the transcontinentals. Germany became the major European source of capital for the transcontinentals, but the German houses were not willing to take the American claims on faith. In 1872 Philip Speyer and Company forced the Central Pacific, by then nearly a decade old, to issue its first stockholder's report "such," Speyer's agent, Henry Schuester wrote, "as was made by every other R.R. in the world over fifty miles long." Schuester threatened, Huntington reported, not to "buy or recommend his friends to buy any of our securities."[82]

The Central Pacific joined other American roads in the production of one of the nineteenth's century great fictional genres: the annual stockholder's report. Corporate reports were designed to sell stock and bonds; they gave information for a purpose, which some of the dimmer lights in the railroad hierarchies did not always understand. Either from unusual honesty or from normal carelessness, Leland Stanford listed all the company's debts, the principal and interest owed the federal government, in his draft of the 1872 Central Pacific annual report. In a sentence in which the reader can almost hear Huntington's long-suffering sigh, he wrote, "I shall strike the interest out unless I get the reasons why they were put in as this report is to help the sale of stock and this item of say $80,000,000 is not in that direction."[83]

The railroads would have liked to have a monopoly of information, but they did not. The greatest threat to them was the Associated Press. To a modern reader a small antebellum newspaper might seem nothing but an archaic version of Google News: a compendium of articles clipped from other newspapers. The process took time and was the result of innumerable choices by separate editors, so there was no telling how far or where a particular piece of news would spread. As a means of relaying information, it was slower than private correspondence.

The New York Associated Press originated from a consortium of seven New York newspapers that banded together in 1846 to centralize the gathering and dissemination of foreign news. The Associated Press had its own reporters, but its major role was to collect and cull news published elsewhere. It was a combination of low tech—passenger pigeons released from incoming ships—and high tech: telegraph lines that sped information to New York, and then out of New York to newspapers that subscribed to the service. By the 1850s the NYAP had gone national with regional associations funneling news into New York, which then redistributed a digest to subscribing papers. The service's great power came from the special low rates it received from Western Union and its control over which papers received the digest.[84] After the war it survived conflicts between its regional affiliates and reached an accommodation with an emerging rival, the United Press, to maintain a monopoly on telegraphic news transmission.[85]

Commercial and political news formed the bread and butter of the Associated Press. The power of its agents, and for that matter of the Western Union operators who transmitted the news over the lines at night, was limited but real. Major news items almost always went through, although scandals embarrassing to Republican politicians might be suppressed. Minor news items, such as lawsuits against railroads or political attacks that might affect securities, were left to the discretion of Associated Press agents.[86] Investors became extraordinarily attentive readers because the Associated Press was creating a national market by making information about prices and conditions almost instantly available.[87]

James Simonton was manager of the Associated Press, and he haunted Collis P. Huntington, Jay Cooke, and other railroad men because he had power beyond that of any single newspaper editor or publisher. The Associates of the Central Pacific believed that Simonton, who was also partial owner of the *San Francisco Bulletin*, hated them. Most of California hated them; what distinguished Simonton was that his hatred could cost them money. Simonton could have articles unfavorable to the Central Pacific published in the *Bulletin*, and then he could have them selected for the AP digest that went out over Western Union to all members of the Associated Press. Such articles hurt Huntington's ability to borrow. "We have large amounts to pay and it is very difficult to get money here and then such articles as was published in the S.F. bulletin of Jan. 19 . . . are republished in the New York Sun and then that paper sent every where by Simonton hurts our borrowing money here (N.Y.) no doubt more than there (San Francisco)." By 1871 Huntington was convinced that the Western Union operators had orders not to send any information favorable to the Central Pacific.[88]

At least in the short term, a newspaper was able to make or ruin, deflate or inflate, the value of securities. The men who ran the transcontinentals cared nearly as much about newspapers as about their securities because newspapers and financial papers were connected. "I seriously wish that some legislative measure could be passed, which would make the shooting of reporters wholly justifiable on sight, punishable by a fine not exceeding ten dollars," Charles Francis Adams, president of the Union Pacific, wrote to Charles Perkins of the Burlington.[89] William Mahl, who in the 1880s became Collis P. Huntington's right-hand man, claimed Huntington avoided the typewriter and had all of his correspondence written out in longhand because printed pages reminded him of newspapers, and newspapers always "failed to make an impression."[90] What Huntington said, however, was never an infallible guide to what Huntington did. He read newspapers very carefully.

The "lies told and retold" in the press made investors nervous and hurt railroad securities. The rise and fall of securities measured the impact of information, but at the same time their rise and fall was itself information that could be manipulated. When falling bond prices indicated that an investment was risky, Huntington intervened to buttress bond prices so that they seemed to shout security. "The news from Cal as published in this morning papers is not very satisfactory," Huntington wrote Hopkins in September of 1873, "and it will all be telegraphed by Simonton to Europe in hopes of hurting our securities in that market." Huntington countered by buying Central Pacific securities: "today something over 100,000 of CP bonds and the market closed 100⅛ bid and none offered. This will go by Reuter's news agency over the cable tonight and an advance of ⅞ since yesterday on the

C. P. in this market will more than counter balance any political news from Cal that they can send."[91]

Cooke had not gone into the Northern Pacific planning to deceive investors. He promised that this would be a safe, pay-as-you-go proposition. He had assured his partner and brother-in-law, William Moorhead, who opposed taking on the Northern Pacific, that he had no intention of carrying "a great transcontinental railway upon our backs." As Harris Fahnestock understood the proposal, "We do not propose to advance money at all in this construction, but to work upon a strictly cash basis and gauge the building of the road by the funds on hand, the condition of the country and to keep in view the idea of making it self sustaining."[92]

Anthony Trollope traveled through the United States during the early 1870s when railroad promotions like the Northern Pacific were everywhere in the press and in private conversation. Trollope took in the talk, the promises, the fantasies, and the utter carelessness of such promotions and distilled them in 1875 into his great novel *The Way We Live Now*. Trollope put his fictional South Central Pacific and Mexican Railway under the direction of a group of arbitrary, powerful, greedy, heedless, and not particularly bright men who, but for their noble birth, could have been pulled from many actual western railroad boards of directors.[93] Trollope grasped the greed, the corruption, and the misplaced hopes that started the railroads off in life with debts that their traffic could not sustain.

Jay Cooke was no Augustus Melmotte, Esq., the financier of Trollope's novel, not least because Melmotte was a shadowy figure and Jay Cooke was well known. Yet read more than a century later, Cooke's correspondence exudes a salesman's confidence reminiscent of Melmotte. When talking to investors, he said one thing; when talking to his partners, he said another. He probably believed both. Cooke told himself and others that the Northern Pacific was a perfectly safe investment. "The more I look at them," he wrote Moorhead in 1871, "the better I am satisfied that they are the best bonds in the world."[94] But more astonishing than regarding the bonds as a safe thing, Cooke regarded the Northern Pacific as a relatively small thing. Like so many men coming out of the Civil War, everything they did later was dwarfed by that gigantic struggle. Jay Cooke had dealt, and continued to deal, in thousands of millions of dollars through his marketing of government bonds. The Northern Pacific seemed to him, in the words of William Moorhead, "a mere bagatelle." A man who had handled those thousands of millions would "look upon fifty millions of dollars as comparatively a small amount."[95] Cooke put 10 percent of all his firms' profits into an account for "Old Patriarch Jacob," which he distributed to charity. Cooke listened to his God, but he should have listened to his partner, Harris Fahnestock. Fahnestock was a relatively young man in the 1870s. Later pictures of him—small, dapper, with a Vandyke beard—give him the quality of a human exclamation point. He was a man who insisted on being heard. He never considered the Northern Pacific a small thing; he understood the dangers it presented all too well.[96]

Fahnestock understood that Cooke was lying to his partners, lying to his investors, and, perhaps most dangerously of all, lying to himself. Fahnestock was in reality what bankers presented themselves to be: an honest and prudent man. He recognized that the House of Cooke was on the edge of a whirlpool, and he wanted to pull back. Fahnestock's letters to Cooke grew blunter and more hectoring as the Northern Pacific's drafts on the House of Cooke grew greater and greater. The original contract limited such drafts to $500,000, but the management of the Northern Pacific was as careless as it was incompetent. Cooke eventually replaced the road's hopeless president, J. Gregory Smith (like Leland Stanford of the Central Pacific, an ex-governor), with George W. Cass, but, despite his promises to his partners, he advanced funds far beyond the promised limit. Fahnestock wanted to force the Northern Pacific to resort to the market to finance its short-term debt, but the railroad continued to come to Cooke.[97] By the summer of 1872, as workers built between the Red and Missouri rivers, the Northern Pacific's debt to Jay Cooke and Company had reached $1,583,000, more than three times the agreed-on limit of $500,000.[98] By the summer of 1873, when the road reached the Missouri with an additional sixty-six miles built between Puget Sound and the Columbia River, the debt had reach nearly $7 million. The security for the loans was the bonds Cooke was finding it more and more difficult to sell.[99]

Fahnestock could not have been clearer about what Cooke was doing and where it would take him and the firm. In June of 1872 Fahnestock had told his senior partner that Cooke was "morally liable to every man & woman holding the bonds for the proper economical application of all the money received and for verification of all the statements contained in our publications." Fahnestock enumerated the deceptions that Cooke had perpetrated on "a class of investors who have been influenced by [Cooke's] personal recommendation." Cooke had assured investors of "the intelligence vigor and economy of the management. We know that it has been inefficient, distracted . . . and extravagant to the last degree." He had described the land grants as rich and valuable, but a large proportion were "practically valueless either for cultivation or for lumbering," and the rest were "less valuable than the public have been led to believe." Publications promoting the bonds had promised rapid marketing of the lands for the security of investors. The railroad had as of June 1872 received exactly $338.76 in cash for the lands. The Northern Pacific had claimed a comprehensive system to promote immigration; such claims were lies. Such extravagant claims, he wrote, had actually deterred capitalists from investing, and Cooke was selling not to "moneyed men" but "almost exclusively to persons who rely upon our recommendation rather than upon their own judgment." Fahnestock saw "discredit if not . . . ruin" ahead.[100]

The ruin Fahnestock feared would, like railroad promotion, be transnational. Canada too had an election in 1872, and the Canada Pacific became a threat to John Macdonald's Conservative Party. The Canada Pacific was centered on Quebec, its terminus, and offered nothing to powerful Ontario interests. Those interests responded by chartering a second railroad, the Inter-oceanic Railway, and promoting it as a road free from American influence. The choice between the Canada Pacific and the Inter-oceanic thus became a choice between Quebec and Ontario framed as a choice between American intervention and Canadian independence, which was in turn framed as a choice between the Conservatives and the Liberal Party. Framed this way, the Conservatives would lose Ontario.

The Conservatives reformulated their position. They chartered both the Canada Pacific and the Inter-oceanic Railway, allowing both roads to dip into the United States, but funding neither. Macdonald's cabinet publicly denounced American participation in the Canada Pacific. Privately, however, the Conservatives continued to accommodate Hugh Allan. Macdonald's Conservative Party, like Grant's Republican Party, which was dunning Cooke, needed money for the 1872 election. Macdonald's ally George Cartier approached Allan for campaign funds. If Allan gave the funds, he would get the presidency of the new consolidated company and the contract to build the road. The contract would bring fifty million acres of land and a $30 million subsidy. Allan informed his American associates in the summer of 1872 that their stock would "have to stand in [his] name for some time." The Americans were not worried; their plan was to retreat into the shadows, let Parliament debate, and then emerge "stronger than ever." It seemed a good plan. Allan contributed $350,000, and this money, spent liberally for votes, allowed Macdonald and the Conservatives to squeak through the 1872 election. When the proposed merger failed, in large part because the Inter-oceanic continued to contend that Allan was a wedge for Northern Pacific participation, Macdonald arranged a whole new company—the Canadian Pacific, with Hugh Allan as president and with representatives on the board from all the provinces—to build the railroad.[101]

Only in January of 1873 did Cooke mention a "hitch" in Canada; rumors were circulating that Allan would dump the Americans.[102] Cooke remained sanguine; intermediaries assured him that the exclusion of the Americans was more "form than substance." He recognized that they needed "to manage Allan," but he also knew that because "Canada and England are both jealous" of the connection with the Northern Pacific, Allan had to act cautiously. Allan's attempt to raise English capital from Morton, Rose and Company would, as Cooke correctly judged, fail. In the end the Canadian Pacific would have no choice but to cooperate with the Northern Pacific.[103] Cooke continued to believe that Sir Hugh was "highly friendly and if he could act independently would act at once in cooperation with the Northern Pacific."[104]

On April 2, 1873, as the Crédit Mobilier investigation continued in the United States, the Honorable Lucius Seth Huntington, member for Shefford in Quebec, rose in the Canadian Parliament and accused Hugh Allan of having advanced large sums of money to the Conservative Party in exchange for a railroad charter. Government ministers had accepted the money knowing that Allan was merely a front man for a company owned and controlled by Americans. Virtue came late to Mr. Huntington in such matters. The preceding fall he had been corresponding with Jay Cooke about investing in the very railroads he now saw as a threat to Canadian sovereignty. Macdonald himself moved to establish a committee to investigate.[105] In the words of the governor-general of Canada, the Pacific Scandal of 1873 involved charges of "no less a crime than that of having sold Canada's most precious interests to certain American speculators, with a view to debauching the Canadian constituencies with the gold obtained as the price of their treachery."[106]

Macdonald was initially confident that he could delay and control the investigation, but he had to take care of potentially damning evidence.[107] Hugh Allan, a man whose imprudence, in Macdonald's words, "almost mounted to insanity," had put quite a bit in writing, including how he came to be promised the charter.[108] The recipient of much of this correspondence was George W. McMullen, a Canadian businessman who had acted as an intermediary with the Americans. Allan bought back the correspondence for $37,500 in American dollars. McMullen got $20,000 immediately. The second payment was to be made when Parliament adjourned without ever seeing the letters.[109] It would never come.

On July 4, 1873, the *Toronto Globe* and the *Montreal Herald* published the letters that Hugh Allan thought he had bought from George McMullen. This was followed on July 17 with an account from McMullen that linked Macdonald and his government directly to Allan's payments to the Conservative Party in exchange for the charter.[110] John Macdonald had been drunk a good deal of the fall of 1872 and did not remember—or claimed not to remember—all he had done or agreed to do, but he also unfortunately put some of his agreements in writing. He had clearly promised Allan the railroad charter, and Allan received it, but only after promising Macdonald a purge of the Americans.[111] Macdonald might have evaded direct blame if the secretary of John C. Abbott, the man who had arranged the purchase of the McMullen letters, had not rifled Abbott's safe and sold letters he found to the Liberal Party. They were published as evidence of the truth of McMullen's story.[112]

Things spun out of control in a wonderfully bizarre Canadian way. Macdonald got drunk and disappeared. He returned, as he always did, the master of parliamentary politics. He managed to keep Parliament from any more than a token meeting in August and secured the investigation by a royal commission dominated by his political allies. But his hold grew shakier as both public support and the support within his own party weakened. He put his faith in the age and ineptitude of the royal commission, whose elderly judges lacked, as the governor-general put it, "the disemboweling powers which are rife in young cross-examining counsel."[113] The witnesses' bowels stayed safely intact. Their testimony droned and meandered like a fly circling a warm room.

The commission did its best to sedate Canada. It took evidence—contradictory, equivocating, and in many cases simply perjured—and then published it. It offered no summary and no conclusion. When the governor-general sent the account off to the colonial secretary in London, he reported, "A greater amount of lying and baseness could not well be crammed into a smaller compass."[114] In early November, Macdonald resigned. His government fell, and he passed over into the parliamentary opposition.[115]

By the end of the summer of 1873 the western railroads had, within the span of two years, ended the Indian treaty system in the United States, brought down a Canadian government, and nearly paralyzed the U.S. Congress. The greatest blow remained to be delivered. The railroads were about to bring down the North American economy.

VI. THE LONG WINTER

At the beginning of 1873, if maps were to be believed, railroads crisscrossed the continent. Harbors on the Pacific Coast opened their mouths to receive the trade of Asia. Quiet places like San Blas, Acapulco, and Guaymas in Mexico and San Diego in California prepared to become bustling cities. Places that barely existed as organized non-Indian communities, Tacoma in Washington Territory and Granville, Port Simpson, and Waddington Depot in British Columbia, became potential railroad termini and imagined the world at their door. San Francisco, the only city worthy of the name on North America's Pacific Coast, trembled before the attempt of the Central Pacific Railroad, which regretted its earlier decision to terminate at Sacramento, to get a government grant of Goat Island in San Francisco Bay. If the

Associates succeeded, they would create their own port and leave San Francisco isolated and commercially irrelevant.[116] There were maps to detail these routes, congressional or parliamentary bills in the United States, Mexico, and Canada authorizing massive transfers of land, money, and credit to support them, stock certificates signifying ownership of the roads, and bonds representing money lent to these roads. All that was lacking on most of these roads was tracks and trains.

All western railroads, actual and imagined, were highly leveraged operations. They had accrued more debt than they could pay through operating profits and depended on continued borrowing to meet their obligations. Any diminishment in their ability to borrow meant disaster. Shut off the flow of capital to operating railroads, and they would rust, rot, and shrivel. Today, when what remains of the old transcontinentals is so resolutely material—the lines of their tracks, the old engines and cars often lovingly restored in parks across the West, the stations that have become restaurants or museums—it is easy to forget that they were as much matters of information and trust as they were constructions of wood, steel, and stone. When railroads failed, what first broke down was not the machines and tracks but the networks of trust that provided the funds that built the railroads and fueled the economy that set people and goods in motion.

By late 1872 the ability to draw in new funds to keep this cycle of borrowing going was coming to an end. European investors were losing their enthusiasm for unfinished American railroads. The federal government's policy of refunding its debt by retiring wartime bonds and gradually removing greenbacks from circulation was tightening the money supply. The large negative trade balance that the United States had with Great Britain was causing gold to flow east across the Atlantic, thus cutting down available American capital.[117] Much of Europe's move to the gold standard and the resulting rise in the price of gold further increased the movement of gold out of the United States. James Lees summarized the situation in a letter to William Ralston of the Bank of California:

The enormous amount of European capital sent to this country [i.e., the United States] of late years (a great deal of which has been wasted in extravagance and ill spent in wild cat enterprises such as Railroads through deserts—beginning nowhere and ending nowhere) bearing interest which has heretofore been reinvested here but now will probably be remitted together with heavy trade balances against this country will all tell on our gold supply. To meet this demand we probably have less than at anytime within the last 25 years, so that the whole thing looks very serious to me indeed.[118]

William Ralston knew more about the Central Pacific than anyone but the Associates. When the Associates wrote overdrafts on his and other banks, Ralston knew it. When the Central Pacific bought locally on credit, he knew it. Merchants exchanged the railroad's notes at the banks for ready cash, with the banks discounting the notes; the difference between the face value and what the merchant received was an interest charge. If the Central Pacific failed to pay a note, the merchant or contractor who cashed it at the bank was responsible to the bank. The "ring" of men surrounding the bank, as Mark Hopkins of the Central Pacific complained, "know *all about* our business here." They knew what the Associates owed, whom they owed it to, and what rates they were paying. There was "nothing but the perplexities of it" that they didn't know.[119]

Above all, Ralston knew that the Associates were trying to sell the road. Huntington offered the Central Pacific, a road capitalized at $135 million, which claimed to have $59,644,000 in paid-up stock (which, of course, it did not) and nearly $7 million in annual net earnings, to A. A. Cohen, Michael Reese, and the ring of financiers centered on the Bank of California for $20 million with only $2 million to $4 million down.[120] Cohen's partners offered $11 million, and Huntington broke off negotiations.[121] Huntington contemplated merging the Central Pacific with the Union Pacific, but that too failed.[122]

Ralston and Cohen knew that the Central Pacific was a road that had greater debts and obligations than assets and revenue. In times of easy credit, the Associates could borrow new money to meet old obligations. When credit tightened, they were in trouble. In December of 1872 the Associates of the Central Pacific faced payments of slightly more than $2 million in interest due on January 1, 1873, alone; in addition, they had considerable floating debt. This was not public knowledge. Their annual report listed only $2,722,244 in interest payments due for the entire year and does not seem to have listed the floating debt at all. They owed the three San Francisco banks with which they did business $1,850,000, all of it subject to call, and all the bankers were professing to be in need of coin. The failure to pay any part of it would bring an immediate demand that they pay all of it. And, finally, there were taxes. "It seems to me," Hopkins wrote, "financial dishonor is unavoidable—and that can scarcely fail to bring a general collapse."[123]

Knowing the road's condition, Ralston demanded more collateral. In December of 1872 he got Stanford to promise that Huntington would place either one million dollars or 200,000 pounds sterling with Lees and Waller in New York for credit on their San Francisco account. Stanford's preference in any crisis was to do nothing. Actually, at any time, his preference was to do nothing. "If damned," Mark Hopkins wrote, Stanford "will be condemned for leaving undone those things that he might have done."[124] Although Stanford saw Huntington in New York soon after making his promise to Ralston, Huntington claimed that Stanford neglected to tell him of the agreement. Stanford intercepted telegrams to Huntington about the crisis, and Huntington discovered them only by accident. Stanford had found them so disagreeable that he was not going to show them to Huntington. It "was not," Huntington noted wearily, "safe to do business with him or in other words trust him to do anything."[125] Huntington was unable to borrow in New York, and only when A. A. Cohen persuaded Michael Reese to borrow £50,000 sterling at 1¼ percent interest per month, which Reese then lent to the Associates at slightly higher interest, was the railroad granted a reprieve.[126]

Jay Cooke, too, felt the pressure, but he maintained his characteristic optimism about eventual success and denounced Fahnestock for his constant "croaking." In the early 1870s the United States was still a largely agricultural country, and the natural rhythms of planting and harvest acted like the moon on financial tides. Farmers withdrew money or took out loans to finance planting and harvest in the spring and fall, and to meet these demands country banks withdrew their deposits from their correspondent banks in New York. In winter and summer unused funds flowed back to New York because of the interest its banks offered. The city banks, in turn, lent this money out to businessmen, investors, and brokers, but it was liable to "call" at any moment.[127] When Collis P. Huntington told his associate Mark Hopkins, "Call for as little money in April as you well can, because April is usually the most unsettled and hardest month in the year in which to get money, unless it is Oct," he was referring to this seasonal ebb and flow of money that made commercial capital more abundant in winter and summer and much scarcer in fall and spring.[128]

Spring and fall were the seasons of financial crisis. Borrowers were liable to have their loans called in, and bankers needed to make sure that the securities they held were liquid and easily converted into the money that their own depositors required. This was the principle that Jay Cooke insisted informed his own banking methods. He was sanctimonious about it, and his letters to his partners concerning it sounded like sermons.

I have passed through so much trial and tribulations during the last 33 years in banking that I cannot but feel that our duty to God, who has so graciously blessed us in all things, and our duty also to our customers and our government, is that we should keep our hands entirely free from all loans investments or enterprises that are not cash at an instant's notice even in the midst of a fearful panic.[129]

What Jay Cooke preached, however, he no longer practiced. The loans to the Northern Pacific could not be turned into cash when in the fall of 1872 New York speculators attempted to capitalize on the shortage of currency and corner greenbacks. Extorting extravagant charges from those in need of cash, they were on the verge of causing a banking panic in New York. As drafts from the Northern Pacific and associated railroads continued to flow in and its deposits continued to flow out, the New York branch of Jay Cooke and Company faced disaster. It had to borrow, but borrowing was virtually impossible because no one had cash to lend. Cooke's political connections saved him. The assistant secretary of the Treasury, William Richardson, happened to be visiting Cooke's estate at Ogontz, outside Philadelphia, when the crisis broke. Cooke persuaded him to buy back government bonds in New York, releasing greenbacks into the system. Through his brother Harry in Washington, Cooke made sure that the Treasury monitored the situation, relieving the shortage, making borrowing possible, and saving Cooke and Company. The episode shook Cooke.

You could hear the thunder and feel the wind by early 1873. Collis P. Huntington was a hard man, tough, remorseless, seemingly as impervious to the world around him as a rhinoceros, but in early 1873 he wrote Hopkins, "Things look bad. I am doing all I can [to] get matters straight and think I shall succeed but I am not well and I do not think that I have had twelve hours sleep in the last three weeks."[130] A "kind of nervous unrest" came over Huntington. He feared he would soon be unfit for business.[131] He was ready to "get out of all active business." It was time, he advised Leland Stanford, to "retire and enjoy" their gains even if they sold the Central Pacific for only half its real worth.[132] The Crockers had already departed. After Edwin's stroke, the Crocker brothers left the company entirely, although Charley would return in 1873 when the other Associates could not meet the final payment owed him for his share.[133]

It didn't matter where one turned in 1873. In the United States, Canada, or Mexico, the same grandiose plans, continental ambitions, secret negotiations, and financial maneuvers that tied together political leaders and corporate promoters of the transcontinentals were unraveling. The heady mixtures of nationalism, greed, necessity, and ambition were inexorably slipping out of control.[134]

The political connections that saved Jay Cooke in 1872—an election year—did him less good the following fall. Cooke's voluminous correspondence breaks off in 1873, and although he later denied it, he must have known that the storm would break. He cut his asking price for bonds. His attempt to organize a new syndicate to buy the remaining seven-thirties (as the 7.3 percent bonds were called) at 83 instead of par failed.[135] The clearest sign of his trouble was his absence from Gibraltar, his estate on an island in Lake Erie. He routinely came to the island for several weeks in the spring and fall when the fish were running. Fishing and praying were the hallmarks of Gibraltar, and when Cooke was not in residence he made the estate available to Protestant clergy. The ministers were there on September 18, 1873, when news reached Gibraltar that their "loved and generous host had failed." On September 15 Cooke was entertaining President Grant at his Ogontz estate. On September 19 he was issuing orders to close his mansion at Gibraltar. His fall was that rapid.[136]

William Richardson certainly knew that a crisis was coming, but only in the dim way of a man who might dismiss a tidal wave as a high tide. "Anticipating the usual autumn stringency," the Treasury Department had sold gold and accumulated currency to ease the squeeze in the fall by purchasing bonds and thus supplying cash to the markets. This was more necessary than ever because, in the words of the economist William Timberlake, declining reserves in New York banks meant that nearly "constant volume of circulation and deposits was perched on a smaller and smaller pivot of reserves." Richardson did purchase bonds as the panic set in, but he "did not think it well to undertake to furnish from the Treasury all the money the frenzied people may call for." "Confidence," he said, "was to be entirely restored only by the slow cautious process of gaining better knowledge of true values . . . and by conducting business on a firmer basis, with less inflation and more regard to real soundness and intrinsic values." His abandonment of Treasury Secretary Boutwell's policy of letting "the economy grow up to the Civil War money stock" represented an abandonment of Cooke, who until his death denounced hard money and the gold standard as a source of suffering and ruin.[137]

With the refusal of the Treasury to intervene, the full impact of the annus horribilis fell upon the railroads. The advances to the Northern Pacific Railroad made the House of Cooke incapable of meeting the call of country bankers who tried to withdraw their funds to finance the harvest. The tightening money market left Cooke and his partners incapable of borrowing the money they needed. When on September 18, 1873, the New York branch of the House of Cooke shut its doors, the other branches followed.[138] Their failure triggered the Panic of 1873, which led to the depression that paralyzed the economy. Credit tightened, and prices fell. The coal and iron industries suffered along with the railroads; half the American iron foundries had closed by the end of 1874. Bankruptcies doubled, from 5,183 in 1873 to 10,478 in 1878.[139]

Above all, it was a railroad depression. In 1874 new railroad construction in the United States fell to 1,911 miles, and both passenger and freight revenue began to decline.[140] Between September 20, 1873, when the House of Cooke collapsed, and the end of the year, twenty-five railroads with $150,233,250 in outstanding bonds defaulted. In 1874 seventy-one followed with a bonded debt of $262,366,701, and another twenty-five having $140,448, 214 in outstanding bonds defaulted in 1875. Railroad stock prices fell by 60 percent between 1873 and 1878.[141] The fledgling transcontinentals halted where they were, usually in the middle of nowhere.

Governments fell with the railroads. The depression cost the Republicans their control of Congress in the elections of 1874. In Canada, Allan surrendered the charter of the Canadian Pacific in late October 1873. For Jay Cooke the Canadian Pacific had never been anything more than the tail of his Northern Pacific dog. By September that dog was for all practical purposes dead, and by then railroads were falling all across the continent.[142]

In Mexico the railroads died with a whimper rather than a bang. Edward Plumb, the agent of New York capital in Mexico, having successfully negotiated a contract with President Lerdo, believed that the next session of the Mexican Congress would bring the approval he coveted. He still believed that on October 11, 1873, when he received in Mexico City a shipment of New York newspapers current to September 27. They had "the details of the financial storm which so suddenly and violently has swept over the U.S." Plumb hoped "the worst is now over and the atmosphere may become all the more clear after the storm." But the financial skies would not clear for years, and Plumb's failure to get his contract approved by the Mexican Congress actually came as a relief. An opposing Mexican company argued that the financial crisis in the United States made it impossible for Americans to raise the necessary money and that Mexico would do better to seek English capital. Plumb was certain his rivals could not raise the necessary funds, but Congress's decision to give them the contract left him relieved that he had "not to take up such a load at present."[143]

VII. STORIES OF THE FALL

It would be edifying to see the Panic of 1873, as Secretary Richardson did, as a reinstitution of financial discipline, business rectitude, and true values.

Sinners and the righteous, however, tumbled down into this particular economic hell together, and those who survived were less virtuous than lucky. Overcapitalized, mismanaged, and often ill conceived, all the transcontinentals were fit for perdition, but the Central Pacific and the Union Pacific survived.

The Union Pacific survived thanks to Jay Gould. During the panic, he purchased stock in the Union Pacific, which was tottering on the brink of bankruptcy. In cooperation with Sidney Dillon, its president, he immediately executed a scheme to save the road from defaulting on its bonds. He did so, characteristically, by threatening to default. He had Dillon announce to the income bondholders that they would not be paid. Dillon offered to take their bonds in exchange for new sinking fund bonds at lower interest. This could have been a quite legitimate piece of finance, but Dillon and Gould secretly formed a pool to buy the income bonds that many holders were now eager to sell. They also secretly intervened in the market to boost the price of the sinking fund bonds. They took no risk. Union Pacific guaranteed that any losses the pool suffered would be made up by the company. It was a wonderful piece of insider dealing; Gould profited, investors lost, and the savings were used to lower the floating debt.[144]

Collis P. Huntington saved the Central Pacific only through ruthlessness and blind luck. More than once, Huntington teetered on the edge of defaulting on notes that would have brought the whole pyramid of debt tumbling down upon him.[145] At the end of September, overwhelmed by work and worry, even he seemed ready to succumb: "I stay in my office not knowing just what to do."[146] He let his eastern road, the Chesapeake and Ohio, fail, which brought down the Central Pacific's bankers, Fisk and Hatch. This should have been the end of the Central Pacific, for Fisk and Hatch had lent the railroad $3 million that it could not repay. Fisk and Hatch had hypothecated these bonds to larger banks, and when these bankers found out how much the Central Pacific owed, they realized that the bonds they had taken as diamonds were really so much glass. They were persuaded it would be best to stay quiet and grant Fisk and Hatch a reprieve: three years to repay their loans. They would not force Fisk and Hatch to call in the Central Pacific loan, which would have driven that road into receivership. While this saved the Central Pacific, Huntington summed up the downside: "it has hurt us as it has destroyed their [Fisk and Hatch's] power to borrow for us. And then our owing them so large an amount hurt us as it was known to their largest creditors who are prominent bankers."[147]

Everyone agreed to lie. The utilitarian fictions of capitalism are apparent when the annual report for the Central Pacific Railroad for 1873 and the report of the railroad's bankers, Fisk and Hatch, to Central Pacific bondholders in January of 1874 are compared with the less imaginative letters exchanged among the Associates. On January 1, 1874, Fisk and Hatch published numbers that assured investors that the Central Pacific had a large surplus from earnings, more than enough to cover its bonded debt (it didn't mention other debts). The Central Pacific, the bankers reported, maintained "undiminished, its accustomed prosperity in management, resources, and revenues." The Central Pacific's annual report for 1873 remained as reassuring as ever: "the financial and business prospects of your Company were never brighter." In November of 1873, however, Hopkins wrote Huntington that it was "impossible to save out of it (revenues) enough to [pay] the C.P. January interest." In December he had resigned himself to trying to pay the interest by not paying workers or taxes, by "robbing Peter to pay Paul."[148]

Two different stories were told about the result of the debacle of 1873. The railroad journals, as business journals must, found the bright side. Railroads might fail, promoters might fall, and investors might lose, but the tracks themselves survived. In 1877 the *Railway Age* gave such an account. Investors have lost, but the American public has won because the United States "has the railroads. They are built and in operation, and the owners cannot take them away, even if they want to."[149]

Had personal losses secured a larger good—a national railroad network? Had, in effect, misinformation and financial corruption worked for the benefit of the nation? In answer, John Murray Forbes, whose Burlington roads were edging west, told another story. He complained that the loans had gone out to collections of rails, ties, bridges, and rolling stock "called railroads, many of them laid down in places where much of it was practically useless."[150] Charles Hassler, whose *Weekly Financial Report* was closely followed by investors, wrote that "one of the great causes, if not the main cause," of the disaster in railway affairs was the "concealment of truth." Only through fraud had some of the lines been built, and it was "quite likely" that the country would "be better off without them."[151] The country had acquired a set of poorly built railroads without the traffic to sustain them. They would continue to deteriorate unless good money followed bad to maintain and improve them.[152] Modernity is as much a product of disaster as of success; both can bring the new into being.

A RAILROAD LIFE

◆—◆—◆

WILLIAM HYDE

L ike so many others who used the railroads to reimagine and to remake the American West, William Hyde was an engineer, and engineering, as he once wrote Mark Hopkins, was "but the servant of Investment."[1] Hyde was an especially eager servant: ambitious, busy, and self-promoting. He desired to rearrange the western landscape for personal profit and national progress; in him, the two were always, almost innocently, connected.

Personal profit and national progress was one of those pairings that seemed natural in the nineteenth century and suspect a century or more later. The pairing of the organic and the mechanical was another. Like so many engineers, Hyde never clearly separated his organic metaphors from his work of designing and building machines: railroads, steam plows, and yet unnamed contrivances that could mobilize steam to run cars on rubber tires. The central metaphor of the transcontinentals was biological; they were trunk lines, and trunk lines needed branches with freight rates so low "as to ripen into life millions of dollars worth of development."[2] Development was but the fruit of the transcontinentals, and the trains would carry to market the fruit they had called into being across rivers, mountains, and even arms of the ocean like San Francisco Bay. Nature and the machine were not yet enemies.[3]

Hyde was ultimately a failure as an engineer. He survives not through his machines but through his letters. Those letters trace lines of power like those in a diagram of a steam engine, but hardly as orderly. The lines of power in the letters originate from the sites of Hyde's writing, places where transformations were plotted and undertaken: San Francisco, Washington, D.C., and Los Angeles.

The first letters in Hyde's letterbooks were from San Francisco, where in 1871 he was the chief engineer for the Terminal Central Pacific Railroad. The Terminal Central Pacific was designed to take advantage of what Hyde calls the "great blunder" of the Central Pacific "of officially making Sacramento their initial point and selling the right to go to San Francisco to the Western Pacific R.R. Co. which Co. made as great a blunder by making San Jose their initial point leaving open for competition the air line route of which ours is the completing link to the California Pacific Co. between Vallejo & Sac." The plan for the railroad shifted at various times, but in all its variations it amounted to dredging, scraping, filling, and building until trains would eventually run across the bay from Vallejo on a stone embankment to wharves and warehouses built on the shoal and tideland around Yerba Buena Island or, as it was most often referred to, Goat Island, where the spans of the Bay Bridge now connect.[4]

San Francisco never embraced the development of Yerba Buena, regarding it as a threat to its own growth. In any case, San Francisco did not have the power to deliver Yerba Buena to the railroad, although it might have had the power to deny it. The Terminal Central Pacific needed greater leverage to transform Goat Island than it could get in San Francisco. The railroad had a corporate charter from California, but Yerba Buena was federal property, and in the nineteenth century the key sites for any American transcontinental were places where the roads never ran: Washington, D.C., Boston, and New York City. Hyde went to Washington as chief lobbyist to get the government to give his employers some or all of Goat Island. If a railroad controlled the island, it could make it, rather than San Francisco proper, the great embarkation point for Pacific commerce. San Francisco would be at its mercy.

To secure control Hyde went to Washington, D.C., to lobby Congress. It is hard to say whether any of his correspondents ever believed the letters that Hyde wrote them from Washington. A century and a half later, knowing the railroad would never be built and reading the letters in the Stanford University Archives, one finds it hard to imagine that they did. Even the far more powerful efforts of the Central Pacific to make up for its blunder ("I went to see the President yesterday," Collis P. Huntington wrote to Mark Hopkins concerning *their* attempt to get Goat Island, "and had a very full talk with him"), failed to wrest it from the federal government.[5] Hyde's letterbooks are full of his verbose, repetitive correspondence; each page yields equal quantities of self-deception and self-promotion. Senators whose help he believed he had obtained in one letter always disappointed him in the next. He wheedled, whined, and then denounced a company so tightfisted with its own worthless stock that it wouldn't even give him sufficient cash and paper to bribe the necessary lawmakers and pay off government clerks.[6] I am dealing, he told his wife, "with all the elements that win battles in Congress: Greed, Ambition, Lust for Money and Power."[7] And yet he was always sure that they were on the verge of success.

Then, quite suddenly in May of 1869, he went over to the enemy, the Southern Pacific, at first an offspring of Central Pacific interests and eventually the child that mastered its parent. He had just two months earlier denounced his new employers as a monopoly, but now he was fully and eagerly at their service, although after a year and a half he still had "no defined sphere or duties or acknowledged position."[8]

Eventually Hyde found a niche in Los Angeles, not yet a site of much power, but instead a site to be transformed. At first he was merely a political manager in a fight to secure a subsidy from the city for the Southern Pacific, but by 1872 he was at last doing what made him happiest.[9] He was building a railroad. Not much of a railroad—really, a branch line posing as a section of the trunk—but it was iron rail and wooden ties and workmen to regulate and ships to unload. He was in his glory, and he was in love. His letters reflect his contentment as a tool of capital.

Southern California, no matter how much it may disappoint later, no matter how its inhabitants always seem unworthy of its charms, exerts an initial attraction on some so strong that even Hyde called it love.[10] William Hyde, already passionately in love with his wife, wrote her letters that incorporated the land around him so thoroughly that they read as if he and she and Los Angeles had formed a ménage à trois in which she only knew the third party through her husband's descriptions. "My precious lover, . . . Los Angeles is a delightful place—and under certain circumstances you and I would find life joyous there. . . . I think of you constantly and kiss you over and over again in my goodbye embrace. Darling, goodbye."[11] "My darling wife, I have just been looking at your picture and such a thrill of love went through me that I kissed it over and over again. I do love you so much. How I wish you were here to see this wonderful country and to be by me. . . ."

It was a perfect nineteenth-century relationship. What he adored was what he sought to transform. He had rivals for the land, but he dismissed them. They were unworthy. Fresh from bribing congressmen, and saving his own railroad expenditures "for the day of the election," he recognized their corruption at once casually and self-righteously. "There is a Spanish element here which if made to vote must be paid for it—and the most money carries their votes. They have no interest nor care for a cause but if their votes are wanted pay will get them. . . . Isn't it disgraceful? At the election granting county aid to this little San Pedro Railroad there were gangs of these men driven into corrals and then let in to vote in small parcels and when their votes were cast were paid their money. The idea of their holding the franchise is disgraceful."[12] And later that month, in another letter to his wife, he reported, "I rode off for the upper part of the Los Angeles river and the immense plains of the San Fernando passed the old mission of the same name—an immense straggling adobe building tiled over—groves of olive trees in the enclosure and a crowd of old Indians hanging around. The whole country is as yet unsettled. . . ."[13] The railroads would change all this.

He was a man in deeply over his head. Not because he did not know about building railroads, but because he did not, despite his Washington experience, fully appreciate the men he worked for. He wrote Leland Stanford that John Downey, like Stanford an ex-governor of California and the kind of minor promoter who would eventually be as thick as the chaparral in Los Angeles, "has already shown the cloven hoof," and has become more and more selfish.[14] He wrote Collis P. Huntington that he had never in his life seen a rural community like Los Angeles: "All high and low seem to be on a coin basis."[15] Cloven hoof? Selfish? Coin basis? He was working for Collis P. Huntington and Leland Stanford; John Downey was an altar boy in comparison; Los Angeles was a community of saints. At the very moment Hyde wrote, Huntington was floating a complicated scheme to Stanford and Mark Hopkins that involved bribing enough people to control the San Francisco board of supervisors, having San Francisco vote a bond issue to buy a rival to the Southern Pacific that would secretly be controlled by Huntington, Hopkins, and Stanford, and then using the bonds to buy the Southern Pacific at a tidy profit to the partners even after the million-dollar bribe was paid.[16]

The bribes, Huntington believed, would pay dividends; he was not sure about the money Hyde spent. Hyde did not understand the economy of corruption. The Associates wanted to know how he spent their money and what he got for it. Hyde had not provided the details. Huntington did not understand the need to spend so much money to win an election when none was being spent against him.[17]

Hyde, in turn, could not understand why the Southern Pacific did not push the Los Angeles branch line, but the Associates were near drowning in deep financial waters, and every penny of their own money now mattered to them. The papers were full of rumors, accurate for once, that Huntington, Stanford, and Crocker wanted to sell the Southern Pacific to the very man, Tom Scott, who backed the men who opposed Hyde in Los Angeles.[18] The deal fell through, but the Southern Pacific and the Central Pacific were both on the market and their owners feared collapse.[19] Hyde's perennial dogged-ness and optimism seemed very much like a species of blindness. By the time the crisis came, Hyde was out of work.

CHAPTER 3

FRIENDS

[W]e must take care of our friends.

—COLLIS P. HUNTINGTON[1]

FOR A RAILROAD to survive, it had to have friends. Friendship became the preferred mode for a whole set of homosocial relationships in business and public life. The correspondence of the Associates of the Central Pacific Railroad reads like a Quaker meeting: Friend Huntington, Friend Stanford, Friend Crocker, and Friend Hopkins. The men who ran the railroads had journalists who were friends and executives in other corporations who were friends. They had bankers who were friends, but above all they had politicians who were friends. "Friend" was, perhaps, the key word in Gilded Age governance and business. On "being asked the secret of political success," John Morrissey, "prize fighter, professional gambler and member of Congress . . . replied, 'Stick to your friends, and be free with your money.'" As a lawmaker told the reporter George Alfred Townsend, "measures lived or died on friendship." It was not only good to have friends; it was essential.[2]

Both Tom Scott and Collis P. Huntington knew the necessity of friendship. Scott and Huntington emerged from the Panic of 1873 like survivors of a train wreck. Scott, true to form, did not so much stagger as strut. He had taken over the Texas Pacific, which had been rechartered in 1872 as the Texas and Pacific to build from Shreveport, Louisiana, to Marshall, Texas. From there it was to take the most direct route along the 32nd parallel through El Paso and, by the most direct and eligible route, to San Diego, with a potential branch from Fort Yuma on the Colorado to San Francisco. It was the last road to receive a substantial federal land grant: roughly eighteen million acres.[3] It had also seized the corpses of its failed predecessors—the Memphis, El Paso, and Pacific and the Texas Western, which became, confusingly, given later events, the Southern Pacific (of Texas) as distinct from the Southern Pacific (of California)—and consumed their federal and state land grants. It then very nearly became a corpse itself. The grants came with deadlines that the road failed to meet, but Scott had friends. Congress and the Texas legislature granted extensions.[4]

Scott had endorsed notes for the California and Texas Construction Company—the Texas and Pacific's equivalent of the Union Pacific's Crédit Mobilier. When it failed, Scott could not cover the notes, but he remained, as he always did, publicly sanguine and confident. In November of 1873 the *American Railroad Journal* reported that Scott had assured the holders of the notes that if they would give him from two to twenty-four months, they all would be paid. He believed "that Congress will extend aid to his enterprise, not by indorsing the company's bonds, but by lending to the company government bonds, under such guarantees of payment by the company as he can show is sufficient."[5] It was astonishing that in the very year of the Crédit Mobilier, Scott, dragging the corpse of a similar construction company, persuaded creditors that he could induce Congress to offer him essentially the same arrangement that had plunged the Union Pacific and Congress into scandal. It was vintage Scott. It was also belief in the power of friendship.

In 1873 Huntington was neither as flamboyant nor as well known as Tom Scott, but he was equally determined and growing more confident. Before the panic, a fearful and demoralized Huntington had tried to sell out to Scott, but Huntington was perversely reinvigorated by the economic disaster that destroyed railroads all across the country and yet, seemingly miraculously, had left him and the other Associates standing. Scott, despite his bravado, was a mere mortal after all, and if Scott intended to regroup and drive the Texas and Pacific toward California, then Huntington was ready to fight him.[6] Huntington, too, had friends.

The Associates had bought the Southern Pacific, then a paper road chartered to run down the coast, just as they bought virtually everything that ran on two rails in California. They moved its route to the Central Valley and made it the equivalent of an expensive night watchman guarding the approaches to the Central Pacific's West Coast monopoly. If they couldn't sell their railroads, they would protect them, and their initial goal was to stop the Texas and Pacific from entering California. Their ultimate goal of making the Southern Pacific a transcontinental with branches extending into Mexico was a result of confronting Tom Scott, and not the cause.[7]

Their confrontation revealed not only the power of friendship but also its moral ambiguity in Gilded Age politics. Political friendship was itself virtually always corrupt; friendship facilitated the movement of public goods to secure private favors, but leagues of friends also mobilized to prevent such transfers, sometimes for the public good and sometimes because they wished to have the spoils themselves.

In the 1870s Scott and Huntington both relied on friendship, but they seemed to have been cast from different molds. Huntington had none of Scott's charm and none of his grace. Scott could seem unctuous, but Huntington showed little desire to please. In private Huntington was often wry and funny, but in public he came across as a self-satisfied and willfully obtuse bully. Scott, the public man, left few private papers. Like Jay Gould, Scott preferred conversation to correspondence. He did not like to leave tracks. Huntington, however, living in New York and dealing with his Associates in California, had a voluminous, frank, and very often incriminating correspondence. Even during his lifetime large numbers of his letters leaked into the public domain and were published by his enemies. He had no choice but to be shameless when his own writings revealed so much to be ashamed of.

The differences between the two men were the products of self-fashioning, not of background. They sprang from the same pinched and narrow corners of rural America. Huntington grew up in Poverty Hollow in Harwinton Township, Connecticut. The death of Scott's father explained his early exile from home. The young Huntington was taken from his impoverished family by the town overseers and bound out to local farmers. Both the young Scott and the young Huntington became clerks. While Scott rose in the Pennsylvania Railroad, Huntington went west with the Gold Rush and became a Sacramento storekeeper. Both became spectacularly dishonest and assumed that others were the same. They regarded those who opposed them as evil men. At the height of their conflict, they assumed this about each other, even as each appreciated the other's skill.

What most differentiated Scott and Huntington in the early 1870s was that Scott knew a lot about railroads and Huntington initially knew very little. Unfortunately for Scott, and fortunately for Huntington, knowing the railroad business was not that great an asset for building transcontinentals. The transcontinentals were not so much about earning revenues from moving people and freight as about finance and politics. Finance and politics were in the late nineteenth century about networks, and networks, in turn, were functions of family, friendship, and information. Huntington's second wife, Arabella, captured this later in 1889 when she teased her much older husband for "sitting on [his] chair and making money all the time—like an old spider."[8] It was a nice image of Huntington, weaving his financial web. It was the web that mattered. Without the web the spider was just a hungry arachnid and Huntington merely a storekeeper.

Huntington and Scott knew what modern scholars sometimes forget: the federal government did not leave the railroad business to the market and the states to regulate, and their most decisive competition often took place in Congress. Their political lobbies connected politics and business, but these were only part of a second, much larger web of politicians, newspapermen, bankers, and businessmen. The webs ensnared what the railroads needed to survive—subsidies, friendly legislation, newspaper stories that made it easier to market the railroads' securities, and favors of all kinds.

The strands of this web were as strong and as gossamer as anything a spider wove. The strands had to be nearly invisible, and they could not reveal the spider. By and large the strands were made from information that helped friends and hurt enemies. To manipulate information railroads bought newspapers, but this was only a phase of the business. As they grew more sophisticated, they preferred to cultivate rather than employ individual newspapermen and publishers.[9] The railroads' everyday means of cultivating newspapers were free passes, printing contracts, and advertising, often above going rates, but they also recruited newspapermen as agents and lobbyists and lent them money. All were prophylactics against bad news. Huntington, Scott, and Gould often wrote articles or had them commissioned, but their value depended on disguising the source; the value of a lie depended on the apparent rectitude and disinterestedness of the liar.[10]

In practice there was little rectitude and less disinterestedness in the newspaper business. In 1886 Isaac Bromley, a newspaperman and a lobbyist, prepared a memorandum on New York newspapers and their attitude toward the Union Pacific for the road's president, Charles Francis Adams. The *Times* was hostile, largely because Wall Street bears were using it to drive down Union Pacific stock. The *Indicator* and the *Graphic* were friendly, but only because Wall Street speculators were using them to bull Union Pacific stock. The *Stockholder*, a Gould organ, was quiet until Gould decided where his interests lay. The *Financial Chronicle* would do whatever it was asked as long as it had "a reasonable share of advertising." The *Financier* had little influence, but such as it had was for sale: "its purpose being black-mail." The *Sun* was in Bromley's pocket, publishing what he sent. The *Star* did "as Huntington directs." The *Tribune* was friendly but useless. No one except Republicans read it and the Republicans already backed the funding bill the Union Pacific desired. The *World* was hostile only because the *Star* was friendly, and William Dorsheimer, the *Star*'s editor, had "opened a personal warfare on Pulitzer." And so it went for page after page.[11]

Newspapers were the basins that caught the news, but there were ways to prevent, or at least slow, the arrival of information the railroads wanted held back. When the Associates filed suit against A. A. Cohen, the San Francisco businessman often so central to their affairs, it turned into an embarrassment because Cohen used the trial as a trumpet to blast his charges against the Central Pacific across the country. Huntington acted to confine the publicity. "I have no doubt," Huntington wrote Hopkins, that "[if] the A.P. agent was seen much of this stuff could be kept back." Huntington's lobbyist, Richard Franchot, once succeeded in getting the Associated Press reporter in

Washington on the Central Pacific payroll until the Associated Press editor Simonton suspected as much from the changing tenor of his stories. At their most ambitious, the Associates unsuccessfully sought in 1875 to get exclusive Associated Press membership for the *Chronicle*, a paper they then controlled, by offering double the going rates and thus cutting off the hated *Bulletin* and *Call*.[12] Such interventions were necessary because, as Huntington wrote to his then-asssociate, David Colton, "Capital is always timid," and the timidity of capital created the need for constant reassurance and continual good news both political and financial. Such interventions were also difficult. By 1883 the Associates were subsidizing the *Bulletin* and the *Call* as well as country newspapers, only to have the *Chronicle* and the *Examiner* turn against them.[13]

Nineteenth-century Americans were not shocked by the corruption of the press; neither were they surprised that businessmen cheated, lied, and stole; what worried them was the corruption of the republic.[14] In the Gilded Age, Americans feared that the republic had become corrupted—diseased, decaying, and dying. They identified the source of this corruption as monopoly, and they made monopoly synonymous with the corporation.

The corporate monster—Monopoly—had appeared before the Civil War as the Bank of the United States and had been slain by Andrew Jackson, but it reincarnated as the transcontinental railroads. The monster moved into the halls of Congress, but instead of devouring a rotten republic as the Jacksonians had feared, it announced that it just wanted to be friends. What was supposed to be a tragedy—the decline of republican virtue and then the death of the republic—became instead a farce. That is how Mark Twain cast it in *The Gilded Age*. The republic didn't die; it became a collection of Senator Dilworthys. Congress met and Congress debated and Congress passed laws, but its public business had become seemingly inextricably involved with private gain.

And yet this formulation was both too simple and too cynical, because this age of corruption was also an age of reform. The Gilded Age spawned powerful movements for social reform and fierce anticorporate politics without, however, yielding the kind of simple battle lines between the masses and the classes that the most ardent reformers hoped would emerge. In part, this was because there was rarely a single railroad interest. There were multiple competing railroads, and they made Congress and state legislatures places in which to compete. And, in part, it was because reformers, too, became part of the networks that corporations created. Networks connected friends, and while a reformer might be one railroad's enemy, he could as a result become another railroad's friend.

Often missing from Gilded Age friendship was what seems to us its defining and necessary element: affection. It is not that these men never liked each other. When Mark Hopkins died in 1878, Huntington wrote, "I liked him so much and his death has hurt me more than I can tell. If I had not so much to do for the living I would stop for a time and think only of the dead."[15] But Friend Huntington despised Friend Stanford. "I am disposed to think," Huntington had written Charles Crocker in 1871, "Stanford will go to work for the railroad company as soon as the horse races are over. Of course, I do not expect anything until then."[16] And he once wrote Stanford himself, "I wish you would tell me whom to correspond with in Cal. when I want anything done; for I have become thoroughly convinced that there is no use in writing to you."[17] The other Associates shared his disdain. Their writing on Stanford is a chronicle of amazement, dismay, and irritation at his greed, laziness, ignorance, and ineptitude.[18] Mark Hopkins thought Stanford's key quality was his intellectual torpor. "He could do it," Hopkins told Huntington of some necessary task, "but not without more mental effort than is agreeable to him."[19] Men who had once been Stanford's friends were even less generous. Ex-Senator Conness of California railed against Stanford as "this immensely stupid man," who had forgotten that he "had helped make his fortune."[20]

David Colton was certain that Stanford and Hopkins disliked him and would blackball him as an Associate when the special five-year agreement that made him one of them was up. It was this certainty, as well as his financial desperation, that led him to embezzle. But even as Colton embezzled, he employed the language of friendship. When friends of the Central Pacific failed to pass critical legislation in 1878, Colton was alternately lachrymose and indignant—"we have got no true friends outside of us five."[21]

The elimination of affection from corporate and political friendship in the Gilded Age was its genius. The key figures of the Gilded Age networks of finance, government, journalism, and business had stumbled like so many vampires on a cultural form (friendship), drained it of its lifeblood (affection), and left it so that it still walked, talked, and served their purposes in the world. Friendship was a code: a network of social bonds that could organize political activity. Affection was not necessary.[22]

Friends did favors for one another and worked toward common goals. On a rare occasion when Leland Stanford addressed railroad workers as friends, he explained that they "were engaged in a common enterprise" and ought to be bound together with a "common bond of sympathy."[23] The key attributes of friendship were such bonds of sympathy, reciprocity, loyalty, and a presumption of mutual independence.[24]

Friends were loyal, and loyalty, as friends themselves observed, could not be purchased even if it could be rewarded. Friends of the railroads were not agents, bought and paid for. Friends sometimes differed, but it was the long-term relationship that counted. Nor, given the finesse and secrecy involved in congressional committee work and negotiations, could friends be easily monitored; they could only be trusted. Friends had to be prepared for betrayals. "Destroy when read." The phrase—sometimes boldly scrawled, sometimes a simple notation—is a staple of the archived correspondence between railway officials and politicians. The letters resting so undestroyed in the archives testify to both a misplaced confidence in railroad friendship and evidence that friendships were always provisional.

When friendship faltered, the ensuing denunciations often focused on honor and loyalty. Among the Civil War generation of the North, treason was the ultimate sin; loyalty was the great virtue. The language of war became the language of business. Senator John H. Mitchell of Oregon was a friend of Henry Villard, the receiver for the Kansas Pacific and later president of the Northern Pacific. In between his terms in the Senate, Mitchell was a lawyer and lobbyist for the Northern Pacific, and he saw his subservience to corporate interests in moral terms. "I do despise a traitor," he wrote Villard, and "you will receive my suggestions in the spirit in which they are made that is of entire devotion to you and your interests while in your employ."[25]

Friendship was where the kind of men found in an Edith Wharton novel obtained their footing. In a Wharton novel the businessman husbands or fathers—so necessarily present and as necessarily alien to the love affairs and friendships, to the flirtations and conversations, around which the novels revolved—only blundered and did damage. The female characters created inchoate networks too insubstantial to support the ponderous men whom they accidentally ensnared. But in the hotel rooms, clubs, and offices men spun out their webs of friendship. The material networks—the bands of steel that girded the continent—also depended on inchoate networks that mirrored the secrets, courtships, and flirtations of drawing room and dining room. The cultural connections of business and politics central to the railroads were the domain of friends.[26]

These inchoate connections, however, demanded material support. The railroads could and did grant political friends direct payments in the form of "loans" or cash, but such payments were unimaginative and often unnecessary.[27] They caused problems in case of investigations, such as that of the Pacific Railway Commission in 1887, which discovered vouchers for large sums of money without receipts to show where the money had gone. Huntington discovered a better way to fund such payments. He demanded rebates of 2½ or 5 percent on the prices charged by those doing business with the Associates. Expecting the rebates, suppliers raised the prices on the goods that they sold the Central Pacific and the Southern Pacific, but that did not disturb Huntington. The rebates were paid in cash and became a slush fund that was used for, as Huntington's assistant William Mahl put it, "payments for which it was thought just as well not to take any receipts."[28]

The railroads had numerous other ways of disguising favors. When Senator William Stewart of Nevada chaired the Pacific Railroad Committee in the Forty-third Congress, the Central Pacific gave him fifty thousand acres of land in the San Joaquin Valley, the whole transaction disguised with a dummy trustee.[29] William Barnum, a senator from Connecticut, was a manufacturer and a member of the Pacific Railroad Committee in 1877. "I bought the 1000 wheels of Barnum," Huntington wrote Hopkins. "He is in the U.S. Senate and does about what I want to have him have done. Reason why I bought the wheels."[30] The railroads could also offer senators and representatives employment as lawyers during their terms and as lobbyists after they left Congress.

But the cleanest and cheapest ways of helping friends was by giving them what the railroads often got in return: information. "Your letter touching the disposition to be made of outstanding land grants but anticipates a wish to know your opinion and have your views," Senator Roscoe Conkling wrote Huntington in 1880. A week later Conkling, in a letter marked private, asked Huntington for advice on Central Pacific stock. "I shall buy as much as I well can if I can know that you would think well of the purchase." By the end of the year, the $60,000 that Conkling had invested with Huntington had grown to $84,000.[31]

These were all, in effect, retail transactions. Sometimes the railroads tried to get their friends wholesale. William Carr, a.k.a. Uncle Billy, a.k.a. Boss Billy, had metamorphosed from something of a thug into an original incorporator of the Southern Pacific. He was a political fixer and an intimate of Stanford. Carr controlled federal patronage in San Francisco under Republican administrations, and he had considerable influence over some California congressmen. By 1875 he had received $60,000 in Southern Pacific bonds for his services to the Associates. Huntington and Colton debated how much he was worth in the future for "it was very important that his friends in Washington should be with us, and if that could be brought about by paying Carr say $10,000 to $20,000 per year, I think we could afford to do it, but, of course, not until he had controlled his friends."[32] Payments also went directly to the political parties. There were rumors in 1876 that Scott had offered the Democratic and the Republican national committees each $300,000 for resolutions in support of the Texas and Pacific and large sums to individual congressmen.[33] The techniques of friendship that began in Congress and legislatures were quite flexible. They could be extended outward to the press, to judges, or to anyone in a position to help or hurt the railroads.

I. THE LOBBY

At the political heart of the networks that Thomas Scott and Collis P. Huntington created were lobbies. They extended their lobbies until they were larger and more far-reaching than anything previously seen in American politics. The lobby as a means of supplicating favors from the government had long antedated the transcontinentals. What made the western railroad lobbies different was their evolution into a means for one corporation to fight another corporation. The lobby made politics a realm of economic competition between corporations.

Before the Panic of 1873 railroad lobbies were small and often operated through independent lobbyists—or strikers, as they were called. The strikers knew key things and key people. Lobbyists formed the so-called Third House of Congress. Given the increased scale of public business that came with the Civil War, lobbyists, often reporters or ex-politicians, helped to move legislation and thus avoid gridlock, but at a price.[34] The Civil War and Reconstruction created a golden age for strikers. Uriah Painter so adeptly combined reporting for the *Philadelphia Inquirer* and the *New York Sun* with lobbying and speculation that the legions who did not love him called him "Uriah Heep," "this singed rat," or "that persistent falsifier."[35] Harry Cooke had been his tutor. In a country where gold, stocks, and bonds rose and fell on war news, a reporter's knowledge of troop movements was information that could become money. Painter used information and became the tool of others in using it.[36] Painter's work for the Cookes blended finance, information, and politics in ways that would grow standard for the transcontinentals.[37]

Strikers, however, were dangerous servants to corporations, and after 1873 railroad corporations moved to marginalize them and replace them with larger and more elaborate lobbies.[38] "The damned strikers are so numerous," Collis Huntington had written Charles Crocker in 1870, referring to bills he sought to get title to Goat Island, "that if we should endeavor to put the matter before Congress this session I have no doubt it would cost us more than it would be worth, but I will feel of them and see what can be done."[39] Displacing the strikers was a gradual process. Tom Scott came to Washington with a formidable political reputation. His enemies described him as standing in the smoke of political battle like a Davy Crockett of corruption: "a one man power, who sets up and pulls down, and rules with omnipotent sway. Able, unscrupulous, shrewd, knowing how to make the interests of thousands of imitators of a smaller pattern run in the same groove with his own, he has probably done more to corrupt legislation, debauch politics, make bribery a science, elevate it to the rank of profession and enshrine it among the fine arts, than any man in this country."[40] Scott remained quite involved in the Texas and Pacific lobby, running it at key junctures, but he did not simply replace strikers with his own personal power. He built an organization.

Tom Scott's evolving relationship with Uriah Painter, who served Scott first in the Pennsylvania Railroad, then in the Union Pacific, and finally in the Texas and Pacific, reflected the changes taking place in lobbying.[41] Scott was initially deferential, writing Painter as late as 1873, "I . . . feel assured your interests can be better conserved by standing by us rather than by using your influence in favor of adverse measures. I would be pleased to hear from you from time to time as to any proposed measures to be introduced likely to affect our interests."[42] Painter, in turn, was heady with the power Scott's corporations commanded in Washington. When Secretary of the Treasury Boutwell threatened Scott's interests, Painter denounced Boutwell as "cross and malignant" and then turned on Grant. "You can secure fair play or ruin him," he wrote Scott of the president of the United States, "and I would not be kicked around like an old hat, while I had the power to command respect. . . ."[43]

By 1874, however, Painter, the feared striker, was casting himself as a victim of "rich corporations" that refused to grant him his due, and by the end of the decade he was denouncing men he had once served.[44] When loyalty went unrewarded and trust failed, the outrage was real. In Painter's papers there is a bundle of correspondence—his letters and the replies—that he took care to preserve and keep together. The issue they addressed was not the railroads per se but the closely related affairs of the Pacific Mail, the steamship service that provided the only real alternative to the Pacific Railroad in travel from the West Coast to the East and whose rates often determined transcontinental rates. It was a company the railroads tried to control. Jay Gould had proffered an arrangement through Grenville Dodge to Uriah Painter, and through Painter to friends in Congress. Congressmen were to derail legislation in such a way that certain securities were to rise in value. Part of the profit would go to the friends of Painter, Dodge, and Gould. They killed the measure Gould wanted killed but apparently not in the manner Gould wished, and so the securities were not delivered. Painter was outraged. It was a question of "honor." This was not "honest dealing." There would be a price to pay: "a man's broken word here is a barrier to further credit." Dodge said he could do nothing, and it was useless to threaten Gould. Gould refused to act.[45] Strikers no longer inspired fear; they were growing domesticated and sought scraps from corporate tables.

When Grenville Dodge enlisted Uriah Painter in Gould's scheme in the late 1870s, Dodge had become, among many other things, a corporate lobbyist in the service of Gould and Tom Scott. He had gone from being a Civil War general and chief engineer for the Union Pacific to being an Iowa congressman. He had become a lobbyist for the Union Pacific and then moved on to the Texas and Pacific in 1874 when Scott hired him as chief engineer. He also served as the chief lobbyist for the Texas and Pacific, even though he never fully severed his ties with the Union Pacific. Dodge could still be odd and erratic. When caught up in the Crédit Mobilier, he panicked and temporarily abandoned his work on the Texas and Pacific to hide in St. Louis.[46] Such lapses, however, did not prove fatal; Dodge, who was adept at promotion, particularly self-promotion, overcame them. During the Civil War, he had considerable success in organizing spies and informants, a talent that proved useful as a lobbyist. He remained an ambitious, audacious, and apparently convincing liar. It was always safest not to trust what Dodge said. The problem was that often some unknown part of it was true.[47]

Collis Huntington built his Central Pacific/Southern Pacific lobby around Richard Franchot. Franchot, who had been a railroad president, a congressman, and a general, was as cynical as he was able. A master of detail, he did not overwhelm Collis P. Huntington, his friend and employer, with details. Franchot's letters rarely took up more than a page or two. In 1880 Vice-President William Wheeler, in the process of wheedling a pass "as a personal favor" for his nephew from one of Franchot's successors, claimed that if Franchot, who died in 1875, had lived, he would have been the next senator from New York. There is no reason, however, to believe that Franchot would have wanted to be a senator.[48] He already held high and lucrative political office in the Central Pacific.

The transcontinental railroads needed men like Dodge and Franchot because the bonanza of grants and laws garnered in the 1860s had left them interested in virtually every branch of government. Dodge listed his own efforts for the Union Pacific in 1870 in Homeric detail. In Congress there had been the junction bill, "a bill amending the Wyoming Laws," the "Bridge Bill," and the perennial question of the Union Pacific's payment of interest on government bonds. In the courts he had had to look after the Davis suit to prevent the courts from appointing a receiver for the road, the Cheyenne case, and the Evanston townsite case. He had to work to get a reversal in a land case, *Freeman* v. *U.P.R.R.* In the Department of Interior, he had to secure "the order from Secretary Cox as to our right inside of Reservations," and he had to watch over decisions as to the right of parties to unsurveyed lands within reserved areas. In Treasury he had to shape "the modification of the construction of the interest law." In the War Department there was the matter of the reduction of the military reservations. And then there was "the Reversal of Commissioner Drummonds' decisions against us," the railroad's right to coal mines, the exchange of government bonds for company bonds, and securing patents for railroad lands. These issues involved "hundreds of thousands of dollars and thousands of acres of our best lands."[49] It was no different for the Central Pacific. There were, Collis P. Huntington estimated in 1876, currently "35 bills in the senate and the house that we are interested in."[50] Getting the original privileges had not demanded a lobby; regulating them, maintaining them, and denying them to others increasingly did. In the 1870s no lobbies were as large as those of the Central Pacific/Southern Pacific and the Texas and Pacific.

Beginning in 1874 Tom Scott's Texas and Pacific lobby grew in order to obtain subsidies from Congress, and Huntington's Central Pacific/Southern Pacific lobby grew in order to deny the Texas and Pacific those subsidies. In evaluating the struggle between the two corporations, it is best to keep the vulnerability of each in mind. Both the Southern Pacific and the Texas and Pacific were so dependent on credit that they resembled two large and angry men trying to fight while on life-support. Both corporations carried immense debt, and both depended on steady infusions from existing subsidies, bond sales, and loans. Each flailed at the other, each trying to maintain its own lifelines while cutting off those of its opponent.

Scott was clever, persistent, and increasingly desperate. Like a man whittling a stick, he pared and sharpened his requests as the 1870s wore on. He first asked that the United States accept Texas and Pacific bonds as security for an equal amount of U.S. Treasury bonds, thus allowing him to build the railroad on the credit of the United States. He reduced that request to a guarantee of interest on the railroad's own bonds, and in 1878 there emerged a hodgepodge of bills with a medley of subsidies from a guarantee of interest to the government's payment of $20,000 in greenbacks per mile in exchange for an equivalent in Texas and Pacific bonds. Scott originally wanted the funding based on the trunk and all its branches. He later reduced it to the trunk line itself. In all their forms, his bills remained, as an opposing congressman said, "substantially a proposition to build this road . . . on Government credit without making them the property of the Government when built. If there be profit, the corporations may take it; if there be loss, the Government must bear it."[51]

As the Texas and Pacific and the Southern Pacific built up their staffs in Washington, D.C., Huntington complained in 1877 that the fight "grew more and more expensive each year."[52] In the 1870s and on into the 1880s congressional committees, if not blind, were nearsighted. They had no staffs.[53] To influence the committees and provide information, the Texas and Pacific and the Central Pacific employed ex-congressman, some of whom had made reputations as reformers, to know more than the committee members knew. The Central Pacific hired S. C. Pomeroy of Kansas, J. R. West of Louisiana, George Julian of Indiana, Lyman Trumbull of Illinois, and Franchot himself. For more specialized tasks, they employed attorneys, such as John Flagg, who took care of land matters for the Central Pacific in the late 1870s.[54] They also cultivated men whose jobs gave them the opportunity to snoop, overhear, and intercept telegrams and letters. When Uriah Painter went to work for Tom Scott, he made it a point to take care of doorkeepers and telegraph operators.[55] Huntington recruited John Boyd, who eventually became the chief Central Pacific lobbyist, while Boyd was an assistant doorkeeper of the House in 1868.[56] Huntington and Richard Franchot helped secure George Gorham the position of secretary of the Senate. Gorham also became a close friend of Senator Conkling.[57]

Dodge recognized that lobbyists were not enough to secure desired legislation. He knew that friends of the railroad in Congress remained partisan politicians, answerable to constituents and local party machines. To have any hope of getting his subsidies, Scott had to expand the scope of the lobby well beyond Washington, D.C. Dodge quite characteristically took credit for professionalizing the lobby and widening its scope. Dodge viewed Washington as a volcano: laws, regulations, and subsidies spouted from the Capitol dome like lava, but the force that propelled them was generated deep within the country. Influencing Congress demanded being on the ground in D.C.—in the lobby—but it also meant creating pressure on congressmen in ways that seemed to come from their constituents. Such pressures took the form of newspapers that crossed congressmen's desks, and the letters, petitions, and resolutions of their constituents and party members that piled up on them.[58]

To create such pressure, the railroad lobbies could not just gather information; they had to manufacture it. In March of 1875 Dodge explained his strategy as if it were the antithesis of lobbying:

> There was no success here until I changed my whole policy, by reaching men from their homes not in Washington and let me say to you that all the members [of Congress] who have been brought to us have been brought in that way and not by men who have been here in Washington in our interest and under our pay. . . . What strength the T & P have had here has been secured from the fact that it has been relieved, almost entirely, from what is known as a lobby.[59]

Dodge was not eliminating the lobby: he was expanding and perfecting it in ways that played to the dual identity of congressmen as both friends of the railroad and partisan politicians. Dodge found that his old Republican colleagues claimed to be sympathetic to the Texas and Pacific but were unwilling to go against the antisubsidy resolutions of their constituents in party conventions and state legislatures.[60] To compensate, Dodge sought to develop countervailing strength in the Democratic South by selling the Texas and Pacific as a southern transcontinental. Dodge turned Scott's debts and failures into strengths. Scott's numerous creditors saw in a subsidy their source of payments and became his champions. The Texas and Pacific was only a small road of 320 miles when the Panic of 1873 halted it, but it projected branches that, either directly or through connecting lines, would link it with St. Louis, Galveston, Houston, San Antonio, Vicksburg, Memphis, and New Orleans.[61] From each branch, actual and projected, hung fruit: work for subcontractors, business and rising property values in the towns it connected, and opportunities for new feeder lines. Those who hoped to harvest this fruit became friends of Tom Scott. All of them could serve as dummies for railroad ventriloquists, conveying the Texas and Pacific message to Congress.[62]

II. ANTIMONOPOLY AND PARTY POLITICS

After 1873 the Associates would look back fondly on the Civil War and its immediate aftermath as the years when national politics were synonymous with Republican politics. Then the railroads could safely hitch their fate to the Republican Party. In 1873 Mark Hopkins wrote Huntington, "When we commenced, eleven years ago, Congress and Legislatures were gentle steeds. Bless me how they rear and tear now."[63] The rearing and tearing was owing partially to the resurgence of the Democrats. Huntington had begun to recognize the need for new tactics as early as 1871 when he proposed, "Some of us ought to act with the Democratic party. I think there is little difference between them now; it is only the seven reasons: the five loaves and two fishes."[64] He thought the Associates' reputation as Republicans had hurt them in their losing fight to secure Goat Island in San Francisco Bay as their terminus.[65]

Hopkins recognized that the Democrats' demand for a cut of railroad favors and railroad money was not the only change in railroad politics. Something else was happening, and it alarmed Richard Franchot, even though he initially thought it was a temporary disturbance. In 1870 Franchot had written Huntington, "[Congress is] very much demoralized on R.R. and as scary as the very devil and I should not be surprised any day they bolt like a drove of sheep." With the "country press . . . howling[,] . . . members are very weak kneed in regard to legislation in favor of great monopolies. . . ."[66] But Franchot dismissed this as a "spasm of virtue." When it "is over," he assured Huntington, "all will be well again for reasonable propositions in aid of Rail roads, and I think in course of session we will get what you require for SPRR." Until then they still had "good friends," whom they "could rely on."[67]

After the Crédit Mobilier scandal broke, Franchot was no longer so dismissive of reform. In one of his more effusive letters to Huntington, he stressed the vulnerability of their railroad friends to assault by the press. "Now I repeat what I heard from good men every day," he wrote in a prose nearly as vivid, garbled, and ungrammatical as Huntington's, "and there is some truth in it for the press is omnipotent for good & evil in politicks." "[A]ll our R.R. friends," he told Huntington, are near despair. "The newspapers come down on them and they have not a newspaper in the land to defend them. They feel that the vast capital at stake in R.Roads in this country is allowed to be jeopardized for the want of an organ and they ask friends to stand up for them to be pelted down by the press of the country without raising a hand or a dollar to defend them."[68]

It was the Grangers, quickly the premier organization of American farmers, who panicked Franchot. They took their name from the Patrons of Husbandry or the Grange and became, in the words of one of their supporters, "a power which no party can afford to ignore."[69] Their rise marked the beginning of postwar antimonopoly politics, but their ideological roots tapped older Jacksonian fears of special privilege, corruption, land monopoly, and tenancy. Their chief target in the 1870s was the railroads.[70]

Historians have long recognized that Granger demands for railroad regulation in the early 1870s arose most powerfully from businessmen—merchants and wholesalers—in towns and cities of Illinois, Iowa, Wisconsin, and Minnesota who felt that railroad rates favored their competitors in other places.[71] Railroads had the ability to disrupt existing market networks and determine whether existing towns and businesses prospered or died. "A railroad," Henry George wrote, "approaches a small town as a robber approaches his victim. The threat, 'If you do not accede to our terms we will leave your town two or three miles to one side!' is as efficacious as the 'Stand and deliver,' when backed by a cocked pistol."[72] But George grasped only the first episode of railroad clout. The physical presence of a railroad merely created a greater strength: the power to set rates.

The moral and political core of the Granger and antimonopolist critique of railroad corporations was that they had become an embodiment of special privilege and discrimination. Antimonopolists argued that all of the bulwarks of freedom in the United States were under assault from corporations that were, by their very nature, monopolies. "Monopoly" was the key word in the reform vocabulary, and it is essential to understand what late nineteenth-century Americans meant when they used the term. A monopoly was, first of all, a private entity granted special privileges by the state. It was thus almost by definition corrupt since antimonopolists believed that special privilege "in the last analysis rested upon legislative, executive and judicial favoritism." Such privilege could take the form of tariffs, land grants, loans, or other subsidies that favored a few and hurt many, or corporate charters that gave the railroads public aid without concomitant public control. By the 1870s special privilege and monopoly had become synonymous with corporations.[73]

The second mark of a monopoly was the ability to destroy, limit, or distort competition. The competition in question was not simply that between the railroads themselves or railroads and other forms of transportation; it was competition between all those businesses that used the railroads. By manipulating rates, the railroads could decide who succeeded in business and who failed. They could discriminate among individuals, offering favored shippers lower rates or rebates. They could discriminate among places, giving towns equidistant from the same destination different rates. They could discriminate among things, putting similar kinds of cargo in different categories and charge them different rates. The railroads' ability to discriminate—to use another key word in the antimonopolist vocabulary—against republican citizens violated both equity and basic rules of the market.

Monopolies in other businesses hurt their competitors and their consumers, but railroad monopolies hurt everyone because through their ability to set rates they could dictate the very terms of all competition. In the late nineteenth century laissez-faire was still making its strange transition from a doctrine of radicals and democrats to a doctrine of conservatives fearful of popular politics. The classical liberalism of Thomas Jefferson or Adam Smith feared government intervention in the economy as always and necessarily favoring the rich. This liberalism valued property because its possession bestowed more than access to things. It gave independence, "a stake in productive wealth, a chance to exercise initiative, do valuable work and earn standing in a community."[74] These values seemed precisely what corporations and corporate property threatened. They made people dependent.[75] The embrace by Gilded Age conservatives of laissez-faire, however, made property not the means to freedom but the reward of freedom. Conservatives embraced the rich; they did not fear them.

Monopoly's distortion of competition led to a third criticism of monopoly. An enterprise became a monopoly when it encompassed an activity that citizens could not normally avoid, and so gained an ability to extort what antimonopolists sometimes termed rents but more often a tax. A tax was any taking of a portion of the value of a product that was not the result of an addition of value to that product. In a republic the ability to tax belonged to the legislature, made up of representatives of the people. It was a public right. Antimonopoly was originally a producer ideology. Producers such as farmers were entitled to the value of what they produced, but landlords, middlemen of all kinds, bankers, and railroads claimed the lion's share of the profit from products to which they had contributed little or nothing. They, in effect, levied private taxes. The vanguard of antimonopolists followed this through to the logical conclusion. Any business whose profits came from the power to tax—that is, to claim a share of a product's value without altering it—was illegitimately claiming a public or state function. Public functions belonged to the people and their representatives, and such businesses should be nationalized.

Antimonopolism was a political movement that sought to reshape American politics, but the transcontinental railroads had narrower political ambitions. They wanted to control only those aspects of the political system that were critical to their interests. They regarded politics as simply another phase of business. They corrupted government, the public press, and financial markets, but their politics never went much beyond seeking profit. Although most railroad men denounced and feared antimonopolists in general, in practice the reformers became just another political grouping that could, in certain circumstances, prove useful. Few antimonoplists initially imagined that men like Tom Scott could under certain circumstances enlist on the side of competition or that Collis P. Huntington could march under the banner of antisubsidy.

Railroad men learned that normally the worst place to challenge antimonopolists and reformers was in elections. Charles Crocker complained in 1883 that the railroads' intervention in conventions and primaries made the men they opposed their enemies, while the men they succeeded in nominating "are so anxious to prove that we did not help them, that they are the worst men we have to deal with . . . for they are very anxious for an opportunity to show that they have no love for us."[76]

The Associates' electoral record in California from the completion of the Central Pacific into the mid-1880s was abysmal. The victory of Governor Henry Haight, an antisubsidy Democrat, in 1867, was followed by the 1871 election of Newton Booth, an antimonopolist Republican. When Stanford tried to defeat Booth's run for the U.S. Senate, he turned to the Democrats. Booth not only won, but Stanford undercut the pro-railroad Republican machine and alienated the railroad's important friends, Senator Sargent and George Gorham. In 1879 voters, over intense railroad opposition, approved a new California constitution providing for railroad regulation and in 1882 elected George Stoneman, an antimonopolist Democrat, as governor. In 1886 Charles Sherrill wrote Huntington in frustration, "In regard to California . . . for the last fifteen years we have met with more opposition from the representatives of that State than from those of any other State in the Union."[77] Powerful railroads often could not command their home state's delegations. Tom Scott and the Pennsylvania Railroad had enormous influence within the Pennsylvania Republican Party, and Simon Cameron's son was an incorporator of the Texas and Pacific, but Speaker of the House Randall from Philadelphia was, at least publicly, an antisubsidy Democrat.[78]

Elections, however, were the beginning, not the end, of politics, and railroads learned, as Charles Crocker put it, to "manage men after the election."[79] John King Luttrell, a Democratic representative from California, was a member of the critical Pacific Railroad Committee in the mid-

1870s. Huntington wanted David Colton to make him a friend: "I hope you will get some one to convince him that we are good fellows, and that should not be a hard thing to do, for I have no doubt of it myself."[80] It was an interesting, perhaps intentional, double entendre. "Good fellows" in the underworld slang of New York City was then, as now, a term for a criminal who thought there was honor and loyalty among thieves.[81] When Luttrell refused the carrot, Huntington picked up the stick. In 1875 he dismissed Luttrell as "a wild hog." Colton was to "*Beat him.*" But how? Beating him with a Republican would create animosity against the railroad among congressional Democrats who were becoming a majority in the House. In Nebraska the Union Pacific learned to influence Democrats in a Democratic district and Republicans in a Republican.[82] Direct electoral intervention to defeat an enemy with a member of the opposing party was usually a last resort and often a failed one. If Colton could not prevent his nomination, then Colton was to put a railroad Democrat up against him in the general election to split the Democratic vote and thus more obliquely elect a Republican.[83]

The Associates were always persistent. Luttrell metamorphosed into an "honest man." He introduced a bill to authorize the Central Pacific to build east, gobbling up the Texas and Pacific land grant as it went. It is a "fight [that] will cost us much money," Huntington wrote, "but I think it is worth it." Huntington asked Colton to thank Luttrell "for the good work that he . . . has done in Washington." Huntington welcomed Luttrell's reelection.[84] On leaving Congress, Luttrell occasionally lobbied for the railroad.[85]

Recruiting men like Luttrell involved a kind of seduction. It often took place in hotels such as the Willard or over private dinners. Collis P. Huntington seduced E. J. Ellis, who had earlier been seduced by Tom Scott. Ellis could have been a character in a Wharton novel, but he could also have been an invention of Mark Twain. Both fished different parts of the same social pool. In 1879 Ellis was thirty-nine years old, and he was as importunate as he was impecunious. A veteran of the Confederate army, an ex-prisoner of war, a graduate of the law school at Louisiana State University, he was also a Democratic representative from Louisiana between 1875 and 1885. He was a "Redeemer," freeing the South from Reconstruction, and complicit in a politics that spilled African American blood and broke the back of African American suffrage in Louisiana. He was also a member of the Pacific Railroad Committee and a friend of Collis P. Huntington, who was a Republican and a former abolitionist.[86]

By December of 1879 Ellis was a particularly desperate and indiscreet friend. "In February of this year I met you for the first time," Ellis wrote Huntington. "I had a long conversation with you about the R.R. interests of the South looking to the Pacific Ocean." Until January of 1879 Ellis had been "a strong advocate of Tom Scott," but realizing that the standoff in Congress threatened any transcontinental railroad for the South, Ellis tried to get the Texas and Pacific to compromise with the Southern Pacific. It refused. This, Ellis said, "opened my eyes to the real but occult designs of the T. & P. scheme, it was merely an extension of the Penn Central" through to St. Louis. Only then did Ellis turn to Huntington and the Southern Pacific as the real hope of New Orleans for a connection to the Pacific.

Ellis's conversion to the Southern Pacific, however, did not spring solely from his devotion to the South. "[A]t that interview a transaction occurred which bound me to you personally and identified me with your personal fortunes such ties as cannot be broken or disregarded." Huntington had proposed to advance him "a certain sum per annum," and Ellis agreed, "*voluntarily*" (Ellis underlined the word), to serve Huntington's "interests in any way shape, manner and form." Huntington had made 80 percent of the annual payment. Ellis desperately needed the remainder now. His position as a member of Congress had destroyed his law practice. He had pledged more and more of his salary to meet his debts. By December of 1879 it was pledged into May of 1880. He would not "embarrass or inconvenience a friend for . . . selfish purposes," and if the request caused Huntington any inconvenience, he should "dismiss it from [his] mind and thoughts," but since Huntington had fixed no date for the payment, he thought he should ask.

"But enough of this," he wrote. When he could locate his family in D.C., he would come to New York "to know fully your views and wishes with regard to measures pending here. I desire to know your exact will with regard also to the Northern Pacific and its proposed extension." He saw no reason to give them an immense land grant "gratis." Huntington, of course, also saw no reason why a rival road should be given a grant. "I am sincerely and always, your friend," Ellis wrote in closing.[87]

Huntington insisted that the Associates never offered bribes for official favors, and this was a lie; what he meant was that they did not bribe friends like Ellis. Friends reciprocated favors. Huntington also said that when the corrupt are in power "bribery may be the last and only means left to honest men."[88] Railroads resorted to bribery—a quid pro quo—only when their network of friends was insufficient to a crisis at hand. When railroad men offered bribes, they believed the fault lay with the recipients. Huntington and his friends remained "honest men."

Railroads often bestowed favors with praise of the recipient's honesty. Senator William Stewart of Nevada is, Huntington wrote, "peculiar, but thoroughly honest, and will bear no dictation, but I know he must live, and we must fix it so that he can make one or two hundred thousand dollars. It is in our interests and I think his right."[89] Similarly, Roscoe Conkling was a quintessential friend, whom Huntington considered "decidedly the greatest man in the United States Senate."[90]

Conkling was one of those powerful and ridiculous figures who dominated the Gilded Age Senate. He possessed some of the same "moral grandeur" that Twain gave to his Senator Dilworthy. He brought to Congress what his enemy, the equally powerful and equally ridiculous Senator James G. Blaine of Maine, described as "his haughty disdain, his grandiloquent swell, his majestic, preeminent, overpowering, turkey-gobbler strut." Cartoonists seized on the turkey-gobbler strut, and Conkling could never shake it. He hated Blaine. When Blaine, who was implicated in the Crédit Mobilier and other railroad scandals, became the Republican candidate for the presidency in 1884, Conkling refused to campaign for him, announcing that although a lawyer, and often a railroad lawyer, he did not "engage in criminal practice." Blaine lost New York by a hair and with it the election. Conkling was a great hater, but he was also a consistent friend. Oliver Ames of the Union Pacific wrote in 1874 that Conkling "has always been in the interest of the Central Pacific and ready at all times to work for whatever they wanted." Conkling's high-mindedness centered on his opposition to land grants to roads that might compete with the Central Pacific.[91]

Huntington rewarded and protected such virtue. He once asked Stanford to "arrange something out of which he [Conkling] could make some money (something handsome). You will have to be very careful how you do it, as he is very sensitive, but, of course, like the rest of us, has to eat and drink." The Central Pacific fed him well even as it reassured him of his virtue.[92] Huntington even contributed to Conkling's lasting monument, a statue by John Quincy Adams Ward still standing in Madison Square in New York City. At least one of the other statues in the square—Chester A. Arthur—is fitting company.[93]

Railroad men and their friends knew that the uninitiated easily mistook reciprocity for bribery and that the system could not be opened to public scrutiny. Senator Cole of California was a recipient of Central Pacific "loans," and when he broke with the road in 1875 Huntington considered suing him "for the money he owes us," but feared "it would admit of liability to open up some questions that would possibly hurt us, because they would probably be misconstrued."[94] When J. N. Dolph was elected to the Senate from Oregon, he asked for, and got, reassurances from Henry Villard of the Northern Pacific that his "interests will be properly taken care of." Villard also assured him, "I shall take good care that your identification with our interests shall not embarrass you in the least as senator."[95]

The railroads tried to place their friends and lobbyists at critical congressional choke points where bills could be delayed, stopped, or advanced. The key points were the Pacific Railroad Committees of the House and the Senate. These committees were not prime congressional assignments, and so railroads faced little competition from other interests in securing them. Ways and Means in the House and Appropriations or Judiciary in the Senate were also critical committees for the railroads, but these were sought-after appointments and hard to secure.[96]

Winning control of the Pacific Railroad Committees did not ensure legislative success for the railroads, but without control of these committees a successful political offensive in Congress was impossible.[97] Lobbyists did their most effective work in committees. They excelled at preventing quorums, amending legislation, delaying reports, sidetracking legislation to other committees, or "antagonizing" bills by introducing similar legislation to split the vote. As Woodrow Wilson wrote in the 1880s, a bill on leaving the "clerk's desk to a committee-room . . . crosses a parliamentary bridge of sighs to dim dungeons of silence whence it will never return."[98]

To get their friends on committees, the railroads had to try to influence far more important politicians. The Gilded Age Senate and House were very different places, varying in size, their rules, and the length of terms of their members. Each demanded different tactics. In the House the rapid turnover of members in the 1870s, and the power of the Speaker meant that railroads recruited friends more opportunistically. Ideally, the railroads could influence the Speaker, who determined the composition of critical committees and was in many ways more politically powerful than the president.[99]

In the Senate, with its longer terms, weaker leadership, and greater ability of members to influence their committee assignments, it paid the railroad to cultivate long-term friends. No senator exercised the kind of control that the Speaker did in the House, but influential senators like Roscoe Conkling had significant power in the party caucuses that staffed the committees. Although turnover in committees from session to session remained high in the 1870s (about 50 percent), it was far less than in the House. By 1883 the Senate began making committee appointments for an entire two-year congressional session instead of a year at a time, rendering railroad friends there all the more valuable.[100]

III. THE SOUTHERN TRANSCONTINENTAL

Throughout the 1870s Collis P. Huntington and Tom Scott fought to control the Pacific Railroad Committees; these were the epicenters of their long war over who would control the southernmost transcontinental. Although they had neither national interests nor any transcendent principles at stake, Scott and Huntington still sought to influence the selection of and the actions of the Speaker of the House, and Scott even tried to intervene in the selection of the president of the United States. Like a brawl spilling in from the next room, their battle played a role, either marginally or centrally, in some of the most important political conflicts of the 1870s.

When in 1874 Tom Scott renewed his attempts to gain a subsidy to push the Texas and Pacific to California, he had a huge burden to bear in the popular reaction against the Crédit Mobilier and railroad subsidies in general, but he also thought he had a formidable advantage.[101] In the elections of 1874 the Democrats had captured the House of Representatives, and they would retain control for eight of the following ten years. Scott and Grenville Dodge thought reasonably enough that a Democratic House rooted in the South augured well for a subsidy for the Texas and Pacific, a southern road.[102]

Scott had "his railroads running out of Washington in almost every direction," and virtually the first thing Grenville Dodge did was to urge Tom Scott to grant passes to any congressman who might be of use to them.[103] Politicians loved passes. The files of every nineteenth-century railroad make it possible to gauge when a congressional session was about to begin and when it was about to adjourn by determining when the requests for passes began to arrive. They came from congressmen, cabinet officers, and bureaucrats. They came from judges, including Supreme Court justices, and military officers. They came from the vice-president. They came from the president. In the state legislatures they were handed out like party favors. It was not a peculiarly American custom. In Canada they went to members of Parliament and ministers and to members of provincial parliaments and important officials. All friends had them, and even the friends of friends requested them. In 1870 Huntington reported that having sent a senator two passes for friends the preceding week, the senator responded by asking for six more. In 1874 the Central Pacific had carried 6,186 "deadheads," as nonpaying passengers were called.[104]

Eventually passes became so burdensome that roads tried to restrict them, but the policies they instituted made the assumptions that lay behind the issuing of passes even clearer. Passes ideally were to go only to proven friends or prominent candidates for friendship. Sidney Dillon of the Union Pacific phrased the policy discreetly as passes only for those who "should deal with us fairly."[105] As receiver of the Kansas Pacific, Henry Villard was more direct. They went to "parties that have been or can be useful to us."[106] And W. P. Clough, counsel for the Northern Pacific, was frankest of all: "I have always been guided by the principle of not advising the issuance of any transportation, for which a full and complete equivalent, in some form, was not in immediate sight."[107] But the distribution of passes to politicians, their friends, and those doing substantial business on the roads proved hard to control. Charles Francis Adams considered them "Congressional blackmail."[108] No railroad could deny passes when their rivals passed them out; as T. F. Oakes of the Northern Pacific wrote, "ultimately we will be forced to do as our neighbors do or lose our business." The Interstate Commerce Commission forbade them in 1887, but that did not stop railroads from issuing them to powerful friends.[109]

Dodge and Scott set out to make the Texas and Pacific a sectional issue, a mark of justice to the South. Dodge's strategy was to mobilize the southern press in order "to pound" the opposition. The idea was to use arguments that played on the sectional disparity between government aid to the North and West as compared with that to the South. Dodge recruited the journalists and supplied the figures. He sought to frame the issue so that instead of representing aid to a private corporation, the Texas and Pacific subsidy would stand for sectional justice in the wake of the Civil War. In part the tactic was ideological—to break down the old southern emphasis on a narrow reading of the powers of the federal government. The goal was to bait the northern press into attacking the southern proposals, thus unifying the South in their favor and giving an opening for northern friends of the railroad to sponsor some sort of sectional compromise.[110]

Dodge worked hard to implement this strategy. He circulated petitions for the road in key congressional districts, solicited influential men in the South to work on congressmen and to get resolutions in favor of the road from southern legislatures. As Dodge wrote Scott in 1875 regarding the circulation of petitions in one congressional district, their operative was not to "rest until he had the name of nearly every voter there on a petition by some pretense or other."[111]

It was a clever tactic, and it put Huntington on the defensive. In the early years of his war with Scott, Huntington spent much of his time responding to Scott's initiatives. Scott often outwitted him, but Huntington was a quick study, and he had a great advantage. Scott was trying to advance legislation; Huntington only wanted to stop it. And as Huntington later wrote, it is "very much easier to stop legislation than it is to procure it." "[W]ith a certain sum of money," he claimed, "I can stop almost any legislation when the same amount will not pass the bill."[112] Huntington put his own men to work in the South organizing opposition to Scott.[113]

Dodge realized that the Texas and Pacific's bills would never pass if antimonopolists united against them, and he quite adroitly moved to present bills promising subsidies to a corporation as bills that would end the Union Pacific/Central Pacific monopoly on transcontinental traffic. Dodge's "careful hard work" secured a resolution from the National Grange—or the "communists," as Huntington called them—for "reasonable aid" to the Texas and Pacific. Scott marched forward under the banner of antimonopoly. He also organized conventions at St. Louis and Memphis to produce resolutions for public aid to the Texas and Pacific.[114]

In the mid-1870s this strategy seemed on the verge of success. Scott's bills failed in the lame-duck session early in 1875, but Dodge hoped that with an incoming Democratic House a bill would go through.[115] Scott, however, needed a sympathetic Speaker. Despite Dodge's success in flying the flag of antimonopoly in the South and West, northern Democrats had mobilized voters by attacking government subsidies and corruption, which made Tom Scott, a famous corruptionist seeking subsidies, anathema to them. And Dodge to his dismay found southern Democrats more interested in capturing the presidency in 1876 than in getting a Speaker sympathetic to southern railroad connections. No candidate for Speaker could make an obvious deal with Tom Scott.[116]

Scott's response to the dilemma was so byzantine, so full of what seemed like feints and betrayals, that it is hard to be sure what happened. The affair was encapsulated in Scott's relation to Congressman Samuel J. Randall, a near neighbor and personal friend in Philadelphia, and a man with his own taint of corruption. Randall was an opponent of subsidies and one of the two leading candidates for the speakership. In the summer of 1875 he accepted the offer of Beverly Tucker, who was both his friend and a noted friend of the Texas and Pacific, to tour the South to drum up support for his candidacy. Tucker traveled that summer on the separate payrolls of both Randall and Tom Scott, pushing two seemingly antithetical products: the antisubsidy Randall for Speaker and a subsidy for the Texas and Pacific. Randall had promised Tucker a "fair" Pacific Railroad Committee, one that would allow the subsidy bill to get to the House floor for a vote. Tucker, however, not only failed to sell Randall in the South but news of the combination of Randall and Scott drifted north, and hurt Randall there.[117]

When the House Democrats voted in the fall of 1875, Randall lost to Michael Kerr of Indiana, another antisubsidy Democrat, who had the support of Collis P. Huntington. Randall attributed his loss to the suspicion that he had made a deal with Scott. And so it would seem that the election was a triumph for Huntington and a defeat for Scott. But things were not so simple. Randall received fewer votes than expected from the southern states supposedly most enthusiastic about the Texas and Pacific. And some of Randall's supporters suspected that Scott's machine had used the *New York World* to circulate rumors about a deal between Randall and Scott in order to discredit Randall while actually soliciting support for Kerr. In reality Scott did more than that. He arranged with William Hurlbert to buy the *New York World* from Manton Marble. Marble was the power behind Kerr's throne. According to the terms of the contract, Marble would receive an additional $100,000 "within thirty days after the adoption by the Congress of the United States of any bill or bills securing the endorsement by the United States Government of the Texas and Pacific R.R. . . . or any other practical guaranty in subsidy to said road."[118]

In 1876 Kerr gave Scott his majority on the House Pacific Railroad Committee. It included James Throckmorton, a member of the board of directors of the Texas and Pacific. The committee, as Huntington reported, "was set up for Scott," and in early February a subcommittee recommended a favorable report on the Texas and Pacific bill.[119] Huntington, however, now played his own reform card and responded with antisubsidy resolutions from state legislatures that he hoped would control Thomas Platt of New York and Gilbert Walker of Virginia and block the bill when it came before the full committee.[120] Just to be sure, Huntington paid Platt, who was usually considered Jay Gould's man, $5,000. By March he thought his efforts and the strong antisubsidy feeling in the country and Congress had stripped Scott of his committee majority.[121]

The critical blow against Scott may have been more subtle. As always, railroad politics came down to committee rooms, arcane rules, the exchange of favors, and the fidelity of friends. Nearly invisible acts had great import. In 1875 a Central Pacific lawyer, Harvey S. Brown, disposed of $9,000 in Washington in two months, with the money going to a "certain party in Washington." Where the money went is not clear, but Joseph McCorkle, an ex-congressman from California said that Brown had promised Dr. Hambleton, who was on the Central Pacific's payroll, $5,000 to give to L. Q. C. Lamar, a friend of the Texas and Pacific, chair of the House Pacific Railroad Committee and later secretary of the interior. All Lamar had to do was delay the favorable report on the Texas and Pacific by his committee. Brown denied any arrangement with Hambleton; it was, however, during this session, when Scott seemed to have the votes to pass his Texas and Pacific bill through Congress, that the bill came out of committee too late for a floor vote in the House. Dodge and Scott then failed to get the necessary two-thirds vote for the suspension of rules to bring their bill to a vote.[122] If Lamar betrayed Scott, he did so because friendship could not prevent duplicity. "You know it is so easy for a person to be a friend and not a friend in a measure before Congress," Grenville Dodge later wrote to Tom Scott, "that no one can tell whom to count on in any emergency or on an amendment."[123] At the time it seemed a temporary setback. In hindsight it was a crucial defeat.

Huntington had turned Scott back, but Scott's political abilities, his willingness to spend money, and his knack for creating alliances between men of antithetical principles dismayed and worried Huntington, who complained in 1876 that "the devil, the communist, and the Pa. R.R. have united against us." This was high praise of Scott's political ability to link corporations, corruption, and reform, but Huntington, too, was becoming adept at this game.[124] When Scott raised the flag of antimonopoly, the Southern Pacific hoisted the flag of antisubsidy. In December of 1875 Congress passed the Holman Resolution, introduced by the same Indiana congressman who during the Civil War had denounced the Pacific Railway Act of 1864. The resolution renounced corporate subsidies. Grenville Dodge thought the vote largely for show, but it was still a sign of the strength of reformers—and the Southern Pacific Railroad.[125]

In the summer of 1876 as, in Huntington's words, the "liveliest fight" he was ever in grew more and more expensive and the Texas and Pacific was still unable to grasp the prize, Scott invited Huntington to meet him at Beach House Sea Girt below Long Branch, New Jersey, a "lovely house out of the way of the 'thousand and one' people."[126] Jay Gould, who wished neither side well, but who was alarmed at the ancillary damage being done the Union Pacific as it sought a compromise on debt repayment with the government, attempted to mediate. There was a truce, then renewed war, further negotiations, and, in late December, what seemed briefly like peace as the two sides worked out an agreement that would need congressional legislation to be effective. On the surface the agreement, as first announced, seemed a capitulation by Scott. The Texas and Pacific and the Southern Pacific would meet a hundred miles east of El Paso, with the Southern Pacific receiving the Texas and Pacific land grant west of the junction. Scott had given up California, Arizona, and most of New Mexico, and each road would work for a federal guarantee for interest on its bonds and for the bonds of the roads' branches.[127] Huntington offered Gould a share in the construction company that would build the Southern Pacific, and Scott agreed to help pass a sinking fund bill to resolve the Union Pacific debt.[128]

Neither Scott nor Huntington observed the agreement for long. Scott had won over two members of the Senate's Pacific Railroad Committee, Senators Spencer of Alabama and Walker of Virginia, to secure control of that committee. How he won them over is indicated by Huntington's conviction that they could be "switched back with the 'proper arguments.'" He put "proper arguments" in quotation marks to designate the phrase as a euphemism for quite improper arguments.[129] When the Pacific Railroad Committee altered the compromise bill that Huntington, Gould, and Scott had agreed upon, Huntington blamed the alterations on Scott. He didn't like changes regarding how the Southern Pacific connected with San Diego, but more dangerous were provisions about rates and regulations.

Scott had cleverly used the treaty between the railroads to create both a subsidy bill and, in an odd way, a reform bill. The bill made the linked lines an "open highway" with the Texas and Pacific and the Southern Pacific promising to charge freight received from each other and from all other connecting roads the same rates as freight originating on their own lines. The bill also gave Congress an unspecified "control" of those rates. And, as icing on the cake, it prohibited "any combination, agreement or contract" between the Southern Pacific and the Central Pacific. Huntington had, in effect, promised to lobby for a bill that produced a new road regulated by the government and that prohibited the coordination of the two halves of the Associates' California monopoly: the Central Pacific and Southern Pacific. The government had the right to examine the books to make sure there were no such contracts. If Huntington opposed the bill openly, Scott would cite it as proof of the Central Pacific's desire to preserve its monopoly, adding an even greater aura of antimonopoly reform to his own request for subsidies.

When on January 24, 1877, the bill was reported out of committee, Huntington remained on the surface its friend. In Washington, he told Hopkins, "it is understood that I am for it," but he began setting backfires against it and urged Hopkins to send messages to congressmen promising to build the Southern Pacific with no subsidies. His real aim was to "strangle" the bill.[130] He also moved to make sure that such a bill would not emerge from committee again. He lingered at the Willard Hotel for two extra days in March 1877 "to fix up R[ailroad] Committee in the Senate." Tom Scott was there doing the same thing, but, wrote Huntington, "I beat him for once certain."[131]

Scott responded to the failed compromise by raising the stakes. He would try to control not only the Speaker of the House but also the president of the United States. Kerr's death in August of 1876 and Randall's accession to the speakership forced Scott to begin all over again in 1877 when Randall ran for reelection as Speaker. Once more Randall's supporters faced the dilemma of reconciling southerners who wanted a subsidy with antisubsidy Democrats. Once more Randall indicated that although he might personally oppose the bill, he would appoint a Pacific Railroad Committee that would advance it to the floor of the House for a vote.[132] He even suggested that he would vote for the Texas and Pacific if the South wanted it.[133] Once more threats materialized that made it critical for Randall to win over the Texas and Pacific. Rumors circulated that the Texas and Pacific would deliver enough southern Democrats to elect a Republican Speaker in exchange for Republican support for the subsidy.[134] Voters were confused. As one wrote, "The *New York Sun* says Mr. Randall is the 'uncompromising enemy of the Southern or Texas Pacific Railroad.' The *Richmond Dispatch* says Mr. Randall desires to be speaker because he favors this project. Can you advise me without doubt, what his views are upon this question?"[135] The Associates thought Scott opposed Randall. Randall won the election, and Scott, once more, got a majority on the House committee. Antisubsidy congressmen complained that Randall played both sides, saying "he was opposed to subsidy and then made the Committee in favor of subsidy."[136]

But during the winter of 1877 the contest over the speakership was cast into the shadows by a much larger battle. The deadlocked presidential election of 1876 brought the business of Congress to a standstill. As the constitution mandated, the election would be decided by the House. Tom Scott's role in resolving the election of 1876 demonstrated at once the reach and the limits of the railroad lobby and corporate power in politics. Had the Texas and Pacific lobby been stronger, there would have been no need for Scott to intervene in the contested election for president between the Republican Rutherford B. Hayes and the Democrat Samuel Tilden. He would have already received his subsidy. Had the lobby been less powerful, he could not have attempted to intervene. In December of 1876 two newspapermen, Henry Boynton and Andrew Kellar, had proposed an arrangement between Scott and Hayes. Scott would persuade enough southern Democrats in Congress to support Hayes to give the Republican the election, and Hayes would, among other things, obtain the Republican votes necessary to subsidize the Texas and Pacific.[137]

It was an audacious proposal, and when Congress appointed an electoral commission to decide the election, Scott tried to influence the commission decision on the disputed votes in Louisiana. Dodge warned him that he had overstepped and should avoid "entangling alliances." Dodge thought it possible that the commission might "accomplish something, but if it does not it is very liable to make enemies on both sides and will not they strike back at us in every way they can[?]" "Our Southern policy," Dodge thought, "should be based solely upon material improvements. The moment we drift off into political matters, we are liable to cause the south to lose sight of the T & P."[138] As great a historian as C. Vann Woodward thought that Scott had won Hayes the presidency. The explanation has since been discredited, but not because Hayes was not approached and not because Scott did not try. Hayes never made any promise beyond a tepid support for internal improvements, and Scott could not persuade southerners to exchange the presidency for a railroad.[139]

Such grand failures always seemed to energize Scott, and in the wake of Hayes's election, he reinforced his lobby and sought new friends. In 1876 Scott supposedly had two hundred lobbyists, many of them ex-members of the House and Senate, at work in Congress.[140] Two years later he had "every old political . . . Bum of the South in his employ . . . at $250 per month up."[141] In December of 1877 Huntington found out that two friends of the Southern Pacific—Senators Howe and Ferry—were no longer on the Senate's Pacific Railroad Committee. Huntington was "not happy." Ferry was a particularly expensive friend to lose; even after losing his committee post, he drew on Huntington for $10,000 in cash as a "loan." Replacing Howe and Ferry were Senator Stanley Matthews of Ohio, President Hayes's brother-in-law and a friend of the Texas and Pacific, and Senator William Windom of Minnesota, a friend of the Northern Pacific since Jay Cooke's days. Because the Northern Pacific and the Texas and Pacific had a common interest in securing and protecting their subsidies and breaking the Union Pacific/Central Pacific monopoly, his appointment gave Scott "control of the Senate."[142] Scott once again took the offensive, with his forces pouring out from their headquarters—which the Central Pacific's lobbyists called "the menagerie on 13th St."[143] Huntington, however, knew the critical congressional choke points for railroad legislation. After a visit by Huntington to Washington in early 1878, Charley Sherrill, his chief lobbyist, requested $1,500. On February 10 Sherrill wrote I. F. Gates, "I got the check cashed . . . and payed the fifteen hundred dollars to Senator Windom and hold his receipt for same."[144] Senator Windom of the Pacific Railroad Committee had become a friend of the Southern Pacific.

Pervasive corruption did not keep the barrier separating friends of the railroads from reformers from becoming more and more porous. By 1878 an innocent observer might have thought this corporate warfare between the Texas and Pacific and the Southern Pacific was really a fight between two sets of reformers. That a man was ideologically opposed to great corporations did not mean he could not be of service to them. In 1878 C. H. Bardwell, a journalist and enemy of Tom Scott, solicited Huntington to back the antimonopolist Greenbacker Seth Yocum in Pennsylvania to defeat ex-governor Andrew G. Curtin, a Scott ally and the Democratic nominee for the House. When Yocum won, Bardwell again intervened, asking Huntington to protect Yocum from Scott's efforts to deny him his seat. At the time the Greenbackers were expected to hold the balance of power in organizing the House, and the organization of the House remained critical to the great battle Huntington was waging against Tom Scott's Texas and Pacific.[145]

Despite Scott's gargantuan efforts, the Texas and Pacific and the Southern Pacific deadlocked in Washington, D.C., and both opened new fronts to vanquish the other. Scott supported reform efforts in California to get a strong railroad commission to regulate the Central Pacific and the Southern Pacific. And in 1878 the California Railroad Commission handed Tom Scott a great gift by disclosing the enormous floating debt carried by the Associates' railroads. Huntington, unwilling to sell Southern Pacific bonds at prices well below par, had instead acquired heavy short-term liabilities on the Central Pacific. Using the *New York World* and pamphlets sent to bankers to spread the news, Scott thoroughly alarmed investors and badly hurt Huntington's ability to borrow.[146]

Hitting the Southern Pacific on financial markets was critical for Scott, because the Associates, too, had adopted new tactics. They pushed forward efforts to get charters from the Arizona and New Mexico territorial legislatures to construct a railroad to Texas. To obtain these charters, they mobilized their own cadre of political hacks in need of employment and sought friends in the territories.[147] Among them was John C. Frémont, rising like a zombie from the political dead. On becoming territorial governor of Arizona, he immediately requested $2,500 from the Southern Pacific. He assured Crocker that he thought the interests of the territory depended on the success of the Southern Pacific.[148]

In 1878 Scott fell sick, and the end game began. Scott continued to wage railroad war into 1879, but his friends started to desert him, and his once impressive organization fell into disarray. Samuel Barlow, a railroad promoter in his own right and a power in the Democratic Party, sent Richard Taylor to Washington to help the Texas and Pacific in 1879, but a dismayed Taylor reported at the end of the session that although the measure had "every element of success, equity, sectional feeling, local interests, hostility to Huntington and Gould, politics, . . . all have been frittered away. A large part of the foundation on which I attempted to build has proved imaginary." The Texas and Pacific had lost too many friends.[149]

The defeat of the Texas and Pacific revealed the ultimate moral ambiguity of Gilded Age politics. The defeat of Tom Scott took down one of the most corrupt, and also one of the most able, men of his time. The defeat of the Texas and Pacific was therefore a victory for reform, except that some antimonopolists, such as the Southern Grange, were allied with Scott, and the man who ultimately defeated him, Collis P. Huntington, was as corrupt as Scott. He needed his "boys" to defeat Scott, and the "boys," Huntington reported, "are very hungry and it will cost considerable to be saved." In March of 1879, as Congress adjourned after a last "desperate struggle" over the Texas and Pacific, John Boyd, who was in charge of the Southern Pacific's efforts in the House, reported that month's expenses to Huntington. The total was $12,585. The largest category was bills received, which ran to $12,345, and under that was the cryptic notation "$125 × 85," which yields a total of $10,625—the bulk of the monthly expense. There seems only one likely explanation for a single notation repeated 85 times: the cost of a vote.[150]

How much Scott and Huntington spent in the 1870s is impossible to determine. In 1887 when a special railway commission investigated the affairs of the original transcontinentals, it found expenditures of $4,818,355.67 on the books of the Central Pacific Railroad for which there were insufficient vouchers to show where the money had gone. This represented only money from the Central Pacific, not from the Southern Pacific or other corporations that the Associates controlled. It did not represent employment, passes, investment opportunities, gifts of land, or the numerous other ways that railroads had of rewarding friends. "There is no room for doubt," the commission concluded, "that a large portion of this money was used for the purpose of influencing legislation and of preventing the passage of measures deemed to be hostile to the interests of the company, and for the purpose of influencing elections."[151] By way of comparison, the railroad paid $29,812.54 in federal taxes during the same period. Its legal expenses were $2,361,154.00. It paid state and local taxes of $5,857,380.[152]

IV. REFORM IN THE GILDED AGE

Railroads could enlist reformers to serve their interests in battles against other corporations, but reformers could also ally with railroads to pass reform legislation. Because railroad politics involved competition between railroad corporations in legislatures, Congress, and various bureaucracies, there was rarely any single railroad interest. Legislation that hurt one corporation might very well be supported by rival corporations, and in such calculations of interest lay possibilities for reform.

The details of such railroad politics were mundane and tedious. A major battle involved the question when and how the Land Office should issue and the railroads accept patents (or title) for the land in their grants. Until the government issued patents, towns and counties could not tax the land. Settling these issues took nearly two decades as the railroads stopped bills in committees and delayed action in friendly courts. Reformers found themselves entangled in seemingly endless procedural questions.[153] In the most extreme cases, these issues stretched out over a generation.[154] Almost 90 percent of the Central Pacific's land in Nevada and Utah was patented only after 1893.[155]

Railroads did not want patents when they thought the land of little value and feared taxation, but they very much wanted patents when they thought more valuable land might be forfeited. By building too slowly or not building at all, some railroads had failed to fulfill the conditions of their charters, and antimonopolists in Congress pressed for the revocation of these land grants in the 1880s. Several secretaries of the interior stopped issuing patents in order to prevent railroads from selling lands to which they were not entitled.[156] With the danger of forfeiture looming, railroads that had avoided getting patents in order to avoid taxation now reversed position. They complained about the inefficiency of the Land Office in issuing patents. Most claimed that they had always wanted patents and had always been willing to pay taxes.[157]

Like battles to secure subsidies, battles over land grants and title produced alliances between antimonopolists and corporations. The Central Pacific backed legislation to restore unearned land grants to the public domain. It was a way to strike at the Atlantic and Pacific, the Northern Pacific, and other rivals.[158] Other railroads, in return, backed reforms that hurt the Central Pacific and the Union Pacific. The latter two desperately wanted to defeat the Thurman Act, which required them to pay into a sinking fund to retire the debt they owed the government. Both railroads mustered their lobbyists and friends against the bill. Senator Newton Booth, the reform senator from California and the Associates' old adversary, knew their methods and charged that the Gordon bill, which the Pacific railroads hoped to substitute for the Thurman bill, would make the Senate "*particeps criminis* in the fraud that the men who hang around our doors would perpetrate." When passed, he proclaimed, the Gordon bill should go not to the president of the United States but to the "presidents of the companies. . . . It is the coin and mintage of their brains. It was approved in advance."[159]

"The men who hang around our doors" were a lobby grown too obvious and ubiquitous. The political networks the railroads had created were, it turned out, at their best when nearly invisible, appearing only when they were in action and motion. It was as if they were some strange railroad whose trains, tracks, stations, and telegraph wires were all visible when a train passed, but then disappeared. To render them visible was to weaken them. Or, to change the metaphor, flies should never see the spider.

When the Thurman bill passed in 1878, Gould and Huntington blamed each other for being too much in evidence, but it was not just that their own lobbies had failed. Others had succeeded. Some of the most effective arguments for the Thurman Act came from competing railroads, which, unlike the Union Pacific and the Central Pacific, had not received government bond guarantees. An unsigned memorandum in the files of the Chicago,

Burlington, and Quincy, a road that was no friend of the Union Pacific, aptly summarized the case against the Union Pacific. The Union Pacific was "paying to a few wealthy men who own the $36,000,000 of its capital stock, which never contributed a dollar to the construction of the property, 8 per cent annually on the par value of the stock or 12½ percent on its present market value." The Burlington lobbied in favor of the Thurman Act.[160]

Tom Scott also helped push the Thurman bill forward. Scott, Huntington wrote Crocker, had "worked up a feeling against the C.P. beyond what you have any idea."[161] Scott supposedly controlled five crucial votes in the Senate.[162] Senator William Wallace, a conservative Bourbon senator who voted for the Thurman Act, has been cited as an example of how little ideology mattered in the Senate, but Wallace can more persuasively be seen as evidence of how much friendship with Tom Scott mattered. Wallace was probably one of Scott's senators whom Huntington had in mind when he blamed Scott for the defeat of the Gordon bill and the subsequent passage of the Thurman Act.[163]

The Thurman Act marked a victory for reformers, if in the end an empty one, but it was also a victory for the Burlington system and Tom Scott. Other reform measures resulted from similar alliances. Reform, too, could be evidence of railroad politics and corruption.

The linkage of corporations and politics through organized friendship put some of the culture's highest values at the service of some of its most mendacious ends. That the politics of friendship were corrupt made the language of honesty, probity, and fair dealing all the more necessary, not only, or even primarily, to mask the corruption but rather to assure the participants that they still operated within a known moral universe.

The "inwardness," to use a nineteenth-century term to denote things whose meaning was not apparent on their surface, of legislation, newspaper stories, or administrative decisions makes it necessary to look beyond final votes and even earlier roll call votes in Congress to understand how corporations played politics. The announced intent of a bill was not always its real purpose. The public opposition of representatives often hid private support. They would publicly vote against a bill while privately making sure that it had the votes necessary to pass. Much of this duplicity was embedded in the loyalty of friends. There was sometimes honor among thieves. Collis P. Huntington may have been mocking the railway commission investigating the Pacific Road in 1887, or he may have been lying, or he may have been seeing the world from the peculiar perch of Collis P. Huntington, but when asked to explain why the railroad had spent so much money in Washington, he said it was to bring moral influence to bear.[164]

A RAILROAD LIFE

———◆———

ELIAS C. BOUDINOT

Indians were a difficult people to classify. Some resisted railroads, some rode them, and some desired to build and own them. On the far extreme were men like Elias C. Boudinot, who became a willing tool of the Atlantic and Pacific Railroad. Boudinot was a striking man; people did not forget him. He looked like Wild Bill Hickock, who looked like Buffalo Bill, who looked like George Armstrong Custer. Boudinot had the same handsome features, the same shoulder-length hair, the drooping mustache, the same impassive stare—not at the camera, but slightly away. Except that Boudinot's hair was not blond. Elias C. Boudinot had a New England mother, but he was still a Cherokee Indian. If the competition were not so stiff, Boudinot might be ranked among the great scoundrels of the Gilded Age. It was fitting that a Cherokee scoundrel should bear a resemblance to a variety of white scoundrels and showmen who came to personify the West in popular culture.[1]

Boudinot was the son of Elias Boudinot, the editor of the *Cherokee Phoenix*, murdered in 1839 for his role in the Treaty of New Echota, which had led inexorably to the Trail of Tears. He was the nephew of Stand Watie, the Cherokee who was the last Confederate general to surrender during the Civil War, and he was himself, despite his New England mother and New England education, a delegate to the Confederate Congress.[2] He came out of the Civil War with a need to recoup his fortune, and he blended business and politics in a familiar Gilded Age manner.

In arguing for the abolition of Indian Territory, treaties, and the special legal status of tribes, Boudinot quite characteristically made himself exhibit A. He had once trusted in treaties, he claimed. He had relied on the exemption from U.S. tax laws in Indian Territory provided by the Cherokee Treaty of 1866, but Congress had passed laws in violation of the treaty, and the courts had upheld them. Boudinot had lost his property for back taxes. This had taught him, so he maintained, that treaties were a charade; sovereignty could not stand against either the U.S. government or corporations; and the Indians' only hope was the end of Indian governance in Indian Territory, the end of common land holdings, and the acquisition of citizenship. This was, his opponents countered, a recipe for disaster, and time would prove them right, but Boudinot always claimed that he was acting in the best interests of the Cherokee and other Indian peoples.[3]

Elias C. Boudinot was the founder of Vinita in Indian Territory, which, although the Atlantic and Pacific Railway never wished it to be so, became for a time the de facto western terminus of the railroad. The Atlantic and Pacific was from beginning to end a road of troubles. It was as unfortunate in its friends as in its enemies. It had both in Indian Territory in the early 1870s. Nobody among the so-called Five Civilized Tribes of Indian Territory was more enthusiastic than Elias C. Boudinot.[4]

Charming, well spoken, garrulous, courtly, mendacious, and violent, not surprisingly Boudinot became involved with the railroads. His Cherokee opponents, which included the vast majority of Cherokees, labeled him a traitor and an opportunist, but this did not stop his lobbying in their name for territorial government, railroad grants, and the division of Indian lands. He claimed his life was in danger, and it probably was.[5] The son of a murdered editor, he made sure he was on the right side of the pistol in tribal disputes. He was said to have murdered the editor of the *Tahlequah Telephone* as the victim sat at his desk. Boudinot had not liked an editorial.[6]

Boudinot denied that he was an agent of the railroads, but he had close ties to the corporations whose land grants depended on either Indian cessions or the dissolution of Indian Territory. The Missouri, Kansas, and Texas Railway—the KATY—claimed in its annual report that Congress had granted the road a 100-foot right-of-way and 4,121,600 acres of land. The asterisk in the report noted that this land was "subject to temporary Indian occupancy, under Treaty stipulations." Translated, this meant that the land remained Indian land until the Indians ceded it, which no tribe in Indian Territory proved willing to do. The railroad, in fact, had no land beyond its right-of-way except for what the Indian nations, or their citizens, would provide them through lease or other rights of occupancy, or until this land was restored to the public domain by laws like the ones Boudinot was urging. Dozens of territorial bills would come before Congress in the 1870s and the 1880s to accomplish this end; some of them were written by the corporations themselves.[7]

Although the land grants lay in abeyance, the railroads still sold bonds based on them to European investors, and the railroads themselves moved into Indian Territory. Boudinot drove the first spike in Indian Territory when the Missouri, Kansas, and Texas pushed south of the Kansas border on its way toward Texas in 1871. He saw opportunities. The Missouri, Kansas, and Texas had agreed to build a depot jointly with the Atlantic and Pacific at the townsite sure to arise where the Atlantic and Pacific, heading west, crossed its tracks. Relying on the Atlantic and Pacific survey, it calculated the crossing at a place called Big Cabin, in the northeastern corner of what was then Indian Territory and is now Oklahoma. Since it built its line first, the Missouri, Kansas, and Texas erected a depot there and awaited the coming of the Atlantic and Pacific.[8]

And in July of 1871 the Atlantic and Pacific appeared, but not at Big Cabin—instead, it went a few miles north to Vinita, which consisted of a fence enclosing about two thousand acres of prairie some thirty-four miles from the Missouri border. Elias Boudinot had put up the fence, claiming the use of the land as a Cherokee citizen. The loan for erecting the fence had reportedly been arranged by the Atlantic and Pacific. Boudinot was to have one-third of the profits from the townsite.[9]

Vinita: it was as if the Atlantic and Pacific had been haunted by John C. Frémont, who had been among its founders. Boudinot had named his fenced prairie after Vinnie Reams, a sculptress more beautiful than talented. She was the "young lady artist" who in 1871 "petrified," as Mark Twain put it in *The Gilded Age*, Mr. Lincoln into a statue with an expression that indicated he was "finding fault with the washing." This is the statue that now stands in the Capitol rotunda. In Paris during the summer of 1869 the young Vinnie Reams had had a dalliance, and perhaps an affair, with the much older Frémont, who had remained in France while his family toured

Europe. He occupied his time trying to seduce Vinnie while fighting off charges that agents of another fledgling transcontinental of which he was a partner, the Memphis, El Paso, and Pacific, had defrauded French investors. That road was supposed to tap "the great commercial route from Guaymas and the interior at Santa Fe" and then intercept "the traffic of the great River of Colorado," which had as little traffic to speak of then as now.[10]

By the early 1870s Frémont was a man so expert at transmuting opportunity into spectacular disaster that he was not only capable of squandering a gold mine but actually did squander one. Frémont had gained fame as the Pathfinder exploring the West and helping bring California into the Union. He had been the darling of the nation, but his California activities ended in his court-martial, and on his later expeditions what had earlier seemed daring now seemed only recklessness and ignorance. Men straggled out of the mountains bearing tales of cannibalism. In 1856 Frémont had been the Republican candidate for the presidency of the United States. He lost. He became a Civil War general and nearly lost Missouri before Lincoln sacked him. Ulysses S. Grant served under him. Grant found him a man of mystery: "You left without the least idea of what he meant or what he wanted you to do."[11]

Frémont lost Vinnie Reams as he lost control of the various western railroads that he helped organize. The Leavenworth, Pawnee, and Western, renamed the Union Pacific, Eastern Division, to confuse it quite purposefully with the Union Pacific, had come to nothing because of, as Frémont put it, "estrangements" between Frémont and his partner. The estrangements led to a chain of events that culminated in a murder, in which Frémont was not involved.[12] In 1871 the man who had aspired to be president of the United States was the president of the Memphis, El Paso, and Pacific and a criminal.[13] In Paris the French courts, trying Frémont in absentia, convicted him of fraud. His agents had forged documents, given false information, and swindled roughly six million dollars from investors of limited means. Frémont had no intention of delivering himself up to French authorities. That Frémont's railroad crumbled at the touch surprised few who knew him. "Fremont is entirely unreliable in money matters," Jay Cooke wrote his brother Harry in 1871, "and it injures any one to have any connection with him."[14] The Memphis, El Paso, and Pacific ceased to be a railroad and became merely became a scandal. The Atlantic and Pacific would fail; not even Frémont's departure could save it. The Southwest Pacific reverted back to the state of Missouri when Frémont failed to make the first payment, and he sold his stake in the Union Pacific, Eastern Division. In its own way this unbroken record of failure was impressive.[15]

Even with Frémont gone, a kind of corporate dalliance on the prairie persevered, but all in all it was perhaps better not to have named a railroad junction after one of the participants in a failed, and maybe even an unconsummated, romance. Things did not go well in Vinita. Agents of the various railroads were soon throwing opponents' rails into ditches. Mr. Bond, the acting general manager of the Missouri, Kansas, and Texas, disliked the Atlantic and Pacific's Mr. Kellat, whose "manner and matter of . . . conversation were more like that of an insane man, or man mad with passion, rather than that of a gentleman representing a respectable Railroad Corporation." His actions were "a glaring case of Celtic ignorance and impertinence."[16] Things went downhill from there. The Missouri, Kansas, and Texas trains ceased stopping at Vinita, which everyone agreed reduced its utility as a railroad junction. The Atlantic and Pacific armed its employees and resorted to lawyers.[17] When it and the Missouri, Kansas, and Texas eventually did connect at Vinita, the connection was actually between an Atlantic and Pacific passenger train and a Missouri, Kansas, and Texas cattle train whose passenger accommodations were not exactly what travelers had been led to expect. The Atlantic and Pacific was supposed to build west from Vinita, but in the winter of 1872–73 the contractor's horses died, halting construction. And then it was 1873, the annus horribilis, and funds for the road dried up.[18] Most significant of all, the Indians refused to cede the lands that would free up the road's land grant. Vinita became an unintended terminus.

Indians remained stubbornly athwart the line of empire, defying the isothermal and the Atlantic and Pacific, and all the Atlantic and Pacific could do was howl. In its pamphlets it created a literary parody of the Indian Territory inhabited by the Cherokees and other southern tribes. The actual

Indian Territory was dotted with farms and ranches, towns and schools. It had newspapers and legislatures and courts, all run by Indians. For C. J. Hillyer of the Atlantic and Pacific, however, Indian Territory was a wilderness, and "[a] railroad and a wilderness are incompatible things, and cannot long co-exist. Either the wilderness will be subdued or the railroad will die of starvation." Indians were too few and too barbaric, he argued, to support a railroad or a modern society. "We might as well for all business purposes, build a road for three hundred miles through a tunnel or a desert, as through the fertile Indian country in its present condition."[19] Hillyer played off of what John Benson, a Cherokee, called the chief mistake of legislators and the American public regarding Indian Territory: "that the Indians of this territory are but savages, and that their country can be monopolized by railroad speculators and governed by the appointees of the president of the United States instead of those of their own selection." Benson favored connections with the larger economy, and he favored development. He just wanted development to take place under the governments of Indian nations and under Indian control.[20]

Boudinot hung on by proxy. He built a hotel in Vinita, a place where he felt acutely uncomfortable as people do when they think the other residents want to kill them. He rented the hotel to a white man. The Cherokees ruled this illegal and finally tore the hotel down in 1879. Boudinot sued; he continued to lobby Congress to turn Indian Territory into a standard American territory with territorial government; he traveled in Washington high society; he caned Cherokee representatives who denounced him. For years he was a familiar figure in Washington, D.C., but by the time of his death, in 1890, he had returned to practice law in Fort Smith, Arkansas, and was living on his ranch in Indian Territory.[21]

CHAPTER 4

༄ ∞◯◯∞ ༄

SPATIAL POLITICS

But a little practice and a little study of field geometry
will enable any one of ordinary intelligence without any
engineering knowledge whatever . . . to lay out a railway
from anywhere to anywhere.

—ARTHUR WELLINGTON, *The Economic Theory of the Location of Railways*[1]

THE RAILROADS MADE nineteenth-century Americans realize that space
was political.[2] It was a disconcerting recognition because space and
politics seemed categorically different. Space was natural; it was what existed
in the world separate from humans; politics was cultural, one of many different arrangements humans created to deal with one another. Space always
seems the most natural when it is the most static, when it is measured simply
as the distance from here to there. Measures of distance differ from society
to society, but distance, the stuff being measured, seems a creation of the
natural world changing only as continents drift and mountain ranges rise.

Conventional representations of railroad lines rendered them static and
thus a mere overlay on a natural space. The gorgeous maps printed in the
late 1880s by the *Engineering News* depicted the American railroad network
and its recent expansion as a jungle of multicolored railroad lines, their
trunks crossing and their branches sometimes intertwining. They captured

the growing extent of railroad space, but they could not capture the way this expansion changed space itself since, like all maps, these were static.[3] The deeper meanings of railroad space remained invisible unless the trains were put in motion. Emphasizing motion was essential to creating a spatial politics.

The railroads made space political by making the quotidian experience of space one of rapid movement. A railroad train in motion was a snorting, smoking, roaring thing; for all the beauty of its movement, it was an assault on the human senses, which registered that it was the train's movement that mattered. But it wasn't just the train that moved; the things the train connected seemed to move with it. The British novelist Anthony Trollope while visiting the United States in the 1860s wrote, "The town that is distant a hundred miles by the rail is so near that its inhabitants are neighbors; but a settlement twenty miles distant across the uncleared country unknown, unvisited, and probably unheard of by women and children. Under such circumstances the railway is everything. It is the first necessity of life, and gives the only hope of wealth." Trollope captured why the locomotive had "been taken to the bosoms of them all as a domestic animal."[4]

What Trollope grasped was that space itself took on different forms according to how movement was measured. The speed of the train determined the time of the journey and the experience of space. Substituting time for distance made space political, but only to the extent that politics determined which places got railroads and which did not.[5]

A further step was necessary for the full fruition of spatial politics: people had to measure space primarily by cost. Measuring space by cost rendered it radically unstable. It changed every time a freight rate changed. It became apparent that whoever controlled this measure of space gained considerable power and advantage. And once this became apparent, the struggle to control and regulate those measurements not only irrevocably entered the realm of politics but moved to the center of nineteenth-century American politics. North Americans realized that the building of railroads had created the hardware of the railroad network, but just as critical to the operation of railroads was the software—the time schedules and tariffs (rates) that managed movement of people and things through space—and the administrative apparatus that kept track of railroad cars, determined routes, and set prices. These formed the heart of a railroad politics that was fundamentally a spatial politics.

I. ABSOLUTE SPACE

In 1869 Butler Ives, a thirty-nine-year-old engineer in the employ of the Central Pacific, helped complete a first draft of western railroad space. He had been in the field surveying the route of the railroad for three years, in some cases working far to the east of where the Central Pacific would run. The country he traveled was often Indian country. Ives was a romantic who feigned a cynicism that often became an ill-concealed form of boasting, as when he described the work of laying out the route across the Great Basin: "For 150 miles of the distance we had day camps or for every camp in that distance we had to haul water with mule teams from 10 to 15 miles for cooking & drinking purposes & some of that was brackish. I found it a good place to take the romance out of some enthusiastic young engineers I had in my party." But at other times his own romance was all too apparent, as when he led his party east of Ogden and into the mountains.

> The country for 150 miles east is but a succession of Mt. Ranges with very narrow valleys along the streams. There is but little timber except on the higher slopes of the Mts while most of the country is covered with good grass. The streams are filled with trout and the Mts. with game rendering it one of the best sections of country I have ever been in for camping purposes. I have carried my old shot gun on the pommel of my mule's saddle all summer. Have killed one brown bear, one antelope & geese, ducks, grouse, hare etc. without number. We have had trout whenever we took the trouble to fish for them.[6]

Ives, who was from Michigan but had long lived in California, took pride in his ability to live in these western places. "They keep me out on this infernal region of Salt & desolation," he wrote his brother, "because I am familiar with the country and don't fear the Indians which is a bugbear to most people in this country. In fact, I am sort of a vagabond pioneer of the

R.R. Co. singled out for difficult jobs with a carte blanche to do pretty much as I please."[7] His skills were transportable, but the local knowledge that he developed was not. That did not matter, however, because the whole point of creating railroad space was to make such local knowledge superfluous. A passenger train would cover those 150 miles in less than a day without any need for the travelers to find or carry water or to camp.

"Vagabond pioneer" was a role Ives played; he was really a very modern figure, a professional engineer whom a corporation employed for a salary. He carried with him not only his shotgun but his tools of abstraction—the "old solar compass" and two barometers. He knew he was using these tools to measure and transform space. His work helped make the East, once so far away, near, whether he measured his separation in time or in money. "I don't know how things will shape with me when the road is finished," he wrote his brother. "If I can get time I will come & see you. It will not cost me much for I am a deadhead on both roads."[8] He was a company man with company benefits.

Ives's correspondence largely stopped in 1869, and then, in the way that documents and history truncate fuller lives, there was in 1872 a final letter from Jonathan Valentine, a superintendent of the Wells Fargo Express Company, to the superintendents of the Union Pacific. "We forward tomorrow express addressed to Detroit, Mich. the remains of Mr. Butler Ives who was one of the Pioneer Engineers in surveying and locating the route of the present overland railroad, the C.P. and U.P. lines. As a tribute to Mr. Ives attainment as R.R. Engineer, and character as a gentleman, and as a courtesy to Railroad Managers, we forward the remains free and will esteem it a favor if the U.P. & American Cos. will cooperate with us."[9] Ives was dead; he was just cargo, but he remained a deadhead. His corporate privileges were intact; the railroad did carry him home.

Ives passed away five years before the first edition of Arthur Wellington's *The Economic Theory of the Location of Railways* appeared. Wellington served as an engineer on the Mexican Central Railway and the Mexican National Railway, but his most impressive production was his book, which would go through five revised editions by 1891. Like Ives, Wellington was an engineer who reduced local knowledge to numbers, a universal language of elevations, grades, curves, and the power that a steam engine could muster. He did this to create railroad space.[10]

Wellington was an enumerating modernizer, and a very intelligent one, who wanted to lay out the physical infrastructure of railroad—its tracks, bridges, tunnels, stations—so that movement yielded the highest possible revenues. He thought methodically about the connections between infrastructure, movement, and revenue, and his skill lay in keeping all three elements in play at once. He was engaged in a perpetual act of translation. He translated geography into a kind of hybrid space—at once abstracted and physical. I will call this hybrid space absolute space; it was both geometric and natural. It came into being when workers altered an existing landscape by driving a railroad through it. The track created an axis. Looking down the track, engineers could measure a linear space and the length of journeys; looking outward from the tracks, surveyors could find the series of square sections that made up the railroad's land grant.

The Canadian Pacific in the years immediately following its completion in 1885 formed a nearly pure example of absolute space as a paradigm of order and control. The Canadian Pacific laid out its stations every eight miles. Why eight? Apparently eight miles was the maximum distance at which a farmer could make a roundtrip with a wagonload of grain on level terrain in a single day. A farmer along the line halfway between stations would still be able to make his journey and be back by dark. At every second station there would be "depots, section-houses, and water tanks" as well as the various sidetracks necessary to load, unload, and switch trains. And roughly every one hundred miles, the train would reach a divisional point with railroad shops and yards, which inevitably meant jobs and larger towns. The Canadian Pacific was imposing a pattern here that would determine the movements, routines, and opportunities of people not yet in the country.[11]

Besides the railroads, only the state could structure space on this grand scale. Together the Canadian and American land surveys and railroads marked out the shapes of what was to come. It was as if Manitoba, Alberta, Saskatchewan, and all the places like them across half a continent were a child's coloring book with the patterns presketched. Farmers could add color and variety, but the lines of their fields, the locations of their roads, the places where they would take their crops and buy their supplies—all of these had first been determined by the survey grid and later elaborated by the railroads.[12]

W. C. Van Horne was the primary architect of railroad space on the Canadian Pacific. He was a striver. As an old man, he remembered how he had aspired to be a general superintendent of the railroad, any railroad. He imagined that a general superintendent "must know everything about a railway—every detail in every department," and Van Horne, as much as any man, did. General superintendent may have been his original destination, but general superintendent was a local stop and Van Horne became an express. He was a general superintendent before he was thirty. He "took no holidays and . . . worked nights and Sundays. . . . And not any of this could be called work, for it was a constant source of pleasure."[13] An American lured north to run the Canadian Pacific, and eventually rising to be its president, Van Horne became an ardent Canadian nationalist, in part because Canadian nationalism was the fuel for the Canadian Pacific.[14] Van Horne was a man conditioned to think about railroad space in terms not only of the thousands of miles that the Canadian Pacific spanned but also of the inches and feet involved in the design of a car, or the square footage of a warehouse or grain elevator.

Van Horne recognized the power of spatial arrangements—how, for example, the precise arrangement of sidings and the buildings along them in Manitoba could influence the price that wheat grown in the province brought a continent away. The Canadian Pacific leased rather than sold land adjoining sidings, and that allowed Van Horne to mandate the kinds of structures that could be built there. By replacing numerous small buyers and their small single-story warehouses, in which high- and low-quality wheat were promiscuously mixed, with "two or three suitable elevators at every grain station on the line," which separated wheat by grade and loaded wheat mechanically rather than manually, the railroad could exert control over the quality of wheat.[15] Van Horne reduced the harvests of tens of thousands of western Canadian farms into a small number of graded classifications that enabled a buyer in Liverpool to know what he was getting when he purchased Manitoba wheat. That gave it an advantage over wheat shipped from

Duluth, Minnesota—the Northern Pacific's terminus—which was "very variable, sometimes . . . 'No. 1 Duluth Hard Wheat' means one thing at one time and quite a different thing at another, and this has had the effect of injuring its reputation and reducing its value in the World's markets." Rigorously graded Manitoba wheat would bring a premium on world markets, and the railroads as much as the government had to take responsibility for ensuring uniform grading.[16]

II. RELATIONAL SPACE

Absolute space, in turn, yielded a second kind of railroad space: relational space. Relational space came into being only when the geometrical measures of absolute space, calculated in inches, feet, or miles, were related to other abstract measures such as time or cost. Relational space was the railroad space of movement that arose when humans calculated their journeys not in miles and feet but in hours and minutes or dollars and cents. Railroad distance measured in miles between two points was stable; distance measured in time or money was often radically unstable and a matter of bitter dispute. It formed the heart of the entire railroad enterprise.[17]

Like Ives, Arthur Wellington was both cynical and touchingly naïve. He was scornful of much engineering practice, but he still thought that, if engineering was rightly defined, railroad problems were ultimately still engineering problems. Western railroads in particular were primers on where not to locate railroads. The Kansas Pacific never left the prairies and the Great Plains, but it contained "numerous and heavy grades, distributed over the whole of it."[18] The Mexican Central had rejected a route that would have put it through Silao, Guanajuato, and León. It decreased its tributary population per mile even as it added "nearly 500 miles of extra haul" between Mexico City and El Paso.[19] The Western Pacific took the shortest route between San Francisco and Sacramento, but an alternate route, taken by the California Pacific Railroad, was shorter "in the sense of economy and transportation," which is to say it was a "dead-level road," while the other had a maximum grade of fifty feet to the mile.[20]

Wellington measured the success of railroad technology by its ability to move freight at minimal cost. By these standards the technological success of most western railroads was open to question. As Wellington pointed out, "a little practice and a little study of field geometry will enable any one of ordinary intelligence without any engineering knowledge whatever . . . to lay out a railway from anywhere to anywhere." There was "no field of professional labor in which a limited amount of modest incompetency, at $150 a month, can set so many picks and shovels and locomotives at work to no purpose whatever."[21] Many engineers built railroads badly, and it might take years to discover the hidden costs of steep grades, sharp curves, missed sources of traffic, and the failure to keep a line as level as possible.

Once built, a railroad's absolute space became part of the local geography ideally suited for mapping and conventional description in a railroad guidebook. *The Pacific Tourist*, designed to entertain and inform, provided railroad travelers information about towns, sights, stage connections, and a rudimentary history. Its readers encountered a set of maps, anecdotes, descriptions, statistics, and illustrations all set firmly in absolute, three-dimensional space. Archer, Wyoming, "is 508 miles from the starting place (Omaha), with an elevation of 6,000 feet above tidewater. This station is a side track with section house nearby." Cheyenne, the "Magic City of the Plains," was "516 miles from Omaha, elevation 6,041 feet."[22] The *Railroad Gazetteer*, "For Gratuitous Distribution on Railways, Steamers and Stages" of the Central Pacific, meticulously located for its captive audience of travelers tunnels, snowsheds, and exceptional sights by their distance from San Francisco and their elevation.[23]

What distinguished railroads from the natural geography through which they ran was their centrality to measures of value; they transformed everything around them. There is no such thing as a badly placed river or a mountain, although humans may wish they were located elsewhere. They are where they are, but engineers located railroads for human purposes. There were good locations and bad. To determine the line between "the utterly bad and barely tolerable" in railway location, Wellington relied on a second abstract measure: the dollar. Wellington thought engineering should not be considered the art of construction but rather "the art of doing that well with one dollar, which any bungler can do with two after a fashion." How to build a railroad was widely studied, but "the larger questions of where to build and when to build, and whether to build them at all" had been neglected.[24]

The first step in the engineer's job of giving maximum value to railroad movement was to reduce the natural complexity of a road to a mathematical simplicity that would indicate the optimum route over which a single engine could pull the maximum number of fully loaded freight cars a given distance at the lowest cost. Through the 1880s, with the coupling technology then in use, the maximum length of a freight train was fifty to sixty cars. On most lines, however, the real limit was lower, often much lower, and was set by the number of cars a locomotive could pull up the ruling grade.[25] The ruling grade was not necessarily the maximum grade. If a train had to approach a grade at low speed or from a standing stop then this "virtual" grade might be the ruling grade while a steeper grade approached at high speed might be more easily surmounted. Numerous short steep grades forced railroads to run smaller more frequent trains, and the cost of doing so was far greater than running large trains. This ability to limit the length of trains was, in Wellington's view, "the whole objection to gradients."[26]

Ideally, a railroad should follow the most level terrain, using nature to reduce the grade as much as possible. Curves, as long as they were not excessive, were tolerable. *Railway Location* was nearly a thousand pages long by the late 1880s, but its essence was clear: railway location was primarily about gradient and traffic. If there was a "fundamental law for location," it was "*Follow that route which affords the* EASIEST POSSIBLE GRADES FOR THE LONGEST POSSIBLE DISTANCES, *using to that end such amounts of distance curvature, and rise and fall as may be necessary, and then* PASS OVER THE INTERVENING DISTANCES ON SUCH GRADES AS ARE THEN FOUND NECESSARY."[27] Engineers should choose routes that concentrated grades into a limited number of places of steep ascent where helper engines could assist.[28]

Wellington's concern with the ruling grade was, of course, not the whole story, but it was most of it. His second concern was traffic, which also reduced down to a maxim: the layout of railroads should secure the largest possible tributary population and, whenever possible, link major centers of population.[29] Wellington thought engineers paid far too much attention to what he called the minor details of railway location—relatively small variations in distance, curvature, and the rise and fall of topography less than the ruling grade of the road. These "minor details" did influence the cost of moving people and goods and at the extreme could cripple a line, but improvements should be made only when they were justified by increases in business, gross receipts, or savings in operating expenses greater than the costs of improvements.[30] Such calculations should be made conservatively, never estimating an increase in traffic more than two to five years in the future.[31]

Wellington's calculations of movement took him into the realm of relational space, which was the wonderland of modernity. It rendered what was close distant and the distant near. For Wellington its key measure was cost of transport, and that did not vary "in direct ratio, or in anything like direct ratio" with distance. Other items—"grades, . . . cost of construction, terminal expenses, volume of traffic, whether cars return full or empty"—had more to do with the actual cost of service. In any case, Wellington thought the price of transportation had nothing to do with the cost of producing it. It was, he believed, simply a function of what people were willing to pay.[32]

Calculations of cost disrupted the clichés about the annihilation of time and space that governed people's initial reaction to the railroads. Margaret Irvin Carrington had captured that first reaction in 1869 when she wrote that with the transcontinentals and the Atlantic cable "the Christian world and all civilized people [may] rejoice that the islands of the sea and the barbarism of Asia have been brought so near to our homes that with only a single wire to underlie the Pacific, the whole earth will become as a whispering gallery, wherein all nations, by one electric pulsation, may throb in unison, and the continent shall tremble with the rumbling of wheels that swiftly and without interruption or delay transport its gospel and commerce." The Pacific Coast was by 1869 only four days from Omaha, and "[a]n officer of the army recently returned in forty hours over a distance which required a march of sixty-four days in 1866."[33] But Carrington did not speak of the shifting costs of such trips.

Railroads reduced the cost of movement, but they also rendered it dramatically unstable. Ignore the instability, and the whole world did seem to be collapsing together. The Senate Select Committee on Interstate Commerce reproduced this orthodox vision when it reasoned that a mechanic in Massachusetts had only to work a single day to pay the cost of transporting the food he would eat for a year one thousand miles from the western prairies. "If the mechanic will give up one holiday a year . . . he is placed alongside of the prairie, and distance is eliminated from his condition."[34] Such calculations, however, ignored fluctuations in costs and differences in costs between one destination and other. When rates rose, or when they sank faster for one place than for another, seemingly fixed places grew not closer but more distant. This was relational space, and it became the heart of antimonopoly politics.

The measures of relational space were the timetable and the tariff. Both translated distance into other abstract measures—time and cost—but to get the full measure of relational space they had to be read together. The whole purpose of the timetable was to translate distance from miles into time. Going eastward from San Francisco in November of 1871, a passenger left San Francisco at 7:00 in the morning and reached Sacramento at 2:00 in the afternoon. It was after midnight when she reached Reno, and roughly twenty-four hours after leaving San Francisco she was at Humboldt in Nevada. Nearly another day would pass before she reached Ogden. People moving through space had to orient themselves by time—when the train departed, when it arrived, how long it was in transit—and compare the savings in time with other means of transportation. The timetable's measures of space were always shifting: schedules changed, stations were added or dropped, new technologies increased the speed of the train and thus shortened the time between places, and weather delayed the train and thus increased the time. Ultimately this orientation in space by time changed time itself. The Central Pacific Railroad in November of 1871 had to specify that the schedule operated on Sacramento time because each city, operating on sun time, had its own time. Eventually, in 1883, the railroads promoted and enforced standard time to coordinate their schedules. Lives took shape around this.[35]

Just as the timetable translated space into time, so the tariff list translated distance into money. This was a relatively simple translation in the case of passengers. It depended largely on the class of travel, but it was a much more complicated translation in the case of commodities. The cost of shipping varied from commodity to commodity and was always changing. Here is where relational space grew most important. When the price of movement between two places fell, then those places drew closer together. When it rose, they grew farther apart. Since the prices, or tariffs, that the railroads charged fell as a whole throughout the late nineteenth century, space had shrunk. The average rate per ton-mile on freight declined fairly steadily on both the Central Pacific and the Union Pacific between 1870 and 1885, with the rates in 1885 roughly one-third of what they had been fifteen years earlier.[36] Things were, however, more complicated than they seemed.

The overall decline in freight rates and comparisons between American and European freight rates became something of a stock answer to complaints about American railroad tariffs, but they were not answers that stood up well to scrutiny. In 1897 the president of the Atchison, Topeka, and Santa Fe informed the Kansas legislature that the average rate charged per ton-mile by his system had fallen 55 percent between 1882 and 1896.[37] The average rate per ton-mile, however, was not a particularly revealing statistic. Because railroads charged more for short hauls than for long hauls and because they discriminated between commodities (charging less for bulk goods like coal or wheat than for luxury goods like coffee or tea), a change in the length of the haul or an increase in the amount of lower classifications of freight would produce a decline in the average rate per ton-mile without much alteration in rates. The expansion of the Santa Fe after 1882 and the rise in Kansas coal, corn, and wheat production would in and of themselves have gone far to reduce average rates. An American Statistical Association forum in 1897 concluded that "the low average freight rates per ton-mile in this country are due chiefly to the enormous amount of long distance freight traffic."[38]

The average rate per ton-mile told little about the fall in the cost of transportation in relation to the fall of commodity prices. It appears that falling rates for the transportation of corn and wheat at best mirrored the falling prices for those commodities. The railroads charged what the crops would bear. Real rates may have fallen in the 1870s, but the price of transportation maintained either roughly the same proportion to the value of the crop or actually claimed a higher proportion from the 1880s into the 1890s.

Real railroad rates spiked proportionately to corn and wheat prices during the depression of 1893–97.[39] The Atchison's statistics did not answer what C. E. Prevey later called the "ethical question regarding the fairness of rates." Prevey wondered whether "the reduction in average rates per ton-mile [has] been at the expense of the railroad companies and a direct gain to the public, or does it consist in merely doing less work for less money?"[40]

Falling prices and average rates were not the issue; comparative prices and discrimination between shippers were the issues. Because prices did not fall evenly, distance did not shrink evenly, and this gave rise to the chronic discontent of those who used the railroads. It did not matter to wholesalers in Spokane, for example, if they seemed to grow closer to Chicago as their rates decreased over time if the rates to ship from Chicago to Seattle fell even faster. In such a case, they were at a disadvantage. They were in comparison to Seattle growing farther away from Chicago even though Seattle was 229 miles west of Spokane. Similarly, the special rates granted to Winnipeg brought that city closer to eastern Canada than any other place on the Canadian prairies.[41]

III. THE THINGS THEY CARRIED

If one thinks of the railroad tracks, bridges, and stations that made up the railroads' absolute space as hardware and rate tables that governed their relational space as software, it is easier to understand how railroads could project order and create disorder in such a way that the very concepts blurred. The physical capacity of railroad lines steadily increased. The limits of the technology—the need of locomotives for coal and water and the restraints on how far farmers could profitably haul goods by wagon—shaped a seemingly uniform railroad space, but technological restraints were to some extent plastic.[42]

Over time everything on a railroad swelled. Freight cars increased in size from 10 tons in 1870 to 15 and 20 tons, reaching 40 tons in the early twentieth century, even though these large cars rarely carried a full load.[43] The increases in car size as well as in train size were the fruits of steel rails, which allowed heavier loads, rebuilt and ballasted lines, better brakes, better couplers, and more powerful locomotives. The Pennsylvania was the gold standard of railroad lines, and the one that kept the best records. Its average train carried a payload of 94.3 tons in 1863, 116.8 tons in 1873, and 196 tons in 1883. Western lines, not as well built or as well equipped, almost certainly averaged far less.[44]

As railroads built more tracks, and as trains increased in length and in number to carry more freight, they required more freight cars. Freight cars remained inexpensive individually, with their cost remaining steady at about $500 from the Civil War to 1900, but collectively they were a major drain on the railroad. To take just three representative western railroads over this period—the Central Pacific, the Northern Pacific, and the Chicago and North Western—the number of freight cars on each road increased, respectively, from 3,200 to 5, 850 (Central Pacific), 0 to 16,726 (Northern Pacific), and 5,982 to 35,194 (Chicago and North Western). And on each the large majority of freight cars were the simplest: boxcars and flatcars.[45]

As railroad tracks connected more and more places, movement often spawned disorder. The timetable disguised this disorder not simply because trains were often delayed but because it disguised the fact that many trains were not scheduled. Passenger trains, express trains, and scheduled freights usually did move along smoothly enough, but by the 1880s most western freights were unscheduled and put together as cargo required. For these trains the railroad was less a single line through space than a contraption that looked like an old Tinkertoy.

Imagine each stick of the Tinkertoy as a division of 100 to 125 miles, and at the end of each division—the round connecting piece of a Tinkertoy—was a railroad yard. This division point was the key marker in the absolute space of railroads. Now imagine a freight car bound from San Francisco to Cleveland or from Vancouver to Quebec. The car moved in divisional increments. A locomotive moved it from San Francisco to Sacramento, at which point the engineer put the engine in the roundhouse and the cars with their cargo in the yard, and a new train was made up. The car might sit there for a day or more before going on to the next division at Reno, where the process was repeated. And so a freight car proceeded across the country. The bigger the division point—at Ogden, where the cars moved from the Central

Pacific, to the Union Pacific or Omaha/Council Bluffs, where it moved to one of the Chicago lines—the longer the possible delay. In Chicago it could take a week or more to move out of the yards.[46] And none of this took into account bad weather, accidents, or the endless hours spent on sidings waiting for other trains to pass. It was impossible to simply divide the distance traveled by the speed of a freight train—11 miles per hour to 18 miles per hour—and get the duration of the trip.

In 1886 William Van Horne traced nine freight cars moving through mountainous British Columbia westbound from Donald to Port Moody. The first six cars to depart took from six to nine days to make the entire journey; they spent most of their time sitting in yards and sidings. It took these cars five to seven days to travel the 121 miles between Kamloops and North Bend. The next week the last three freight cars made the entire trip in half the time—in from three to four days. During the same period cars going east over the same track took between two and five days between Port Moody and Donald. "It is not necessary to run our freight trains very fast to make first rate time," Van Horne admonished his divisional superintendent. "It is only necessary to keep cars full watch to see that they are not scattered along the road or delayed at Divisional Points."[47]

The inefficiency of normal railroad movement played to the genius of nineteenth-century railroad owners, who were usually able to find occasions for profit in their own ineptitude. Insiders organized independent fast-freight companies—each with its own colored cars reflected in its name, such as the Blue Line or the Red Line—to move freight continuously across the country. A fast freight attained no greater speeds than any other freight, but it kept moving instead of pausing every hundred miles. Insiders skimmed the cream of this traffic for years until management created internal fast-freight divisions.[48]

Changes in technology produced additional opportunities to divert profits to insiders or well-connected customers. When, by the end of the century, refrigerated cars were beginning to be used for chilled beef and fruit, the railroads left their purchase to fast-freight lines. In 1890 American railroads owned 8,500 refrigerator cars; the fast-freight lines and the so-called shipper lines, such as the Armour Packing Company, held 15,000.[49] They, too, became a way to drain off the most profitable traffic, often for the benefit of railroad insiders.[50]

Fast-freight companies profited by keeping goods in motion, but value also accrued at those places where movement stopped so that shippers could load goods and customers could take them off. With all else equal, farmlands with ready access to railroad stations, warehouses, and elevators had greater value than farmlands too far from a railroad for an easy haul. Towns competed so desperately for railroad connections because railroads increased not only business but also property values. There was money in knowledge of where a railroad was going or, better yet, where a railroad would erect stations, elevators, and, warehouses and where it would establish its divisional points with yards and repair shops. Both those running the railroad and those in existing towns knew this.

There were two kinds of urban places in the West: market centers, which very often existed prior to the arrival of the railroads, and railroad towns, usually divisional points on the railroad that owed their prosperity and even existence to the railroads' location of roundhouses and shops within them.[51] In both the railroads created value, in both the railroads, either the corporation itself or, more often, privileged insiders, sought to monopolize as much as possible the increased land values that they created. The degree of railroad control varied significantly.

The Canadian Pacific was one of the few roads that succeeded in allocating this profit to the corporation. In choosing possible division points, the railroad selected the site that allowed it "to secure a large enough interest in the adjacent real estate to recoup" its expenditures on shops and sidings.[52] In the words of the *Toronto Globe* in 1882, the managers of the Canadian Pacific had "a say in the existence of almost every town or prospective town in the Northwest. Individuals rarely have an opportunity of starting a town without their consent and cooperation."[53] When landowners at Grand Valley, Manitoba, tried to negotiate a better price for a future townsite, the railroad found more amenable men at what would become Brandon.[54] When the Canadian Pacific's superintendent Alpheus Stickney and chief engineer Thomas Rosser tried to use insider knowledge to engage in private land speculation, Stickeny was replaced by Van Horne, who then fired Rosser.[55]

American railroads usually allocated speculative profits to corporate officials and board members. James J. Hill insisted that his roads did not engage in townsite development. They didn't. He reserved that for himself. When the St. Paul, Minneapolis, and Manitoba, the mother road of the Great Northern, built to Devil's Lake, North Dakota, it destroyed many existing townsites simply by avoiding them.[56] This left open the opportunity for Hill and other railroad officers to use the Northwest Land Company, in which Hill held half the stock, to develop towns on behalf of the railroad.[57] In this Hill did what Charles Perkins of the Burlington and Missouri had done and what Frederick Billings of the Northern Pacific did. Either individually or through land companies, insiders took advantage of their access to information and profited from expected booms in land prices at towns where railroads located stations and divisional points.[58] In the words of the geographer John Hudson, writing about the Dakotas, "the successful towns were those platted by railroads or their designated agents."[59] Or as Charles Francis Adams complained, "town site schemes are jobs from beginning to end. I have never struck them anywhere . . . that I did not find some sacrifice of interests of the company at the bottom of the whole thing."[60]

Railroads could bully small towns by threatening to move their shops elsewhere, but transcontinentals rarely had the same kind of leverage over large market centers such as Denver, Salt Lake City, or San Francisco. The Associates failed in their efforts to overcome San Francisco and control the juncture of rail and shipping on the Pacific Coast by creating at either Goat Island or Oakland a port/terminal where they owned all the surrounding real estate. And later in the century Los Angeles defied the Southern Pacific and defeated that road's attempt to make Santa Monica into the port for the city of Los Angeles. Denver did not wither because the Union Pacific passed to its north, and the city soon had the Kansas Pacific and the Denver and Rio Grande. The Northern Pacific controlled Tacoma, but Seattle emerged as the leading city on Puget Sound, and it had secured its independence even before James J. Hill and the Great Northern made Seattle a terminus. The arrival of the Canadian Pacific in Vancouver, which had easy water connections to Puget Sound, forced the Northern Pacific to grant Seattle rates equivalent to Tacoma's.[61] Kansas City was never under the domination of a single railroad. Despite all of the Union Pacific's efforts, Omaha remained Omaha, and the reasons behind the bitter struggle of the Union Pacific and the Central Pacific to dominate Ogden was often a mystery to people who saw Ogden. It never posed a threat to Salt Lake City.[62]

There were exceptions. The decision of the Mexican railroads to bypass Matamoros, once a major entrepôt in northeastern Mexico, caused that city to wither. Its population had dropped from 40,000 in 1882 to less than 4,000 by the end of the 1890s.[63] And Vancouver, British Columbia, might seem the great exception to this, but here the Canadian Pacific did not displace an existing market city so much as create a regional market city where none had existed before. When the Canadian Pacific announced in 1884 that its terminus would be "in the immediate vicinity of Coal Harbour and English Bay," it began a process that would transform what was first the site of Gastown and "Gassy Jack" Deighton's hotel and saloon into Vancouver, British Columbia. It did so, however, only after a lengthy and bitter struggle. The Canadian Pacific received a land grant of roughly 6,000 acres near its terminus. Private owners coughed up an additional 175 acres to the railroad. L. A. Hamilton, the "CPR's surveyor and later land commissioner," determined the layout of much of the future city, and the goal was quite straightforward: "to give the greatest possible value to our [CPR] own lands and therefore the least to any other." And from all of this the Canadian Pacific prospered. It did not rush to sell off its holdings, and it imposed stringent terms on buyers. The assessed value of its holdings steadily rose as the city grew, from roughly 1,000 people in 1887 to about 20,000 in 1900.[64]

The railroads could not dictate to larger cities, but they still could profit from the value that railroad movement created there. In negotiations with San Francisco, the Associates obtained 60 acres at Mission Bay for the Southern Pacific and the Central Pacific. Sixty acres of largely submerged land might seem a pittance relative to the immense land grants held by these two railroads, but that wasn't how the railroads did the math. For accounting purposes, the Central Pacific valued the 12 million acres in land grants it controlled at $30.37 million. It valued its half share in the Mission Bay tideland at $285,000, or $9,487 an acre. In other words, 1 acre in San Francisco equaled 3,795 acres of land outside San Francisco.[65] This was one possible calculation and a low one. In its annual report the Central Pacific put a much higher valuation on its lands in Sacramento, Oakland, and Mission Bay. These 670 acres of urban land were worth $7,750,000 exclusive of improvements. Urban lands totaling a little over a section (640 acres) were thus worth roughly 25 percent of the entire value of the rest of its land grant.[66]

Freight traffic rather than passenger traffic gave lands value in the nineteenth-century West. Western railroads were freight roads carrying the basic commodities of an agricultural and increasingly industrial nation. Where there was no access to ocean or other water transportation, the railroads were the primary carriers of grain, other agricultural produce, livestock, coal, lumber, and minerals. The remainder of their traffic was manufactures, merchandise, and a variety of miscellaneous goods. The proportion of these things varied across the West, but taking the systems that ran through Kansas as a fair sample of the western railroads, the figures for 1890 were a total of 29.3 million tons of freight, of which 8.5 million tons (28.9 percent) were agricultural products, 3.5 million tons (11.9 percent) were animal products, 8.2 million tons (27.9 percent) were minerals, and 3.0 million tons (10.1 percent) were forest products. The western roads were even more heavily commodity roads than those in the East. Nearly 80 percent of their freight traffic came from field, farm, mine, and forest.[67] Although more traffic in Kansas flowed west than east, the cargoes were not simply raw products flowing east and finished products flowing west. In 1888 raw materials such as coal and semifinished goods such as lumber made up a significant portion of the freight going westward.[68]

Businessmen, farmers, and railroad officials all over the West recognized that the price of moving things—railroad rates—did not vary evenly with distance. If they did, there would be no distinction between the most important markers of relational and absolute space. The shorthand for making the cost of transportation proportional to distance was pro rata, and the railroads objected to it strenuously and effectively. Thomas Kimball of the Union Pacific summarized the critique in early March of 1877: the "popular assumption is that the cost of transportation is strictly on the basis of uniformity as to miles, and that compensation should be on the same basis of uniformity as to miles, and that compensation should be on the same basis regardless of the length of haul." But, Kimball argued, local traffic was more expensive because the costs of "switching, handling, dropping and picking up cars, and returning cars" were far greater per mile on short hauls than on long hauls.[69] This explained the logic behind the distinctions railroads made in the rates for short hauls and those for long hauls, but it did not establish the justice of particular railroad rates.[70]

The struggle to define and implement fair rates became the center of spatial politics. A century and more later the details of these rates, the state and federal commissions created to investigate them, the political campaigns that took place around them—in short, the very stuff of spatial politics—seem as dreary and arcane as they are distant. But examine these details, and the power of the corporations—and the fear it inspired—becomes apparent. It was visible whether shippers reacted with fury or resignation to the influence railroads had over them. When his Idaho lumber company lost its special rates and its markets to the Montana Improvement Company, reputedly owned by Northern Pacific insiders, O. A. Dodge asked the railroad for either a restoration of his old rates or, if the Northern Pacific had deemed it "advisable to do all the lumbering business," a fair price for his property.[71] His business was at the mercy of the railroad. If it decided to cut him out of the market, he was resigned. All he could do was ask for compensation.

But more victims protested. When the Pacific Railway Commission investigated subsidized railroads in the West in 1887, the anger was palpable even though it might be hard to imagine that the rates for Spreckels sugar or canned vegetables created deep emotion. In the late 1880s Lincoln, Nebraska, was a wholesaling center and a rival of Omaha. When the Union Pacific compiled statistics on stations west of Omaha, it was the only one where imported goods far exceeded exports. Lincoln had connections with three major railroad systems, but of these only the Union Pacific had direct connections to the Pacific Coast. A Lincoln wholesale grocer testified before the commission that by charging wholesalers in Lincoln a higher rate for California products—particularly Spreckels sugar and canned fruit and vegetables—than they charged wholesalers in Omaha, the Union Pacific gave the Omaha wholesalers "the advantage of us and it is the destruction of our business." The comparative prices of sugar and canned goods became evidence of the "extending influence of corporate power." It was. And it helped make the monopoly power of corporations the chief political question of the day.[72] Charles Francis Adams admitted that he did not see how anyone could "enter upon any manufacturing industry on the line of a railroad corporation which makes a plaything of its tariffs," and he thought the Union Pacific had played with its rates far too much.[73]

Railroad rates affected the structure of entire industries. Most western commodities needed processing of some kind before they reached their final markets: wheat had to be milled into flour, timber had to be cut at sawmills, ore had to be smelted, cattle and sheep had to be slaughtered and turned into meat and by-products. Where businessmen located mills, stockyards, and smelters often depended on the intricacies of railroad rates. When railroads charged higher rates for hauling wheat than for hauling flour, they were encouraging the growth of mills near the site of production. When they charged higher rates for flour than for wheat, they encouraged millers located near the sites of consumption. When they raised prices on dressed beef so that a refrigerated carload of forty slaughtered carcasses cost as much to ship as a carload of twenty live animals, even when the cost of the refrigerated car was only one-third more, they favored Chicago as against more westerly stockyards and slaughterhouses.[74]

Setting rates was difficult. Even the railroads had very little knowledge of their true costs and thus the profit on any particular item. When in 1877 Collis P. Huntington asked his general superintendent A. N. Towne for the "cost of hauling freight per train per mile," Towne, who described himself as a "high tariff and low speed advocate," replied that "this is a problem difficult of solution and it cannot be arrived at with any degree of accuracy as a rule, a basis for one road would not be at all applicable to another." The "profoundest Railroad Mathematician, Mr. Fink," had written that such a calculation demanded "fifty eight items of expense all of which vary on different lines of road and enter more or less into different combinations."[75]

In fact, railroads did not base their rates on the cost of service, which they were incapable of determining.[76] When the imminent arrival of James

J. Hill's Great Northern in Butte, Montana, in 1889 threatened to drive prices charged by the Union Pacific and Northern Pacific lower, Charles Francis Adams was uncertain whether it was worth competing with Hill, because he had only "guesses, surmises, general impressions or other vague estimates of the value to us of the Anaconda and Butte business." He certainly could not trust the estimates of his own managers. The Union Pacific and the Northern Pacific were jointly operating the Montana Union Railway in Butte, and after setting prices for the hauling of coal, they offered one supplier a rebate if he *reduced* the amount of coal he shipped under his contract with the Montana Union since Adams thought the road was losing money on every ton hauled.[77]

This combination of ignorance and miscalculation was not unique to the Union Pacific. In April of 1889 William Mahl, an accountant who became Collis Huntington's right-hand man, was in San Francisco examining the books of the Southern Pacific. He reported, "As the matter now stands it is impossible to bring anything to New-York, or to arrive at any intelligent understanding about matters from the books here, and each month's business really requires a special investigation because practices have been changed since the preceding month." There were four separate auditors in the building, and each time one of them picked up a new idea that he liked, he put it in place "without any reference to any definite policy and the result is a constant changing in methods, distribution, etc. which is horrorful in every way."[78] When railroads buried state railroad commissioners under piles of incommensurate, confusing, and often arbitrarily constructed data, they were just doing to others what they did to themselves.

Albert Fink knew more about railroad rates than any other nineteenth-century North American. He studied railroads the way Darwin studied evolution, but whereas Darwin found a simple rule, Fink watched his rules fly apart. He could find no uniform rule for rate making.[79] Fink opposed legislating rates since "transportation tariffs cannot be established by simple arithmetical or mathematical rules; they require the application of quite a number of principles all correct in themselves, and this to a great variety of ever changing facts."[80] For each kind of freight one needed a separate calculation to determine what rate the traffic could bear, hence the multiplicity of rates and categories of freight involved in moving things through space. This was a task that demanded experts.[81]

When forced to offer a governing principle for rates, Fink contended that railroads priced goods according to what a given commodity could bear. But this was an unfortunate phrase, for it implicated squeezing every possible cent from every commodity. What the railroads meant was that they would price a commodity as high as they could without reducing the volume shipped. In practice, this meant that for certain low-value bulk commodities—wheat, coal, lumber—there was a maximum amount that could be charged no matter how long the carriage.[82] Similarly, to fill a train, and thus at least cover fixed costs, it might be necessary to charge some freight only the cost of carriage. In practice, pricing according to what the traffic would bear meant traffic managers and freight agents set rates experimentally and then modified prices as necessary. Prices were educated guesses constructed by trial and error and varied according to immediate circumstances.[83] This did not mean that the agents could not set rates both cleverly and adroitly.

IV. HOW RAILROAD RATES CONSTRUCT SPACE

California provides a good example of how rates constructed space, how space became political, and how for shippers railroad space seemed a kaleidoscope. Lathrop was one pivot around which the kaleidoscope turned in California during the 1870s and 1880s. Surrounded by wheat fields for many miles on all sides, Lathrop—the maiden name of Jane Stanford—was a small, nondescript town in the San Joaquin Valley. But, as Albert Wilbur, the railroad's telegraph operator and later freight agent there in the early 1880s, explained, "it was the most important junction on the C.P. system of railroads." That was a function of wheat. A single district to the south of Lathrop was alone supposedly capable of supplying one hundred cars of wheat every day for an entire year. It was where that wheat did not go that made Lathrop important.[84]

California railroads moved wheat west, not east. Sailing ships departing from San Francisco Bay delivered wheat to its final destination, which was usually Great Britain. Steamboats along the San Joaquin and Sacramento rivers provided by far the cheapest and most efficient way to move freight to San Francisco Bay in the 1870s and 1880s, and Lathrop was about ten miles from Stockton, which except during winter and spring high water, was the practical terminus of navigation on the San Joaquin. The way to secure lowest costs and the least expenditure of energy would be to take wheat by rail to Stockton and put it on steamboats and barges. Nature, as Mark Hopkins had realized when he initially planned the terminus of the Central Pacific at Sacramento, seemed to defeat railroads. They could not compete with steamboats for low-cost bulk commodities. But just as the Central Pacific did not terminate at Sacramento the Southern Pacific line along the San Joaquin Valley did not terminate at Stockton. The railroad wanted to eliminate the river's ability to dictate rates for the whole San Joaquin Valley. On the Sacramento, the railroad operated its own steamboat lines, but on the San Joaquin it first bought out the steamboats, removing most of them, and then moved to keep wheat off the river.[85]

In 1876 the Central Pacific/Southern Pacific charged only local rates for freight within California, but in 1877 the Southern Pacific instituted through rates from San Francisco to Southern California destinations south of Gloster in Kern County, 377 miles away. In the San Joaquin Valley the Central Pacific/Southern Pacific added to its usual first-, second-, third-, and fourth-class rates a local tariff for grain on the Southern Pacific and, more significantly, a port grain tariff for carloads of wheat destined for Sacramento, Stockton, Oakland, and San Francisco. The low special rate extended to the end of the San Joaquin Valley, and it created a relational space measured by cost that compressed the valley, pulling towns comparatively closer to shipping points. No major valley wheat-producing area paid more than $6.00 a ton to move wheat to San Francisco Bay ports for shipment abroad.[86]

The managers of the Central Pacific/Southern Pacific wanted to encourage grain production, but they also wanted to keep wheat off the San Joaquin River and away from Stockton. The goal was to make the combination of railroad fares to get to the river and steamboat and barge fares on the river higher than direct railroad fares to San Francisco and Oakland.

Farmers could get a lower fare to Stockton than to Oakland or San Francisco, but transfer fees to get the wheat from the railroad car to the steamboat added $1.50 a carload, and this combined with the steamboats' own charges of $1.50 per ton or $15 per carload made the price higher than shipping directly to San Francisco. Even at later, much lower steamboat rates of $.70 to $1.00 a ton reported in the 1890s, the railroads undercut the steamboats.[87]

Lathrop was the key to their doing so. Below Lathrop the railroad paralleled the navigable channel of the San Joaquin. In effect, the railroad's special rate charged farmers a great deal to get wheat to Lathrop and very little to leave, as long as their cargo was going to the bay. This was very clear to farmers who shipped from Lathrop. It cost them $1.20 per ton to get their wheat a few miles to Stockton by rail, and this fee, plus the transfer fee and the steamboat fare, raised their shipping costs above the $2.20 that the railroad charged to carry the wheat directly to Oakland and San Francisco. Only those who could haul their wheat directly to docks on the navigable part of the San Joaquin could effectively use the river. For most farmers the railroad had erased the San Joaquin as a source of transportation not because of superior technology or efficiency but because it used its rates to manipulate and control space.[88]

Farmers in the upper San Joaquin Valley encountered another price exacted by the railroad. What the railroads gave in freight going to San Francisco, they took back in freight leaving San Francisco, which was the port of entry for goods coming in by sea and also, because of lower through rates, for transcontinental traffic. Costs ranged from $.05 per 100 pounds for those stations near San Francisco to $1.25 for 100 pounds, or $25.00 a ton, for the farthest valley stations. Again the increase in rates was not uniform across distance. Stations below Lathrop that could use the San Joaquin River paid little more for first-class goods coming in than they did for wheat going out. Stations beyond Lathrop faced a steep escalation in price. Farmers in the San Joaquin Valley shipped wheat at a maximum of $6.00 a ton, but they paid freight rates that topped out at $25.00 a ton for goods they consumed.[89]

Rate reductions had meaning only within the particular spatial patterns of traffic. Thus the California Railroad Commission could appear in 1883 to deliver a ringing victory to the state's farmers by reducing grain rates 35 percent, but their reduction applied only to grain going east, which was not the direction that grain traveled. "For one ton of grain shipped from San Francisco to interior points there are more than a thousand tons transported in the other. Upon the one ton, which is charged for at exorbitant rates, there is a reduction, upon the one thousand, which is the produce of the *labor* and *time* of the producer, *there is no reduction whatever*."[90]

The Southern Pacific and the Central Pacific erased the "natural" advantage of Stockton's location on the San Joaquin River, but they simultaneously justified their rate structure by appealing to nature. In the 1870s the Central Pacific, using short-haul rates, charged three to six times as much to haul goods from Ogden, where it connected to the Union Pacific, to points in Nevada as it charged, using long-haul rates, to move identical goods over the Sierras from San Francisco to the same places. General Manager Towne regarded such rates as part of his duty to ensure "the highest possible earnings and the least possible operating expenses for the Central Pacific."[91] J. C. Stubbs of the Central Pacific justified such rates by claiming it was unfair to have the "artificial" advantages of the railroad trump the natural advantages of San Francisco. In 1881, when the Associates had managed to make friends of two of the three railroad commissioners, the California Railroad Commission ruled that as long as the rate from Ogden to Reno was reasonable, it made no difference if the rate from Ogden to San Francisco was less, even if Reno was two hundred miles closer to Ogden and the railroad had to cross the Sierras to get to San Francisco. San Francisco had the sea, and "[n]o regulation of whatever nature can overcome these differences until railroads can transport persons and property as vessels on navigable water can perform the same service."[92]

Appeals to nature were thus opportunistic. In fact, the Southern Pacific had already overcome Stockton and the San Joaquin River, and by the 1880s it was maneuvering to overcome San Francisco. The advantages that San Francisco Bay gave San Francisco were quite real. From the completion of the first transcontinental, the Union Pacific and the Associates recognized that they were at the mercy of the Pacific Mail Steamship Company. With its connections by rail across Panama, that company could move goods nearly as quickly as the railroads and at a much lower cost. In 1873 Jay Gould of the Union Pacific complained about competition from steamships, saying, "It is outrageous that we have to carry our California business at so low rates."[93] By the late 1880s little had changed. Charles Francis Adams testified before the Pacific Railway Commission that the Pacific Mail Steamship Company "could reduce the rate . . . until it would make the business worthless to us, and yet make something itself" on traffic to the East Coast.[94] This was an amazing statement, one worth lingering over, for it meant that the railroads really were not necessary for much of the freight traffic between the East and the Far West. If the Pacific Mail wished to do so, it could dominate the traffic. The question then becomes why it did not do so?

The first part of the answer is that the Pacific Mail was a lazy and corrupt corporation. It had, as its name indicated, a federal subsidy to carry the mail. It carried coffee and fruit from Central America to San Francisco and sent rice, lumber, flour, and goods from San Francisco wholesalers in return. It also carried manufactured goods from New York and sent wine, lead, rags, and perhaps rice back. It did not carry wheat. That went by sailing ship. The second part of the answer is that the Union Pacific and the Central Pacific, recognizing their vulnerability to rate cutting by the Pacific Mail, offered to pay what amounted to a subsidy for the company to raise its rates. The Pacific Mail consented. It could make more money by doing less.[95]

The subsidy that the railroads paid Pacific Mail remained in operation for most of the period from 1870 into the 1890s; it took the form of an agreement to buy space in its steamers at above-market prices first by the Central Pacific and the Union Pacific and later, as more transcontinentals reached the Pacific Coast, by the Transcontinental Association. The railroads acted as a freight agent, either reselling this space at the prevailing transcontinental railroad rates to shippers, leaving it empty, or, as the Southern Pacific did, shipping the equipment it needed to build in Mexico by sea rather than by rail. In return the Pacific Mail charged rates identical to those of the railroads, did not add new ships, and refused to solicit traffic to compete with the railroads.[96]

Sometimes, when a new group took control of the line, the Pacific Mail would demand an increase in the subsidy from the railroads. The result was

usually a quick capitulation by the railroads, although Gould and Huntington in 1875 attempted to create a competing steamship line to rid themselves
of the Pacific Mail. When, as a result, Pacific Mail stocks fell, Gould briefly
gained control of that company. But the Pacific Mail was itself dependent on
the Panama Railroad, the short line across the isthmus between the Pacific
Ocean and the Gulf of Mexico that was, on its completion in 1855, the first
real transcontinental railroad. Trevor Park, a speculator like Gould, took
over the Panama Railroad and abrogated its contract with the Pacific Mail.
He eventually attached Pacific Mail steamers for nonpayment of debts owed
the Panama Railroad. Gould capitulated and sold out, and the railroads and
the Pacific Mail once more agreed on a subsidy.[97]

There was a second fight, in 1880, over the amount of the subsidy. The
steamship company cut its rates on first-class freight in January of 1880
and prepared to contract for new vessels. They left lower classes of freight
to other steamship lines and sailing ships. The railroads surrendered, raised
their offer of a monthly subsidy to the steamship company from $25,000 to
$110,000 a month, and renewed their agreement. Gould and Huntington
came onto the board of the Pacific Mail.[98] The threat of the Pacific Mail did
much to explain how the railroads constructed space in California during
the 1870s and early 1880s.

Together the dearth of transcontinental traffic and the threat of the
Pacific Mail made the Southern Pacific/Central Pacific system a regional
road. It funneled goods into San Francisco Bay, and it transported goods—
both California manufactures and imports—out.[99] Wheat and flour
accounted for 15 percent of the total traffic on the system into the late
1880s.[100] It carried only a limited set of goods east. Eighteen items—chief
among them sugar, fruit (initially canned), and wine—made up the large
majority of this traffic. The great rise of California exports by rail in the
late 1880s consisted largely of sugar and fruit—canned, dried, and green—
along with a brief spike in grain. Only green fruit shipped in refrigerated
cars gave the railroads a clear advantage over steamships.[101] (See Appendix,
Charts A, B, and C.)

San Franciscans thus did not initially need the Associates railroads to
connect "the City" to the East or the rest of the world, but they needed the

railroads to connect them to the rest of California. Railroads gathered California's products for shipment out of San Francisco and adjacent ports and distributed San Francisco's manufactures and their imports to the interior. The railroads and San Francisco's powerful wholesalers reached an accommodation on the backs of interior consumers. The Central Pacific/Southern Pacific charged through rates only for out-of-state goods going into San Francisco. It charged much higher local rates for all goods—except wheat—shipped within the state. The result was that it was cheaper to ship out-of-state goods by rail into San Francisco and then reship them back to their destination. The railroad's rate structure served the city's commercial dominance, and San Francisco's wholesalers accepted higher transportation prices that could be passed on to interior consumers. (See Appendix, Chart D.)

Frank Norris captured this accommodation in a scene in The Octopus. Norris's character Harran Derrick watched the plows that his father had bought pass through his fictional San Joaquin Valley town of Bonneville on the Southern Pacific on their way to San Francisco, where they will be shipped back to Bonneville. "Think of it," he declaimed. "Here's a load of stuff for Bonneville that can't stop at Bonneville, where it is consigned, but has got to go up to San Francisco first by way of Bonneville, at forty cents per ton and then be reshipped from San Francisco back to Bonneville again at fifty-one cents per ton, the short haul rate. . . . [I]sn't it a pretty mess! Isn't it a farce! the whole dirty business!" As expressed in dollars, a straight line was not the shortest distance between two points in the relational geometry of the railroads.[102]

The transcontinentals, however, chafed under the limits steamship competition imposed. In the 1870s and early 1880s Gould and Huntington adopted two new tactics. They formed fast-freight companies to try to give the railroads a clear advantage for time-sensitive goods, but their more critical innovation was the so-called special contract system, which proved an ingenious way to construct space for the benefit of the railroads. The system created two sets of westbound rates. The rates in the first set were prohibitively high; those in the second were much lower, supposedly about one-half the higher rates. Merchants could, however, get the set of lower rates—the special contract—only if they agreed to ship all their goods by the railroad.

If they received any goods by sea, they had to pay the higher rates. The railroad further demanded that anyone shipping on a special contract not buy or sell from anyone who shipped goods by means other than rail. To enforce the contracts, the railroads demanded the right to inspect their customers' books to verify that they complied with the terms of the contract.[103]

The special contract system explained the sudden preference of San Francisco merchants for long-distance rail shipments in the early 1880s. Through shipments by rail to San Francisco rose from 226,585,940 pounds in 1879 to 387,174,940 pounds in 1883, even as local shipments stagnated in the early 1880s. The rise in through shipments was a mark of the Central Pacific's and Southern Pacific's ability to coerce wholesalers.[104] (See Appendix, Charts D and E.)

Very few individual merchants dared challenge the railroad. As the California railroad commissioner W. W. Foote put it, the Central Pacific "under existing conditions, without competing eastern lines west of Utah, and almost absolutely controlling local traffic within this State, is too powerful an organization to be successfully resisted by any individual or firm."[105] Even if a wholesaler received all its goods by sea, it would still have to use the railroad to distribute to the interior, and the railroad's ability to grant rebates to a rival firm could kill the non-cooperating firm. Foote clearly understood the consequences: "The contract system enforced upon the merchants of San Francisco, by means of which they are forced to pay double prices unless they ship all their goods by rail, partakes more of the nature of a crime than a mere breach of duty. . . ." The special contract was precisely the kind of abuse that the California Railroad Commission was designed to correct, but two of the commissioners elected in 1882 refused to act; they were widely rumored to have become friends of the railroad.[106]

V. THE RISE OF THE OCTOPUS

The fight over the special contract system was an example of spatial politics. The system turned San Francisco's merchants into antimonopolists, and this, in turn, created the Octopus: the only briefly successful Southern Pacific political machine of the era. Behind this paradoxical result was the Blind Boss, Chris Buckley, who headed San Francisco's Democratic machine. Born on Christmas Day 1845, he was a man of transformations. He had been a Republican and became a Democrat; he had once been a drunk but became sober; he had even once left San Francisco for Vallejo, but returned to reign from the Alhambra saloon on Bush Street. In 1882 he claimed to be an antimonopolist.[107]

The San Francisco merchants joined an antimonopoly crusade led by the Democrats that swept the California elections of 1882. The nearly immediate defection of two of their new railroad commissioners had not been what they expected.[108] And they were even more dismayed by two decisions of Judge Stephen Field. The Southern Pacific had nearly crippled many counties by refusing to pay taxes. Litigation culminated in *County of San Mateo v. Southern Pacific Railroad Company* (1882) and *County of Santa Clara* v. *Southern Pacific Railroad Company* (1883), which famously voided the tax bills for charging different rates for corporate and noncorporate owners and ruled that the corporation was a person within the meaning of the Fourteenth Amendment and entitled to all constitutional protections.[109] Field, whom his fellow California Democrat Stephen Mallory White called "one of the most dishonest characters that has ever discharged the function of a judicial office," was also one of the Associates' most reliable judicial friends.[110]

Fundamental democratic principles were at stake in Field's decisions. Governor George Stoneman challenged Field's conflation of corporate persons with actual living and breathing citizens, arguing that the state had a right to distinguish between "the natural person . . . who is a *part* of the Government" and the "artificial person, which is but a creature of the Government." Field's decisions trampled logic and a core democratic practice that stretched back to the founding of the republic: "lodging in the legislature, and the legislature alone, the right to determine taxes."[111]

In 1884 Stoneman called a special session of the legislature devoted solely to railroad legislation. Antimonopolists wanted a clear demonstration of state authority over railroads, and they wanted taxes, including back taxes, from the railroads. They also wanted the Barry bill, which would have outlawed the special contract system and prohibited any discrimination between individuals by the railroad.[112]

The antimonopolist coalition appeared invincible. With a 61–19 Democratic majority in the assembly and a 32–8 majority in the senate, antimonopolists were confident that even if conservative Democrats, who had legitimate doubts about the constitutionality of some of the measures, and representatives of areas that had reasons to support the railroads joined conservative Republicans, the bills would pass. The bills sailed through the assembly, but in the senate, bill after bill ended in a tie, with the Democratic lieutenant governor casting the deciding vote to defeat them. Stoneman and the antimonopolists were thwarted by the Blind Boss, even though Buckley had publicly supported the bills. Nine of ten Democratic San Francisco senators—Buckley's "lambs," "good fellow[s]," who "could gather in a few simoleons without overtaxing" their strength—voted against the antimonopolist agenda. For Buckley a battle between the railroads and antimonopolists was an opportunity that only a fool would let pass. The railroad could taste defeat or it could sweeten Buckley's pot with the necessary simoleons—nineteenth-century slang for the dollar. The Pacific Railway Commission later estimated that the Southern Pacific spent about $700,000 on politics that year. These funds became part of a rich stew of boodle—kickbacks from officeholders in San Francisco, payments from those needing franchises, grants, contracts or other favors from San Francisco, protection money, and more—that Buckley used to keep down San Francisco's taxes, feed his lambs, and make himself a wealthy man.[113] The political marriage of Leland Stanford and Christopher Buckley gave birth to the Octopus.

The Octopus temporarily thwarted antimonopolists, but the Pacific Mail remained the nemesis of the Southern Pacific, and with the arrival of the Atchison, Topeka, and Santa Fe and the Atlantic and Pacific in 1885, the Southern Pacific lost its railroad monopoly. As more and more transcontinentals reached the West Coast, they were unable to agree on the division of payments to the Pacific Mail made by the Transcontinental Association.[114] In March of 1885 the Pacific Mail again flexed its muscles; it lowered its prices, driving rates on the railroads down 40 percent during the last quarter of 1885.[115] Then, in December 1885, the Atchison and the Atlantic Pacific announced their withdrawal from the Transcontinental Association, which formally dissolved in February of 1886. By March transcontinental rates were in free fall, with rates on the Central Pacific and the Union Pacific falling from 1.18 cents per ton-mile in 1885 to .43 cents in April of 1886.[116] The result, Albert Fink thought, was a "wholly unnecessary, thoughtless and unjustifiable difficulty."[117] The through business had by 1885 been "rendered valueless by increased competition."[118] It was so subdivided among competing roads that Charles Francis Adams estimated it formed but 5 percent of the Union Pacific's entire business for 1885.[119] In 1886 it was even worse.

There seemed no bottom to the catastrophe. The managers of the Canadian Pacific thought they could capture the transcontinental trade of the "chief cities of the United States, east of the Rockies." The Canadian Pacific sought to use its "continuous line," its "shorter rail distance and . . . its lighter grades" to absorb the added cost of steamship connections from British Columbia to San Francisco and other ports.[120] It had little choice. There was virtually no through business to carry to or from western Canada. By January of 1887 the general traffic manager of the Canadian Pacific reported "a wholesale slaughter of rates and general scramble for business." Rates plummeted, traffic increased, and net revenue fell.[121]

A single commodity, sugar, reflects the dilemma of the Southern Pacific amid these rate wars. Between 1882 and the early 1890s sugar—which meant Spreckels sugar—was the major commodity shipped east from California by rail. Sugar was by and large not even produced in California. It came from Hawaii and was shipped out of San Francisco.[122] Any threat to sugar was thus a significant threat to the Southern Pacific, and in 1886 the Pacific Mail struck at sugar and at another leading California export, salmon. In February 1886 the Pacific Mail shipped only 105 pounds of sugar. In April it shipped 2,495,735 pounds, largely to New York. It was a shot not so much across the bow of the Southern Pacific as directly into its corporate offices. Sugar shipments by rail fell from just below 120 million pounds in 1886 to just above 70 million pounds in 1887, while sugar shipped east by sea rose from virtually nothing for most of 1885 to roughly 20 million pounds in 1887 and 1888. (See Appendix, Chart F.) The railroad could not afford to lose this kind of traffic. In the fall of 1886 the Pacific Mail proved it could do the same with salmon. Having previously shipped only trivial amounts, it suddenly sent 597,500 pounds east that October.[123] And in 1887 shipments of wine by sea increased dramatically while those going by rail fell. The Southern Pacific lost this traffic to sailing ships.[124] (See Appendix, Chart G.)

Falling rates on land and sea meant that overall traffic increased, but the increase came largely in imports carried at a loss; losing exports to the shipping companies did double damage since it meant having to haul empty boxcars east.[125] In 1886 the Union Pacific carried 35 percent heavier tonnage than the year before and made 26 percent less money.[126] In 1887 the Southern Pacific increased its freight by 10 percent while its revenues supposedly also fell 10 percent.[127] Unable to sustain their losses, the railroads agreed to reconstitute the Transcontinental Association by mid-1887, but it remained fragile. With the passage of the Interstate Commerce Act of 1887, a new railroad organization, the Interstate-Commerce Railway Association, took over the job of arranging freight rates.[128]

The railroads' troubles did not benefit San Francisco. Under the stress of competition, the Southern Pacific had lowered rates from eastern points to interior California towns without apparently lowering rates out of San Francisco. Although through rates to San Francisco were still lower than direct rates to an interior town such as Fresno, they were now higher than the combination of the fare to San Francisco and the fare to Fresno. Such changes put Chicago wholesalers in competition with San Francisco. The declining position of San Francisco wholesalers consolidated their political opposition to the railroads and encouraged them to subsidize steamship lines and turn to tramp steamers and sailing vessels. The Traffic Association of California, founded in 1891, moved aggressively to preserve San Francisco's status as the state's wholesaling center. Dominated by "young men and younger methods" instead of the "old mercantile fossils," the association did not challenge the railroad directly. Its members simply proposed to deal collectively with shippers. They were, in effect, a union of merchants. Their goal was high overland rail rates to the interior and low rates by sea to San Francisco; this was an ironic antimonopoly effort aimed at ensuring San Francisco's preeminence.[129] The merchants became formidable opponents of Chris Buckley and the Octopus.

VI. REGULATING SPACE

In the nation, as well as in California, the construction of relational space became a focus of antimonopoly politics. Antimonopolists in the 1860s and 1870s initially sought to reassert the primacy of absolute space. They advocated uniform charges by the mile within each class of goods as the easiest way to make rates transparent and fair. And, true to their liberal roots, antimonopolists embraced competition as the way to secure such rates.

The first consequence of the building of multiple lines in a single territory was the creation of a basic distinction between competitive and noncompetitive points. The competitive points were where railroads crossed or converged or came close enough together that a day's wagon trip could reach two or more lines. Competitive points tended to draw steadily closer in the relational geography of railroads, while the noncompetitive points drifted farther and farther apart. As S. F. Pierson of the General Ticket and Passenger Agents Association put it, the result of rate discrimination between competitive and noncompetitive points was "to tax unduly the business where no . . . competition exists."[130]

It is easy to see why many inhabitants of noncompetitive points thought that the only hope was to attract another railroad. Many did just that. In 1888 Charles Francis Adams estimated that less than 5 percent of the stations on the Union Pacific were noncompetitive.[131] Competition worked to lower rates most effectively at large transfer points with considerable traffic, but overall it did not eliminate inequities; it just changed their logic and form.

Many antimonopolists soon regretted the results of competition. Peter Dey, president of the Nebraska State Railroad Commission, explained why merchants preferred stable, reasonable rates over rate wars that caused rates to fall precipitously. If any merchants bought new goods to profit from a rate cut, they all had to do so or be undersold. But this also meant they had to sell those goods they already had in stock at the new, lower price, taking a loss on these goods whose cost included the earlier, higher freight rates.[132] Not only did losses offset gains, but present instability sowed future instability as warring railroads secretly promised customers cut rates in the form of rebates during ensuing months, ensuring further chaos.[133]

Competition encouraged pools. A pool was a formal organization among competing roads to divide the revenue of a certain class of traffic—the transcontinental traffic, the traffic in Colorado or Utah, or the traffic passing to and from the Union Pacific to the Chicago roads at Omaha. As Charles Francis Adams explained, "[t]he vital element of a pool is the payment of all money received into a common fund and the return of the money, in fixed proportions, to each party in the pool." These divisions of revenue were predetermined. It made no difference how much traffic a road was actually carrying, although the percentages would be periodically adjusted to reflect the changing tonnage of each road. A pool made numerous railroad companies act as if they were a single company. It demanded a "unity of management," consistent, its advocates argued, "with the public interests." The most ambitious pools established "a permanent executive department . . . to see that the resolutions passed and agreements made are faithfully carried out." They also had a "judiciary department, consisting of a board of arbitration," to settle disputes. The roads agreed to submit their books to a pool commissioner to make sure that they were turning over the promised revenue.[134] Pools offered a means of private corporate regulation. Neither they nor price-fixing were illegal under common law, but neither were their agreements enforceable in court.[135]

Charles Francis Adams had initially been one of the most enthusiastic advocates of pools. In 1879 he had joined Albert Fink in managing the most famous pool of all by accepting the position of chair of the board of arbitration of the Eastern Trunk Line Association, a railroad pool that encompassed virtually all of the major lines east of the Mississippi. In the West the famous Iowa pool controlled the distribution of traffic to the roads connecting with the Union Pacific at Omaha, and other pools multiplied across the region in the 1870s and 1880s. The Union Pacific, for example, had pools "everywhere" before the Interstate Commerce Act outlawed them in 1887.[136]

Because there was no way legally to enforce the agreements, pools tended to be transitory. They were vulnerable to false bookkeeping, solicitation of traffic off the books at lower rates, rebates to preferred customers, and other manipulations. They fell apart as a result of cheating, the conviction of one member that it could defeat the others in open competition, and the invasion of a pool territory by a new road. Eventually even the famous Iowa pool declined and fell apart. Each case of cheating, each incident of aggression, each cutting across of lines or invasion of new territory, made it harder to reconstitute a pool.[137] Once a pool dissolved and competition resumed, the outcomes were limited. The railroads could reconstitute a pool, or fight until only one remained, or one railroad could buy out the others. All, as Adams contended, eventually "resulted in combination."[138] In order for pools to work, they needed to be state sanctioned and state enforced.

Although pools imposed stability only at the cost of higher rates, some customers, and even some reformers, considered them better than the alternatives if they could be managed honestly. William Felker, an attorney who served as a Colorado railroad commissioner, testified before the Pacific Railway Commission in Denver in 1887 that he favored railroad pools, if they were honest, because they brought predictability and allowed merchants to plan, but he added that he had never known of an honest one. Charles Francis Adams did not differ on the situation in Colorado. He wrote his general manager in 1887 that the Colorado pool had been "arbitrary, excessive in rates, and refused to observe the signs of the times." It would bring "a popular reaction."[139]

The particular dishonesty of railroad pools that Felker had in mind involved the rebates that freight agents offered favored customers in order to increase their road's share of traffic. Rebates were the children of competition. A railroad with a monopoly, like the Central Pacific in Nevada, might discriminate between places or among types of freight, but it had little reason to offer rebates.[140] A railroad facing competition, however, had reasons to offer special rates to its most valued or powerful customers or to places it wanted to build up. The railroads defended rebates as necessary and legal, but they also found them expensive and a source of unending trouble. They could not, however, afford to eliminate them, unless their competitors also eliminated them, or they would lose traffic.

Under competitive conditions, a tariff list gave a shipper merely general information about what the going rates were in sending a given quantity of goods from point A to point B. Only a fool regarded railroad tariff tables as the actual rates paid. As Joseph Nimmo, the chief of the U.S. Bureau of Statistics put it, "published freight tariffs supplied no information whatever to the public as to the actual rates charged."[141] Published rates, Albert Fink testified in 1880, were "not carried into practical execution." They were "often disregarded almost as soon as they [were] made."[142] At a competitive point a shipper confronted published rates, discounted rates quoted by local freight agents, or rates quoted by the "armies of agents" sent out by fast-freight companies, which ran their own cars. These quoted rates were not, however, the rates at which goods traveled. Those were secret because privileged shippers got private rebates.[143]

If the rebates offered to privileged customers had been open to everyone, they would have amounted to a lower special rate on goods, but because they were secret and not a subject of direct public knowledge, they became matters of rumor, innuendo, and gossip.[144] A shipper knew what he paid, but he had no idea what railroads were charging other customers.[145] Rebates were abhorrent to antimonopolists because they were discriminatory, secret, and in violation of the railroads' common law and statutory duty to offer equal access to all customers.

Competition, rather than making railroad space seem legible and fair, increased the sense of disorientation, inequity, and outrage. The net effect of competition and accompanying discrimination was to make cities and towns all over the West the equivalent of railroad cars that were moving constantly backward and forward through relational space at the whim of the corporations. With distance a function of cost, one day a town was closer to its suppliers and customers than a rival town; the next day it was farther away. Westerners wanted to rein in the railroads, but their attempts to do so by luring even more railroads west through local subsidies in order to force rates down only exacerbated the situation. The more competition exacerbated discrimination, the more reformers turned away from it as a panacea and looked toward public regulation.

Regulation faced difficulties of its own. In 1887 Charles Perkins of the Burlington engaged in an exchange of letters with William Larrabee, the Republican governor of Iowa, a leading antimonopolist. Among the many and often contradictory things Perkins said about pricing was that railroads based their prices, or at least should base them, on the costs of doing business plus a reasonable profit measured in terms of the return on capital.[146] Larrabee retorted that much railroad stock represented no real capital investment and that much of the actual capital had come from public subsidies in the West. This made it difficult, if not impossible, to calculate a "reasonable profit." And, he pointed out, because costs went down with each ton carried, predetermined rates designed to ensure reasonable profit could never reflect the actual cost of any shipment.[147]

Agreeing on fair and reasonable profits was practically impossible. Not only did it involve agreeing on the capital actually invested in railroads, but it also demanded reliable data on railroad costs. The railroads' failure to keep statistics that would allow the allocation of costs, and the high proportion of fixed costs, opened up the possibility of manipulation by apportioning costs to particular items of traffic. Economists sympathetic to regulation thought that basing rates on cost of service was, as Edwin Seligman wrote, "neither practised nor practicable."[148] Finally, if fair meant nondiscriminatory, then railroads had to renounce their quite reasonable assertion that certain kinds of discrimination were necessary to the construction of railroad space. If the railroads could not assign lower rates to low-value, high-bulk products such as wheat or coal, then the railroads' utility to the nation was diminished.[149]

The rates railroads charged and the discriminations they practiced became part of spatial politics. They called into question the relationships between corporations and the governments that gave them life and, more critically, the relationship between citizens. Those whom the railroads favored had advantages over all others. A whole series of words that held basic values of the republic—"equity," "freedom," "nondiscrimination"—became words that took on a spatial meaning. As the railroads made and remade space in the late nineteenth century, they pulled cars as full of politics, ideology, and social relationships as of lumber, wheat, and coal.

A RAILROAD LIFE

ALFRED A. COHEN

A. A. Cohen had a wicked tongue. When he turned it on the Associates of the Central Pacific Railroad, he memorably described Charles Crocker as "a living, breathing, waddling monument of the triumph of vulgarity, viciousness, and dishonesty."[1] He added, regarding his days of intimacy with the Associates, "I was compelled to come in constant contact with many men whose habits, whose manners, whose mode of thought and whose conversation were not calculated to advance me either in my own esteem or in that of my fellow citizens, but I thank God, who tempers the wind to the shorn lamb, that I was not required to cooperate with 'General' David Colton."[2] Yet, before and after he flayed them, he was their friend.

A. A. Cohen had connections. In the 1860s he was a lesser member of the Bank of California ring that controlled much of the investment in the Comstock Lode and San Francisco. Through the ring, he knew D. O. Mills, William Ralston, Lloyd Tevis (whom Collis Huntington thought the ablest man on the West Coast), William Sharon, and Michael Reese. Those were, at the time, the richest men in California. Through the ring he also came to know the Associates of the Central Pacific Railroad, who would become the richest men in California. He sold the Associates the Oakland Railroad and Ferry in 1868 and the Alameda Railroad and Ferry in 1869, when the Associates were forging their California monopoly. He continued to manage these properties until final payment was made and they were consolidated with the Central Pacific in 1870. In the early 1870s he tried to form a syndicate with Mills, Ralston, and Tevis to buy either the Southern Pacific or the Central Pacific, but his partners knew too much about the actual condition of the road to pay what the Associates were asking. To Cohen's dismay, no trade was ever made.[3]

Still, Cohen remained a friend of the Associates until the middle of the decade even as the Associates demeaned him, irritated him, and disappointed him. In the early 1870s Huntington had considered making Cohen an Associate, and Stanford seemed to agree, but in his usual bungling manner, he changed his mind and angered Cohen, who, as a result, did "not feel very friendly to the Associates." An offer to make him the railroad's attorney was a poor consolation prize.[4] Hopkins, who was becoming a man who spent far too much time with his pets, wrote cryptically that Cohen was "one of the dogs that fetch as well as he carries."[5] Relations between our "Israelite friend," as Huntington called Cohen behind his back, and the Associates were souring.[6]

The language of friendship and the networks it sustained were nonetheless too important for Cohen to abandon lightly. In a letter in March of 1875 Cohen wrote to "Friend Huntington" reminding him that it was "a bad plan to throw off our old friends" and asking for railroad passes for himself and his wife, but the salutation on the letter thanking Huntington for the passes was "Dear Sir."[7] Friendship was essential to business, but by fall the Associates no longer considered Cohen a friend. Someone, apparently Crocker, told Huntington that Cohen was cheating them on a contract to transport coal by ship for the Central Pacific, and Cohen solicited a friend, D. O. Mills, to write in his defense.[8] By the beginning of 1876 these charges had resolved into a personal quarrel with Charles Crocker, "accompanied by acts of hostility on Crocker's part."[9]

Friendship had gone bad. With years of knowledge and a deep well of resentment, Cohen turned railroad reformer. He accepted employment as a lobbyist to advocate, as a later lawsuit by Associates put it, a bill "to regulate the rate of charges on the plaintiff's railroads." Railroad politics were complicated, and Cohen's sudden turn from railroad owner and railroad attorney involved more than a sudden change of heart. Outraged, Huntington considered "him a lower man in my opinion than [he] had heretofore supposed lived on the face of the earth."[10]

Huntington's outrage sprang more from his fear of Tom Scott of the Texas and Pacific than from his hatred of Granger laws like the Archer bill, which Cohen was advocating, although that hatred was deep enough. Scott was, at first glance, an odd ally for a born-again railroad reformer like

Cohen. But reform and corruption were often allies in railroad politics. In Sacramento, Cohen was lobbying for the Archer bill, which set maximum rates and sought to end the rate discrimination in favor of long hauls, with an animus that surprised the Central Pacific's superintendent, A. N. Towne. Since San Francisco was the main beneficiary of long-haul discrimination, the well-connected Cohen's devotion to reform was more than a little puzzling. Relatively few businessmen in San Francisco at that time shared it, both because it would hurt their commercial dominance and because the Southern Pacific, for all its faults, had a San Francisco terminus and favored San Francisco with through rates. The Southern Pacific was then engaged in a bitter battle with Scott's Texas and Pacific, destined for San Diego. The goal was to become the southern transcontinental.[11] The key to the puzzle was that the very threat of regulation hurt Southern Pacific bond sales, and that helped Tom Scott. Scott, Huntington wrote, has "a stronghold of the newspaper press of this country with Cohen to send fals [sic] telegrams over here with Scott to circulate them."[12]

The Associates defeated the Archer bill, although a weaker bill passed, and set out to ruin Cohen through the same networks that Cohen was using to assault them. Huntington wrote Hopkins that he wanted to brand Cohen a thief and send it out as "news altho . . . it would not be to many who know him." The Associates published their charges that he was a thief in order, in Cohen's words, "to crush the defendant, to blacken him in the esteem of his fellow-citizens, to hold him up to execration as a dishonest agent." Only after defaming him did they sue him over claims he had cheated them in the sale of property connected with the purchase of Cohen's railroads and in his contract to carry coal for them.[13]

The suit was a big mistake. Cohen knew far too much about the Associates, and he knew how to reveal his knowledge in ways that could do the most harm. Cohen had a powerful ally in James Simonton, the editor of the *San Francisco Bulletin*, enemy of the Associates and, most significantly, manager of the Associated Press. Simonton made sure that stories on the Cohen trial achieved wide circulation, and Cohen used the trial as a stage for revealing and ridiculing the Associates' business methods, weakness, and scandals.

He had Crocker, and E. H. Miller Jr., the company treasurer, on the stand, and he questioned them about the Contract and Finance Company, which was the Central Pacific's Crédit Mobilier, and the matter of the company books that had disappeared just as Congress prepared to investigate. He had Crocker, who supervised the building of the railroad, testify that he did not know who was the last president of the Contract and Finance Company. He made Crocker look like a fool, which was not all that hard to do. As Huntington said of his Associate in another context, "It is very difficult for any one to be interviewed by an unfriendly newspaper man without getting hurt, and Mr. Crocker, of all the men I know, is not the most unlikely to get hurt."[14]

Cohen, no doubt, took pleasure in his ridicule of Crocker, but his target in all this was the financial markets, and he did not confine his activities to the courtroom. He wrote a pamphlet deconstructing, lie by lie, false statement by false statement, exaggeration by exaggeration, the case Huntington made for the Southern Pacific.[15] But it was not just the broadsides that Cohen fired; there was the constant harassing fire. "[T]here is something over the wires nearly every day to the associate press in the interest of Cohen or say against us," Huntington reported in May.[16] Such things took a toll on credit and bond sales. By June the damage was becoming heavy, and Huntington wanted to settle, but the damage rolled on into the summer and fall.[17]

In October, Cohen, who until that point had not acted as his lawyer, delivered his summation to the judge, which he then published as a pamphlet. It was a masterpiece of nineteenth-century vitriol. The Associates lost their suit, and they were unable to quiet Cohen. The pamphlet called attention to the mansions that the California Associates (but not Huntington) were building on Nob Hill. Mark Hopkins and Leland Stanford had jointly bought a block bordered by California, Powell, Pine, and Mason streets, and Crocker and Colton built nearby. Huntington's own New York living standards in the 1870s were such that his real estate agent complained that he could not sell his New York house until Huntington fixed the "very bad smell that pervades the ground floor" caused by rot from leaking pipes.[18] Huntington would have much preferred that his Associates not flaunt their wealth by building mansions that testified to their gains. Cohen turned on the mansions with glee. Crocker's new home had so much drapery, tapestry, and cloth that "visitors shall be filled with doubt whether it is designed for a haberdashers shop or a stage scene of a modern furniture drama."[19] In December, Cohen devoted an entire pamphlet in the form of a play to Stanford, the president of the road. In *The California King* Cohen mocked him as "sullen, remorseless, grand, and peculiar . . . with the ambition of an Emperor and the spite of a peanut vendor."[20]

By the end of the year, Huntington had had enough. He was in Washington in early January of 1877 making arrangements for the coming session of Congress and staying, as usual, at the Willard Hotel, but Cohen was on his mind. He wrote Hopkins,

> *I saw Cohen last week in New York and I had a talk with him, a friendly talk, and got him and Stanford together. He said he wanted no quarrel with us etc. And I take it we want none with him. He called at our offices in New York twice, once after he had talked with Stanford and he told me that S. told him that S. thought they had better let the whole matter rest until they returned to Cal. Cohen seemed very good natured and I think wants to be friendly with us, and I think it well for us to be on good terms with him. Life is to [sic] short for us to have many quarrels on our hands with all our other business. I think it would be well to ask Crocker to make friends with Cohen, not saying that I suggested it.*[21]

Cohen had the ability to inflict damage, but the reality of the Central Pacific monopoly was that, if and until Scott's Texas and Pacific reached California, he could hurt the Associates without helping himself. That there was no hint of affection remaining between Cohen and the Associates was not a bar to renewed friendship; they could be friends without liking each other. Only hatred was personal. Cohen had stung Crocker and Colton, and they wanted him banished to the outer reaches of this particular capitalist kingdom. Henceforth, as Colton said, they would "do business with this man as we do with a stranger or not at all."[22]

And so Cohen remained a reformer, and more damage ensued. He continued to be active in the push for regulation that resulted in the ratification of the California Constitution in 1879 with a powerful railroad commission.[23] In August of 1879 he spoke at Platt's Hall in San Francisco, denouncing the railroad as a "rapacious corporation" and warning voters that unless they elected strong and knowledgeable men to the railroad commission, it would come to nothing.[24]

But Cohen was a businessman, and reform did not really pay. He continued to send out feelers to test whether a truce was possible. When Cohen was returning from Italy in 1878, he asked Huntington for a pass to San Francisco and recommended he take a trip on the railroad through Brenner Pass in the Tyrol mountains.[25]

And eventually they reached a truce. In the early 1880s Cohen once more became a lawyer for the Associates, although Huntington suspected he was doing them damage even as they employed him. He knew too much and too many people, and he could say things that hurt them.[26]

The truce came about in part because the long battles had taken such a toll on those on both sides of the Texas and Pacific and Southern Pacific fight. It had turned Colton's hair gray, and he could sleep only "three hours out of 24."[27] He was dead before 1878 was out. Hopkins, already sick, had traveled to Yuma under the care of a Chinese herbalist. Yuma was then the end of the line for the Southern Pacific, and there Hopkins died.[28] By the fall of 1878 Tom Scott was so exhausted and seriously ill that he had to leave Washington.[29] The fallout from all of this was not only Cohen's truce with the Associates but a falling out among the Associates themselves, or rather between the surviving Associates and the family of David Colton, the man whom Cohen had so despised. Ellen Colton, the widow of David Colton, had sued the Associates for defrauding her after they had found that her deceased husband had embezzled from them for years.

In 1884 Cohen fell silent, cut down by a stroke, his speech and memory gone. He amazingly recovered, however, and testified before the Pacific Railway Commission in 1887. He was smart, and he was funny.[30] He also acted as Leland Stanford's lawyer before the commission. He defended the

Associates and the Central Pacific, but there were moments when a man less obtuse than Stanford must have wondered about Cohen's layered meanings. "I think that your question, Commissioner Anderson, confuses the witness," Cohen interjected at one point to stop a very confused Stanford from digging an even deeper hole for himself. And, at another point, Cohen confessed to the commissioners that "there is a little misapprehension as to the answer of Governor Stanford yesterday with respect to the net earnings of the road." Cohen hoped he and the other lawyers could correct it. They could.[31]

Cohen renounced his earlier crusade against the Central Pacific as his "early ebullitions of temper, when [he]was young and green." He would, he told the commission, be glad to explain "what I thought I then knew, and what I have since found to be facts." This was a common change of heart, Stanford assured the commission. "[T]here was a time in this State when it seemed that everybody was against the railroad, but I have lived long enough to see almost every one of these people in this State a friend of the railroad." It was good to have friends.[32]

CHAPTER 5

⌒⌒⌒⌒

KILKENNY CATS

There once were two cats from Kilkenny
Each thought there was one cat too many.
So they fought and they fit
And they scratched and they bit
And instead of two cats, there ain't any![1]

IN JUNE OF 1884 Charles Francis Adams became president of the Union Pacific Railroad. Fifteen years earlier, the year of the Union Pacific's completion, he had published his *Chapter of Erie*, which made his name as a railroad reformer, and he had been appointed to the Massachusetts Board of Railroad Commissioners, one of the first and the most famous of the state commissions to regulate railroads. He would serve for ten years.[2] In 1878 he had been named a government director on the board of the Union Pacific and then had rejoined the board as a regular member in 1882.

Adams had often been critical of railroad practice, particularly Union Pacific practice. Western railroads issued too many securities, received too little money from them, and, as a result, carried large loads of debt. They were too often corrupt and run for the profit of insiders. Poorly constructed and poorly managed, these railroads expanded too quickly into regions without the traffic to sustain them and duplicated their rivals' tracks where there was traffic. Adams came to the Union Pacific to rescue it from its latest bout with disaster and to change the normal practice of western railroads. "I do not believe in fighting," he wrote. "I do not believe in wasteful construction. I do not believe in destroying business by foolish competition. We are coming to all these things with considerable rapidity."[3]

Adams knew that he was taking on a "concern . . . in bad repute, heavily loaded with obligations, odious in the territory it served."[4] He became president in the midst of the Panic of 1883–84, after workers on the railroad had just forced the management to rescind wage cuts. Congress was demanding the immediate payment of money due the sinking fund established by the Thurman Act. George Edmunds of Vermont, the chair of the powerful Senate Judiciary Committee and a man whom Adams would come to detest, forced Sidney Dillon, whom Adams privately referred to as "the old thief," from the presidency and anointed Adams as his replacement. If the move was not made, Edmunds would issue a report on the road that would destroy the little credit the Union Pacific had left and recommend that board members be charged with misdemeanors for illegally paying dividends.[5]

Still, Charles Francis Adams Jr. took the job willingly. He was forty-nine, ambitious, and a child of privilege. His grandfather was John Quincy Adams, the sixth president of the United States. His great-grandfather was John Adams, the second president of the United States. His father, also Charles Francis, had merely run for president and served as ambassador to England. When Adams had left the Union army, he had given what he regarded as his men's assessment of him. They "don't care for me personally," he wrote. "They think me cold, reserved and formal. They feel no affection for me, but they believe in me, have faith in my power of accomplishing results, and in my integrity." These he regarded as "old family traits."[6] He did not lack confidence.

Many of the Union Pacific's problems could be traced back to Jay Gould. Gould and Adams had circled each other since 1869 when Gould had been Adams's target in *Chapter of Erie*, a book that until the end of his life Adams regarded as "a careful piece of literary work." The Adams family was as illustrious and well connected as any in the United States; Gould rose from poor beginnings. Adams was a successful author, a reformer, an intellectual, a man of the world, who had "faith in publicity," the establish-ment of facts "by a fair-minded public investigation" and the appeal "to an enlightened public opinion."[7] Gould was notoriously quiet and secretive. He said little, and the little he said was often purposefully ambiguous and misleading. Adams wanted transparency. Gould lived his life in a fog often hard to penetrate even now. Adams's correspondence and writings are volu-minous. He said, if anything, too much. Gould left little behind him but his wealth. Adams wanted the railroad out of politics; Gould knew that the railroad depended on politics.

In some ways, however, Gould and Adams were not so different. Adams denounced Wall Street and gamblers, but his fortune as much as Gould's depended on paper—on the timely acquisition and sale of securities and speculation in property. Adams rarely speculated in Union Pacific securi-ties, however. He considered himself the representative of the New England investors in the railroad.[8] Both Gould and Adams had the same grim view of western railroads as hopelessly overbuilt, badly managed, and in need of reordering.

In the 1880s Adams appeared, as one scholar has put it, as "The Man on Horseback," while it was "difficult to exaggerate the depth of vituperation heaped on Gould by his contemporaries." Joseph Pulitzer regarded Gould as "one of the most sinister figures that have ever flitted bat-like across the vision of the American people." He was a vampire sucking the blood of legitimate enterprises.[9] Adams, on the other hand, in his own eyes and those of his supporters, was not just a man of principle and probity but also an efficient modernizer. He had brought order to Massachusetts railroads. He regarded the men who ran railroads in the 1870s and 1880s as his social, intellectual, and professional inferiors. They were dinosaurs: dangerous, dimwitted in all but moneymaking, and doomed to a deserved extinction.[10]

I. CREATIVE DESTRUCTION

The Union Pacific encapsulated virtually everything that Adams thought was wrong with railroads. The "posture of affairs" of the Union Pacific was, "to say the least, dangerous," Adams wrote. "The difficulty of our position is simply this, that on any honest basis of capitalization the road would, even at the lowest rate which has ever been proposed, return not only a fair, but a large profit."[11] Jay Gould did not differ on the essentials. In 1887 he rather disingenuously told the Pacific Railway Commission, which a coalition of antimonopolist congressmen and congressmen in league with Wall Street bears had delegated to investigate federally subsidized railroads, that the Union Pacific "would be all right if it were capitalized on a moderate basis" but that it could not compete with new roads costing $12,000 per mile.[12]

In calling the Union Pacific overcapitalized, Adams and Gould meant that its outstanding securities had a greater par value than its actual assets. Late nineteenth- and early twentieth-century economists made a distinction between actual capital and capitalization. Capital was "tangible assets, such as real estate, rails, locomotives and cars . . . good will . . . contracts, alliances, and reputation." In short, all the assets of a corporation "intended for continuing productive use."[13] Capitalization, on the other hand, represented the firm's outstanding securities: "the aggregate of this paper certification of value, taken at par."[14]

In a well-run corporation funded debt and other securities—money obtained from stocks and bonds—translated rather easily into capital assets, and overcapitalization signified the acquisition of debt without the parallel acquisition of equivalent assets. The commonplaces of transcontinental financing—the giving away of stock, the selling of bonds at deep discounts, and the insider contracts for construction—virtually ensured that these roads' capitalization was far in excess of their assets. A company with low capitalization could charge lower rates and required less income to pay interest and reasonable dividends than a company with high capitalization.[15] This was the problem that Adams was describing in the case of the Union Pacific, but the real question was how the Union Pacific came to be overcapitalized.

The concept of overcapitalization is now largely unfashionable and a little archaic. The idea of leverage has largely replaced it. Even in the nineteenth century Jay Gould argued that the value of securities, like the value of assets, was simply what people were willing to pay for them. Sometimes it was wise to accrue large debts to acquire assets; sometimes it wasn't. Time and the markets would make it clear whether accruing debt was wise. The issue was one of risk. If you could borrow at high rates and still make a profit with the borrowed money, then you were simply being an entrepreneur, a risk taker, and a person to be admired, not condemned.[16] Leverage, however, has not completely shed the older meanings of overcapitalization, which was partially a moral concept pointing toward the real possibility of duplicity and fraud. Modern leveraged buyouts with their extensive acquisition of debt still have the taint of reckless men putting shareholders' and employees' interests at risk.

Charles Francis Adams and Jay Gould were sophisticated men; they knew that overcapitalization might seem to be only about numbers—the tallying of assets and debts—but that it was also about stories. When Adams used words like "fair" and "honest," his modifiers hinted at their opposite—unfair and dishonest—and a story that Adams, the great advocate of transparency, wanted kept quiet because acknowledgment of the road's tainted past could do him no good. Gould, on the other hand, when called to testify before the Pacific Railway Commission, told stories, which was unusual. Adams was a man too often taken with his own cleverness. He often did not know when to keep quiet. Jay Gould was a famously quiet man. It was best to pay attention when both men acted out of character, and when Gould, in particular, was as oddly garrulous as he was in his testimony on overcapitalization.

Jay Gould, widely suspected of looting the Union Pacific, wanted to shift attention elsewhere in his testimony, and so he told a story that made overcapitalization the story of risk, the monetary cost of a heroic past. When the Union Pacific was built, he told the members of the Pacific Railway Commission in 1887, it paid "as high as $5 or $10 a piece for ties, and the iron rails, I think, cost $300 a ton, and men had to take their lives in their hands to go out there. You know the Indians were after them." With a minimum of 2,640 ties to a mile, Gould conjured up a road whose ties alone cost from $13,200 to $26,400 for each mile built. With iron at $300 a ton, an additional $26,400 would be necessary to build a mile of road. The unassembled, ungraded road—without spikes, wooden trestles, fishbars, bolts, buildings, ballast, and the labor to assemble them—already supposedly cost from $39,000 to $52,800 a mile. Listen to Gould's story, and overcapitalization was simple. The Union Pacific might as well have been originally built of gold. When pressed by an incredulous commissioner about the cost of the ties, which as it turned out actually cost from 65 to 90 cents apiece, Gould meandered off into a story about a scalped conductor.[17] The scalped conductor was real, but he was also an allegorical character in a parable about risk. The reason the railroad cost so much was that such a risky enterprise forced promoters to promise great rewards and pay high prices. Economists in more mundane ways still tell Gould's story. The high cost of capital in the Pacific Railway—the difference between the face value of securities and what people actually paid for them—can be taken as investors' rational calculation of risk.[18]

Gould knew all about risk, but he was also a magician. Like any magician, he sought to create an illusion by attracting spectators' eyes to one thing and away from the action that actually achieved the desired result. Gould told simple stories of a heroic past, not complicated stories about exchanges of paper. Slight, perhaps smiling, speaking softly as he always did, the small, dapper man sitting at number 10 Wall Street testifying before the Pacific Railway Commission told stories and performed railroad finance. Gould was, as usual, giving the information he wanted to give, withholding more, letting people draw their conclusions, thinking, with good reason, that those conclusions would not only be wrong but also forward his interests.

Gould drew attention to risk in order to attract it away from fraud. He focused on the late 1860s and not the late 1870s. That was the magician's trick. It concealed the secret that both he and Adams, in a rare moment of agreement, wanted kept quiet: overcapitalization was more the result of fraud, deception, and insider dealing than of entrepreneurial risk taking. Twenty years earlier Charles Francis Adams had argued that overcapitalization was a "tax on trade" to be paid eventually by the nation's consumers who would have to add bloated transportation charges to the cost of goods so that railroads could pay their interest and dividends on capital never actually received.[19] Now Adams wanted to forget that fraudulent past. As if he could: every Union Pacific train carried its consequences, and every Union Pacific customer paid its freight.[20]

Pacific Railway Commissioner E. Ellery Anderson, a corporate attorney, gave the basic plot of fraudulent finance in his questioning of Leland Stanford in 1887. The techniques in the Union Pacific and the Central Pacific were, after all, the same.

> . . . it seems to be the general belief that the present weak condition of the Central Pacific Railroad Company is due to the fact that the contract with Crocker & Co., and the contract with the Contract and Finance Company, and the contracts with the Western Development Company, and the contracts with the Pacific Improvement Company have drained the company of its resources; that certain individuals have procured to be issued to themselves enormous quantities of stock and bonds of this company, and have paid dividends on the stock, and have made the interest charge on the bonds exceedingly heavy, and the origins of its difficulties lies there entirely, and nowhere else.[21]

Anderson's story of innumerable pieces of paper exchanged in complicated ways did not have the resonance of a scalped conductor.

Jay Gould was better than any other man alive at selling for very high prices financial paper that he acquired at very low prices. Gould's detractors accused him of boosting Union Pacific stock prices at the cost of the road's long-term health. He cut expenses and paid dividends, but the price was the deterioration of the road. He made a killing on the stock market and left a decaying and decrepit property to others.[22] The centerpiece of Gould's efforts was his acquisition of the Kansas Pacific in 1880.

In a continent full of looted and mismanaged railroads, the Kansas Pacific may have been the sorriest of the lot. It had issued "stock and bonds of every possible description . . . to those concerned, up to the full estimated earning capacity of property," and, as it turned out, beyond. The result was numerous, contentious, and divided claimants whose financial paper promised them assets and dividends that did not exist and who could not agree how to divide what did exist.[23] What made this relict of greed and incompetence a threat to the Union Pacific was section 15 of the Pacific Railway Act of 1864, which gave the Kansas Pacific, and other branches of the Pacific Railroad, pro rata rates for traffic it shipped along Union Pacific tracks. A shipment on the Kansas Pacific destined for Ogden that joined the Union Pacific tracks at, say, halfway between Omaha and Ogden should cost the

Kansas Pacific rate plus half the fare the Union Pacific normally charged between Omaha and Ogden. The Union Pacific, however, charged its full rate on top of the Kansas Pacific fare. No shipper with a choice would pay such a premium, and the Kansas Pacific, losing traffic, pressed for enforcement of the law in Congress and the courts.[24]

If the Kansas Pacific succeeded, it would harm the Union Pacific and, more critically for Gould, hurt Union Pacific stock prices. Gould's solution was to bring the Kansas Pacific and the Union Pacific under common ownership. To do so, he had to make arrangements both with Henry Villard, who represented the largely German holders of the Kansas Pacific's senior securities, and with the holders of more junior and less valuable securities. The Germans had a first mortgage on the last 245 miles of Kansas Pacific track that ran into Denver, a mortgage on half the company's lands, and a third mortgage on the rest of the road.[25] The junior security holders controlled the stock as well as bonds with precious little security behind them.

Gould's first move was quite orthodox and responsible. He organized the junior security holders, who recognized that they were going to get neither the face value of their securities nor all the back interest due them. Instead, as Commissioner Anderson of the Pacific Railway Commission later explained, they would put these securities "into a common fund and ascertain among themselves what each security was fairly worth, and scale them down in the reorganized system, taking some at 50 and others at 30 and others at par. . . ." In exchange they received pool certificates. Reorganization would involve an issue of a new security that would be exchanged for those in the pool in proportion to each pool member's holdings. In Gould's words, this new consolidated mortgage would "fund all this heterogeneous mass of securities into one uniform security, and at the same time . . . make a saving in the annual interest charge, and also in the principal of the debt."[26] The so-called St. Louis pool reduced the junior securities from their par value of $17,330,350 to $4,855,300 and thus substantially lessened the capitalization of the company.[27] This was supposedly the diuretic that purged watered securities from the system.[28]

Unless the bondholders represented by Villard joined the pool, however, Gould's efforts would be in vain since the Germans could foreclose on the most critical and valuable assets of the road. The negotiations between Gould and Villard in 1878 and 1879 devolved into something resembling a street fight. The struggle made Villard's reputation as a financier. Although Gould eventually succeeded in a suit to remove Villard as receiver because of conflict of interest, Villard and the bondholders retained the power to foreclose and moved to do so.[29]

Gould's attempt to demoralize the Germans actually discouraged his allies, the junior bondholders and stockholders. In March of 1879 Gould, seemingly magnanimously, moved to buy them out. He acquired a majority of the Kansas Pacific stock. In the stock and bond market of the time, the face value of a stock share—usually $100—was par. A stock selling at par was thus 100. A stock selling at 3 sold at 3 percent of its par value or, put another way, brought 3 cents for every dollar of par value. Gould bought Kansas Pacific stock, which had been selling at anywhere from 3 to 12, at an average of 12½. In the spring of 1879 he withdrew the stock from the pool, while reselling shares of the remaining pool securities to associates such as Russell Sage, Sidney Dillon, and Frederick Ames, all major holders in the Union Pacific.[30] Villard's bondholders really did not want to take over and run the Kansas Pacific, and so, although Villard regarded Gould as totally untrustworthy, he resumed negotiations.[31] In April, Gould granted the bondholders back interest and expenses. He recognized two of the three first mortgages in full and reduced the interest on the third only from 7 percent to 6 percent. There would be little water squeezed out from the first mortgages.[32]

Gould could now join the Kansas Pacific to the Union Pacific, but he changed directions. Having successfully boosted Union Pacific stock from a low of 13 to around 80, and with a reviving stock market, he sensed new opportunities. He had second thoughts about merging the Kansas Pacific with the Union Pacific. The latter would have to pay a premium.[33]

Gould moved easily from being an agent of the Union Pacific to being an agent of the Kansas Pacific because he was always first an agent of Jay Gould. That he, Dillon, and Sage controlled the Kansas Pacific and were leading figures on the board of the Union Pacific did not excite any moral qualms in Jay Gould—but then few things did. In the autumn of 1879 Gould offered the Kansas Pacific to the Union Pacific. The price was high: dollar for dollar.

A share in the Kansas Pacific and a share in the Union Pacific would each bring a share in the new consolidated railroad. In its November meeting the Union Pacific board, feeling betrayed, angrily refused to pay a premium for a road that over the previous ten years had on average not made enough money to pay the interest on its debt.[34] Gould told them they would be sorry. They soon were.

Gould had two tools for inducing remorse. The first one was the Denver Pacific. Arthur W. Hoyt rode it to Denver in 1879. He described it as a "single track RR poorly located & poorly built with high grades and bad curvature, part of the distance over rolling prairie and part on level ground." It was, however, the only way to connect the Union Pacific to Denver.[35] An even more formidable tool was yet another broken-down would-be transcontinental: the Missouri Pacific. Around it Gould grouped a collection of other roads that had proved chronically unable to meet their interest payments: the Kansas and Nebraska, which became the Kansas Central, the St. Joseph and Pacific, and the Central Branch of the Union Pacific, which was one of the original independent chartered branches of the Union Pacific proper. Unprofitable as they might be individually, they could form a system that would rival the Union Pacific.[36]

Gould was playing a difficult game. He wanted to give value to large amounts of Kansas Pacific and other securities that he could not readily dispose of on the open market, and he didn't want to drive down his Union Pacific stock. He bulled Kansas Pacific stock prices into the 80s by the end of 1879, and in January of 1880 it would vault above par, but these prices reflected the expectation that the Union Pacific would acquire the Kansas Pacific, and the rise was almost certainly the product of a "made" market: the prearranged sale of small amounts at inflated prices. Any attempt to unload large amounts of the stock would cause its market to crash.[37] Most of Gould's other securities were not even being sold on the stock exchange.[38] As Charles Hassler, a financial writer, later testified, quotes in the financial papers were "no guide at all" to actual prices. The only true guide was actual sales in some volume on the stock exchange. Quotes only signified that someone was putting in a bid for small amounts of stock in order to keep up the price, or that a single buyer was attempting to acquire a large number of securities. The idea was to peg a price higher and higher with nothing offered, until the "lambs" came in to try to make purchases thinking there was a real rise in value. Then some of the securities could be unloaded to them at five to ten times their worth.[39] The rising quotes for Gould's stock were the equivalent of salting a mine.[40]

In January of 1880 the Union Pacific and Gould resumed negotiations. Gould resigned from the board of the Union Pacific so that there would be no obvious conflict of interest in the sale of the Kansas Pacific. Dillon and Sage, however, remained on the Union Pacific board, which agreed to buy the Kansas Pacific, Denver Pacific, and Gould's smaller Kansas roads. The newly merged roads became the Union Pacific Railway Company to distinguish it from the old Union Pacific Railroad Company. The board then elected Gould a director of the new railroad.[41]

There followed a complicated series of stock exchanges on which Gould and his partners made a large profit.[42] The water that had been sucked out of the Kansas Pacific through the St. Louis pool was pumped back in so that its debt was hardly reduced at all, and the Union Pacific increased its debt by $39 million through its purchase of the Kansas Pacific, Denver Pacific, and other lines.[43] The Pacific Railway Commission accountants later described the Kansas Pacific's books as "simply disgraceful," but they could trace enough transactions to waver between horror and admiration: "The controllers of the shares in the three companies constituted a ring which managed the business with highest skill and cunning."[44] With the stock market booming and investors believing that the end of the Kansas Pacific's threat to the Union Pacific made the Union Pacific a stronger railroad, Union Pacific stock remained high. Gould sold, as did Henry Villard, who had also speculated in Kansas Pacific securities.[45] Gould realized immense wealth from a railroad that he saddled with immense debts.[46]

Gould took his profits from the Kansas Pacific and built the new system around the Missouri Pacific that the Union Pacific feared. Gould's enemies were never sure what he was up to; Collis P. Huntington still thought he was only "as usual lighting down upon one thing [or] another and sucking some portion of its lifeblood, and then taking wing again for some other carcass."[47] In this case, Huntington was wrong. By linking the Missouri

Pacific, the Wabash, the KATY, and the Texas and Pacific, Gould was system building.

The Union Pacific staggered forward under the load Gould had imposed, and by the time Adams became president, it was in desperate straits. The penalties imposed by Congress after the Crédit Mobilier scandal left the company, as Adams phrased it, "in the position of a man whose hands are tied fighting against men armed to the teeth. We cannot lease; we cannot guarantee; and we cannot make new loans on business principles, for we cannot mortgage or pledge; we cannot build extensions; we cannot contract loans as other people contract them. All these things are prohibited to us; yet all these things are habitually done by our competitors."[48]

Gould's policy of paying dividends to maintain stock prices left the Union Pacific with a deteriorating infrastructure as well as a massive debt. The Union Pacific had refused, despite losing its original constitutional challenge to the law in the Supreme Court, to pay into the sinking fund established by the Thurman Act to cover its debt to the government while it litigated other aspects of the act. Gould's maneuvers also had made the Union Pacific a vulnerable and tempting target for Chicago roads posed to advance from the east. Charles Perkins of the Burlington recognized that the Union Pacific's "life depends on high rates more than that of any Company." In 1884 the road was on the brink of receivership.[49] Adams called on the personal credit of the Union Pacific's executive committee to obtain the loans that saved the road.[50] Dividends ceased and stock prices fell.

Adams the president could not say what Adams the reformer knew. His first task was to convince the public and the government that the road was now in the hands of honest men. But to rescue the railroad, he also had to avoid antagonizing Gould and Sage, who were dangerous enemies. He was compelled to obfuscate or justify practices that as a reformer he had attacked.[51]

II. THE COLTON TRIAL

Making large amounts of money from roads that could not pay their debts was something of an art form in the 1870s. The men who owned the other half of the Pacific Railway in the 1870s were as adept as Gould, but more self-righteous. Collis P. Huntington claimed that the builders of the railroads—himself included—had "profited very little by the building of the roads." In the kind of fearless non sequitur that he made a specialty, Huntington thought the people of California had failed to recognize the selflessness of the Associates because Stanford, Hopkins, and Crocker had taken out "something over five millions to build three dwelling houses for the communists and agrarians to look at."[52] How people who had "profited little" could take out five millions to construct mansions so large that they looked like small villages seemed a puzzle, but Huntington was, perhaps inadvertently, making a significant point about railroad financiering. The Associates did not make money from the Central Pacific or the Southern Pacific, although these were the basis of their fortunes; they made money from the Contract and Finance Company, the Western Development Company, and the Pacific Improvement Company. San Francisco bankers knew that money flowed to the Associates, not to the railroads. As late as 1877 David Colton found that San Francisco bankers would not lend the Central Pacific and Southern Pacific money without the personal notes of the Associates behind the loan.[53]

The Colton trial provided a primer on how to put very little into a railroad and take very much out. When on November 14, 1883, the Colton Trial opened in Santa Rosa, the county seat of Sonoma County, California, it shared headlines in the San Francisco newspapers with the capture of Black Bart, "the notorious stage robber," who had robbed his last stage a few miles from Copperopolis, California, on November 3. The shared headlines were a nice coincidence because Ellen Colton, the widow of David Colton, one of the Associates, contended that Leland Stanford, Collis P. Huntington, Charles Crocker, and the estate of the deceased Mark Hopkins had betrayed her and left her "in the condition of a man attacked by a highwayman upon the roadside." As it turned out, David Colton had embezzled from his fellow Associates, and the Associates had responded by taking securities—stocks and bonds—from his widow and leaving her, like the doggerel verses Black Bart left with the victims of his robberies, her dead husband's worthless note for a million dollars.[54]

The accounts of the trial focused on corruption: Colton's defalcation (to use the preferred nineteenth-century term), the remaining Associates' response, and the widespread payments to public officials that surfaced in the Colton–Huntington correspondence that Ellen Colton's lawyers submitted as evidence. It was a trial full of sentimental Victorian nastiness. Colton's embezzlement was simple and easy to grasp. On his father's seventieth birthday, Colton had sent him a touching note full of premonitions of Colton's own death. "Enclosed," he wrote, "please find a check for $365, being a dollar for each day in the year that makes you three-score and ten." The check was from the Rocky Mountain Coal and Iron Company, part of the Associates' properties that he managed. Colton had stolen the money he gave to his father.[55]

But buried deeper in the trial was a more revealing and elusive corruption. Among the securities Ellen Colton surrendered to the Associates were those of the Western Development Company (WDC), which was the successor of the Contract and Finance Company. It was a construction company and a banking company that performed feats of financial magic. It concealed, transformed, and transferred assets so that debts incurred by the Associates' properties could end up as money in the pockets of the Associates. The Associates never paid for their stock in the WDC; instead, they lent funds that had been gained through the old Contract and Finance Company to the WDC, which paid them the going interest rates on the West Coast— as high as 12 percent—on these funds. The WDC was a screen to obscure the activities of the men who ran the Central Pacific and Southern Pacific from bondholders and bankers.[56]

The Associates, seemingly such ordinary, bulky Victorian men, were chimeras able to change form at will, and by changing form, they created value. As Colton's lawyers argued, the Central Pacific, the Southern Pacific, the WDC, and others "were but convertible terms with these four or five movers in them, and they were fused constantly one into the other, and there was no distinction. The corporations were the individuals, and the individuals were the corporations."[57] The Associates proffered a deal, went to the other side of the table, put on another set of hats, and accepted the deal. In the books and ledgers of these companies, trades that appeared to be between a wide variety of entities were not what they seemed.

Ellen Colton's lawyers sought to demonstrate how business was conducted in this internal house of mirrors. In 1871 the Central Pacific began to make deposits into various sinking funds, as required by law, to pay off its bonded debt. To keep the deposits from sitting idle, the Central Pacific starting in 1872 lent the WDC the money in the sinking fund at 10 percent per year. The loans then went into the individual accounts of the Associates. As collateral for these loans, the Associates in 1875 transferred from their WDC accounts 17,577 shares of Central Pacific stock. Subsequent loans in 1876, 1877, and 1878 followed the same trajectory. By the end of its own corporate career in 1879, the WDC had borrowed over $3 million from the sinking funds. Most of the debt was settled by letting the Central Pacific keep the collateral.[58]

Promoters had learned that the values of stocks and bonds were not necessarily determined by what people would pay for them on an open market. Jay Gould testified that there was no market for either Central Pacific stocks or Southern Pacific bonds in the late 1870s. By transferring them to the Central Pacific, the Associates had their cake and ate it too.[59] "Now as to the sinking fund," Huntington wrote Colton, "we very likely have done what was best for us up to this time . . . ; but what we have done is not a thing to talk about, and I do not think there is a careful business man in the world outside of our five selves who would say it was well invested, while we know it is."[60]

Who was harmed by such a maneuver? "It may be a transaction open to censure by proper parties," the Associates' attorney Hall McAllister admitted. "It might be very pertinent with reference to parties who are interested in the Sinking Fund in calling these defendants to account." But while bondholders might have reason to complain, Ellen Colton did not. David Colton helped arrange these transactions. Betraying bondholders was not the issue in the Colton case. Ellen Colton lost.[61]

Disguising the movement of money, however, created unintended opportunities within the corporations for further fraud. As the Contract and Finance Company was being merged into its successor, the WDC, Charles Crocker asked J. O'B. Gunn to examine the books. The Associates had known what they did not want Congress to find in the old Contract and Finance Company books, but what Gunn found surprised them. It took

Gunn only a few hours to find "where [John] Miller had stolen $300,000."
It took longer to find that as much as $900,000 (the Associates made vari-
ous estimates) was missing. John Miller, as it turned out, was not really John
Miller, he had been Ambrose Woodruff. The Associates got back roughly
$400,000, but the rest was gone for good. Miller/Woodruff knew too much
and apparently had the memoranda to prove what he knew. The Associates
did not want him testifying, and, in Miller's words, "through the testimony
of the witnesses from the railroad company [he] was declared innocent of
all crimes." In his later testimony before the Pacific Railway Commission
Miller remembered their kindness. The commission got little from him.[62]
But even an honest Miller might not have been able to follow the cash.
William Mahl, whom Huntington sent out from New York to examine the
Southern Pacific's books in 1889, found them virtually incomprehensible.[63]

The profits from the stocks that the Associates retrieved from Mrs.
Colton were still flowing in as the trial unfolded. Huntington had done
his best to make sure that the Central Pacific paid dividends in the 1870s,
even if he had to borrow to do so. There were two reasons to borrow to pay
dividends. The first was that dividends delivered cash to the Associates who
owned virtually all the stock. The second was that it made the Central Pacific
appear to be a solid, dividend-paying road. When the U.S. railroad auditor
Theos. French examined the Central Pacific's book in 1879, he found that
it borrowed "money, ostensibly for investment in branch lines, steel rails,
&c.," but "really for payment of dividends to stockholders."[64] French never
pushed his concerns. The Central Pacific put him on the payroll.[65]

In 1880 Huntington began strategically selling, and when necessary
buying back, small amounts of stock to create a market largely among European investors. The Associates issued $5 million in new stock and put the
money into the same general fund from which they paid dividends.[66] It was
something of a Ponzi scheme, for new investments were used to provide
dividends on old and thus boost security prices. Prices for Central Pacific
stock went as high as 105½ in 1881, and Huntington had maintained them
in the high 80s and low 90s as he disposed of the stock. He worked hard at
it, and it irritated him that, as was so often the case, his Associates did not
recognize his art.[67]

By 1883 Huntington had finished selling out the Associates' majority interest in the Central Pacific, which at the time leased the Southern Pacific. The European shareholders who controlled the road delayed transferring the shares into their own names, fearing liability for the company's debt under California law. The stock remained in the names of dummy stockholders designated by the Associates who, in turn, designated the Associates as voting proxies for the shares.[68]

The new Central Pacific stockholders thus had little control over the board of directors or the Associates. As Huntington put it, "we shall have to take the stockholders more into our confidence than heretofore, and while we can prattle about the road and its business, we need not say anything more than our credit requires, or than we care to."[69] The British were sheep the Associates sheared not once but twice. In 1885 Associates reversed the lease of the Southern Pacific to the Central Pacific. The Southern Pacific now leased the Central Pacific for ninety-nine years. The Associates, having reaped a fortune from the sale of their Central Pacific stock, still maintained operational control of both roads.[70] With no need to placate the British investors and owning little stock themselves, they cut the Central Pacific's dividend in half for 1884 and then eliminated it entirely until 1888. Prices for the Central Pacific fell as low as 26 by 1885 and then hovered in the 30s and low 40s. Too late, foreign investors realized that what had happened to them was more serious than the general decline of railroad stocks during the downturn of the early 1880s.[71]

Neither the Associates nor Gould simply destroyed, although it might have been better if they had. The money they made from weakening existing corporations went into what Adams identified as another great flaw of western railroads—overbuilding. The Associates transformed the Southern Pacific from merely a road to hold off Tom Scott into a new transcontinental. Lower prices on capital, steel, labor, and new technologies allowed them to build new railroads at less cost than the old.

Trading a poorly built road on a difficult route for a much more efficient road on a better route was the kind of creative destruction Joseph Schumpeter praised, but investors were more inclined to see fraud. There was not enough traffic for two transcontinentals in California, and so the Associates diverted traffic from the Central Pacific to the Southern Pacific. Since the Central Pacific and the Union Pacific formed a single route, this also meant taking traffic from the Union Pacific. In Adams's view the Central Pacific had become a mere "bob tail road, ending at Ogden."[72] In 1884, the first full year in which the completed Southern Pacific ran to New Orleans, the reported earnings of the Central Pacific fell by 40 percent from the preceding year, from $8,094,149 to $4,872,734. By the spring of 1886, the Sunset Route of the Southern Pacific was carrying 93.7 percent of the freight traffic moving by rail from California to New York. This was a large percentage of relatively little traffic. It was an internal transfer of business that moved gains to insiders—the Associates—and away from new investors. It also gave the Associates the added benefit of reducing the amount of money the Central Pacific had to pay into the sinking fund provided by the Thurman Act.[73]

III. TERRITORY

Americans, Mexicans, and Canadians built an extraordinary amount of railroad in the 1880s. It came in two great spurts, the first beginning at the end of the 1870s and then slowing down in the economic downturn of 1883–84. A second expansion came at the end of the decade. The vast bulk of railroad building in the late 1870s and early 1880s—nearly 75 percent in the peak year of 1882—took place west of the Mississippi, in western Canada, and in northern Mexico. The railroad mileage of the Pacific states (Idaho, Utah, New Mexico, and Arizona as well as Washington, Oregon, and California) increased from 4,461 miles in 1879 to 7,961 miles in 1884, while the mileage of the interior western states (the states between the Mississippi and the Rockies, except Louisiana) rose from 22,959 in 1879 to 32,741 in 1884.[74] Mexico's lavish concessions to American railroad promoters in the north were responsible for most of the 5,866 kilometers (3,645 miles) of Mexican railroad in 1885.[75]

In 1881 the Union Pacific/Central Pacific route was the only railroad to the Pacific Ocean; by mid-decade it was one of many. Starting in Canada and moving south, there was the Canadian Pacific, the Northern Pacific, and the Oregon Short Line—a new Union Pacific route to Portland—that allowed the Union Pacific to divert westbound traffic from the Central Pacific. South of the original Pacific Railroad were the Southern Pacific, which reached New Orleans in 1883, and the Atchison, Topeka, and Santa Fe, which reached Guaymus through its Sonoran connection in 1882, before breaking through the Associates' defenses to reach San Diego in 1885. In addition, the Denver and Rio Grande had breached the Rockies and reached Salt Lake, providing another connection to routes farther west. The Frisco and the Atlantic and Pacific, which the Frisco controlled, had reached Needles, on the California border. The Burlington had had plans to go all the way from Chicago to the Pacific but thought better of it and stopped at Denver; it proved a good decision since its through freight from Denver in 1878 was only 86 cars and its westward freight to Denver only 759.[76] The Chicago and North Western also stopped east of the Rockies.

In addition to the roads connecting the continent horizontally, there were new north–south roads linking it vertically. The Mexican Central, which ran from El Paso to Mexico City and was completed in 1884, was part of the Atchison, Topeka, and Santa Fe system. The old Palmer/Sullivan concession yielded the Mexican National Railway, an extension for all practical purposes of the Denver and Rio Grande, from Laredo to Mexico City. It was finished in 1887, but by then it had passed to English bondholders and became the Mexican National Railroad.[77]

The men who built these railroads did not so much have plans as convictions. William Strong, the president of the Atchison, Topeka, and Santa Fe in the 1880s, thought the power of a road depended upon its length and territory.[78] These long trunk lines were spears, skewering a country and pinning it to a wall for later skinning and division. "A new line," as Charles Francis Adams said of the Canadian Pacific, "claims all creation."[79]

Watching these railroads career across the Rockies filled Collis P. Huntington with astonishment, even though he had built one of them. "[I]t is a great country west of the Rocky Mountains in acreage," Huntington wrote ruefully, "and very few people on this side [the East] know how little business there is there."[80] Jay Gould thought it would not be long before "another crop of receivers will be in court." To Adams, who assumed control of the Union Pacific in the midst of the building, it was simply "a period of madness."[81] Still, on they came. By 1885 it appeared that traffic "just sufficient" to maintain the Union Pacific and the Central Pacific when they had a monopoly on the business in 1881 would have to support seven roads. The Union Pacific and the Central Pacific had only 31 percent of the total tonnage at the end of 1886. Lower rates would not increase the traffic sufficiently to restore the old business.[82]

In 1885 Charles Francis Adams had a chance to inspect this western railroad progress firsthand. He left New York at midnight on April 17, 1885, eventually picking up the Chesapeake and Ohio and going south and west along the patchwork of roads Collis P. Huntington had put together to form the eastern half of a national system that connected with the Southern Pacific at New Orleans.[83] Adams hated New Orleans; he hated it generally and particularly. He hated its heat, filth, and vermin. He hated the St. Charles Hotel. From New Orleans he boarded the Southern Pacific for El Paso, where he would take the Mexican Central for Mexico City.

Huntington, Adams had concluded, was in trouble. At night, when Adams could not see beyond the darkness that surrounded his private car, he relied on his body to record the bumps and jolts and his map and watch to gauge the time between stations and thus the speed of the train. In the daylight he surveyed the country, counted passing trains, and looked for tank cars carrying water. He talked to conductors and porters and counted passengers. The line to New Orleans was a wretched ragtag of mismatched pieces. Much of it was poorly built; some still had iron rails. The swaying cars and the lack of speed translated into money that Huntington would have to spend east of the Mississippi. And in 1885 Huntington could not command such capital. "[T]his system," Adams wrote, "I think must go to pieces in bankruptcy." And between 1885 and 1887 much of the system did fall piecemeal into receivership; Huntington unloaded his interests.[84] Ocean transport remained more efficient than rail. The Southern Pacific connected to New York and the East through the Morgan Steamship line running out of New Orleans.[85]

Adams took the Southern Pacific's Sunset Route out of New Orleans. The Sunset Route and the Texas railroad map in general were the fruits of the Associates' victory over Tom Scott. Jay Gould, having gained control of the Texas and Pacific from the sick Scott and made it part of his new Missouri Pacific system, also inherited Scott's old war with the Associates. In 1881 Gould sued his rivals, arguing that since the Southern Pacific had built on the Texas and Pacific right-of-way in New Mexico, the Texas and Pacific owned the Southern Pacific. During the trial Gould's lawyers called the Southern Pacific an octopus; the Southern Pacific's lawyer, the Associates' old friend Senator William Stewart, called the Texas and Pacific an incubus. It was a trial in which perhaps only the invective was accurate.[86]

East of San Antonio, Adams missed a connection that put the train a day behind schedule; it was symptomatic of the inefficiency of the little lines Huntington had stitched together to reach New Orleans from San Antonio. These eastern Texas roads, Huntington had admitted, included "the worst" he had "ever traveled over."[87] Adams was impressed with the country, which was rich, fruitful, and prosperous. He thought San Antonio "one of the most attractive places that [he] had ever seen in America." West of San Antonio the road improved and the country declined. Huntington, needing a Texas charter, had reached an arrangement with Colonel Thomas Peirce of the Galveston, Harrisburg, and San Antonio that gave the Associates effective control of that road.[88] The Associates contracted with Peirce to link San Antonio and El Paso, and he, in turn, hired their latest corrupt corporate jack-of-all-trades, the Pacific Improvement Company, to do the building. Peirce paid them in stocks and bonds that left the Southern Pacific in control of the new line.[89] The new road traversed difficult country, but despite a washout at Eagle Pass that cost Adams another twenty-four-hour delay, he thought the road good. Once they hit the Rio Grande, the country was, however, "absolutely unproductive"; the small herds of cattle in the gorges did not indicate much for the road to haul. In a day's travel Adams passed only one freight locomotive, and it pulled mostly empties. The country was without wood and water. The trains ran on poor-quality coal brought up from Mexico, and, lacking enough artesian wells, the railroad had to haul tank cars with water for the locomotives. With no agriculture, with no minerals, and with only cattle to be split with the Texas and Pacific, the Southern Pacific had to depend on through traffic. How "the Southern Pacific, sustains itself at all," Adams wrote, "is a greater and greater mystery to me."[90]

By 1885 its rival, the Texas and Pacific, could not sustain itself. It could not pay interest on its debts, and large portions of the road were decrepit.[91] The Southern Pacific was a better road than either the Central Pacific or the Union Pacific, but that did not make it necessary or profitable.

By May 3 Adams was in Mexico City after a "very interesting . . . and . . . instructive journey." He traveled the Mexican Central. Thomas Nickerson, who had been president of the Atchison until 1880, remained president of the Mexican Central.[92] The Mexican Central was an American road, but Mexico was "a more thoroughly foreign country than [Adams] ever was in before. It is half Indian and half Moorish; and the whole journey from El Paso to the City of Mexico is an insight into a new life." Like the Southern Pacific in West Texas, the Mexican Central in northern Mexico was a very good road through nowhere.[93] Adams thought that what little business northern Mexico might provide would be drained off to New Orleans when Palmer finished the Mexican National, which reached the United States at Laredo. If the Mexican Central leased the new road in self-defense, it would be left with eight hundred miles of useless road to El Paso.[94] In this Adams was wrong only because the Mexican National insisted on building a narrow-gauge road on which it was difficult to interchange cars and traffic.[95]

Adams's pessimism was not much relieved as the zigzag journey continued. He traveled the Southern Pacific across the Southwest to Los Angeles, then up to San Francisco, and took the Central Pacific east to Salt Lake City. Then he went north on the recently built Oregon Short Line, a subsidiary of the Union Pacific, to Portland, then east again on the Northern Pacific to St. Paul, down to Omaha, and then west to Denver on the Union Pacific and its connector, the Denver Pacific. He returned on the Kansas Pacific. He thought the Northern Pacific was in a hopeless position given the Canadian Pacific to its north, the lack of traffic in the United States, and the prospect of a difficult and expensive construction over the Cascades to complete its direct link to Tacoma.[96] Except for western Canada, he had seen most of the vast territory that had recently been opened up by the transcontinentals.

What Adams did not know was that the Canadian Pacific was in the midst of a financial crisis that forced it to turn to the Canadian government for more aid.[97] Like the American transcontinentals, the Canadian Pacific was built ahead of demand across a difficult and sparsely populated territory with such a heavy debt that it had problems meeting its fixed interest charges to the Canadian government. Even before it was complete, it was offering part of its land grant in exchange for retiring $10 million of the debt it owed Canada. This was the same attempt to exchange a gift for forgiveness of a debt that the Pacific Railway had tried, except in the Canadian case it would work.[98] As with the Union Pacific, the government's lien on its lines and its own precarious financial condition made it difficult for the Canadian Pacific to sell bonds on its branch lines.[99] And as with the American roads, antimonopoly opposition—in this case the "Grits," the equivalent of the American Grangers—hurt its ability to sell land and bonds.[100] The Canadian Pacific responded by cutting necessary investments and upkeep to make the road appear profitable. It had not been in full operation for a year, before instructions went out in 1887 "to make a good showing in the working of the railway this year . . . even if we are unable to keep up the property in what we would regard as a first class condition."[101]

Surveying this massive creation of railroad space, Adams was appalled. He seemed to scour the dictionary for synonyms for "insanity," "illness," and "sin" to describe the actions of the railroads as they overbuilt and cut rates. His most common description was "mania for railroad construction."[102] Such "unnecessary, and I might almost say unpardonable construction"[103] and the resulting rate cutting, were "most ill considered."[104] This was "insanity," and it created "foolish competition."[105] He lived in a world where the "lunatics" ran the asylum.[106] The battle between the Atchison and the Southern Pacific had precipitated a "period of madness."[107] The St. Paul and Chicago, Burlington, and Quincy "have set every one crazy on the subject of railroad extension west of the Missouri River. . . . They are all daft on the subject of construction, and the epidemic has got to run its course."[108] He despaired over railroad managers. "[T]here is no limit to the follies they would commit."[109] The consequences of the accumulating madness and folly were obvious: "we will be cutting and slashing at each other like fiends."[110] The effects would be what they had been before: "when the madness passed away the country has been strewn with the wrecks of half finished railroads."[111]

Adams condemned the first stage of overbuilding as he was about to participate in the second. Too many trunk lines built in the early 1880s had so divided the transcontinental traffic as to make it practically worthless. In the late 1880s the trunks grew branches to garner new traffic. When the U.S. census recorded the number of people per mile of completed railroad in 1840, it was 6,194. In 1880 the number was 571. By 1890 it was 375.[112] By the end of 1889 more than 20 percent of the United States' railroad mileage of 161,000 had been constructed in the last four years. The states and territories west of the Mississippi, excluding Louisiana, kept pace. They had only 24 percent of the country's population in 1890, but they had 43 percent of the railroad mileage. The Pacific group now had 11,473 miles, while the western group had 58,536. In Mexico, Americans had laid 11,500 kilometers (7,146 miles) of track by 1896 and owned 80 percent of the securities issued by Mexican railroads. The Mexican Central alone built 1,200 miles between 1880 and 1890.[113]

The best example of this second wave of overbuilding came in Kansas. The line that divides western Kansas from central Kansas resembles the weaving path of a drunk careening from a starting point just west of the 98th parallel in the north and tilting west as he goes south. The drunk was following the line of twenty-five inches of annual rainfall, the amount needed to guarantee a crop.[114] East of this line in central Kansas were three of the major wheat-producing counties in the state—Saline, McPherson, and Barton, where building made sense. The population of central Kansas rose from 451,000 to 657,000 people between 1880 and 1887, most of the increase occurred between 1885 and 1887. The real question involved the wisdom of building into western Kansas—the bulk of the state—and on into Colorado.[115]

The history of western Kansas did not give much promise. Prompted by the Burlington's plans to build along Prairie Dog Creek in northwestern Kansas, Charles Francis Adams had a preliminary survey run for two routes from the North Fork of the Solomon River west across rolling plains "entirely destitute of wood and water" to the main line of the Kansas Pacific at Monument and Gopher. He found stockmen along the route. There had been a migration of farmers into the country during the unusually wet years between 1879 and 1882, but drought had driven them out. Still, in 1885 five railroads—the Atchison, Topeka, and Santa Fe, the Union Pacific, the Missouri Pacific, the Burlington and Missouri, and the Rock Island—were poised to expand into western Kansas north of the Arkansas River. The railroads were like racers on a starting line in a race none of them particularly wanted to run. They would run only because they feared their rivals would run without them; it was thus not in their best interests to break first.[116] County boosters offered subsidies, and railroad engineers traced new routes, often along obscure creeks toward desolate towns, even though three of them—the Union Pacific, the Atchison, Topeka, and Santa Fe, and the Missouri Pacific—already ran through or into the region. Adams feared that the railroads would "go to work constructing like madmen."[117] They were, he wrote Perkins at the end of 1885, about to enter upon a "Kilkenny cat period of existence which can result in but one thing; that is immense waste of opportunity and wealth. If it should not result in ruin, it will be fortunate."[118]

Caution was not a key attribute of Jay Gould. The Union Pacific had leased the Central Branch, which ran between and parallel to the Union Pacific and the Kansas Pacific trunk lines through "a very rich region," to Gould's Missouri Pacific, in return for Gould's promise not to build lines that competed with the Union Pacific in central and western Kansas.[119] Forbes of the Burlington was skeptical about an agreement with Gould, who had "as many aliases as a London professional thief." Forbes was right. By 1886 Gould was building the Kansas and Colorado Railroad toward Pueblo under the subterfuge that it was not part of the Missouri Pacific. It paralleled a new extension of the Atchison, and both competed with the Kansas Pacific.[120] In retaliation, the Atchison laid plans to build into northern Kansas and attack the Central Branch.[121] On every side there were men whipping runaway horses because, looking around them, they saw other men doing the same and thought there must be a reason.

Railroad war had begun. The Atchison and the Missouri Pacific both bolted west from the Great Bend of the Arkansas paralleling each other about two miles apart to Greeley County on the western border. It was the "maddest specimen of railroad construction of which" Adams had ever heard, but he joined it, vowing to "carry this war directly into Africa."[122] Not to build was to die "a slow death of inanition." He would carry out "a bold, clear cut, aggressive policy."[123] In January of 1887 Adams was considering seventeen different new lines and branches in Kansas, many of them useful only to preempt other roads or to threaten their business.[124] In this he imitated the Atchison's and the Burlington's practice of "covering by their charters and by bonded aid all the territory which is, or at any future time might be tributary to their roads." At Colby, in the far northwestern corner of the state, the Union Pacific met the Rock Island, which in 1888 finished building across the corner of Kansas and into Colorado. It was well beyond the 99th meridian.[125]

By 1889 six different companies had completed seven separate lines in western Kansas between the Great Bend of the Arkansas River in the south and the Nebraska border, an area about 120 miles wide.[126] Three of these lines ran to the Rocky Mountain Front or beyond. The hope was, as P. P. Shelby, the general freight agent of the Union Pacific, wrote, that "[i]mmigration will more than offset any decrease caused by new competing lines." The railroads did carry people into western Kansas, and then they carried them out again. The railroads watched the population of western Kansas fall by nearly half between 1887 and 1897 as drought and depression struck.[127] Even Senator Ingalls of Kansas, the corrupt Candide of the prairies, admitted that the result of expansion was that "[e]mpty railroad trains ran across deserted prairies to vacant towns."[128] In 1878 Kansas had had 2,427 miles of railroad, about one-half the mileage of New England or New York.[129] By the end of 1890, Kansas had 8,900 miles of railroad, more than either New York (7,745) or New England (6,840). It had more railroads per square mile and more than four times the railroad per capita than New England, a region with more than three times the population.[130] (See Appendix, Map B.)

Kansas was an exaggerated version of the entire West. The average number of tons carried per mile of railroad in the region south of Nebraska and east of Arizona peaked in 1886 at 1,482 and steadily declined to 1,312 by 1892. The receipts per ton-mile also declined. The states to the north and west, where there was less building, did better, but even there the average number of ton-miles stagnated after 1886 and plunged after 1892 when depression hit in 1893. In 1896 the western railroads carried fewer tons per mile than they had in 1887.[131]

In 1888 Adams delivered a jeremiad that pretty much summarized the great expansion of the 1880s:

> *The railroad situation in my opinion is as bad as bad can be. I think we are all going to the devil, and going together. Nevertheless during the next six months, I think things will be better rather than worse. After that, the deluge. I do not believe that there is any power on earth,—and certainly I am sure there is none in the heavens over the earth,—which can save from destruction a system which is managed on such vicious principles and is so devoid of all that basis of good faith by which only the business of civilized communities can be successfully conducted, as the railroad system of this country now is. It is plunging to destruction just as fast as it can go. The contempt I feel for the railroad men of this country as a whole I make no effort to express as language is wholly inadequate for the purpose. I should never have conceived it possible that a great system could have outgrown the men in charge of it as our railroad system has during the last twenty years. It is wallowing in the mire.*[132]

IV. RATIONALIZING IRRATIONALITY

When numerous informed people engage in an activity that most of them think is mad and self-destructive, an explanation is necessary. The economist C. Knick Harley advanced a useful theory as to why railroads engaged in what seemed premature and destructive construction. Harley argued that it is necessary to separate two different things—the actual building of a railroad and the exclusive right to build a railroad into a new territory—to understand why overbuilding occurred. The exclusive right to build a railroad was more valuable than an actual railroad in a newly settled agricultural region because an actual railroad in such a region would lose money until the population grew thick enough to provide the traffic necessary to turn a profit. The right to build, however, allowed a railroad to refrain from laying tracks until population and economic activity had reached an optimally profitable point. Cooperation and respect of each other's territory remained the optimal strategy for the long run. In 1880 John Murray Forbes had succinctly stated the ambitions of the Chicago, Burlington, and Quincy in these terms: "PEACE, getting fair returns for capital and avoiding putting a cent more capital into the country than its real growth forces us to do at a profit." That road, however, became perhaps the most aggressive road in the West because, as in a game of prisoner's dilemma, while long-run cooperation may have been the best strategy, the worst fate was to trust a partner who proved duplicitous. Under Forbes's successor as president, Charles Perkins, the Burlington usually presumed duplicity.[133]

In Harley's view agreements not to compete were inherently unstable because once settlement in regions without railroads reached a point where a railroad could make a profit, albeit less of a profit than if building were delayed, then it became impossible to hold territorial agreements together. The incentive to build into a rival's unoccupied territory, or into an occupied territory with an increasing population, was economically rational—a calculated response to rising costs of cooperation and the rising gains of "preemptive capture of unbuilt lines."[134]

Harley's analysis is quite useful, but incomplete. His model omitted much actual nineteenth-century railroad behavior. First, he ignored the reality that many railroads remained largely speculative enterprises meant to make a profit through their financing. In such cases the actual state of development of the territory they built into was not their central concern. As C. P. Huntington put it in regard to the Atchison, Topeka, and Santa Fe's Sonoran Railroad, as long as the Atchison could "float securities so as to build railroads at a profit, their paying or non-paying after completion has very little to do with their building."[135] And since building a railroad increased land and mineral values in the area adjacent to it, there were always speculative opportunities for those with prior knowledge of a route.

Second, the creation of weak overcapitalized railroads created targets for railroad managers who thought they could build more efficient and less indebted lines. By building lines well under the cost of the transcontinentals, the Chicago roads could undercut them and capture their traffic. In 1885 the Burlington chartered the Chicago, Burlington, and Northern to build toward St. Paul; this was, in Adams's words, a shotgun fired into a hornet's nest and "opened a race of construction and counter-construction, attack and reprisal, which will change the whole map of that country." Adams told Charles Perkins that he thought it "one of the most ill considered railroad acts which have come within [his] range of observation."[136]

Third, it was not always established railroad corporations that decided to build. "Railroad sharpers" were ready to build a local line and then force one or another company to buy it to keep it out of a rival's hands. Adams reported that the soil teemed with projects designed to get rival companies by the ears.[137] Such projects, in turn, were sweetened by bond subsidies voted by every Kansas town that wanted a road or competing roads.[138]

Fourth, Harley assumed that managers carefully assessed the business their firms would gain or lose if they built. But, as Alfred Chandler has argued, managers did not make their moves based "on any careful estimate of the demand for transportation."[139] As the second building boom of the 1880s came to a close, Adams admitted that the Union Pacific had not taken enough time to get information about the regions in which they constructed railroads.[140]

Finally, Harley assumed that once a railroad expanded into a territory that could provide a modest profit, further expansion ceased until a similarly promising territory became available; expansion would not extend into far more sparsely settled regions. This was very often not the case. New railroads had a billiard ball effect. As each road lost traffic in one area, it ricocheted off to seek new traffic in another area. It was a battle between the Burlington and the Wabash east of the Missouri in 1880 that prompted the Burlington to renew expansion west of the Missouri at the expense of the Union Pacific to make up for its losses.[141] This building culminated when the Burlington system reached Denver in 1882.[142] Building in Kansas triggered building farther west in Colorado, Wyoming, and Oregon, with companies seeking to compensate for losses elsewhere.[143] Railroads could come less as opportunists than as refugees. As Adams wrote, should the Chicago, Burlington, and Quincy and the Chicago and Northwestern "build into our territory, and we should have to sustain that loss . . . we would recoup ourselves by active development elsewhere."[144] Conflict in one region had the disconcerting habit of spawning conflict in others.

The actual causes of overbuilding thus seem less the rational calculations of managers than the consequences of an overcapitalized, speculative, corrupt, and increasingly unsteady system. Railroads caromed across the continent, creating systems that in toto made no rational sense but that could yield vast personal fortunes through construction, speculation, and financial manipulation.[145]

Only the scale of overbuilding differed in Canada and Mexico, where subsidies tempted railroads to expand. In 1876 Porfirio Díaz, who had received substantial aid from American investors seeking access to Mexico, seized power from the elected president, Sebastián Lerdo de Tejada. Although Díaz occasionally played the anti-American card for domestic effect, he created the kind of oppressive order that American financiers appreciated. By 1896 the Mexican government had allocated subsidies in cash and bonds worth $107,743,660 to the railroads.[146]

American promoters rose to the bait. The Associates projected the Mexican International to reach from Eagle Pass, Texas, to Mazatlán on the Pacific, but the road never made it farther than 350 miles, reaching Durango in 1892. Although Huntington claimed in June of 1882 that he had instructed John Frisbie Jr., Díaz's railroad adviser and a man already on Huntington's payroll, not to bribe government officials, he sent Frisbie $25,000. Frisbie, in turn, gave some of that to Ramón Fernández, governor of the Federal District and a close adviser to Diaz. Huntington created the usual insider construction company and, in the usual manner, granted stock to José I. Limantour, Díaz's finance minister; Manuel Romero Rubio, Díaz's father-in-law; Ramón Fernández; and the wife of Geronimo Treviño, the governor of Nuevo León.[147]

In Díaz's railroad sweepstakes the key concessions were the routes to Mexico City: the Mexican National and the Mexican Central. William Jackson Palmer and James Sullivan received a subsidy of $11,929,870 in certificates convertible to 5 percent bonds to build the Mexican National from Laredo to Mexico City. Díaz adroitly deflected opposition by allowing the states to negotiate individual agreements with the new railroads. The Mexican National and the Mexican Central spent lavishly to the great advantage of local elites who realized how much they had to gain from American railroads. The subsidy to the Mexican Central eventually totaled

$26,609,003.[148] In addition the Atchison, Topeka, and Santa Fe, aided by a subsidy of 7,000 pesos per mile, built from Nogales to Guaymus in 1882, creating its first outlet on the Pacific.[149]

In both Mexico and the United States, not only the same factors but the same people were involved in the schemes, successful as well as unsuccessful, to build railroads. Matías Romero secured a concession for a railroad from Mexico City to Oaxaca, and ex-president Grant agreed to join him in that enterprise. The Mexican Southern in an attempt to build across the narrow Tehuantepec Isthmus, attracted Grant, Huntington, and a powerful coalition of American promoters. Gould also promoted the International Mexican Railway Company (not to be confused with Huntington's Mexican International), a 680-mile road for which, according to an engineer sent out to examine its route, there was no business. Gould eventually merged it with the Mexican Southern. In 1884 a business partner of Grant's son in the firm of Grant and Ward squandered both the senior and junior Grant's investments and fled. Grant was left a bankrupt; the firm's creditors, unable to collect their debts, failed, helping to precipitate a banking panic. Mexico voided the concession to the Mexican Southern.[150]

V. SUPERHEROES OF BAD MANAGEMENT

The entrepreneurship so apparent in the 1880s involved innovations that combined financial manipulation, the waste of capital and labor, and the construction of railroad lines that fulfilled little or no discernible need except the enrichment of the promoter. Henry Villard was the king of bad entrepreneurs. In his attempts to recover money for German bondholders, Villard had gone up against two of the great freebooters of American capitalism: Jay Gould and Ben Holladay of the Oregon and California. Personally, they could not have been more different. Gould was small, quiet, dignified, and happiest with his orchids and his family. Holladay was, in Villard's description "a genuine specimen of the successful Western pioneer . . . illiterate, coarse, pretentious, boastful, false and cunning."[151] Villard bested Holladay, stripping him of his holdings. Gould's acquisition of the Kansas Pacific came at a price that satisfied the German bondholders. The rise in

Kansas Pacific securities also netted Villard his first fortune, giving him a financial standing he previously lacked.[152]

Villard went on to become a superhero of bad management—powerful, daring, able to destroy railroads at a single blow. He encapsulated virtually everything that Charles Francis Adams saw as willfully destructive in western railroad building. Centering his investments on the Pacific Northwest, Villard gained control of the Northern Pacific, a weak corporation that he made both bigger and weaker.

Villard secured the money to do this from Europe, New England, and Wall Street. Influential people in each of these places regarded him as one of them. His marriage to Fanny Garrison, the daughter of the abolitionist hero William Lloyd Garrison, gave him New England connections that he cemented through the unlikely route of becoming secretary of the Social Science Association in Boston. This allowed Villard, who in his old age took to writing about himself in the third person, to undertake the "investigation and study of public and corporate financiering, including that of railroads and banks. The subject of railroad securities especially interested him." Villard came to know Charles Francis Adams, who admitted his ability and never trusted his judgment, and William Endicott, a Boston banker and investor who was crucial to his enterprises.[153]

But it was Villard's German connections that proved the key to his success. Germans trusted Villard because he was German born, fluent in the language, and familiar with American railroads and finance. He was admittedly fragile and prone to go to pieces in a crisis, but that was true of many of the men who operated in Wall Street and railroad circles. The obvious strengths of the charming, well-connected Villard masked his deficiencies.

Beginning in the late 1870s Villard and his representative Charles Bretherton, borrowing in New York, Frankfurt, and London, began assembling a transportation empire in the Pacific Northwest. He bought out successful firms, such as John Ainsworth's Oregon Steam Navigation Company, which controlled the Columbia River, and unsuccessful firms like the Oregon Steamship Company. With the help of English speculators and investors, he acquired Holladay's old properties. He created the Oregon Improvement Company, which began building a line from Portland to the still uncompleted Northern Pacific at Wallula. When Frederick Billings, then president of the Northern Pacific and its largest stockholder, refused to sell that railroad and insisted on building to both Portland and over the Cascade Mountains to Tacoma, Villard countered with the famous Blind Pool. Participants invested in Villard, not knowing what he would do with their money. He acquired control of the Northern Pacific in the spring of 1881. Yet another new company, the Oregon and Transcontinental Company, became a corporate bag to hold the Northern Pacific, the Oregon Steam Navigation Company, and other Villard properties under a single ownership.[154]

Villard, like most of the other financiers, knew little about running railroads. He ran, as one scholar has put it, "a loose, almost haphazard operation, almost totally unconcerned about cost accounting."[155] He once summoned Colonel George Gray to talk about branch lines and then forgot to tell him the "chief point" for which he had summoned him.[156] Villard loved to hear himself talk, and he savored the praise of others. His writing was really speaking, for he dictated his letters, which often ran from ten to twenty pages. His subordinates might not hear from him for weeks and then be buried under an avalanche of prose. "My multifarious business occupations do not permit me to follow up my correspondence regularly," he explained to Herman Haupt, the general manager of the Northern Pacific, who was trying unsuccessfully to install a system modeled after the Pennsylvania Railroad, "and I am compelled to avail myself of odd moments of leisure to attend to it. This I state simply by way of explaining the delay even in the acknowledgment of your letters." However shaky his business skills, however careless about details, he was confident of his financial abilities. He was at home with the Northern Pacific.

Villard's letters exuded a garrulous optimism. They were full of preening self-promotion. As an ex-journalist, he liked to quote others, particularly when they were full of praise for Henry Villard. During the good times, the letters virtually crowed. Making money seemed effortless, and Villard resurrected many of the old schemes of the transcontinentals. The Oregon and Transcontinental, acting like the Crédit Mobilier or the Contract and Finance Company, would build branch lines for the Northern Pacific.

The branch lines, organized as separate companies, would issue 6 percent bonds to pay the Oregon and Transcontinental twice the cost of construction as well as giving that company a majority of their stock. The Oregon and Transcontinental would, in turn, pay for the lines by issuing 5 percent bonds; the difference in interest in the bonds they were receiving from the branch lines represented further profit. The Northern Pacific would secure the deal by giving the branch lines traffic guarantees that would yield the earnings necessary to enable them to pay the interest on the bonds. Success would bring rising stock prices. How could they lose?[157]

Well, they might lose because the Union Pacific was extending the Oregon Short into the Pacific Northwest, and there was not enough traffic for both railroads. To counter this, Villard spun further but abortive plans. In combination with the Vanderbilt interests and the Chicago, Burlington, and Quincy, Villard would form a pool, acquire a majority of Union Pacific stock, and put the Union Pacific "in harmony" with the Chicago, Burlington, and Quincy and the Northern Pacific.[158]

As things began to go sour, the letters grew even longer, full of explanations, self-justifications, and accusations. When William Endicott in 1882 criticized Villard's initial formulation of the pool to buy the Northern Pacific, Villard modified it but insisted that "sometimes rashness of this kind is really the greatest prudence." Endicott protested Villard's plans to sell bonds to raise money for dividends on stock, which, in turn, would raise the price of the stock. He argued against using the solvent, low-debt Oregon Railroad and Navigation Company to guarantee the debts of his more dubious acquisitions, weakening the company in the process.[159]

In both good times and bad, Villard obfuscated and lied. The lies and their contradictions were often barely separated in the letterbooks. He had, he wrote the Boston banker Henry Higginson, promised to issue no new securities, and what he said "was strictly true at the time," but the situation had changed. There was always a "but" with Villard.[160] He would occasionally admit the falsifications, but they were necessary for the good of the company. It was as if he was channeling Jay Cooke.[161]

The core problem with the Northern Pacific was at once simple and common; it cost too much to build, and it brought in too little revenue.

Villard's financial maneuvers made a bad situation worse. He sold bonds, and then he sold new stock. He borrowed more money, putting up stock as security. When the stock fell, the lenders wanted more collateral. Villard chose to intervene in the market to support the stocks, which cost still more money. As financial markets constricted and interest rates rose, the situation became desperate. Cynics said that although Villard had shown he could spend money, it was not yet apparent that he could make any. Villard's optimism and capacity for self-deception took in even the skeptical. Endicott questioned Villard's tactics but continued to encourage friends and clients to buy Villard securities into the disastrous summer of 1883. He pointedly asked Villard whether there was any reason he should not give this advice.[162]

It was not a good time to ask Villard anything. By the summer of 1883 he was operating in two parallel universes. The first was a world of public acclaim as he organized an elaborate and expensive excursion to the West to celebrate the completion of the Northern Pacific. He brought three hundred guests from Europe and the United States at a cost of approximately $300,000 to join the Montanans who came to witness the ceremonial completion of the road. There were the usual politicians—Ulysses S. Grant, Secretary of the Interior Henry Teller, and Carl Schurz, the most prominent German American politician in the country. But there were also illustrious Europeans. The British parliamentarian and historian Lord Bryce advised Villard on the British delegation, which unfortunately included the young Lord Onslow, who having snubbed the journalists, became the running joke of the summer in American papers. "Our Noble Deadheads," one newspaper called him and his companions, making them into archetypal British parasites and twits.[163] The great German social thinker Max Weber was there, as was the not so great American social thinker E. L. Godkin, who edited the *New York Evening Post*, which Villard owned.[164]

The guests were full of praise for Villard, which was why they had been invited. The journalists on the trip praised not just his vision but his integrity: "the best of your deeds is to have shown how, out of his own head, a man may coin millions for himself and for others without lowering his standard of high integrity or betraying the confidence of others."[165] The Germans and German-Americans sent him a letter calling the Northern Pacific one of "the great works of civilization by which not only this country but other nations will profit."[166] The guests on train 4 were, by these standards, subdued. They simply thanked him for the opportunity to witness "completion of the greatest commercial enterprise of history."[167]

The flattery of the guests paled before the demonstrations along the way, particularly those in St. Paul and Portland, the effective termini, and Tacoma, the terminus to be. The St. Paul celebration on September 3 with its parades, speeches, and dinners set the extravagant tone for what followed.[168] The city of Bismarck celebrated with short speeches by Sitting Bull and General Grant. As the party moved west, the Crow Indians encamped and staged dances for the party at Grey Cliff.[169] In Portland the celebration stretched over two days, September 10 and 11.[170]

The great ceremonies at St. Paul and Portland bookended the joining of the tracks on September 8 at the junction of Little Blackfoot Creek and Independence Creek, sixty miles west of Helena. Fittingly, the completion was an illusion. The tracks had actually connected on August 22 at Gold Creek.[171] Endicott, with more admiration at the beginning of the summer than he would be able to muster at the end, had once written Villard, "I cannot quite make up my mind whether it is you or Barnum or Forepaugh that has 'the greatest show on earth.' I suppose that you have no doubt on that point."[172] By the end of the summer Endicott had no doubt either.

For each public achievement and celebration there was, as a kind of counterpoint, a business disaster. By August the Northern Pacific and Villard's other companies were sinking like stones on the stock market. As the line was completed and the excursion departed, so did Henry Higginson. Endicott had reported him demoralized, and Higginson asked Villard to repay his loans. Immediately Villard responded in a huff: it was "just such a feeling of unfounded distrust as crops out in your letter which caused the entirely unwarranted break in our securities."[173] As the journalists praised his integrity, Villard wheedled, obfuscated, and lied. He maneuvered to hide the large interest charges on construction expenses, and he attempted to deceive investors into thinking that the expenses were a funded rather than a floating debt.[174]

The two worlds could not remain separate forever; they reunited when

Villard returned east to face the financial crisis. He claimed simultaneously that anyone who had read the corporate reports would have known of the heavy cost of construction for some time, and so this could not be the reason for the stock's fall, and that he had not realized the extent of these expenses. In the kind of sentence that pretty much summed up his managerial style and that of many of his contemporaries, he wrote, "[T]he trouble was not only that the cost was much greater than was expected but that it was almost impossible to know at any one time what it would be. Hence it was unpractical to make provision in advance for current requirements and no measure of permanent relief could be resorted to until the whole of the road was actually completed."[175]

Villard managed to be both rescued and disgraced. The banking house of Drexel-Morgan headed an investment syndicate whose loans saved the whole structure from collapsing. There was no room, however, for Villard in the new, enfeebled Northern Pacific. He thought of himself as a "tragic" figure. Officially he resigned, but actually, as the British press put it, he, "to use an expressive though unpolite English term, . . . was 'kicked out.'" Leaving under a cloud of mismanagement and financial irregularities, he was replaced by Robert Harris. Harris negotiated a pooling agreement with the Union Pacific to split the traffic from the Oregon Railroad and Navigation Company, which nonetheless soon became an object of rivalry between the two roads.[176]

At the end of 1883 Villard, who always had "fits of nervous depression when the seasons change," wrote an *Et tu, Brute* letter to Endicott full of self-pity but not remorse: "I am already so accustomed to getting kicks and cuffs instead of thanks that I perhaps ought not to be surprised at the tone of your letter."[177] He saved, eagerly, almost compulsively, the letters of condolence and praise he received in the wake of his downfall. They compose three thick files in his papers.[178] He retreated to Berlin with his family. He had not, as Adams wrote, "outgrown his grand ideas."[179] Nor had he taken any responsibility for the failure. In a statement to the stockholders, he blamed it on the engineers, and the chief engineer, Adna Anderson, replied in outrage to "certain assertions that differ so widely from the actual facts." Villard replied that he had no intention of blaming Anderson, and then blamed him anew. More controversy ensued. None of this was astonishing; what was astonishing was that he could ever again secure financial backing to return not only to railroading but to the Northern Pacific.[180]

VI. A SYSTEM THAT DID NOT BURY ITS DEAD

Capitalism was supposed to be the most ruthless of systems, punishing failure and lavishly rewarding success. Charles Francis Adams took the traditional view, when he wrote that the transcontinentals were engaged in a Malthusian struggle.[181] As usually happened in the nineteenth century, Malthus proved a bad prophet. Competition did not lead to the demise of overcapitalized railroads. The law preserved insolvent railroads as corporate zombies—the undead who preyed on the living. The original goal of receivership was to pay off a corporation's creditors, and if the corporation died in the process, so be it. By the 1870s, however, the courts were reluctant to dismember roads to satisfy creditors. Selling a road off piecemeal would sacrifice, as a legal memorandum for the receivers of the Kansas Pacific put it, "the right of the public to claim the use and service of a Railroad upon offer of private compensation."[182]

This was a compelling claim, but the issue was less whether railroads should continue to operate than whether failing railroads should damage healthy ones and who should bear the burden of reorganization. Because a railroad in receivership could suspend its interest payments, receivers could lower rates to increase their road's traffic. Competitors had little choice but to respond with cuts of their own, which increased their own chances of receivership.[183] In 1884 receivership underwent further evolution in the famous Wabash, St. Louis, and Pacific Railway case. The Wabash was part of Gould's new system and like much of that system could not pay its debts. Its managers, not its creditors, sought court protection. The court made the managers the receivers. The legal pendulum had swung to favor managers over creditors.

Theoretically, receivers should have squeezed creditors and stockholders to eliminate water from the corporation. In practice major reorganizations before the depression of 1893 were as likely to increase fixed charges as to lower them.[184] Reorganizations were more likely to restructure rather than to reduce debt. Innovative new securities such as income bonds, where payments depended on the earnings of the company, and preferred stock, which offered the holder priority payment of dividends before common stock, did not promise annual payments and thus lessened the danger of default.[185]

Competition had created a spectacle of a railroad dog chasing its own tail. Railroads sought consolidation and stability, but all that competition yielded was a crazed, emaciated, and vicious dog. Attempts to escape this conundrum, to calm the dog, make it obedient to the public good, and have it prosper in the process, led more and more people to think that predictable, fair, and reasonably efficient railroad transportation could not be left to competition and market forces. As one specialist would put it retrospectively in the early twentieth century, "unregulated railway enterprise inevitably results in discriminatory practices."[186]

MISE EN SCÈNE

LABOR IN NATURE

Nineteenth-century North Americans accepted that the most modern of industrial products could be set in the midst of what they regarded as the most primeval nature. In the United States, in particular, intellectuals and popular writers alike regarded the machine in the garden as a defining symbol of the republic, marking Americans as both a people of progress and a people of nature. In photographs, paintings, and travel narratives, the forests, mountains, plains, and prairies dwarfed the powerful machines that penetrated them, and the machines, in turn, dwarfed the men who operated them, when the men appeared at all. The workers were so diminished paradoxically because they were so threatening. They were the serpents in this garden.[1]

Railroads actively promoted western railroad journeys as modern journeys into the sublime. The elimination of workers from such journeys did not need much explanation. By definition, the sublime overawes humans who view it. The sublime is not a place of work. The 1879 edition of *The Pacific Tourist* made the transcontinental trip seem both an inspirational immersion in nature and a journey utterly devoid of physical effort or discomfort. It would "make even the most desponding or prosaic feel there is beauty in prairie life." In sight of the mountains, "[w]ithout scarcely asking the cause the tourist is full of glow and enthusiasm." The traveler had encountered the sublime. "[E]ach individual seems but a little mite, amid this majesty of loneliness." And all this is before the traveler even entered "the mighty wonders of the Far West."[2]

As they crossed the desert, *The Pacific Tourist* reminded travelers lounging, talking, and reading in the palace car of the luxury they enjoyed compared with "the great suffering of those who attempted to cross . . . without adequate preparation and the consequent burning thirst they and their animals have endured," but the work of crossing the desert was not a thing of the past.³ While the travelers lounged, men did dangerous work all around them, but such men were hidden in full view. They were on the track crews and construction crews the train passed; they were in the yards and stations. Engineers and firemen ran the locomotives, and brakemen worked the top of the cars. Except for conductors and porters, the railroads actively tried to keep the men directly responsible for running the train separate from the passengers. When they appeared, passengers complained, and the Canadian Pacific banished trainmen from the smoking cars and sleeping cars.⁴ The consumption of travel by passengers and not the production of travel by workers became the quintessential railroad experience.⁵

In the spring of 1879 William Emerson Strong, an army officer, left Chicago to see the Grand Cañon of the Arkansas only recently penetrated by the Atchison, Topeka, and Santa Fe and the Denver and Rio Grande. Strong was a nineteenth-century traveler attuned to the western sublime. He knew what to look for, and he possessed the language to describe it.

> *Three-and-a-half miles from Cañon city we turned abruptly, the base of a ragged precipitous spur from the main range—a little valley lay at our feet and beyond loomed up in majestic grandeur the lofty dead wall which marks the entrance to the royal gorge. Rapidly now we approached this marvelous cañon—this deep, dark and awful pathway of the Arkansas River through the heart of a solid granite mountain.*⁶

Strong did not ignore labor. He rode on the equivalent of a construction train: an unobstructed flatcar without a roof, where a wind blew the engine's smoke away from his party. He traveled with, among others, "Mr. Clark Lips, the principal contractor," who gave him the dates of construction from "October 1, 1878 . . . to about May 1, 1879, and the number of men employed from two hundred and fifty to three hundred," as well as the cost of grading and laying the eight miles of track through the canyon: "a trifle less than one hundred and forty thousand dollars to the mile." Strong saw beyond Lips's statistical reduction to the details of construction: the roadbed "cut from a solid granite wall" and the difficulty "experienced in getting a foot hold." He admired how the company lowered "[m]en, machinery and supplies . . . from the cliffs to the bed of the river by means of ropes, and often a distance of from one thousand to fifteen hundred feet." With the road finished, travelers "saw at several points the great snubbing [*sic*] poles still standing on the edge of precipices and although thirty inches in diameter and from forty to fifty feet in height appeared to us, even through strong fieldglasses, not larger than ordinary fishing rods. It hardly seemed possible that men had ever been lowered to the bottom of the cañon from those heights."

With the construction workers gone and only their artifacts and accomplishments remaining, the technological and the natural merged for Strong.

> *The railroad bed through the cañon, and in fact of the entire line, was equal to any I had ever seen. The work was skillfully and artistically done. The rails were of steel and the ties of oak. [The track, open for but a few months, had been] hitherto considered by the ablest engineers impracticable—in fact impossible. Until within a few months of our visit, the dark recesses of the mighty gorge were unexplored except at one or two points near the entrance, which had been reached in midwinter. . . . By the energy, enterprise and skill of a Railroad Company the difficulties were surmounted—the cañon was conquered, and from the platform of a palace car the traveler could see the wonders and beauties which for all time hitherto have been hidden from mortal eye.*[7]

The skill and energy of workers became those of "a Railroad Company," and the results blended it with nature. As when Leland Stanford drove the last spike, at the final moment owners and promoters, men who had done no physical labor, stepped forward to perform the final symbolic work and take the credit.

Yet if we return to Promontory Summit to look closely at the famous Russell photographs commemorating the completion of the Pacific Railroad, we find workers. As if insisting on a presence soon to be rhetorically denied them, they swarmed over the facing locomotives. But even here the Chinese workers were already fading out of the pictures, present in laying the final rails at the beginning of the series of photographs and then gone from the final, culminating shot. Pictures of workers in yards and shops and other industrial settlings remained abundant, of course, but instead of noticing the labor that went into the operation of railroads in nature, Americans and Canadians emphasized the labor railroads displaced.

Industrial workers—the men who produced the technology and operated the machines—were banished not just from the sublime but also from the pastoral, the settled or middle landscape that was neither wild nor urban.[8] And this was more mysterious because the pastoral clearly involved human labor. The famous Currier and Ives print *Westward the Course of Empire* pictured the creation of the pastoral and puts the railroad at its center. The engraving was full of human life. The Indians observed and retreated. The settlers built and the signs of their work—the schoolhouse, the newspaper, and the railroad station in the foreground—were the signs of progress. The locomotive was the engine of progress, and it called into being the very labor that created the garden, but that labor was agrarian and not industrial. Passengers are visible on the train, but the viewer can see no railroad workers.

Why some workers and not others? Nineteenth-century Americans thought labor was itself natural, and its result was to "finish" nature and apply the last touches that turned it into the garden. "The spontaneous energies of the earth are a gift of nature," Thomas Jefferson wrote in a characteristic passage, "but they require the labor of man to direct their operation. And the question is so to husband his labor as to turn the greatest quantity of this useful action of the earth to his benefit. . . . The plow is to the farmer what the wand is to the sorcerer. Its effect is really like sorcery."[9] Jefferson, like Emerson later, saw both nature and the nation as realms of becoming as yet incomplete. Jefferson posited a natural world that was only partially finished and that human labor and technology completed. Jefferson and the agrarian tradition went further. Through labor in nature it was not only the natural world but human beings who were finished. The farmer's finishing produced the pastoral and in doing so the farmer produced himself as an independent republican citizen. Work in nature was thus doubly transformative, but only certain kinds of work done in certain kinds of ways.

Here was the problem: in western nature industrial workers did the wrong work in the wrong place. American conceptions of nature met their ideological limits. Jefferson had distrusted industrial workers as completely as he celebrated farmers. Whereas labor on the land ennobled, wage labor in industry degraded. In the antebellum United States, Republican Free Labor had expanded the realm of ennobling to include craftsmen and other small independent producers as well as farmers, but industrial workers remained both few and suspect. After the Civil War they grew far more numerous but no less suspect. Railroads catapulted industrial workers into nature, but they seemed out of place. Although their work in nature was essential to the creation of a western pastoral, they were not transformed by it. They remained wageworkers and not autonomous producers. Industrial workers remained threatening, foreign, and degraded. The labor of creating the railroads thus could be fully celebrated only if it was transitory. The results could remain, but the workers had to disappear. The images of the moving construction camps, the hells on wheels, the instant towns of saloons and whorehouses could be winked at as temporary local color. Workers should similarly vanish; otherwise they threatened what they had called into being.

Workers, however, absent though they became from tourist literature and descriptions of the sublime, did not vanish. They were everywhere for the simple reason that the railroad could not run without them; if they ceased work even for a season, the railroad would inexorably crumble into two streaks of rust pointing west across the continent.

CHAPTER 6

❧

MEN IN OCTOPUS SUITS

They [the stockholders] frequently awake at an eleventh
hour to a realization that the underpinning of their
stockholdings is entirely rotten, that assets have no foundation
in fact, and that the respective companies are to all intents
and purposes positively bankrupt.[1]

—*THE FINANCIER*, 1893

SINCE THE LATE nineteenth century writers and scholars have used the transcontinental railroads and the men who controlled them to encapsulate their age. They have become symbolic, although what they symbolize and the valence of the symbol have shifted, sometimes radically. They began as Robber Barons, standing for a Gilded Age of corruption, monopoly, and rampant individualism. Their corporations were the Octopus, devouring all in its path. In the twentieth century and the twenty-first they became entrepreneurs, necessary business revolutionaries, ruthlessly changing existing practices and demonstrating the protean nature of American capitalism. Their new corporations also transmuted and became manifestations of the "Visible Hand," a managerial rationality that eliminated waste, increased productivity, and brought bourgeois values to replace those of financial buccaneers. These images often have not so much replaced each other as existed side by side. By the twenty-first century, you could dress Huntington, Villard, and the rest most any way you wished: they were so many portly male Barbies.[2]

Observers and scholars have tried to capture the railroad corporations that these men created through organic metaphors—the Octopus, the Visible Hand—and organic metaphors invite evolutionary trajectories, which lead to a triumphant corporate form: businesses, which in both size and capitalization, were larger than anything known before. They held multiple units whose operations covered vast amounts of space. They demanded not only specialized personnel but salaried managers arrayed in hierarchical organizations.[3] Managers staffed the positions below president and the board of directors, while the board and the offices of president and treasurer were the domain of "either investors or spokesmen for investors." Each group had a different goal for the corporation. Managers preferred long-term stability and the health of the organization; presidents and the board favored maintaining dividends over new investments in the road. The speculators sought profit from construction companies and other ancillary operations and the manipulation of securities.[4]

The corporate form, however, dictated that some functions would win out over others. Speculators, financial buccaneers, and personally run railroads yielded to professional corporate managers. At any time entrepreneurial figures could arise and change the functioning of the whole system; once the revolution had occurred, however, corporate evolution reverted to its course, returning the corporation to its ultimate managerial form. By 1880 according to the standard account, Alfred Chandler's *The Visible Hand*, the managerial corporation was dominant and other railroads moved to conform to its practices. All there remained to accomplish was interfirm cooperation and system building.[5] In these histories form followed function, and railroads pioneered the inevitable triumph of the American corporation.

There are two major problems. The first is that although there were certainly managerial corporations and the earliest ones were railroads, not all American railroads were managerial corporations by the 1880s. The second is that if corporations were the functional response to multiunit businesses whose operations covered vast amounts of space, then American corporations should be much like those elsewhere faced with similar conditions. They are not. In different countries railroad corporations were products of different societies, histories, and legal regimes. Successful economies did not necessarily reproduce the U.S. corporate model; economic growth did not depend on doing so.[6] Great Britain, Germany, and France managed to institute reforms in law and corporate governance that contained the kinds of fraud and insider manipulation that made controlling U.S. corporations so lucrative in the late nineteenth century. Their reforms came long before those in the United States. There were multiple solutions to problems and many possibilities for corporations.[7]

If we distinguish more sharply between form and function, we can see American railroad corporations as containers that could hold different kinds of purposes. Most of the men who organized western railroads, and many of the managers of those railroads, knew how many ways people could use corporations. Categorizing businessmen as managers, speculators, or entrepreneurs makes them ideal types—personas rather than actual people. Actual people had several different personas either at different times or simultaneously. Tom Scott was, depending on the place and moment, a salaried manager, an investor, and a speculator. Were Henry Villard or Collis P. Huntington or Leland Stanford investors or speculators? It was not always easy to say. Was Jay Gould a speculator? Well, certainly, but he was also by some accounts a knowledgeable railroad manager.[8] All of these men could shape-shift as opportunity warranted.

These men also knew a big truth that has no place in evolutionary models: corporate failure as well as success could be lucrative. It was possible to wreck these trains and walk away with millions. Others would have to clean up the mess. The smooth internal functioning of these corporations was not necessary to their persistence. They could be internally chaotic, financially undisciplined, prone to failure, and tremendously attractive for insiders nonetheless. Attached to this big truth was a little one: if failure could be lucrative, then ignorance, incompetence, and disorganization were not incompatible with the corporate form.

Incompetent managers and dysfunctional corporations are compatible with evolutionary metaphors only if the bad managers disappeared along with the dysfunctional corporations. Supposedly only the fit survive. And so the one constant in the otherwise contradictory literature that makes railroads a model for American corporate success is to make them fit. Whatever the railroads did—rob, create, organize—they supposedly did it ruthlessly and effectively. Believing this is easiest if writers and scholars watch from a distance and do not descend into the bowels of these corporate beasts. If the goal is to have great villains or powerful heroes, don't read the mail of the men who ran the transcontinentals.

Frank Norris's *The Octopus*, which appeared in 1901, the year after Collis P. Huntington's death, was the literary apotheosis of the power, ruthlessness, and efficiency of the transcontinental railroad. The novel leaped from the mechanical power of the locomotive to the soulless power of the corporation: ". . . the galloping monster, the terror of steel and steam, with its single eye, Cyclopean, red, shooting from horizon to horizon . . . symbol of a vast power, huge, terrible, flinging the echo of its thunder over all the reaches of the valley, leaving blood and destruction in its path; the leviathan, with tentacles of steel clutching into the soil, the soulless Force, the iron-hearted Power, the monster, the Colossus, the Octopus."[9] The fictional Southern Pacific in Norris's novel was the Pacific and South West Railroad, and its president, Shelgrim, was "a giant," a man with "an ogre's vitality," who had "sucked the life-blood from an entire people." He was a man who could destroy whole states and yet know in detail, and sympathize with, the travails of a bookkeeper. He insisted that he only rode and did not control the railroad. It was a creature of "[f]orces, conditions, laws of supply and demand," the equivalent of nature itself.[10]

Spend time in Collis P. Huntington's correspondence, and all this is laughable. He and his Associates were not giants; their railroads were not forces of nature.[11] And the Southern Pacific had no operative as terrifyingly competent as S. Behrman. Everything the Southern Pacific could do Norris encapsulated in S. Behrman.

> *If the freight rates are to be adjusted to squeeze us a little harder, it is S. Behrman who regulates what we can stand. If there's a judge to be bought, it is S. Behrman who does the bargaining. If there is a jury to be bribed, it is S.*

Behrman who handles the money. If there is an election to be jobbed, it is S.
Behrman who manipulates it. It's Behrman here and Behrman there.[12]

S. Behrman was a fiction, but he was also a composite of men who were real enough: W. H. Mills, Creed Haymond, W.W. Stow, Boss Billy Carr, and others who looked after Southern Pacific interests in California during the 1880s and 1890s. Behrman did what actual railroad operatives did. What made Behrman an implausible character was how competently he did it. Looking for Behrman's equivalent in archives is like looking for Superman and finding only Clark Kent. The agents of the Southern Pacific were not only fallible; they were often bumbling.

The actual Octopus was a sadly conflicted monster. Those tentacles of steel were as likely to be slapping at each other or poking into the monster's own cyclopean eye as to be securing prey; the soulless force of the corporation actually amounted to a group of divided, quarrelsome, petulant, arrogant, and often astonishingly inept men. With the possible exception of the Canadian Pacific, it was true of all of the transcontinentals; it was true of most western railroads.[13] There was an Octopus, but it was usually less fearful than funny and fantastic. It was like watching a group of fat men in an Octopus suit.

Much of the modern history of corporations is a reaction against the Robber Barons and fictions such as the Octopus. More mundane corporate types replaced Shelgrim and Behrman, but looking for entrepreneurs and managers who embodied Behrman's competence and efficiency is as futile as looking for the Octopus. Examining corporations through nineteenth-century western railroads is like looking at them through a funhouse mirror. It is certainly possible to see, particularly in Charles Francis Adams's Union Pacific, an example of the managerial corporation, but it exists in a seemingly monstrous form. There were attempts at bureaucratic rationality, but they ended up either comic or frightening. Entrepreneurs were certainly present, but whether any corporate success, let alone larger social good, emerges from their efforts is not always readily apparent.

In all these cases, to discover anything about the workings of the nineteenth-century railroad corporations, it is necessary to go inside these organizations. And so on to the funhouse.

I. THE VISIBLE HAND

Corporate organization and bureaucratic rationality have become markers of modernity.[14] Railroads helped pioneer both. This is the truth of organization charts with their hierarchies of work and responsibility. But there is also another truth. As Charles Perrow, perhaps the leading scholar of organizations, has put it, "One must know the hierarchy to survive it."[15] Surviving it could mean subverting it. The actual chart could not only mask disorder; it could be a source of disorder, a guide to what had to be subverted in order to satisfy personal ambition.

One of the most impressive and influential organizational charts in the West was the work of the Chicago, Burlington, and Quincy. It borrowed the basic "decentralized line-and-staff divisional form" from the Pennsylvania, and this became typical of western roads. The chart did two things. First, it divided men by occupation and arranged them hierarchically. Second, the railroad replicated these hierarchical networks over space by splitting their long lines into divisions, often named for a town or geographical feature, of 100 to 125 miles.[16]

In each division there were trainmen who worked on the moving train. There were trackmen and sectionmen who repaired the track. There were shopmen who repaired and manufactured equipment. There were stationmen, the baggagemen and telegraphers who worked around the station, and there were yardmen who assembled and disassembled trains at division points. These workers did not normally go beyond the bounds of their division. Each division also had a superintendent, a master mechanic, and other officers. Overseeing them all was a general superintendent and his staff, generally located in a major city along the line. The road's higher administration often worked in a separate corporate office, sometimes far distant from the railroad. The officers who oversaw the day-to-day operations of the road for the Union Pacific, for example, were either in divisional towns or in the offices at Omaha, while the financial officers, the president and vice-presidents, and their staffs were located in Boston.[17] In essence, railroad corporations developed hierarchical organizations, repeated this basic organizational form within separate spatial divisions, and put the whole under a single centralized office.[18]

On paper all of this was quite impressive, but an organization chart did not necessarily describe actual practice. Like so many railroad publications, the railroad organization chart was often a fiction, and the charts dissolved into particular networks of dependence, cronyism, and kinship. Job classifications were hopelessly porous.[19] The organization chart depended on managerial capacity—the ability to communicate orders and monitor their implementation—honesty, competence, and, ultimately, intent: for what ends was the railroad being operated? It also demanded subordination. Those on the bottom rungs of the ladder were supposed to do what those on the upper rungs told them to do.

The charts often attributed capacity, honesty, and subordination that did not actually exist. Western railroads were giant corporations employing thousands of men, but into the 1880s they were less tightly centralized organizations than collections of fiefdoms. To a remarkable degree, upper-echelon corporate officers in the late nineteenth century failed to establish their authority in either the hiring of workers or the formulation of work rules along the railroad. There were no clear standards for any position. A system that was supposed to yield "the most honest, most reliable and most capable" men often worked out differently. Gifts to foremen and superiors became customary; they were an extension of the kind of corrupting friendship that shaped railroad politics.[20] To rise to the level of a construction foreman or section boss was to gain control over some small division of railroad space and the men who worked within it. Master mechanics, trainmasters, stationmasters, and superintendents had larger domains and greater power. Even a brakeman often controlled half of a freight train when it came to "levy[ing] tribute" of a dollar "for the division" on those who sought to catch a ride on a freight.[21] The railroad workforce was the product not of an imaginary idealized labor market but rather of "patronage, favoritism, nepotism, and extortion."[22] There would be attempts to centralize, standardize, and control these organizations, but they had not succeeded by the 1890s.

The struggle of executive officers at the upper levels to gain control over subordinates, mirrored a second struggle at the lower levels: that of workers to gain—and maintain—control over their own work. This struggle was over rules. Workers fought over the petty injustices and tyrannies that made a workingman's life so frustrating and over the work rules that controlled the length and dangers of their days. These disputes over hiring and firing, the length of a workday, what a foreman could and could not demand, and the rules that determined how a job was done and under whose discretion were the very stuff of workers' lives. They marked an attempt to carve out a republic of work within the corporate kingdom. Foremen resisted in order to preserve their own prerogatives, and corporate executives persisted because for them the principle that ownership meant control was at stake. He who paid, they proclaimed, got to say how things were run, but for workers this was a principle that undercut the manhood of republican citizens. It was not a principle suitable for a democratic society.

Work is always a matter of praxis, and there is no understanding workers' actions without paying attention to the details, but work was also more than a practical affair. It was ideological and political. It was in the details that workers perfected tactics and worked out larger principles that would give them substantial control over work.

The brotherhoods preceded the Knights of Labor and would survive them. The brotherhoods had essentially taken the classifications of skilled work on the railroad, particularly in the so-called running trades, and made them the basis of their own organizations: a Brotherhood of Locomotive Engineers first formed in 1863 on the Michigan Central, a Brotherhood of Railroad Brakemen arose in 1883, and a Brotherhood of Locomotive Firemen arose in 1873. There was a Switchmen's Mutual Aid Association and an Order of Railway Conductors. While the Knights sought an overarching organization that would take in all workers, the brotherhoods "modeled themselves after older fraternal orders" and benefit societies. They recruited the skilled and semiskilled workers who had always proved easier to organize and more difficult for employers to coerce than unskilled workers.[23]

The brotherhoods were never eager to strike, and the monopoly of skill they assumed that they possessed often proved imaginary, but they were not paper tigers. They were quite effective in small work actions, and most effective of all in what amounted to the guerrilla warfare they waged around work rules. The railroads laid out no clear standards for any position, and executives reasoned that if subordinate officials were to be responsible for results, they should have liberty to select those who worked under them and determine their duties. The Northern Pacific's manual for its workers in 1883 ran to 105 pages, but the bulk of it had to do with trying to govern the priority and management of numerous trains running on a single track. It took only eleven sentences to describe a brakeman's duties outside of his responsibilities as a flagman.[24] In this lack of specificity, the brotherhoods found their openings.

The virtual absence of clear rules about work and the variety of technologies employed on supposedly unified systems allowed skilled workers to institute their own practices and to a remarkable degree impose them on the companies. Neither workers nor management ended up happy with the original system that gave foremen and master mechanics authority over hiring workers and governing their work. Charles Francis Adams certainly recognized the problems caused by "the bull-headed blundering of some subordinate bent on having his own way," and he wanted to hammer into managers' brains that they were mistaken if they thought "their sweet wills, and their sweet wills alone, are to rule" in matters of hiring and firing.[25] But when Charles Francis Adams met with the Knights of Labor in Denver in 1885, he found that the "sweet wills" of officials were already under attack from below. Adams wanted to solve the problem by standardizing job criteria and bringing hiring and wages under the control of the general superintendent, but centralization challenged not only foremen but workers themselves.[26]

Conflicts between workers and management were so time-consuming because they centered on particular practices and because particular practices came from both the organization of work and the nature through which the railroads ran. Like many others, William Pinkerton chafed under the wage cuts, the petty tyrannies of foremen, and the physical demands of the job. In thousands of daily dramas a workingman confronting a superior might be forced to swallow his pride or he might quit on the spot. Pinkerton worked as a fireman, fueling and managing the pressure on the locomotive and acting as a second set of eyes for the engineer on the Southern Pacific in the early 1880s. When Pinkerton boarded his engine in Los Angeles, his engineer told him, "You are not worth as much money on this trip as you were when you began." His wages had been cut. Pinkerton dismounted and ran into Master Mechanic Gregg, who had lowered the pay for firemen working on the specific engine type—"the monkey-motion of Stephens"—that Pinkerton was operating. Pinkerton stood on the platform reading the bulletin announcing the wage cut while Gregg berated him for delaying a passenger train. When Pinkerton finished, his "inexperience," as he explained tongue in cheek, led him "into the error of abusing the master mechanic." Gregg promptly discharged him. The locomotive, the train, and all the passengers sat for several hours before a new fireman arrived.[27] Multiplying such incidents along a line created no end of problems and inefficiencies that higher management sought to eliminate. Pinkerton did not need to confront Gregg to disrupt the workings of the railroad. When workers, with the support of their unions, complained, they could slow the turgid administrative machinery of the railroads to a crawl. Their complaints, Adams told the Knights in 1885, already took up a great deal of his general superintendent's time. They were meant to.[28]

In these confrontations skilled workers had an advantage: they usually understood the details of railroad operations better than managers did, because they, in part, created the machines they operated. The "Stephens" behind Pinkerton's monkey-motion engine was Andrew J. Stevens, a New England mechanic who migrated west and beginning in 1870 worked in the Sacramento shops of the Central Pacific, where he experimented with new designs and built prototypes. They tended to be large locomotives with large tenders, thus demanding more work from firemen. It is no wonder that a cut in wages infuriated Pinkerton.[29] Specific details and large principles were not easily separated, and this made railroad conflicts so esoteric and so bitterly fought.

Andrew Stevens was exceptional, but many lesser versions of him were working on western railroads in the 1870s and 1880s. Railroad technology remained a process of developing and passing on innovations without patents. It developed much like open-source software today. Mechanics tinkered with locomotives. They redesigned them and on some roads manufactured their own, developing distinctive and individualized machines, which workers recognized and named. Innovators collaborated and disseminated along "an informal but effective network of technical experts." Master mechanics and the workers under them created a "pool of techniques" and innovation that the original builders of locomotives in eastern factories often tapped. As a young man, Terence Powderly, the head of the Knights of Labor, worked as a machinist in the shops of the Delaware, Lackawanna, and Western in Scranton, Pennsylvania. To Powderly a finished or repaired engine was "a beautiful piece of machinery [that] stands on the track almost a thing of life."[30]

Workers were honestly attached to these machines. On the Union Pacific the practice of assigning a particular crew to each locomotive persisted into the 1880s. Engineers took great pride in their locomotives, decorating and personalizing them. Although the engines did not need to rest when the crews rested, they sat idle rather than being taken out by a new crew. This struck higher management as absurd, but master mechanics also resisted the change. The workers' ability to prevent machines from being used as machines was an assertion of power that could also check the companies' desire to treat humans like machines, particularly as locomotives became larger and more powerful. Pinkerton's fit of pique over his cut in pay foreshadowed the strain put on firemen by bigger locomotives, demanding more fuel.[31]

This informal technical network was, however, already weakening after the Civil War as the Patent Office grew increasingly liberal in issuing patents, limiting the informal diffusion of technology. But these changes did not necessarily give an advantage to the corporations.[32] The railroads, almost comically and without embarrassment, stepped into Granger and antimonopolist clothing to cast themselves as innocent victims of monopolies created by patent holders. They battled powerful patent holders such as George Westinghouse as well as their own skilled workmen. Simultaneously, however, the railroads were also creating a new system that placed technological change in the hands of educated and professionalized engineers, a system that would not be fully in place until the end of the century.[33]

Because work rules and compensation could not be easily separated, the more complex work rules became, the more the brotherhoods stood to gain in negotiations. Setting wages for most workers assigned to a specific site—a section, a station, a yard, or a shop—was a simple calculation of setting a rate of pay for each hour worked, but setting compensation for trainmen was more difficult. Railroad trainmen could not be paid by the hour, because it was not at all clear when they were working and when they were not. Since so much of their freight traffic was unscheduled, railroads always had to have crews available to depart on short notice. Trainmen were told that their "entire time belongs to the Company." They could not take on other work when they were off duty. They always had to be ready to depart. When a locomotive and crew did depart, they did not necessarily proceed directly to a set destination and then return. A scheduled train crew might face a considerable, but predictable, layover; an unscheduled freight crew might sit somewhere for days awaiting a new train or might have to deadhead—that is, to ride as an extra crew on a departing train. The railroads always balked at paying for idle time, even as they demanded that train crews remain idle as a condition of their jobs.[34]

By the early 1880s trainmen and managers alike had agreed that the basic unit of compensation would be some measure of mileage, but this yielded new disputes. As Henry B. Stone, the general manager of the Chicago, Burlington, and Quincy, argued, "Nothing . . . could be more fallacious than the claim that a mile run on one railroad should be paid at the same rate as a mile run on another, and that a mile run on one part of a large system should be paid at the same rate as a mile run on another part, regardless of all other circumstances."[35] Variations in equipment, schedules, and types of trains, whether the trains were through or local, and whether they ran on main or branch lines all resulted in differing amounts of labor. Freight trains, except for livestock trains, always ran more slowly than passenger trains, and thus their crews worked longer hours on runs of similar distance. Scheduled freight crews, however, had it better than unscheduled, or wild, freights whose runs took longer still, because they had to yield the right-of-way to virtually all other traffic and thus spent hours on sidings.[36]

Nature, too, influenced practice and therefore how men organized work. The frequency of snowstorms, hills, and mountains, traveling at night rather than during the day, and the strain and danger of moving freight and switching cars on slopes all added up to distinctions in labor. Workers on the Northern Pacific in 1893 gave a detailed geography of difference. Edgeley, North Dakota, was "a very hard place to do switching. . . . The 'Y' there is about ¾ of a mile away from the station and it is a very steep grade." On runs west of Mandan "the topography of the country, and the difficulties under which the work is performed, justify the higher rate" of pay. Near Fertile "two very bad hills" were hard on short crews. The run in Canada from Winnipeg to Portage "is in continual snow. They have to run a snowplow nearly everyday ahead of it." Each division was different; each run was different, sometimes very different. In Washington Territory the Palouse branch was "a branch peculiar to itself." And natural differences mattered not just because of work but also because of where workers had to live. Wallula "being a very undesirable place to live in" meant that its workers deserved more hours paid at overtime rates. Specific differences in compensation had to be added to balance the scales. Equity demanded the recognition of difference.[37]

Recognizing difference was not the same thing as agreeing on how to compensate for it, and the result was the endless negotiations over work rules that served the brotherhoods so well. The railroads would have preferred to have it both ways. They wanted a standard run and a standard workday. If crew members finished a run in under ten hours, they would owe the company the remaining hours in labor. In 1893 J. B. W. Johnson, a conductor on the Northern Pacific, presented the brotherhoods' counter to the railroads' logic of compensation. Once the trainmen had completed their assigned trip, they deserved extra compensation for any other work done that was not an integral part of their original run. The company could not unilaterally decide to compensate by miles when it was to their advantage and by hours when that was to their advantage. If pay was going to be normally determined by hours worked, a man should be "perfectly free to follow his own will wherever it may take him, or engage in any other business outside his hours of work." No railroad, as Johnson knew, could effectively run its operations if its train crews were not always on call.[38]

Two ways of bridging this difference emerged. The first depended on paying trainmen by the run and then equalizing the difference between the runs with so-called arbitraries. Arbitraries were fictitious miles added to long runs or runs made under difficult conditions; they were the wage equivalent of constructive mileage—imaginary miles added to the actual haul of branch lines to increase their share of the revenue. It appears that engineers negotiated the first systematic schedule of arbitraries on the St. Paul and Manitoba in 1885. The agreement paid the engineers by the run with the average run defined as 100 miles at an average speed of 10 miles per hour. The standard day for a train man thus became 10 hours (100 miles at 10 miles per hour), and all work above 10 hours qualified as over-time. If an actual run was over 100 miles, then workers would be compensated for the extra distance at a specified mileage rate.[39] Pinkerton's wages as a fireman on the Southern Pacific, which contained some large divisions, also included arbitraries. He received "$2.97 a hundred miles and allowed an excess mileage of 200 for 150," or, in other words, if his run was 150 miles, he was paid for 200.[40]

In the West arbitraries served the brotherhoods well. Until 1894 both the Northern Pacific and the Union Pacific trainmen could appeal directly to the general manager in regard to disputes over work rules, and on the Northern Pacific, so the general manager claimed, such appeals took up "more than half his time." By coupling grievances with demands for extra compensation, workers and their representatives made small but cumulatively substantial gains, since "the determination of these matters at these meetings necessarily takes the form of a compromise . . . with the net result that the men have continually gained ground."[41] After ten years of negotiating with the brotherhoods on the Northern Pacific, the managers of that railroad found that the incremental changes in the work schedules had helped to increase the wages of trainmen more than 20 percent by 1893. Other classes of employees, without elaborate work rules, had gained far less, and section workers nothing at all. The situation was similar on the Atchison, Topeka, and Santa Fe.[42]

II. MEN AND BOYS: MANHOOD AND MANAGEMENT

The struggle over work rules in the 1880s and 1890s pitted executives and middle managers against both foremen and workers, but what of the managers themselves? Just as Norris read the power of the locomotive onto the corporation that owned it, so there has been a tendency to read out early bureaucratic behavior and bureaucratic psychology from the organizational chart, as if hierarchical organization created a hierarchical psychology or as if the lines on charts actually regimented behavior. Railroad managers certainly saw themselves as professionals, and they treasured organization. They formed associations, met regularly, and claimed a professional identity. But it is dubious to assume that they shared, or created, a set of values as orderly as the chart and aligned around the efficiency of the companies they served.[43]

If any nineteenth-century transcontinental railroad president could have walked out of the railroad offices into the pages of Alfred Chandler's *Visible Hand* as an advocate of modern hierarchical management and the imposition of bureaucratic organization, it was Charles Francis Adams. Lecturing at Harvard College, he portrayed the late nineteenth century as a time in which the old freebooters of American capitalism were yielding to a new generation of managers and college-educated professionals. Organization was now everything, and he told Harvard undergraduates that the genius of the modern corporation was that "the individual withers, and the whole is more and more." His job, as president of the corporation, was to keep the whole operating in harmony.[44]

Privately, with that combination of arrogance, unforgiving intelligence, and condescension that so endeared him to others, Adams welcomed the changing of the guard. The railroad in general had "outgrown the men in charge of it." In the beginning there were few "what we would call educated men connected with it," and the men who ran the roads had the "peculiarities of self-made men." They could not organize, they could not delegate, they lacked sufficient staff, and they could not grasp the changes in scale that had taken place. "Their minds all run to extreme simplicity, and to the primary relations of employer and employe [*sic*]." Unfortunately, they now ran railroads of thousands of miles rather than fifty miles and with thousands of employees. Most saw their lines once a year, if that, and their employees regarded them as "capitalists having no interest whatever in them or the property except to draw money from them and it."[45]

The virtues Adams wanted in his managers were the supposed virtues of the new bourgeoisie. When he named J. K. Choate as general super-intendent of the Colorado Division, he wrote an avuncular letter telling him, "You will have to learn to be cautious of speech, careful in attention to detail, sure of your position, and then quiet and firm in execution. I especially hope that you will have no quarrels. They do not pay. The man who passes his life in continual contention uses up a very large portion of his energy in so doing. You will need it all for your work."[46] Adams's ideal managers were to be the vanguard of the triumph of "bureaucratic values" in their preference of "rationality and peace" over "passion and violence" in a new middle class.[47] They supposedly embodied the values of this class: tolerance, charity, cooperation, respectability, and a desire to persuade rather than to force.[48]

There was much about the Union Pacific and the modern railroad corpo-ration that Charles Francis Adams did not share with the students at Harvard College. Privately Adams described the Union Pacific as "the worst school for railroad management that the country now possesses. The traditions of the Union Pacific are uniformly and wholly bad."[49] The corruption and dishon-esty that the original management had sown, Gould and Dillon had fertilized, and it now sent roots down through the whole enterprise. Adams soon ceased to be surprised by cases of small-scale fraud. "Like master, like man," he wrote after one revelation. "The large operations of Messrs. Gould and [Russell] Sage in the stock market just as certainly led to a system of peculation and job-bery throughout the organization in its subordinate parts as an example of sharp dealing and dishonesty leads to more sharp dealing and dishonesty."[50] He was alarmed by the "nastiness" involved in the Oregon Short Line, a road built through financial circumlocution to avoid the limits Congress had placed on the Union Pacific. There was "nothing clean" about the road. The thefts began with high officials in the Union Pacific and extended downward: "everyone there has been stealing right and left from us and robbing the public to a degree."[51] S. H. H. Clark, the longtime general manager and intimate of Gould, "did not know what a railroad was. . . . [T]he man was utterly incom-petent and not over honest."[52] Adams eased him out.

The more Adams discovered about the Union Pacific, the more he dis-dained it.[53] C. E. Perkins of the Burlington hit closer to the mark than usual—and displayed the anger and petulance that Adams often provoked—when he claimed that Adams "suspects everybody less stupid than himself of not being honest," but fraud was virtually everywhere in the Union Pacific even if the problems went beyond fraud. Adams complained that the Union Pacific was managed "as if it were a small corporation operating perhaps one hundred miles of road. . . . Too many people have interfered with the duties of one another for the simple reason that no one has well defined duties, but from top to bottom the one man power has prevailed."[54] "[T]he incompetence of the general management" from 1878 to 1884 exceeded belief. "The land department, I am satisfied, is managed far from satisfactorily. I have grave doubts as to the honesty with which it has been managed." Adams thought the whole Colorado operation was "tainted with fraud," and doubted whether there was a "single sound spot in our whole Colorado system."[55] The mechanical department was "in very bad shape," as he discovered when twenty-five locomotives had to be condemned and scrapped at one fell swoop.[56] He had little confidence in his chief engineer's "capacity or mental alertness," but at least he was honest and vigorous.[57] The commercial department needed "thorough, radical overhauling."[58] He had not "one iota of confidence" in the freight and passenger agents. "I do not believe in their capacity or in their judgment."[59] He was "dissatisfied with the Operating Department" and "utterly dissatisfied with the Construction Department."[60] The conductors, he believed, stole "50 per cent of the collections on the trains"; the bookkeepers could not be trusted; the workers, whom at first he had praised, he soon thought were a sullen, resentful mob. He eventually came to regard his employees who joined the Knights of Labor as so many felons.[61]

The road was still full of "Gould-Hopkins-Clark" men, and S. R. Callaway, the general manager Adams brought in to reform the system, seemed unable to delegate responsibility, recruit competent subordinates, or reorganize administration. You, Adams wrote Callaway, are "trying to do the work of great numbers of incompetent men yourself, instead of weeding them out. . . . Why, I have even expected you to tell me that you are convinced after long examination that our conductors were stealing, therefore, you had decided to dismiss them and in future you would run the trains and collect the fares yourself."[62] By 1887 Callaway, rightly convinced that Adams had lost faith in him, was ready to depart.[63]

Seventeen years after its completion, the Union Pacific was "floundering in the mud." Despite its huge capitalization, it was poorly ballasted and ill equipped, an "'easy riding road' without any improved appliances whatever." There were no coherent standards for its locomotives or freight cars. Its shops were "badly located and ill-equipped. We have got no coal shutes, artesian wells, or sufficient equipment."[64] How the Union Pacific "struggles along under the vast and unending deluge of incompetency which rolls to and fro over it, is a thing which has been, and is, a standing puzzle to me," Adams declared.[65] Only in 1889, in a rare fit of optimism, did Adams think he saw improvement with business "handled with more energy and intelligence" and "the good effects of character in those in control." For the first time he saw any "indications of a system" in the general traffic manager's department, and other departments had also improved.[66] Clouds erased this ray of sunshine soon enough as the incessant quarrels of subordinates caused him to lose faith in yet another general manager. A few months later Adams was lamenting that the constant change he had brought to the Union Pacific "ought to have ruined it." The losses involved in replacing the incompetent with the inexperienced were too great.[67]

Outside of the Chicago roads, disorganization seemed the common condition of most western railroads. In 1881 Herman Haupt, the general manager of the Northern Pacific, found that many of his department heads refused to speak to each other, either officially or personally, and it took a detailed personal investigation to find out what it was that the departments were supposed to do.[68]

The problem, however, was not just one of organization; it was more fundamentally an issue of culture. There was no sharp boundary between managers' business lives and other aspects of their social lives. It was hard to inculcate a bureaucratic competence when it was at odds with deeply held cultural values of manliness and masculinity. For the men who ran the railroads in the 1880s, these views were rooted in the Civil War. The Union army had provided many men who later worked for the railroads with their initial experience in large organizations—with regimentation, duty, and bureaucracy, with command and subordination. The military's lessons were, however, paradoxical. The military experience bred a deep distrust of the very hierarchy that defined it, yet large organizations like the railroads seemed to demand such hierarchy, and railroad officials appealed to their military experience and used military analogies—war, attack, defense, treaties, seizure of territory, surrender. They militarized corporations in metaphor if not in fact. In the railroads, as in Charles Francis Adams's army, "the constitutionally unqualified were to instruct the uninformed."[69] The rivalries and jealousies that rent the Union army played havoc with railroads. In Adams's war, as in his railroad, "the regimental quarrels were incessant; the spirit of insubordination was rife and in the air."[70] It is no wonder that these veterans transformed the actual processes of war into the metaphors of the railroad business.

The connection between the experiences of war and railroading went deeper than metaphor. Men who knew the war as soldiers also often carried away a sense of themselves distinct from their positions as subordinates or superiors. It involved their sense of themselves as men. They had not entered the Civil War cynically; they did not fight it cynically. It had been a war, as the historian James McPherson has phrased it, for cause and comrades. For many of them the meaning of the war transcended the horrors they had witnessed. The war had given him, Charles Francis Adams concluded, "that robust, virile stimulus to be derived only from a close contact with Nature and a roughing it among men and in the open air."[71] Courage mattered. Loyalty mattered. Honor mattered. Personal pride mattered. Soldiers, and their culture, defined these as masculine values. The Gilded Age substituted gain for cause and friends for comrades.

A Civil War battlefield sometimes seemed a convention of men destined for the transcontinentals. In the wake of his defeat in the battle of Chickamauga in 1863, General William Rosecrans found himself besieged in Chattanooga, Tennessee. Rosecrans would become a promoter of Mexican railroads; his chief of staff, the future president James A. Garfield, would be caught up in the Crédit Mobilier scandal following the war. William Palmer, who created the Denver and Rio Grande, was serving as a Union officer. Henry Villard, later president of the Northern Pacific, was there as a reporter. Tom Scott arranged the logistics of the movement of troops along the railroads that rescued Rosecrans.[72]

The railroads threw men whose values and temperament had been forged in battle or in proximity to battle together with men who had not served, and men too young to have fought in the great struggle. As veterans endeavored, often unsuccessfully, to ennoble moneymaking, their subordinates, mere children during the war, seemed to their superiors still children after the war: weak, unruly, willful, and hard to control. Their manliness had not been so fearsomely tested, and their elders could be quick to remind them of that. When the mother of one of his young subordinates in the Union Pacific wrote about the hardships of his life, Adams told her, "[Y]ou will, I fear, have to talk in vain to men of my generation. . . . [T]he hardships and dangers incurred by your son seem to me quite trifling in comparison with my own recollections of four years active service, summer and winter, in Virginia."[73]

Neither veterans nor their juniors easily fit the mold of bourgeois and bureaucratic rationality that supposedly defined the emerging corporation. Adams's subordinates were not men eager to persuade or cooperate. They were less manly, with its connotation of discipline and self-restraint, than masculine, with its aura of force, aggression, and sexuality. The standard interpretation is that leisure became the domain of a masculinity exiled from an increasingly regimented business world, but Adams located masculinity at the heart of corporate culture.[74]

The actual operation of railroads had as much to do with a code of masculinity, zealotry, honor, and revenge as with careful calculation of self-interest or the company's interest. Adams thought that "nine quarrels out of ten, costing large sums of money, are brought about by the fact that subordinates as a rule have no sense of the responsibility of their positions."[75] Adams wrote to Jay Gould, "[T]he average railroad official is . . . so jealous of what he is pleased to call the prestige or honor of the company to which he belongs that he is always ready to involve it in complications which may cost it millions, either through competition or false competition rather than see it bear the loss which may not amount to ten thousand dollars. About nine tenths of the railroad misfortunes of the country, so far as my experience goes, may be traced to this fruitful source."[76] The "average railroad man" has "no judgment, less discretion, and less conscience. As a rule, I fancy the best way to deal with him is to club him."[77] Clubbing him, of course, put Adams within the club he was combating.

It was a hard club to avoid. When Thomas Cooley, then a receiver but the future head of the Interstate Commerce Commission, contacted Adams about recruiting "good men to take hold of the Wabash road," Adams cautioned, "[R]eally capable and intelligent men are hard to find." Railroads were "full of men capable of development and worthy of promotion," but the organization killed them. "In railroad, as in other life, I fancy the good die young. They certainly don't mature visibly."[78]

Adams's attempts to change this culture only led to frustration. His effort to keep the Union Pacific "in harmony" drove his general managers to nervous breakdowns and early death. He wanted men able to adjust to the West, but he also wanted eastern college-educated men.[79] His Harvard and MIT men often did not last. He drily wrote how regularly his managers were overcome by a "spasm of economy" which compelled them to dispense with the services of "various minor officials." He added, "[T]his fit of economy almost always strikes some young men whom I regard of decided promise, who have been sent out by me. The uniform certainty with which they have been let out under these circumstances is something which would require . . . a wide philosophical generalization to explain."[80] When C. S. Mellen, his general traffic manager, wondered why young easterners were concentrated in a few departments, Adams went through the organization, department by department, to detail how his desires to place college men were thwarted. He ended with J. S. Tebbets of the commercial department. Tebbets is so disturbed, Adams wrote, by any "connection with the East, with Harvard college and myself, that he has shown a strong desire to fill all vacancies which might arise in his own department by the appointment of men who could neither read, write, nor cipher. He was determined that no one should suspect him of any weakness towards education. His only regret was that he had ever had any himself."[81]

Adams thought of himself as the future, but he stood for what was an older Victorian attitude of manhood defined by control and self-restraint that he thought should inform commercial life. "Pride, prejudice and anger," he wrote, "should have nothing whatever to do with business," but Adams's managers were aggressive and testy. They were, in his terms, "boys" who "lost their temper . . . so that they go in for it regardless of the degree to which their clothes will be torn." They had "no regard whatever for the interests entrusted to their care."[82] Far from being throwbacks, they anticipated a new ideal of masculinity. Pride, prejudice, and anger were part of their makeup, and they were proud of it. They would not be pushed around.[83] Adams both protested this—proclaiming railroad men "disposed to be altogether too 'smart'" and vowing "to jump very hard on any of our young men who resort to trickery, chicanery, smartness, or underhand dealing"—and promoted it.[84]

Daniel McCool was the kind of railroad man who betrayed Adams's hopes for maturity and revealed why railroads expanded against the best managerial judgment. In 1885 McCool, fresh from the Michigan Central, became the new general manager of the St. Joseph and Grand Island, a road recently reorganized from the bankrupt St. Joseph and Western Railroad and controlled by the Union Pacific.[85] In southwestern Nebraska the Grand Island and the Union Pacific were surrounded by much stronger roads, but McCool took the bait offered by the citizens of Geneva, Nebraska. He agreed to accept a subsidy to build to Geneva, making it a competitive point with the Burlington. This was a hostile act, and the Burlington gave notice of its intent to build a branch line from Fairmont through Geneva south to Hebron. McCool had started a fight that he could not finish. The Burlington could crush the St. Joseph "all to pieces." But the only solution Adams could see to ill-considered expansion was more expansion. If he could not restore the status quo or make a deal with the Burlington, he would extend the Grand Island into new territory to make up for business lost to the Burlington and later to the Rock Island.[86]

McCool was "nervous, and by temperament, excitable." He acted rashly.[87] For McCool business involved manliness. He protested that he did not like "to be obliged to lie down and be walked over," and Adams retorted that "this is far less disagreeable than to be first knocked down, and kicked in the face after you are down."[88] Adams's advice, "which strikes oddly on railroad ears," was "to stand upon distinctly higher moral plane. Gradually, they will have to meet on it."[89]

Adams himself was not always prepared to be either businesslike or moral. Antagonized by both the North Western and the Burlington, each of which crossed the Union Pacific's lines in Nebraska to invade each others' territory, Adams wrote Callaway, "It is very well to be Christian, and better yet to be businesslike, but we must not, as yet, cease to be human."[90] When pushed, Adams often pushed back. In the midst of a dispute over Rocky Mountain business, John J. Hagerman of the Colorado Midland threatened to build to Salt Lake. Adams reported, "I replied that he might go to Salt Lake or the Devil, but he must not threaten me in my own office. It was pure impudence. The interview was a quite lively one."[91]

III. A POLITICAL ANIMAL

Charles Francis Adams at least tried to make the Union Pacific a managerial corporation and to forge men like McCool into bureaucratic managers. He wanted the Union Pacific to become a corporation that made money by providing efficient transportation at a profit. He did not engage in stock manipulation. He did not engage in townsite speculation. He did not create subsidiary companies to drain off resources from the railroad. He did not rack up huge corporate debts to create personal profits. Which is not to say that Adams was honest. He bribed politicians, but he did so as an Adams: claiming to do so for the good of the corporation, or rather for that of its stockholders, and not for himself and a select group of insiders.

Adams was in current terms a manager, not an entrepreneur. The man who preceded and succeeded him, Jay Gould, has been resurrected as a Schumpeterian entrepreneur. He was a system builder who forced other railroads to imitate him and thus changed the whole nature of their operation.[92] Joseph Schumpeter measured the success of capitalism by taking a view that emphasized increasing productivity over the long run, but the engine for long-run success was the ability of entrepreneurs like Gould to amass vast fortunes in the short run. What was immediately good for Jay Gould, Leland Stanford, Collis P. Huntington, Henry Villard, and the rest was ultimately good for everybody.[93]

There is, however, something paradoxical in this logic. The rewards to entrepreneurs come quickly, but judgments about the utility and worth of their innovations come much more slowly. There arises a kind of evaluative shortcut in which all those who engaged in creative destruction—changing the nature of existing systems—and reaped great rewards were, ipso facto, heroic entrepreneurs, producing a better product and a more efficient way of doing things. They contributed not only to their own wealth but to the efficacy of the system and the larger material advantage of humanity.[94] A successful entrepreneur who created inefficient and prodigiously wasteful corporations becomes impossible, a contradiction in terms. By definition, the market is always right. Because of bad luck or bad timing, some good entrepreneurs might fail, but all bad ones did. But how do we know whether the market is right in rewarding particular entrepreneurs if we can only judge their innovations over the long term?

There is also something odd in Schumpeter's emphasis on entrepreneurial success as a product of business acumen. Not only was the successful entrepreneur supposedly not good at politics, but this was also supposedly a trait of the entire bourgeoisie, which Joseph Schumpeter portrayed as being "unable to take care of its political class interest."[95] Schumpeter denied what American railroad men knew. There was no separating business and politics.

That railroads were political animals was the truth of *The Octopus*, even if the power Norris attributed to them did not necessarily always exist. That leads us back to S. Behrman and his real-life counterparts in the employ of the Southern Pacific. *The Octopus* raised questions that later critics of the Robber Baron school, dismayed by its exaggerations, largely dismissed. They threw the baby out with the bathwater. They did not spend much time on a central contention of the Robber Baron literature: that many entrepreneurial fortunes had as much to do with corruption of the political process as with success in selling transportation, and that such entrepreneurial success had long-term costs for society. Examining these costs will occupy a later chapter, but first it is necessary to explore in more detail how the Southern Pacific intervened in politics.

Frank Norris envisioned the Southern Pacific as the epitome of the malevolent corporation—achieving through fraud, insider dealing, and political connections what it could not achieve through market competition. Norris had one of his characters complain,

> *They own us, these task-masters of ours; they own our homes; they own our legislatures. We cannot escape from them. There is no redress. We are told we can defeat them by the ballot-box. They own the ballot-box. We are told that we must look to the courts for redress; they own the courts. . . . They swindle a nation of a hundred million and call it Financiering; they levy a blackmail and call it Commerce; they corrupt a legislature and call it Politics; they bribe a judge and call it Law. . . .*[96]

Leland Stanford was the president of the Central Pacific Railroad and its public face from its founding until his death. He was also the first president of the Southern Pacific Company, incorporated in Kentucky in 1884 as a holding company for the Associates' interests, until Huntington forced him out in 1890. In California people assumed that Stanford's public presence connoted private authority and that he had created and ran the railroad as he ran California politics. In reality, neither Leland Stanford nor Collis P. Huntington knew—or initially cared—much about operating railroads. The difference between them was that Huntington admitted it, telling General Manager A. N. Towne in 1880, when the Central Pacific was well into its second decade, "I have very little knowledge of the details of operating railroads."[97] This was not false modesty. Stanford knew even less.[98]

Before 1884 Stanford's experience as a Civil War governor seemed to do him little more good than his lack of experience as a railroad man. The political agents of the railroad complained about their own ineffectuality in controlling California's electoral politics. Stanford's friendship with Christopher Buckley, beginning with the special session of the legislature in 1884, changed all that. Stanford and Buckley not only blunted the antimonopoly offensive but solidified railroad power. Between 1884 and 1892 the Octopus was quite real.[99] In 1885 Stanford bought his way into the U.S. Senate. He was a Republican, but this was not a sign of Republican hegemony. Stanford needed Buckley, a Democrat, to help protect railroad interests during the years the Republicans were not in power. Just as Buckley's Democratic loyalties did not extend much beyond the city of San Francisco, so Stanford's Republican loyalties never diluted his primary obligation to Leland Stanford and the Southern Pacific. In 1886 it was rumored that Stanford gave enough railroad support to the nativist American Party to give the Democrats the legislature in a three-way election. The legislature elected the Democrat George Hearst to the U.S. Senate. He was the owner of the major Democratic daily in the state, the *San Francisco Examiner*, and ally of the Blind Boss.[100]

The late 1880s were halcyon, if very expensive, days for the Octopus. The railroad ruled through an alliance with San Francisco's Democratic and Republican political machines, assorted friends, and businesses dependent on it. San Francisco's Republican machine sent as its delegates to the state Republican convention "the toughest element San Francisco could well produce outside the State's Prison." The Southern Pacific and its allies gave California the 1889 "Legislature of a Thousand Drinks" and the 1891 "Legislature of a Thousand Scandals."[101]

All of this seemed to buttress the view of the Southern Pacific as a very corrupt, but coldly efficient, corporation. It did not appear so, however, from the inside. For his Associates "efficient" was never an adjective that could appear in the same sentence with Leland Stanford. That Stanford got credit for Huntington's success in making them all incredibly rich offended Huntington's vanity, a trait that, if it existed earlier in his career, he had suppressed.[102] Huntington's disgust with Stanford had only grown as both of them aged. "He has never made any money," Huntington wrote of him, "but has had a good deal made for him and knows no more of its value when he gets it than he does of the way in which it was obtained."[103]

Stanford's deficiencies appeared most starkly in Southern California. The Associates and Gould had settled the differences between the Texas and Pacific and the Southern Pacific out of fear, not so much of each other, but rather of a new combination formed by two lines that had spent time in receivership—the Frisco and the Atchison, Topeka, and Santa Fe. Together, they shared ownership in a third bankrupt railroad, the Atlantic and Pacific, whose charter provided an entry into California. Huntington feared for California; Gould feared that the Frisco was going to strike into northern Texas and disrupt his new system there. Gould and the Associates approached the

Seligmans, Gould's longtime bankers, who controlled the Frisco. The Seligmans agreed to help them buy enough Frisco stock that together the Seligmans, the Associates, and Gould controlled that road and, through it, the Atlantic and Pacific. After the predictable betrayals and disagreements, the Seligmans reaped a healthy profit on the stock sale; Gould, with a controlling share in the Frisco, stopped its expansion into Texas, and Huntington had the Atlantic and Pacific halted at Needles, on the border of California. Stuck at Needles, the Atlantic and Pacific was a dead end and deadbeat road unable to meet its costs, which amounted to $2,300,000 per annum. Its local traffic amounted to only about $800,000, and so it needed $1,500,000 in "earnings from through traffic and rebates" to break even. Traffic from the Frisco and Atlantic and Pacific could supply, at best, half of this, and the Southern Pacific supplied it with precious little eastbound traffic.[104] Blocked from entering California over the Atlantic and Pacific, the Atchison took matters into its own hands. In 1885 it bought and completed the California Southern to San Diego. The route was difficult and expensive and was made more difficult by the Southern Pacific's opposition.[105]

By 1887, however, the Southern Pacific's opposition to the Atchison had grown distracted and ineffective, and Charles Crocker and his son, the only ones who seemed to be paying attention, were near panic. The Atchison penetrated Los Angeles, and Crocker, obese, diabetic, and soon to be dead, blamed Stanford's utter ineffectuality as president. Stanford was convinced that Southern California would never be the source of significant growth for the Southern Pacific.[106] As the Atchison prepared to build toward San Francisco, Charles's son, Fred Crocker, even urged the consolidation of the Southern Pacific and the Atchison.[107] Southern Pacific managers were convinced that the Atchison was building so aggressively, cutting rates so recklessly, and absorbing losses so cavalierly because they "had some deep laid plans which they were working out." Charles Francis Adams did not think so. "[T]hey have," he wrote, "no plan whatever; they got into this thing without intending to while playing a little game of bluff, and the contest . . . [had] worked results which they by no means anticipated."[108] They were content to continue what Adams called "this grotesque Chinese battle" because they saw in the struggle an advertisement for Southern California and stimulation to immigration from which they would benefit later. The Southern Pacific could continue to resist because many of the passengers whom the Atchison delivered to Los Angeles at ridiculously low fares then paid full local rates on the Southern Pacific to travel through California.[109]

The Crockers' inability to rally the Associates was a sign of the toll that death, illness, corruption, vanity, and desire were taking on the Southern Pacific. In October of 1883 Huntington's first wife, Elizabeth, died of cancer, and then in March of 1884, during a European trip, Stanford's only son, Leland Junior, died in Florence. These dual tragedies briefly brought Huntington and Stanford closer together, but their aftermaths soon drove them farther apart. Huntington sought consolation in a new wife and an old railroad. The old railroad was the Chesapeake and Ohio, whose first bankruptcy neither deterred Huntington's ambitions for it nor changed the fact that it was overextended and mismanaged. The new wife was Arabella Worsham, whose background was as dubious as the Chesapeake and Ohio's. When Huntington married Arabella in 1884 he was sixty-three, and she was somewhere near thirty-three, though no one was quite sure. Arabella was one of those mysterious nineteenth-century widows who were as public as their origins and first husbands were obscure. Huntington and Arabella had known each other for years. Rumor had it that he was the father of her teenage son, Archer, and he was certainly the source of the capital she used in buying Fifth Avenue properties, refurbishing and redecorating them, and then selling them. She redecorated on a grander and grander scale after her marriage.[110]

Arabella's marriage to Collis took place scandalously soon after the death of his first wife. They married in the bride's Fifth Avenue parlor, and the ceremony had more than a whiff of the Gilded Age mélange of corruption, reform, and friendship. Henry Ward Beecher, the most famous Protestant clergyman of his generation, presided. Beecher had been one of the nation's most prominent abolitionists during the Civil War, but by the 1880s he was more noted for the scandal surrounding his alleged adultery with a parishioner. His social conscience fluctuated as wildly as his affections. During the 1877 railroad strike Beecher proclaimed that a workman who could not live on bread and water was not fit to live, but by 1884 he had drifted back to reform, warning of the dangers that consolidated railroad capital presented to the republic. That would seem to make him an odd man to preside at the wedding of as consolidated a piece of railroad capital as Collis P. Huntington, but after the ceremony Huntington slipped Beecher an envelope containing four thousand-dollar bills. This could buy a lot of bread and water. They were friends, and it was fitting that Huntington's marriage so closely echoed Huntington's politics. When Beecher died in 1887, plutocrats and Knights alike found something to praise.[111]

The Stanfords could not so easily replace their only son, whom Jane had conceived on the verge of middle age.[112] In their grief the Stanfords decided on an elaborate memorial: a private university in California that would bear Leland Jr.'s name. The deep loss of the Stanfords is still visible in the nineteenth-century sections of Leland Stanford Jr. University. The Stanfords' grief was touching. It was also mad.

The university displayed the emotional vulnerability of the Stanfords, but it also revealed an egotism and arrogance that remains astonishing even in a state not known for reticence. The mourning parents erected a tomb for Leland Jr. on what became the Stanford campus, reserving space for themselves when they died. Constructed by Italian craftsmen, the tomb is granite and marble, and upon its completion its cost was higher than the 1880 assessment for the original 1,640-acre Stanford ranch on which it sat.[113] They also built the memorial chapel, destroyed in the earthquake of 1906 but rebuilt, that contained the portrayal of Leland Stanford Jr. being borne into heaven by an angel. In the stained-glass window all eyes are on young Leland as Christ sits relatively ignored above.

Literally to cap it all, there was the triumphal arch designed by Augustus Saint-Gaudens and erected at the end of the milelong Palm Drive that still forms the main entrance to the campus. Today only the pillars remain, but originally a sculpted frieze showing the procession of civilization in America wound around a massive arch. It began with a female figure of Civilization giving a torch to Columbus and ended with the mounted Stanfords—Leland apparently wearing a pith helmet and Jane riding sidesaddle—entering California with a locomotive at their back. They entered through the Sierras, which were held up by Titans. This represented a trip of exploration for the railroad that Stanford actually never took. In between Columbus and the Stanfords came Pizzaro, Cortés, Washington, and figures representing agriculture, industry, and the arts. The arch radiated hubris too great even for California. The earthquake of 1906 brought it down, and it was never rebuilt.[114]

Leland Stanford's election to the Senate in 1885 was a similar expression of grief and egotism by a man who seemingly could no longer bear California with its memories of his son. A. A. Sargent, who was again a friend of the railroad and Huntington, was the railroad's candidate. He found, however, that the Republican caucus, which would control the election in the legislature, had suddenly and surprisingly endorsed Leland Stanford, who had not previously been in contention. Stanford had bought the seat and broken the code of loyalty to friends.[115] W. H. Mills, a Huntington partisan, thought this was "the great mistake of Governor Stanford's life" and "added nothing to his honor. He was not a figure in the United States Senate and he had no capacity for defending his own position."[116]

Many rich people in the Gilded Age employed interior decorators; what made the aging Associates and their widows different was that they married them. Mary Frances Sherwood Hopkins, the widow of Mark Hopkins, found solace with an interior decorator much younger than herself. Edward Searles was more than two decades her junior, and their marriage, too, caused waves that rocked the Southern Pacific. When her adopted son Timothy Hopkins, who was close to the Stanfords, objected to the marriage, the widow Hopkins disinherited Timothy. Her representatives, Thomas Stillman and Thomas Hubbard, got Timothy dismissed as treasurer of the Southern Pacific and kept off the board of directors. Huntington cooperated. He thought Timothy Hopkins "somewhat venomous, although too small to be dangerous and . . . only irritating."[117] Searles proved more than irritating. His attorneys wanted to look at the books, which, as Charles Crocker put it, "shows a spirit that may bring about a want of harmony."[118] The want of harmony was already too evident.

Hopkins *was* venomous, but Timothy's own desire for a share of the Hopkins fortune kept him only irritating. Years later, when the United States filed suit against the Stanford estate to try to recover money lent to the Central Pacific, there were rumors it would go after the Hopkins estate as well. It brought a letter from a C. Dunham to Attorney General Richard Olney, marked, of course, personal and confidential. After his mother disinherited him, Hopkins had consulted Dunham because Hopkins believed that Dunham had damaging information about Searles. And Dunham admitted that his "knowledge of some of the latter's [Searles's] eccentricities and weaknesses and of the whereabouts & way to reach certain unwilling witnesses who could testify minutely in regard to such weaknesses, would be of great service to Mr. Hopkins." Since Hopkins did eventually settle with Searles, blackmail may have worked. But Dunham's letter was not about Searles's weaknesses; it was about Hopkins's knowledge of what Hopkins had called the "plunder" and "stealings" of the Associates. Hopkins admitted that he was fighting for his share of the stolen goods and that the "receiver is as bad as the thief," but he nonetheless gave Dunham detailed accounts of the stealing. Embittered against Huntington and Stanford, he said that if they were not protected by the statute of limitations, there was enough evidence "to send them to prison for life."[119]

By 1887 both Crocker and his son, Charles F., were desperate to have Huntington concentrate on the West. They wrote with increasing concern and near panic about the rapid development of Southern California, the opportunities for combining railroad building and land speculation, and the aggressiveness with which the Atchison was cutting the Southern Pacific out of a rapidly increasing and lucrative business.[120] Charles Crocker warned Huntington not to think that the Southern California boom was "a temporary affair"; power and population within the state were shifting. He urged Huntington to come west to view the situation firsthand.[121]

More was involved than Stanford's inattention to Southern California. If Stanford's inattention to business could have killed a railroad, the Southern Pacific would have died long before. They were expending money in regions that Crocker doubted would ever give a return, even as they lost regions that promised rich traffic. The Associates were building in the San Joaquin Valley and Mexico. They needed money to prop up hopeless Texas roads that in Crocker's words "don't seem to do much."[122] In December of

1887 Charles Crocker drove the last spike completing the California and Oregon. Railroads now connected Portland and San Francisco, but since overbuilding was reaching into the Pacific Northwest, that did little to raise the Associates' financial standing.[123] In the winter of 1887–88 the Southern Pacific began to pull back its construction crews, even though Crocker thought the price would be losing "our grip on Southern California and possibly on Northern also." The Southern Pacific had "frittered away a good deal of money without building much of any road . . . that is going to return us good interest."[124]

Europeans were reluctant to buy bonds or to finance more of the Associates' western roads.[125] Unable to raise money from his usual sources, Huntington turned to the Drexel, Morgan Company, which had previously rescued the Northern Pacific from Henry Villard. Pierpont Morgan was not interested. Huntington's financial plan for expansion, he wrote, "would throw upon us a responsibility to the public in the way of management etc. [more] than we feel able just now to assume."[126] Unable to market securities issued on the new roads, Crocker vacillated between urging a cessation of all building and suggesting that the Associates sell their own marketable securities and use their own money to build new roads in California.[127] Huntington's decision to borrow on money markets when he could not sell bonds led to an accumulation of short-term notes and the postponement of paying bills that had by 1889 hurt the Associates' credit.[128]

With the plunging rates of the late 1880s, traffic was increasing, but the Southern Pacific and Central Pacific were losing some of that traffic because they did not have sufficient motive power to move the cars over their tracks, and Crocker feared that when they obtained locomotives, they would not have the coal to fuel them.[129] Thanks to competition with the Pacific Mail, the Atchison, and the Canadian Pacific, much of this traffic was already being carried at a loss.

Charles Crocker died in the summer of 1888, and, given that his last year was a sustained lament over the state of the Southern Pacific, it must have seemed that the railroad might not long survive him.[130] Crocker was buried in Oakland. Huntington did not attend the funeral, but Thomas Edgar Stillman and Thomas Hubbard, representing the Searles/Hopkins interests, were among the mourners. They immediately wrote Huntington suggesting a change of regime in the Southern Pacific.[131]

Huntington was ready. He had decided to liquidate his eastern railroad interests after the Chesapeake and Ohio collapsed into receivership for the second time in 1889, and he wanted revenge against Leland Stanford.[132] Huntington was not a man much bothered by corruption, but corruption paid for with Southern Pacific money was supposed to advance the interests of all the Associates and not simply those of Leland Stanford. Huntington had long despised Stanford for his stupidity and carelessness, his selfishness and greed, his laziness and his immense self-regard, but he hated him for his betrayal of A. A. Sargent in the election of 1885.[133] When Huntington heard of Stanford's efforts to seize the nomination, he telegraphed Stanford, "IT IS REPORTED THAT YOU ARE IN THE FIELD AGAINST SARGENT. I CANNOT BELIEVE IT." Stanford had humiliated Huntington, who had promised Sargent the railroad's support.[134]

The California senatorial election of 1885 ended the tentative reconciliation between Huntington and Stanford, but it took awhile for an open split to emerge. Huntington felt an obligation to elect Sargent that may have been indistinguishable from an obligation to demonstrate his own potency. Initially, he swallowed his pride and flattered Stanford to get California's remaining Senate seat for Sargent in the next election, but Huntington was suspicious that the railroad's operatives did not work hard for a Republican legislature. When the legislature went to the Democrats and the seat to George Hearst, Huntington seethed with anger and resentment.[135] Years later he still could not let these incidents go. He voiced disgust with Stanford's "having used . . . much money for political purposes, which should not have been used." This "very long and unsavory story . . . the people of California" already knew too well.[136]

Once launched, the war between Huntington and Stanford would continue until Stanford died. Few roads had as dysfunctional an upper management as the Central Pacific and Southern Pacific. In other roads when one faction triumphed, the other left. Gould and Adams entered and departed the Union Pacific; Villard came and went in the Northern Pacific, but the Crockers, Hopkins, Stanfords, and Huntingtons, for all their bitterness and mutual hatred, always ended up where they started: within the Southern Pacific. The Associates and their heirs were so intertwined that they could never be rid of one another.

The split became public in 1890 as Stanford began preparations for his reelection to the Senate. Fred Crocker, who following his father's death controlled along with his brother a quarter interest in the Southern Pacific and its affiliated companies, was a vice-president of the corporation. He had lost all faith in Stanford's management. Huntington, having largely sold his eastern railroad interests, cultivated Edward Searles. Huntington, Crocker, and the attorneys representing the Hopkins/Searles interest met with Stanford in New York at the end of February 1890. Huntington supposedly had documents showing that Stanford had bought the Republican nomination and the election in 1885. Men from both parties agreed that California's Senate seats were, in W. H. Mills's words, "always for sale," but what was known was not necessarily to be talked about. If Stanford did not resign, Huntington would publish the documents. That Huntington, who had spent his career denouncing every account of his own wrongdoing as blackmail, was willing to blackmail Stanford was no more surprising than that Stanford was susceptible to blackmail. If Stanford resigned, Huntington would remain silent and Stanford could return to the Senate and nurture his quite mad hope to become president of the United States by gaining, among other things, the support of the antimonopoly Farmers' Alliance. Crocker just wanted "Stanford out of the active management and [he] believed the easiest and best way to get rid of him was to allow him to return to the Senate."[137]

The bargain struck in New York made Huntington president of the Southern Pacific Company, and he took office in April of 1890. Getting Stanford back into the U.S. Senate was supposed to be done quietly and without disturbance. Crocker, although he "did not approve of Stanford's business methods," did not want the company's dirty linen washed in public. Surprisingly, Huntington could not hold his tongue. He inserted into his otherwise conventional acceptance of the presidency of the Southern Pacific a line that found its way into newspapers across the state and nation: "In no case will I use this great corporation to advance my personal ambition at the expense of its owners, or put my hands in its treasury to defeat the people's choice, and thereby to put myself in positions that should be filled by others."[138]

Huntington growled and sniped, but he was too unpopular in California and national politics and railroad politics were too intertwined for him to make any serious attempt to strike at Stanford. Both he and Stanford needed a congressional bill for the Central Pacific to extend its debt to the government that would come due beginning in 1895. Stanford may have been a ridiculous and inept senator, but he was a Republican senator and should Huntington weaken him, the Republicans could lose an important seat. The Republican leadership made it clear that if this happened, they would punish Huntington by punishing the railroad.[139]

IV. GOING OFF THE TRACKS

Huntington's war against Stanford might be dismissed as a quarrel between two vain and very rich men, but it was actually a symptom of the Southern Pacific's larger and deeper dysfunction. Huntington hired W. H. Woodard, a correspondent for the *Los Angeles Times*, as his supposedly secret political agent.[140] Woodard described his job as "watching the friends of Senator Stanford both in and out of the Ry [Railway]." His terminology was quite exact. Like the Union Pacific, the Southern Pacific might seem to be a corporate bureaucracy, but its management was really networks of friends attached to one faction or another of its owners. There were, Woodard wrote, "Stanford men, Huntington men, Crocker men, and some railroad men."[141]

The coalition that had displaced Stanford fractured immediately. Charles F. Crocker, who liked to be called Colonel and whom Huntington pointedly called Fred, was the first vice-president, and the only Associate living permanently in San Francisco, and he aspired to be the Southern Pacific's president.[142] In the view of his many enemies, Fred Crocker could not see things in combination, and so he was incapable of having a plan. "I have never yet detected in his mind," Mills wrote Huntington, "an ability to perceive that what is accomplished makes the next step absolutely necessary and inevitable." One idea could displace another, but the two could not coexist or form a connection. "[H]is policies proceed from his stomach rather than from his brain." Huntington did not know how to handle him. "Sometimes he is alright, and a few hours after, without any apparent reason, he is all wrong."[143] Distrusting Crocker, Huntington initially relied on the second vice-president, A. N. Towne, who also remained the western general manager of the Southern Pacific.[144] Both Crocker's and Stanford's men regarded him as Huntington's "spy and detective upon all the others."[145]

The result was that rumor, innuendo, and gossip reigned in an utterly fragmented administration. Nothing could be accomplished expeditiously.[146] The departments "seem[ed] to be independent of each other with the head of each depending on his 'pull' with one or more of the owners."[147] The eastern and western segments of the company were under different management and quarreled incessantly. By March of 1893 A. C. Hutchinson of the Atlantic system was in a blood feud with Towne, infuriated by Pacific division trains that arrived chronically late in El Paso, the connecting point between the two great divisions. Making up time forced Hutchinson to run his trains at greater speed, which meant "increased expense & a great increase in chances of accidents."[148]

The energy of the executives went into eliminating their enemies.[149] Woodard wondered rhetorically, "Can it be expected that Mr. Charles Crocker will quietly submit to the removal of his men and confirm to the community here his inability to keep old and trusted officers in employ of the Company against Mr. Towne or, as they put it, Mr. Huntington?"[150] The answer was obviously no. Crocker and his allies systematically stripped Towne of responsibilities until, although general manager, he was left with only the operating department and some of its collateral branches. He had no authority over most coal purchases, and he lost control of the traffic department to J. C. Stubbs, who returned to the road at Huntington's behest and became third vice-president of the Southern Pacific Corporation. Towne retaliated by undermining Stubbs at every opportunity, which left Stubbs feeling betrayed by Huntington.[151]

This infighting took its toll on both the company and Towne. In February of 1893 Towne went to see Mills, broke down, and "continually wept . . . saying in measure that he had lost your [Huntington's] confidence."[152] And he had. Huntington blamed Towne for the road's difficulties. William

Mahl, the ultimate Huntington loyalist, was dismayed at how Towne ended up being regarded by both sides "with distrust and apprehension."[153] The quarrels spilled over into the press, where letters depicted Crocker as isolated and powerless.[154] The more powerless Crocker felt within the administration of the corporation, the more oppositional he became.[155] He had combined with Huntington and the Hopkins interests to oust Stanford, and now he moved to ally with Stanford to block Huntington. Huntington, in turn, denounced Crocker—he "opposes everything as his father did before him"—and softened toward Stanford, whom he wanted to "be in perfect accord with me [Huntington]—in short not interfere with my way of doing things."[156]

What seemed a single corporation was the tool of four men—and eventually four families—who grew increasingly divided, bitter, and distrustful. The Stanfords, Huntingtons, Crockers, and Hopkins/Searles interests could not disengage, because their fortunes were mingled in the Pacific Improvement Company, the descendant of the Contract and Finance Company and the Western Development Company.

In his unpublished memoir, William Mahl wrote of C. E. Bretherton's visit to Huntington sometime in the late 1880s. Bretherton was the representative of the English stockholders of the Central Pacific, who had watched their investment decline precipitously in value. Bretherton talked and Mahl "listened with much interest to a point of view of our people's affairs and practices held over there [i.e., in Great Britain] and complaints about its shortcomings." The main complaint was that the affairs of the Associates were arranged so that the Pacific Improvement Company, the Associates' insider construction and finance company, "took the cream and [left] only the skim milk for the railroads; also that the properties were not managed as corporations, but at the will and pleasure of individuals who filled certain positions."[157]

Bretherton cited as an example "Mr. Huntingtons [sic] office at Mills Building, 23, Broad Street." The names on the doors of the various offices bore only the name of the occupant, not of their corporate affiliation or position. Mahl—the designer of forms, the standardizer of stationery, the skilled auditor and accountant—might have been expected to bridle at such a description. Instead, he accepted it as true, but he argued that it was all for the best. What Bretherton failed to understand, Mahl insisted, was that all of the officials in the office "had in mind solely the interests of Mr. Huntington as an individual and affairs in which he was concerned, and that in all our acts, we always had in mind individual money for which we had a higher sense of responsibility than could be had for de-individualized money, that is, money which did not belong to any particular individual and towards which our sense of responsibility would be greatly diminished." This did not convince Bretherton, whose clients had good reason to think of Huntington as the Lisbon earthquake of American finance.[158]

Bretherton rightly identified the Pacific Improvement Company as the real source of the Associates' wealth. Its nickname within the Southern Pacific offices was the Personal Interest Company. Even if investors placed representatives on railroad boards, they did not know about the affairs of the PIC and other corporate entities critical to the railroads. The PIC held the securities of the Southern Pacific and Central Pacific; it controlled, either directly or indirectly, the construction of their roads and facilities and their subsidiary lines. It profited from their operations, and it was the private preserve of Huntington and the other Associates.

Mahl provided the best account of how the PIC worked. The PIC had no capital of its own. The Associates had provided the company with its initial capital through the usual mechanism of depositing cash, stocks, and bonds in its treasury, receiving interest in return. The PIC hypothecated the securities they had borrowed to raise the capital to build the Associates' railroads and other enterprise. Often they borrowed from the Central Pacific, which the PIC used as a bank. When the PIC had finished work, it was paid for its efforts in securities, which sometimes had little or no value at the time of issue. These securities were then equally distributed among the Associates and redeposited in the PIC.[159]

Taking low-value securities for expensive work might seem an unlikely road to wealth, but this was merely one in a series of transactions. Charles Bretherton gave an example of how PIC debt was turned into cash for the Associates as they continued the kinds of maneuvers they had perfected in the 1870s. The PIC borrowed money from the Central Pacific and, having run up a debt of over $4.5 million, settled by surrendering its collateral: largely Guatemala Central Railroad bonds—"property situated in a third rate Spanish-American republic"—and Southern Pacific Steamboat bonds. These bonds had no market value. The Associates thus received par value from the Central Pacific for bonds with no market value. When the bonds came due, the Central Pacific's board, still controlled by the Associates, did not demand their redemption, which might have caused difficulties. They instead agreed to extend them.[160]

The PIC usually had large debts but only limited liquid assets; cash tended to be drained off into the Associates accounts. In 1893 Mahl estimated it owed $36 million while claiming assets, most of them not liquid, of $90 million in securities, land, streetcar lines, hotels, waterworks, mines, ships, and railroads.[161] Because the PIC was leveraged and had so many illiquid assets, it performed something of a high-wire act that could be terrifying in times of financial crisis.[162]

The Southern Pacific was thus dysfunctional on multiple levels. Having established an administration in which "pull" determined which officials succeeded and which failed and then having multiple and dueling centers of power at the top—Huntington, Fred Crocker, and Stanford—the Southern Pacific reaped what it had sown.[163] The increasing chaos of the Southern Pacific's political operations did not stand in contrast to its corporate governance. It was a direct reflection of it.

The Blind Boss, Chris Buckley, had badly overstepped in the 1890 election. He had betrayed the Democrats to ensure a Republican legislature and Stanford's election. When Huntington took control of the Southern Pacific, he abandoned Buckley, and the Democrats also turned on the Blind Boss.[164] Even more critically, San Francisco businessmen turned on him. Their tool was the Wallace grand jury, impaneled by Judge William T. Wallace. The grand jury was illegally constituted and packed with anti-Buckley men. Some its members had studied under the Blind Boss, and they had learned well. Eventually, the California Supreme Court disbanded the grand jury and voided its indictments, but by then the indicted Buckley had departed San Francisco for "reasons of health." He went first to Canada and then to London. He eventually returned, but he never recaptured his old power.[165]

The departure of the Blind Boss and the arrival of Collis P. Huntington, who announced that he was getting the Southern Pacific out of politics, did not mean that the Southern Pacific would no longer use government to protect its interests. As Huntington put it, "I am out of politics, but I am not out of doing what I can for California, and I also expect in every way possible to protect the rights of the Railroad Comp'y."[166] The true interest of California, he also made clear, was "that of her great industrial interests."[167] Collis P. Huntington thus entered California politics while insisting that he was saying good-bye. Along with Buckley's actual farewell, that ended up creating three competing Southern Pacific political operations: Stanford's, Huntington's, and Crocker's. Their collective ineptitude in the 1890s ended the reign of the Octopus.

Only in fiction did the Octopus have a Shelgrim and a Behrman ruthlessly in charge. Norris's "galloping monster, the terror of steel and steam," was real enough, but when the Southern Pacific came barreling down the track, there was often only a group of fat men in an Octopus suit fighting over the controls.

A RAILROAD LIFE

WILLIAM MAHL

Illiam Mahl's unpublished memoir of a railroad life resides today in the University of Texas Archives. Its author was one of the country's first organization men, but the memoir is incomplete and haphazardly organized. Such organization as it possesses is based less on the systems Mahl worked for than on the leading men Mahl knew. Mahl worked for Albert Fink and Collis P. Huntington. He worked for Tom Scott; he worked for E. H. Harriman, the man who became the twentieth century's paramount railway tycoon. Mahl wrote his memoir as an old man, and there is an old man's air about it: the repetition, the stories tailing off so a reader turns the page only to find that there is nothing more. On the surface it is one of the blandest documents in the railroad archive. It is an accountant's memoir; it is a loyal corporate servant's memoir: a hagiographic account of the pleasures of working for Collis P. Huntington, a man, in Mahl's words, whose "strong personality, experience and good judgment had impressed itself upon all of us."[1]

On closer reading, however, both Mahl and his memoir become more interesting. Mahl morphs into a paradox: an enigmatic, bureaucratic Candide. His reader is left unsure whether the memoir is an artful construction—a wonderful satire—or whether it is hopelessly naïve.

Collis P. Huntington is the axis around which the memoir spins. Mahl typically told stories of Huntington's corruption, distrust, secretiveness, and vindictiveness to provide evidence of how he was wise, kind, and honorable. He described Huntington's creation of a slush fund to pay off politicians and then cited it to defend Huntington's honesty.[2] He illustrated Huntington's grasp of human nature with an anecdote of how Huntington kept Mahl from finding out about the desire of the Kansas and Texas to hire Mahl for a job that he very much wanted and that would have paid him more than Huntington did. Even when Huntington, thinking that Mahl had betrayed him, turned on him, Mahl remained devoted to him. "[B]y his suspicious nature," Mahl wrote, Huntington thought "that every man had his price," and he came to think that the Crocker and Stanford faction had discovered Mahl's price. But "[t]here was no occasion for Mr. Huntington to have ever doubted in the slightest degree my loyalty to him," Mahl wrote. And instead of being resentful, Mahl was pleased that before his death Huntington decided Mahl had, after all, been loyal.[3]

Such stories dominate the manuscript and overshadow Mahl's account of his career. The child of German liberals who fled the failed revolution of 1848 and settled in Texas, he entered the shops of the Louisville and Nashville Railroad in Bowling Green, Kentucky, as an apprentice. It was 1860, the brink of the Civil War, and Mahl was seventeen. Another German émigré, Albert Fink, was general superintendent of the road, and Mahl came to his attention. Although at first disdainful of "quill drivers," Mahl took a course in bookkeeping at Boyd's Commercial College and rose rapidly through the railroad ranks. By the end of the war he had begun his "inquiries into the cost of railway operations." His work allowed the Louisville and Nashville to begin to determine the cost of carrying passengers and freight.[4]

From the Louisville and Nashville, he went to the Lexington and Frankfort whose general superintendent sent him to Altoona and Philadelphia to study the methods of the "Pennsylvania Railroad Company . . . in those days considered as the highest type of working organization and in accounting for its expenses." On his return, he instituted Pennsylvania practices on the Lexington and Frankfort, which in 1869 merged with the Louisville and Frankfort to become the Louisville, Cincinnati, and Lexington.[5]

Mahl's early career trajectory thus conformed nicely to the Chandlerian narrative of how economic rationality and efficiency came to the railroads, but only to a point. It diverged when Collis P. Huntington entered the picture. Huntington had built his career on deceiving others, manipulating railroad finances, and running overcapitalized corporations about whose day-to-day operations he knew little. He assumed that this was how all railroads were run, and when he acquired the Louisville, Cincinnati, and Lexington as part of his Chesapeake and Ohio system, he set to work to find the particular corruption that explained why that road's operating expenses were such a high proportion of its revenue. There was no corruption—only competitive local conditions from other railroads and river transportation—but Mahl could never convince him of that. Mahl left the road, and Huntington installed new managers who promised to get operating expenses down to 50 percent of revenue. And they did by crediting themselves with revenue they did not really have and by not paying bills that they did have. Mahl predicted it would take about twenty-four months for their accounting practices to catch up with them. And two years later the railroad went into receivership, along with the rest of Huntington's Chesapeake and Ohio system.[6] Instituting the methods and forms of the Pennsylvania did not necessarily create an honest or efficient railroad.

Mahl returned to Kentucky in 1874, and in February of 1882 Huntington hired him and brought him to New York as a general agent to look after his properties in the lower Mississippi valley and the West. The work was not glamorous. In May of 1883 Mahl was writing to Huntington comparing the cost of the printed stationery forms used on the Central Pacific and explaining how costs could be reduced substantially by changing paper quality, creating a standard system, and printing the forms in large lots.[7] Such things were Mahl's talent, but Mahl also was, within the moral universe of the corporation, an honest man. Huntington wanted an honest man precisely because Huntington was dishonest and thought most other men were like him. Huntington believed he was being cheated by the small roads he had acquired in Louisiana and Texas to finish the Southern Pacific. He had a great deal of money invested there, and everybody seemed to be getting money out of these roads but him. He sent Mahl down to find out "what is the matter." Mahl found more than fraud; he found accounting techniques that concealed as much as they revealed and could only confuse managers and lenders to the detriment of the road. His solution was systematization, clarity, and surveillance. Managers of subsidiary roads had to know that Huntington was watching them.[8]

Mahl believed in good accounting. During the Civil War he "began to appreciate that accounting, for which up to this time [he] had but little appreciation, could be developed as a science for the supervision and control of the operations of a railway and that good accounting could be synonymous with good management." Good management depended on good information.[9] It was in part a matter of the correct form. In 1885 Mahl issued the first annual reports for Huntington's Texas roads and for the Chesapeake and Ohio. He eventually expanded this evolving format, piece by piece, to the Southern Pacific. His reports "gave the reader a clear and comprehensive account of the Company's affairs and condition." Such reports remained rare in American railroading.[10]

These reforms took time. Into the 1890s there was still little in the annual reports of the Southern Pacific that allowed an investor or a banker to see "the relation of [the] two divisions [east and west of El Paso] to their capitalization."[11] Mahl ordered and clarified the statistics. He not only tried to make finances more transparent to the public, he also gathered and organized internal data in ways that showed managers the consequences of different strategies. He prepared charts showing how much the Southern Pacific lost through decreases in rates as against how much was gained by the increase of traffic at lower rates.[12]

What he preached in the 1860s, however, he found it still necessary to preach in the 1890s when he acknowledged, "Good accounting is rapidly becoming synonymous with good management, and the successful railroad manager of to-day appreciates that fact that good accounting is essential to good discipline and results." He still had to use "becoming" rather than "has become."[13] The trouble with good accounting and transparent reporting was that it made visible, to railroad commissions and investors, what the railroad wished to be invisible.[14] This was why the practices railroad men encouraged with one hand, they sometimes blocked with the other.

But the corollary of good accounting for Mahl was not the hegemony of accountants or the centralization of authority in the accounting department; accounting was necessary, but not sufficient, for good management. An efficient railroad required not just good information but an administrative system with clear lines of responsibility that could make use of that information. Railroads needed to give managers both authority to innovate and responsibility for the results. Accounting allowed results to be tabulated and tracked. Accountants were to be subordinate to managers. Mahl wanted each department to have its own staff of accountants with "the head of the department free to collect, for his information, any special data in respect to cost, services, etc., which he deemed desirable, and in whatever manner suited him best." The auditor coordinated the accounting of the various departments by prescribing "the manner and method, in which the accounts to be rendered by them to the Accounting Department shall be met." Mahl was proud of the order that he brought to the corporate accounts and books of the Southern Pacific, but the struggle was ongoing. He was creating small islands of order in a railroad sea of disorder. In the early twentieth century he would be appalled by the books of the Union Pacific system when, under Harriman, he was placed in charge of those accounts.[15]

All of this can seem reassuring. Professionalization, standardization, and efficiency increased with the growing scale of the economy and the corporations that dominated it. Honesty came as a necessary by-product. Information had to be accurate and transparent if managers were to manage the system effectively. Mahl was not a glamorous figure. His career was not exciting, but the end result seemed impressive and reassuring. Yet, to say that railroad professionals were displacing the old financiers was going too far.[16] Like everything in Mahl's memoir, this drive for transparency and efficiency had troubling paradoxes. Mahl's larger goal was not operational efficiency, but rather financing. "The operations of a railway," he admitted, "interested me only insofar as I could marshal their earnings or assets as the basis of additional credit on which to borrow money to extend its enterprises."[17]

Mahl was personally honest, but he was only tactically honest as a servant of Huntington and the Southern Pacific. Mahl's job was not to protect the interests of investors. It was to protect the interests of Collis P. Huntington. The reports of the Southern Pacific and Central Pacific remained transparent only to a point. Investors might know the affairs of the railroads more clearly than ever before, but they did not know the affairs of other corporate entities critical to the railroads. The Pacific Improvement Company, which was so involved in the operations of the Central Pacific and Southern

Pacific, which held their securities, and profited from their operations, was the private preserve of Huntington and the other Associates.[18]

Mahl's duty was to "guard well the things that were committed to [him]." He tried to avoid the necessity of withholding information and lying by making a point of never knowing more than he needed to know and of never stating things too definitely.[19] When he wrote or spoke, he learned to read and speak like Huntington. When asked to draft a circular on the jurisdiction of high officials in the Southern Pacific, he "succeeded in the master's art of using 'flexible' terms." Huntington "did not like expressions or terms which were definite except under certain circumstances and conditions, and inclined to phrases which were susceptible of modification in construction."[20] This was actually an admirable tactic for instructing managers. It was less useful for describing financial affairs.

In figures such as Mahl the complications and ambiguities of nineteenth-century corporations appear. He was both a corporate modernizer and a man who contributed, sometimes brilliantly, to subverting the interests of the corporation while advancing that of its owners. He was no more a stage in the evolution of the corporate bureaucrat than the Southern Pacific was a stage in the evolution of the corporation.

There was a second Mahl in the railroad archives and, briefly, in Mahl's memoir. Mahl's youngest son, John Thomas, also chose a railroad life. John Thomas reflected the changes that professionalization did bring to the railroads. His father had begun as a young apprentice; John Thomas graduated as a civil engineer from Columbia University. But the old networks of friendship and kinship so apparent on the early railroads still held. He became engineer of maintenance of way on the Southern Pacific's lines east of El Paso, and then chief engineer of construction. He named his first son after his father.[21]

The kind of tension between railroad generations apparent in Charles Francis Adams's dealings with his younger subordinates appeared within the Mahl family in the letters between father and son. William thought his son extravagant. John Thomas was, apparently, borrowing money from his father to invest in Mexican railroad bonds. William, the apostle of order and predictability, lectured John Thomas on the uncertainty and unpredict-ability of life and railroads. John Thomas's sister, Alice, was tubercular and fragile, and that only increased William Mahl's anxiety over the dangers of life. John Thomas tried to be dutiful and obedient. He, after all, owed his position to his father.[22]

Mahl's letters read like the nagging, inevitably condescending letters of a father asserting authority over a son; they are a mixture of love and admonition, but in hindsight they became something else. The letters were premonitions of a train of disasters. John Thomas's wife died suddenly of appendicitis, leaving him with two young children. Her death caused John Thomas's own tuberculosis to worsen at a time when his father was bedrid-den with typhoid fever. John Thomas went to Phoenix for the desert air, but kept the news from his ailing father. When his parents found out, his mother went to Phoenix and found him so ill that she put him on a train to take back to New York to see specialists, but his heart failed. He died on the train in North Carolina on March 30, 1901. He was thirty-one years old.[23]

His mother took his personal effects, and there is, presumably as John Thomas left it, a relic of his railroad life, frozen in time in the University of Texas Archives. It is a small wallet embossed with the name J. T. Mahl. William Mahl preserved it with his own personal papers. The wallet became a professional life reduced to its ephemera.

There was a reminder of the dangers of the work, and perhaps a gesture toward his father's cautions: a card that reads, "In case of wholly disabling or fatal accident immediately notify Kimball C. Atwood, Secy. of the Preferred Accident Insurance Company of New York, 256 & 257 Broadway, N.Y. Signed J. T. Mahl, Houston, Texas, policy no. 216848."

There was a pass for the year 1900 on the Houston and Texas Central for Mr. J. T. Mahl, Car & Party. There were numerous cards granting franking privileges or free telegrams on Western Union, and then there were more railroad passes.

A pass for the Houston East & West Texas, expires Dec. 31, 1900
A pass on the St. Louis Southwestern Railway, Cotton Belt Route, 1900

A pass on the Houston and Shreveport Railroad Company, 1900

A pass on the San Antonio and Gulf Railroad, the Alamo Route, 1900

A pass on the San Antonio & Aransas [sic] Pass Railway, the Mission Route, 1900

A pass on the Southern Pacific, Sunset route

A pass for the Southern Pacific Company, Pacific system

A pass on the St. Louis Southwestern Railway company of Texas

These latter passes were for 1901, longer than J. T. Mahl's life would last. Going through them is like picking a dead man's pocket.[24]

CHAPTER 7

❧⟶⟨⟨⟩⟩⟵❧

WORKINGMEN

*We complain that our rulers, statesmen and orators have not
attempted to engraft republican principles into our industrial
system, and have forgotten or denied
its underlying principles.*[1]

—GEORGE McNEILL, 1877

N 1880 A. E. Touzalin, then the general manager of the Burlington and
Missouri, published an unsigned letter in the *Nation*. "Out West," he
wrote, "where we have the Grange element to contend with and a middle
class who rise to political power through the injustice and prejudices of the
Grange element, we especially need the moral support and political help of
our men in all contests against corporations. We do not get this support by
merely paying daily wages earned." He emphasized, "There is no business
or profession where the interests of the employer and the employed should
be more closely identified. There is none where this is less the case than is to
be found on most of our Western roads." Citing the extraordinary demands
put on railroad men in the West, where the "strain on the nervous system is
severe," he suggested insurance plans, special loan funds for home purchase,
reading rooms, and hospitals.[2]

Charles Francis Adams endorsed these proposals, becoming an advocate of what would later be known as welfare capitalism. In its heyday in the early twentieth century, it was a prescription for defeating unions. And, in part, that was Touzalin's aim. Touzalin thought that hospitals and insurance plans would wean workers away from their own organizations, particularly the railroad brotherhoods, one of whose great appeals was the insurance that they offered. The suggestion for reading rooms carried with it not only the whiff of uplift but a quite specific attachment to the YMCA, which following the great railroad strike of 1877 created its Railroad Department with substantial funding from the roads. The YMCA sought to undercut a working-class culture of drink, camaraderie, and a tough manliness and replace it with a more restrained, Christian culture of manhood geared toward individual self-improvement. This vision of a working class was not all that different from the cultural goals of the Knights of Labor, but the YMCA intended its policies to undercut political radicalism, prevent strikes, and merge the workers' interests with those of the corporation.[3] The suggestion that corporations aid their workers in buying homes went to a conviction that family men with property at risk would be more conservative, more reluctant to strike, and more willing to support the corporations than workers with less at risk.

But Touzalin's main worry, and a legitimate one, was an antimonopoly alliance against the railroads that would include their own workers. Such an alliance became the explicit goal of both the Knights of Labor and the Farmers' Alliance. Touzalin knew that his suggestions would not be popular among many western railroad men. He most likely wrote anonymously because he anticipated, and feared, the reaction of Charles Perkins, soon to become president of the Burlington system. Perkins did suspect that Touzalin was the author and predictably dismissed the letter as "rubbish." Equally predictably he sought to "kill this seed before it sprouts." Perkins was an intellectual troglodyte who reduced everything to the "laws of supply and demand." He believed in the "discovery and fixing of economic truth." Although he could be surprisingly flexible in actual labor negotiations, he opposed the suggestion that the company had any obligations toward or interests in its employees beyond the wages it paid them for the work it received.[4]

Touzalin, however, was a practical man who knew that the railroads could not afford to be indifferent to their workers' politics and social life. He knew that the railroads depended on politics and thus on workers' votes as well as their labor. Although Perkins saw in Touzalin's suggestions a taint of obligation, Touzalin meant something else. The railroads did favors for political friends; they had to make friends of their workers, too.

Charles Francis Adams had passed on Touzalin's letter to the *Nation* both because he, too, prided himself on being a practical man and because Touzalin's suggestions corresponded to his wider Comtean beliefs. In 1865 Adams had chanced on an essay by John Stuart Mill, the English utilitarian, on Auguste Comte, the French founder of positivism. Adams claimed, "[T]hat essay of Mill's revolutionized in a single morning my whole mental attitude." He went from "the theological stage, in which [he] had been nurtured, and . . . into the scientific."[5] Mill's essay was both a sympathetic account of Comte and a critique that sought to blend Comte's positivism with a defense of the very nineteenth-century liberalism and the eighteenth-century revolutionary tradition that Comte hated. Mill threw out some of Comte's more cracked social theories but retained Comte's positivism, which recognized that "all phaenomena without exception are governed by invariable laws, with which no volitions, either natural or supernatural, interfere." What Adams seems to have taken away was an odd unstable mix, as much Mill as Comte.[6]

Adams's intellectual life became an ongoing series of amendments, exceptions, and additions to what he took to be a founding Comtean charter. Mill allowed Adams to remain in many ways a quintessential liberal who envisioned society as composed of autonomous subjects each seeking advantage. When he thought workers on the Union Pacific were acting too collectively and taking the brotherhood of man too seriously, for example, he recommended countermeasures to encourage "individuality among the workers."[7] Mill, however, also allowed Adams to combine this liberalism with his sense that organizations were replacing individuals as basic social units. Progress would come from recognizing the laws of human society. Adams adjusted easily enough to the idea that cultivated minds would lead human society in recognizing these laws, never doubting that his mind was among the most cultivated. But whereas Comte dismissed laissez-faire and the "so-called rights of the individual"—the hallmarks of Gilded Age liberalism—as purely "metaphysical," Adams, reading Comte through Mill, could hold on to them as corollaries to social laws, an "inference from the laws of human nature and human affairs." He could have both his liberalism and his positivism.[8]

Social laws yielded for Adams a constrained individualism; instead of blindly pursuing self-interest, humans in society would seek the "cooperation of mankind one with another, by the division of employments and interchange of commodities and services." Human society, in short, sounded a lot like a railroad corporation. Cooperation was the source of progress; and it reached its fulfillment when "the true methods of positive science were applied to society."[9] In Mill's view the market might be a temporary practical necessity for settling workers' share of production, but it was certainly not a moral ideal, and society was striving for a moral ideal whose model was the military, since until "laborers and employers perform the work of industry in the spirit in which soldiers perform that of any army, industry will never be moralized and military life will remain . . . the chief school of moral cooperation."[10]

Adams, too, regarded the dominance of the market as but a phase of human existence and looked elsewhere for principles of social organization. In the late nineteenth century progressive liberals like Mill as well as radical writers like Edward Bellamy, who borrowed heavily from the Knights of Labor, praised the army as a social model. This stress on cooperation and the unwillingness to see the market as a template for society distanced Adams from Perkins, but ideals of a cooperative society based on military analogies, particularly when embraced by ex-military officers, conveyed a rather constricted view of cooperation.

A corporate officer commanding laborers had a more sanguine view of the army of labor than did the actual laborer. According to the military analogy, workers were soldiers and their job was to take orders. They had no control over their work, how it was done, or when it was to be performed. In selling their labor, they had passed through a filter that negated the social rules that governed the rights and duties of republican citizenship. They became a different kind of being; they were no longer, in the workers' terms, men. Their opinions did not matter. They were to do what they were told. Conditions they would never accept in their civic or public life were to be the conditions of their working lives. Employers might be benevolent, but that was the employers' decision.

I. CONTROL OF WORK

When Touzalin wrote about the extraordinary demands the railroads put on the nervous systems of workers and recommended insurance and hospitals, he was writing elliptically about the details of work. The details of work killed men. Long hours and dangerous work produced deaths and injuries. The Kansas Pacific monthly reports during the 1870s made the human cost just an addendum to calculations of monthly revenues. The juxtaposition makes for odd reading, but it did quite literally, if inadvertently, measure in blood the cost of profit. The net earnings of the Kansas Pacific main line and Leavenworth branch in December of 1877 were $80,440.46. Then came the casualties. On December 1, Michael Menahaw, a brakeman on train number 6, was thrown from the top of the car by a sudden motion of the train while switching at Junction City, Kansas. He bruised his right arm and hip. Cornelious (*sic*) Anderson, a colored brakeman in the steel rail gang, was thrown from a handcar and run over on December 7. The car passed over him, seriously injuring his back and hip. On December 13, Edward Smith, another brakeman on train number 6, had his hand mashed in making a coupling near Mirage, Kansas. "The coupling was a difficult one to make on account of one of the cars being a foreign one. The brakeman had but two fingers on his hand and had his lantern on his arm, which doubtless contributed to the accident." It was also doubtless that Smith had already lost his other fingers in a previous accident. The absence of one or more fingers was a mark of a brakeman. On December 23, "E. A. Morphy brakeman on no. 8 fell between first car and engine as train was pulling into a siding. As he attempted to step from ladder into the engine tender, he slipped, the tender being covered with frost, and fell between the car and the tender." Luckily, the engineer saw him fall, and reversed engine, so that the train did not run over him. Morphy suffered severe bruises.[11]

The monthly injury lists—men falling from cars, hands mashed coupling cars, men crushed between cars or scalded by steam—became monotonous. Only the names changed.[12] Most were injured, but some, like John Retsorf, died.[13] A single miscalculation, a single piece of bad luck, a single piece of faulty equipment, and a world of horrors ensued. John Retsorf—at least that is how his name was rendered by a clerk who never knew him—was a worker on the Kansas Pacific who on October 11, 1877, was switching trains in Hugo, Colorado. He "stepped in between the second and third cars from the engine to uncouple them, and in running along between the cars his foot caught between the rails, dragging him under and between the cars, which ran over him, cutting off both feet and lower part of legs, and crushing left hand, arm, and shoulder." Imagine him there. One moment a man was doing his ordinary work, the next moment his feet were lying separate from his body and blood spouted from his legs. "He was immediately sent to Denver by special train where an amputation of his legs and arm was performed. He survived several days after the amputation and hopes were entertained of his recovery, but in this we were disappointed as he died on Oct. 24."[14]

Coupling cars was a detail of work, as was setting the brake on a moving train; these were details to which only workers gave much attention. In 1890, the first year the Interstate Commerce Commission gathered reliable statistics, roughly half of the 9 percent of all trainmen who were injured annually were hurt coupling cars. The chief culprit was the drawbar. A drawbar was a simple mechanism used to attach one car to another. *The Car Builder's Dictionary* defined it as "[a]n open-mouthed bar at the end of the car in which the coupling links enter and are secured by a coupling pin."[15] Its design forced brakemen or yardmen to place their bodies between railroad cars and put their hands between couplers to insert a pin as they came together.

It is astonishing how long the primitive and dangerous link and pin technology survived. In 1887 the Yard Master's Mutual Benefit Association sent out a flier to railway officials whose preamble began,

Whereas the old style of link and pin coupling has for the past forty years not merely subjected yardmen and brakemen to extra hazardous risk in the perfor-

mance of their respective railroad duties, but has been the direct cause of death
and accident to many thousands of railroad employees, thereby entailing on their
unhappy families widespread misery and other incalculable misfortunes . . .[16]

Automatic couplers had been available since the 1870s, and some states
began requiring them in the 1880s. With automatic couplers kept in good
repair, virtually all coupling accidents were preventable. The railroads' own
tests of safety couplers demonstrated this.[17] The railroads, however, refused
to rush adoption. They continued to maim and kill to avoid expense and the
difficulty of standardizing equipment. The Northern Pacific responded to
dangerous technologies and faulty equipment with convoluted statements
of the obvious. "The coupling apparatus of Cars . . . is liable to be broken,
and as, from various causes, it is dangerous to expose between the same the
hands, arms, or persons of those engaged in coupling. . . ." They admonished
their workers to be careful and warned that the common requirements of
railroad work—getting between moving cars, stepping upon the front or
rear of moving engines—were strictly prohibited and done "at their own
peril and risk." The Northern Pacific banned unnecessary whistle blowing
on the Sabbath and profane language any day, but it slaughtered workers
day in and day out.[18]

Brakes ranked second only to drawbars in the dangers that they presented. Initially railroads stopped trains by means of a series of mechanical
brakes mounted on top of cars. Brakemen moved along the roofs of the cars
setting and releasing the brakes by turning wheels at each end of the car
according to commands communicated by the train's whistle. To brake a
train properly required considerable skill. A brakeman had to apply light or
medium pressure. Tighten a wheel too hard, and wheels skidded, flattening
the wheel but not effectively slowing the train.[19] A brakeman could not simply tighten the brakes and move on. The Northern Pacific told its brakemen
never to leave a brake on for more than three minutes since it damaged the
wheel. Instead, they were to move back and forth from car to car setting and
releasing the brakes. This was difficult in good weather when they needed to
have one eye out for tunnels, bridges, and beams in snowsheds that might
knock them from the cars; it was near suicidal on a winter night in the

mountains with below zero temperatures, ice on the cars, the wind blowing, and the snow falling. Realistically a brakeman could control only three cars, but most freights never had this level of staffing.[20]

But the issue of automatic brakes bared the complexities involved in purely technical solutions. George Westinghouse in 1869 developed an automatic brake relying on compressed air that allowed an engineer to stop an entire train with a lever in the locomotive. The system also automatically set the brakes on a runaway car. Because air brakes could stop short trains quickly and reliably, they allowed increased speed. The possibility of more safety and greater speed, in turn, increased consumer pressure for their use on passenger trains. Brakes, not more powerful locomotives, initially made passenger trains faster.[21]

Automatic braking systems came much more slowly to freights. In 1883 the Northern Pacific mandated a maximum speed of 18 miles per hour for its freights, and it only slowly and gradually introduced air brakes in the late 1880s. Charles Perkins of the Burlington resisted automatic brakes on freights because increases in speed would allow more wear on tracks and equipment, further increasing costs. Also, until all railroads adopted automatic brakes, the interchange of freight cars between lines added time and expense to switching trains. Workers had to sort the cars with air brakes to put them all at the front of the train so that their hoses could be connected to each other and the locomotive.[22] All of this assumed that the brakes on cars interchanged with another line were actually functioning and in good repair. To be forced to pay royalties to Westinghouse, who adroitly used the patent system to achieve a near-monopoly, and then to endure these difficulties added insult to injury.

The far western railroads began to put air brakes on their freight trains in the 1880s because much of the terrain they traversed was mountainous with relatively steep grades.[23] Steep grades kept trains shorter and obviated one of the problems with air brakes, which stopped long trains unevenly, causing the rear cars to jerk, shudder, and sometimes jump the tracks. The roads did not, however, place full faith in the automatic systems, which were hard to maintain. They still employed brakemen who could set hand brakes in an emergency. As L. S. Anderson explained after an Idaho freight's air brakes failed and it plowed into another, the fault lay with the brakemen since air brakes were "likely" to fail "at any time," and experienced "[t]rain men certainly should be able to control a train with the hand-brake, if they are attending properly to duty."[24]

By the early 1890s there was considerable pressure in state legislatures to mandate both automatic couplers and air brakes on all cars, and when statistics gathered by the new Interstate Commerce Commission made the toll of accidents visible, the carnage became too much even for conservative politicians to accept. In 1893, the year the first national safety legislation for the railroads was enacted by Congress, 1,567 trainmen died and 18,877 were injured. Senator Henry Cabot Lodge of Massachusetts thought the failure of railroads to prevent such accidents amounted to inhumanity. It was as if, Lodge wrote, the casualties from the bloody Civil War battle of Shiloh were exacted from railroad workers year after year. The battle analogy was gripping and deceptive. It encouraged people to think that the dead and injured accumulated by hundreds in spectacular accidents instead of incrementally, day by day. If work was war, it was closer to the guerrilla conflicts of the twentieth and twenty-first centuries than to the Civil War. As the details of the Kansas Pacific reports indicated, workers died and were injured in mundane and predictable ways as fragile human bodies worked to control moving machines.[25]

The companies resisted any attempt by Congress to legislate technological standards, but resistance to implementing new technologies did not rest solely with the corporations; in the case of brakes, workers also suspected the new technology.[26] Railroad brakemen had good reason to distrust technological fixes. To work properly, automatic breaking systems had to be regularly inspected and kept in good repair, but the law mandated only the gradual addition of cars with automatic brakes; it did not mandate inspection and regular service. Nor did many brakemen have the technical skills to inspect the often complicated mechanisms themselves.[27] Automatic brakes therefore potentially threatened to diminish the number of brakemen's jobs without increasing safety. In response, skilled workers continued to rely on manual brakes while stressing the virtues of experience over a naïve reliance on technology. For the brakemen the technology was secondary. The real battle was over control of work: who would decide on change, and how would it be implemented?

II. THE KNIGHTS OF LABOR

In his belief that the current conditions of industrial capitalism were but a passing phase, Charles Francis Adams was close to a man who was his, and other railroad men's, nemesis—Joseph Buchanan. Railroad officials considered Buchanan far more dangerous than Terence Powderly, the Knights of Labor's grand workman, who was, they thought, able and "very conservative in his views."[28]

In the 1880s Buchanan lived in Denver, where he was an editor and a labor leader. The closest he seems to have ever come to a direct meeting with Adams was on July 14, 1885, when Adams visited Denver as president of the Union Pacific Railway. That evening there was a meeting—a séance Adams called it—between the executive board of the Knights of Labor in Denver, of which Buchanan was a leading member, and Adams. Adams found the Denver executive board distasteful. It had a strong "hoodlum" element. Three or four of them, he thought, could "not be dealt with in any reasonable way. They have got to be bought if they can not be broken down." But he didn't meet Buchanan, who was probably in Canada attending the general assembly of the Knights.[29]

Although a provincial city, Denver was, like the rest of western North America, the product of global capital flows, global markets, and global labor migrations. And it was no more isolated intellectually than it was economically. In 1885 both Adams and his absent adversary Buchanan drank from international streams of political and social thought and mixed the results in a way that was thoroughly American.[30]

Born in Hannibal, Missouri, Joseph Buchanan was no more systematic a thinker than Charles Francis Adams, but he too ordered his economic thinking around a larger cultural ideal of cooperation. He was, like Henry George, whom he admired, a typesetter, turned newspaperman, turned publisher, radical intellectual, and organizer. He was very much a sentimental Victorian, who wrote of his having to talk to his wife by the light of an open stove door to conserve the last two candles so that he could set type. But such Victorian touches often came with a western accent, as when his wife met him at the Denver railroad station with pistols in her purse to protect him from a lynch mob. Buchanan was a radical, but a rather catholic one whose mind functioned as a kind of hotel where any, and it sometimes seemed all, of the advanced ideas circulating among workingmen in the 1880s could find lodging. He believed deeply in the solidarity of the working class, but he was also a racist prone to vicious ravings against Chinese workers. He was nominally an anarchist who for a period printed the current cost of dynamite on the masthead of the *Labor Enquirer*, but he was against propaganda by the deed—violence—and for political organization. His idea of anarchism amounted to little more than an attraction to a cooperative society, and he was more consistently a socialist. He himself was a teetotaler who unfortunately and flamboyantly fell off the wagon at the 1885 Knight's convention in Hamilton, Ontario, giving his enemies within the Knights—whose internal politics were as vicious as those of the railroads—an opportunity to secure his expulsion from the national executive board for actions unworthy of a Knight. Although banished as a drunk (which he was not), he could nevertheless be a proud, self-righteous moralist, which did not make his relationship with the head of the Knights, Terence Powderly, who could be as priggish as any man on the planet, any easier. But Buchanan could also be a pragmatist, a skilled negotiator, and a superb strategist who knew what was possible and what was not.[31]

By the time that Adams ascended to the presidency of the Union Pacific, bringing with him his paternalist program, the Knights already dominated the road, thanks to Joseph Buchanan, who embraced that organization's Gilded Age incarnation of American republicanism and the ideal of "citizen-as-producer and producer-as-citizen."[32] When the general manager of the time, Silas Clark, had cut wages on the Union Pacific in the spring of 1884, the men in the Denver shops had gone to Buchanan and asked for aid. Buchanan helped them organize the Union Pacific Employe's (*sic*) Protective Association. Within days the UPEPA spread down the line. When Clark, falsely claiming that the wage cut was not his idea, backed down, success brought in more recruits. Buchanan led the UPEPA into the Knights. The

Union Pacific violated the May agreement, fired leaders of the UPEPA, and instituted a second wage cut, but the machinists again struck, and Buchanan negotiated another victory.[33]

In 1884 and 1885, as Adams struggled to right the wobbly Union Pacific, the Knights of Labor seemed unstoppable in the West. In February of 1885 Jay Gould cut wages of the men in the Wabash Railway shops by 10 percent. This followed a 10 percent cut the preceding fall on the Missouri, Kansas, and Texas, and it precipitated a strike on the Wabash and eventually on the Missouri Pacific and the Missouri, Kansas, and Texas. The Denver Knights, fearing a Gould victory could endanger their gains, funded an organizing drive led by Buchanan that created new Knights assemblies along the Missouri Pacific from Kansas City to St. Louis. Gould retreated and rescinded the wage cuts. When Gould's managers reneged on the March agreement, Buchanan forced Gould to concede again in September of 1885. Not all strikes were successful. A strike Buchanan opposed on the Denver and Rio Grande failed in the spring and summer of 1885, but the victories over Gould helped instigate a boom for the Knights of Labor, whose numbers nationally had spiked from 111,000 in 1885 to 729,000 by July 1, 1886.[34] Buchanan had made the Union Pacific the most thoroughly unionized railroad in the country. In 1885 Adams estimated that of the 15,000 employees of the Union Pacific, 10,000 were members of the Knights of Labor, with more in the skilled brotherhoods.[35]

Adams was unusual in that he met with the Knights and negotiated with them, even though he regarded their complaints as "few and trivial."[36] The "trivial" complaints involved issues of seniority, the discharge of men for belonging to the Knights of Labor, the reinstatement of men following a strike, uneven restoration of wages, work rules, injuries on the job, and the like. It was typical of Adams that he carefully investigated these complaints. He found that the Knights' accounts were by and large true and that his foremen had lied.[37]

For workers, seniority, wages, hiring and firing, and safety were hardly trivial; they were the bread and butter of union politics. Labor shortages in the West had allowed workers to sustain a regional advantage in pay into the 1880s, and when railroads squeezed them, as they did in both Canada and the United States, they organized to maintain their early advantages. Doing so demanded a say in the details of work.[38] When Adams resolved the difficulties presented to him, the Knights considered him friendly.[39]

Adams, for his part, saw himself conceding particular points but not general principles. He recognized that what was at stake in his dealings with the unions was whether management or "labor organizations" would be "controlling the operations of the road."[40] He conciliated the workers, but he still considered them vicious children. He feared and deprecated them. They still considered the company, if not Adams, their enemy. Adams was shocked to find the depth his own workers' hatred of the corporation, particularly in Wyoming. By 1886 Adams had concluded that the Union Pacific's workers in Wyoming were "peculiarly rough, lawless and undesirable."[41] His new general manager, S. R. Callaway, who succeeded Clark in 1885, wrote Adams that at the Rawlins shops the Knights demanded the reinstatement of a man who had told the foreman to go to hell when instructed to clean up around his bench. At Carbon, Wyoming, the scene of trouble since the fall of 1884 when the company had discharged coal miners for joining the Knights of Labor, the men were still out on strike at the beginning of 1885 because, so Callaway claimed, the company would not discharge "all Finlanders and Chinese." At Laramie the foreman came to meet Callaway "with his head all mashed up." When he "remonstrated with the men" about a task they had not done, "they set upon him and hit him over the head with a bolt." The "bully" wielding the bolt had already gained "eminent distinction of having fought a bull dog on his knees with both hands tied behind him." Callaway did not "know how it would be possible to bring about a greater state of demoralization than that which seems to exist today. There seems to have been no care whatever, [sic] taken in the selection of the employes."[42] Isaac Bromley, whom Adams hired and dispatched west in 1885, reported "a hostile attitude to the Company" and that "jealousy, distrust and suspicion, in all matters proceeds upon the assumption that the Company is greedy, avaricious, and tyrannical, with no interests in common with its employees, but on the contrary determined to oppress and crush them." Bromley thought that "a man's employment by the Company is proof prima facie . . . of his hostility to its management."[43] And in the kind of surrogate manliness that often appeared in railroad correspondence, Callaway telegrammed his satisfaction at the Knights' encountering Pinkertons in Cheyenne, Wyoming, and backing down when "confronted with large number [of] sixfooters with Winchester rifles."[44]

What made the Knights particularly dangerous was what Touzalin had feared: their links to antimonopoly politics. Buchanan was a Colorado delegate to the Antimonopoly Conference of 1883, which eventually led to the Greenback-Labor Party, and in 1884 he had run the Colorado campaign of General Benjamin Butler, presidential candidate on the Greenback-Labor ticket. That campaign failed badly in Colorado. He later led the drive to organize Colorado's workers around the Prohibition Party in 1886.[45]

The strength of antimonopoly sentiment in Colorado and elsewhere, however, could not be gauged by tallying third-party votes. Antimonopolists never successfully united under a single party, but voters did back antimonopoly candidates who were present in all the parties. A series of streams instead of a single river, antimonopoly politics became ubiquitous, linked, and incredibly fluid. Adams got a better sense of antimonopoly strength in Colorado and the depth of antirailroad feeling when in 1885 he asked the Union Pacific's lawyers to investigate the company's legal and political options in dealing with a potential strike in Colorado. Adams wanted a military force to suppress strikes, but he learned there was too much antimonopoly sentiment in the West to depend on state aid, and inadequate grounds for demanding federal aid. A. J. Poppleton, the Union Pacific's lead attorney in the West, outlined the issues. The Knights had enemies in Colorado—Buchanan was not paranoid in his fear of lynch mobs—but they also had considerable popular support. Theoretically the governor of Colorado had the power to suppress a "mob" or a "riot," and the laws seemed broad enough for Poppleton to equate a strike with a riot, "but when it comes to work them out practically there may be more difficulty experienced" because in Colorado public sympathy was with the strikers. Federal law was more promising. The federal government had the power to suppress "insurrection, violence, unlawful combination, or conspiracy" against the laws of the United States. Unfortunately for the Union Pacific, antimonopoly forces in Congress had, in the wake of the Great Strike of

1877, passed an act making it unlawful "to employ any part of the army of the U.S. as a posse comitatis [*sic*]" except when expressly authorized by the Constitution or by an act of Congress. This created "much difficulty," but Poppleton thought that the charter of the Union Pacific, an act of Congress requiring the railroad to carry U.S. mail and other government freight, created an opening for the use of federal troops. Adams was willing to go further. If the rationale for bringing in troops to protect the property on which the government held a lien failed, he would bankrupt the road and put it into the hands of the courts, which could then call on the federal government to suppress the strike.[46]

The difficulty the railroads faced was abundantly clear in the Knights' triumph over the Missouri Pacific. Workers had beaten Gould in 1885 not only because the brotherhoods of skilled workers, the shopmen, and less skilled workers who flocked to the Knights had united but also because they had curtailed violence and brought local and state government officials to their side. Strikes were political, and public opinion mattered. Violence cost workers sympathy, and the violence of workers could never match the violence of the state. To eschew violence was not to eschew force. Workers went beyond persuasion: boycotts, threats, the killing of engines, and physical barricades were all tactics that approached violence but did not involve the physical attacks on scabs or Pinkertons that often brought disaster. If there was going to be a resort to violence, then the winning side would be the one whose use of force was legitimated by the state. When the Missouri Pacific Railroad demanded that local authorities at Sedalia deputize Pinkerton detectives to protect railroad property in the strike of 1885, town officials instead deputized brakemen, conductors, and other workers. Residents of the communities along Gould's lines saw the corporations as alien institutions, but they regarded the workers as neighbors and citizens who shared with them a wider antimonopoly sentiment.[47] Seeing no imminent threat to life and property, the governors of Missouri and Kansas refused to dispatch the militia. Workers enforced peace and order against the private violence of corporations.

The Knights made common cause with other antimonopolists, but they were not antimonopolists pure and simple. They were a peculiar labor union, but they were above all a labor union. They linked their union to antimonopoly politics by what amounted to three great grappling hooks. The first was common ideological roots in American republicanism. The second was an abiding distrust of railroad corporations in particular and corporations in general, which led many of their members to see the railroads as little more than a privileged conspiracy to rob them of their wealth and manhood. And the third was hatred not just of contract labor but of contract laborers. In the West this took its most virulent form in Sinophobia, which was unfortunately not some excrescence disfiguring western antimonopoly; it was an essential part of its worldview.

III. CONTRACT LABOR AND THE CHINESE

It is hard to find a clearer and more concise statement of the core principle of antimonopoly than the claim of George McNeill, an official in the Knights, that the ultimate goal of the Knights of Labor was "to engraft republican principles into our industrial system."[48] That such statements sound hopelessly utopian in the early twenty-first century marks the sea change between how Americans now think about work and how nineteenth-century workers thought about it. Like McNeill, many workers believed that in a democratic republic the same principles that governed organized social and political life should also govern people's working life. And the Knights, however unevenly, took republican sacrifice and the equality of white men seriously. In 1884 the Knights told the Union Pacific that they regarded themselves as "a band of brothers." When hard times came, they "did not wish to have a portion of the force dismissed." Workers on the Denver and Rio Grande took the same position in the spring of 1885. Instead of layoffs they wanted to have the work of all proportionately reduced.[49]

The Knights, like other antimonopolists, embraced technological progress, self-improvement, and material prosperity, but this did not mean that they believed the primary purpose of an economy was to produce maximum wealth. The true object of a republican economy should be to produce republican citizens with the income necessary for independence and the leisure to devote to improvement and family. Monopoly thwarted this object, and workers, like many farmers and businessmen, embraced antimonopoly and regarded the railroad corporations as their real and symbolic enemies.[50]

What added to the corporation's danger was its connection with unfree labor, which the Civil War had supposedly eliminated. Before the Civil War, the ability to make contracts was what differentiated free men from slaves.[51] The contracts that labor contractors offered immigrant workers—Europeans, Chinese, and Mexicans—flew in the face of the "free labor" whose triumph the North had supposedly secured. To the Knights the contracts offering foreign workers a loan for passage and work on arrival amounted to a kind of debt peonage that put low-wage workers at the mercy of contractors.[52]

A. C. Beckwith supplied labor, largely Chinese, to the Union Pacific coal mines. The surviving contracts do not detail Beckwith's relationship with either the Chinese or white workers, but the Union Pacific always represented to the miners that they were "in the employ of Beckwith, Quinn, & Co.," and that company seems to have followed the common practices of other contractors: the railroad paid the wages of the Chinese workers directly to Beckwith, Quinn, and Company, which deducted any necessary charges before the Chinese miners received their money. A decade later contractors of Japanese labor, some of whom were Japanese and some white, had perfected a system that involved a kind of death by a thousand cuts. The contractors garnished a daily fee of ten cents from each railroad worker they supplied out of a wage of a dollar to $1.15 a day. They took an additional dollar a month from each worker as a translation fee, charged the workers a medical fee, and deducted money for remittances to Japan.[53]

These fees were merely a beginning. Because Beckwith, Quinn had possession of Chinese wages, it could advance credit against these wages, a huge advantage in securing the trade of the Chinese. A verbal promise by the Union Pacific to make it paymaster for white miners, and the acquisition of the Union Pacific's company stores in the Wyoming towns of Rock Springs, Almy, and Carbon, allowed them the same advantage in securing the trade among white miners.[54] Beckwith, Quinn became a combination employment agency, travel agency, loan shark, and merchant.

Beckwith, Quinn by and large followed a template developed during the construction of the Central Pacific by the Six Companies of San Francisco for recruiting large numbers of workers to labor in remote places. The Six Companies were the coordinating body of the six, and later seven, benevolent associations of the Chinese in San Francisco. Merchants dominated these associations, and they supplied Chinese workers to the Central Pacific and later to the Southern Pacific. The Six Companies recruited most of the needed workers from Chinese already present in California, but when recruiting new workers abroad, they advanced them the cost of a ticket plus interest, which the workers contracted to pay back. The Six Companies arranged for the employment of these indebted workers, and the workers' employers, in turn, agreed to garnish the money owed the Six Companies from the workers' wages.[55] The interest the Six Companies gained was far less lucrative than collateral agreements to supply isolated workers with food, clothing, and other necessaries. Unlike white workers, Chinese and, later, Japanese workers did not get board as part of their railroad employment. They were dependent on contractors.[56]

The Knights of Labor and other organized workers racialized contract labor and used it to demonize "nonwhites" as naturally dependent and thus the tools of bosses, but contract labor *was* exploitative. Contract labor turned the contracts that Americans had fetishized as both the symbol and the guarantee of freedom into weapons to use against workers. It was as if vampires, far from recoiling from the cross, had seized it and made it their own. Labor contractors using European, Asian, and Mexican workers operated across the North American West throughout the late nineteenth century.[57]

The demand for contract labor on western railroads during the construction boom of the late 1870s and early 1880s was enormous.[58] In 1881 Henry Villard, rushing the Northern Pacific toward completion, received a telegram reporting a "great lack of men on grade toward Lake Pend d'Oreille, only about seven hundred where three to four thousand are needed."[59] He was already negotiating for Chinese contract labor.[60] But European as well as Asian immigrants came west as contract laborers. In 1883 the Canadian Pacific was simultaneously building sections along Lake Superior, across Manitoba, and in British Columbia, and it was short of men in all three regions.[61] East of the Rockies contract laborers were more likely to be Europeans—Italians or Slavs. Just as bankers acted as intermediaries to provide the railroads with international capital, so the padrones, as the contractors were often called, procured labor on an international market.

Organized workers constructed a history of railroad labor that made not just contract work but nonwhite workers a mark of decline, but to do so, they had to ignore the presence of nonwhite contract labor from the beginning of the transcontinentals. When William Pinkerton, the railroad memoirist, remembered the "vast shifting army that builded the great railway lines of the United States," he made that army white. In the cartoons of Thomas Nast, Irishmen like Pinkerton retained the simian features used to mark their antebellum marginality, but the Irish had already become white, and often ferociously and defensively so. In Pinkerton's version the railroad army had disbanded with "the last tie having been laid, the last spike driven, and the last bolt fastened in our own great railway systems."[62]

The railroad army, however, never disbanded; instead, its composition changed. Pinkerton had originally worked with men whom he considered white. As the railroads continued to expand, they recruited workers Pinkerton despised. "In the places where they toiled but a half a generation ago, one sees to-day gangs of dwarfed Italians, taciturn Greeks, and 'Bohunks' from the crowded and oppressed European countries."[63] Pinkerton deliberately constructed his narrative as a tale of triple declension: from early freedom to corporate oppression, from manhood to dependence, and from whiteness to darkness. In order to create this trajectory, however, Pinkerton had to ignore the roughly eleven thousand Chinese who worked on the Central Pacific during the peak periods of construction in the late 1860s.[64] Pinkerton was a man of large intelligence and narrower sympathies. He saw his fate as conjoined with that of other workers—but not all of them.

When Callaway blamed the strike at Carbon on the refusal to discharge "all Finlanders and Chinese," he touched both on the expansive definition of nonwhite prevalent in the nineteenth-century West and on the common hatred of all workers perceived to be contract workers. But, ultimately, the West had few anti-Finnish riots and no successful campaign to ban Finns. It was the roughly 180,000 Chinese who emigrated to the United States between 1849 and 1882 who came to be the ideological embodiment of worker declension—supposedly inferior men who became the tools of an oppressive corporation. The face of the contract laborer became Chinese, and the Chinese contract laborer morphed into a more plastic form: the coolie.[65]

Whites created the coolie long before any Chinese worker hoisted a rail or lifted a sledgehammer on the railroad. The coolie, at various times, was imagined as a surrogate of the slave and as an alternative to the slave. The coolie was neither black nor white and could be molded as a threat to either or both. The coolies were migrants but Sinophobes eventually successfully argued that they could not, and should not, ever be American immigrants.[66] Creating coolies was not just, or even primarily, the work of workers and antimonopolists in the West, but they enthusiastically equated Chinese with coolies as the term came to be defined following the Civil War. Coolies emerged as the most dangerous subset of contract labor—virtual slaves, racially inferior, and inalterably alien. What the Chinese were—free immigrant labor—became submerged beneath the invented and imagined coolie.

In the West hatred of the Chinese was pervasive. It cut across class lines. The Chinese occupied a strange space where they were both essential and exotic. The newspaper writers whom Henry Villard carried west to celebrate the completion of the Northern Pacific regarded them as at once necessary and alien.

> *The Chinese camps became more and more frequent (Idaho, Jocko River, Clarks Fork) and at every watering place and "wood up station" he stands at the side of the train, bareheaded, stolid, indifferent, in his blue blouse and baggy trousers with his hands in his pockets and his scant and ridiculous que hanging over his shoulder and down in front of his garments altogether perhaps weighting ten ounces and his shoes four pounds. Hundreds of him along the line, waiting patiently for the next order to move on. And then back of Ah John for millions of acres stands the virgin forest of spruce and pine and tamarack. We glide through them for miles and miles. . . .*[67]

With their character so obvious that it was discernible from the window of a train—"stolid," "patient," "ridiculous," and waiting only for orders—the Chinese had already been reduced to caricature.

The orders that the Chinese awaited were to build railroads. In 1882 there were reportedly fifteen thousand Chinese at work on the Northern Pacific in Washington Territory, with another six thousand working on that line in Idaho and Montana. That same year roughly six thousand Chinese arrived to work on the Canadian Pacific in British Columbia. And this does not include those working on the Southern Pacific system.[68] Few white workers wanted the construction jobs these Chinese held; but most non-Chinese workers feared that, once the roads were finished, they would move into other work along the lines.

In March of 1886 John Cooke, the secretary of the Knights of Labor assembly in Huntington, Oregon, demanded the dismissal of all Chinese employed by the Oregon Railroad and Navigation Company. He denounced their "complete monopoly of the various branches of unskilled labor on the Pacific Coast" and then, echoing the kind of republican and Lincolnian language that had presaged the Civil War, spoke of the "irrepressible conflict" between "civilization and barbarism." The Chinese were a "curse," and the Knights acted "to protect our interests our country and our race."[69] This easy transition from job competition to a crisis of civilization that endangered the republic and "our race" was typical of the Sinophobia that by 1886 dominated the Pacific Coast.

Workingmen did not invent Sinophobia, and not all Knights were anti-Chinese, but Sinophobia eventually sank its deepest root among western workers, particularly among the western Knights. In part the anti-Chinese movement in the West grew out of actual labor competition, especially during the depression of the 1870s, but this was hardly the whole explanation. Sinophobia took root in places where there were very few Chinese. Charles Francis Adams could be loose with figures, but he claimed that of the "20,000" Union Pacific employees, only 300–400 were "Asiatics."[70] Yet by 1885 workers had taken to calling the Union Pacific the "Great Chinee" company.[71] This was a function of contract labor. Adams could deny that men employed by the Oregon Railroad and Navigation Company were Union Pacific employees just as he could deny that workers provided by A. C. Beckwith were Union Pacific employees. The linkage of corporations and Chinese was, however, by 1886 so powerful that it would not be broken apart by arguments about numbers.

The welding of anticorporate and anti-Chinese politics first flowered in San Francisco, which produced the seeds that spread out along the coast into Canada and inland along the railroad lines. In the twentieth century even Sonora would sprout its own indigenous Anti-Chino League. The anti-Chinese movement did not depend on the actual presence of Chinese in any numbers, because the Chinese were less fellow human beings than a powerful ideological construct.[72] Their degradation represented the fate of all workers should the corporate/coolie partnership be allowed to persist; degradation gained them hatred rather than sympathy.

In the late 1870s Denis Kearney, a San Francisco drayman and petty entrepreneur, demonstrated the political possibilities of anti-Chinese politics by using it to promote an insurgency within the Democratic Party. He captured the Democratic ward clubs and incorporated them into the New Workingmen's Party, whose slogan was "The Chinese must go." The Workingmen were both antimonopolist and racist. The two were often synonymous. They placed clauses in the new 1879 California constitution denying Chinese the vote and prohibiting their employment on public works. By then anti-Chinese politics were by so pervasive that they faced little opposition in doing so.[73]

Focusing only on Kearney and the Workingmen can make California's anti-Chinese politics seem little more than a response to Chinese labor competition during the depression of the 1870s, but the logic of the anti-Chinese movement was broader and deeper. The Special Committee on Chinese Immigration, whose *Report to the California State Senate on Chinese Immigration: Its Social, Moral, and Political Effect* appeared in 1878, can serve as a primer of the arguments made against the Chinese and an illustration of how widely diffused they had become in California. Although some of the facts the report cited were quite true, the report carefully selected them from a larger, more diverse testimony to weave an account of irreversible Chinese moral degradation and its threat to the American public. It was a story built on sex and a kind of prurience that imagined Chinese women, themselves degraded and abused, as ensnaring white children. Even though the committee estimated that only 3,000 of 100,000 Chinese then in California were women, the report put prostitutes who were "held in slavery by their own people for the basest purposes" at the center of their analysis. The committee's attempts to elicit testimony that Chinese immigrants in general were in fact coolies, and thus virtual slaves, failed, but they rescued their argument by equating the exploitation of these women with slavery. The trope of slavery allowed the Chinese to be both victims and a danger.[74] Exploited themselves, they weakened white society. Advocates of Chinese exclusion paid little attention to white men who patronized Chinese prostitutes, but, like Terence Powderly, the chief workman of the Knights of Labor, they claimed that Chinese women infected "thousands of boys" with venereal disease. These boys of from eight to fifteen would, so doctors held, eventually infect their wives and, through them, their children.[75]

Moving quickly from the real but limited evils of prostitution in California, the argument located the problem in the Chinese as a whole. They were, the committee wrote, quoting Bayard Taylor, "the most debased people on the face of the earth. . . . [T]heir touch is pollution, and harsh as the opinion may seem, justice to our own race demands that they should not be allowed to settle on our soil." The committee report repeated arguments that the Chinese degraded work, but such arguments were a capstone, not a foundation of the report. The report was not the product of workers. The author was Creed Haymond, who was then an antimonopoly Democrat but who would evolve into the Southern Pacific's leading lawyer.[76] Nor were such sentiments peculiar to the United States, let alone California. They were echoed in Canada.[77]

Constructing the Chinese as a debased race made Sinophobia one of the flavors in the stew of American racism, but Sinophobes added a distinctive aspect to the hatred of the Chinese. The other "inferior" races—Indians, Mexicans, blacks—would supposedly disappear under competition with whites. It was, however, whites who would retreat before the Chinese. Employed by the railroads and other corporations, the Chinese would drive wages down to levels that would undercut the ability of white workers to support their families, and this would unleash a cascade of catastrophes. "They crowd our men of families out of employment, and leave them to want and destitution. They make hoodlums and criminals of our boys, and drive our girls to worse than death by working for wages which to them means starvation."[78] The Chinese were doubly unnatural in that they did not have families and that they threatened republican families. "Home life, as we understand and honor it, is unknown to them."[79]

For working-class white westerners what we consider issues of gender (manhood and family), what we consider issues of class (control over work), and what we consider issues of race (anti-Chinese politics) leaned on each other like poles in a teepee.[80] In order for some workers to defend what they regarded as core values, they believed they had to demean and attack other workers. Workers' vision of themselves depended on those they despised. The Knights' motto that an injury to one is an injury to all served only to emphasize that "all" did not include Chinese. Joseph Buchanan would make this quite explicit when, to exclude the Chinese, he altered his belief from the brotherhood of man to "The Brotherhood of Man, Limited."[81]

The Knights, with good reason, have been praised in other contexts as "a beacon of racial enlightenment on a dark sea," so why were they so viciously racist toward the Chinese?[82] It was not because of any deficiency in the Chinese as workers. The Knights admitted that the Chinese were good workers—his "only virtue is his industry"—but being industrious was not enough. Their hard work made them, as the California Knights declared, "a menace to free labor and free men."[83] There was an element of self-loathing in the contempt of the Chinese. The Knights were hardly reconciled to the place of wage labor in a republican economy, and when they attacked the Chinese they often repeated slurs previously directed at wageworkers in general. The Chinese were "ignorant, conscienceless . . . corrupt . . . crafty . . . criminal . . . depraved." Too "timid" to be men themselves, they threatened American manhood, the virtue of American families, and the nation itself.[84] These were precisely the charges often leveled against wageworkers in the American republic.

In the denunciations of Chinese workers as workers, there is more than a casual resonance with Jefferson's famous denunciation of urban workers. "The mobs of great cities," Jefferson wrote during the 1780s in his *Notes on the State of Virginia*, "add just so much to the support of pure government, as sores do to the strength of the human body." Men who worked for wages were a source of the "degeneracy" that was a "canker" on the body politic.

When E. L. Godkin's *Nation* denounced immigrant workers following the great railroad strike of 1877, which produced widespread violence, as men "who carry in their very blood traditions which give universal suffrage an air of menace to many of the things which civilized men hold dear," he simply updated this language. Even Adams, for all his initial paternalism, echoed such sentiments. Unions, Adams thought, only made workers worse. It was the same everywhere "when brotherhoods are endeavoring to secure any result. . . . They are as cruel and merciless as wild beasts, when it comes to the question between them and their employers."[85]

The Knights, whose papers could refer to "the stigma of being a hireling," took the general abuse of wageworkers and translated it into racial abuse. The Chinese were quite literally scapegoated. They were credited with and then punished for attributes assigned to all industrial workers and which white workers feared in themselves. There was a sense among workers in the West that certain work under the conditions enforced by railroad corporations was inherently degrading, and these were the jobs the Chinese occupied. William Pinkerton, for example, described punishing physical labor of maintenance and repair performed by section workers, in the kind of grandiloquent language to which he was partial, as a job "where the sweat from one's body dropped tinged with blood; where a man's soul withered and his heart contracted, and he became a machine, inert, callous, dead."[86]

White workers transformed themselves from being a threat—an ignorant and vicious working class—to being victims. They marked certain kinds of work as inherently degrading and other workers as inherently degraded. Degraded workers hardly counted as men. They were tools of bosses. Having racialized the danger they faced, white workers then racialized resistance. Resistance was the marker of whiteness and manhood; the mark of nonwhites was dependence, long the great danger to the republic. The supposed consent of the Chinese to their own oppression made them both inferior and dangerous. The Chinese would first deprive workers of their manhood, then weaken the families that were the fruits of that manhood, and finally undermine the republic that depended on their manhood.[87] As in so many other things, gendered constructions lay behind racialized constructions of dangers to society.

Americans deeply believed in uplift, but once the Protestants largely abandoned their efforts at conversion, the Chinese ceased to be targets for uplift. They didn't qualify. They could not be reformed, because they were inassimilable: "separate, distinct from, and antagonistic to our people in thinking, mode of life, in tastes and principles." In 1870 western Republican congressmen had taken the lead in making sure that Asians could not become naturalized citizens. This made Asian immigrants by definition unable to participate in the rituals and duties of the republic.[88]

The next step was to halt immigration almost entirely. Friends of the railroads in Congress and the provisions of the Burlingame Treaty with China had been enough to stop the passage of bills restricting Chinese immigration in the 1870s. The renegotiation of the Burlingame Treaty with China allowed proponents of Chinese exclusion to press forward, but Collis P. Huntington, who very much favored Chinese immigration and Chinese labor, remained confident that his friends in Congress could defeat immigration restrictions on the Chinese. He underestimated the strength of the anti-Chinese forces not only in the West but nationally.[89] Only a veto by Chester A. Arthur stopped the first version of the Chinese exclusion bill in 1881, but Arthur accepted a second version in 1882 with a ten-year rather than a twenty-year moratorium on immigration and a ban on Chinese citizenship. Collis P. Huntington denounced the "outrageous act" against "that peaceable and industrious people" and then moved characteristically from high principle to immediate self-interest. He worried that the act gave the Canadian Pacific an advantage in securing the steamer trade from China.[90]

Neither antimonopolists in general nor the Knights of Labor in particular were satisfied with the Chinese Exclusion Act; they launched a wider political attack on contract labor. And here, too, they were politically victorious. In the United States the Foran Act of 1885 banned and rendered null and void all contracts "to import alien workers for 'labor and service.'" Parliament eventually passed a similar Canadian act, the Alien Labor Act of 1897. Practically, however, the Foran Act proved hard to enforce. Contract labor did not vanish.[91]

Chinese exclusion forced contractors to find new sources of supply, and the Foran Act caused them to develop new subterfuges.[92] Contractors and

the railroads piously promised to observe the act. "As importation of contract labor is strictly forbidden by law," an 1898 agreement between the
Japanese labor contractors Tsukane and Ichiro Hirota and the Great Northern Railroad read, "we will never attempt to hire Japanese residents outside
of the United States."[93] But between 1891 and 1900 over 27,000 Japanese
workers, virtually all of them unskilled, entered the United States, and others entered Canada. They worked as far east as Minnesota.[94] Labor contractors simply taught the men they recruited to lie on entry.[95] The Oregon
Short Line, the Union Pacific, the Southern Pacific, the Great Northern, the
Northern Pacific, and the Canadian Pacific all competed for Japanese labor,
and a variety of labor contractors competed to supply them.[96] Contractors
solicited workers from outside the continental United States and battled on
the docks to keep rivals from stealing them away. As C. T. Takahashi of the
Oriental Trading Company began an account of subterfuge and thuggery by
one of his competitors, "When we brought a shipload of Japanese laborers
over from Hawaii last spring Remington sent about sixty men of the most
desperate character. . . ."[97]

The Foran Act did not end contract labor, but it did weaken it. The railroads never completely trusted the contractors, and they could not legally
hold the workers to their contracts. The railroads suspected that the contractors shifted workers from one line to another to drive up wages.[98] Contract
labor worked best in isolated places where workers had few options; elsewhere workers could still quit a job whenever they chose. They could not be
forced to work for the length of a contract.[99]

Chinese exclusion and the Foran Act should have rendered the Chinese
and contract labor dead issues. Legislative success, however, only exacerbated anti-Chinese sentiment. There was far more violence against the Chinese in the West following the passage of the Chinese Exclusion Act in 1882
and the Foran Act in 1885 than before it. The exclusion act had created a
new category of illegal alien that thrust the Chinese into a netherworld. They
were subjects "barred from citizenship and without rights," and until they
proved otherwise, every Chinese could be regarded as illegal.[100] There was
a quite real, if relatively small, movement of the Chinese into the United
States from Mexico, where the Chinese were actively recruited for railroad

work in Sonora.[101] Far more Chinese came across the border from Canada as the Canadian Pacific neared completion.[102] Once they had entered the country, it was impossible to tell new and illegal Chinese residents from old and legal Chinese residents. All were vulnerable because Chinese exclusion criminalized what had been normal movements of labor. Yet outside of U.S. ports there was little state capacity to enforce the law. Sinophobes regarded ineffective enforcement as proof that the Chinese and corporations were conspiring to flout the law and mock the will of the people. All over the West the new laws only increased the potential for violence.

IV. ROCK SPRINGS

Corporations were, in fact, happy to subvert laws excluding the Chinese and to recruit Chinese workers, but their capacity to do so was limited. The Union Pacific recruited Chinese from Oregon for their Wyoming coal mines only to find that they came in insufficient numbers to keep the desired ratio of three Chinese for every white miner at Rock Springs. In 1885 there were 331 Chinese miners and 150 whites at the Rock Springs mines because during the preceding two years the company had "not been able to get Chinese enough to keep up the proportion."[103]

As the Union Pacific complained about the inability to recruit sufficient Chinese, the San Francisco Trades Assembly raised the stakes from exclusion to abatement. In 1882 the assembly established the League of Deliverance, whose goal was through threats and actual violence to drive the Chinese from the West. The league quickly degenerated into a confidence scheme in which local organizers pocketed contributions, but it succeeded in moving anti-Chinese rhetoric up another notch. In 1884 and 1885 talk of abatement and violence was very much in the air. Western Knights wanted abatement for its own sake and as a way to attract membership.[104]

Wyoming Territory, which had comparatively few Chinese, was an unlikely place for anti-Chinese violence to erupt, but Rock Springs contained all the necessary elements. It had some Chinese workers in a territory with strong antimonopoly sentiments and a history of corporate corruption. It had the Knights of Labor and the determination of the Union Pacific

Railroad to demonstrate to its workers that, while it was willing to practice corporate paternalism, managers, not workers, controlled the terms and conditions of work.

The Chinese presence at Rock Springs was a legacy of Jay Gould's control of the Union Pacific. In 1875 coal miners in Rock Springs had struck the Union Pacific. It was a small strike in a distant place. Butch Cassidy and his Hole in the Wall gang, second-rate desperados but desperados still, operated nearby. Rock Springs was still a collection of dugouts, tents, and cheap buildings gathered near the railroad tracks of the Union Pacific along Bitter Creek on the high desert. Rock Springs existed because of the convergence of coal and the railroad. Despite the town's name, its water came in by tank cars. It was dreary and dirty beyond the normal dreariness and dirtiness of any coal mining town, but Rock Springs also offered testimony to the power of the railroad to create new industries on the edges of the world economy in places where even state authority remained tenuous.[105]

The strike of 1875 was a seed that spawned a much bloodier aftermath. What fertilized and watered that seed came from far beyond Rock Springs. In creating the town, along with its sister coal mining towns of Almy and Carbon, the Union Pacific marked them with its signature blend of mismanagement and corruption. The Union Pacific began in 1868 by subcontracting mining on its coal lands to the Wyoming Coal and Mining Company, whose board contained the Union Pacific president Oliver Ames and five of his fellow Union Pacific board members. Wyoming Coal sold the coal that it mined at Almy, Carbon, and Rock Springs to the Union Pacific at six dollars a ton for the first two years of the fifteen-year contract, and then gradually dropped the price to three dollars. This initial price was three times the going price paid to independent producers. That was business as usual. What the railroad lost, insiders gained. To ensure that the firm did not face significant competition in other markets along its lines, the railroad gave the company a 25 percent discount on the price it charged for hauling coal, thus allowing it to undercut competitors at the point of final sale. To mine the coal, the company brought in experienced miners born a quarter of a world away. Many of them were Irish and more were British—Welsh, Cornish, and Scots—who had previously mined in

Missouri, Kansas, Pennsylvania, or Iowa. The leadership of the Wyoming Coal and Mining Company, however, proved no more capable of running a coal company than a railroad. They could not adequately supply the Union Pacific, which had to buy additional coal from outside operators.[106]

The ineptitude of the Wyoming Coal and Mining Company, and the way its greed got in the way of his far more efficient avarice, was one of the many things that appalled Jay Gould about the Union Pacific after he gained control of the road in 1874. Gould wanted to boost Union Pacific stock, and to do so he needed to pay dividends. He canceled the coal contract and moved to create a direct Union Pacific monopoly over coal. He also refused to haul coal from independent Wyoming mines along the railroad's route.[107] He even sought to cut both the Rocky Mountain Coal and Iron Company, which the Associates of the Central Pacific owned, and the Weber mines in Utah out of local markets by restricting their access to coal cars at key times.[108]

The miners were not, strictly speaking, wageworkers. They were contractors paid by the ton. In 1875 Gould cut the price paid to miners to a dollar a ton. Gould contracted with A. C. Beckwith to provide Chinese workers to replace recalcitrant whites, and miners struck, seeking a restoration to $1.25. Gould brought in more Chinese. Beckwith provided Chinese labor both to work in the mines and to serve as section hands on the railroad. The Chinese went to work at the reduced payments the whites had refused, and payments continued to fall thereafter. The price for coal at Rock Springs in 1885 varied according to the difficulty of working the seam, but the standard price had fallen to 74 cents.[109] The Chinese worked hard, learned quickly, and cost the company about $32.50 a month compared with $52 for white miners who still dominated supervisory positions. Rock Springs sprouted a Chinatown, and the Chinese came to outnumber the whites.[110]

During the first ten years that the Chinese worked at Rock Springs, there was little overt conflict, but beyond Rock Springs the meaning of being Chinese was changing, and the political potential of anti-Chinese agitation was growing. The "Chinese Question," as Isaac Bromley of the Union Pacific reported to Charles Francis Adams in 1885, was "the most prominent topic west of the Missouri River."[111]

Adams did not want trouble with the Knights of Labor in 1885, and he regretted that the Union Pacific even had coal mines. He thought the company had no more business mining coal than it had raising wheat, noting, "If we could get rid of those mines by giving them away, it would, in my opinion probably result in the company's making enormous amounts of money every year as a carrier of commercial coal."[112] Getting rid of the mines would also shed the vexatious issue of strikes in the coal mines and the antagonism the company endured for using Chinese miners at Rock Springs. Adams did move to divest himself of the Colorado mines, including the mine at Louisville, which were still involved in the lingering Colorado strike, but he held on to the Wyoming mines.[113]

Like seemingly every labor issue along the Rocky Mountains and the Great Plains in 1885, the Colorado coal strike led back to Joseph Buchanan. When Buchanan organized the Union Pacific Employes Association in 1884, it became Knights District Assembly 82 under the leadership of Thomas Neasham, an English immigrant, while Buchanan became head of District Assembly 89, which contained virtually all the other Knights of Labor locals in Colorado, including the coal miners.[114] In 1884 Buchanan led the miners in Knights District Assembly 89 in a strike that stretched across Colorado and into New Mexico. The miners quickly reached agreement with the small mine operators but not with the Union Pacific Railway, the Atchison, Topeka, and Santa Fe, and the Colorado Coal and Iron Company, which had once been part of the Denver and Rio Grande and was still its major supplier.[115]

The agreement with the small mine owners was yet another sign of the tightening connections between the Knights of Labor and the wider anti-monopoly movement in Colorado. District Assembly 89 of the Knights of Labor and the owners of smaller mines created a conciliation board that they intended to function much like a railroad pool: raising coal prices and keeping them stable in Denver and other urban centers. This agreement benefited both the miners and the small mine owners. It was based on a mutual antipathy toward the Union Pacific and other railroad corporations, which could, by virtue of their ownership of the railroads and coal mines, set prices that would drive independent operators out of business, depress

1. Henry Villard Henry Villlard, at the center with his hat on his knee, posed with members of the party that he brought west to celebrate the completion of the Northern Pacific in 1883. Villard was intimately familiar with the failure of the transcontinental railroads. *(National Portrait Gallery, Smithsonian Institution; gift of Henry Villard)*

2. Collis P. Huntington "Of our modern Forty Thieves," Ambrose Bierce wrote, "Mr. Huntington is the surviving 36." Huntington was the driving force behind the Southern Pacific. *(National Portrait Gallery, Smithsonian Institution)*

3. John C. Frémont Frémont, in railroads as in many things, was a man not to be trusted. *(National Portrait Gallery, Smithsonian Institution)*

4. Charles Francis Adams The grandson and great-grandson of presidents of the United States, he was president of the Union Pacific Railroad. *(Courtesy Department of Special Collections and University Archives, Stanford University Libraries)*

5. James J. Hill The president of the Great Northern, the last of the nineteenth-century transcontinental railroads. *(National Portrait Gallery, Smithsonian Institution; gift of the Old Print Shop)*

6. Locomotives Pushing Snowplow Eight Southern Pacific locomotives pushing a snowplow in the Sierras in 1891. *(Courtesy Department of Special Collections and University Archives, Stanford University Libraries)*

7. Completion of Northern Pacific The celebration at Fargo during Henry Villard's triumphal tour on the completion of the Northern Pacific in 1883. This was one of many celebrations; meanwhile Villard's Northern Pacific could not pay its debts. *(Villard Arch, Fargo. Henry Villard Collection, Baker Library Historical Collections, Harvard Business School, olvwork359135)*

8. Royal Gorge of the Arkansas This William Henry Jackson photograph, c. 1885, shows the tracks of the Denver and Rio Grande running into the narrow Grand Cañon, or Royal Gorge, of the Arkansas River. Workers and equipment were lowered by ropes from the rim to construct the roadbed and track. *(Milstein Division of United States History, Local History & Genealogy, The New York Public Library, Astor, Lenox and Tilden Foundations)*

9. Monopoly versus Farmers and Labor Entitled "The Tournament of To-Day.—A Set-To Between Labor and Monopoly," this cartoon is from the August 1, 1883, issue of *Puck*. Capital is mounted on a locomotive with a shield labeled "Corruption" and a spear labeled "Subsidized Press." (*Puck, August 1, 1883. Courtesy Department of Special Collections and University Archives, Stanford University Libraries*)

10. "In the Hollow of His Hand" Carried by the railroads, Charles Crocker and Collis Huntington support Leland Stanford, who, in turn, holds the Railroad Commission and a figure who appears to be a railroad commissioner in the hollow of his hand. (*The Wasp, February 19, 1881, vol. 6, no. 238. Courtesy Department of Special Collections and University Archives, Stanford University Libraries*)

11. Laramie, Wyoming An Andrew J. Russell photograph of the Laramie Hotel, Laramie, Wyoming, in 1869; this is how the town appeared from the Union Pacific tracks when H. K. Thomas was station-master. *(Photography Collection, Miriam and Ira D. Wallach Division of Arts, Prints and Photographs, The New York Public Library, Astor, Lenox and Tilden Foundations)*

12. Laramie Shops This Andrew J. Russell photograph of the Laramie machine shops from the Southwest is a good example of an industrial island that the railroads had to create to maintain themselves. These shops were hotbeds of labor organizing. *(Photography Collection, Miriam and Ira D. Wallach Division of Arts, Prints and Photographs, The New York Public Library, Astor, Lenox and Tilden Foundations)*

13. Poster: Atchison, Topeka, and Santa Fe An example of the transnational reach of the transcontinentals. *(Baker Library Historical Collections, Harvard Business School, olvwork365688)*

14. Poster: Northern Pacific For hubris, grandiosity, and repeated failure, few corporations could surpass the Northern Pacific. *(Photograph album commemorating German investments' role in completing the Northern Pacific Railroad. Henry Villard Photograph Album, 1883, Baker Library Historical Collections, Harvard Business School)*

15. A Picture for Employers A typical anti-Chinese cartoon. Sinophobes framed the issue for employers as a choice between a white workingman's family and degraded Chinese who supported neither homes nor families. *(Puck, August 21, 1878. Courtesy Department of Special Collections and University Archives, Stanford University Libraries)*

16. Central Pacific Train at Auburn Depot This photograph of two Central Pacific trains at the Auburn, California, depot by Alfred Hart c. 1865–66, captures the small size and limited carrying capacity of early western railroads. *(Courtesy Department of Special Collections and University Archives, Stanford University Libraries)*

17. Across the Continent This famous Currier and Ives lithograph by Fanny Palmer places the railroad among the symbols of American progress and marks it as a carrier of civilization. *(Courtesy Department of Special Collections and University Archives, Stanford University Libraries)*

wages, and allow the railroad mines or favored companies to monopolize the market and control access to it. Corporate domination did not necessarily lower prices for the consumer. Whereas the Union Pacific controlled the coal market, wholesalers could not sell coal without "whacking up," that is, paying the Union Pacific or, as Adams suspected, a corrupt agent of the company for the privilege.[116] Middlemen who whacked up in turn charged their customers more, and their customers then retrenched, cutting the market for coal.[117]

In 1885 the miners at the Union Pacific mines in Carbon, Wyoming, demanded that the conciliation board mediate disputes between them and the Union Pacific, and S. R. Callaway reported that the Knights "have got all the storekeepers and many outsiders into their organization and apparently intend running the Union Pacific Railway."[118] Adams blocked this move by recognizing the miners at Carbon as members of the Union Pacific Employes Association, which made them part of District Assembly 82 headed by Thomas Neasham. It was separate from Buchanan's District Assembly 89, the Denver executive board of the Knights, and the Colorado conciliation board.[119]

Adams was uncharacteristically optimistic on September 1, 1885, when he wrote to F. P. Alexander, one of the Union Pacific directors, "I fancy the labor trouble, for the present at least, is quiescent. This is a great point gained. I can turn attention to getting our finances in shape and carrying out the work of reorganization."[120] Settling things at Carbon certainly seemed more important than quieting the issues at the Rock Springs mines, where the majority of miners were Chinese and the Knights were weak.[121]

The premise of the anti-Chinese movement was that the Chinese shared nothing with whites, but this was not the truth of a coal mine.[122] At Rock Springs whites and Chinese shared the dangers and details of the work itself, and what sparked the immediate conflict between them was the mutual recognition that there were many ways to die in a coal mine—by explosions, runaway mine cars, asphyxiation, cave-ins, and more—and that some places were safer than others. Knowing those places was a matter of skill and experience. Good miners knew that the best places for supports to prevent cave-ins varied with rock strata, depth of the mine, and the size of the coal seam. Workers believed that they were the best judges of safety. They knew where the air was good or bad; they knew that to stint on mine timbers or place them badly was to save costs and increase production at the risk of miners' lives.[123]

It was a safety issue, a work rule, that set in motion the conflict at Rock Springs in September of 1885. Isaiah Whitehouse had been working in entry number 7 at the Rock Springs mine, but he left to go to entry number 5 because the air was bad. "The rooms were not fit for a man to work in. They would kill a man if he had to stay in them. I could not maintain my family and have my health." Whitehouse could have improved the air by digging a crosscut or breakthrough to ventilate the room, but only if the company offered him customary compensation for digging the airway. The company refused. Foremen told miners that if they would not dig an airway for free, the room would go to the Chinese. The Knights accused the company of using the Chinese to upset "time-honored usages" and to introduce "insidious innovations."[124]

Such company policies were signs of how the erosion of "time-honored usages" was costing skilled and independent workers control of both their work and their sense of themselves. The miners, the Knights' Neasham argued, would be unworthy of the name of American citizens if they "tamely submitted" to the treatment doled out to them by the company. For employees to be forced to sign papers allowing the company to control where they worked and how they worked and to assess penalties when they complained or refused was an attack on the independence that was at the root of workers' identity. As one Rock Springs miner put it, a man was asked to sign away "his free speech, his liberty and his manhood."[125]

On September 2, 1885, the day after Adams had expressed his confidence in labor peace, Isaiah Whitehouse began to work his new room in mine number 5. Dividing a mine up into "rooms" was an old British practice, and Whitehouse was English. Born in Staffordshire, he had come to Wyoming by way of Pennsylvania two years earlier. He was a family man and a delegate-elect to the Wyoming legislature. Whitehouse's presence led to a quarrel with a group of Chinese miners over who had the right to work the room. James Evans, the mine superintendent, had assigned the Chinese the same room that a pit boss had given Whitehouse. The Chinese, except for the phonetically rendered Leo Qarqwang, and Leo Mauwick, were unnamed, as they usually were in surviving records.[126]

The dispute between Whitehouse and the Chinese began as a conversation, a very rudimentary one, given the language differences, and escalated into an argument whose seriousness became clear enough when a Chinese worker swung a pick at Whitehouse and Whitehouse knocked him down. More men came rushing in, and the swinging of picks and shovels at human bodies rather than at seams of coal became general. This spark had by afternoon blazed into an armed mob that marched on the Chinese section of Rock Springs. They shot down fellow workers in the streets and burned others alive in the houses where they had taken shelter. Both murderers and victims were overwhelmingly immigrants. The murderers were English, Scots, Welsh, Swedes, Danes, Irish, and, in smaller numbers, Poles, Bohemians, and Hungarians. Their victims were Chinese. What struck observers was the contrast between the violence of the riot and the utter calm that followed. Rock Springs' Chinatown burned and then smoldered; bodies lay where they had fallen, and amid the stench of death, hogs devoured human flesh. Residents of Rock Springs could hear gunshots in the hills, but inside the town a "Sabbath-like quiet reigned." Roughly fifty Chinese died either in the riot or after the mob drove the survivors off into the high desert and mountains. The Chinese lost not only their lives but their savings from years of work in America; supposedly $200,000 was stolen or burned with the houses.[127]

Labor unrest soon spread to Evanston and its nearby mining town of Almy, and eventually even to Carbon, where no Chinese were employed.[128] The rioters also drove James Evans out of town and threatened Mormon strikebreakers whom the railroad tried to recruit.[129]

News of all this came quickly to Boston, and Adams's notations in his diary about the struggles in Wyoming made it clear how utterly incommensurate railroad lives could be. Adams learned of the massacre as he prepared to leave for Newport, and further dispatches arrived as he kept what used to be politely called bankers' hours—in his office by midmorning and often out by midafternoon. As Adams mulled the negotiations that would shape the fate of men, both white and Chinese, who spent their days underground, he tracked the New England weather and walked in the woods and along beaches with his wife, children, dogs, and friends. He could spend part of a workday afternoon reading Carlyle. He enjoyed his baths and lunched at his clubs. There was nothing wrong with this. Quite the opposite; it was precisely the kind of life with its leisure, family, friendships, comforts, and self-improvement that the Knights imagined for workers and that was so utterly beyond their reach.[130]

No one would be punished for the murders; no one would even be tried. Local papers reported that "the unanimous opinion of the people" sustained the white miners, and, after ritual condemnation of the killings, the grand jury and the Wyoming press blamed the Union Pacific for the violence. S. R. Callaway, the general manager of the road, thought "the sympathy of the entire community west of the Missouri River seems to be with the men against the company." In a period all too familiar with mass violence, the parallel between what was happening in the West and what was happening in the South was inescapable. Charles Francis Adams was quick to connect killings of Chinese in the West with the murders of blacks by the Ku Klux Klan and other white terrorists. If Rock Springs had been in the South, "the whole Republican press of the country would have rung with it. The wheels of Congress would have been set in motion, and the 'untamed spirit of the rebellion' would have been denounced in unmeasured terms." Rock Springs was "the most atrocious, cold-blooded, systematic . . . massacre anywhere in this country, not done by savages." The "savages" Adams had in mind could have provided him with some other examples, but he was really not interested in that.[131]

The parallel with the South was a good one, and while it allowed Adams to take the high moral ground, it was also double-edged.[132] If the battle was going to be understood in terms of Reconstruction, the Knights of Labor had already won.[133] Just as the South regained the ability to subordinate African Americans, so the West was winning the right to subordinate Chinese. Adams's own general manager reported that the Knights had adroitly shaped the issue so that attention was diverted away from the massacre and that the Knights "appear before the people as a defender of American labor against the encroachment of capital and Chinese labor combined." Terence Powderly, the general master workman of the Knights, accused the Union Pacific of using the massacre, which he condemned, to deny employment to the Knights in Rock Springs.[134] The low and brutal murders at Rock Springs, as is often the case in such instances, were soon obscured in a fog of high principles.

Adams's high principles, however, dissipated as quickly as did the Knights' brotherhood of man. In early October he was defining the struggle as an issue "between law and order, civilization and Christianity on the one side, and massacre and riot, socialism and communism on the other."[135] Adams denounced the Knights for protecting murderers, although he "never for a moment supposed that those guilty of the massacre . . . were necessarily members of that organization, or acting under its orders."[136] Three days later Adams decided that the Chinese would have to be sacrificed. "You cannot operate a railroad successfully in the face of an all-pervading public sentiment, no matter how wrong it may be. Railroads are commercial enterprises; they are not humanitarian, philanthropic, or political." A railroad was not in the business of propagating ideals, although—and here he retreated to the old clichés—it would "spread them gradually, in the natural course of events"; meanwhile, it was "essentially and always a business and not education or missionary machine."[137] It was also, he admitted, a company held in "odium," and that imposed a "heavy burden" in Wyoming.[138]

Instead of a general conflagration with civilization at stake, the murders spawned a series of local strikes, negotiations, boycotts, and federal interventions that sputtered and flared without every igniting the general conflict that Adams thought, and often hoped, would erupt. Because the murderers went free and the Chinese returned to Rock Springs under the protection of troops, the murders settled little. Coal production quickly recovered.[139] The Knights' intervention at Rock Springs only bared their own divisions. When Thomas Neasham visited the Rock Springs mines following the murders, he quickly found himself at cross-purposes with the miners. Neasham, who like Terence Powderly did not believe in strikes except as a desperate last resort, claimed that he urged the miners, who wanted the Knights to shut the Union Pacific down, to return to work. The miners retorted that it was Neasham who had earlier urged them *not* to return to work unless the Chinese were banned from the mines and there had been a thorough investigation of the white miners' grievances. The company rejected this demand, and the miners threatened that any Chinese who entered the mines would not come out alive. In the interim the Knights agreed to provide aid to the miners, and Adams moved toward mines operated by Chinese and machinery.[140]

Adams's ultimate goal was to replace the miners and slide them right out of Wyoming, but he did not attack the Knights in general.[141] He cautioned Callaway that the Knights were "a formidable labor organization in the ranks of our employees." They needed to be recognized and dealt with.[142] They were also politically potent. Callaway told him that the Colorado House was "composed largely of Knights of Labor candidates, who are pledged to support all kinds of anti-railroad measures."[143] This was the alliance between workers and the antimonopolists that Touzalin and Adams had feared in 1880.

V. WORKERS' MARGINALISM

Confrontations between labor and capital gripped the attention of the nation in the 1880s, but relatively little attention went to an intellectual revolution that was gripping the young discipline of economics. Charles Francis Adams may have known something of it, but probably not until much later; Arthur Hadley of Yale, whom Adams promoted in railroad circles, would become a leading American marginalist.

Marginalism was, in the words of John Bates Clark, its great American exponent, an expression of the law of diminishing returns, the "one law that governs economic life." He might have called it the law of the final increment.[144] Clark's theory of "the variation of economic results" explained how the first increment of land, labor, or consumption was the most valuable and every additional increment declined in value. "Bread given to a man in a succession of slices," Clark wrote, "nourishes, pleases, and ultimately gluts him. If he must eat it, the nth slice is worth nothing to him, and the following ones less than nothing."[145]

This seemingly technical doctrine had broad social and practical implications. Marginalism discarded the labor theory of value on which classical economists, Marxists, and working-class radicals based their reforms and their social logic. When union leaders like Eugene Debs, then of the Brotherhood of Locomotive Firemen, demanded an "honest distribution of wealth according to the contributions of labor," he presumed that the value of the labor in any particular product could be calculated.[146] The marginalists agreed with Debs that workers' wages should be based on the contributions of their labor. Nor did they quarrel with Debs, or with Marxists for that matter, on whether labor was social. Clark recognized labor "as a distinctly social element." The marginalists, however, asserted that labor fell under their universal law. It had no fixed value. What mattered was what an employer would pay an additional worker to procure a new increment of production. The marginalists argued that the market determined the worth of that increment. Wages thus depended on that marginal productivity and would "be determined precisely by the laborer's value to the highest bidder."[147] There was no appealing this; it was an economic law. The value of labor would be much closer to the price paid for the last laborer hired than for the first.

There is no evidence that workingmen read the marginalists, but in the late 1880s some moved to what might be called a workingmen's marginalism. There was among the American working class at the end of the nineteenth century a strong vernacular intellectual tradition apparent in the pages of labor newspapers. Some writers for the *Union Pacific Employes' Magazine* grasped the essence of marginalism even if they would not have recognized the term. They accurately identified it as a doctrine that assured class conflict. One columnist wrote, as a hypothetical worker out of employment seeking a job from an employer, who would grant a job "if I can produce for you a tithe more than you will pay me in wages; no, if I produce a tithe less."[148] Employers would hire additional workers only if it was to their gain. With the deflationary tendency of the late nineteenth-century economy and a surplus of workers, the price of labor and the wages of workers would continually fall. The wage paid the last worker hired would become the governing wage. In bold language that workers could easily understand, the writer spelled out the consequences for workers.

So long as they [i.e., the workers] recognize the right of a man to hire them, they must recognize his right to refuse. He will rarely refuse when it is to his gain. The amount he will pay is regulated in a measure by that and the number seeking his service. Consequently by recognizing this right to hire they indirectly recognize his right to fix the pay, for it can never be above what he demands as gain, no matter how wasteful his management may be, on which the hired service might improve; the servant is helpless before the recognized right of the employer. . . .[149]

This was American marginalism as it appeared to workers. What American marginalists saw as inevitable and a matter of law, workers saw as a matter of class privilege, power, and choice. The employers' logic was true, but only within the economy as currently organized. And if workers accepted it, and if "the ownership of the earth centralizes as rapidly for another generation as for the past decade they must teach their posterity to be prepared to get off the earth at any time the owners of it demand, or accept any terms for the privilege of remaining that may be offered, for certainly they will teach their children to be law observers, if they do fail to teach them to be law makers."[150]

In Europe marginalism was often a doctrine that justified state intervention and welfare economics. If, as the marginalists argued, the first increment of social utility for any given person was the greatest in value in terms of both need and satisfaction, then to many British marginalists it logically followed that the greatest social welfare would be achieved by redistributing wealth downward. Since the rich got less social utility and satisfaction from each increment than the poor, redistributing wealth to the poor was thus the best way to maximize social utility.[151] American marginalists rarely accepted this logic. Such a redistribution of wealth was in American terms agrarianism, a label for all plans to redistribute wealth downward. Both the railroads workers and the antimonopolists were, in this sense, agrarians. As long as they were, it was hard to see how the railroad corporations and their workers would make common cause, no matter how much managers like Touzalin might wish for such an alliance.

A RAILROAD LIFE

WILLIAM PINKERTON

William Pinkerton was a vernacular intellectual—shrewd, thoughtful, and grounded in a quite particular knowledge and experience—who wrote the best of the nineteenth-century railroad memoirs. An Irish immigrant, he went to work on the Choctaw extension of the St. Louis and San Francisco Railroad—the Frisco—in the late 1870s, taking a subcontract on culvert work with a man named Murphy, who was "a typical old-time grader." Like many of the men who built the railroads, Pinkerton was young and mobile. He and Murphy earned their money and then blew it all on a spree in Fort Smith. They returned to the Frisco to earn the fare to Canada, where Murphy had heard that great money was to be made on the Canadian Pacific. There was, however, no work for them on the Frisco, and they parted ways.[1]

It was the beginning of a railroad life, and, as Pinkerton wrote, his "first experience with that vast shifting army which builded the great railway lines of the United States."[2] That army was, however, ill disciplined and increasingly rebellious and resentful. For picaresque and sentimental as Pinkerton's memoirs were, their purpose was to "make plain the abuses practiced by the great railway corporations of the United States against their employees."[3] He suffused *His Personal Record* (taking the title with purposeful irony from the personnel record used to blacklist railroad workers) with a celebration of workingmen's skills and an abiding hatred of railroad corporations.

Pinkerton recorded these abuses with a fine eye and prose that might now be called cinematic for he, and other writers like him, recorded motion as the essence of railroad work and a railroad life. In this his memoir differs from the extensive collections of photographs of nineteenth-century railroads. Photographs, seemingly so fully of a moment, necessarily reify and thus distort the work and lives that they seem to capture. Each is but a single frame, and everything in them is frozen and stationary. When the camera's eye focused on the turntable, which allowed workers to turn cars and engines, the tracks radiated out from the turntable like petals on a mechanical flower. Yet in such a picture nothing moved. The turntable did not turn; the train and the yardmen stood motionless.[4] Similarly, the camera stilled all motion in a picture of the shops at Laramie. It is, like virtually all railroad pictures, of shops and workers, a still life. All was quiet.

But Pinkerton's stories were about the railroad in practice, which was, of course, all about motion. Trains moved; workers ran and jumped on moving cars; shopmen worked with whirring belts and drills and saws that bored and cut. This is what photographs missed, and what Pinkerton captured. Pinkerton worked the yards at Oakland, Kansas City, and along Puget Sound. These yards were not still lifes; they were the beating heart of the railroad. Trains moved in and out of the yards; workers made and repaired cars and locomotives in the shops.

When workers like Pinkerton thought about movement, they thought about work: not just trains moving up and down mountains, but shorter bursts of motion as trains switched cars, adding them and dropping them off, or the small movements involved in coupling cars together with iron pins. When they thought about such things, they thought not about contemplative human bodies at rest but rather about bodies at work—bodies themselves part of nature—yet actively mediating between machines and the external natural world. When they thought about the sublime, they thought about the workers' sublime.

After Pinkerton quit a job on the Denver and Rio Grande, he decided to visit Leadville, Colorado, a mining camp then rising toward the peak of its prosperity. It was a journey, a movement, partially by rail. He could not make the whole journey by train, because a necessary tunnel was not yet completed. Where the tracks stopped, he and a companion had to step out onto a trail that included rope ladders and planks that quite literally hung off the sheer face of a cliff above the Grand River.[5]

At the end of this trail, Pinkerton joined a large group of men waiting for the construction train to Leadville. Their numbers were "so great as to effectually awe the train crew, and no attempt was made to levy the usual contribution." The final grade into Leadville was steep, and the train had to be split in two. When those in the rear cars realized they would be left behind, they rushed forward.

> *One man—I had talked with him a few minutes before and learned that he was a blacksmith—stepped between the draw-bars in attempting to climb on the cut attached to the engine. The engineer received the signal to go at the same instant and slacked back, catching the man between the bars. He did not utter a sound, but I remember the look of terrible agony, of utter despair, in his white face, as he clutched the iron that was pressing out his life, straining at it in an endeavor to hold it back. In a second the engineer slacked ahead, and the poor fellow leaped from the track like one springing from the path of threatening danger, to fall lifeless beside the rail. . . . It was merely an incident. One more life had been extinguished in the unfeeling, unfriendly struggle. That was all.[6]*

The incident, briefly told, is rich in technical details—the drawbars used to connect the cars, the cut (several cars attached together), how the engine slacked back on a grade before moving forward, the work the dead man did—and it is also rich in natural details, but not the ones we expect. There is only the description of the human body in agony—no sound, the white face, the body straining at the bar crushing it between cars, the way the dead body seems to leap rather than crumple. The human body—the nature within us—and the labor it did was at the center of Pinkerton's account.

Pinkerton, an industrial worker in nature, stepped outside the usual representations of nature and technology. He did not mention the mountain scenery, the vast distances captured in the tourists' gaze. He could not take his eye off the foreground—the dying body of a man being crushed by a train. He concentrated on the technology, which he knew intimately, on bodies and machines in motion, but he hardly celebrated them. Technology and nature were awesome, dangerous, and uncaring. This was the workers' sublime.[7]

The dead worker had been a blacksmith, perhaps employed in the railroad shops; Pinkerton had been a grader, and over the course of his railroad life he would do more work as a grader, work as a laborer loading railroad cars, as a stevedore unloading railroad cars and loading ships, as a wiper lubricating and cleaning engines. He became a brakeman, a fireman, an engineer, a switchman, and conductor on a freight train. Besides the Frisco and the Denver and Rio Grande, he worked for the Southern Pacific, the Northern Pacific, the Montana Union, the Oregon Short Line, and the Atchison, Topeka, and Santa Fe.[8] He acquired skills, but there was no upward progression in his railroad journey. Pinkerton bounced all around and up and down the organization charts.

But no single job Pinkerton held could define him; his actual life took him all over not only the West and the organization chart. The chart could not contain him. He could be, depending on the moment and the opportunity, a brakeman, a fireman, an engineer, or a conductor, or a switchman. Pinkerton and the thousands like him posed the problem the brotherhoods faced when they tried to believe that there was a monopoly of skill within the bounds of a union of specialized workers. This was a fiction.

The great expansion of the railroad networks in the 1880s created opportunities for Pinkerton and thousands like him. The West demanded labor, and without a system of tracking workers, a man's past would not necessarily follow him. Pinkerton's railroad youth was so peripatetic because in the 1880s young men could obtain railroad work in the West relatively easily. Pinkerton changed jobs because he was fired and because he quit. He lost rank because he was blacklisted and because he was hurt. In moving from road to road and in and out of the skilled trades, he was not atypical.[9]

But as Pinkerton aged and married, the labor market tightened and the personal record, the catalog the companies compiled of a worker's history, became more ubiquitous. Pinkerton feared the personal record not just because of his involvement in strikes and his frequent insubordination; he feared it mostly because he was aging, and an aging worker was a vulnerable worker. Companies offered insurance plans and company hospitals, but Pinkerton regarded them as frauds designed to shield the companies from liability and to undercut the appeal of the brotherhoods, whose insurance plans were central to their own recruitment efforts. Many workers shared his suspicions.[10] Offering to pay benefits with one hand, the company sought with the other to limit them by hiring younger workers who would be less likely to make claims on their insurance or use the hospitals. Physical examinations did help reduce accident rates, but they also reduced claims against relief funds.[11] Companies could use physical exams to weed out applicants with what Pinkerton regarded as trivial ailments incurred on the job and to terminate longtime employees who threatened to draw on a relief fund.[12] Companies used hospitals as centers of surveillance. On workers' discharge from the hospital, the Northern Pacific issued black forms to those who would be taken back on the payroll; doctors issued red forms to those who would be terminated.[13]

Their personal histories came to haunt workers. Whatever the abuses of hiring by foremen and master mechanics, they did not create a permanent record. When Charles Francis Adams sought simultaneously to centralize hiring on the Union Pacific and to educate and weed out recalcitrant workers, he quickly realized that he needed "some sort of examination as to their character, qualifications and previous employment."[14] By 1895, when W. H. McCord of Stanford University—a college founded with a railroad fortune—wrote the Illinois Central to ask about its hiring practices, the Illinois Central sent him a blank application form of the kind that William Pinkerton detested. To a worker approaching middle age, it was full of dangers. His name? This would allow the railroad to trace his previous employment—including strike activity. If he gave a false name, then he would have to falsify his family because the form asked for information on his family members. If he was caught in any lie, he could be fired. The form demanded the names of any roads he had previously worked for and why he had left. Here Pinkerton saw the blacklist. Offending one road antagonized them all.[15]

But the key piece of information the railroad sought, seemingly the most innocent, was to Pinkerton the most dangerous. The railroads needed to know the worker's age. By the 1890s railroads refused to hire anyone over the age of thirty-eight for any position below an executive and above a laborer. A man who lost his job at thirty-eight and looked for another had to lie or sink to the section gangs. Pinkerton's bitterness boiled up out of his prose:

A railway employee amenable to the age limit . . . knows he cannot leave his present position and obtain another if he has attained the proscribed age. He will submit to reduction in wages, he will stifle his resentment at the impositions practiced upon him, chafe at the restrictions and bow his neck to the slavery his employer demands. In rendering its employees subservient, dependent; in chaining them hopeless to one position, one spot, for years; in imposing conditions against which an employee cannot rebel without losing his employment, and with it all hope of finding another position at this chosen vocation, the primal purpose of labor unions—independence—is weakened, if not entirely broken.[16]

And yet the aging bodies that threatened to betray them and cost them their livelihood were also the repositories of railroad workers' skills. Railroad work demanded a bodily knowledge that could register the connections between machines and the physical world around them. In a story he told to show the value of a "seasoned" man, Pinkerton recounted how one day a freight that he worked while serving as brakeman on the Oregon and California was "tipping over the hill into Leland" in Oregon. They were going, Pinkerton thought, "a little too fast for a starter." As an experienced brakeman, he liked to feel the air brakes working when they first started down a grade. He began to pinch them up a little, setting four brakes, but with no effect. Only when the whole crew set to work on the manual brakes did they succeed in stopping the train on a flat stretch of track in Leland. The train did not feel right, and as it left Leland, Pinkerton moved from car to car, clutching each brake wheel and looking down to check the angle cocks, "the valve by which the air is cut in and out on a car." On the fourth car, he discovered "some men beating their way by riding on the bumpers between the cars. One of them had his foot on the air pipe, and in endeavoring to steady himself had completely closed the angle cock," which disabled the braking system to that car and all the cars behind it. When the train stopped Pinkerton opened the valve and restored the braking system to the rest of the train. He noted, "[B]ut if my experience had not told me that something was wrong, and we had tipped the hill into Glendale, where we were to meet a passenger train, there might have been a different ending."[17]

Privately, the companies admitted that an increase in new men meant an increase in accidents.[18]

Pinkerton did not resent railroad companies because of some ideological predisposition; he resented them because of their policies, which he regarded as an attack on American workingmen. Pinkerton valued loyalty among workingmen, but who counted as an American workingman depended on race. Japanese, Chinese, African American, and the "dwarfed Italians, taciturn Greeks, and 'Bohunks' from the crowded and oppressed European countries" who replaced American-born and northern European workers on construction crews were not American. When they took jobs "white" men needed or when they broke strikes, they posed a threat to white workers.[19] Race trumped class for Pinkerton, in part, because for him race was a complicated category; it went beyond descent and included character, whose great marker was independence. White men were independent. Nonwhites were by nature dependent, the ideal tools of bosses, suited to the most demeaning work, and dangerous because the corporations would use them to force all workers down to their status.

Racial lines hardened when work became scarce and the number of available workers increased. Pinkerton was working as a switchman in yards of the Columbia and Puget Sound Railway in 1889 or 1890 at a time when the coal miners at Newcastle east of Seattle were on strike, "and the mine-owners were shipping negroes to take their places." About twenty black workers were crowded into a boxcar waiting for the train to take them to the mines. There was a "railroad ball" with a half barrel of beer on tap in a boardinghouse next to the yards, and the switchmen "concluded it would better suit our convenience to have it nearer at hand." They sent a "committee," of which Pinkerton was one, to claim the barrel and "after meeting and overcoming some opposition on the part of assembled guests," they brought it to the switch shanty.[20]

After drinking for a while, they "decided to have some fun with the negroes," and they carried the keg to their boxcar where the men in the car were soon "enjoying themselves greatly." By then Pinkerton and two companions, "none of us sane or sober," decided to make the blacks "the victims of an excellent joke, as we looked at it." Silently, or as silently as drunks could be, they shut the doors on the boxcar and fastened them from the outside. All went quiet inside the car, which stood on a wharf. Pinkerton and his companions' plan was to signal the switch engine back and bump the car off the wharf and into the waters of Puget Sound, where the "car would have been submerged many times its depth."[21]

The men imprisoned in the car began to fear their fate, and one began beating on the door demanding it be opened. The other two men were ready to proceed according to plan, but the "gravity of the situation struck" Pinkerton "like a lump of ice between the eyes." He "realized that we were about to commit murder by wholesale, and in a most cruel and savage form." He told his companions, it was murder and they would "all hang for it." He dashed the signal lantern to the ground and ran ahead to stop the engineer from obeying any signal that followed. "Instead of pushing the negroes into the Sound, we coupled their car into a Seattle freight as an empty. . . . Next morning they found themselves far from their destination. . . . They deserted the car at the first daylight stop, and scattered over the country."[22]

In 1892 Pinkerton, blacklisted and broke, found himself out of work in Pocatello, Idaho, "that Mecca of black-listed and outlawed railroad men," but it was changing. It had been a place where work was easily available, but now it was not to be had. The best he could get was a contract for "shoveling coal at Fossil, Wyoming."[23] While Pinkerton was working at Fossil, the Oregon Short Line, part of the Union Pacific, discharged white section men and replaced them with Japanese. "Prominent in the discussion of this new menace to the American citizen workingman was Buck Bryan, a gentleman of leisure, a collector of fossils, who had some unpleasant notoriety, owing to a certain quickness of trigger and freedom with which he removed objectionable characters from his plan of being." Pinkerton was not able personally to "attest to the badness of Buck, but he had the name of being as bad as they are made."[24]

Buck Bryan held court in Fossil's saloon, and it was into this saloon that the Japanese came. Their reception was "cool." The people of Fossil thought the Japanese "mere accessories in the commission of the outrage against American labor, knowing full well that the mere fact of their willingness to be employed by the railroad company was not in itself a crime. The crime was at the hands of those who sought cheap labor. . . ." As the last of the Japanese workers walked past Bryan, he jumped to his feet "with a yell: 'What in the hell do you mean by trampin' on my foot, you sawed-off savage?'" He lit into the Japanese with a large rolled-up hanging map, the kind with poles at the top and bottom. More startled than in immediate danger, the Japanese fled.[25]

"It was a common thing to chase Chinese laborers out of a community in the west in those days," Pinkerton wrote, "and the difference between them, with their rabbit-like disposition, and the Japanese, was not understood." The workers took the incident as a joke, and laughed, but a discharged white section man ran into the saloon saying the "Japs, reinforced by their comrades, were coming to attack" them. The workers doused the lights in the saloon, "looked to [their] weapons," and filed outside to meet them. The approach to the saloon was over a long plank extending across the ditch besides the railroad tracks. Bryan stood on the plank. "Give me the first shot," he said. "I'll make good citizens of them, damn them!"[26]

Bryan shot at them as they came, and the Japanese broke and ran. A volley from the railroad workers followed, but it was aimed over their heads. The workers returned to the saloon, "where a committee was appointed to wait on the Japs the next morning and deliver to them the ultimatum of the citizens of Fossil. That ultimatum was that they must board the first train that stopped, rice-bags and baggage, and never return."[27]

CHAPTER 8

❦

LOOKING BACKWARD

*The epoch of trusts had ended in The Great Trust. In a
word the people of the United States concluded to assume
the conduct of their own business, just as one-hundred
odd years before they had assumed the conduct of their
own government, organizing now for industrial purposes
on precisely the same grounds that they had organized for
political purposes.*

—EDWARD BELLAMY, *Looking Backward*[1]

IN 1888 EDWARD Bellamy, surely one of the worst novelists of the nineteenth century, wrote, as bad novelists often do, a best seller. The premise of *Looking Backward* was that society had become one big corporation
and all productive property had fallen under collective management. The
United States had reorganized as a giant industrial army; class conflict had
vanished, and the eight-hour day had been achieved. People worked less,
possessed more, and had the leisure to cultivate their talents. The son of a
Baptist minister, and himself an editorialist and a short story writer, Bellamy
began his book in the wake of the Haymarket Riot. He wrote at a moment
when virtually all the ideas that he incorporated in his novel were in the air.
Although people now read the novel as vaguely totalitarian and as an omen

of European communism, it was really very American. It was about the democratization of work. Bellamy plucked ideas not just from the Knights of Labor but from corporate leaders, agrarians, and a small subset of otherwise quite conservative economists who had embraced a theory of natural monopoly. Even the ideas with European antecedents had been thoroughly Americanized. They envisioned a cure to ruinous conflict and competition in an increase in the scale of organizations.

Many of Bellamy's most enthusiastic readers were antimonopolists. Bellamy caught them during a sea change in the movement. Two years before the publication of *Looking Backward*, a journalist, James Hudson, published *Railways and the Republic*, which summarized much of the conventional antimonopoly thinking of the 1870s and early 1880s. As fully as any laissez-faire economist, Hudson believed in competition, but the import of the word was changing. For old-fashioned liberal antimonopolists like Hudson, competition remained a moral value, rooted in a sense of equity, individualism, and freedom and in a hatred of special privileges bestowed by government.[2] Attacks on special privilege in the form of railroad land grants and unfair railroad rates targeted distortions of competition. Reformers, and courts, justified railroad commissions as legitimate tools for restraining the anticompetitive practices of railroads, which were "a restraint on individual freedom." When the Supreme Court upheld these commissions in the so-called *Granger* cases of 1877, it marked the railroads as a specific class of property "clothed with a public interest" and holding monopoly power, in the sense that the public had no choice but to make use of their services.[3] The court countenanced regulation of railroad rates because the railroads threatened competition and by threatening competition limited individual liberties.

"Discrimination" provided the critical link between competition and the threat to freedom. The idea of discrimination entered most powerfully into American political discourse in the late nineteenth century not in regard to race or gender but rather in regard to the prices railroads charged their customers. That overall railroad rates were falling was not the issue. When the Senate Select Committee on Interstate Commerce reported its investigations in 1886, it concluded that the "essence of the complaints" against railroads was "the practice of discrimination in one form or another." The "great desideratum is to secure equality."[4]

Railroads discriminated in three ways. They discriminated among people when they offered one shipper a lower rate than a competitor. They discriminated among places when, all things being equal, they charged more for shipment from one place than from another. They discriminated among things when they offered lower rates on one form of a product than on another, such as when they charged less for wheat than for flour or less for live cattle rather than for frozen beef. All of these forms of discrimination involved movement; they were all forms of spatial politics.

Charges of discrimination had resonance because they touched both the material interests of millions and the basic notions of republican equity. Because railroads were chartered by the state, because the government used its powers of eminent domain to aid the railroads, because governments granted land to railroads and extended some railroads credit, and because the railroads were public highways under common law, their obligations to the public were much greater than those of normal businesses. Critics claimed it was unjust for railroad corporations to set rates that discriminated against the citizens of the governments that gave them life.[5] "When railroads charged more to some shippers than to others and more per mile from one place to another," then, as Hudson argued, "the equality of all persons is denied by the discriminations of the corporations which the government has created." Wealth was "not distributed among all classes, according to their industry or prudence, but is concentrated among those who enjoy the favor of the railway power; and general independence and self respect are made impossible." When such influences undercut "the establishment of a nation, of intelligent, self-respecting and self-governing freemen," the result was "little better than national suicide."[6] Hudson denounced discrimination among things as "prescriptive and unreasonable," discrimination among places as "burdensome and dangerous," and discrimination among persons as "corrupt and criminal."[7]

When Bellamy rejected economic competition as wasteful and dangerous, he was universalizing a much more particular argument made by corporate leaders and some university economists—call them railroad intellectuals—that railroads were a natural monopoly.[8] Railroad intellectuals turned antimonopoly on its head. What antimonopolists designated the solution—competition—became the problem. The rapid increase in railroad mileage in the 1880s, and the resulting competition for traffic, made railroad abuses worse, not better. Competition made railroads weaker even as it intensified complaints about the discrimination they practiced against their customers.[9] Cheap transportation would come from "directing the largest possible volume of movement through the fewest possible channels" and not from encouraging the duplication that created competition.[10]

The moral and political core of antimonopolism was the assault on special privilege and discrimination. Antimonopolists argued that all of the bulwarks of individual freedom were under assault from corporations that were, by their very nature, monopolies. Hudson had conflated the moral meaning of competition as a sign of liberty and antidote for discrimination with a newer sense of competition as simply a tool for restraining prices. The conflation of the two meanings exasperated the easily exasperated Charles Francis Adams, who had already accepted the demotion of competition from a moral imperative to simply a technical factor that helped establish "a relationship between prices and costs."[11] Mr. Hudson was, Adams wrote, "a newspaper man; which means he is no thinker."[12] Everything Adams had learned about railroads in his years as a reformer and president of the Union Pacific could be encapsulated in the idea that "[c]ompetition and the cheapest possible transportation are wholly incompatible."[13] Bellamy combined Adams and Hudson. He kept Hudson's attack on discrimination and universalized Adams's belief that competition in railroads was inefficient and destructive into a belief that all economic competition was ineffective and destructive.

Adams and the railroad intellectuals admitted that their defense of monopoly was counterintuitive. Most Americans regarded competition as "a nostrum at once universal and infallible." Competition, however, helped neither railroads nor their customers.[14] Adams, who by 1886 was president of the Union Pacific, had played a major role in popularizing this critique of competition, but by 1885 he was promoting not his own books but a book by Arthur Hadley, a young professor at Yale. Hadley's *Railroad Transporta-*

tion was not particularly original, but it was wonderfully clear and succinct. Adams believed that even congressmen could understand it, and he liked to send them copies. Hadley became a marginalist and had the marginalist's faith in competition, but unlike many of his colleagues he made an exception for railroads and telegraph companies. "All our education and habit of mind," Hadley wrote, "make us believe in competition." Competition in a free market theoretically made the price of goods "proportional to their cost of production." When the price fell below the cost of production, producers would cease to produce and prices would rise to a point that stimulated renewed production. When any endeavor proved profitable, new producers would arise and the competition among them would lower or stabilize prices. But, Hadley argued, competition among railroads did not work this way. A railroad was a natural monopoly because competition made it less rather than more efficient. When prices fell, railroads continued to solicit traffic, even when they had to carry it at a loss, because their high fixed costs meant they lost even more if their equipment lay idle. "Business at any price rather than no business at all" was their motto.[15] Eventually, of course, some would fail. Followed to its logical conclusion, competition would leave only one road standing, thus creating the monopoly it was supposed to prevent.[16]

Hadley gave a simple calculation that showed why fixed costs made competition disastrous for railroads. Imagine a situation where railroad A connects two places. It carries 100,000 tons of freight at $.25 a ton between those places and earns $25,000 a month. It costs $10,000 to run the trains; the remainder goes to interest, maintenance, and general expense. This $15,000 is a fixed charge that does not vary with traffic. Now imagine a railroad B that builds a parallel line and cuts the rate to $.20. Railroad A must meet the rate. When B reduces its rate to $.15 to gain traffic, A must do the same. The new rate does not allow railroad A to pay interest, but it can still pay for repairs. Railroad B cuts further to $.11. "If," Hadley explained, "you take at 11 cents freight that cost you 25 cents to handle, you lose 14 cents on every ton you carry. If you refuse to take it at that rate, you lose 15 cents on every ton you do not carry. For your charges for interest and repairs run on, while the other road gets the business."[17]

Hadley's analysis was accurate enough in regard to western railroads, whose immense initial costs and limited traffic made the duplication of routes seem a species of insanity, but this was not necessarily all that was wrong with them, nor would it necessarily be permanently wrong with them.[18] Adams, the manager, as opposed to Adams the railroad intellectual, knew that this was not the whole story. Adams admitted that without the immense fraud that had inflated the cost of the Union Pacific, it could have made money. Many of its fixed costs, after all, were for interest on money it had never actually received. And Adams the manager who complained about the inefficiencies of the Union Pacific would have been simply rearranging the deck chairs on a sinking ship if the real problem had been enormous fixed costs about which he could do little. Fixed costs were a huge problem on western railroads, but they were not necessarily inherent in railroads themselves. When in the early twentieth century Louis Brandeis quite surgically dissected railroad rates, he demonstrated what the correspondence of managers had already revealed. Railroad accounting was incapable of giving a clear picture of costs. And later studies demonstrated that, on mature railroads, the ratio of variable to fixed costs was almost the reverse of what Hadley posited.[19]

Bellamy could sound like Charles Francis Adams in his denunciation of competition, but he appealed to a vanguard of antimonopolists, who were ready for nationalization of natural monopolies such as the railroads and telegraph. In 1888 Joseph Buchanan, Charles Francis Adams's old nemesis in Colorado, had moved from Denver to Chicago to edit a labor newspaper, the *Chicago Daily Star*. He proposed a union of all reformers on the basis of the "one thing that all the elements indorse: . . . Government ownership and operation of the railroads and telegraph."[20] In the Canadian prairies antirailroad politics—and calls for state ownership—thrived and their target was the literal monopoly of the Canadian Pacific.[21] In Mexico the *científicos* of the Mexican bureaucracy demanded federal oversight of the railroads that Mexico would eventually nationalize.[22]

Nationalization became a part of the Omaha platform of the Populist Party in 1891, but it tended, like the Populist Party, to thrive in states where the railroads had managed to block or hamstring regulatory reform. In states with strong or dominant antimonopoly wings in existing parties, antimonopolists remained Democrats and Republicans and were satisfied with regulating railroads. Where antimonopolists had failed to control one of the existing parties and commissions remained weak or corrupt, many, but not all, antimonopolists tended to become Populists or endorse nationalization.[23]

Unlike Mexico and Canada, the United States never permanently nationalized any of its railroads, but that the three countries would take different tacks with their railroads was not at all clear or certain in the late nineteenth century.[24] To corporate managers and antimonopolists alike, railroad corporations and railroad competition seemed destructive and dangerously out of control, but paradoxically only the expansion and replication of the corporate form seemed a solution to corporate abuses.

I. BENEVOLENT TRUSTS

The vanguard organizations of antimonopoly in the 1880s—the Farmers' Alliance and the Knights of Labor—saw the imitation of corporations as the first step toward eliminating corporate abuse and power. The Farmers' Alliance "organized farmers from 'the business standpoint.'"[25] When Texas farmers created cooperatives to market cotton and other commodities and when California farmers created fruit exchanges, they imitated the scale and structures of corporations.[26] Charles Macune, the leading figure in the Texas Farmers' Alliance, made the Alliance the equivalent of a corporation: farmers would organize "'for the same reason that our enemies do': for 'individual benefits through combined effort.'" Once organized, famers would act pragmatically, as antimonopolists did in Congress, opposing some corporations and allying with others.[27]

In California, Marion Cannon, a banker and bean farmer in Ventura County and the head of the California Farmers' Alliance, was a leading opponent of the Southern Pacific, which controlled "bean warehousing, marketing, and shipping" across the region.[28] He eventually became a Populist congressman, and he was also an ally of the future Democratic senator and antimonopolist Stephen White. But if Cannon and bean farmers opposed the Southern Pacific, citrus growers embraced the railroad when it encouraged their cooperatives.[29] Similarly, the Farmers' Alliance and the

National Cordage Company would in the 1890s form the ill-fated National Union Company to monopolize the jute bagging industry and secure guaranteed low prices to Alliance members.[30]

The Alliance sought to defeat monopoly by creating "benevolent" trusts such as the National Union Company and by pushing government ownership of "natural monopolies" such as the railroad and telegraph. Their model for government ownership was the Post Office when—and this may be impossible for modern Americans to imagine—the Post Office was a model of efficiency, expertise, and dependable service.[31] The Farmers' Alliance had in its Ocala platform of 1890 advocated the nationalization of railroads but only as a last resort, if the state commission system failed to rein in railroad abuses. The California Populists demanded the "absolute and unconditional" government ownership of the railroads, and they wanted it "as speedily as possible." The St. Louis convention of the Populists, which grew out of the Farmers' Alliance, endorsed nationalization in 1891, and with Marion Todd's *Railways of Europe and America*, the Populists added their own analysis to a large library on what was wrong with the railroads and how to fix them. According to Todd, the question had become "Whether the Railways shall own the people or the people own the Railways."[32]

The Knights of Labor both attacked monopoly and rejected existing arrangements of wage labor as an adequate basis for an equitable economy or a just republic.[33] They embraced a zeal for small independent producers in agriculture and an equivalent zeal for large cooperative enterprises in industry. Like Henry George, Terence Powderly of the Knights attacked the railroads because they, as the first large corporations and as the largest private landholders in the United States, embodied monopoly, and monopoly was the enemy of working people and the republic. George convinced Powderly that the land question was a battlefield on which monopoly must be defeated.

Today both Powderly and George, if they are remembered at all, suffer under the immense condescension we bring to those who backed now unfashionable losing causes. Powderly seems the faintly ridiculous head of a labor organization that did not confine membership to laborers and was tainted with men's club silliness. The Knights of Labor with its grand social pronouncements, secular theology, rituals, odd officers—master workman, worthy foreman, unknown knight, statistician of the assembly—looks like a left-wing Elks Club, at once grandiose and ineffectual.[34]

But both Powderly and George were as imbued with the romance of progress as the railroad men they opposed. Neither wanted to go back to the past or thought he could go there. It was the future that was at stake. Powderly was never an ideologue. He was remarkably, even tediously, empirical. He believed the Knights always had "to ascertain the full facts" before acting.[35]

Powderly argued that since the government had enriched railroads in the name of the public good, it should now act on behalf of the working poor, providing them not only with land they could claim under the Homestead Act but with the means to set up farms. The government should also limit the size of farms to what an owner could cultivate with his and his family's labor.[36] Powderly embraced the Homestead Act and small producers not because he wanted to return the entire economy to a world of independent producers but because he adopted Henry George's view that wages would be no higher than the highest returns a laborer could obtain on the worst land available for cultivation. Unless workers had access to land, excess labor would drive down wages.[37] Powderly in the early 1880s proclaimed the land question as "the one great question of the hour." Workers, as he admitted, never really warmed to his analysis, but for him it was the first step toward the larger goal of allowing workers to transform industry into a democratic enterprise.[38] The Knights' effort to create a more democratic and cooperative society was the dream that Bellamy drew upon.

II. WAITING FOR NATURAL MONOPOLY

Railroad men also embraced centralization. Charles Francis Adams, Charles Crocker, Charles Perkins, Jay Gould, and Collis P. Huntington all thought that the future lay in railroads' coalescing into a few massive regional systems or even one system. Whether this would happen through a process of elimination, through consolidation, or through legalized pools with railroads determining rates under government supervision seemed the only matter of dispute.[39]

The question they faced was what they were to do until that day arrived.

The only immediate solution either executives or railroad intellectuals could offer for the railroads' problems was pooling, but railroad pools had already proved to be failures. Bitterly competitive, the railroads fought one another while seeking parties—the government or bankers or both—that could restrain their own most destructive tendencies.

Vanguard monopolists also turned toward politics for the solution to their problems. They needed the state, but they had not yet completely abandoned liberalism. They, too, had in their ranks people still devoted to competition as the cure for all economic and social woes. The antimonopolist James Hudson and the Burlington's president, Charles Perkins, had opposite opinions of the railroads, but both of them believed that competition was the universal panacea. Even they, however, let the state in through the back door. The market would make everything right only if the state would force corporations to compete fairly in the market. Competition and fairness were not the natural condition of the market. They had to be imposed from the outside.

During the 1880s antimonopolism had secured more regulatory success through politics than the corporations had, and antimonopolists would continue to advance in the early 1890s on both the state and the federal levels. The election in Texas of the Democratic antimonopolist governor, James Hogg, who served from 1891 to 1895, and the creation of the Texas Railroad Commission, probably the most effective in the West, were both antimonopolist triumphs.[40] The Southern Pacific and Gould's Texas Pacific considered Texas the most effectively organized antirailroad state along their routes. Similarly, in Iowa the strength of antimonopoly in both the Democratic and the Republican parties had yielded a successful railroad commission.[41]

In Congress the antimonopolists also had success. The 1880s are not usually associated with reform, but the Foran Act with its prohibition of contract labor was an antimonopoly and labor reform as, for all its racism, was Chinese immigration restriction. The Thurman Act, which forced the original transcontinentals to create a sinking fund for paying back their government loans, was an antimonopoly reform bitterly opposed by the Union Pacific and the Central Pacific, although supported by their corporate rivals. The rescission of railroad land grants and the successful attacks on illegal corporate control of the public domain all pointed to the political potency of antimonopoly coalition, even if the coalition was fractious and unstable. And in the 1880s the long battle over the Reagan bill to regulate interstate commerce and provide federal regulation of the railroads and the fight for the eight-hour day had strong political support that seemed destined to overwhelm corporate opposition. These were straws on the wind that Bellamy detected.

III. LABOR'S DEFEATS

In the late 1880s it was certainly possible to talk about the clash between the forces of capital and those of antimonopoly, but doing so involved a bird's-eye view. On the ground in the West, the forces of monopoly and antimonopoly milled rather than massed. From a distance both sides looked formidable. Closer up they appeared divided, jealous, and ill disciplined. They were as likely to turn their arms on each other as on their supposed enemies. The attacks each side launched could be ferocious and the damage inflicted great, but the results of these tremendous battles were often ambiguous. Large battles, such as the Knight's second strike against Gould's Southwest System and the Great Upheaval that enveloped it, and the Burlington Strike rightly capture most historical attention. Beside them events such as the investigations of the Pacific Railway Commission seem mere skirmishes, but skirmishes can reveal much about the complexity of antimonopoly and the lay of the land.

For all his ideological fervor, Joseph Buchanan remained a pragmatist. The first question he asked about any strike was whether the strikers could win. When workers on Gould's Southwestern System went out on strike for a second time in March of 1886, the odds were heavily against them. Martin Irons, who led the strike and was vilified for it, warned the Knights that they were walking into a trap laid by Jay Gould.[42]

The Knights struck in 1886 because the managers of the Gould system, which included more than 4,100 miles of track and stretched over five states as well as Indian Territory, refused to honor the agreement of 1885. They kept their promises to the most powerful workers—the trainmen—

but they refused to restore the pay cuts made to the most marginal railroad workers—the section hands and yardmen. After agreeing to a meeting to hear the Knights' grievances, General Manager Herbert M. Hoxie of the Missouri Pacific disappeared when the Knight's delegation arrived in St. Louis.[43]

What changed between the success of the Knights in 1885 and their renewed struggle with Gould in 1886 was the legal status of one of Gould's major roads—the Texas and Pacific. The Texas and Pacific went into receivership in December of 1885 for failure to pay interest on bonds owned by another of Gould's roads, the Missouri Pacific. By throwing the road into receivership, Gould turned its employees into federal employees. The court could deputize the railroad's officials "making interference with the work of the deputies interference with the laws of the United States and any action might be declared to be in contempt of court." Railroads in receivership claimed the right to abrogate existing labor agreements, and they appealed to the courts to mobilize the armed force of the state to combat strikes.[44]

The Knights thought the Texas and Pacific receivership was part of "a systematic method for the purpose of breaking up of the Knights of Labor" on the part of "contemptible and blood-sucking corporations and their governmental allies."[45] Strip away the rhetoric, and there was the recognition that Gould had maneuvered so that he would have the government on his side. The strike could not be won in Texas. If workers on the Gould system outside of Texas walked out in sympathy, they would sacrifice themselves in a hopeless cause. The paradoxical result of the bad management, financial plundering, corporate manipulations of the courts, and descent of railroads into receivership was their growing strength vis-à-vis their workers. It allowed Gould to tell Powderly, "[T]he contest is not between your order and me, but between your order and the laws of the land."[46]

The situation of the Knights demanded discretion, but they chose valor. Gould's managers precipitated the strike by firing the local assembly leader of the Knights in Marshall, Texas, C. A. Hall, after he left work with his foreman's permission to attend a district meeting of the Knights. The Knights demanded his reinstatement and struck. Outsiders had trouble seeing the connection between the proximate cause—the firing of one worker, whether justly or unjustly, because of his absence from work—and the consequences that flowed from it: the eventual economic paralysis of an entire section of the country. Gould and his managers made the firing of Hall seem the sole reason for the strike, and the Knights never gave the public an adequate explanation of their actions. Hoxie contended that the Missouri Pacific was an innocent victim of an obscure dispute on a line that, since it was in receivership, was not even part of the Gould system. The Knights' larger list of grievances and Hoxie's refusal to hear them vanished. As a public relations tactic, Hoxie's claims were clever, but both management and the workers knew better. The small incident that detonated the strike and the very large bomb that it triggered were intimately connected. For the workers the issue was their right to organize in order to control their own labor by shaping work rules and having these rules observed by management. For management the principle, as enunciated privately by Hoxie, was simply who was going to control the railroad, Gould or his workers.[47]

As so often happened, the issues were personalized and framed in terms of manhood. After the strike was lost, a story circulated among the Knights of a brakeman coming to Hoxie's office with a request for a pass. He entered, left the door open, kept his "hat on his head in true brakeman style," and in a loud voice asked whether Hoxie was in. General Manager Hoxie looked up from his desk and replied, "Yes sir, Mr. Hoxie is in." The brakeman took the written request for his pass from his pocket and spun it across the desk. "Hoxie looked up in amazement, and said: 'Now, young man, would it not look better for you, when coming into a gentleman's office, and especially so when asking a favor, to remove your hat, wipe your feet, and inquire in a quiet voice, 'Is Mr. Hoxie in?'" The brakeman considered this, took back the letter, went out, and closed the door. He then came in again, wiped his feet, took off his hat, and inquired politely and softly whether Mr. Hoxie was in. "'I am Mr. Hoxie,' replied the general manager; 'what can I do for you?'" "You can go to hell, you round-shouldered son-of-a-bitch,"* retorted the brakeman. "I don't want none of your favors—I'm from Texas."[48]

The Knights' decision to strike for the defense of principle and the

---

* The original says "h——l" and "son-of-a-gun." I have restored the more likely language of the brakeman.

weakest among them was as precipitate and disastrous as it was admirable. The Knights were badly divided, and Powderly learned of the strike only by reading the papers. His own subsequent actions were so vacillating, careless, and indecisive that Gould was able to cast the strike as a struggle between Powderly and Irons.[49]

Gould let workers take the initiative, and roughly fourteen thousand of them walked out or were subsequently laid off along the Gould system. As the strike dragged on from February into March and April of 1886 with the Brotherhood of Locomotive Engineers refusing to support it and farmers and businessmen growing alarmed by their inability to ship or receive goods, workers found their support increasingly shaky. Although in many towns the civil authorities remained sympathetic to the Knights, or were even Knights themselves, the courts opposed them. The Texas courts became their most formidable enemies, but the Missouri and Kansas courts were also free with injunctions, and they deputized Pinkertons and other detectives hired by the railroads.[50] The railroads had achieved a near-monopoly on "legitimate" violence, and when workers and their supporters countered with violence of their own, the situation only grew worse. As pitched battles erupted in Fort Worth and East St. Louis, opponents portrayed the strikers as dangerous mobs. The failure of arbitration by the governors of Kansas and Missouri and their subsequent condemnation of the strike cost the Knights more support.[51]

Affairs had arrived at precisely the point Joseph Buchanan had foreseen when in 1885 he opposed sympathy strikes and recognized the dangers of fighting railroads in receivership. He had made three points. The first two were obvious. The Knights could shut down every shop along the Gould system, but they were scarcely organized outside of the shops, and it would take time—too much time—for this to affect operations if the engineers refused to strike. Second, if they resorted to force to stop the trains, they would be met with counterforce that would inevitably escalate. He acknowledged the workers' potential for violence. They could beat the Pinkertons and railroad detectives, and fighting for "Betty and the babies," they might even defeat the militia, but this would only draw in the federal government, and the workers were no match for the army. Third, and most critically, with each escalation of violence the strike would become less and less a contest with the corporations and more and more a battle with the state. The violence would be revolutionary, and Buchanan knew that workers unwilling to vote for revolution were unlikely to be willing to fight for one.[52]

Public sympathy in swinging away from the strikers did not swing toward Gould. Something more complicated happened. In Texas the strike retained the support of organized farmers, and the workers still drew considerable sympathy in the railroad towns, but important elements of antimonopoly businessmen, who found themselves cut off from necessary merchandise, split with the strikers.[53] In Missouri the most detailed study of the strike in a railroad community—Sedalia—found less a decline of antimonopoly sympathy than a fissuring. Hatred for Gould and the railroad was pervasive, but the growing economic toll of the strike brought resentment against the Knights whose leader, Martin Irons, was cast as Gould's equivalent—an outsider seeking to dictate to the community and deny local people opportunity. This was the double-edged sword of antimonopoly. It could also be turned against organized workers.[54] When businessmen created a law and order league to protect property, they were not, in their minds, coming to the aid of corporations—although they were pledged to protect railroad property—but instead trying to steer antimonopoly back onto a more conservative track. They tried to persuade workers to join them in attracting other railroads to Sedalia to break the Missouri Pacific's and Gould's hold on the town. For them competition remained the cure.[55] In the subsequent election, both the Democrats and the Republicans in Kansas struck antimonopoly themes.[56]

In early May the executive board of the Knights abandoned the strike. The defeat of the Great Southwest Strike dealt a body blow to the Knights, but it did not make other railroads feel secure. Frustrated by his own dealings with the Knights, Charles Francis Adams wanted a climactic struggle brought on by his workers where he thought he could get public opinion on his side.[57] Adams had already threatened the Knights, telling them that he would drive his road into bankruptcy in order to get the court orders for federal force that he needed, but Adams never got his climactic strike. Although Union Pacific workers offered some aid to the men striking against Gould, they did not strike themselves. The Union Pacific remained a thoroughly organized road with strong chapters of Knights up and down its line who G. M. Dodge felt "dictated to the Chiefs." The Union Pacific's spies within the Knights found they remained organized and ready to strike if necessary. The Chicago, Burlington, and Quincy, fearing the strength of the Knights, quietly gathered the names of Knights on its lines and moved to break the order. The only question among its executives was how to do it. In the fall of 1888 Adams reported Denver to be a "seething center of [labor] discontent." Similarly, in 1887 Charles Crocker had described the workers on the Southern Pacific in Texas as "a bad lot . . . encouraged to insubordination and unreasonable demands by the drift of public opinion and the enactment of anti-corporation laws by the Legislatures. It seems to be in the air!"[58]

By the time the general executive board of the Knights called an end to the Great Southwest Strike against Gould, on May 4, 1886, it had already been eclipsed by a second, greater catastrophe.[59] The strike had helped spark what became known as the Great Upheaval—a tsunami of 1,400 strikes against 11,562 businesses in 1886. And many of these strikes, in turn, merged with a national campaign for an eight-hour day. The *Union Pacific Employees' Magazine* argued that an eight-hour day would increase the number of employed and create great well-being among workers; any reduction in pay would be temporary since pay would soon be forced up to former levels and beyond.[60] The walkout became another sign of the fatal ambivalence of Terence Powderly toward a movement he led. Powderly, not unreasonably, saw labor's great assets as the ballot and its willingness to imagine a cooperative society as an alternative to competition. Strikes were a desperate last resort, and he condemned the general strike that his members pushed so enthusiastically. He feared class conflict. As often happened, Powderly went unheeded by large numbers of the men he ostensibly directed; 350,000 workers had walked out on May 1.

In Chicago the eight-hour strikes had merged with other labor actions, including a major strike at the McCormick Reaper Works, where on May 3 the police fired into a crowd of workers, killing six. And then on the rainy evening of May 4, amid a dwindling crowd, an unknown bomber tossed an explosive device in the midst of the police. The Haymarket bombing, and the wild police shooting that followed, took the lives of seven policemen and at least three civilians. It spawned endless rumors of anarchist plots, a period of what the economist Richard Ely would call "police terrorism" in Chicago and what Brand Whitlock, a Chicago journalist, saw as "one of the strangest frenzies of fear that ever distracted a whole community." The bomber was never found, but eight Chicago anarchists were demonized, convicted, and condemned in a shameful trial. Four would eventually be executed, and one would commit suicide in his cell. The eight-hour strikes petered out, and many of the employers who had conceded eight hours now reneged.[61]

The Haymarket Riot inflicted dire wounds on the Knights and the anti-monopoly alliance. On May 14, 1887, during a western tour, Terence Powderly gave a public speech at the Mammoth Rink in Denver, which could hold five thousand people. A ticket costing twenty-five cents admitted both a gentleman and a lady, and Powderly drew a crowd of more than three thousand. He and the Knights remained formidable enough that the governor of Colorado and the mayor of Denver were in attendance and preceded Powderly on the stage. Thomas Neasham introduced him. Powderly, despite bad lungs, was a compelling orator able to fill not only halls but hours. The *Union Pacific Employees' Magazine* gave full coverage to his speech, and even though the editor summarized parts of it, the small print of the article filled six pages of two columns each. Powderly spoke for over two hours.[62]

The speech gave a flavor of the man—his sense of high principle, his mastery of the intricacies of labor politics, and his ability to fixate on the wrong target. He spoke "quietly, slowly, earnestly, with every mark of the greatest sincerity." Listening to Terence Powderly was like listening to a man, eloquently and sincerely, condemning the termites in a burning house. Part of the talk was homilies—he believed in progress, in "the greatest good to the greatest number," in America, and in temperance. But mostly his speech was a "frank, manly avowal of principle and severe denunciation of the red flag element." When he proclaimed that he was "no anarchist . . . no communist" and that he was "a Knight of Labor and an American," there was tremendous applause for several minutes.[63] He praised education, opportunity, and denounced foreign ownership of American land. It was a labor sermon.[64]

By socialists and anarchists, Powderly meant not only the accused Haymarket bombers, but District Assembly 89 in Denver and Burnette Haskell, who had taken over Joseph Buchanan's old paper the *Labor Enquirer*. The *Union Pacific Employes' Magazine* occasionally ran columns praising socialism, but Haskell's *Enquirer* was stronger stuff. He maintained the socialist and anti-Chinese leanings of Buchanan's *Enquirer* and added a dressing of vituperation. Haskell had viciously attacked Powderly's leadership. There was much to attack, but many of Haskell's accusations were ridiculous and nearly hysterical.[65]

Powderly did not come to Denver simply to defend himself against Burnette Haskell; his speech was part of a larger strategy of shoring up the declining Knights. He made denunciations of socialists and anarchists the glue to hold together middle-class antimonopolists and the Knights, but it was a weak bond. In Denver the conservative press as well as antimonopolists praised Powderly. Denouncing anarchists and praising Americanism was political pabulum; it was not food for a strong coalition. Powderly's speech only exacerbated labor divisions in the city. The *Labor Enquirer* gladly responded and was, in turn, denounced in a flurry of resolutions of Knights' locals. The hatred of "anarchists"—the enemy within—sometimes seemed to exceed the hatred of corporations. By September the *Magazine* claimed to prefer the executives of the Union Pacific not only to Haskell but to Joseph Buchanan.[66] The western middle-class and working-class alliance against corporations hung tenuously together in the late 1880s, but fear of anarchists and socialists—and the two were often hopelessly conflated—divided antimonopolists among themselves and diverted their focus.

If the Knights' decline had not been so noisy, tumultuous, and violent, it might have seemed that their brief period of power was a mirage, a worker's dream without real substance. But the wreckage of the fall was everywhere. Haymarket, the loss in the Great Southwest Strike, and the failure of the eight-hour-day movement were bad enough, but Powderly's abandonment of striking stockyard workers and his failure to mediate quarrels with trade unionists within the Knights made things worse. The Knights, who numbered a minimum of 729,000 in 1885, had shrunk to only 260,000 members by 1888, and the number was still dropping fast.[67]

The defeat of the Knights left their current and former members bitter not merely at Gould and the railroads but also at the brotherhoods, which had refused to support them. The brotherhoods had become a kind of castle keep, a bastion of labor devoted to protecting only the privileged few. The Brotherhood of Locomotive Engineers refused to honor the strike against Gould. Its leader, P. M. Arthur, said that he did not consider his brotherhood a labor union at all and that it would not cooperate with the unions of other workers. Arthur had recruited engineers to replace those Gould system engineers who refused to man their trains, and in the wake of the Great Southwest Strike he and his engineers were widely despised.[68]

And then in February of 1888 the Brotherhood of Locomotive Engineers struck the Burlington. The Great Burlington Strike of 1888 pitted perhaps the best-managed western railroad against engineers whose skills, so Arthur claimed, were "superior to that of any other body of men on the continent."[69] In the down-the-rabbit-hole world of nineteenth-century railroad labor struggles, the strengths of both sides became their weaknesses. Unlike the Texas and Pacific, the Burlington was a profitable road, and because it was not in receivership, its workers were less vulnerable to injunction. Best of all from the workers' standpoint, the Burlington was widely hated by its rivals for its aggressiveness and success. And because it competed with numerous roads coming out of Chicago, farmers and merchants could still ship and receive goods even with the Burlington largely shut down by the strike. The Burlington, for its part, was challenging a powerful, stable union, but one whose members overestimated their monopoly on skill and whose conservatism alienated them from other workers.[70]

The strike came because the Burlington was only *comparatively* the best-run road in the West; it still shared the common dysfunctions of its rivals. When its general manager determined policy, his decision did not necessarily influence lower ranks of management. Although the engineers had demanded uniform pay rates and an end to lower pay for new engineers, the Burlington had negotiated a compromise agreement around work rules in 1886 that governed the pay its workers were to receive for various runs. Henry B. Stone—talented, bluff, stubborn, arrogant, and quite deaf both literally and figuratively—was the Chicago, Burlington, and Quincy's general manager in 1888. He was unable or unwilling to make his subordinates abide by the work rules and pay schedules agreed to for various runs. Agreements were meaningless if managers ignored them. Compensation at uniform rates by mileage would, engineers thought, solve the problem of officers unable to unwilling to monitor more complex agreements.[71]

Many of the roads running out of Chicago already paid by the mile.[72] This was the rough equivalent of pro rata, but neither workers nor managers on the Burlington thought all railroad miles were equal. The Brotherhood of Locomotive Engineers' negotiating committee was candid about one reason that the engineers wanted the mileage basis: it would allow older engineers whose aging bodies had sustained the physical toll of years of railroad work to move off the more arduous runs on the main line and take easier runs on the branch lines without suffering a cut in pay. These engineers still had growing families to support; they could not otherwise afford to give up the more lucrative runs that seniority and experience had gained them.[73]

C. E. Perkins, always more flexible in practice than in principle, and G. W. Holdrege, the general manager of the Burlington and Missouri, were willing to concede a mileage basis, but Stone resisted. He claimed that the mileage system would create new inequities and increase the cost of wages. He also did not want to appear to be weak by yielding to the workers and admitting his own failure to enforce existing agreements.[74]

Neither the workers nor management had very precise ideas about the cost of switching from a trip to a mileage basis at the time that the negotiations took place. By the time the Burlington management crunched the numbers, it found it would actually be paying the engineers less than they currently earned if it switched to a mileage basis. The engineers asked for 3.5 cents per mile for passenger engineers and 4 cents per mile for freight engineers.[75] On the mainline of the Chicago, Burlington, and Quincy they were already making 3.44 cents, and freight engineers averaged 4.23. On the branches, wages were lower. On the Burlington and Missouri, the situation was actually reversed: engineers on branch lines earned more than main line engineers. But even here passenger engineers would get only a small raise, and many freight engineers would get a cut.[76] By the company's own calculations, the full-rate engineers would have received less under the new system.[77]

The demands of the firemen and engineers did not make much sense if the issue was wages; the deeper issue was control over work. This was clearest in a second demand that the engineers regarded as nonnegotiable: that the Burlington cease its policy of paying firemen recently promoted to engineers lower wages than regular engineers during their first two years of service. This change would cost the company money, but more critically it would inhibit the production of a surplus of younger engineers who provided a constant temptation for officials to "run things cheap" by discharging old engineers and replacing them with new men at lower wages.[78] A surplus of engineers also made it harder for older engineers who lost their position on one road to gain a position on another.[79]

Stone, who along with his superintendents and master mechanics thought the workers were bluffing, got his strike. The engineers' and firemen's committees, just as committed to their own manliness, mistook disarray among management and the necessary delays this involved as management's trifling with them. Both sides dug in, and disaster, as so often happened in the railroad business, followed. The strike, which did not fully peter out until the summer, hurt the company badly; for the strikers it was a catastrophe.[80]

Both sides found themselves deserted by their nominal allies. The Knights, who dominated the shops, refused to join the strike, and many engineers and firemen on connecting roads refused to boycott Burlington cars.[81] The Brotherhood of Locomotive Engineers put too much faith in its monopoly of skills. Taken together, men it had expelled over the years, men who had lost their jobs to younger men, men who had been blacklisted by other roads, and men who not finding work as engineers had become firemen formed a large pool of potential replacements. Many of these men had reason to hate the brotherhood; some of them proved willing to turn scab. The Burlington, for its part, found that the General Managers' Association of Chicago, which had done much to bring solidarity to the struggle against the Knights and had acted effectively in earlier Chicago strikes, refused to support them. Competing roads agreed to boycott Burlington cars and were stopped only by the Burlington's getting an injunction against the Wabash and the Union Pacific; other roads actively sought to take business from the Burlington. Only after a bitter struggle and with much traffic lost to rivals did the Burlington break the union.[82] The strike, as a director later said, was about the rights of property. The directors had refused "to delegate to the unions the power to run the road without owning a share in it or having any right to interfere in its management." To prevent the Brotherhood of Locomotive Engineers' return, the Burlington instituted many of the social welfare proposals that A. E. Touzalin had proposed, and Charles Perkins condemned, at the beginning of the decade.[83]

The Great Burlington Strike proved a costly victory and bared, for any who needed more evidence, the deep divisions among the western roads. The willingness of the other roads to act as scavengers and treat the Burlington as so much carrion was a sign of the bitter railroad competition that continued to rage in the West and the lack of corporate unity. The Burlington ran at a substantial loss and had to cut dividends.[84] Stone eventually left the railroad, after having risen to a vice-presidency, and, in an odd career for a deaf man, ran the Chicago Telephone Company. In 1897, displaying the same determination and obtuseness that he had shown in the strike, he died on the Fourth of July examining a "bomb," as the newspapers called fireworks, that he thought had failed to explode. It exploded, killing him instantly.[85]

IV. BEARS

The Burlington's victory hardly seemed a victory for railroads in general. To regain traffic the Burlington cut rates, and this only contributed, using the phrase of the times, to the general demoralization of rates. Interspersed in the same railroad correspondence that traced the labor difficulties of the Great Upheaval of 1886 and the Burlington strike of 1888 were letters detailing the dismay and panic of western railroad men as renewed rate wars and competitive building caused western railroad stocks to plummet.[86]

In some ways the greatest power that antimonopolists possessed lay in the most unlikely place: capital markets. Antimonopolists might not be able to kill or even control the corporations, but they could weaken and hurt them. Wall Street bears, corrupt politicians, and worried investors became their odd bedfellows. This strange alliance appeared most clearly in the genesis of the Pacific Railway Commission.

Among the many problems facing the Union Pacific and the Central Pacific was the large debt that these roads owed the U.S. government. The debt, which would begin to come due in 1895, hurt the ability of both the Union Pacific and the Associates to borrow. The Thurman Act had supposedly taken care of the repayment of these debts: by 1886 the Union Pacific was annually paying 25 percent of its net earnings, about $7 million, into a sinking fund invested in U.S. bonds, but a combination of deflation, the success of the United States in retiring its debt, which lowered the interest on U.S. bonds, and the government's tardiness in crediting the company's accounts, meant that the U.S. bonds in the sinking fund brought in only about 2 percent instead of the anticipated 6 percent.[87] The debt had not appreciably diminished.[88]

The Union Pacific and the Central Pacific, sometimes separately and sometimes in tandem, attempted to renegotiate this debt; these efforts did not go as well as they might. At the close of 1886 Charles Francis Adams wrote to General J. H. Wilson, a member of the Union Pacific's board, "I sit helplessly by, and observe the progress of disaster." The disaster in question was the so-called funding bill to settle the debt. Adams watched the legislation that he sponsored slip so thoroughly out of his control that it transmuted into a bill that he tried to kill.[89]

The coalition that defeated his funding bill included antimonopolists, who distrusted the railroads, congressmen sympathetic to labor who feared that Gould would regain control of the Union Pacific, former friends of the railroad who felt neglected, and Wall Street bears who sought to drive down Union Pacific stocks for their own profit. Adams tried to make the whole defeat a plot of the bears. Senators had unintentionally "been like jumping-jacks under the hidden manipulation of Wall Street influences. Men in Wall Street have pulled the strings and these Senators have jumped up on their legs and waved their arms exactly like manikins."[90] Some of the jumping senators had interests of their own to pursue.

In the late 1880s the railroad lobbies were not what they had been. The Central Pacific retained its lobby, but under Adams the Union Pacific had cut back on its operatives. As Huntington would do in California a few years later, Adams announced that he wanted the Union Pacific out of politics. But Adams, no less than Huntington, cared about legislation. His goal was for laws benefiting the company to have "the appearance of not coming at all from the Union Pacific."[91] This was an ideal tactic, if the company could secure such legislation. But it could not. Both the Central Pacific's all too visible lobby and the Union Pacific's nearly invisible one proved to be problems.[92]

Adams blamed the failure to get legislation on the Southern Pacific lobby, which he thought did more harm than good. On hearing of the death of Charley Sherrill, Huntington's chief lobbyist, in January of 1887, Adams wished "it might be the beginning of a succession of obsequies in the case of each of which [he] could designate the person whose corpse should occupy the hearse."[93] Sherrill had certainly embarrassed Adams, but he knew what Adams had forgotten: the railroads ran on friendship. Isaac Bromley, the Union Pacific lobbyist in Washington, tried to convince Adams that a larger lobby, distasteful as this might be, was necessary. He reported that the average congressman saw the Union Pacific funding bill as "a measure for the benefit of a great corporation," and one that offered little to his constituents. A paid lobby could make it clear to congressmen "that some of their constituents would be benefited by the passage of this bill. In short, that it 'means business' for somebody who can 'mean business' for them." The Union Pacific had the name of employing a lobby, Bromley argued, so it might as well have the game.[94]

Senator George Edmunds of Vermont took it on himself to intervene in the Pacific Railroad debt debate.[95] Adams came to regard Edmunds as an "ill-mannered bully, and by all odds the most covertly and dangerously corrupt man [he] ever had opportunity and occasion carefully to observe in public life," but Edmunds had originally wanted to be Adams's friend.[96] Adams had consulted him in 1885 on changing the Thurman Act so that the Union Pacific could invest its sinking fund money in its own bonds in order to get a higher return and generate money for expansion. Edmunds had cautioned against it, saying that if he did so, someone would then demand a higher rate of payment from the company. Adams ignored him, and when the Union Pacific pushed legislation in the following session of Congress, Edmunds became that someone he had warned Adams about. He introduced an amendment increasing the rate of payment to 40 percent of net profits. Edmunds had sabotaged the bill.[97]

Adams and John Boyd, Sherrill's successor as lobbyist for the Southern Pacific, had to sabotage Edmund's sabotage, getting the 40 percent provision removed. But the Wall Street bears were still active, and they got a provision into the bill for a commission to investigate the Pacific Railroad.[98] Edmunds, switching sides, vociferously opposed the commission. He had his principles, and one was that no outside commission should investigate congressional corruption. That should be left to men like himself who were experts in such matters.[99] Senator Preston B. Plumb of Kansas had also once been a friend of the Union Pacific. He had come to hate Adams and the railroad because, as Plumb put it, the Union Pacific was "a selfish crowd who never divided with anyone." Plumb added the investigation of land grants and taxation to the commission's instructions.[100] An alliance of Wall Street bears, corrupt senators, and antimonopolists had not only blocked the desired funding bill; it secured the Pacific Railway Commission to investigate corruption in the original Pacific Railroad. The debt the Union Pacific and the Central Pacific owed the government and the validity of parts of their land grant became matters of public discussion.[101]

Having failed to stop the commission, the Union Pacific and the Southern Pacific, which now leased the Central Pacific, tried to control it. Adams wanted to meet with President Cleveland personally. He sought confirmation of the appointment with the president in code, "knowing from experience that the wires are not reliable."[102] Adams failed to control the composition of the commission, which pretty much ensured that the resulting testimony would be embarrassing. The corporations could endure embarrassment; they enlisted their lawyers to make sure that the results did not become dangerous. The Associates recruited Alfred Cohen to sit by their side as the commission heard testimony in 1887. When Charles Crocker began to reveal too much, Cohen intervened to tell the commission that Crocker was a little confused, and had mixed up his dates and his facts.[103] After that, Crocker got sick and avoided further testimony.

The heavy lifting came with Leland Stanford, who at first failed to appear and then asserted that the government actually owed the Central Pacific money, presenting the commission with what amounted to a bill.[104] Why the government should pay any of the items Stanford submitted, which were not part of the original legislation aiding the railroad, was a basic source of wonderment, but some of the calculations were themselves as revealing as they were amazing. Included was $17 million the government supposedly owed the Central Pacific for loss of business to competing lines that had also received aid from the United States. And Stanford added almost $20 million, the loss to the railroad from having sold its government bonds at below par.[105]

Submitting the bill was a mistake. Having made his claims, Stanford had to defend them, and putting Stanford on a public platform meant things were nearly certain to go from bad to worse. The commission kept Stanford testifying for days. At first the answers of the befuddled Stanford were just embarrassing, but Cohen soon realized they were becoming dangerous. Stanford had no coherent answer when Commissioner E. Ellery Anderson, a railroad lawyer and a reform Democrat, ignoring the question of why the government should refund any shortfall on the sale of bonds, pointed out that the Central Pacific had in fact paid the Contract and Finance Company for its work by giving them the bonds at par value, so any loss on subsequent sales fell to the Contract and Finance Company and not the Central Pacific. This led to embarrassing questions about the disappearance of the Contract and Finance books, and then Stanford refused to produce other books. Cohen began to intervene more frequently, at first to compromise with the commission and then to try to halt the flow of questions and disastrous answers.[106] Cohen asked that Stanford, which is to say Cohen, be given a chance to correct his testimony in writing. There was, Cohen feared, "a little misapprehension as to the answer of Governor Stanford yesterday with respect to the net earnings of road."[107] Cohen objected that the questions were confusing the witness.[108] Sometimes Stanford's answers were contradicted by the board minutes of the Central Pacific approved by Stanford. In such cases Stanford retreated to a failure of memory.[109] He couldn't remember, for example, the purpose of a seemingly memorable personal voucher for $171,781.89 charged to the general expense account on December 31, 1875.[110] With the damning evidence pouring in, Cohen decided the silence of his clients was the last and best resort.[111] Cohen had Stanford and Charles Crocker Jr. refuse to answer any of the questions about payments to legislators and officials or about other mysterious vouchers. Cohen would take the issue to court.[112]

The legal issue was whether Stanford and his Associates had to testify on the $4 million in vouchers with only vague receipts that the commission rightly suspected had gone to friends of the railroad. Hearing the case during the commission's hearings was Justice Stephen Field, a Californian, one of the nation's most distinguished jurists and a longtime friend of the railroad. He ruled that Stanford did not have to testify. Whatever the merits of Field's decision, it protected, among others, Stephen Field. Field kept further details from emerging, but more damage was done by the commission's reading the Huntington/Colton letters into the record, bringing the old politics of friendship once more into public view. When the commission grilled Huntington, Cohen could not persuade him to shut up. His performance was fiercer but no more convincing than Stanford's.[113]

The report the commission issued late in 1887 was worse than Charles Crocker expected.[114] Huntington now took over efforts to limit the damage the report could do. He agreed to finance a New York newspaper, the *New York Star*, for the ex–lieutenant governor of New York in exchange for his getting President Cleveland to reject the report, but this too failed. The president endorsed the report with its charges of "malfeasance, breach of trust and fraud." Huntington had succeeded only in adding a failing New York newspaper to his investments.[115]

The railroads kept trying to get their funding bill. In 1888 Huntington turned to the Republicans, promoting a scheme in which the land grant railroads would give the Republican party $300,000–$400,000 to carry New York in the 1888 presidential election, and they, in return, would get to name the secretary of the interior and other officials, who had much to say about land titles, taxation, and whether the railroads had met the terms of the grants. Adams wanted nothing to do with it.[116] In December of 1888, following the election, which the Republicans won, Adams had a conversation with Huntington that left him with a "bad taste." Huntington was "even more cynical, coarser-fibred and openly canting in his talk than ever before," but Adams was not sure what the "old scoundrel" was driving at. It was clear only that it would cost the Union Pacific a contribution of $50,000 for Huntington to get the funding bill passed.[117] By then, Huntington and Adams were not in this fight together. Adams found his efforts to pass the Outhwaite bill, which would have amended the Thurman Act and created new terms for the payment of the Union Pacific debt, blocked by, among many others, Collis P. Huntington, as well as the Burlington and the Northern Pacific. For different reasons, each subverted the clean bill Adams wanted.[118]

With few friends, Adams turned to bribery. He regarded this as his duty to his stockholders. He took cynical satisfaction when the bribes failed to achieve their ends. The $20,000 he gave to the Democratic and the Republican national campaign committees as a down payment of $50,000 each for moving his legislation forward proved fruitless.[119] And then in 1889 Senator Plumb of Kansas and Senator Edmunds of Vermont once again stood in the way of legislation that the Union Pacific wanted. Their opposition was not the only reason why legislation stalled in Congress, but the two men were formidable obstacles. Plumb, in particular, was "very adroit and effective at this sort of obstructive policy." He "wanted something," but none of Adams's attempts to fulfill his requests for railroad lines and stations in Kansas turned out to be what he really wanted. Adams finally turned to a Kansas intermediary, Morrison Mumford of the *Kansas City Times*, to contact Plumb. Plumb was "very plain" with Mumford. He wanted money, "big money." It was expensive to live in Washington, he said, too expensive for a senatorial salary. This kind of exchange was probably not what Plumb's colleague Senator Jonathan P. Dolliver of Iowa meant when he eulogized Plumb as "strong, rugged, honest, caring little for personal appearance, and having in mind the accomplishment of his purposes," but it might have been. Plumb was certainly honest in voicing his desires. Adams delegated John Thurston, the company's general attorney in Omaha, to handle negotiations with Plumb, but no direct negotiations between Plumb and Thurston took place. Instead, Plumb enlisted Senator J. J. Ingalls of Kansas as his intermediary.[120]

Each state in the Union is entitled to place in the National Statuary Hall adjacent to the rotunda of the Capitol Building in Washington, D.C., two statues of people notable in their history. There are statues of Samuel Adams and Ethan Allen. There are statues of Henry Clay and Andrew Jackson. And there are some more surprising statues. There is a statue of the traitor Jefferson Davis, and there is one of John James Ingalls from Kansas.

J. J. Ingalls was a Republican senator, serving from 1876 to 1890. His official political legacy is a *Collection of his Writings . . . Essays, Addresses and Orations*. They are now mostly laughable in the way twenty-first-century op-ed pieces will probably be laughable a century hence. There are the bland certainties, the *tout est bien* quality of knowing that J. J. Ingalls is senator and Kansas is well served, that those who are rich should be rich, that the poor deserve to be poor, and that all is as it should and must be. Ingalls was the kind of senator who thought Roscoe Conkling an honest man, and began a speech on Kansas with the phrase "Kansas is the navel of the Nation." But buried in the pomposity and flattery is what he calls an epigram. "The purification of politics is an iridescent dream. . . .This modern cant about the corruption of politics is fatiguing in the extreme. It proceeds from tea-custard and syllabub dilettantism and frivolous sentimentalism."[121]

Ingalls thought himself cut from presidential timber, and considering the presidents of the late nineteenth century, he might have been. In 1889 he was also acting vice-president of the United States, as close to the presidency as he ever came. In late January of 1889, John Thurston, after traveling to Washington to consult with Ingalls, met Charles Francis Adams Jr. at the Knickerbocker Club in New York. He conveyed a proposition from Ingalls that left Adams, hard as it is to picture, "speechless."[122]

Ingalls was up for reelection in two years and feared the rising tide of agrarian discontent in Kansas. The Kansas Republicans were divided over the Union Pacific debt extension bill, and Ingalls wanted it resolved and out of the way. To do this, he had to satisfy his colleague Plumb. Plumb wanted $25,000 in cash and $25,000 more when the bill passed the Senate. He also wanted the freedom to vote against the bill and offer hostile but meaningless amendments. Plumb had cultivated a reputation as a railroad reformer and antimonopolist by seeking a law to ban the granting of railroad passes. Plumb claimed to accept no passes, preferring to be "independent and under obligations to no one." Ingalls intimated that unless Plumb was satisfied, Ingalls, too, would oppose the bill. The situation, in Adams words, was that he had "two Senators of the United States—one of them acting Vice President,—colleagues,—and one of them very deliberately negotiating the sale of the other, and urging it on me, the President of a railroad company, as a thing, most desirable to be consummated for reasons connected with his own political future."[123]

Adams consented to the purchase, but he negotiated terms. Plumb would get no money until the bill passed the Senate in a shape acceptable to the Union Pacific. The Union Pacific did, however, place $25,000 in Ingalls's hands to "disperse for the furtherance of his own political ends." Adams claimed that he thought of this and other bribes as a kind of congressional experiment. He did not think the bill would pass. He did not think the money would be paid over. He was acquiring useful knowledge. His attempts would "demonstrate the fact that [he] could never work the funding bill through Congress. The job called for a workhorse of a wholly different build from [his]." And so it did. The bill did not pass; the final payment was not made. The bill demanded friendship, not bribery. It demanded a railroad lobby. Adams, as was so often the case, could diagnose the problem. He just could not execute the remedy.[124]

V. THE INTERSTATE COMMERCE COMMISSION

In the late 1880s the battle between antimonopolists, who sought to control and regulate the railroads, and railroad managers, who sought to lessen killing competition, resulted in a fragile truce whose fruit was the Interstate Commerce Commission. The commission became the great hope of railroad men like Charles Francis Adams for restraining competition. That one of the most ardent supporters of the Interstate Commerce Act was Senator George F. Edmunds of Vermont indicates how tangled and potentially dubious a piece of legislation this was. Edmunds could go both ways, becoming a willing corporate servant when his price was met or an ardent reformer when it was not. During the negotiations around the Interstate Commerce Act, Edmunds emerged in full antimonopolist mode speaking of the "tyranny

of . . . corporate management and corporate combination." It is no wonder
that as the bill took shape, it was never entirely clear whether it was an antimonopoly measure or a way to weaken the thrust of antimonopoly; whether
it was a railroad measure or a blow at the railroads. Neither the antimonopolists nor the railroad men could completely agree on this.[125]

Congress passed the Interstate Commerce Act in 1887. It marked the
culmination of the long antimonopoly crusade of John H. Reagan of Texas,
who had worked to attract railroads to his district in the early 1870s and
who in 1878, as a member of the House of Representatives, had introduced
a bill "to regulate interstate commerce." Reagan, the ex–postmaster general
of the Confederacy, never repented of his treason and was as thoroughgoing
a racist as other white men of his time and place. He was, however, an eloquent antimonopolist whose bills were aimed at "the unjust discriminations
of common carriers," although he consistently defended the presumably just
right of these common carriers to discriminate on the basis of race.[126]

Virtually all railroad men opposed the Reagan bill, but many of them
came to see some sort of regulation as inevitable, and a few saw it as desirable. There was a spectrum of railroad opinion. By 1887 Leland Stanford
was an undistinguished senator from California. He had sunk so low in the
opinion of his Associates that Huntington's cipher name for him was "nox-
ious."[127] He rarely spoke in the Senate, but on January 10, 1887, he rose to
denounce any federal attempt to regulate the railroad corporations as unjust
discrimination against what were innocent associations of citizens as natural
as farmers gathering to raise a barn. Everything in the railroads had "come
from private sources," Stanford claimed, and the government had no right
to single them out for regulation.[128]

These were the kinds of assertions that might have left listeners as slack
jawed as if Stanford had claimed locomotives ran on moonbeams, but the
correspondent for the *New York Tribune* reported that few senators could
actually hear him: "His voice is scarcely audible ten feet away, his manner
betrays embarrassment, his enunciation shows he lacks practice in public
speaking, and he seems to lack confidence in himself." But the speech was
money talking. As the reporter put it, Stanford "was worth listening to; the
possessor of fifty millions always is."[129]

Even as reactionary a figure as Charles Perkins, who publicly denounced regulation, privately saw it as inevitable and worked to pass legislation for a national board of railroad commissioners. The board won Perkins's approval for the same reason that railroad men came to accept a commission to regulate interstate commerce: such boards could investigate but they lacked direct enforcement powers. The railroads believed, and Reagan feared, that members of expert boards would be in railroad terms "reliable men" or in Reagan's terms "salaried apologists of the railroads."[130]

When the Republicans controlled Congress in 1882, the railroads tried to gut the Reagan bill and substitute a measure inspired by Charles Francis Adams that would legalize federal enforcement of pooling agreements. An infuriated Reagan denounced the substitute measure but in a way that revealed the complexities of the Gilded Age Congresses that crafted these bills. Reagan voiced disgust at the corruption of Congress while expressing the antimonopolist sentiments that the same Congress contained. Reagan feared that the "imbecility, corruption, or fear of offending the managers of these corporations" would allow the railroads to master both the government and the economy and reduce the masses of the people to "serfdom, poverty and vassalage." An "aristocracy of wealth with monopolies and perpetuities which are forbidden and denounced by all our constitutions" threatened to overwhelm the republic, "breaking down . . . all the bulwarks of civil liberty, and to the destruction of all manhood; of that personal freedom and independence which is the pride of every American citizen; and of civil liberty itself." If Congress did not act to curtail the railroads "our weakness and moral cowardice" would create "a class of rulers and masters," and "instead of being citizens of a great, free republic," Americans would become subjects.[131] In this rhetoric the stakes of spatial politics of railroads were apparent.

Reagan turned aside the railroads' efforts in 1882, and after that momentum was on his side. The introduction of his bill became a nearly annual ritual, and these bills often passed the House only to die in the Senate. Reagan, however, had made the regulation of interstate commerce a national issue the railroads could not avoid. After 1882, with an antimonopoly majority in the House, the question was not so much whether there would be federal regulation as what form it would take.[132] Railroad men recognized that they were losing their ability to defeat it. Even the Senate committees, the great bastions of railroad friendship, began to weaken. In January of 1886 the Senate Select Committee on Interstate Commerce reported that "upon no public question are the people so nearly unanimous as upon the proposition that Congress should undertake in some way the regulation of interstate commerce."[133] The differences between Reagan and his most formidable congressional opponents had by 1886 boiled down to how precisely the prohibitions in the bill were to be worded, and how they would be enforced. The rival Cullom bill contained the commission that Reagan so distrusted. Then in October of 1886 the Supreme Court in *Wabash, St. Louis & Pacific Ry. Co.* v. *Illinois* ruled that the states could not regulate interstate commerce. This left a vacuum that it was clear only the federal government could fill.[134]

As passed, the Interstate Commerce Act of 1887 was as much a product of the conference committee put together by the Democratic leadership as its ostensible parents: Representative Reagan and Senator Shelby Cullom of Illinois. Much of what Reagan advocated—the public posting of tariffs, outlawing of pools, and fines against guilty railroad officials—would eventually end up in the conference version, but the act took Reagan's specific prohibitions of rebates and short haul/long haul distinctions and either attached conditions or made the requirements vague. They had to be "reasonable" and not "undue or unreasonable." Prohibitions that antimonopolists wanted etched in stone, the law made a matter of the commission's and courts' discretion.[135] Although many railroads continued to oppose it—and the Atchison, Topeka, and Santa Fe and the Burlington both hired Richard Olney, the future attorney general under Cleveland to lobby against it—there was much in it to reassure railroad men. In the phrase "under substantially similar circumstances and conditions," a cynical Charles Francis Adams thought, "there is much labor cut out for the commission, and they are big with litigation for the courts and fees for the lawyers."[136]

Ultimately, the price Reagan and the railroads paid for the bill's passage was the elimination of what each regarded as the essential element for successful regulation. The law's embrace of a commission gutted Reagan's core conviction that state courts and local institutions were the best remedy for railroad abuses.[137] Reagan, in turn, insisted on language specifically banning railroad pools, and government-enforced pools were the key prescription of railroad intellectuals for curing excessive competition.[138]

Still, Charles Francis Adams hoped the bill would improve the way that railroads behaved. Anything, Adams thought, would be an improvement. "Our method of doing business is founded upon lying, cheating and stealing:—all bad things." Rebates in particular were "a canker eating into the very vitals of railroad prosperity." The current system, he held, is "so bad, so rotten, so corrupt, that it cannot long continue. A thorough shaking up will in my opinion lead to nothing but good results." If it worked, the Interstate Commerce Act would be a "blessing."[139]

Collis P. Huntington opposed the Interstate Commerce Act, but he hardly panicked. Like Adams, he recognized the imprecision of the act. He put his hopes in the possibility of amendment and repeal and the ability of the railroads to influence the commission for their own purposes. He presumed, correctly enough, that the first result of the act would be to raise rates.[140] Until the commission made the law's meaning clear, "every company must construe it for itself." Huntington conceded that pools could no longer be called pools "but there is, I suppose, a way of dividing up the traffic that is just as good as a pool."[141]

VI. THE INTERSTATE-COMMERCE RAILWAY ASSOCIATION

For the Interstate Commerce Commission to work to the advantage of railroads, it could not stand alone. It had to be a stepping-stone to greater railroad cooperation and consolidation. The new commission needed to cooperate with the railroads. Worried this would not happen, Charles Francis Adams set about to make it a reality.

At the end of the 1880s it still was not clear how powerful the ICC would be. In 1888 two of the United States' most prominent railroad intellectuals, Arthur Hadley and Adams, provided bookend evaluations of the commission. Hadley, the Yale professor, wrote in January in the *Quarterly Journal of Economics*. In December, Adams gave a widely reported speech at the Commercial Club in Boston. Hadley was enthusiastic. "Never, perhaps, has an important body of new law been so rapidly created and so generally obeyed." In his estimation, "[t]hus far, the career of the Commission has been a brilliant success. Instead of nullifying the law, they have made it enforceable." The commission's particular success had been its attack on the chicanery, low dealing, and discrimination that had brought such public censure upon the railroads. The commission struck "at some of the worst abuses in American railroad management."[142]

But to read Adams in December was seemingly to encounter a different law and a different commission. He doubted whether the law was "in all respects . . . well-considered or beneficent." It had not "produced the good results that were hoped from it." He did not think the commission had been able to touch the double-dealing, cheating, and subterfuge that Hadley had praised it for attacking. The ICC could not touch "the covetousness, want of good faith and low moral tone of those in whose hands the management of the railroad system now is—in a word, in the absence among them of any high standard of commercial honor." Freight agents and railroad managers were too clever for the ICC, and they found "dishonest methods of rate-cutting . . . secret systems of rebates, . . . indirect and hidden payments made to influence the course of traffic . . . unprecedented in the whole bad record of the past." Especially in the lines west of Chicago, there was "an utter disregard of those fundamental ideas of truth, fair play, and fair dealing which lie at the foundation not only of the Christian faith but of civilization itself." The short haul/long haul clause that Hadley thought the ICC had handled so adroitly was, for Adams, a disaster. "Under the operation of the act, the smaller local railroads through the country are being ground out of existence." The result was that "contrary to every design of those who framed the act, its provisions have lent a new impetus to just those forces which it was intended to check." Adams feared that with the ICC failing so spectacularly, "the physician should conclude that they had fallen into the vulgar error of not giving enough of his sure-cure remedy, and so proceed to double the dose."[143] What the ICC needed to do was cooperate with the railroads in forming a "railroad clearing house" that would establish a set of reasonable and firm rates that the ICC itself would enforce.[144]

Adams and Hadley had not drifted as far apart as it might seem. Much of Hadley's praise for the ICC was actually praise for how close the commissioners were to Arthur Hadley in recognizing that the railroads were natural monopolies. Praising the ICC served as a kind of teaspoon of sugar to allow it to swallow his subsequent suggestion that the commission modify the act's explicit prohibition on pooling. The ICC had implicitly adopted the railroads' theory of pricing—what the traffic could bear—and was wisely making sure it was "impartially and equitably" applied. The difficulty Hadley foresaw was maintaining the railroad peace in the East and Midwest that followed the passage of the act in 1887. Rate wars would inevitably begin again since powerful rings of shippers like meat packers or corporations like Standard Oil would force concessions. With rate wars, regulation would become more difficult, and all the gains Hadley praised could be lost. Hadley urged the commission not to prohibit practices "which are popularly complained of, and whose cessation would involve great loss to the railroads," but which "really do little harm to anyone." By this he meant pooling or its equivalent.[145]

Adams ultimately made the same point. His criticism of the ICC was a criticism of those antimonopolists who naïvely hoped to stop centralization even as the operation of the commission accelerated it. Privately, Adams expressed surprise at how quickly the ICC had matured and potentially powerful it had become, and, at least in his own account, he persuaded Jay Gould that the ICC could be the "compelling power" needed to discipline the railroads. Adams, characteristically, did with criticism what Hadley did with praise. He criticized the railroads far more harshly than the commission, and this served as a prelude to his suggestion of how the commission could be useful: by relaxing the prohibitions on pooling, it could allow the railroads to collaborate while eliminating the cheating and bad practices that had always defeated pools in the past.[146] Adams's position was not that different from the one that John Reagan himself eventually came to hold. Reagan, as head of the Texas Railroad Commission, preferred to have railroad commissions set general freight rates, but the next best alternative was a system of pools, whose rates were approved by state commissions and enforced by them.[147]

The Interstate-Commerce Railway Association was Adams's tool for collaboration. Adams designed the association to ensure the cooperation of the railroads running west of Chicago and to have those roads align their interests with those of the ICC. The need for such cooperation was apparent across the West. Railroad war—often instigated by the expansion of the Atchison, Topeka, and Santa Fe—was ubiquitous in Kansas, Texas, Colorado, and California. The mileage of the Atchison system had increased from 2,799 in 1884 to 7,010 in 1888.[148]

The situation was not much better in the Pacific Northwest and in Montana. After Villard's fall, the Northern Pacific began in 1885 to move tentatively toward cooperation with the Union Pacific. Instead of rate wars, they sought to arbitrate. Instead of competitive building, they sought to consolidate, sharing track. Or, at least, that is what their presidents said they sought to do, but neither events nor their railroads were fully under their presidents' control, and what presidents said and what presidents did were often not identical.[149]

In 1887 and 1888 the two roads repeatedly seemed to reach agreement, and just as repeatedly things fell apart.[150] The negotiations began as an attempt to fix territories. They moved to an agreement to use the Oregon Railway and Navigation Company, which the Union Pacific leased in 1887, as a jointly owned instrument to develop the Pacific Northwest with disputes settled through arbitration. This evolved into a track agreement in which each company agreed to sell the other access over its tracks in the Northwest.[151] But these agreements were inherently unstable. When the Northern Pacific finally succeeded in 1887 in completing its Cascade division, this direct line over the mountains into Tacoma made, as Frederick Ames of the Union Pacific noted, "their interest antagonistic to" the Union Pacific's. It also exacerbated the rivalry between Portland and the cities on Puget Sound. The completion of the Associates' line between Portland and San Francisco added another American route to tidewater in the Pacific Northwest.[152]

The negotiations between the Union Pacific and the Northern Pacific proved so lengthy and so inconclusive that Villard had returned as chairman of the board of the Northern Pacific while they continued. Virtually everyone involved carried on the negotiations with a maximum of personal animus. Adams regarded Elijah Smith of the Oregon Railway and Navigation Company, whom he called "the Prophet," with "a strong sense of antipathy, anger and contempt." He claimed not to have the same "feeling of contempt, not unmixed with loathing," toward Villard that he had toward Smith, but seeing this in his letters demands an eye for distinctions in scorn beyond most readers. Villard sent Adams a letter that Adams thought best to stop reading after three pages because if he kept going "it would be impossible that either business or personal relations could hereafter exist between us." Returning the letter didn't do the trick. Animosity continued to grow, although Adams had moments of lucidity, as when he wrote, "[The] position which Mr. Villard and I are holding towards each other seems to me umittigatingly [sic] absurd. I cannot for myself see how there is any divergence in interest between us, and yet we are continually acting as if the widest possible divergence existed."[153] But mostly Adams despised Villard as a "broken man, nervous, . . . half-beside himself with irritability." Villard thought that Brayton Ives, once Villard's ally and now his adversary within the Oregon and Transcontinental, was "worry[ing] Villard into his grave; and the spectacle is an edifying one. He has my best wishes."[154]

Given Adams's dangerous financial maneuvers in the Pacific Northwest and the Union Pacific's renewed building, his participation in the Interstate-Commerce Railway Association was a kind of financial detoxification. Adams wanted the association to prevent him from doing virtually everything he was doing. He wanted the bankers and the government to discipline him and his rivals.

The Interstate-Commerce Railway Association took shape in meetings in the library of J. P. Morgan's mansion in New York in January of 1889, following an initial meeting of railroad presidents in Chicago to create an organization to serve as the "clearing house" for rates. It would unite the railroads west of Chicago in one large organization. This initial meeting had drawn the ire of antimonopolists, who cast the presidents as a "pack of conspirators." It was this antimonopoly criticism that strengthened Adams's resolve to cooperate with the ICC.[155] The railroad men interpreted the Interstate Commerce Act as prohibiting only the paying of money by one railroad to another to maintain prices. It did not prohibit agreements to set prices per se. Adams, as chair of a committee to draft the bylaws of the organization, arranged a separate evening meeting with the members of the ICC in a "hot, stuffy and inconvenient parlor" of their hotel after they refused his invitation to dinner at the Union League Club. The commissioners, although suspicious, gave their approval to the association. The Interstate-Commerce Railway Association would act like a pool in setting standard rates and giving each company "its due share of the competitive traffic," but it would inform the ICC of its activities and use the ICC as its enforcement arm. The association would mediate disputes, but should mediation fail and an offense against the association involve "the violation real or apparent of the provisions of the Inter-State Commerce Act," the executive board would notify the ICC and provide evidence of the violation.[156] In presenting this plan, Adams framed the choice as between anarchy and organization.[157]

Opponents of the railroads saw in the meetings at Morgan's mansion the arrogance of monopoly, but both the *Proceedings* of the conference between railroad presidents and bankers and Charles Francis Adams's account in his diary radiated the querulousness, desperation, and divisions of the railroad presidents. Tension between railroad financiers and railroad managers bubbled over. When Adams said that final arbitration of disputes would be by three experienced men from the executive board, Ransom R. Cable asked whether it was to be "men experienced in the sale of bonds or the operation of a railroad." When he expressed his own preference for managers, A. B. Stickney, the founder of the Chicago Great Western, snapped, "I think that is what we do not want."[158]

But the very fact that they were quarreling over how to arbitrate and not whether to arbitrate confirmed the necessity for an authority larger than their corporations. The association required the arbitration of disputes—the same demand the railroads were resisting from their own workers—and this seemed, in the words of Marvin Hughitt of the Chicago and North Western, "to give over entirely the management of the properties to arbitration."[159] Arbitration would not work without outside compulsion, particularly since powerful roads, among them the Southern Pacific, did not take part in the conference and since the organization, as Hughitt had observed, could never work without them. Adams, who chaired the meeting, agreed. The new organization needed a "railroad Bismarck."[160]

There were, however, no Bismarcks immediately available. Adams was elated at the ICC's approval of the new association, but he dismissed Thomas Cooley, the ICC's chairman, as a "second rate Judge, somewhat past the period of usefulness, and long since wholly past the period of growth." The ICC's approval gave the organization some protection, but Cooley's views amounted to no more than "respectable rubbish." The presidents sought their Bismarck among the bankers. Although it would be impolitic to say so publicly, it was the bankers who could stop the suicidal overbuilding and creation of parallel lines by refusing to provide financing. J. P. Morgan pledged on their behalf to "do everything in their power to prevent the negotiation of any securities for the construction of parallel lines or the extension of lines not unanimously approved by the Executive Committee."[161]

The Interstate-Commerce Railway Association imagined that together the government and bankers could save the railroads from themselves. They would run as smoothly and rationally as industry did in Bellamy's *Looking Backward*. That notion was as fanciful as the novel.

MISE EN SCÈNE

THE DEATH OF JOHANNA GROGAN

When the unnamed blacksmith died, crushed between cars before William Pinkerton's eyes, Pinkerton regarded the death as otherwise unnoted, but sometimes the men who ran the railroads remembered the dead. Not much haunted Collis P. Huntington, but the death of Johanna Grogan disturbed him. His workers died by their dozens and hundreds; the dead and injured men's families descended into poverty and desperation without notice in his letters, but Huntington remembered Johanna Grogan after the special hauling his private car along the Atchison, Topeka, and Santa Fe tracks struck her in Missouri on May 26, 1890.[1]

Huntington had to go out of his way to find out who she was. She was employed at a hotel in Baring, Missouri, for $2.00 a week. She gave all the money, except what was necessary to clothe her, to her parents, who lived in a log cabin on a farm of 135 acres, much of it worthless swamp land a few miles outside Baring. The farm had a makeshift barn with a thatched roof and a mortgage of $700 on it, which, it turned out, had been embezzled from the school fund by the county clerk who had used county funds as capital in making private loans. The clerk, in the words of Johanna's father, Michael Grogan, "done the same to a good many more; when he was about to be found out he shot his brains out." This threw the mortgage into something of a tangle. The Grogan family had come from Chicago and had ten living children, the youngest of whom was a year old. The agent from the Atchison, Topeka, and Santa Fe who visited their farm wrote that although the father was industrious and the family well thought of in the community, the farm didn't pay. He also noted that neither the wife nor the children wore shoes. On the day the train hit her, Johanna was going home "to prepare to go to Chicago to visit an uncle whom she had not seen for a number of years." She was taking advantage of a cheap rate—$1.00—from Baring to Chicago. The Atchison was drumming up business for its new route. The agent noted Johanna's wages, the amount of the mortgage, and the cost of a ticket. The details that mattered mostly had dollar signs.

Johanna was walking the track, as rural people usually did, to cross a bridge, and before starting across, she looked back and saw the engine at the depot. A number of trains were idling at Baring, and she assumed they were switching cars. She had no idea that there was a special among them, and she was nearly across the bridge when she discovered that the engine was upon her. The engineer, seeing her, sounded the whistle, but the result was not what he intended. Startled, she panicked, "and she lost all control of herself and she seemed impeded in trying to get off the track."

The accident was, her family agreed, her own fault "for going down the track, although this is a short way to get to their place and it seems they all take that road in going to and from Baring." The railroads assigned blame, and the poor accepted it, and this created room for charity. But, to be fair to Huntington, he had offered to pay for Johanna's treatment as soon as he had seen the poor girl with her right leg "cut off and mashed above the knee." The train took her back to the station, and a Dr. J. G. Welch was called. He proved an unfortunate choice because after examining her for fifteen minutes, he asked the conductor if she was badly hurt; "it was evident from his excited manner and his actions generally that more competent service was necessary." They took Johanna to a hotel in Baring, called in other doctors, and more of her leg was amputated. If any in Huntington's party held themselves responsible, they did not say so, but as the trip continued they did complain of Dr. Welch's incompetence. Over the course of the next week or so, Dr. Brown made thirteen visits, Dr. Welch was in nearly constant attendance, and Dr. Philpott, the local surgeon for the Atchison, Topeka, and Santa Fe, made three visits. Despite their efforts, infection set in, and Johanna Grogan died. All the physicians submitted bills, as did Mr. Gibbons, who kept the hotel, and the undertaker, Mr. Froggs.[2]

Huntington had offered to pay for her care, but when the bills came in he balked. Poor Johanna Grogan, worth so little in life, became a source of profit in death. The doctors' bills came to $486; the hotel bill for $76 and the $60 to bury her brought the total to $622. These were piddling amounts by railroad standards. Huntington would not have looked twice if these had been costs of lobbying. Still, Johanna Grogan would have had to work for nearly six years to earn what her week's dying had cost her, and Huntington thought the bills "outrageous." The bills were a sign of small-town men's "disposition to impose on [his] good nature in the Grogan matter."

The bleeding, grievously injured girl who had excited Huntington's sympathy was now less a person than a precedent. That his train had killed her did not matter. He owed her nothing. His sorrow for Johanna Grogan yielded to self-pity for being "in a position where [he] could not possibly protect [him]self from swindle so long as [he] manifested a willingness to show substantial sympathy." The Atchison, Topeka, and Santa Fe sent its lawyers to knock down the bills, and they did so; only Dr. Welch, who enlisted on his behalf a justice of the peace, also named Welch, refused to settle.[3]

Like Huntington, the officials of the Atchison, Topeka, and Santa Fe began to see themselves as the real victims of the accident. They did not want a summons served on Huntington by Justice of the Peace Welch, and they "most certainly [did] not want to see him robbed." It was not just Huntington; for their "own safety in such future cases, some stand should be taken."[4] The railroad regarded Dr. Welch's case as blackmail.[5]

When he returned from vacationing in the Adirondacks, Huntington thanked President Manvel of the Atchison, Topeka, and Santa Fe for his efforts to be "just & fair all around." His own offer to pay, he explained, "was not an impulse, but a feeling that every humane man understands." His humanity, however, had to be balanced against manhood. "Since I am liable for nothing I most certainly do not wish to be imposed on by outsiders." Johanna's death had become a contest between a small-scale chiseler and a man who had never been overscrupulous in accumulating his millions. Welch was out of his league.[6]

Still, the death nagged at Huntington. He had the Atchison, Topeka, and Santa Fe use its lawyers to negotiate with the county to lessen the amount Grogan owed on the mortgage whose principal had been stolen from county funds. Eventually, he gave Grogan the money to settle the mortgage. Grogan, who "did not want to trafic on my poor girls death to make money," had denied the solicitations "by almost every lawyer within ten miles of [him] to give them the case for a percentage of what they would collect."[7] A man who spent so much of his life dealing in large frauds found that the dead girl had enmeshed him in the petty frauds of a Gilded Age county. He saw neither justice nor irony in this.

CHAPTER 9

❦

COLLAPSE

Assuredly, this is a complex world.

—CHARLES FRANCIS ADAMS[1]

B Y THE END of the nineteenth century, there were many people who wanted to murder western railroad corporations, but suicide seemed their more likely fate. Nationalization amounted to a death penalty for the railroads, but even those who wished to spare them wanted them neutered so that they would trot tamely under the guidance of state commissions. The railroads, for their part, continued their own rush toward receivership, and here they had no one to blame but themselves and the perverse conditions of their industry. They had already shown that they could wreck both their own financial house and that of the nation.

Railroad managers seeking shelter found few safe stations between 1890 and 1896. In Kansas, where antimonopoly had been relatively weak, a new People's Party scored a tremendous victory in 1890, denying J. J. Ingalls his reelection. Senator Preston B. Plumb died the next year. Ingalls's fears had come to pass. The People's Party marked the beginnings of Populism, which quickly became a regional presence in the South and the West. Rooted in the antimonopolism of the Farmers' Alliance and the Knights of Labor, the Populists threatened both established parties and the railroads. In 1890 the railroads could not predict that the Populists in Kansas and elsewhere would not achieve effective railroad regulation.[2]

Populism had a powerful but limited appeal. With the exception of elections in which Populists fused with Democrats, they never attracted a majority of the working-class vote outside of the mountain West, in large part because of their support of prohibition and women's suffrage.[3] In 1896 the Populists fused with the Democrats to nominate William Jennings Bryan, an antimonopolist but not a Populist, for president. His defeat marked the practical end of the party.[4]

In the early 1890s there was overwhelming political hostility to the railroads all over the West, but the ability of the Populists and the larger antimonopoly movement to turn that hostility into meaningful law and regulation was decidedly mixed. Sometimes, as in Kansas, they could sweep elections and still not achieve effective railroad regulation.[5] In 1890 Nebraska produced a People's Party when the Knights of Labor and Farmers' Alliance joined to counter railroad control of politics, and the Republicans and the Democrats alike maintained significant, if usually minority, antimonopoly wings.[6] Antimonopoly Democrats and Populists combined to elect a Populist senator in 1893 to replace the Republican Algernon Paddock, a friend of the Union Pacific and recipient of its "loans." Antimonopolists had a clear majority in the legislature and elected the governor, but party rivalry and mismanagement prevented them from accomplishing much.[7] In 1894, despite the success of Populists and antimonopoly Democrats in electing a governor, the Republicans carried the legislature, electing John M. Thurston, a Union Pacific attorney, as senator.[8]

On the Pacific Coast, California and Oregon, like Texas and the Midwest, had strong antimonopoly traditions within existing parties, and this dampened the growth of the Populists. In California in 1892 the Southern Pacific confronted a resurgent antimonopolism with its core vote in the Democratic Party. Oregon had a strong antimonopoly tradition in both parties. In 1886 Sylvester Pennoyer, an antimonopolist Democrat and Sinophobe, won the election for governor and was reelected in 1890, but the failure of antimonopolists to control both houses of the legislature led Pennoyer himself to endorse the formation of a third party. In 1892 the People's Party emerged in Oregon. It appeared like a comet targeting the federal judiciary and the railroad, and it disappeared just as quickly. Oregon antimonopolists produced anti-Chinese legislation as well as antirailroad legislation, but the federal judiciary struck them both down as unconstitutional.[9]

The still sparsely populated and less agricultural portions of the West— Colorado, Nevada, western Washington, and Montana—were among the few places where workers, particularly miners and railroad workers, enthusiastically embraced Populism. The biggest reason was silver, whose overproduction had crippled the economy of the region. The Populists recognized deflation as the curse of the era and wanted an inflationary money policy. Going off the gold standard and coining silver at the ratio of sixteen ounces of silver to one of gold was one way to achieve this. Such a policy would stimulate silver mining and the industries that depended on it. Some Republican officeholders in Nevada, Montana, Idaho, and Washington became Silver Republicans and urged the full monetization of silver. In Washington State antimonopoly Democrats and Populists controlled the state in the mid-1890s, capitalizing on unusually high voter turnout and enthusiasm.[10] In Colorado the Populist governor, Davis H. Waite, proved a loyal ally of labor.[11]

As a bulwark against this rising tide of political opposition, the western railroads initially had the Interstate-Commerce Railway Association. It was a kind of railroad Alcoholics Anonymous supposed to suppress their self-destructive tendencies. Their hope that bankers such as J. P. Morgan would impose discipline was an attempt to seek professional care. Relying on the association turned out to be as effective as committing a drunkard to a saloon. The railroads kept all their old faults and learned new ones.

I. AN ALCOHOLICS ANONYMOUS FOR RAILROADS

In late 1890 the Interstate-Commerce Railway Association died at the hands of the corporations that formed it. It was two years old. Among the hands around its throat were those of Charles Francis Adams and the bankers— Peabody, Kidder; Baring Brothers; and others—who had taken over the Atchison, Topeka, and Santa Fe. Adams was the father the Interstate-

Commerce Railway Association; the bankers were supposedly the saviors not only of the association but also of the Atchison. In the end, they dispatched both.

By 1888 the Atchison had driven the first transcontinentals, the Union Pacific and the Central Pacific/Southern Pacific, to distraction and desperation. Under William Strong, the Atchison fought the Southern Pacific in California, Mexico, and Texas. It also challenged Jay Gould and his system in Kansas, Colorado, Texas, and Indian Territory. In 1887 it had taken to fighting its friends. The Burlington and the Atchison shared investors and had a long history of cooperation, but when the Atchison decided to build from Kansas City to Chicago and become the only transcontinental with direct connections to the large eastern trunk lines, it alienated the Burlington, a road always ready and willing to retaliate.[12]

The Atchison regarded its own expansion as delayed revenge for the invasion of the West by other Chicago roads. The Rock Island, the Chicago and North Western, the Burlington, the Chicago, Milwaukee, St. Paul, and Pacific, and others had expanded into the most heavily settled and lucrative agricultural regions west of the Missouri, while the transcontinentals still remained dependent on these roads for access to Chicago, the railroad hub of the nation.

Even though many of its enemies were vulnerable, the Atchison by the late 1880s had too many fights on too many fronts. The Southern Pacific under Stanford had resembled a gladiator so debilitated that he had to lean on his sword to stay upright. But quite suddenly, the Southern Pacific's feared enemy, the Atchison, keeled over and crawled from the field. It had collapsed under the weight of paper. Building railroads without much regard for how to pay for them or for the traffic they might carry, neglecting to provide or maintain the equipment necessary to run trains on vastly extended systems, and accumulating large and often disguised debts were not traits peculiar to the Southern Pacific.[13] The vast quantities of new stock the Atchison had sold declined in value even as the bonds it sold increased its fixed costs. In 1884, as a much smaller road, it had a reported profit of over $5 million, whereas in 1888, having more than doubled in size, it had a deficit of nearly $3 million.[14] In 1888 the Atchison paid $2,361,300 in interest charges on leased lines alone. It carried as assets large payments due it from branch lines, but there was little chance the money would ever be paid. It was living in a fool's paradise, paying out real money and taking in worthless IOUs.[15] By 1888 critics and stockholders encircled President William Strong and demanded a change in management.

In 1889, as Atchison stock prices were plummeting, the banking houses that had helped sell the roads securities (and held large amounts of them) forced Strong out. Led by Kidder, Peabody, they installed Allen Manvel of the St. Paul, Minneapolis, and Manitoba as president.[16] With an annual interest obligation alone of over $9 million and earnings of only $6.3 million the preceding year, the Atchison sorely needed reorganization. The bankers persuaded bondholders to accept a voluntary reorganization in order to lower interest payments and eliminate the large floating debt. They also instituted a new, supposedly state-of-the-art bookkeeping system that replicated that of the Pennsylvania Railroad.[17]

Charles Francis Adams deemed all of this a good sign. "When the Atchison road was taken by the bankers out of the hands of the railroad men into their own, I supposed that we should see at least one management which would always be on the side of conservatism and forbearance." There were agreements with Gould and Huntington, who toyed with the idea of merging the Southern Pacific and the Atchison, to stabilize rates and curtail the wars of expansion in Texas and California. The Southwestern Railroad and Steamship Association and the Trans-Missouri Freight Association of 1889 joined the growing number of associations designed to limit competition within the confines of the Interstate Commerce Act.[18]

In 1889 it appeared that the western railroads had embraced order. They had taken what to some of them had appeared a defeat at the hands of anti-monopolists—the Interstate Commerce Act—and used it to try to control the rate cutting, overexpansion, and internecine competition that was ruining them all. They turned what had become increasingly testy relations with investment bankers into a collaboration that could work for the benefit of both the banks and the railroads.

But it was not as it appeared. When Allen Manvel left James J. Hill's St. Paul, Minneapolis, and Manitoba to take over the presidency of the

Atchison, Topeka, and Santa Fe in 1889, he wrote Hill, "I could write a small book of 'Revelations' now and it will be a large volume before I get thro."[19] It became an enormous volume. Manvel was a railroad man. He knew it was about the books. The books were where railroads hid the bottle. It turned out to be where bankers hid the bottle too.

In the case of the Atchison, the bankers—supposedly the great advocates of transparency and accountability—were complicit in the fraud.[20] The consortium of bankers who had reorganized the Atchison in 1889 sang a song of fiscal responsibility, and its refrain was sweet and simple: the Pennsylvania system.[21] That system allowed much more refined measures of fiscal health than simple profit or loss. It forced distinctions between construction costs and operating costs and how expenses were to be allocated to each account. And, as refined by Albert Fink, it classified operating expenses in a way that allowed distinctions between fixed expenses and operating expenses, with the "operating ratio" measuring "the percentage of gross revenue . . . needed to meet operating costs." It made cost per ton-mile the major measure of railroad efficiency.[22] Such reforms promised much because for most western roads bookkeeping remained formidably opaque. In 1888 John H. Davis and Company, a brokerage firm that was one of the first to employ a financial analyst, reported in its April circular that Gould's Missouri Pacific system had set a new standard in inscrutability with a report that was so "vague [and] confusing" that it was "a credit only to the technical skill of the company's bookkeepers" in disguising information.[23]

The Pennsylvania's accounting system, however, presumed rather than required honesty, and the accounting practices of the Atchison in the early 1890s became quite literally a textbook case in deception and fraud. The textbook was that of William Morse Cole, a professor of accounting at Harvard.[24] The company's report over the four years between 1889 and 1893 showed "a fairly steady growth of gross earnings, net earnings, and net earnings per mile."[25] Were these earnings real? The financial press told readers that they were. In 1893 the *Commercial and Financial Chronicle* assured investors that "statistical analysis" refuted "unfavorable rumors."[26]

It was hard work for a professor of accounting at Harvard to decipher the books and determine the accuracy of the Atchison's rosier figures. Cole was suspicious of the road's construction, equipment, and improvements accounts; there was "what looks like an attempt to hide the fact that there is a discrepancy." Totals in these accounts increased mysteriously from one annual report to the next without explanation, but this was apparent only if a reader carefully compared the reports. Often, the published figures were incomplete and confusing—"the road reports some items for the consolidated system and others for the Atchison system proper." In some years, without explanation, the report included the Colorado Midland and in some years left it out. The report exaggerated the assets of the road and tried to conceal the failure to maintain track and equipment. The Pennsylvania's accounting system did allow Cole to go beyond the rosy bottom line where earnings were "steadily increasing" and notice a decrease in earnings per train mile and that every other element of the accounts was "doubtful or distinctly unfavorable."[27]

Cole's analysis was retrospective; the actual errors, fraud, and misstatements in the accounts remained safely concealed until the Atchison fell into receivership in December of 1893. Then an auditor appointed by the receivers did the forensics, and what had happened became clear enough. The Atchison credited $4 million in rebates to shippers as an asset under the heading "Auditor's Suspended Accounts, Special." Not only were such rebates illegal under the Interstate Commerce Act, but rebates "should have been deducted from earnings" and not credited to them in a special account. The road created purely fictitious assets and credited sums that "had no foundation in fact" to their accounts. The books carried uncollectible balances from dissolved pools as assets. The cash balances, bills payable, and accounts receivable were all inflated with fictional assets or bad debts. The road understated interest charges. Although Cole had no illusions about the desire of all railroads to bury facts and leave others open to misinterpretation by "the unskillful" or optimistic reader, the Atchison reports boldly ventured into "actual misstatements of clear fact." These misstatements "were on matters about which the outsider could get no information from the reports," and they served "to hide actual losses and make them seem profits." When the company did attempt to explain its figures, the efforts were "not convincing"; they reflected a deliberate attempt to obscure "the poor economy of the management."[28]

Not only did the new management cook the books; it continued Strong's policy of expansion. Baring Brothers of London were part of the consortium that controlled the Atchison, and the Atchison appeared to have added the failing Colorado Midland to its system only to protect the investment of Baring Brothers in that road.[29] The Atchison's renewed expansion into Chicago undercut the Interstate-Commerce Railway Association, which was supposed to contain expansion and the duplication of routes. With the Atchison proceeding to Chicago, Adams decided that the Union Pacific must go to Chicago, not by building there but by brokering an agreement with the Chicago and North Western. The agreement would destroy the association.[30]

In the fall of 1889 Adams was excited by the Union Pacific's partnership with the Chicago and North Western, a road largely controlled by the Vanderbilts. It was the largest of the Chicago roads in mileage, with seven thousand miles of track, slightly larger than the Union Pacific and second only to the Pennsylvania Railroad nationally. Its branches extended into the Dakotas, Nebraska, and Wyoming. By cooperating with it, the Union Pacific would "do away finally with the Missouri river as an artificial barrier in western railroad traffic."[31] Publicly Adams denied that the agreement violated the Interstate-Commerce Railway Association compact, but privately he gloated over a formidable combination. The agreement "practically brings together in close association the two largest railroad organizations of the west." Adams envisioned an even larger combination with other Vanderbilt roads, including the New York Central, which would make the Union Pacific part of a truly transcontinental system with outlets on the Great Lakes, the Gulf of Mexico, and eastern ports.[32]

There was no reason to expect other western lines to acquiesce in the Union Pacific/Chicago and North Western alliance. Jay Gould was particularly outraged.[33] When rival roads demanded action by the Interstate-Commerce Railway Association, the association found the Union Pacific and Chicago and North Western in violation of the association's bylaws. The Union Pacific and the Chicago and North Western thereupon withdrew from the Interstate-Commerce Railway Association. Although the association lingered, it was clearly on its deathbed. When it continued to call meetings, Jay Gould wondered whether the Missouri Pacific should be present or should "simply send flowers for the corpse."[34]

II. BANKERS

Investment bankers had long been complicit in the bad practices and corruption of the western railroads. That bankers did not like to be deceived did not mean that they opposed deception. During the great boom of the 1880s, they had vouched for, and thus given value to, paper that investors would otherwise not have touched, and they had sought to bolster this dubious paper with even more dubious reports. Among the most important banking houses for the railroads, particularly for the Associates of the Southern Pacific, were the interlocking firms of the Speyer family: Speyer Ellisen of Frankfurt, Speyer and Company in New York, and Speyer Brothers in London. Speyer and Company had in the early 1880s encouraged arranging the Central Pacific's books to "make as good a showing as possible to facilitate the negotiation of bonds." The Associates had done so thorough a job that they had deceived even themselves. "[I]n some way or other, I do not remember just how it came about," Huntington prefaced one explanation to Charles Crocker of the mixing and reallocation of the earnings of subsidiary roads. Neither the Speyers nor the Associates knew the true allocation.[35] And as long as the bonds sold and the railroads paid interest, no one really cared.

After the severe downturn of 1883–84, it became apparent that the bankers were no longer so willing to go along and get along. The immediate cause of a souring of relations between the Southern Pacific and the Speyers was unsurprisingly Leland Stanford. The usual procedure of the Associates was to sell their bonds through a pool established by Speyer and Company, which had the exclusive right to market the bonds at a set price. The bankers also lent money to the Associates with the bonds as collateral. It was in the interests of both the Associates and Speyer and Company to maintain a base price for the bonds, and they did so by buying up any privately held bonds that came on the market. The Associates did retain the right to sell bonds that they held personally on the California market, but the California market was small and their bonds were supposed to stay there. Doing their best to sustain Southern Pacific bonds on a bad market in 1883, Speyer and Company found bonds appearing on both the New York and the European markets that were being sold for a California account. They told Huntington that they suspected, correctly enough, that the bonds "emanate from [his] associates and friends in California." The bonds came from Leland Stanford. He was, in effect, forcing his bankers and Associates to buy his bonds to maintain market prices. Huntington could not remember when he had "been so much annoyed," which, given his relationship to Stanford, meant he must have been ready to chew on the furniture. By December, Speyer and Company was ready to break ties with the Associates.[36]

That in the 1880s the accounting and financial affairs of the Central and Southern Pacific were opaque in court, opaque before the Pacific Railway Commission, and opaque to the California railroad commissioners was less surprising than that they were a mystery to the corporations' own bankers. When Speyer and Company asked for details on expenditures on sundry expenses of over a million dollars, William Miller, the Central Pacific accountant, "explains about a small increase in taxes!!!" When they asked about $3.5 million dollars spent on equipment and construction materials, Miller "kindly gives us details of $159,500!!! & ignores all the rest. We must confess that we cannot consider these any answers to our questions."[37] The Speyers recognized that investors were growing weary of the practices of American railroads and their bankers. In the fall of 1883 Speyer and Company had informed the Associates that it was "most difficult to put the figures (for the Southern Pacific) in a favorable light" for the bondholders. The Speyers knew that information published by Poor's *Manual* and provided by the railroad was "quite wrong." They knew, too, that the bonds of the Southern Pacific could never have been issued on their own merits, and would have been worth less than 20 percent of their present price "if it had not been for C.P. support & even more having Speyer's name on the prospectus."[38]

The Speyers insisted that henceforth "the books & general arrangements be properly kept. There is here now a great outcry by the public against

American R.R. accounts & information being withheld & we believe the Companies that will meet the views of the British public in this matter will profit by it. . . . The whole office arrangements in San Francisco are wretched." British investors had found the reports for previous years "utterly misleading," and from the information available to them, Speyer and Company found the accounting rife with mistakes and deceptions. It thought that the administration of the sinking fund established to repay the government debt was corrupt and that trustees had to be appointed with their first loyalty to the bondholders and not to the Associates.[39]

All of this was perfectly true, but it condemned the Speyers nearly as thoroughly as the Associates. Bankers and railway promoters had their hands so deeply and lucratively in each other's pockets that it was hard to disengage. The bankers made large profits off the sales of securities that also enriched promoters, and the promoters borrowed heavily from the bankers. The collateral for these loans was often the same securities that the bankers sold or securities they would sell in the future. A break in the price of securities would be disastrous for everyone.[40]

How, given fraudulent and incomplete information and their complicity in selling securities worth a fraction of their asking price, did the bankers maintain the trust of European and eastern investors? Their greatest asset was the so-called long depression of the late nineteenth century. Falling returns on investments in Europe and low interest rates in the 1870s and 1880s drove European capital to seek higher returns in developing countries such as the United States where investors encountered lies, deception, fraud, and large and repeated defaults. Bankers had led many investors into this hazard, but this made the bankers all the more necessary.

Bankers, as the German banks did through Henry Villard in the case of the Kansas Pacific, began to exert considerable leverage on railroads in receivership in order to protect the interests of bondholders. To sell securities in the late 1880s, bankers became far more solicitous and rigorous in trying to pry detailed and accurate information from the railroads. They might still deceive investors, but they did not want to be deceived themselves. These new demands had annoyed Charles Crocker no end. Crocker wrote that he knew that Huntington liked "Speyer & Co. as much as I dislike them, for

I assure you, I do not like them. They always make such conditions and ask so many questions, and demand this and that thing to be done, which is very annoying to me, though it may not be to you."[41] By 1885 Speyer and Company was examining the Southern Pacific's and Central Pacific's bond issues closely, and it grew more and more insistent on explanations for the figures the Associates submitted.[42]

American railroad promoters knew that bankers connected them with European capital, and they knew that others besides Americans sought European capital; what they did not know until 1890 were the ramifications of this. In 1890 they learned. The name of the lesson was Argentina.

The Argentinean Pampa with its rapidly expanding grain and livestock production, its frenzied and subsidized railroad building, its private and public corruption, its dispossession of native peoples, and its heavy foreign immigration was a virtual doppelgänger of the North American West in the 1880s. Buenos Aires and Chicago emerged as parallel places. Each depended on an immense, flat, grassy interior. Each had benefited from a wave of recent conquest that had dispossessed and displaced indigenous inhabitants. Each depended on heavy infusions of outside capital. Both were ports; both were railroad centers. Railroads carried wheat and cattle for distribution and slaughter. In 1890 it turned out that these parallel places were connected.

Capital connected the Pampa and the Great Plains; capital connected Chicago and Buenos Aires. More particularly the London banking house of Baring Brothers connected them. Railroads in Argentina depended on new loans and investment to cover the fixed debt from old loans and investments and the cost of imported equipment. This made them twins of North American transcontinentals, which also needed steady infusions of new capital. Baring Brothers of London sold Argentinean bonds and made heavy investments in Argentina's railroads and land. And for a while this brought the bankers large profits.[43]

In 1889 foreign investment in Argentina, seeking even greener fields, declined while Argentinean export revenues fell with the price of wheat on world markets. The Argentineans began having difficulty meeting their interest payments, which in 1890 amounted to 40 percent of the country's foreign expenditures. The existing British loans, payable in gold, began to look more and more risky as the collateral held for them fell in value. Argentinean securities held by Baring Brothers became negotiable on London markets only at a heavy loss. With declining wheat prices and declining investment, land prices fell; provincial banks that had made domestic loans with land as security failed, and the government collapsed. The tragicomic finale came when new government officials seeking additional loans met delegates from Baring Brothers, who asked the new officials to pay what they owed and release the Barings from existing contracts. Only the intervention of the Bank of England, which assumed Baring Brothers' obligations and then reorganized the firm, prevented the bank's complete collapse.[44] This would seem to have been a disaster in a distant place, but that is not how it seemed to Henry Villard and Charles Francis Adams.

III. VILLARD AND ADAMS

Henry Villard had returned to New York in 1886 bearing bags of German money and the influence of the Deutsche Bank. Villard's railroad career was a series of recapitulations that always seemed to begin and end in the same way. German trust launched him, and Germany was his refuge in disgrace. After his first failure at the Northern Pacific, Villard in effect returned to his German womb and was reborn. He reentered the United States on the wings of German capital. Someone, after all, had to guide German foreign investments in the late 1880s, when about 17 percent of the 667 million marks that Germans invested annually went to the United States. Villard acted as an intermediary between the Deutsche Bank, other German banks, and American railroads, engineering a series of bond sales that benefited both him and the bankers. In late 1886 he returned to New York as the Deutsche Bank's agent to negotiate the purchase of securities from Drexel, Morgan, and Company.[45]

In New York, Villard recapitulated earlier moves that took him from being an independent operator to holding a position of power in the Northern Pacific. Like so many of his railroad contemporaries, Villard mixed greed with heedless optimism and thought the result was vision. John Ainsworth, from whom Villard bought the Oregon Steam Navigation Company in

1881, had recognized very quickly that Villard "never prepares for nor anticipates disasters or disappointment, but presumes always on a greater increase of business than the growth of the country will warrant."[46] He returned to the Northern Pacific boardroom in the fall of 1887 and was put on the Northern Pacific's finance committee. He later claimed that he had returned from a sense of duty to rescue his old company from disaster. In the fall of 1888 he declined a nomination to the road's presidency, successfully urging the election of Thomas Oakes instead. By 1889 Villard was chairman of the board. Once again channeling Jay Cooke, Villard promoted third mortgage Northern Pacific bonds, which he marketed through syndicates that included "August Belmont, the Rothschilds, the Northern Pacific Directors and himself." Drexel and Morgan snapped up the bonds at a premium, and in yet another demonstration of hope trumping experience, the Deutsche Bank had to close the subscription in Germany immediately after opening it. Applications for the $4.5 million offered covered the issue several times over. The Deutsche Bank doubled its purchase of bonds the next year.[47]

The Northern Pacific had always been notable for selling more paper than transportation, and that did not change. The success in selling third mortgage bonds led to the issuing of yet more bonds—$160 million of the 5 percent consols, or consolidated bonds—which were designed to run for one hundred years and fund new lines as well as retire the higher-interest first and second mortgage bonds and the old Oregon and Transcontinental bonds now largely held by Villard's new holding company, the North American Company.[48] As long as European money was readily available, the plan seemed sound, but Frederick Billings, a longtime power in the Northern Pacific who was all too familiar with the difference between Northern Pacific plans and Northern Pacific execution, was cautious. He wanted the purpose of the new bonds explicitly stated and a floor set on them below which the directors would not be allowed to sell. "Let us," he wrote, "make no mistakes."[49] The Northern Pacific immediately made mistakes of the most fundamental kind. In its attempt to retire the first mortgage Oregon and Transcontinental bonds, officials miscalculated the number of bonds involved. Then, as financial markets tumbled in 1891, Drexel and Morgan reneged on its earlier agreement for marketing the new consols. A renegotiated agreement greatly increased the cost.[50] Billings died in September of 1890 and was not there to object.[51]

Just as with the Atchison and the Union Pacific, Chicago became the siren beckoning the Northern Pacific to disaster. The Northern Pacific had leased Wisconsin Central to gain direct access to Chicago. It built an expensive new terminal and then created a new company, the Chicago and Northern Pacific, to manage its interests east of the Mississippi and south of Duluth. To do this, it took on new fixed costs. It did all these things never thinking of Argentina.

John Sherman and the U.S. Congress also gave little thought to Argentina. Sherman was a senator from Ohio, the less famous brother of the Civil War hero General William Tecumseh Sherman. He had succeeded Salmon P. Chase, when Chase became Lincoln's secretary of the Treasury. Sherman would also become secretary of the Treasury as well as secretary of state under Rutherford B. Hayes, but he spent most of his career in the Senate, where he was often a friend of the railroads. He was known as the "financial statesman," of the Republican Party, and he yearned for, but never achieved, the presidency.[52]

John Sherman was an odd man to have his name attached to two of the most famous, and least successful, antimonopoly measures of the late nineteenth century: the Sherman Silver Purchase Act and the Sherman Antitrust Act. Sherman was not an antimonopolist, but he recognized that by 1890 antimonopolist strength in Congress necessitated compromises beyond the Interstate Commerce Act, and the result would be the two acts passed in July of 1890 that bear his name. In making a case for political compromise, one should avoid John Sherman. If Henry Clay was the Great Compromiser, John Sherman was the Not So Great Compromiser. The Sherman Silver Purchase Act failed to achieve the intent of the original bills it replaced, and the Sherman Antitrust Act aimed at capital but hit labor.

The Sherman Antitrust Act, for all its failings, was a radical piece of legislation. It forbade—until the Supreme Court reconsidered and decided otherwise twenty years later—*all* combinations in restraint of trade and attempts to monopolize all or part of interstate trade. From one vantage point, it was a "revolutionary" attack on price-fixing.[53] It paradoxically rejected laissez-faire in the name of restoring competition. The market was supposed to prevent monopolies, but when monopolies arose in the market, the government had to intervene to reproduce the very market that had produced monopoly.

To vanguard antimonopolists and the railroad presidents who believed in natural monopolies, however, the Sherman Antitrust Act threatened the ability to set prices created by the ICC. The Harrison administration quickly used the law against the Trans-Missouri Freight Association, and the railroads defended themselves by saying that their regulation was preempted by the ICC. Two lower courts upheld their position. The arrival of the new Cleveland administration in 1893 seemed to further decrease the danger. Richard Olney, the Burlington railroad attorney who became attorney general, refused to enforce a law that he believed "to be no good."[54]

Olney, however, could not stop the government's appeal of the Trans-Missouri Freight Association case from proceeding. It wound its way through the courts, and the Supreme Court finally heard it in 1897. The court ruled that the defunct association had illegally acted in restraint of trade and that the railroads were subject to the Sherman Antitrust Act.[55] Their price-fixing was illegal.

The second piece of legislation to bear Sherman's name was the Sherman Silver Purchase Act. In the 1870s and 1880s Greenbackers and Silver Republicans regarded Sherman as a foe, but he was central to the compromise—opposed by advocates of free and unlimited coinage of silver—that produced the act of 1890.[56] The debate on the bill did not directly concern railroads, but the bill would have a more immediate impact on the railroads than the antitrust act because it would quickly affect their attempts to raise capital.[57]

Congress passed the Sherman Silver Purchase Act just as the Argentinean crisis reached its apex. The events had no logical connection; the timing was quite contingent. In history, contingency matters. Argentina panicked investors; the Sherman Silver Purchase Act added to their panic. The railroads did not see any of this coming.

Despite the breakup of the Interstate-Commerce Railway Association, Charles Francis Adams had been uncharacteristically sanguine at the beginning of 1890. Unlike virtually all other railroad men, Adams wore his pessimism like a badge of honor. His journal entry for January 1, 1890, which reads like a travel brochure, was unusual, even remarkable. The Union Pacific now had "8,000 miles of road [and] . . . a whole fleet of steamers." It covered "the continent from the Missouri to the Pacific and from the Lakes to the Gulf." Adams thought that if his current "confoundedly dusty and prosaic" work was successful, the future of the road would "be very different from the past." Although he took no pleasure in his job, he thought success was at hand.[58]

As the year wore on, Adams's journal entries grew more familiar: venomous, despairing, and, at once, self-accusatory and self-justifying. They were accounts of a corporation that had lost its grip by a man who was losing his grip. All Adams believed he had accomplished was a delusion. He thought he "had perfected a good local organization." He had eliminated the floating debt, and he thought he had brought expenses under control. But he wrote, "[I had been] just shouting before I was out of the woods; and to-day these woods lie about me thicker and more tangled than ever before." The story he poured out in his journal was a "contemptible tale of intrigue, incompetency, lying, stealing and betraying."[59]

The essence of the story was simple. After Thomas Potter's death, Adams had appointed a weak and indecisive man—W. H. Holcomb, or "old flabby-guts," as Adams came to call him—vice-president and executive head of the company. Holcomb was immediately beset with a conspiracy led by Charles Mellen (no relation to William Mellen of the Northern Pacific), a more able man who felt himself passed over. Omaha had become a "hot-bed of intrigue" and corruption. Adams, who thought that the constant administrative changes and reforms during his tenure had demoralized the company, decided he had to support Holcolmb, but poor Holcomb floundered, demonstrating a "flabby incapacity and indecision in the presence of the conspirators." While its executives intrigued against each other, the road deteriorated. A railroad Adams had thought on the verge of a new era was instead the same old Union Pacific. He discovered in June that Sidney Dillon's nephew had secured a no-bid contract that would milk the road for $8,000 a mile above the "proper cost" of the new line from Seattle to Portland. He quashed the contract, but it was yet another sign of the continuing rot within. The road was so poorly managed that during the winter it had barely "escaped a complete collapse." Locomotives "unfit for service could hardly get the train over a track." There was "hardly a pretence at regular train service."[60]

Initially, Adams raved more than he acted. His subordinates were as "sorry a pack of knaves and incapables as [he] want[ed] to see." Mellen was a "shallow fool," but Adams could not spare him: "he is a tool that cuts, and of such I have had few." Chambers H. McKibben, one of the educated young men Adams had sent west, was a "liar, libertine, ingrate, drunkard and thief." But above all there was Holcomb, whose "gross, inexcusable, and still inexplicable incompetency" had ruined all of Adams's plans. Adams saw himself as a Frederick the Great or Marlborough or Napoleon whose brilliant plans had come to naught through the failure of some "wretched lieutenant."[61]

Adams was ready to resign. His long journal entries dripped with self-pity and self-loathing, but "in the dreary little parlor of that dismal Millard House in Omaha" Frederick Ames and Edwin Atkins, both members of the board, persuaded him that he must stay on. And so, in July, Adams wrote, "I wearily bowed my back, and took up my heavy burden."[62] The burden was a dysfunctional railroad with a large floating debt that was unable to pay its fixed costs. Adams would have to sell securities to save it; that was a challenge in the best of times, and 1890 was not the best of times.

There was a manic-depressive quality to Adams's account of the last six months of 1890. He was manic when he traveled west and saw the line. The Pacific Northwest fired his imagination, and the young men he met there gave him hope. He "felt what a great thing the Union Pacific system was."[63] When he came east, discouragement and despair met him at the station. He sat in Boston and received numbers, and the numbers were not good. In September, Adams told Grenville Dodge, who, despite Dodge's age and illness, Adams hoped would succeed him, that he intended to resign, but he went west again, and this time even Omaha buoyed him up. He persuaded himself that what excited him was actually running the road, "the management of the property, the development of the system, the contact with the officers." It was only the finances and dealings with Wall Street that depressed him.[64]

The problem was not lack of traffic. The Union Pacific was "overwhelmed with traffic; trains were daily running into each other and a carnival of accidents prevailed." The problem was that traffic drove up expenses faster than revenue. Expenses were running $500,000 over the preceding year. By Adams's account Holcomb had done nothing to cut expenses and improve the road's performance. The problem in Adams's mind was ineptitude and inefficiency, and remedies came too late.[65]

The Union Pacific was so vulnerable because it had been unable to sell securities since the preceding March. It had acquired majority control of the old Oregon Railway and Navigation Company from Villard, but to pay for its stock it resorted to $4.5 million in short-term notes that it intended to redeem by the sale of 5 percent bonds. Until those bonds were sold, it had huge floating debt.[66]

The answer as to why the Union Pacific was unable to sell securities was not a single trail to a single cause. There were too many bonds for too many roads on the market in early 1890, and Adams did not want to discount the bonds too heavily. He preferred to wait. That there was no reason for an investor to trust the Union Pacific was apparent from Adams's correspondence, but investors did not have access to his correspondence, and they had bought securities from even worse railroads, including earlier versions of the Union Pacific. Still, two of the main lines of explanation for the failure to arrange bond sales led back to Washington and to Buenos Aires.

The Argentinean crisis spooked British and other European investors, who saw all too many parallels between Argentina and the United States. This was hardly an irrational reaction. The West *was* a larger version of Argentina. By the autumn of 1890 the crisis that began in Argentina had ricocheted through London and struck North America—"assuredly," Adams wrote, "this is a complex world." The Sherman Silver Purchase Act in June of 1890 and the fear of a devalued dollar only heightened the anxieties of already nervous European investors, who were liquidating their American investments. Unable to sell their bonds, the railroads had to borrow. The securities they depended on for collateral were falling rapidly, and they were trying desperately to maintain security prices to avoid margin calls for more collateral on their loans. Bears on the New York market smelled blood, and they attacked, further driving down prices. Europeans increased their sale of American securities, and European banks called in their loans. It was not only the Union Pacific that was in trouble. In the autumn of 1890 Henry Villard's private correspondence, always a fine barometer of trouble, reached a pitch somewhere between panic and hysteria.[67]

This was the situation in which the crisis within the Union Pacific came to a head. When, in the past, Adams needed money quickly to meet fixed obligations, he turned to the House of Baring as his "last and most reliable resource in times of financial trouble." In November in 1890, when Thomas Baring was en route to New York, Adams claimed that he still had no clear idea that Baring Brothers was on the verge of failure. He expected Barings to lend the Union Pacific money. Adams claimed to be shocked when Baring refused him. He felt "that the game was up."[68]

Adams had suspected since April that Gould was "getting ready to make a drive at the Union Pacific, and probably me personally."[69] Adams had alienated Gould by his alliance with the Chicago and North Western, but the animosity was older than that. Gould had been Adams's target in *Chapters of Erie*, and Gould had a "long memory" and was "very astute."[70] Adams thought Gould had control of the Associated Press, and newspaper attacks on the Union Pacific were a sign that "the whole pack, headed by Gould are now at work to pull me down."[71]

Rumors circulated that Jay Gould was seeking to control the Union Pacific to save it, and with it the entire American railroad system, but this was possible only if Adams could be gotten out of the way. Gould, of course, denied the stories, but Adams recognized his own obituary. "He was gunning for me, and he had dropped me."[72] The wounded Adams's last hope was that the Chicago and North Western and the Vanderbilt interests would save him. While he waited for his answer at the Knickerbocker Club in New York, Adams wrote cover letters to go out with his just completed *Life of Dana*. Hughitt of the Chicago and North Western came with the expected answer. He told Adams that the Vanderbilts "were not enterprising." They would not help the Union Pacific.[73]

It remained only to negotiate the terms of surrender. Adams had already sent Edwin Atkins to arrange the preliminaries. Atkins found Gould "as he always is—gentle and persuasive." Adams himself was present for the surrender on November 20, 1890. There was no choice; "the alternative was bankruptcy."[74] On Thanksgiving Day, Adams wrote a long account of the debacle. He had come to the Union Pacific presidency to rescue it from the legacy of Jay Gould. He arrived as a reformer and sought to make it an honest road, an efficient road, a profitable road free of floating debt and watered securities. He had failed at all these things, and now the bitter dregs of his failure was turning the road over to Gould—"the little wizard . . . quiet, small, furtive, inscrutable." Gould was polite. The talk was pleasant. Gould outlined a scheme for saving the road once he took control. "There being nothing more for me to do there," Adams wrote, "I got up to go." Gould showed him out.[75]

And there the account should have ended, but Adams, who was a writer as well as a businessman, was in no more control of his writing than of his business. He wrote on, and what was meant to demean Gould only diminished Adams. Gould, Adams wrote, was "smaller, meaner, more haggard and lined in the face, and more shriveled up and ashamed of himself than usual;—his clothes seemed too big for him, and his eyes did not seek mine, but were fixed on the upper buttons of my waistcoat. I felt as if in the hour of my defeat I was over-awing him,—and as if he felt so, too." Adams congratulated himself that he had "been equal to the occasion." He had asked no favors. He sought to convince himself that losing to lesser men did nothing to diminish him, while they remained lesser men.[76]

All that was left was Adams's resignation. On November 26, 1890, Adams "ceased to be Pres't. of Union Pacific, and so ended [his] life of railroad work." That same day Houghton Mifflin Company released his biography of Henry Dana, and he began a second life as historian and author. As he left "Gould, Sage, and the pirate band were scrambling on deck."[77] In hindsight Adams regarded his "railroad downfall" as "blessed," an act of "a kindly Providence" that rescued him from the "[d]isgust and discontent for and with [his] position."[78] But these were reflections in his *Autobiography*; they were a retrospective and, for all their admission of failure, self-serving. Adams desperately wanted to preserve a vision of himself as someone too good for the railroads. To see Jay Gould, Sidney Dillon, whom Adams had succeeded as president, and Silas Clark, whom he had eased out, take over was so much salt in his wound. Adams received the usual thanks from the board, but it was hard to imagine a more thorough repudiation of his tenure.[79]

As for the Union Pacific, its underlying problems remained. It survived the crisis in the fall of 1890 by resorting to short-term loans, many of them provided by Jay Gould. The road then sought to refinance with new consolidated bond issues and, when those failed to sell, with trust notes backed by piles of paper that would bring nowhere near par on the market. The bankers who had promised discipline provided nothing of the sort. J. P. Morgan agreed to handle these notes.[80]

IV. THE SECOND FALL OF HENRY VILLARD

The Argentinean crisis threatened to bring Villard as well as Adams down. Villard kept his panic private.[81] Publicly, it was as if the Northern Pacific kept a storehouse of phrases and incantations from the days of Jay Cooke to use in times like these. Thomas Oakes declared at the end of 1890, "I never had stronger faith than at present in the value of the Northern Pacific property. There is no property in the West, not even the Chicago and North Western that compare with it in earning capacity, gross and net per mile."[82] For the moment statistics seemed to support him. The net earnings per mile of road for fiscal year 1889–90 were the highest in the Northern Pacific's history. That would not last. They declined for the next three years.[83] A major reason for their decline was the lease of the Wisconsin Central by the Northern Pacific. It was a weak line whose service was "abominable." Its acquisition alienated the powerful Chicago roads, and William Mellen, the Northern Pacific's general manager, feared that the Wisconsin Central would deliver far less traffic to the Northern Pacific than the Northern Pacific would lose through the competing alliance of the Chicago and North Western and the Union Pacific. By 1892 the lease of the Wisconsin Central was losing the Northern Pacific $917,000 annually, and the losses were rising.[84] (See Appendix, Chart H.)

At the end of 1890, however, no one yet knew what a drain on resources the Wisconsin Central would prove to be. To meet the present crisis, Villard enlisted John D. Rockefeller and retained the support of the Deutsche Bank. With their help the road met its interest payments.[85] He had steered at least $27 million into the Northern Pacific and the allied Oregon Railway and Navigation Company by the end of the year.[86] He had weathered the storm that sank Charles Francis Adams.

Villard spent that new money and more. By 1891 the Northern Pacific was constructing new lines or extending old ones in Washington, Idaho, and Montana and undertaking expensive repairs to the Stampede Tunnel through the Cascades.[87] It did so despite early reports that new lines were not earning their keep, that the system's earnings per mile were falling, and that the Northern Pacific's increasing expenses were due not to labor costs or material but to the heavy cost and light revenue of the new railroads.[88]

As the road's fixed costs grew and its floating debt followed, prices for both old and new bonds fell.[89] Improvements, too, continued to drain the road. The Northern Pacific had pledged that there would be no expenditure of over $50,000 without the consent of the board and none under $50,000 without the consent of the president, but the promises were not kept.[90] Adding to the Northern Pacific's travails were the roads it had acquired in its contest with the Union Pacific and the Canadian Pacific and in anticipation of James J. Hill's pushing his Great Northern into the Pacific Northwest. When in the summer of 1890 the Northern Pacific first acquired majority ownership of the Seattle, Lake Shore, and Eastern and then leased the company after guaranteeing its bonds, it acquired a bankrupt and unfinished road that had not been able to run a train over much of its route the preceding winter because of snow. It had been, as was customary, set up to create profits for an insider construction company that Northern Pacific officials described as a "circus," and its financing had been so loose that it had issued bonds on its sidings.[91] The Northern Pacific and Manitoba, which the Northern Pacific leased as a Canadian extension, was also badly managed, poorly built, and neglected.[92]

The Northern Pacific had grown very overextended by the spring of 1891, but the road was in a position where it could neither retreat nor stand still. There was always pressure on managers to put money into the roads. Their existing facilities were often incomplete and unable to handle what they presumed would be constantly increasing business. Borrowing and building were symbiotic. Borrowing allowed building, and building by providing more collateral for mortgages allowed more borrowing. With security prices falling and with loans being called in, Villard had to borrow simply to survive, and he became more and more inventive in creating collateral for consolidated bonds. He agreed to a scheme to count improvements on existing tracks as collateral. Investors had little security beyond the Northern Pacific's word.[93]

Villard, of course, saw none of this as a failure of management. He was convinced that the problem was the Sherman Silver Purchase Act. A Cleveland Democrat, he would devote considerable political effort toward its eventual repeal in 1892.[94] The act had never pleased free-silver advocates; it had not provided the cheaper money the backers promised and the country needed; it had only aroused the fears of European investors. Its passage had done no good; neither would its repeal.

V. THE PANIC OF 1893

By the summer of 1893 the transcontinentals were barreling down the track; having expanded mileage, they were cutting rates, and they rushed forward although nearly every signal they saw was red. The ICC failed to prevent their rush to destruction. The ICC's sponsor, Shelby Cullom, feared that the refusal of the courts to accept its rulings as binding meant that the ICC "must become practically a nonentity or a full blown court."[95] The Interstate-Commerce Railway Association had failed, and the organizations Jay Gould helped create to succeed it never proved effective. The railroads charged full speed into the Panic of 1893.

That panic led to the deepest depression in American history until the Great Depression of the 1930s. The depression affected the entire economy, but the railroads precipitated it. As Joseph Schumpeter later wrote, it was "primarily a crisis of the roads themselves—roughly one-quarter of which (measured by capital) went into the receivers' hands."[96] Among them were most of the transcontinentals.

Many of the men actually managing the railroads now recognized, at least privately, that they were heading for a cliff, and their knowledge took a toll. In the early summer of 1893 William Mellen of the Northern Pacific knew how bad the situation was, and he was sick. Railroad men routinely took to their beds in times of trouble, but after treatment by a doctor in New York, Mellen declared himself "entirely restored" and ready for a trip of inspection to the Pacific Northwest in July.[97]

On that trip Mellen fell ill again in a way that oddly echoed the troubles of the railroad that employed him. His pain, suffering, and occasional fears of impending disaster were met with an incongruous optimism, consultations with the best doctors—"a very clever man"—misdiagnoses, and inappropriate remedies. Mellen, like the railroad, grew sick in style, traveling from Spokane to Tacoma and to Victoria, British Columbia, on private cars and then a steamer. He consulted doctors as he went. The doctors blamed his heart palpitations, his "fearful pain," and his cold sweat on *cholera morbus*, what is now called gastroenteritis. The original attack they blamed on watermelon; his flatulence in Tacoma seemed to confirm the diagnosis. He took morphine and purged himself. His last conversations at night and his first in the morning concerned the daily reports that showed the Northern Pacific's revenues running from $25,000 to $30,000 a day behind those of the preceding year. Traffic was dropping precipitously. He said he had grown to love the Northern Pacific "and could not bear to think of it being overwhelmed by misfortune." A day touring Victoria seemed to refresh him, but by evening he was sick again, which led to a warm bath, compresses, mustard plasters, stimulants, and more morphine. J. W. Kendrick, the chief engineer traveling with him, was "much startled" when Mellen's Canadian doctor disagreed with the earlier diagnoses by American doctors and told him that "the difficulty was with the heart rather than with the stomach." Still at 11:00 P.M. on July 26 the doctor was convinced that he was recovering nicely. By 12:00 he was dead. His last words were "Goodbye, oh my poor little family."[98]

Mellen died as the Northern Pacific was negotiating to halt the rate wars that were crippling it. The Great Northern, the new transcontinental that grew out of James Hill's St. Paul, Minneapolis, and Manitoba, had with stunning bad timing built through a vast section of the country with virtually no traffic. With the collapse of silver mining in the West some of the most lucrative freight in Idaho and Montana vanished. If it wanted to carry anything at all on its new tracks, the Great Northern had to capture the relatively meager through traffic to Spokane and Seattle. To do so it cut rates.[99] The Canadian Pacific, too, had plenty of incentive to capture transcontinental traffic in the United States because it had virtually nothing to haul over most of its route in western Canada. A traveler on the Canadian Pacific in the summer of 1890, M. V. B. Stanley, reported to Thomas Oakes that this was a route that "commenced nowhere and ended nowhere." The pamphlets touting the benefits of the Canadian Pacific were "full of misrepresentations, and lies from beginning to end." Except for the region around Winnipeg,

> *nearly the whole distance between North Bay and Vancouver there are grasses or wild bushes on either side of the road. With the exception of some grand scenery in the mountains, it is a dull gloomy, dismal route, and tiresome for want of habitations. . . . The grades of the road are heavy, the curves are numerous and it is a very dangerous road for travelers. The bridges are too light and frail for the purposes they are supposed to serve.*[100]

Northern Pacific engineers, who kept a close tab on the progress of the Great Northern, admitted that it was a better-engineered road with lower grades over much of its route. But they were confident that the Northern Pacific ran through richer country and that improvements on it could erase the Great Northern's advantage, when, and if, the Northern Pacific mustered the funds to make those improvements.[101] The Northern Pacific was by and large pleased with its ability to hold off the Great Northern. "There has never been," Oakes gloated in June of 1893, "such an example in failure to obtain business upon the completion of a new line as presented by the Great Northern Company."[102]

Business, however, was never just business in the late nineteenth century; it was deeply personal, involving judgments of manhood and character. The management of the Northern Pacific and the Canadian Pacific hated James J. Hill, and he reciprocated. Thomas Oakes petulantly declined to attend a St. Paul dinner honoring the completion of the Great Northern and was privately gleeful that the "advent of his road [the Great Northern] has hardly been noticed by the public. This is a very bitter pill for Mr. Hill to swallow."[103] Hill's rivals blamed the railroad problems in the Pacific Northwest on Hill's personal failings and a vindictiveness and envy that amounted to madness.[104] Wall Street, Oakes claimed, thinks Hill is "out of his mind. Even his friends are disturbed about his mental condition."[105]

Hill did have a capacity to alienate, and Northern Pacific managers eagerly reported each new account of enemies he made. William Mellen had reported that Hill's failure to keep his promises to merchants in Spokane had led him to be routinely referred to as "Mr. Ananias Hill," after the biblical figure who was struck dead for lying.[106] The president of the Canadian Pacific, William Van Horne, had long known Hill and considered him "full of spite against both the Canadian Pacific and the Northern Pacific Companies, and towards the officers of both these companies." Van Horne thought Hill arrogant and prone to bluff. He believed Hill was raising on deuces in the rate war. He wanted to call him.[107]

Hill's faults did not make the Northern Pacific any stronger. In late July of 1893, like a raven croaking at the window, Jay Cooke, now old and only a privileged passenger on the road he once controlled, sent a message to Thomas Oakes. Cooke thought that "the arrangements made with the Wisconsin Central and other roads out in Puget Sound were disastrous to the Northern Pacific," but he just wished the resulting controversy could have been "settled, quietly, 'within the family.'" Cooke praised the "general management" of the road. A vote of confidence from Jay Cooke was still the kiss of death. Within weeks the road would be in receivership.[108]

Virtually everyone but Henry Villard blamed Henry Villard for the Northern Pacific's fall.[109] In 1893 he departed in his usual manner. His resignation was accompanied by a long self-justifying lament to Oakes. He had been made "the scapegoat and this to such an extent as to render it an open question whether any other man of position in the financial world was ever subject to more misrepresentation, slander and abuse than [he had] been for a long time past." He had resigned because his "self-respect rebels at the thought of being subject to still more vindictive falsehood and calumny."[110] Villard blamed the demand for the monetization of silver to increase the money supply for panicking European investors, who feared a devalued dollar and who ceased to supply the steady flow of funds that Villard needed.[111] When the Farmers' Loan and Trust Company pushed the Northern Pacific into receivership, it also accused Villard and other directors of fraud.[112]

Never satisfied with just leaving the company, Villard also left the country in November. "Our old friend Villard" sailed for Egypt, E. L. Godkin wrote James Bryce,

> in disgrace. He has been kicked out of every enterprise he was connected with here, and is universally denounced as a visionary, if not worse, who has made money at the expense of other people. . . . I am told the Germans are now as furious with him as the Americans. . . . The unfortunate truth is that of six companies of which he was forefront, every one has either gone to smash or depreciated enormously in value, and the losers naturally ask how it is that he has so much? How vain is human greatness![113]

By the time Villard left the Union Pacific, Allen Manvel of the Atchison, Topeka, and Santa Fe was dead. Worn out by the strain of refinancing the Atchison, he died in February of 1893.[114] It had been hard work cooking the books, and it did not end well.[115] The railroad barely survived him. Amid the usual lies and reassurances about its financial health and bright prospects, it grew shakier and shakier. In December of 1893 it gave way, sliding into receivership.[116]

In between the bankruptcy of the Northern Pacific in the summer and the Atchison's failure in December, the Union Pacific went into receivership in the fall of 1893. After Adams surrendered to Gould, the Union Pacific's corporate life was dominated by the old and sick. The road went through a series of financial crises averted at the last minute by new infusions of cash, until by 1893 declining revenues, falling securities prices, and the flight of European capital doomed it. By then Jay Gould was dead of the tuberculosis that had left him so shrunken at his last interview with Adams. Coming to New York to try to stem yet another financial crisis, Frederick Ames—the last of the Ames family in the Union Pacific—had a stroke and died in his stateroom. Sydney Dillon died in June. Silas Clark, as skittish as a dove, panicked and resigned as president of the Union Pacific, until George Gould,

Jay Gould's son, coaxed him into returning. In the autumn the bloated and mismanaged road sank down into receivership.[117] The Gould interests maintained control through the receivers, in a way that even Richard Olney thought looked bad.[118]

VI. THE STRUGGLES OF THE OCTOPUS

No one would have predicted that the Southern Pacific would be one of the roads to survive the Panic of 1893. It had the same faults as the other transcontinentals and was no better managed. In essence, the Southern Pacific got lucky. It had more guns at its head than any other transcontinental, but ultimately no one pulled the trigger. Admittedly, there was skill involved in this, but it was not managerial skill. It was the ability to bluff, deceive, wheedle, and even steal. These were Collis P. Huntington's skills. Following a transcontinental that survived is as revealing as following those that failed; the stories are not that different.

Collis P. Huntington had great abilities within a narrow compass. He had become a man of New York and Washington, D.C. He was a New York financier who became a railroad manager when he displaced Stanford as president of the Southern Pacific in 1890. That Stanford ran the railroad badly did not mean that Huntington would run it well.[119] His coup against Stanford made him captain of a mutinous and ill-rigged ship that faced the same financial storms as the other transcontinentals.

The Southern Pacific survived the financial squalls of 1890 and sailed into the unsettled weather that followed. Huntington, like Villard at the Northern Pacific, proceeded to make a bad situation worse, expanding in Texas, Mexico, and California. Everywhere he misjudged the future.[120] Into late 1892 he was confident that Mexican bonds would become the Southern Pacific's strongest securities, and he sought subsidies and land grants in Mexico.[121] He argued that the Southern Pacific had to continue to expand in Southern California to compete against the Atchison.[122] He pushed the long delayed coastal route to serve counties still not linked to the railroad.[123] He participated in the general scramble for traffic that led to another breakdown of the reconstituted Transcontinental Association. Rates to the West Coast went into a freefall.[124] This, in turn, again ended the subsidy to the Pacific Mail, a company that Huntington then sought to control.[125]

Huntington overreached and misjudged in politics as badly as in business. The death of Senator George Hearst in 1891 had made one of California's U.S. Senate seats available, and Michael de Young became Huntington's candidate for the Republican nomination.[126] The Huntington/de Young alliance paired two of the state's most powerful institutions—the Southern Pacific and the *San Francisco Chronicle*. It also paired two of the most hated men in California. De Young was Jewish, and his election would have been difficult under any circumstances, but Huntington made it more difficult by relying on two anti-Semites— W. W. Stow and W. H. Mills—to elect him.[127]

Stow and Mills disliked each other as much as they disliked de Young, and in them Huntington had wedded the smug with the secretive.[128] A reliable prelude to any new disaster was a long, detailed letter, often sycophantic, from Mills assuring Huntington that "everything here well in hand."[129] Stow was Mills's opposite: he was pathologically secretive and churlish and demanded almost complete independence. Stow informed Huntington that he had no intention of explaining his actions or taking orders. "I am almost as mulish as you are, when I understand a subject, and I won't attempt to deal with it unless I do, I can't take orders."[130] Stow's rules of politics were simple: "I always try to take care of two parties; first my client and second the party who has done him a favor." This took money, and Stow did not want to draw directly on the company treasurer for "legal expenses" as Huntington had suggested. That left "records that may be exceedingly troublesome."[131] The money would need to be disguised. Mills agreed to support Stow, who was "so very sensitive as to being let alone," but quietly so that Stow would not know he was being supported.[132] Huntington expressed confidence in both men even though they had no confidence in each other.[133]

In August de Young, suspecting that Stow was subverting him, called Stow into his office to tell him that he would spend his fortune and the next twenty years on wreaking vengeance against those who opposed him. Stow replied that de Young had a paper but that he had a shotgun, and if the *Chronicle* attacked him, he would certainly kill de Young. In other cities such language would have been hyperbolic, but de Young was presumably sitting in the very office where his brother had been killed and he himself had been shot.[134]

The outcome of the election was what seemed impossible at the outset: the election of an antimonopolist Democrat Stephen White. White exemplified both the breadth of Californian antimonopoly and its weakness. He was anti-Chinese, although he defended Chinese clients, a free trader, and a person seemingly not much bothered by inequities of the world that did not afflict him. He saved his public discontent for the corruption of politics that had sent both Leland Stanford and George Hearst to the U.S. Senate, and he became an enemy of both.[135] He blamed corruption on the railroads and favored the Australian ballot and direct election of senators. Privately, he could see no reason why railroads should not be nationalized and treated the same as public highways.[136] Honesty in government, free trade, and curbing corporate power were the heart of his antimonopolism. His election gave the Southern Pacific a dangerous enemy.

The Southern Pacific did not really need enemies; mismanagement and a sinking economy were doing damage enough. After 1892 its gross transportation revenues steadily fell. In 1890 it had 6,061 miles of railway with transportation revenues of $48.3 million. The next year the revenues reached $50.5 million and then dropped until 1898, when it had revenues of $43.9 million on 6,744 miles of track.[137] Part of the problem was the immense stretches of line with virtually no traffic. As. W. G. Curtis explained in 1895, "on 45 percent of the entire road mileage west of El Paso one train or less is run each way daily carrying freight. Many of these trains carry small loads, but still must be run to perform the service required by the public."[138] Huntington reported in 1897 that local traffic in Louisiana and East Texas kept the whole Atlantic Division from New Orleans to El Paso afloat, which was hardly a ringing endorsement for a transcontinental.[139]

Huntington seemed to think the cure was yet another railroad. Early in 1893, without the knowledge of his Associates, he became involved with an engineer, E. L. Cothrell, in negotiations to complete a Mexican railroad already in progress across the Isthmus of Tehuantepec. Eventually, when

Europeans secured control of the road, Huntington narrowed his plan to constructing ports at either end of the line.[140] The whole endeavor was a telling and tacit recognition that the most efficient passage between the Atlantic and the Pacific would run through either Mexico or countries to the south.

To finance expansion and improvements, Huntington first took on a dangerously large floating debt, and then to reduce it and to finance more branch lines, he in 1892 undertook negotiations with the Speyers for issuing $38 millon worth of Southern Pacific bonds on a new 5 percent mortgage on branch lines.[141] When the Speyers refused to take the whole issue, Huntington late in 1892 dramatically altered the negotiation by adding new lines to the mortgage and raising the total to $58 million.[142] William Barney, representing the Speyers, wrote Huntington that this was impossible. "Times have greatly changed and people nowadays are more discriminating." Europeans would not touch a $58 million bond issue even from a solvent and well-managed road and certainly not from the Southern Pacific, whose earnings, despite Huntington's assurances of prosperity, were in sharp decline.[143]

Huntington could not have picked a worse time to haggle over the terms of a bond sale. In the spring of 1893 he had to eat crow and negotiate a much worse deal. The Speyers dropped the price that they would give for Southern Pacific bonds by 2½ points, demanded that the Southern Pacific issue only $38 million worth of bonds over the next ten years, and required that Huntington accept all the other conditions he had earlier rejected. Even on these terms, they were not sure they could form a syndicate and create a market.[144] They told Huntington that he "could not have selected a more unfavorable moment than the present one to make an advance negotiation."[145]

It was as if someone had set the calendar back twenty years. On June 17, 1893, N. T. Smith, the treasurer of the Southern Pacific, wrote Huntington to report the worst week he had ever seen in San Francisco. As depositors withdrew their money, the banks frantically called in loans and refused to make new ones. The Southern Pacific paid some loans and extended others at an increased rate of interest. They delayed paying all the bills they could and tried desperately to get the pay car out.[146] When it went out late, angry workers prevented it from moving to the next division until they were sure they had received all their pay.[147] The Pacific Improvement Company (PIC) with its heavy floating debt was particularly vulnerable. The Speyers saved the PIC with a loan of $3 million in June, but this still left uncovered the interest payments that the Southern Pacific owed for July 1.[148]

Unable to sell his new bonds, Huntington borrowed from the Speyers, offering to mortgage everything from the Mexican International to his Newport News Shipyards as collateral.[149] On June 21 he delivered a proposal for yet another loan to the Speyers. His timing, once again, was impeccably bad. It was the day that Leland Stanford died.[150] A man whose presence had been such a problem for his Associates managed to make his absence an even greater problem. He died before he could sign the papers securing another PIC loan; what was worse, he died owing large amounts of money and having left most of his estate in trust for Stanford University.[151] Huntington asked Jane Stanford to sign the papers and help save the PIC. Her lawyers listed a formidable set of reasons why she could not and should not help Huntington. They were not certain that the estate was even solvent, and they argued that Mrs. Stanford's personal share of the estate was too small to help Huntington even if she, as Huntington suggested, threw it into a "vortex from which no return could be expected." She had a survivorship trust, but it was for property intended for the university, and she had "no power to divert [it] from the purposes specified." As executrix, she could not favor one set of creditors—those Huntington was trying to hold off—over other creditors on Stanford's estate. Finally, executors were forbidden by law to sign promissory notes; Mrs. Stanford could sign as an individual, but her lawyers advised against this.[152]

Mrs. Stanford's shortage of cash and inability to draw on the PIC inevitably attracted public notice.[153] Some creditors panicked, threatening suit, and Crocker could not reason with them, because "at such times people do not reason." He regarded Huntington's suggestion that they borrow money on real estate as laughable. There was no market for real estate.[154] San Francisco banks were failing, and Crocker feared a general run that would end with all the banks closing their doors. As Huntington demanded money, and Crocker worried about financial collapse in California, it was as if their letters were written in two mutually incomprehensible languages. The daily receipts of the Southern Pacific did not even meet the road's daily liabilities.

"We are in a position of having suspended payment here . . . and nothing but personal consideration for, and faith in us individually, has so far prevented a number of parties from bringing suits." Crocker halted all construction and improvement and announced that he would supply no more support to the PIC.[155]

And with this the game should have been up for the Associates. The shrinking value of the Associates' securities led to demands from lenders for more collateral on the PIC's loans. Without more collateral the PIC would go under. If it went under, the railroads, whose bonds it held, would go under. So, too, would the Associates, who as the economy declined had both to provide collaterals and to endorse personally the PIC notes, thus taking responsibility for their payment. The end of the PIC would be the end of all of them for, as Huntington explained to Fred Crocker, "default of course you understand will reach our personal property outside of the property of the company."[156]

The dead Leland and the mournful Jane Stanford loomed over Huntington. To pay Stanford's debts and to satisfy his bequests, the Stanford estate needed money. Jane Stanford announced her plans to withdraw from the railroad business and liquidate her assets.[157] Huntington responded that she could not withdraw; the estate was committed to large contracts that had to be fulfilled. He retreated to the ground where the old Associates had rallied despite all their differences and enmities. "If we all stand together I think we shall get through. If not we shall all be harmed alike."[158] He coupled such alarms with forecasts of calm water ahead: "We all feel sure the bottom is about reached and that a few more collaterals will take us outside the breakers." It was no wonder that Crocker thought him delusional. Over Huntington's objections, Crocker began negotiations to turn the PIC over to its creditors, since it was "useless to attempt to keep up this business without resources to meet obligations."[159] A great deal of the PIC's indebtedness was in the form of time loans, but as these came due, they were either not being renewed or turned into call loans that had to be paid on demand, and, as Crocker wrote, "it would be a miracle if some one of them were not in the hands of parties inimical to our interests," who could bring them down by bringing suit.[160]

In the best of times Huntington had few scruples; in a crisis he had virtually none. If Crocker was going to scuttle the PIC, Huntington was going to make sure that there was nothing of value on board. He suggested stripping that company of its most valuable assets—real estate, railroad materials, steamships, and anything else useful to the railroads—by selling them to the Southern Pacific in exchange for ten-year notes paying 5 percent.[161] While seeking to shortchange his creditors, he stole from his partners. When Crocker weakened and gave Huntington stock to use as collateral to meet the demands of lenders, Huntington, in need of cash, sold it.[162] Crocker was outraged. "I am not willing," he wrote, "to continue making myself personally responsible for your acts and the debts you incur without our knowledge or consent."[163] Undeterred, Huntington also sold stock belonging to the Stanford estate.[164]

Jane Stanford could sink the railroad and the PIC by withdrawing her quarter share; to stop her, Huntington mortgaged virtually everything the PIC owned. When, in March of 1894, Mrs. Stanford's lawyers demanded all the securities in the estate's name held by the PIC, there were virtually no unhypothecated securities.[165] Jane had other troubles. Although he acted unwillingly and under pressure, Richard Olney, the attorney general of the United States, prepared a suit against the Stanford estate to recover the loans to the Central Pacific that had never been repaid. Because California incorporation law made individual stockholders responsible for corporate debts, Jane and her new university were now vulnerable and so, too, were the Southern Pacific and the PIC.[166]

In a panic, cash was everything, and to obtain it, Huntington borrowed all that he could. In the brief windows when money loosened, he and Crocker secured new loans and extended old ones.[167] In November of 1893 the Associates borrowed $2 million from the New York Mutual Insurance Company for the PIC, but they had to put up personal notes as well as collateral. Trust was in short supply.[168] At the beginning of April 1894 the PIC was in debt for over $16 million, but it had cash in the bank that it had received from its loans. This it would, in turn, lend the Southern Pacific for coupon payments to keep the railroad out of receivership.[169] Paying interest with borrowed money and hypothecating every negotiable asset could not go on forever. In living from day to day, Huntington averted immediate disaster but sowed the seeds of future trouble.[170]

Ultimately the fate of the Southern Pacific and the PIC rested with the Speyers, who remained the Associates' major lenders and agents for their bonds. They were very unhappy bankers. They had made loans to meet interest payments and avoid default.[171] In exchange for these loans, they insisted on pushing to the front of the very long line of Southern Pacific and PIC creditors. They demanded that all earnings beyond payment of workers and necessary supplies be sent directly to them from California to pay overdue loans.[172] They, however, reloaned these payments nearly as fast as they were made.[173] For every grace the Speyers granted, Huntington paid a price. When he asked the Speyers to release to him securities that they held as collateral in exchange for other, less readily negotiable securities so that he could procure new loans in New York, they did so, but only on the condition that Huntington guarantee payment of dividends on the Central Pacific and pay them hefty commissions and interest.[174]

The Speyers no longer trusted Huntington. By the end of 1893 his failure to maintain daily payments on the advance granted him by the Speyers' London house had "enormously shaken [their] confidence." They could not and would not advance him more money, and they looked forward to January 1, 1894, when interest payments on various railroad bonds were due with "very grave anxieties." If Huntington could not keep "such solemn engagements" has he had already made, they were "afraid to place confidence in other arrangements he may make as regards issue of Southern Pacific 5's," the new 5 percent bonds of the Southern Pacific. They demanded to know the extent of both his corporate and his personal debts.[175]

The line between confidence men and financiers was always blurry in the nineteenth century. That border provided Herman Melville and Anthony Trollope with some of their best material, and by late 1893 and early 1894 the Associates were, more than ever, creatures of the borderland. Desperate for cash and eager to cut expenses, they hatched a new scheme at the expense of British investors. In early November of 1893 they renegotiated the lease of the Central Pacific, which was costing the Southern Pacific, or so Fred

Crocker claimed, $700,000 a year and which made the Southern Pacific responsible for Central Pacific dividends.[176]

This move violated the terms of the loans that Huntington had negotiated from the Speyers, which mandated payment of Central Pacific dividends, and it enraged the British stockholders of the Central Pacific.[177] It was also illegal since the boards of the Central Pacific and the Southern Pacific had common members.[178] C. E. Bretherton, the representative of the British stockholders, proclaimed that the new lease of December 1893 was "a mere naked fraud which ignored the numerous benefits—most obviously the control of traffic diverted to the Southern Pacific—that the Central Pacific bestowed."[179] Huntington moved quickly to reorganize both boards to eliminate duplication. He had to issue several new members a share of Central Pacific stock in order to make them eligible. The board members, including the Central Pacific's new president, Isaac Requa, were in the great tradition of the Associates' boards utterly ignorant of the affairs of the company. They quickly reaffirmed the new lease.[180]

Bretherton, although a member of the Central Pacific's board, did not learn about the terms of the lease until he read them in the newspaper. He regarded this as "almost a slap in the face," and it cost him what was left of his standing with the British shareholders.[181] Bretherton still, however, had standing with the Speyers, and Huntington's new lease had also betrayed the Speyers. News of the lease had led to a fall in the Southern Pacific securities, the very securities that Speyer had been supporting in the market and that the firm held as collateral.[182]

The bankers' letters to Huntington retained only their surface cordiality. William Bonn thought Huntington's age made him incapable of protecting his, and their, interests and told him so. It was time for the seventy-year-old Huntington to transfer the financial management "to younger shoulders." Huntington had grown not only reckless but careless. "In critical times a very much smaller amount than the one you must have borrowed, could break even the biggest concern, and it cannot prove of financial foresight, if anyone exposes himself to such risk." European and American bankers shared information, and the New York banks were alarmed and "gave a very gloomy report" about Huntington and his Associates. All of this made it difficult for the Speyers to persuade German investors not to dump their securities. Far from being reassured by Huntington's optimism, they were dismayed by it. They stressed that they were in no position to market any more of Huntington's securities. They demanded transparency. They wanted a plan, which they would help forge, "whereby books and earnings are kept so . . . that the public clamor for it would be satisfied." They wanted a consolidation of his loans under their supervision.[183]

In London the Speyers laid their cards on the table. "We are afraid," they wrote Huntington, that their letter "will not prove very pleasant reading to you." They would not defend the Central Pacific lease. They reminded him of how much they knew but had not divulged: "the way in which C.P. sinking funds have been invested or allowed to be used for purposes contrary to the spirit and the conditions laid down in the mortgages" and the transfer of leases from the Central Pacific to the Southern Pacific. If Huntington did not revise the lease, they would publicly side with Bretherton. And even if Huntington revised the Central Pacific lease, "it will be very hard work to sell any of [his] bonds here for some time to come."[184]

Huntington was both defensive and conciliatory. On March 19, 1894, he wrote the Speyers at unusual length, which, with Huntington, usually meant obfuscation. He was sure things could be worked out. He did not indicate precisely how.[185] Bretherton, at the urging of the Speyers, came to New York. He would not be reconciled unless the lease was revised and he approved the terms.[186]

When Bretherton saw the annual report of the Central Pacific, it made his anger flare again. The report was "a disgrace to the President who signed it."[187] Bretherton wrote a nineteen-page letter to President Requa. Less a letter than a baring of claws, it was meant more for Huntington than for Requa, whom he knew to be a mere pawn. "I cannot accept the document in question as a truthful presentation of the operations, and position of the Company," he wrote, and then spelled out why. The report's numbers were provided by the Southern Pacific, not the Central Pacific, which lacked the staff to verify them. They utterly misstated the many benefits the Central Pacific provided the Southern Pacific, ignored the diversion of traffic from one road to the other, and the interest-free loans the Central Pacific provided the Southern Pacific. Even taken at face value, the numbers made no sense. The Southern Pacific used a claimed loss of $250,000 a year to reduce an annual rental of $1,360,000 to zero. A lease without a rental was a gift, one the Associates made to themselves at the expense of the stockholders. They maintained their old pattern of "acting as directors of both companies, or in other words, contracting with themselves."[188]

There was much more. The report falsified the income account to disguise the looting of the Central Pacific for the benefit of the Southern Pacific. It concealed the money borrowed to pay dividends. Unable to hide the floating debt, the authors had simply eliminated it from the report. Bretherton detailed the looting of the sinking fund in transactions that were a "thin disguise" for what amounted to a loan to the Associates settled by the Central Pacific's keeping nearly worthless collateral.[189]

All the pillars of the Associates' enterprises seemed to be giving way. Huntington had lost the trust of his bankers. In Sacramento and Washington, D.C., he was losing his influence. Only Mexico's dictator still loved him, and that was because Mexico was even more desperate than Huntington.[190] Díaz was still willing to give Huntington the contract to construct the Tehuantepec ports, but even Huntington was unwilling to take this risk.[191] He asked for more time. Díaz, who was proving to be a most accommodating dictator, gave it to him.[192] But the deal was doomed. In June 1894 Huntington received a letter that described the nearly completed Tehuantepec railroad that would connect his ports as a disaster: sharp curves, steep grades, shoddy construction, rotten bridges, and embankments below high water. In short, like so many North American railroads, it would be both expensive and unsafe to operate.[193]

Beset on all sides, the old bull stumbled on, borrowing from Peter to pay Paul, and then delaying repayment to Peter. He was dunned even by the bank headed by the ostensible president of the Central Pacific, Isaac Requa.[194] Crocker panicked and vacillated. One day he refused to sign notes; the next he relented.[195] In April of 1894 Huntington and the successors of the estates of his old Associates convened and reached an accommodation. It had, Huntington reported, taken only a few minutes. Recognizing they had to act together, they agreed to do "what every body knew before would have to be done." As Huntington put it, "the mountain labored and brought forth a mouse."[196] The mouse soon died. By early May, Jane Stanford was once more refusing to sign notes.[197]

Huntington remained inventive. He took out $2.5 million in a personal loan from E. H. Harriman, who would later form his own railroad empire out of the wrecks of the 1890s.[198] Huntington sought private loans to "keep out of the money market as much as possible." He used private loans to pay down bank loans, and his seeming solvency made New York bankers willing not only to renew some old loans but to extend new ones.[199] He sold some bonds, disposing of $4 million worth to an Illinois Central syndicate.[200] His debts mounted. The Southern Pacific swayed over the pit of receivership that had already swallowed the other early transcontinentals. But it did not tumble.

Salvation came in August of 1896, although at the time it was hard to say whether this was salvation or perdition. In an extraordinary set of transactions, the Speyers once again rescued the Southern Pacific and the Pacific Improvement Company by making both a large loan and pushing forward Southern Pacific bond issues. They, however, retained no trust in Huntington and his Associates. They took literally everything, private and corporate, as security. Huntington had to give them a mortgage on his New York mansion. The Associates also had to allow the Speyers to deduct and keep for payment five years' worth of interest payments for the sale of the bonds.[201] Independent accountants would monitor the Southern Pacific's books.[202]

By the end of 1897 Jane Stanford and the Crockers, discouraged and exhausted, were ready to sell out, but Huntington did not have the funds to buy.[203] Collectively, the Associates would be saved by an improving economy after 1897 and by rapid economic growth in California, particularly in agriculture, which everyone had awaited for so long. For probably the first time, more than three decades after the Central Pacific began construction, it became possible at least to imagine the Southern Pacific as a viable transcontinental and not merely as an overbuilt regional railroad in California.

MISE EN SCÈNE

———◆———

READING THE NEWSPAPERS

When in 1891 his enemies in the Democratic Party and San Francisco businessmen turned on the Blind Boss, Chris Buckley, the resulting battle involved the press and the railroad.[1] Everything in San Francisco seemed to involve the press and the railroad. Denunciation of the bosses morphed easily into denunciations of the Buckley's old ally Senator Leland Stanford, which did not displease Collis P. Huntington, who by then had replaced Stanford as head of the Southern Pacific. San Francisco's editors and publishers despised each other even more than the Associates despised each other, and as Buckley fell, the newspapers attacked their rivals by attaching them to bosses and boodle. The *Bulletin* and the *Call* were particularly eager to attack the *Chronicle*, the city's most powerful paper, and its publisher, Michael de Young, as a tool of the boodlers. De Young retaliated by attacking the *Bulletin* and the *Call* as tools of the railroad. This particularly offended the *Bulletin* and the *Call* because they *were* tools of the railroad. The easiest way for them to demonstrate their independence was to attack the railroad and Stanford, which they did.[2]

All this was business as usual, but Fred Crocker did not understand business as usual. Crocker did not like seeing himself and his railroad denounced in papers that he subsidized. So he cut the subsidies. "I have withstood the slanders, misrepresentations and attacks of the *Bulletin* and *Call* as long as I can," he wrote Huntington, "and do not intend to permit any money that I control in whole or in part to be and sustain these people."[3] W. H. Mills, an ex-newspaperman and the railroad's liaison to the press, tried to explain to Crocker that the *Bulletin*'s and *Call*'s attacks on the Southern Pacific were mere protective coloration. It was also true, however, that their attacks on it were usually attacks on Crocker and Stanford and not on Huntington. Mills was a Huntington man.[4] Huntington restored the subsidies, embarrassing and further alienating Crocker.[5]

When Huntington backed Michael de Young in the Senate election of 1892, the election involved negotiations with the newspapers, which were made more complicated because de Young owned the *San Francisco Chronicle*. Michael de Young was a brave and seemingly reckless man. In 1879 Charles de Young, Michael's older brother and predecessor as publisher of the *Chronicle*, had attacked Isaac Kalloch, the Workingmen's Party mayoral candidate and Baptist minister, as an adulterer. Kalloch responded from the pulpit, claiming the de Youngs' mother had run a brothel, and that the de Youngs were "the bastard progeny of a whore born in the slums and nursed in the lap of prostitution." The next day Charles de Young shot Kalloch, who survived and was elected mayor. When de Young's *Chronicle* resumed charges of adultery, Kalloch's son got a gun and killed Charles in his *Chronicle* office. A jury acquitted him on the grounds of reasonable cause.[6]

The aggrieved son taking vengeance on supposedly slanderous publishers proved an enduring trope. When Michael de Young accused Claus Spreckels, the sugar baron, of abusing his workers and swindling his stockholders, Claus's son, Adolph, shot Michael in the same office where Charles had been killed. De Young survived, but Spreckels, too, was acquitted for reasonable cause.[7] San Francisco seemed to have an open season on de Youngs.

Huntington admired de Young, who, like Huntington, had risen from small beginnings and amassed a fortune. He was even willing to forgive de Young the role he had played in helping defeat A. A. Sargent and elect Leland Stanford, because he thought, among other things, de Young would be more effective than Stanford in the U.S. Senate. So, although the Southern Pacific was subsidizing the *Bulletin* and the *Call*, which were attacking de Young, and although Fred Crocker hated de Young, and although Huntington's own operatives disliked the overbearing de Young, Huntington came to support de Young.[8] He thought that once in the Senate de Young could get the funding bill passed, which was something Stanford could not do.[9]

The Huntington/de Young alliance paired two of the most powerful institutions—the Southern Pacific and the *San Francisco Chronicle*—and railroad support brought much of the country press, which depended on Southern Pacific favors and advertisements, into the de Young camp.[10] Mills also hoped to secure new friends. He needed a Republican legislature to elect de Young, and in exchange for $1,000 a month for thirty months he negotiated a treaty of "amity and comity between the Company" and the most powerful Democratic paper in the state, the *San Francisco Examiner* published by George Hearst's son, William Randolph Hearst. George Hearst was the dead senator whose seat de Young desired, and Hearst was hardly ready to support him, but he was ready not to go after him as hard as he might. The *Examiner* would cease all criticism of the Southern Pacific on important issues but would continue to criticize it on minor issues to the extent necessary to retain the sympathy of the public. It would not, however, encourage any sentiment that would result in hostile action. It would rather "keep within hailing distance of any sentiment that may exist so as to acquire a leadership in public opinion."[11] Huntington waffled. Fearing that other papers would learn of the arrangement and use it against the railroad, he vetoed the compact. Mills, as was his fashion, apologized for having proposed it, only to have Huntington eventually approve it in modified form.[12]

Having gained the far more powerful *Examiner* and *Chronicle*, the Southern Pacific seemed to have lost the *Bulletin* and the *Call,* which demanded a platform "embracing all the living State issues," but it was not so much the railroad that lost them as Huntington. The papers apparently went over to Crocker and Stanford. W. H. Mills saw in the *Bulletin*'s and *Call*'s attacks not assaults on the railroad but rather assaults on Collis P. Huntington. Unnamed friends of Stanford were using the press to attack Huntington's management of the Southern Pacific. They sought to defeat de Young in order to strike at Huntington.[13]

The election was a disaster for the Republicans, for Huntington, and for Michael de Young, and with defeat, the worm turned once more. Stephen White, the leading Democratic candidate for senator and an antimonopolist, had accused his predecessor, George Hearst, of having bought his Senate seat, which was true. W. H. Mills reported that "Mrs. Hearst and Willie" were determined to defeat White when the legislature convened to choose the next senator. The best way to do so was to attack him as a tool of the railroad, and so the *Examiner*, which was taking Southern Pacific money, asserted that White "wore the railroad collar." While some railroad friends in the press were accusing the railroad's enemies of being railroad friends in order to defeat them, other railroad friends in the press really did become the railroad's enemies, at least temporarily. Michael de Young, who blamed very little on himself, thought that Huntington and his agents had "played him for a fool," and he was ready to wreak revenge against the railroad. By January hostile articles began to appear in the *Chronicle*.

When Stephen White was elected by the California legislature, a furious William Randolph Hearst telegraphed from Italy that he was going to fire the whole *Examiner* staff. "Mr. Hearst," Mills wrote Huntington, "is not judicious. Here are a lot of Bohemians running a newspaper whose proprietor is a young millionaire full of extravagant notions as to his consequence in the world. It is not easy to influence a situation of that kind."[14]

⤝⟀⤞

CHAPTER 10

STRIKE

If we could but destroy the money monopoly, land monopoly,
and the rest of them, all would be different.

—EUGENE DEBS, 1894[1]

UGENE DEBS DID not set out to be a radical, and Richard Olney, while hardly a friend of labor, did not always seem its unrelenting foe. Debs did not want to strike, but he led one of the largest and bitterest strikes in American history. Olney had disparaged virtually all the tools he used against the strike, but he used them ruthlessly and effectively. The outcome of the Pullman Strike depended on much more than Eugene Debs and Richard Olney, but they were its public faces.

Eugene Debs built his world upon the same liberal foundation as Henry George. He was born in 1855 to immigrants from Alsace. They settled in Terre Haute, Indiana, which seemed a place that embodied the core liberal values: individualism, progress, and a community organized around voluntary associations. He left school early for the railroad, becoming a fireman, but the railroad did not fully hold him until 1875 when he joined the new Brotherhood of Locomotive Firemen. For him, the brotherhood became the route of personal and social progress. Debs constantly modified his political house, but the Jeffersonian foundation remained intact. Since for Debs "the government will rest upon the intelligence and virtue of the people," a republican economy had, above all, to produce republican citizens. He embraced a nation where a worker "owns himself, is a man, a citizen, and independent." This was quintessential nineteenth-century liberalism: society as a collection of autonomous individuals, each with a moral right to control his own labor. His whole career was an attempt to reconcile liberal ideals of a society constructed through freely negotiated contracts with the world of large corporations and dependent workers.[2]

Debs's antimonopolism assumed that economic combinations that acted against the public interest had to be curtailed. Any special privilege bestowed by the government was anathema, and for Debs, like other anti-monopolists in the 1890s, the words "special privilege," "monopoly," and "corporation" were virtually synonymous.[3] As an official of the Brotherhood of Locomotive Firemen, Debs had often opposed the Knights of Labor, but he gradually embraced a position indistinguishable from that of the Knights, who proclaimed, "There is no basis in the constitution for a charter for special privileges. The spirit of a private corporation is alien to its whole purpose." Monopolies, however, had now proliferated and left the "whole land blackened by their shadow." They had to be confronted.[4] Political rights were no longer enough. Debs, in the words of his biographer, moved to link "traditional political rights with a more democratic economic system." Debs wrote, "All that labor has demanded [is] an honest distribution of the wealth that labor creates. Fair wages, a lesser number of hours for toil. The evaluation of the American idea of citizenship, home and family. Then the wielding of the ballot. Just laws, honest officials, a pure judiciary, the annihilation of trusts and monopolies—in a word, the reign of justice."[5]

There was nothing radical in "just laws, honest officials, a pure judiciary"; but Debs became a radical because in his attack on "trusts and monopolies" he challenged a key fiction imposed and upheld by his less than pure judiciary: that corporations were persons under the law. Debs believed that the courts had destroyed the ability of free men to organize a society and an economy by contract by creating artificial persons—the corporations—whose powers dwarfed those of any actual human being. Freely negotiated agreements between an individual worker and a railroad were a charade.

That was not a negotiation between equals. Only when workers combined into equivalent organizations could they secure their interests.[6]

By 1888 Debs considered the railroad brotherhoods a failure, but at first he desired merely a federation of railroad brotherhoods with strong central control.[7] Like similar efforts to organize corporations, his efforts foundered on what Union Pacific firemen called "home rule." Some workers feared that centralization would take power away from the rank and file and create "a broad opening for bribery and treachery."[8] Why should officers of a national federation prove any more immune to favors from the railroads than many railroad commissioners or politicians?

Faced with opposition, Debs took a hard line. In Chicago in 1889 he helped found a new organization uniting the firemen, switchmen, and brakemen but leaving out the conservative Brotherhood of Locomotive Engineers. The new federation centralized power in a supreme council. He became less and less sympathetic to rank-and-file control, even as he also alienated conservative unionists by attacking P. M. Arthur, the accommodationist leader of the Brotherhood of Locomotive Engineers, and tried to lure away its members. He was remaking the brotherhoods in the image of corporations—or at least imagined corporations—hierarchical, centralized, and unified.[9] Debs desired the kind of overarching combination among railroad workers that Charles Francis Adams's Interstate-Commerce Railway Association had sought to achieve among railroads and the Farmers' Alliance among farmers. He wanted to make workers too strong to be abused.[10]

Debs crossed his Rubicon in 1893. Having resigned his office in the Brotherhood of Locomotive Firemen, he organized the American Railway Union (ARU) and attempted to bring all railroad workers, skilled and unskilled, into a single union.[11] It would be, as his vice-president put it, "like unto a tree" with "each class of men representing a branch of the tree." In all technical matters the branches were separate, "but in all matters of general concern the whole organization operate[d] as one." The union would avoid all but necessary contests with the railroads. Its dues would not be burdensome and thus drive men out. It would, nonetheless, have an employment department, an insurance department, a department of education. It would also lobby legislatures and Congress for laws promoting the health, safety, and well-being of workers. The ARU resonated with the antimonopoly language of improvement, manhood, equity, honor, and citizenship. It marked all of these qualities as the attributes of white men. It did not accept African American members. In seeking hierarchical leadership and the aggregated labor power of its members, the ARU had left the world of contract freedom.[12]

Debs sought, in Nick Salvatore's words, to "transform the face of industrial America."[13] In his labor millennium the union would meet strength with strength, ensuring mutual respect and accommodation and rendering strikes unnecessary and obsolete. Except for organizing labor, however, he did not advocate changing the economic organization of the country. Debs would tame monopoly by imitating it. The railroads were changing, consolidating, and growing in size, and the workers must change to counter and constrain them.[14] Debs found an enthusiastic audience for this message in the West.

Richard Olney's career thrived as a servant of the railroads. He was a New Englander, born in Massachusetts in 1835. He went to Brown University and then Harvard Law School, and was by 1859 a clerk in the office of Benjamin Thomas, an ex-justice of the Supreme Court. Olney married Thomas's daughter and became his associate. He did not serve in the Civil War. He was a Boston lawyer who approached the law much the way he played tennis. His style was often "exasperating." He was aggressive rather than defensive. He appeared awkward and easy to ridicule, but somehow "always returned it where you weren't."[15] Intellectually, he was not subtle; he was often erratic, but he was always practical and always bold.[16]

Personally, Olney was a tyrant. He quite literally hated infants and small animals. He hated big animals, too, for that matter, except horses. He once had a cow shot for trampling his tennis court. Although his daughter married a man he liked, and had her wedding in her father's house, Olney "in a fit of jealous resentment" told her that she should never return to a home she had chosen to leave. Her offense was going to the funeral of her father-in-law in Germany.[17] Olney was a New England Democrat partly from his devotion to laissez-faire and his dislike of protectionism, and partly from simply contrariness, for he lived in a world of business Republicans.[18]

In 1889 Olney became general counsel of the Chicago, Burlington, and Quincy, a western road that was also a creature of Boston capital. Much of Olney's work was protecting it from antimonopolists on state commissions, in legislatures, and in Congress. He would have preferred to abolish the ICC, but he would settle for taming it. "It satisfies the popular clamor for a government supervision of railroads, at the same time as that supervision is almost entirely nominal." He argued that "[t]he part of wisdom is not to destroy the Commission, but to utilize it."[19]

When Olney became attorney general of the United States in 1893, protecting the interests of Charles Perkins of the Burlington was not part of the job description, but it didn't have to be because attorney general was only Olney's day job. He remained on the payroll of the Burlington, and he also seems to have been paid by the Atchison, Topeka, and Santa Fe.[20] Given the number of antimonopolist Democrats, Olney could not appoint only friends of the railroad as U.S. marshals—who formed the enforcement arm of the federal courts—and federal attorneys, but he followed railroad suggestions closely in his appointments.[21] In San Francisco, Olney, who was supposedly influenced by Stephen Field, the U.S. Supreme Court justice and old friend of the Associates, opposed Barry Baldwin's appointment as U.S. marshal, but the California delegation pushed him through. Baldwin was a head of the anti–Southern Pacific San Francisco Traffic Association.[22] Olney joined a cabinet full of men with close ties to corporations, particularly railroad corporations, and with a common hostility to antimonopoly.[23] While Debs was organizing railroad workers, and while the Populists and other antimonopolists were organizing western states, the railroads were organizing the cabinet and the federal bureaucracy.

I. THE COURTS

For many American workers, the hypothetical results of marginalism—the inexorable reduction of wages to the level that the most desperate worker was willing to take—became real in Pullman, the industrial suburb of Chicago in 1894. George Pullman had created a company town to manufacture railroad cars, but he also set out to manufacture railroad workers, the men who produced his Pullman parlor cars and sleepers. His model town was intended to produce sober and clean workers who would be loyal to their employer and conservative in their thinking. Pullman moved the battle over control of work into the worker's home. For many workers, it was a nightmare, an assault on republican manhood even when wages were relatively high. When Pullman in response to the depression of 1893 cut his workers' wages and hours by an average of 25 percent, to such a low level that some could not even pay the rent for his company housing, the workers exploded in fury. Their strike in May of 1894 hit a responsive chord among working people across the country.[24]

In the 1890s the judiciary had not yet settled on the legitimacy of unions and the right of workers to strike. In November of 1893 the *Union Pacific Employes' Magazine* warned its readers against panicking either over the expansive powers that judges were giving to courts of equity or decisions striking at boycotts and sympathy strikes. The intervention of courts was not, it reasoned, a bad thing. To bring a union into court was implicitly to accept the validity of the union, and if the contractual rights of management deserved protection in a court so, too, did the rights of workers. To contest these issues in a court of justice was preferable to a strike, as long as the courts were fair and just. There were decisions, such as those by Judges Taft and Ricks in the so-called *Ann Arbor* cases of 1893, that went against workers, not only prohibiting secondary boycotts but limiting workers' rights to suspend work against corporations "charged by the law with certain great trusts and duties to the public." Even quitting their jobs might open them to legal liability. But there was also the decision of Judge Speer in Georgia that forced receivers there to negotiate with the Brotherhood of Locomotive Engineers and honor existing contracts. There was as yet no judicial coup executed by a united cohort of conservative judges. Judges, too, were struggling with adjusting an older republican culture of contract freedoms to a new industrial order.[25]

Antimonopoly workers hoped that unions and corporations would be treated the same under the law, but the standing of corporations as artificial persons fatally tilted the scales. Union leaders could be indicted for conspiracy simply by acting together for the benefit of their union because the courts regarded them as discrete and separate persons. Corporate leaders acting for the benefit of the corporation, however, were a composite corporate person rather than discrete individuals and thus could not conspire as long as they acted within the corporation. There was little logical reason why a corporation was considered a single rights-bearing person while a union was merely a collection of rights-bearing individuals. The legal reason was that corporations had chosen to incorporate, but in organizational terms there was little difference between a union such as the American Railway Union and a corporation.[26] A union combined the aggregated labor power of its members to increase their collective earnings and maintain their collective security; a corporation combined the capital of its stockholders to increase their collective earnings and to limit their financial liability in a given venture. Both entities ideally sought to maximize the earnings of their members and render their livelihoods more stable and secure. And, occasionally, a judge like Marshall Harlan, a district judge in Nebraska ruling against the Union Pacific in 1894, cut through the obfuscation and said as much:

> *A corporation is organized capital; it is capital consisting of money and property. Organized labor is organized capital; it is capital consisting of brains and muscle. What is lawful for one to do is lawful for the other to do . . . Both act from the prompting of enlightened selfishness, and the action of both is lawful when no illegal or criminal means are used or threatened.*[27]

Most judges, however, recognized no such equivalence. Nor, given the refusal of unions to incorporate, did they have to do so. Unions believed incorporation would open them up to lawsuits and hold them responsible for individual acts by their members. The failure to incorporate brought costs.[28] Judge William Howard Taft ruled in 1893 that by requiring members to join their union brothers in legitimate strikes the constitution of the Brotherhood of Locomotive Engineers "make[s] the whole brotherhood a criminal conspiracy against the laws of their country."[29] To engage in a criminal conspiracy they did not have to commit, or even contemplate, any crimes. By the early 1890s the courts had begun to rule that acts, while perfectly legal when performed by an individual, could be illegal if many individuals combined and conspired to perform them. One worker quitting work was thus legal, but many workers combining to quit work could be illegal. The same rules did not apply to corporate officials who met to cut workers' wages in violation of contracts. The playing field may not have been fatally tilted in 1893, but the courts had the hydraulic lifts in place to force the workers into an uphill struggle.[30]

This was the shifting and unstable ground that Eugene Debs traversed when in 1893 he organized the American Railway Union. His logic, like that of western and southern farmers in creating the Farmers' Alliance, was that what was sauce for the goose was sauce for the gander. Corporations were large and powerful. They could be countered only by organizations of equivalent size and power. He chose to create an organization of similar size and power.

In organizing the ARU, Debs almost eerily repeated the initial success of the Knights of Labor a decade earlier. The Knights had lost many of their locals along the Northern Pacific and Union Pacific by 1893, but they still retained a presence.[31] The overwhelming majority of ARU locals sprang up in places where the Knights' railroad or mixed locals had disappeared or never been.[32] The railroads were the veins through which ARU organizers flowed. The new locals began to spring up along the Union Pacific in September of 1893, and then spread line by line along the Atchison, the Central Pacific, the KATY, and other Texas roads. By January of 1894 there were locals along the Great Northern, the Northern Pacific, and the Canadian Pacific. With the ARU's victory over the Great Northern in the strike of April 1894, locals blossomed virtually everywhere, particularly in California, Canada, and the Midwest.[33] By June of 1894 the ARU claimed 150,000 members in the United States and Canada. Debs believed that if the ARU had to fight, it could win in the West. "There is brawn and energy in the West. Men there are loyal, fraternal and true. When they believe they are right, they all go out and stay out until the fight is over."[34]

But this growth was precarious. The locals that sprang up across the West were signs of worker anger and militancy but not organization. Many of the locals did not have even a post office box, let alone a union hall. The locals were a number and the name, often changing, of a secretary. The only locals that listed a street address were in large cities or towns such as Sacramento, Omaha, Oakland, Salt Lake City, and Los Angeles. Their address seems to have been the home addresses of the secretaries. It was hard to see how Debs could coordinate anything when the vast majority of his locals were represented by only a secretary whose identity might shift monthly.[35]

II. UNION PACIFIC AND GREAT NORTHERN

In the summer of 1893 western railroad workers saw signs of the depression all around them. The collapse in silver production had thrown tens of thousands of men out of work, idled much of the railroad system, filled the railroad yards with tramps and brought many to the brink of destitution.[36] The Union Pacific, the Great Northern, and the Northern Pacific collectively moved to cut wages. And in Chicago, the General Managers' Association consulted with Frank Sargent, head of the Brotherhood of Locomotive Firemen, and P. M. Arthur, head of the Brotherhood of Locomotive Engineers. Both their organizations were separate from the ARU, and both agreed in principle to the necessity for wage reductions. They predicted little resistance.[37]

Arthur and Sargent were neither fools nor traitors; in return for the cuts, the General Managers' Association offered the unions recognition and a comprehensive wage scale that the association would impose on member roads. The opposition to the plan within the railroads came from self-confessed "old fogeys," who vowed never to negotiate with a labor organization, and men like James J. Hill of the Great Northern, who "would not care to be a member of an organization which could order his company to do thus or so."[38] The real sticking point for workers was less wages per se than the Chicago General Managers' move to modify work rules "so as to afford greater latitude to the railroad companies in the management of their affairs."[39] The primary struggle continued to be over the control of work.

In cutting wages, the northern transcontinentals treated the brotherhoods gingerly even as they recognized that, like those of the Northern Pacific, existing schedules and work rules had "objectionable features, as to overtime, privileges, etc. . . . [that] place the Company in a position subordinate to the men."[40] When the Northern Pacific fell into receivership in August of 1893, the receivers ordered a 10–20 percent reduction in employee salaries over $1,200 a year, but deferred action on the mass of employees while undertaking an examination of pay schedules and work rules negotiated by the brotherhoods since 1885.[41] When faced with resistance to wage cuts, Oliver Mink, the Union Pacific comptroller and eventually one of its receivers, backed down.[42] He settled for reducing hours in the shops to thirty-five per week.[43] A 10–15 percent wage reduction followed in September, but only for workers outside the brotherhoods.[44]

The Great Northern took the most draconian actions, but James J. Hill, too, hesitated to take on organized workers. He did not immediately cut the trainmen, enginemen, or shopmen.[45] The cuts thus hit the poorest workers, and they resurrected the old language of wage slavery, by asking how men working sixteen hours a day could support their families on $35–$40 a month paying $11 per ton for coal and $16–$30 a month for rent. Hill replied that they were lucky to have jobs in such hard times.[46]

The initial reluctance to take on the brotherhoods sprang as much from the railroads' distrust of each other as from fear of organized labor. John W. Kendrick of the Northern Pacific thought the Great Northern might encourage the Northern Pacific to cut wages in order "to embroil us with our own men in some way for the purpose of advancing their own interests."[47] Whenever Kendrick tried to meet with Hill's officers, they were always on their way out of town. Kendrick exchanged pay schedules with the Union Pacific so that the two roads could act in concert, but the Union Pacific's schedules were so complicated that Kendrick despaired of any quick wage reduction.[48]

In late November 1893 the Northern Pacific bit the bullet and attacked the brotherhoods, and the Union Pacific followed with cuts across its system. The Great Northern held back until it saw the results of the Northern Pacific's efforts.[49] The Northern Pacific announced a systematic alteration of both salaries and work rules across the line. The two were intimately related because special rules for overtime, for mountain work, for deadheading, for pay while being on call, and for switching all elevated workers' pay, which—combining the pay of conductors, trainmen, and switchmen—had risen 22 percent per train mile between 1885 and 1893. The company aimed to end the brotherhoods' power to control the terms and conditions of their work; it wanted a simplification of the rules, a reduction of wages, and a standardization of wage schedules. The workers recognized the larger goal. The engineers, Kendrick reported, state that "they do not care so much about their reduction in wages, as they do about the loss of their rights." Similarly, the "trainmen east of Mandan object to the schedule principally because they were not consulted. . . ." The switchmen are "very much discontented. They allege as a reason for this that if they concede the Company's right to make any decrease whatsoever in their pay, they must expect that future reductions will be made, and . . . the statement is commonly made that if they submit to this, their condition will soon be no better than serfs."[50]

The brotherhoods did not immediately unite. Kendrick reported, "[The] committees are coming to us from the different orders, and we, apparently, shall not be subjected to the embarrassment of being called upon to receive the federated committee of all the men."[51] Kendrick's hopes proved premature. In mid-January of 1894 the Northern Pacific had to modify the first draft of its new schedule after negotiations with a united brotherhood committee of trainmen and yardmen.[52]

By the time the Northern Pacific acted, it was in receivership, as was the Union Pacific. Despite the legal power of receivers, the *Union Pacific Employes' Magazine* remained sanguine. Receivers were often enemies of the workers, but in receivership workers received precedence over bondholders. The ideal receivership would be one that led to public ownership.[53] The appointment of S. H. H. Clark as receiver on the Union Pacific meant there would be known rather than unknown devils in charge, and the magazine believed courts would protect current wage agreements.[54] Its correspondents were not so sure. Sage Brush, writing from Shoshone, Idaho, saw the courts stripping workers of their liberty, manhood, and dignity, while the workers supported the two old parties that placed such judges on the bench.[55] Workers were right to be skeptical.

When faced with resistance to wage cuts, the Union Pacific and Northern Pacific receivers badly overstepped, giving the ARU its first opening.

The receivers, fearing a strike, secured an injunction that forbade the men from even consulting their leaders in the brotherhoods. The brotherhoods succeeded in modifying the injunctions, but the lengths to which the sympathetic judges would go in supporting corporations were on display.[56] Then in February 1894 the federal judge Elmer S. Dundy issued an injunction that prohibited Union Pacific workers from so much as meeting to discuss the wage cut, let alone striking. It was, Debs said, a "deathblow to human liberty." He attacked the decision as a move to destroy constitutional guarantees and undermine American manhood. The ARU's first victory came in court. Within a month Judge Henry Caldwell had overruled Dundy and ordered the receivers to abide by existing agreements.[57] The receivers had to schedule meetings with the various brotherhoods to renegotiate schedules.[58]

As the Union Pacific case made its way through the courts, the Great Northern had been negotiating with the Northern Pacific to make coordinated cuts across both systems. The two roads were careful not to make the schedules exactly the same and thus open themselves up to charges of conspiracy. Hill considered his only significant obstacle to be the engineers.[59] He continued to reduce the wages of his most vulnerable employees, with the railway carmen taking a second wage cut on March 1 that made their total reduction between 20 and 36 percent.[60] His attempt to negotiate a reduction with the engineers broke down in February, when the men rejected both "the proposed pay schedule and rules."[61]

There was no reason for James J. Hill to cut wages so dramatically. The Great Northern was a vulnerable line with precious little to carry once it left the wheat fields of the Dakotas, but its eastern traffic sustained its profitability. Hill could have cut dividends and left his workers alone. But there was something obsessive and mean about Hill. His memoranda books and diaries record the cost of groceries and coal and the size of fish he caught. Small amounts mattered to Hill. His own obsession with economizing became a conviction that men with far less should economize.[62]

When the engineers and firemen on the Great Northern failed in their attempt to make Hill's cuts temporary and protect the work rules, they agreed to arbitration. The arbitrators, however, only reduced a 10 percent cut to 9 percent. The national brotherhoods opposed a strike. Emboldened by Hill's success, the Northern Pacific renewed its attempt to cut wages. In March workers on the Great Northern, including many members of the brotherhoods, requested the assistance of the ARU, and the ARU dispatched James Hogan.[63]

Hill refused to accept the ARU as a negotiating agent for his workers. On April 13 the union claimed it had intercepted a telegram ordering the firing of ARU men, and the Great Northern went out on strike.[64] Debs proposed "to go over the Great Northern in person; hold popular mass meetings at every point; appeal to the whole people to stand by us in this unholy massacre of our rights." He invoked the language of manhood and proposed tapping antimonopoly sentiment all along the line. If the workers stood up and were men, they would "not want for the support of courageous, manly men."[65]

The sympathy was there. The mayors of Great Falls, Havre, Butte, and Helena warned the Great Northern against attempts to use scabs to take the places of strikers. Their citizens would oppose it. In Great Falls a mass meeting came out in support of the strike and urged the railroad to make a speedy settlement. Members of the ARU requested authorities to deputize them as special police to guard railway property and had already begun patrolling yards and sidetrack at Great Falls. In Crookston, North Dakota, a mass meeting produced a resolution of support, arguing that dividends should be reduced before wages.[66] Marcus Daly, one of the Butte Copper Kings, reported that there was intense bitterness against the railroad, particularly for cutting the wages of men who made only two dollars a day.[67]

Hill's refusal to negotiate had a legal basis. The Great Northern had "existing agreements with a large number of its men," and the leadership of the brotherhoods had denounced the strike. Hill, claiming the workers had been "misled and misrepresented," told them to return to work. Once the ARU and the brotherhoods had settled their own differences, he would negotiate. He blamed the "present troubles" on "the acts of men who are not employed by the company." He said he was always ready to meet with his workers, but only with representatives of men in the actual employ of its company.[68] That Hill had fired ARU leaders made this claim somewhat slippery. Hill denied rumors that he had already hired other workers to replace his employees, but he simultaneously reminded the ARU that men willing to scab had overwhelmed the company with applications.[69]

The ARU brushed aside Hill's assertions. The Great Northern had unilaterally altered the existing agreements; they were now beside the point. Debs insisted that "a large majority of the employees on the Great Northern System," representing "all classes of your employees," had "fully authorized and empowered" the ARU "to act for them in all things touching their differences with the Great Northern Railway Company."[70] On April 23 Debs notified Hill that there was a thirty-three-member committee of Hill's workers, with a five-member subcommittee to do the negotiating, ready to meet him.[71] On April 24 Debs asked Hill to set a time to meet.[72]

Hill sought to delay and seek federal intervention to break the strike in the name of protecting the mails. He wrote to Senator Cushman Davis of Minnesota that "the whole thing would be over in twelve hours if these men knew they are offending against the laws of the country."[73] On April 28 he wrote directly to President Cleveland, complaining that "turbulent mobs" in North Dakota and Montana were interfering with the courts. He did not claim interference with the mails, but interference with steps taken to prevent interference with the mails. "The authority of law and its officers are openly defied and ridiculed." He gave no examples.[74]

Either acting independently or at the solicitation of the railroads, the general superintendent of the Railway Mail Service asked the opinion of the attorney general on a seemingly technical question: what constituted a mail train? If a mail train was any train with a mail car attached, as the railroads contended, then the railroads could secure federal intervention by attaching a mail car to any train they chose. If a mail train was a specific scheduled train designated by the government to carry mail, then strikers could allow that train to pass and avoid federal intervention.[75]

The superintendent, James E. White, did not meet with Olney, who was absent, but the acting attorney general, Lawrence Maxwell, wrote an opinion on the spot. Maxwell was, among his other associations with the railroads, a "director of the Cincinnati, New Orleans & Texas Pacific," and he felt no need to do research or consult precedent. His opinion was everything that White, himself a friend of the railroads and an enemy of the unions, could want. It was "all wool and much more than a yard wide." Maxwell claimed it was "a federal offense to obstruct or retard the passage of any train carrying mail." It did not matter if strikers were willing to let the mail car pass; the whole train had to be allowed to proceed, or those stopping it were subject to "heavy penalties proscribed for those interfering with the United States mail."[76]

Maxwell's decision provided a powerful weapon to the railroads, but one Hill proved unable to use.[77] The peculiar configuration of the Great Northern was the first problem. In 1893 it ran through miles and miles of territory lacking literate inhabitants and U.S. post offices. There was not enough mail to warrant attaching mail cars to more than one passenger train a day. These the strikers could let through without having much of a discernible effect on the strike.[78] The second problem was that Olney was close to Charles Perkins, and he seems to have shared Perkins's dislike of Hill. He actually warned Cleveland against using troops in a dispute between employer and employees, particularly in one "in which the employees may possibly be right." Olney was more worried about Coxey's Army—unemployed marchers on Washington who were seizing trains—than about the ARU.[79]

In the spring of 1894 it was still not entirely clear how fully Olney would oppose the ARU or what weapons he was willing to use. He had refused to use the Sherman Antitrust Act against striking lumber workers in New York, because "the provisions of the statute in question were aimed at public mischief of a wholly different character." To use the act in a civil controversy involving a dispute between employees and employers "wears an appearance of unfairness." In June of 1894 in a commencement speech at Brown University, Olney recognized that the stimulus to movements of workingmen against "the whole organized order of things" was a conviction that "they do not have fair play—that society by its very constitution, necessarily works injustice and inequality. . . ."[80]

Stymied at getting federal intervention and frustrated at the support that the engineers and conductors were giving the strike, Hill on April 25 agreed to meet with Debs and the ARU's delegation without conceding the ARU's right to represent his workers. At the meeting the ARU rejected his proposal for arbitration by a board of "three disinterested railway men," denouncing it as an attempt to delay and divide the men.[81]

Hill replied with his own language of manliness: "Assure all employees who maintain their self respect and act like men that they will be taken care of by the Company."[82] In fact, Hill's sympathizers among the brotherhoods were demoralized. J. Nolan, who had undertaken the original negotiations for the engineers, wrote a long rambling letter, a self-pitying lament, at the refusal of the engineers to act like men and desert the ARU. He thought Hill was showing too much forbearance and denounced the "ARU rabble." The letter ended up in Hill's files, and no one reading it could think that the brotherhood controlled even the engineers on the Great Northern.[83]

Minneapolis and St. Paul businessmen intervened, asking the judges of the Minnesota Supreme Court to appoint the majority of the arbitrators. Hill accepted, after getting a private letter from the head of the committee, C. M. Harrington, saying that he was convinced that the powers of the government had to be invoked to secure a resumption of business and that Debs would not accept arbitration.[84] Hill's acceptance backfired. Debs agreed to arbitration. And Charles Pillsbury, not Harrington, whose child had fallen ill with scarlet fever, chaired the ensuing meeting, where the St. Paul Chamber of Commerce demanded that both sides submit the issues to a panel headed by Pillsbury. In less than an hour the panel, which did not include representatives of the brotherhoods, found in favor of the strikers. They restored 97½ percent of the wage cuts.[85] Hill attempted to exercise his pique by dismissing men who had abandoned their trains, but Pillsbury's commission objected that this was not part of the agreement settling the strike.[86]

III. PULLMAN

In the space of three months the ARU had defeated the Union Pacific in court and the Great Northern with a strike and arbitration. In the midst of the worst depression yet to affect the United States, this was a remarkable achievement. The ARU had conducted a well-disciplined strike with clearly specified ends that were within the power of the strike's object—James J.

Hill—to grant. It had succeeded because there was support along the line among antimonopolist workers, farmers, and small businessmen. Even the business community of Minneapolis and St. Paul was ultimately not willing to stand with James J. Hill. And the federal government had remained neutral. These were the conditions of labor victory.

The Pullman Strike, which for the first two weeks of June remained confined to the town of Pullman and Pullman's employees, replicated virtually none of these conditions except that it, too, was rooted in antimonopoly and, in the West, obtained wide public support. The strike appealed to the railroad workers' best instincts: that an injury to one was an injury to all.[87] When the ARU held its annual convention in Chicago that June of 1894, Debs urged that the union supply money, speakers, and aid to the strikers in Pullman, but otherwise stay out of the strike. His speech to the convention advocated "conservative propositions," but Debs also unleashed the powerful rhetoric of labor republicanism: "When men accept degrading conditions and wear collars and fetters without resistance, when a man surrenders his honest convictions, his loyalty to principle, he ceases to be a man." Debs meant it. The workers believed it. Debs's eloquence trumped his pragmatism, and the convention committed, against his advice, to a nationwide boycott of Pullman sleeping cars. They would not move any train carrying Pullman cars.[88]

The railroads immediately denounced the strike as a sympathy strike that made them the victims of a dispute in which they were in no way involved, but this was only partially true.[89] Because George Pullman did not sell, but only leased his cars to railroads and staffed them with his own crews—the famous Pullman porters—railway workers by targeting only the Pullman cars were directly targeting George Pullman. And although the railroads had contracts with Pullman requiring them to use his sleepers, they had complete discretion over when and where to use them. They were at full liberty to leave Pullman cars off their trains. Even with Pullmans attached to long-distance trains, the strike could have remained limited. There was no need for the vast majority of railroad traffic, locals and freights, to become involved in the dispute.[90]

The center of the struggle was always Chicago, the railroad center of the nation, which had Pullman as a suburb. Here the core struggle played out in June and July, ending with the Seventh Cavalry, Custer's old regiment, deployed on the streets, with strikers ("the mob") depicted as the equivalent of "savages" (the Lakotas) whom the soldiers had slaughtered at Wounded Knee a few years before.[91]

Both sides thought large principles and vast stakes were involved in the boycott. For John W. Kendrick, the general manager of the Northern Pacific, the issue resolved itself "into the question of, whether the roads shall be absolutely controlled by the labor element, or by the managers and owners."[92] Leaving out the word "absolutely," and acknowledging that the Northern Pacific, in fact, was no longer controlled by its owners but rather by the federal courts, whose servant Kendrick ostensibly was, this was a reasonable account of the boycott and ensuing strike. It was about worker control versus managerial dictation. Richard Olney would raise the stakes even higher. He argued that the strike, "if successful, would seriously impair the stability of our institutions and the entire organization of society as now constituted." The ARU contended that it was fighting to protect American institutions, but its proponents would agree that the strike was about the proper organization of American society.[93]

As usual in struggles over large principles, actual events proved messy, ad hoc, and unpredictable. On the western railroads the strike unfolded as a series of often quite personal confrontations and particular decisions made about specific trains in specific places. This was certainly true of the Northern Pacific. "On Tuesday, June 26th, when we attempted to move Train No. 1 from the coach yard to the Union depot," began a letter from the Kendrick to T. F. Oakes, now a receiver of the Union Pacific, "men declined, unless the Pullman cars were removed."[94] The yardmaster who ordered the train moved was named Finnigan, and he, like his subordinates, was a member of the ARU. He remonstrated with the men that they could not strike without giving the road notice and that the Northern Pacific, not the Pullman Company, owned these cars. This was both not exactly true and unpersuasive. The men still refused to move the train. Finnigan reported the refusal directly to the general manager because the superintendent was absent from St. Paul and the assistant superintendent was in Minneapolis.

Kendrick told the yardmaster that he expected him to perform his duty or resign. Finnigan succeeded in persuading the crew to move the train to the depot, and "afterwards reported himself for future duty."[95]

The train left nearly on time, and the assistant superintendent had now arrived at yard. The Northern Pacific was under contract with the Minneapolis and St. Louis Railway and thus obligated to move that road's evening train with its Pullman from the depot. But "one crew after another refused to perform service," and the men were dismissed. The train had moved from the yard to the depot only because the assistant superintendent and the yardmaster manned it themselves. They had to do the same thing for the next Northern Pacific train, the no. 7 bound for Fargo and Winnipeg.

The next day proved a turning point. On the morning of June 27 an ARU committee met with the general manager and the assistant general manager and asked for the reinstatement of the workers dismissed the evening before. Kendrick refused unless they were willing to move trains with Pullman cars attached. This they would not do. Still, the morning and afternoon trains arrived and departed with little trouble. The strike escalated dramatically when the Brotherhood of Locomotive Firemen announced that it had "federated with the ARU" and would not move the Pullman cars. This surprised and alarmed Kendrick, who like other railroad managers did not think that the brotherhoods would strike. Without the firemen, trains could not depart. When train number 1 was ready to leave the station at 4:15 in the afternoon, every fireman assigned to regular road service refused to board the train. The general manager succeeded in persuading a stationary engineer in the yard to serve as fireman, but he filled the firebox so full of coal that it smothered the fire and the train stalled ten minutes after leaving the depot, blocking the main track of the Great Northern. The Northern Pacific had to push the train from behind until it reached Hamline and could coast into Minneapolis. Here the temporary fireman, having sabotaged the train, deserted completely, and since no other fireman could be found, the rest of the crew also abandoned the train.[96] Back in St. Paul the fireman of train number 7 scheduled to depart at 8:00 P.M. deserted the train at the depot. Trains continued to arrive from the west, but they had to be taken into the yards by the assistant superintendent and the yardmaster.[97]

Debs's decision to have all ARU workers walk out until the men dismissed were reinstated was a critical move. What had begun as a boycott of Pullman cars became a strike of the ARU against the Northern Pacific and other roads dismissing workers.[98] In Livingston, Montana, the walkout was nearly total. The only men willing to work were some conductors and a very few brakemen.[99] By June 28 the refusal of the firemen to serve had prevented the departure of any passenger trains from St. Paul. At Elliston, in western Montana, all the employees—conductors, engineers, brakemen, fireman, operators, and clerks—walked out. There was still limited service on the other branches and divisions, but the strike gave every sign of completely shutting down the western divisions as well. Passenger trains remained scattered where the firemen or engineers deserted them or at terminals from which they could not be moved. One train was at Billings; two were at Livingston; one was at Helena and one at Hope. At the end of the day, Kendrick declared the strike general, with nothing moving, and expanding to other lines.[100]

Tracing who walked out and who remained created a diagram of worker solidarity. It varied from place to place. Dispatchers, many, but hardly all, engineers and other trainmen remained loyal to the company, but most firemen and "nearly all the employes in the lower branches of service [were] out."[101] The actions of the men comprised a kind of awkward dance as they balanced their loyalty to one another, their fear of losing work in a depression, their devotion to the ARU, and their anger at Pullman. In Washington State, when the Northern Pacific obtained substitutes for striking firemen, engineers in the mountain division pushed other engineers to refuse to work with new firemen. At Missoula the engineers did not strike, but they would not go out without their regular firemen, who were on strike. In Fargo, North Dakota, engineers also refused to work with new firemen. The switchmen at Seattle struck, but in the face of an ultimatum to return or lose their jobs, they returned and agreed not to go out again on the call of the ARU.[102] At Glendive some men tried to stay neutral, but the Northern Pacific quickly ruled there was no such thing as neutrality. Kendrick wrote that "men who decline service when called upon to perform it are strikers."[103]

The railroads counted on the brotherhoods to support them, but the brotherhoods could not control their members who refused to handle trains with Pullmans. That the brotherhoods were no practical help as the strike took shape was shown in the Northern Pacific telegraphic code for them: "Forsaken," "S.O.B.," and "Titular Anarchy." On June 30, when the Winnipeg train arrived in St. Paul on time, the firemen there refused to serve, and the road could find no engineers. They put two new men on the train, but it was stopped so often by strikers that it took two hours to clear Minneapolis. To move a train to Fargo, the Northern Pacific had to use its assistant superintendent in St. Paul as an engineer.[104] The engineers remained divided. The same day that Kendrick could find no engineers for the Winnipeg train, the engineers on the Minnesota division promised to move trains with any firemen provided them.[105]

As the strike evolved, certain men and places emerged as critically important. The firemen were central. On the Pacific Division, the firemen shut down traffic, although the superintendent there thought the other men were "all right."[106] Grand Forks, a division point, was a critical place.[107] Tangling major yards stopped the flow of traffic, but the strikers' tactic of abandoning trains on the single tracks of the West also created other impromptu blockades that the railroad had to eliminate one by one.[108]

Because the workers' actions seemed so ad hoc, managers were initially confused. Kendrick could not determine whether "there is any method in the manner of the attack of the Union or not." Nor could the Northern Pacific be sure initially whether other railroads would support it or capitalize on its difficulties.[109] There were reports that some lines were being struck while others such as the Burlington, "which operates Pullman cars upon a large scale, has not yet been molested." Kendrick initially suspected that the ARU was striking some roads and letting others alone in order to create divisions among the roads."[110]

Kendrick also suspected that the ARU had struck the Northern Pacific because the Great Northern strike had demonstrated that the population of the northern tier of states was "in favor of anything populistic and anti-corporation."[111] And there was wide popular support for the strike on the Northern Pacific line between the Mississippi and the West Coast. In Tacoma the U.S. marshals and their deputies brought in to support the railroad were shunned. They could find neither lodging nor meals.[112] In Livingston, Montana, W. H. Frances reported to Kendrick that the whole town supported the strikers. Support in Montana was particularly strong in Butte/Anaconda and Missoula. Kendrick summarized the situation as "very disgusting," with the people "either through sympathy or . . . fear, upholding the strike and sympathizing with the men, even to the extent of joining them in their Meetings."[113]

The strike garnered similar popular support along the Central Pacific and Southern Pacific. Except in Los Angeles the ARU organized later in California than it had along the Northern Pacific, but workers flooded into the ARU when organizers appeared in Sacramento and San Francisco in May of 1894. The first week of the strike played out in much the same way along the Southern Pacific as along the Northern Pacific.[114] The ARU struck the Atchison first in Los Angeles, and on June 27, G. D. Bishop, the secretary of the ARU, notified the Southern Pacific of the boycott of all Pullman sleeping cars beginning at noon of the following day. The Southern Pacific's house paper, the *Sacramento Record-Union*, reported passenger trains carrying Pullmans as being delayed or stopped, but the only trouble the company reported was that workers refused to clean the Pullman cars in the Los Angeles yards.[115] Workers in Sacramento stopped one train on the 27th, but on the 28th in Los Angeles all was quiet as the company staged a show of force. There were eight policeman and sixty-five deputy sheriffs in the yard. Trouble came soon enough. At 4:30 Engineer Monroe refused to "pull a string of sleepers to get the Mishawaka out," but then he reconsidered and consented. Engineer Sam Clarke took the Mishawaka to Sacramento. His fireman, however, refused to go, and was discharged and replaced. The next day the ARU struck, demanding the fireman's reinstatement, and by noon the yard was empty.[116] In Oakland on the evening of June 28, the ARU voted to go out but said it would move any train with mail cars only. There, too, police appeared in the yards.[117]

Officially, the Southern Pacific took the same position as the other roads: it was an innocent third party, and Henry E. Huntington, speaking for the company, said that it opposed "the right of any organization of labor to make us a party to a controversy in the determination of which we have no voice."[118] The Southern Pacific, in effect, justified its actions by appealing to the antimonopoly principle that railroads should be a neutral common carrier open to all and discriminating against none. It was a fitting position in a strike that saw antimonopoly legislation—the Interstate Commerce Act and the Sherman Antitrust Act—deployed against antimonopolists. In private Henry Huntington was quite succinct about the company's aim: "We are going to break this strike," and he wanted to obtain laws that would make it impossible for employees ever again to "band together and by strikes interrupt and suspend for a day the transportation of Government mails and Interstate Commerce."[119] His uncle Collis wanted to purge the line gradually of all union men.[120]

The Southern Pacific urged its men to be loyal to the brotherhoods, but the brotherhoods equivocated here as elsewhere. The Order of Railway Conductors and the Brotherhood of Locomotive Engineers agreed "to handle all trains properly manned and protected," but this phrase gave them great leeway as to whether they would or would not move trains. They, too, asked that discharged employees be reinstated.[121]

Sacramento, the destination of the Mishawaka, became the center of the strike against the Southern Pacific. The city was not a terminal point, and was the starting point of only a single route carrying Pullman cars, but the railroad maintained extensive shops there and the ARU was strong.[122] When the shopmen in the Sacramento yards walked out on June 29, the *Chronicle* reported that 2,000 men filed out, joining 1,000 others already on strike. Although Division 10 of the Brotherhood of Locomotive Engineers refused to strike, the engineers also refused to go out on any but their regularly scheduled runs and then only "when perfectly satisfied that it is safe to do so." Each engineer would make that decision for himself.[123]

With the workers, their supporters, their wives, daughters, and girlfriends gathered at the Sacramento depot, the station took on the appearance of a fair.[124] What opponents referred to as the mob was in friendly newspaper illustrations a mixed crowd: the men in derbies and Stetsons, the women in summer dresses, often in small groups, standing, talking, and gesturing. The strikers sensed that Sacramento had become the West Coast equivalent of Chicago "and that if the tie-up is broken at this point the great strike will be lost." Just as the lively crowd was the human symbol of the strike, so the mechanical symbol became cold, immobile machines. The yards and tracks were a jumble of dead locomotives, abandoned trains, and cars switched so cleverly that one of their trucks was on one track and another on a sidetrack with the "switch set the wrong way and the catty cornered car can neither be pushed or pulled." Every switch and crossing seemed blocked by an abandoned car. Despite constant rumors of trouble and reports of burned trestles in outlying areas, there was little violence around Sacramento. Strikers maintained a steady vigilance over the yard, arranging watches of eight-hour shifts and sleeping in the blockaded trains.[125]

Through the first ten days of the action, strikers enjoyed great popular support and favorable coverage in the San Francisco papers, particularly de Young's *Chronicle* and Hearst's *Examiner*. After the strike William Mills, the Southern Pacific political operative, predictably wrote C. P. Huntington a long self-aggrandizing letter in praise of W. H. Mills, but Mills's account shrewdly dissected the role of the press and the state of popular opinion.

The strike, Mills reported, had initially met "with practically universal approval" in California. Mills organized the public defense of the railroad. He could not control the San Francisco dailies, but he took over editing the *Sacramento Record-Union*, working by telegraph from San Francisco. The *Record-Union* set the tone for the small-town papers all over California that depended on Southern Pacific patronage and "looked to its columns for direction." Mills took credit for having "instructed" the public mind and "rectified" public sentiment. This turned out not to be true, and even Mills admitted "that in many localities the Company is unpopular."[126]

Mills blamed Michael de Young, the publisher of the *Chronicle*, and William Randolph Hearst for the sympathetic treatment of the strikes by the press. De Young had demonstrated the possibilities of "journalistic blackmail" to the other papers by publishing what he was paid to publish, which meant he could be on either, or both, sides of an issue. In Mills's view this made the *Chronicle* morally inferior to the *Sacramento Record-Union*, which everyone knew published what the railroad wanted. The difference between the *Record-Union* and the *Chronicle* was the "difference between a wife and a harlot." In this instance, de Young had been driven to support the strike by Hearst. If the *Chronicle* had supported the railroad at the beginning of the strike, it would have "lost ten thousand subscribers" to the *Examiner*, which was attacking the Southern Pacific. What made Hearst's actions particularly enraging was that he was in the pay of the Southern Pacific. Hearst took the Southern Pacific's money and still favored the strikers. Eventually, de Young did become more sympathetic to the railroad, but he did so after "it would be most useful to the Company." In San Francisco the Southern Pacific had only the *Post*, which, as Mills put it, "has been selling out to the Water Company, to the Gas Company, to the Sugar Interest, to the Railroad, and anything or anybody, and the public knows it."[127]

As the first week of the strike paralyzed Chicago and shut down many of the western lines, federal intervention on the side of the railroads was ad hoc and only partially effective. Although in hands of receivers and thus under the jurisdiction of the federal court, the Northern Pacific had merely mixed results in mobilizing federal forces. The Northern Pacific was most successful in Minnesota and North Dakota, where federal judges asserted that no formal injunction was even necessary for marshals to come to its assistance; strikers' interference with the receivers was cause enough. By June 30 U.S. marshals had intervened "to prevent interference with use or possession by Receivers of Company property and to restrain those who refuse to work from interfering with employees engaged to perform their duties." Marshals got trains moving within those states by the end of June, but the line remained closed to through traffic. There was "no use starting out through trains until blockade in Idaho and Montana was raised."[128]

Federal judges and marshals west of the Missouri River proved a mixed bag. In Montana the federal court refused to order marshals to protect the railroad until there was some action that demonstrated a threat to the railroad.[129] The U.S. marshall in Helena, owing to lack of funds and the pressure of local politics, chose to do nothing.[130] In Idaho the federal judge was fearful of reversal and wanted the aid of able counsel in framing his decisions. Even though the able counsel that he wanted was John H. Mitchell of the Northern Pacific, his timidity meant things moved slowly.[131] And at the far end of the line in Washington, the only trains running on June 29 were those carrying militia, although managers thought that with federal protection they could move some traffic.[132]

Federal protection came in the person of Judge Cornelius Hanford, a federal district court judge in Washington, who authorized the U.S. marshal to bring before the court for punishment any persons obstructing operations of the Northern Pacific or interfering with work by employees. These were criteria broad enough to make a conversation a crime. He also ordered that the receivers require all employees to take an oath to support the constitution and laws of United States and to obey all orders of the U.S. court. A refusal to obey a superior's orders would become a violation of the oath.[133] Hanford, whose reputation as an antilabor judge, a drunk, and a corruptionist would balloon following the Pullman Strike, would eventually be impeached after he stripped a man of his citizenship because he was a socialist. He resigned before his trial was complete. Railroad interests supposedly persuaded him to step down before witnesses gave testimony on his corruption that would be fatal to him and dangerous for them.[134]

Elsewhere in the West U.S. attorneys and U.S. marshals were neither dependable nor effective friends of the railroad. At Trinidad, Colorado, a crowd disarmed fifty-two U.S. deputy marshals, and in Raton, New Mexico, the sheriff warned the U.S. marshal not to enter the town with armed deputies.[135] The U.S. attorney for New Mexico told Olney that he did not consider a mere refusal to work on the part of railroad employees to be interfering with the mail. Olney corrected him.[136]

In California the strikers benefited from sympathetic officials as well as from popular support. Although in trials afterwards ARU attorneys would, to acquit their clients, portray the antimonopolist U.S. marshal Barry Baldwin as a tool of the Southern Pacific, he was sympathetic to the strikers. He refused to rule that the strikers' assembly at the Sacramento depot was unlawful in and of itself and implied that the railroad, rather than the strikers, was responsible for the fact that no mail trains went out. He opposed the railroad's requests to call out the militia at the beginning of the strike. He would act to protect the mail, but not until a mail train was made up and the mail loaded.[137] And in Los Angeles the U.S. attorney George Denis, to Olney's later embarrassment and outrage, moved to file an injunction not against the ARU but against the Southern Pacific for refusing to move the mail and for violation of the Sherman Antitrust Act.[138] In doing this, he reinforced the public perception that mails failed to move because the Southern Pacific refused to detach Pullmans from mail trains.[139]

All over the West the failure of marshals either to act or to act effectively and the peacefulness of the strikers frustrated railroad attorneys who wanted much more vigorous federal intervention. In Fargo into early July, according to the Northern Pacific's attorneys, there had been no violence, and the only intimidation had been "moral suasion." There were few examples of strikers destroying property or attacking other workers in the opening weeks of the strike, although strikers certainly threatened scabs and dissuaded them from working. As the Northern Pacific lawyers put it, "Frequently those who announce their willingness to do what is properly required of them . . . desert the service and shirk their duty upon the first attempt of pressure from those whose displeasure they would incur by continuing to perform their duties." Since marshals alone had failed to break the strike, and given every sign that civil officers alone could only gradually do so, railroad attorneys argued that only "the United States Army, distributed along the entire line of the road," could quickly restore operations.[140]

In June and early July the strikers appeared to be loudly and boisterously winning along the western lines, but the strike was actually quietly being lost in Washington. Despite his statements to the contrary, there was never a hint of evenhandedness in Richard Olney's actions. He acted in full cooperation and consultation with the General Managers' Association in Chicago and relied on railroad attorneys for advice on how to break the strike. Olney first moved to protect the mails, using the earlier ruling during the Great Northern strike that any train containing a mail car was a mail train. This decision forced reluctant U.S. marshals to act against strikers if they attempted to block trains with Pullmans and a mail car. On June 28 Olney authorized the swearing in of as many deputy marshals as necessary to protect the mail trains.[141]

Olney forced confrontations that could have been avoided had he acted like previous attorney generals. The ARU announced that it would not interfere with the mails and, for the most part, did not do so. The government could have simply demanded that the ARU allow one mail train through a day on each line. Or it could have ordered the railroads to detach Pullmans from mail trains and remained neutral in the strike. Instead, the government sided with the companies.[142] The companies took full advantage of Olney's ruling. They refused to detach Pullmans from mail cars, and they added Pullmans to local mail trains that did not usually carry them. They moved mail cars from their usual place behind the coal tender to the rear of the train making it impossible to detach the Pullmans without detaching the mail car.[143]

Olney's ruling on the mails proved a powerful weapon against the original boycott, but it was a much weaker weapon against the strike. The strike had shut down rail traffic from Chicago west, and the General Managers' Association wanted the strike broken. It worked closely with the U.S. attorney in Chicago, and even more closely with Edwin Walker, whom on June 30 Olney appointed to assist U.S. Attorney Thomas Milchrist. Walker was the law partner of A. J. Eddy, who was a member of the General Managers' legal committee. He was also a lawyer for the Chicago, Milwaukee, and St. Paul.[144] As Clarence Darrow later said, the equivalent of appointing Walker would have been appointing "the attorney for the American Railway Union to represent the United States."[145]

Olney intervened not so much to enforce federal laws, or move the mail, or protect federal property as to demonstrate the power of the government, its right to intervene, and to break the strike.[146] Olney reversed his position on the Sherman Antitrust Act and the Interstate Commerce Act. Having criticized the use of the Sherman Antitrust Act against labor as a "perversion of the law from the real purpose of its authors," he agreed to pervert it himself. Olney and Walker used both acts to obtain sweeping injunctions in June and July against the ARU. Again there was no pretense of fairness. Walker drafted the bill for an injunction in close consultation with the judges who would grant it. Essentially, the injunction prohibited the ARU from striking. It technically did not forbid men from quitting, but they could do so only if their quitting did not interfere directly with the operations of railroads involved in interstate commerce or carrying the mails. That would prohibit a fireman from leaving his cab or a yardman from refusing to attach a Pullman car.[147]

If ARU members broke the law, they could be prosecuted under criminal statutes, but Olney decided to prevent union actions through injunctions instead of by punishing crimes. Unsympathetic judges saw his actions "as an example of the judiciary making law by equity proceedings"—that is, by use of English common law instead of written law.[148] Olney wanted to take the strike out of the hands of local authorities and criminal courts and use federal troops to suppress the strike. When strikers in Chicago refused to obey the injunction on July 3, the U.S. marshal requested troops, infuriating both John Hopkins, the mayor of Chicago, and Governor John Peter Altgeld of Illinois, who were not consulted. That same day, at Olney's insistence, President Cleveland ordered the deployment of the U.S. Army to enforce the injunction.[149]

The presence of troops did not suppress violence in Chicago, for there had been very little violence; instead, it provoked it. General Nelson Miles, in command of the troops in Chicago, had some sympathy with the workers but none with the ARU. He feared both civil war and anarchy. Miles liked to talk, and he particularly liked to talk to reporters. Later he would write his own account of the strike. Olney wanted Miles to spend less time talking to newspapers and more time shooting strikers.[150]

On July 5 and July 6 there was extensive mob violence in Chicago. The U.S. Strike Commission later found that few strikers participated in the violence in which a mob reportedly made up of the unemployed, tramps, and criminals burned empty boxcars and destroyed $340,000 worth of railroad property. The next day, a clash between a mob and militiamen who had been rushed to the city left four members of the crowd dead and four militiamen wounded. The clash was serious, but the result was hardly anarchy. The total number of arrests over the course of the strike in Chicago was only 515, and the arrests in the city in 1894 were fewer than for 1892 or 1893. As would prove to be the case elsewhere, the first serious bloodshed suppressed the strike. Debs called for a general strike, but it did not materialize. On July 7 Debs and the other principal officers of the ARU were arrested. Debs's arrest and the failure of the Chicago trades union and the American Federation of Labor to widen the strike, coupled with overwhelming force—there were over fourteen thousand troops, police, and deputies in Chicago alone between July 3 and July 10—brought the collapse of the Chicago strike. By July 13 trains were running in Chicago.[151]

Federal troops also crushed the strike in the West, despite local sympathy with the strikers. In Oregon, Governor Pennoyer denounced the Southern Pacific; in Texas, Governor Hogg attacked Olney and the administration's actions in Chicago and elsewhere; in Washington, the Sprague and Spokane units of the Washington National Guard refused to move against the strikers.[152] The ARU had been particularly confident about Montana, which had emerged as perhaps the critical center of resistance in the West outside of California, but federal troops quickly broke opposition there. The black Tenth Cavalry and its white officers deployed against the ARU, which had refused to allow black workers to become members.[153] At Livingston on July 10 federal troops confronted a crowd of several hundred people, which, although it contained old men, women, and children, their commander deemed "a threatening mob." The town's mayor thought the commanding officer, Captain Lockwood, near hysterical and told him to calm down. Lockwood called him a son of a bitch and told him he was running the town. Over the next several days the troops occupied the lines of the Northern Pacific and the Montana Union and broke the blockade. The strike was over in Montana by July 23.[154]

In California breaking the strike proved more difficult. On July 3 the ARU allowed one train through. The train carried Jane Stanford from her ranch in Dunsimore, and it was guarded by ARU men and decorated with flags. The strikers painted "ARU" across the boiler.[155] The union portrayed the train as a gallant gesture toward Mrs. Stanford, but it was also designed to underline the festering differences within the Southern Pacific. It was a slap at Collis P. Huntington and the present management of the railroad, which Jane Stanford hated far more than she did the ARU. Her disdain was reciprocated. In recording the train's movement in the journal of incidents that the company kept, someone wrote "Old Fool" in the margins.[156]

Far more significant than the Stanford train was the Southern Pacific's attempt to break the blockade at Sacramento on July 3. Initially, it all went smoothly enough. U.S. Marshall Baldwin with his deputies, the Sacramento sheriff and his deputies, and the Sacramento police easily cleared the depot of strikers and their sympathizers. There was no resistance. The strike committee's chairman, Harry Knox, urged the men to leave the building. In return for Knox's help, Baldwin agreed to let a few remain to dissuade the crew from moving the train. The master mechanic, the yardmaster, and the yard foreman together fired up one of the dead engines, a big freight engine, no. 1988, and brought it toward the depot, where a Pullman and mail car awaited. The engine began to move at 11:05, but it took time to switch dead engines and cars off the main track to clear it for the outgoing train.[157]

The engineer on the new mail train was Sam Clarke, the same engineer who had already brought a train up from Los Angeles at the beginning of the strike. He brought engine no. 1791 forward after no. 1988 had cleared the track. As the 1791 neared the depot with deputy marshals on board, the crowd in the yard began to chant "scab, scab." When the engine approached a switch from which the effigies of two scabs hung, someone threw the switch sending the semaphore smashing the windows of the cab and diverting the engine onto another track. A large rock flew from the crowd, and it struck just below the window where Clarke was sitting. Clarke ignored it and moved the train back onto the proper track. This, the *Examiner* reported, was the only attempt to injure anyone during the day.

As the train approached the depot, there was movement in the crowd. The strike committee tried to calm the men, and Baldwin and his men signaled the strikers back. The sheriff approached with his deputies, but he had few of them. Most of them had turned in their badges when they were told they were going to have to assist in breaking the blockade. The crowd rushed forward. Men moved quickly, but no one ran. They swallowed up Baldwin and knocked him over as he told them to stand back. When he arose, he pulled his pistol, but men quickly grabbed and disarmed him.

The men delegated to try to dissuade the scabs from moving the train never had a chance to talk to them; they, too, were swallowed up in the crowd moving onto the tracks. Chief of Police Drew on the depot platform tried to halt the crowd, but below him someone quickly uncoupled the Pullman cars, not touching the mail car. As many men as could get hands on the Pullmans pushed them back, and the cars moved away from the depot as if borne on the backs of workers. More men pushed an abandoned Colfax train back onto the main track as a blockade. A heavy freight followed it.[158]

When Marshal Baldwin appeared on the platform, the strikers gave him three cheers. He told them they had interfered with the U.S. mail. According to the *Examiner*, a hundred voices answered, "We will take your mail anywhere," but they would take it only without the Pullman. He ordered them to disperse. They cheered him again. Knox and his committee apologized to Baldwin and offered to get a crew to take the mail to San Francisco, but Baldwin told them the mail train had been interfered with and was no longer complete. The ARU, he said, had made a great mistake. Baldwin now had few choices; he wrote the governor, H. H. Markham, asking for the militia.[159] After midnight the U.S. attorney obtained an injunction against Harry Knox prohibiting him from conspiring to delay the mail.[160]

On July 4 national guardsmen from Stockton and San Francisco arrived in Sacramento.[161] The mustering of the National Guard left the three Sacramento companies, many of whose members were either strikers or had friends and relatives among them, the most conflicted. Guard Company A refused to go to the depot, but the other two Sacramento companies were placed at the front of the column. They had the choice of disobeying orders or, if faced with resistance, shooting and bayoneting their friends, neighbors, and relatives. The strikers blocked their way into the depot. While the officers and Marshal Baldwin debated what to do and who had authority to order the troops to fire into the crowd, the strikers, who wore small American flag pins, urged the soldiers not to act. "Don't you know that we were raised with you; that we are your brothers and that the fight you are making on us is only to enable a hungry corporation to grind its employees down." "Frank," another called, "if you kill me you make your sister a widow." It was unclear to the press in the noise and din whether the soldiers refused orders to advance with drawn bayonets against the crowd, or whether the officers refused to give the order. After a standoff the officers ordered a retreat. "Within two hours," the *Examiner* reported, "soldiers and strikers were wandering off arm in arm, drinking together, laughing together, and having a general good time." During the

Fourth of July celebrations, militiamen mingled with strikers and drank in the saloons.[162]

The failure of the militia restored the situation to a standoff in which soldiers and strikers alike suffered in 100-degree heat. After a quiet Sunday, July 8, passed, the new week began, with reports that the ARU men were arming. Reinforcements for the strikers were visibly pouring in from the north. Despite the injunction, Harry Knox remained free and negotiated with public and railroad officials.[163] Solidarity, however, was crumbling. On July 10, at a special meeting, the engineers agreed to go out on "any and all trains" when called upon. ARU men threatened their "lives and property" if they did.[164]

On July 11 federal troops arrived in Sacramento, and the Southern Pacific launched another attempt to move a train. The engineer, again, was Sam Clarke, but this time the strikers, who had no relatives or friends among the federal troops at the depot, chose to avoid direct confrontation, although there was some skirmishing across the Yolo River by armed men. The train pulled from the depot, proceeding through angry crowds, and crossed over the Yolo Bridge and then over trestle no. 2, which crossed a slough of the river. It had traveled about two miles from the depot and reached the end of the trestle when the locomotive hit a spot where someone had removed a fishplate and spikes and set the loose rail lethally back into place. When the engine hit the rail, it fell off the tracks, crashed through the trestle, and somersaulted into the water and mud below. Several cars followed. Clarke and four soldiers were killed, and the whole tone of the strike changed. Four ARU men were arrested and charged with murder. Soldiers were enraged and eager for vengeance. Public opinion turned against the strikers, but not necessarily in favor of the Southern Pacific.[165] By July 16 the Sacramento strike had been crushed.[166]

In Los Angeles the U.S. marshal, unlike Baldwin, immediately called for federal troops rather than militia.[167] Five companies from Angel Island in San Francisco Bay departed for Los Angeles on July 2, reaching Bakersfield the next afternoon and proceeding on to Los Angeles, where the strikers had completely shut down the Southern Pacific and the Atchison.[168] On July 4 the Southern Pacific began to "pick up the wrecks and blockades," and that afternoon made up the Seventh Street local. A crowd attempted to overturn the baggage car, but the police stopped them. By July 13 military picket lines had replaced striker picket lines. Sporadic resistance continued, but the strikers did not really challenge the troops. Instead, they harassed and attacked scabs. The troops broke the strike. By the twenty-ninth all but one company of soldiers had departed the city.[169]

The unraveling of the Pullman revealed the fractures and fissures among the workers. The strike's public support depended on its nonviolence, which put it in a difficult position when confronted with the overwhelming force of the state. And because antimonopolism was such a diverse movement, including both relatively conservative men such as Stephen White and radical labor, antimonopolists did not always enthusiastically or even fully support the strike. In Los Angeles workers were unable to muster the necessary force to confront troops, so they confronted one another, trying to maintain the lines of solidarity and with it the strike. Their efforts remain preserved not in their own records but in those of the Southern Pacific. The railroad recorded who had struck and who had remained "loyal," but beyond that it sought the relations between them: who had threatened, attacked, intimidated, or tried to dissuade men who had scabbed. The word "scab" itself took on immense power; scrawled as the ultimate epithet on railroad cars and depot and shop walls, it enraged managers. In its derivation from an old English word for "slut," the term was deeply gendered, a slur upon a worker's virtue and manhood. Its implicit claim was that a worker's first loyalty should be to his fellows but that he had prostituted himself to a corporation.[170] The company ordered the word erased as soon as it was found on any company property.

After listing the names of strikers, Southern Pacific officials in Los Angeles wrote, sometimes with dates and locations, the names of employees and those who threatened or insulted them. Frank Baldwin reported that Tony Kaiser and Charles Rowlands confronted him at the foot of Peralta Street and called him a scab. Samuel Martin cited three encounters, providing a kind of geography of confrontation. Young Mike Doyle and two others called at his home one evening, and Doyle told him, "If you ever go to work in that yard, we will beat you to death." Pat Carlon and "a gang" attempted to head him off at the corner of Wood and Atlantic one morning. William Henry standing with a crowd at Fifth and Castro, shouted, "He is a murderer; he murdered Grady."[171] Enforcing the strike involved more than men threatening men. Jack Mulligan's wife "called Jno. Cone a scab to his face."[172]

The strikers attempted to cordon off the scabs, denying them not only the company of workingmen but the commerce of the neighborhood. J. Stewart, designating himself a "committee of one," came to the grocery store of Eiber and Nors to warn them "not to give R.R. Employees credit." There need not have even been a specific threat to any specific person for a comment to find its way into the Southern Pacific's record. F. I. Wilder "made a remark to Smith and Mallard that the whole Sp. Co. was made up of God Damned Sons of Bitches and scabs."[173] But words were no match for soldiers with bayonets and Gatling guns and a surplus of workers desperate for any kind of work in a depression.

When the Pullman Strike broke out, William Pinkerton had married and was working at Rock Springs, Wyoming, driving an engine that hauled coal from the Union Pacific mines. A veteran railroad and union man, he sourly recorded the strike's progress and aftermath. He had joined the ARU and was a delegate to the strike meeting held at Green River. Pointing to the actions of Judge Caldwell in reversing the receiver's pay cut on the Union Pacific, Pinkerton thought the Union Pacific workers would get fair treatment from Caldwell and should stay out of the Pullman troubles. But the strike vote carried, and Pinkerton went out with the rest, for he could not stand the thought of being branded a scab.

The strike was largely peaceful until the sabotage of an engine in Rock Springs. And although Pinkerton had not been active in the strike, he was arrested under the injunction issued by the federal court in Wyoming. His status as an ARU delegate, he supposed, branded him as a dynamiter. He was "kept prisoner in the fort at Rock Springs for ten days" and then sent to Cheyenne for trial. The jail at Cheyenne was still full of men from Coxey's Army, and Pinkerton and the ARU men were confined to a small steel cage about fifteen feet long and four wide. The trial was a charade. The district attorney asked him a few questions and dismissed him. The company, Pinkerton contended, had simply trumped up charges to get influential men out of the way until the strike was crushed. A bitter Pinkerton, contending that the men most eager to strike had been the first to scab, went to Silver Bow, Montana. He obtained employment as a switchman on the Montana Union, but lost it when they discovered he had been a member of the ARU. He then looked for work on the Great Northern, ironically one of the last western lines still to recognize the ARU and not blacklist its members.[174]

For the workers the losses were immense. The Northern Pacific alone had dismissed and not rehired 1,944 men at the end of the strike. The largest number dismissed were in the Pacific Division. Proportionately, Montana, the Rocky Mountain, Idaho, and Pacific divisions appear to have had the greatest losses. The bulk of the strikers were yardmen, shopmen, roundhouse men, switchmen, and firemen. But surprising numbers of engineers, conductors, and brakemen had deserted the brotherhoods and gone out. Over one hundred agents and telegraph operators had also struck.[175]

In California not only did the Southern Pacific discharge strikers; the government pursued them in court. It used 2 defendants as a test case for 132 others that involved virtually all the strike leaders in California, whom the government accused of conspiracy "to retard the United States mails and restrain interstate commerce." The trial took five months. It was prosecuted by H. S. Foote, special assistant U.S. attorney. Foote, as Collis P. Huntington said, "has always been our friend," and Huntington was pushing him for U.S. district attorney.[176] By February 1895 Foote needed money. "As a financier," Henry wrote to his uncle, Foote was "not a success, and he always needs a little assistance, and unless his friends come to his aid, he will become so involved in debt that he can never get out. I suppose we will have to do something for Mr. Foote, but under the circumstances the question is 'how much?'"[177] As a prosecutor, Foote was also not a success. The trial ended on April 6 with a hung jury. Like Pinkerton, the ARU men on the Southern Pacific found themselves blacklisted, but after two years some of the railroads partially relented. Anyone accused of sabotage or active leadership in the strike remained on the discharge list, but others could have their names submitted for reinstatement.[178]

Despite the continuing decline in earnings on the road, the Southern Pacific portrayed the Pullman Strike as a victory. It had supposedly lost

$545,000 because of the strike, but it had used the strike to reduce payrolls and this had made up the entire loss in a year. It annulled all agreements with the firemen; it successfully pressured the engineers, who in the wake of the strike purged their ranks of ARU men, for reductions in pay. The Southern Pacific was gradually imposing the same wages as prevailed in the East. It seemed to have lost its fear of unions, but there was also a renewal of interest among officials in welfare capitalism to counter "a vast feverish spirit of disquiet pervading the labor of the country." The railroad, Huntington admitted, was unpopular, but with prosperity he thought that would change.[179]

IV. THE DECLINE OF THE OCTOPUS

The government had crushed the ARU because the railroads could not do the job themselves. By and large, the western railroads remained what they had been before the strike—bloated, ill managed, heavily indebted, and corrupt. Many of them were in receivership. They were, in a sense, even more creatures of the state thirty years after the end of the Civil War than they had been when the war ended. Many were now wards of the federal courts, and all of them depended on the might of the federal government to control their own workers.

When the equity case against Debs reached the Supreme Court in 1895, it was a sweeping victory for the government and the federal government's right to use injunctions to suppress railroad strikes. The right flowed, the court decided, not from any specific act but from the Constitution itself with the power it gave the government to regulate interstate commerce. The courts did not require legislation to outlaw strikes against interstate railroads, since all such strikes would necessarily interfere with the mails and interstate commerce and thus "could be enjoined, and the injunction could be enforced by the full, armed might of the United States."[180]

The courts were a necessary refuge for the western railroads because otherwise they were politically weak. Over much of the western United States, it was difficult to be a friend of the railroad and win political office.[181] This hurt the Southern Pacific badly because the Associates had two critical pieces of legislation in Washington. Their debts under the original government loans began coming due in 1895, and if not settled with a new funding bill the government could foreclose on the Central Pacific. Second, the Southern Pacific was counting on federal expenditures that would make Santa Monica, which it controlled, rather than San Pedro the port of Los Angeles. To control congressional appropriations, Huntington pursued his usual methods, doing favors for friends of the railroad, like Senator George Vest of Missouri, on key committees.[182] He was lavish with passes to clerks in the departments, from whom he might need information, and to members of Congress.[183] In a fit of unusual discretion, Collis asked his nephew Henry not to number his political letters, because Collis was destroying them, and he did not want traces in the record.[184]

California was thick with opponents of the funding bill. Governor Budd, Senator White, Mayor Sutro of San Francisco, and William Randolph Hearst's *Examiner* and Michael de Young's *Chronicle* all worked against it. Some wanted government foreclosure on the Central Pacific so that the road could be run as a publically owned line. They blocked Huntington's bills.[185]

In his efforts to refund the Central Pacific with a new low-interest, long-term government loan and to get appropriations for Santa Monica harbor, Huntington's most formidable opponent was Senator Stephen White.[186] White was "a terrible fighter" who was convincing Democrats that the future of the party in California depended on beating the railroad in the funding fight and the harbor fight.[187] As in the old days, Huntington went to Washington in 1896. He fumed, rambled, wrote indiscreet things, and cautioned that it "is very essential that these matters should be kept from the public, as they are so liable to be misconstrued." He wanted "good men, who know the right and will do it."[188] When he couldn't find good men in California, he got them elsewhere. In August of 1895 his nephew Henry authorized payments of $2,000 a month to Arthur Brown, one of the first two senators from the newly admitted state of Utah. Brown was later best known for being murdered by his mistress. She was acquitted.[189]

Huntington lost first the harbor fight and then the funding fight.[190] Hearst's *Examiner* sent Ambrose Bierce to Washington in January and February of 1896 to cover Huntington's attempt to secure legislation. Huntington was old and tired. When pressed into a corner, he claimed lapses of memory, lied, and dissembled. He had never had anyone like Bierce listening, condensing, and writing. "Of our modern Forty Thieves," Bierce wrote of the fat old man, "Mr. Huntington is the surviving 36." The effects were devastating, and even the Southern Pacific's disclosure that the *Examiner* had taken railroad subsidies did not stop the bleeding.[191]

The defeat of William Jennings Bryan in the presidential election of 1896 brought the Southern Pacific little solace. Huntington thought Bryan "an unsafe man and on the worst platform probably ever made by any civilized nation." He was "neither better nor worse than any of the other anarchists in the country." But outside of Bryan's defeat, the 1896 elections in California constituted another disaster for the Southern Pacific.[192] Grove Johnson, the only California congressmen who had supported the funding bills, lost. "[H]is defeat," William Herrin, then Huntington's chief operative, wrote, "will naturally cause other friends to be extremely reluctant to publicly acknowledge their friendship to railroad interests." Of the California congressional delegation elected in 1896, six were hostile to the railroads and the other one was "'leery' of the Funding Bill." In the twentieth century Hiram Johnson, Grove Johnson's son, would become the most prominent enemy of the Southern Pacific and governor of California. Nearly four decades of railroad politics had left the Southern Pacific hated in California and without reliable friends. The debts of the bankrupt Union Pacific and the heavily indebted and politically crippled Central Pacific to the federal government would finally be settled in 1899.[193]

MISE EN SCÈNE

FOLLOWING THE DETECTIVES

The Southern Pacific was partial to detectives. When in 1896 antimonopolists elected the Populist Adolf Sutro as mayor of San Francisco, Collis Huntington denounced him as a "pesitiferous cuss" and "as corrupt a man, I think, as there is on the west coast." Huntington had his nephew Henry put a detective on Sutro, hoping to uncover enough dirt to discredit him. He spent the railroad's money for nothing.[1]

Far more often Southern Pacific men employed detectives to follow other Southern Pacific men. In 1895 J. A. Fillmore, the general superintendent, wanting a promotion and seeking to weaken his rivals within the company, among them the assistant to the general manager of the Pacific system W. G. Curtis, put a detective on T. E. Stillman. Stillman was one of the lawyers in charge of the old Hopkins interest and a member of the board. He had apparently been receiving reports that the unpopularity of the Southern Pacific in California was due largely to Henry Huntington. This Stillman denied, but Fillmore thought the information came from Curtis and wanted proof that he could use to ingratiate himself with Huntington and eliminate Curtis. And so he employed a detective.[2]

Nineteenth-century detectives did not skimp on detail. Curtis and F. S. Douty had taken a carriage ride with Stillman, and thanks to the detective we know that during the ride Curtis and Douty had to urinate. We know they got off the carriage to piss by the road. We know that Curtis got through first, and that he stepped over toward the still urinating Douty. We know he said, "Didn't I fix that son-of-a-bitch H.E. [Huntington] with Stillman. I just filled him full." What we don't know is *how* the detective managed to overhear a conversation between men pissing in the dirt.

J. A. Fillmore was quite catholic in his use of detectives. He also had them follow the Huntingtons. An operative with the initials W.J.F. reported on Collis Huntington's visit to San Francisco in October of 1895. The detective was at his "usual position near 1020 Cal. St." when at 9:15 Huntington and Julius Kruttschnitt, the general manager, came out. Most of his report concerned only what a wealthy man did during a business day in San Francisco. He did not work long or hard, but he did ride public transportation. Huntington and Kruttschnitt walked to Powell Street and boarded a streetcar, taking it to Post Street. Two men standing at Post and Montgomery saw Huntington go past. One remarked to the other, "There is the old S.[O.]B. He owns the earth and the people here." The detective wrote this down. Kruttschnitt and Huntington walked down Post Street and entered the Union Trust Company Building.

When Huntington emerged at 12:30, he was with his nephew Henry. They went to the Union Club, stayed there until 1:15 and then walked to the Palace Hotel. They remained there about twenty minutes and then went to the Southern Pacific offices, leaving at 2:35. The detective dutifully followed them from streetcar to streetcar until the two parted. He then followed Collis Huntington to the northwest corner of Van Ness and Pacific Street, where Huntington spoke to a servant girl who was cleaning windows. Huntington dropped his card inside a gate, and proceeded home.

During the afternoon, however, the operative was not alone in following Huntington. Another man standing near the Southern Pacific offices also tailed the Huntingtons when they left, getting on a streetcar when they did and getting off when Collis did. W.J.F. now became a detective following a man following Huntington. W.J.F. described the second man in detail: six feet in height, weight 165–170 pounds, age thirty. He wore "a black cutaway coat and waistcoat and blue striped trousers, brown fedora hat, open face gold watch, turned down collar, green and brown tie, latest style, lace shoes" size 9. W.J.F. thought the second man was Harry Knox. Knox, who was still a leader in what was left of the American Railway Union, had been the strike committee chairman in Sacramento. Fillmore had been the Southern Pacific official most instrumental in breaking the boycott. He would have known Knox well. How the report found its way into Henry Huntington's files and what Harry Knox—if it was Harry Knox—had in mind are among the many things not clear about the Southern Pacific.[3]

CHAPTER 11

ぐ∽ΦΟ⌒

CREATIVE DESTRUCTION

And it has been one great satisfaction of mine through all my
busy life that, while working for myself, in almost everything
that I have done, the public's interest has been served.

—COLLIS P. HUNTINGTON, 1894[1]

IF A WESTERN Rip Van Winkle had fallen asleep in 1869 and awakened
in 1896, he would not have recognized the lands that the railroads had
touched. Bison had yielded to cattle; mountains had been blasted and bored.
Great swaths of land that had once whispered grass now screamed corn and
wheat. Nation-states had conquered Indian peoples, slaughtering some of
them and confining and controlling most of them. Population had increased
across much of this vast region, and there were growing cities along its edges.
A land that had once run largely north–south now ran mainly east–west.
Each change could have been traced back to the railroads.[2]

The railroads' initial contribution to conquest and development was
their transport of troops and their supplies. Native resistance to Mexican,
Canadian, and American state control persisted longest at a distance from
the railroads. The world of isolated posts adrift in a native sea gave way to
a world where troops concentrated by rail to the places nearest an outbreak
to crush resistance. In Mexico the Apaches learned this; in the United

States the Lakotas and Nez Perce learned this. In Canada the Métis learned this.

But conquering and dispossessing Indians did little for the railroads in and of itself; to generate traffic, western railroads had to induce both producers and consumers to move west. Henry George, Terence Powderly, and other antimonopolists were wrong in thinking that the railroad corporations sought to hold land for speculative profit. The men who managed the railroads recognized that the most profitable traffic came from a thickly settled country of small freeholders. Railroads desired an agrarian landscape as much as Henry George, who would have been more correct if he had noted that insiders within the corporations, not the corporations themselves, had skimmed the best lands and townsites for speculative gain.[3]

Actual speculators existed in a complicated relation to the railroads. Beginning in 1867 speculators had bought or preempted the best agricultural land in the San Joaquin Valley; by the time the Associates obtained congressional permission to change the Southern Pacific's route to run through the valley in 1871, they had to settle for lieu lands away from the track along much of its route.[4] Among the largest purchasers of land was E. H. Miller Jr., an old partner of Mark Hopkins, Central Pacific board member, and secretary of the railroad, but few of the other top-fifty land purchasers had direct connections with the railroad. Collis P. Huntington considered these men "land thieves," but the Southern Pacific also enabled them. In some cases the railroad sold and leased them land, and in others, both the railroad and the Associates, acting as individual speculators, bought land from them.[5] (See Appendix, Map C.)

When the Central Pacific acquired the Western Pacific, a railroad running between Sacramento and San Jose, one condition of purchase was conveying the land grant for a token payment to Charles McLaughlin, who had sold that road to the Associates. The second-largest purchaser of Western Pacific Railroad lands in Alameda County was William B. Carr, "Boss Billy," one of Leland Stanford's political fixers, who also acted as an intermediary in a huge sale of Southern Pacific lands.[6] This pattern of land consolidation along the railroad line was similar to what was happening along the Northern Pacific Railroad half a continent away. In the fertile Red River Valley of Minnesota and the Dakotas, the bankrupt Northern Pacific disposed of lands for under a dollar an acre through purchases paid for in depreciated bonds. Many of the buyers were insiders, who created bonanza wheat farms of thousands of acres.[7]

Railroads dealt with speculators, but they preferred selling land to small farmers. In histories of the West the migrations that brought millions to the region in the late nineteenth century are naturalized by comparing them to the flow of rivers or to a storm or a tsunami crashing into the far part of the continent, but this was no unstoppable or inevitable folk migration. We can keep the water metaphor, but denaturalize it. These migrations were more like the directed streams from a fire hose, aimed first here and then there by the railroads, which held and directed the hose.[8] In the West population did not flow evenly across the region; rather, in the words of Richard Overton in 1941, it "definitely followed the rails."[9]

Like so many carnival barkers, railroad publicity bureaus promoted the virtues of the West and cajoled potential settlers to seize the opportunity that the railroads offered. In 1873, at the end of the first wave of migration into Nebraska, the directors of the Burlington and Missouri told their stockholders that the railroad did not deserve "the entire credit for the rapid increase in settlement"—homestead and preemption laws had played a role—but it deserved most of it. Without the railroads the land bordering the tracks would have "remained almost an entirely unoccupied territory."[10] What seemed railroad hyperbole was probably a fairly accurate statement of fact.

Virtually all the big land grant roads invested in publicity bureaus and immigration agencies to attract settlers, but not all such ventures proved immediately successful. The Associates created an effective immigration network only after they reorganized their roads under the new Southern Pacific Corporation in 1883. The collapse of the Northern Pacific badly hurt its early efforts at colonization.[11] The stumbling early efforts of the Northern Pacific and the Central Pacific, however, only highlighted the spectacular success of the roads along the Middle Border, as Americans called the trans-Missouri region: the Burlington, the Union Pacific, and the Kansas Pacific.[12] There was no mystery in this: those roads had fertile land adjacent to already productive agricultural territory and had relatively easy access to markets. In 1878 A. E. Touzalin, then the director of the land department of the Burlington and Missouri, pointed out that if migrants had simply distributed themselves proportionately across the states with available land, the Burlington and Missouri in Nebraska would have received less than one-eighth of the migrants who actually purchased its lands.[13]

That railroads produced settlement is one of two great truths about agricultural settlement in the American West, and it is modified by a second one: somewhere between the 98th meridian and the 100th meridian the possibilities for agricultural settlement narrowed. Here were the semiarid lands of the American steppe. And farther west lay even less promising lands: the most arid sections of the Great Plains, the Rocky Mountains, and then, running south to north, the Sonoran Desert, the high deserts of the Great Basin, the semiarid Columbian Plateau, and, finally, more mountains to the west. Even on the West Coast, only Oregon's Willamette Valley, sections of the Central Valley in California, and parts of the Santa Clara Valley provided the kind of arable agricultural land for which eastern and European farmers yearned. Everywhere else heavily timbered, infertile, or arid lands promised little for small farmers without large investments of labor and capital. Much of the agricultural history of the late nineteenth and early twentieth centuries was simply the attempt of railroad men, boosters, and farmers to extend settlement deeper into the arid regions.

West of the 98th meridian settlers came relatively slowly and in disappointingly small numbers. Californians lamented how little growth the railroads brought them in the 1870s and 1880s even as they watched eastern Kansas boom. In 1891 W. H. Mills of the Central Pacific's land department estimated that far from attracting immigrants, between 1880 and 1890 the Sacramento Valley had *lost* twenty thousand of its natural increase in population. Nevada actually shrank in population after the railroad arrived. Yet over the course of the generation between 1870 and 1900 the cumulative impact of western railroads on the entire region was tremendous.[14] There were 2 million non-Indians in states lying all or in part west of the line of the Missouri River in 1870. The vast majority of them were in eastern Texas, eastern Kansas, and California. In 1900 there were 10.4 million.

It had taken Anglo-Americans roughly two and half centuries to secure the continent up to the Missouri River. They used the railroads to control the remainder in a generation. Canada and Mexico accomplished the equivalents.

Railroad promoters, officials, Fourth of July orators, and boosters all applauded this accomplishment, which was by any standards extraordinary. Leland Stanford, sitting before the Pacific Railway Commission in 1887, took what seemed very much like personal credit for the development of California and then, almost as an afterthought, for the entire West. "It [the Central Pacific] was the first enterprise anywhere in the world which made possible the habitation of regions of country far remote from navigable waters, and has added untold millions to the wealth of the nation."[15] Jay Cooke had helped precipitate a depression and driven the Northern Pacific Railroad into receivership, but he thought that in the end his work had been worthwhile. "Naught but Indians, buffalos etc. existed where now stand great cities & villages, and wherein reside over 6 mil of people with thousands of churches and schools & a constantly growing civilization."[16] In fact, by the end of 1893, W. H. Mills estimated that the Central Pacific, the California and Oregon, and the Oregon and California had disposed of only 20 percent of their land grants, having 12,610,512 acres remaining from an original 15,653,000 acres granted.[17] The large majority of the Northern Pacific grant remained unsold.

In 1877 Ernst von Hesse-Wartegg crossed Nebraska on the Union Pacific. He was for years the German consul in London and later married the opera singer Minnie Hauck. He was a prolific travel writer whose books traced his journeys across the globe. Travel writing in the nineteenth century was much like that of the twentieth or twenty-first. It was crammed with superficial judgments, dubious facts, and stories that only a tourist would believe, but they all gained credibility from authorial experience—this is what he or she had seen and heard—and from the very predictability of the narratives. For all the novelties encountered, the author's journey confirmed the world's order and hierarchy.[18] Western travel narratives also usually confirmed the railroads' order because these writers regularly solicited the roads for passes; they paid their fare in praise.

Hesse-Wartegg knew American railroads before he set foot on them since, as he wrote, the "railroad's steady, beneficial influence on civilization was first recognized in the United States." Even the star-crossed Union Pacific could become an emblem of civilization's blessings. "Built through a dry, treeless, unpeopled desert, the railroad now crosses an agricultural paradise. Civilization sweeps like a storm across the plains and smashes what will not bow down or give way before it. Buffalo, panther, Indian—all flee north to wastes of Dakota and Wyoming, while Nebraska becomes a farmer's dream, the New World's breadbasket." For Hesse-Wartegg civilization meant a familiar world with "small, neat towns of twenty to fifty houses largely built in the last five years and inhabited by German and Bohemian immigrants."[19]

Such quotations can be easily multiplied; the equation of progress with growth, wealth, religion, and "civilization" would not be much altered by adding more examples. They are all part of a long line of "say what you will" justifications of what otherwise might seem unsavory episodes in the American experience. In the end there were more Americans, more American things and products, more American churches and more "civilization," and who could argue with that? In the more pedestrian terms of modern social science, the social benefits of the railroads trumped their costs. For all their failures and excesses, they were a national success.[20]

I. DUMB GROWTH

But were the transcontinentals worth their cost? And did their rapid expansion, on balance, yield more benefits than harm? Americans did argue with the "say what you will" propagandists; that is why the "say what you will" arguments were necessary. Criticisms of nineteenth-century development are neither new nor anachronistic. Nineteenth-century figures as diverse as Charles Francis Adams and Henry George made them.[21] It is necessary to get the criticisms correct. The issue was never the choice between railroads and no railroads. Critics were quite clear about the issues. Should the railroads have been subsidized? Should they have been built where they were, when they were, in the numbers they were, and financed and managed as they were? The railroads seemed unable to achieve a balance between too much and too little. They enabled farmers and miners to produce far more cattle, wheat, and silver than the world needed. They opened up some of the most productive farmlands in the world and some of the most unproductive. Poverty, as Henry George observed, increased in the midst of progress.

Regional lines in California and the Midwest could have handled most of the productive traffic. Rail lines connecting Chicago, Kansas City, and St. Louis with the lands east of the 98th meridian would have allowed the settlement of the prairies and other lines connecting California and western Nevada with San Francisco Bay would have created a sufficient Pacific rail network. Long before the Northern Pacific and the Great Northern arrived, the Oregon Railroad and Navigation Company had given the Northwest a combination of river and rail transportation that allowed the settlement of the great wheat-raising region of the Palouse.

The development of the rest of the region would have been delayed without multiple transcontinentals, but what would have been lost? Mines that glutted the market for silver? The catastrophes that befell both cattle and buffalo on the Great Plains? The suffering of those who settled lands that could not sustain them all over the West? The calamities that afflicted Indians who lost their land, their way of life, and often their lives?

For Joseph Schumpeter the damage capitalism did was the source of its power. In his famous phrase, "creative destruction was its essence."[22] Schumpeter made the entrepreneur's benefits available in the short term, while society often had to wait for its share. The classic deferred gratification of the bourgeoisie was the farthest thing from the entrepreneur's mind. He wanted great wealth, and he wanted it now.[23] As Schumpeter saw it, entrepreneurs must reap more than they sow so that the children of those displaced by their innovations will eat more than their parents. In Schumpeter the abuses of capitalist enterprises, while real, were always transitory; their achievements, at least in the economic realm, seemingly permanent in that they set the stage for further progress as long as the process of creative destruction was allowed to continue. Society needed to be patient.[24]

Calculating social benefits is a tricky enterprise. Most calculations of the social benefits that the railroads brought to the West do not consider social returns for alternative investments and alternative uses of the subsidies. Would the money invested in western railroads have produced greater social returns if invested elsewhere? Second, and more critical to my purposes, the railroads in many, but not all, calculations delivered social benefits without any social costs. In Mexico the railroads amounted to an assault by the landed elite on the rural population. In the United States the social costs of farm and business failures, the dispossession of Indian peoples, the degradation of the environment and the waste of resources tend to be ignored. Social benefit calculators seem to have only plus signs; they do not include minus signs. Finally, the calculations of the benefits of movement are loaded in favor of the railroads. The ability to move across space more cheaply than alternative forms of transportation is counted as an unalloyed good. Thus a failing farmer in North Dakota selling wheat at a loss in Minneapolis–St. Paul ends up in the benefits column as long as he could send his wheat more cheaply by rail than by wagon. This is like giving a greater economic benefit to suicides who slit their wrists over those who blow their brains out because a knife costs less than a gun. That the farmer might have done better elsewhere does not enter the calculation.[25]

In assessing the social utility of the railroads, I want to include social costs harder for economists to measure.[26] I want to be conscious of the price—not necessarily calculated in losses that markets measure—and to consider who benefited and who lost. The issue facing the transcontinental railroads was a simple one. Having built ahead of demand, they had to create traffic in places where there was precious little to sell. Given their high fixed costs, the railroads could not simply wait for profitable traffic to appear. Hauling something, even at a loss, was better than hauling nothing. In attempting to cut economic losses, the railroads helped create both what might be called dumb growth and environmental catastrophes.

Bison became the first victims of dumb growth. This story itself was initially told in the nineteenth century as a triumph and later retold with a note of nostalgia and regret. As Joseph Nimmo summarized it in his 1885 *Report in Regard to the Range and Ranch Cattle Business of the United States,* in a period of less than twenty years "the cowboy has superseded the Indian, and the Texas steer has supplanted the buffalo."[27] Although Nimmo did not know it, in a few more years the cattle business would be in shambles and the cowboy of the open range a thing of the past.[28]

The near extermination of the bison after the Civil War was far more than a simple morality tale. It is rare for a single grazer to so dominate the vast expanse as the bison did, and long before the coming of the railroads the bison were vulnerable. The rise of buffalo nomadism among the Plains Indians had, over time, depleted the herds, less by direct consumption— although this was a factor—than by the competition with Indian horse herds for critical riverine habitat during the harsh plains winters. Horses, and later cattle, introduced disease that sapped the buffalo herds, and in the drought years of the mid-nineteenth century, the weakened herds found that retreat to the east was closed off by increasing white and Indian settlement. In the 1840s and 1850s the opening of the overland trail and increased commercial trade in buffalo hides, particularly along the Missouri River and the rivers draining Hudson Bay, only further depleted their numbers and cut their range. In Canada the destruction of the herds was underway before the arrival of the railroads, but railroads aided the slaughter. By 1872 steamboats were carrying buffalo hides between Winnipeg and Moorhead, which had railroad connections.[29]

Still, at least four million and as many as six million bison survived on the southern plains following the Civil War out of herds that once averaged about eight million.[30] The railroads proved instrumental in their demise by providing a means to get buffalo hides to market in a region utterly lacking water transport. And, as a bonus, their own ex-workers and freighters provided at least part of the labor force necessary to hunt the animals. In the words of William Hornaday, the leading nineteenth-century student of bison, "as soon as the railways crossed the buffalo country, the slaughter began."[31] This is not to say the railroads ever planned, or even foresaw, the slaughter. The Atlantic and Pacific, whose projected route ran through the heart of the southern herd, did not mention bison hides among the products they would carry.[32]

When William E. Connelley, secretary of the Kansas State Historical

Society, recorded the life of George W. Reighard for *A Standard History of Kansas and Kansans* (1919), he located Reighard's early life in western Kansas in a "country of romance and adventure." Reighard was a Union soldier, wounded at Cold Harbor, who left his native Pennsylvania in 1867 and eventually made his way to Leavenworth, where he worked as a government teamster shuttling supplies between Fort Hays, which was on the Kansas Pacific, to Fort Dodge and Fort Supply. By 1871 he had his own mule team, and he alternated between hauling supplies for the construction of the Atchison, Topeka, and Santa Fe and hauling the hides and skins of bison and wolves that he had killed back to the railhead. When the Atchison reached Dodge City in 1872, "he became a member of the large army that exterminated this noble game."[33] Bison cows yielded the best robes, but robes depended on Indians and Métis women to process and tan them. White hunters and skinners were incapable of producing such robes, and by the early 1870s they did not have to do so. This was no longer a robe trade. A new tanning process developed in England created a way to turn green bison hides into strong, supple leather particularly well suited for shoe soles and machine belts.[34] The new market reversed the old valence of buffalo hunting that valued the thick robes of buffalo killed in winter over those killed in other seasons and cows over bulls. Bull hides brought $3.50 each from Pennsylvania tanners in the early 1870s; bison cow hides brought less. Reighard, however, never got more than $2.50 for a bull hide, and by 1874 a glutted market had reduced bull hides to $1.15 with cow hides bringing less than a dollar.[35]

Reighard killed the bison for the "hide and the money it would bring."[36] This was an industrial hunt, from the Springfield 50-caliber rifles and the Sharp's "big fifties" that could kill from several hundred yards away, to the boxcars filled with hides, to the factories with their spiders' webs of buffalo-leather belts running through the air from steam engine shafts to individual machines. Americans seemed frantically impatient with anything that resembled the older crafts of turning animals into products that humans used. The waste of buffalo bothered them less than the waste of time. Colonel Richard Dodge remembered how men eager to speed up the process of skinning spiked the dead buffalo down, made strategic initial cuts in the hide, hooked the hide to a wagon, and then, whipping their horses, peeled the hide away. What was left looked less like a corpse than a stillbirth.[37] If the railroads, as Ernst von Hesse-Wartegg insisted, brought civilization, then the first sign of civilization on the southern plains was its stench as tens of thousands of rotting corpses proved too much for even the wolves to consume.[38]

This harvest of death resulted in surprisingly little cargo. In the years between 1871 and 1879 the hunters reduced the southern herd effectively to zero. Hide hunters supposedly took 3.5 million bison from the southern plains in the 1870s, but these hunters and skinners were only learning their trade and only one in five hides in the early years ever reached market.[39] If at a generous estimate 1.75 million hides reached market over the eight years of the southern hunt, they amounted to 2,450 carloads, which, if spread evenly over eight years, would have been about 306 carloads a year. Concentrated at a few stations, such as Dodge City, and providing a long haul to the east, this was a locally important source of traffic. The Atchison carried only 87,571 tons of traffic in 1871 and so the shipping of roughly 459,500 hides amounting to about 6,400 tons between 1872 and 1874 (as well 1,617,000 pounds of meat in 1873) would have been an important source of freight. The Atchison, however, still went into receivership. In the early 1870s it was an utterly unnecessary road over most of its route. Exterminating the bison did it no good. The whole episode was pathetic. There had been so many bison, and now there were only an isolated few, and so little railroad space proved necessary to carry all that the Americans valued about the species. It was as if lost and desperate visitors to earth reduced what they wanted of its life to a thimbleful and carried it away.[40]

The prelude to the end of the northern herd was the defeat of the Lakotas in 1876–77; the slaughter escalated with the approach of the Northern Pacific to Miles City, Montana, in 1881. Northern Pacific officials had followed both duty and profit in aiding the army's campaign following Custer's defeat in 1876. Without Indian warriors to stop them and the railroad providing transport, hide hunters could break free of Missouri River steamboats.[41] For the Lakotas their defeat and the destruction of the smaller northern bison herd were the twin blows that sentenced them to a more limited and constrained life on reservations.[42]

On the northern plains, too, a species that for centuries had dazzled with its abundance provided relatively little cargo. The Northern Pacific reported shipping 851 tons of hides in 1880–81. Shipments peaked the next year at 2,250 tons, before falling to 1,940 tons shipped from east of the Rockies in 1882–83, the last year for which the road provided statistics.[43] Presuming all the hides were from bison, the total of 5,041 tons amounted to the hides stripped from roughly 360,000 dead bison whose carcasses were left as carrion on the plains.[44] Presuming also that a typical freight car had increased its capacity to 15 tons in the early 1880s, the northern herd produced 336 cars of freight or slightly more than 100 cars a year spread over three years. For the Northern Pacific this was a pittance. In 1881–82, the peak period of the trade, hides amounted to about one-third of 1 percent of the road's total traffic.[45] The slaughter was as thorough as it was economically inconsequential to the railroads. The money gained would not even have paid for Henry Villard's celebratory excesses. Nor was this a world short of leather. In lamenting the slaughter, William Hornaday tried to assign it a large economic value on the theory that Americans would never appreciate anything that could not be assigned a large market value, but the real losses were to the Lakotas, other plains tribes, and all people who would follow. These losses were incalculable. Even Congress recognized this in attempting, unsuccessfully, to halt the slaughter.[46]

II. CATTLE

The slaughter of the bison—which, as Silas Bent informed the Cattle Growers' Convention in St. Louis in 1884, had "infested" the Great Plains—prepared the ground for the open-range cattle industry. This became a second grassland tragedy, as unnecessary and as avoidable as the slaughter of the bison, and even more directly staged by the railroads.

The Civil War and, to a lesser degree, anthrax helped spawn the open-range cattle industry. The Civil War was even harder on cattle than on human beings. There had been 749 cattle for every 1,000 people in the United States in 1860, and, largely because of the destruction of cattle in the South, the proportion fell to 509 per 1,000 in 1870. Only during the 1880s did cattle per capita again rise above the 1860 level, reaching 809 per 1,000 in 1890.[47] In Europe, too, the numbers of cattle declined as the great anthrax epidemic of the mid-nineteenth century decimated European herds and put Great Britain in the market for North American beef. The British market was proportionately more important to Canadian stockmen than to Americans, who enjoyed a much larger home market, but British demand still served to boost prices across North America.[48] Particularly in years of poor corn crops, when farmers did not fatten as many swine, demand for cattle—particularly lower-grade grass-fed cattle—was strong.[49]

In 1870 there were three million beef cattle in Texas, the largest cattle-producing state in the country. Unfortunately, these were also probably the three million worst beef cattle on the continent. Longhorns had evolved to tolerate human neglect and to survive on the open ranges of South Texas. They neither fattened well nor were particularly palatable. Sufficient grass and benign weather allowed Texas cattle to increase to over five million by 1880, a number nearly as large as the next two largest cattle-producing states—Iowa and Missouri—combined. Texas was producing far more cattle than Texans could eat and than their ranges could hold. The decline in cattle numbers nationally created a market. The problem was getting longhorns to it. Texas fever blocked their way.[50]

Texas longhorns harbored two species of the protozoan *Babesia*, both of which caused splenetic or Texas fever. *Babesia* made Texas longhorns a danger to all cattle that crossed their paths.[51] When the longhorns passed along a trail or went into a stockyard also used by local stock, the local stock sickened and died. Having evolved to live with Texas fever, longhorns usually had a mild case when young, and then retained enough antibodies to hold the disease at bay. Longhorns became carriers rather than victims of the disease. Ticks fed on the longhorns, absorbed the disease, dropped off, and laid eggs that yielded young ticks that also carried Texas fever. Although farmers did not know how the disease spread, they quickly and correctly associated it with Texas cattle. Angry, armed farmers and state quarantine laws meant that Texas cattle could not walk to market or to farms where they might fatten on corn. Texas cattle had to move toward railheads outside agricultural districts so as not to endanger far more valuable domestic stock. This is what produced the long drive.[52]

Longhorns walked to Kansas through Indian Territory in order to get to the railroad. Kansas railroads ran into the middle of nowhere, far from angry farmers. Until farmers arrived, they had precious little besides cattle to carry. When farmers arrived, the drive had to find a new destination. Beginning in 1867, Abilene, Ellsworth, Wichita, Dodge City, and Caldwell successively flowered as cattle towns among the muck and manure alongside the Atchison, Topeka, and Santa Fe, the Kansas Pacific lines, and their connecting roads. Each one yielded to a rival as agricultural settlement enveloped it. Remembered as the epitome of the Wild West, these towns were the creatures of a tick.[53] The receipts of cattle at the Kansas City Stockyard from the Atchison gave a sense of the increasing scale of the trade. In 1874 the Atchison shipped only 1,948 cattle to Kansas City, but the number peaked at 207,574 in 1882.[54]

If Kansas cattle towns had served only as a convenient departure point for eastern markets, they would have been even more short-lived than they were. Once the KATY reaching Denison, Texas, and the Texas and Pacific reached Fort Worth, Texas cattle bound to the east could go directly by rail to Kansas City or St. Louis.[55] And from there they could be distributed to farms as feeders to fatten on corn, if farmers were willing to take them. The long drive survived, however, because going north turned out to have unanticipated advantages for cattle and cattlemen.[56]

Shipping longhorns east directly from Texas or on arrival from Kansas proved risky. Railroads tried to segregate Texas cattle from northern stock, but these were western railroads. They kept sloppy records, mixed herds in stockyards, and had far too many railroad accidents that spilled cattle out into the countryside. The result was repeated outbreaks of infection. Railroad incompetence, dealers' lying about a herd's origins, and smuggling from Indian Territory all made Texas fever resilient.[57]

What mitigated the problem was winter. Cold killed the ticks. When Texas cattle were held from shipment until after the first hard freeze or, better yet, when they overwintered in Kansas, they were less of a threat to domestic stock. Livestock dealers could sell them for slaughter or to midwestern farmers for fattening without risk of infecting other cattle.

Holding cattle on the Great Plains had a second, unplanned advantage. Cattle grazed on the central and northern Great Plains put on weight more quickly than they did in Texas. Texas cattlemen began to specialize. Texas became, in effect, a boudoir and nursery: a wonderful place for cows to calve. It was not, however, such a wonderful place for young steers fattening for market. They were better off farther north. By 1870 a cycle developed whereby steers born in Texas, and to a lesser extent cows and calves, walked north to the cattle towns of Kansas, and later Nebraska, where northern ranchers bought herds from Texas cattlemen.[58] In 1871 buyers at Abilene purchased 190,000 head, but the railroads shipped only 40,000 from the town. In 1882 some 200,000 head of cattle exchanged hands at Dodge City, but less than a third of them went to market by rail.[59]

Some stayed in Kansas, but most others went farther north. When George Reighard left his freighting business and returned to Dodge City in 1878, he began to "buy one or two year old Texas steers, run them on the range for two years and ship to market at Kansas City, Missouri." The steers, coming up on long drives from Texas, were cheap, the grass on the public lands and, for that matter, on the railroad lands was free, and the business seemed profitable.[60] A herd of Texas longhorns reached Cheyenne as early as 1868, and the Union Pacific began to promote the possibilities for grazing. It advertised everything between the forks of the Platte as grazing land; its goal was to drain the livestock traffic of Colorado and Wyoming into Omaha.[61] In the early and mid-1870s, as the railroads temporarily soured on the possibility of agriculture west of the 100th meridian, they touted the grasslands as a place where cattle in effect cared for themselves.

West of the 100th meridian for a distance of nearly four hundred miles the Union Pacific railroad passes through the center of the great Pastoral Belt of this continent. This vast region, embracing Western Nebraska, Southern Wyoming and Northern Colorado, forms one of the most remarkable grazing countries in the world. . . . It has been found by experiment that the per cent of annual loss

of stock herded upon the plains without hay, grain, or artificial shelter, is less
than among the carefully fed and sheltered animals of the agricultural States.[62]

In 1875 Grenville Dodge shrank the boundary of agricultural settlement, and thus expanded the boundary of possible pastoralism, by suggesting that the Union Pacific do nothing to encourage agriculture west of Grand Island on the Platte River in Nebraska.[63] Others gave witness to what the railroads proclaimed. Dr. Hiram Latham, whose own ranch investments ultimately failed, wrote an 1871 pamphlet, *Trans-Missouri Stock Raising*, which presented a West of "a billion acres . . . boundless, endless, gateless, and all of it furnishing winter grazing." It was a pioneer of a genre pretty much summed up by the title of General James S. Brisbin's *Beef Bonanza; or, How to Get Rich on the Plains.*[64]

Livestock numbers soared in response, but we cannot be sure of the exact count. In 1886 there were supposedly more than 1.25 million head of cattle in Wyoming, although in 1880 census takers found only about 250,000. Neither estimate was particularly reliable.[65] As western Nebraska, Colorado, and Wyoming filled with cattle, and the Fremont Elkhorn and Missouri Valley advanced west to compete with the Union Pacific, cattlemen in the early 1880s drove them north into Montana, parts of the western Dakotas, and on into Canada, where the advancing Northern Pacific and Canadian Pacific opened up vast new territories.[66] By 1882 Northern Pacific stations at Bismarck, Little Missouri, and Glendive were all shipping cattle. Drovers also brought stock eastward from the ranges of Oregon, Washington, and Idaho where the ancestors of these cattle had originally gone west along the Oregon Trail or come up from California. And by the mid-1880s the railroads were hauling so many "pilgrims" or barnyard stock from the Midwest into the Great Plains that trainloads of cattle going west nearly equaled the trainloads of cattle going east. Some of these cattle were "improved" only in comparison with longhorns; they were often, as one purchaser put it, "a crooked lot, half starved milk calves classed as yearlings and there was scarcely a good one even among the older cattle." A few were shorthorns crossed with Herefords.[67]

As cattle surged onto the Great Plains, shipments on the Union Pacific into Council Bluffs and Omaha increased from 4,780 carloads in 1878 to 6,170 in 1879. Many of these were coming from prairie farms, but shipments east from the Great Plains reached 33,000 head by 1882 and increased rapidly to 63,000 head in 1884. By the early 1880s the Union Division (Nebraska and Wyoming) of the Union Pacific was shipping 9,000 to 10,000 carloads of cattle annually, far more than the 2,100 to 2,700 carloads on the Kansas Division (Kansas and Colorado).[68] By 1885 the number of carloads on the Union Pacific system reaching the Missouri River and points east was 11,522.[69] In the explosion of hyperbole about endless grass and increasing herds of cattle, it was easy to lose sight of the reality that, outside of California and Texas, there were always far fewer cattle both in total numbers and per acre on the western ranges than on the lands east of the 98th meridian.[70]

Like the railroads, the cattle industry was a creature of finance, a phantasm of numbers and calculations so enticing and so disconnected from any underlying reality that numbers ceased to be representations and became their own world. The business was about math, not management. What need was there to manage when the public provided cost-free land that the corporations occupied as well as the grass and water that their cattle consumed? For all practical purposes, the "producer" was the product itself, for cows and steers got precious little help from humans in surviving on the Great Plains. Their owners had only to mark them, gather them when ready for shipping, and send them off to market.

It seemed no more necessary for the promoters of cattle corporations to know anything about raising cattle than for Leland Stanford or Collis P. Huntington to know anything about railroads. John Clay was a Scotsman who spent much of his adult life in the industry. He came to despise some of the men he knew, he condescended to others, and he considered some of them friends. But you can search his reminiscences without finding many whom you would trust with your money. Clay began his career by falling in with Rufus Hatch, no relation to the Hatch—"the good Mr. Hatch," as Clay put it—of Fisk and Hatch, which had helped finance the Central Pacific. Rufus Hatch was "the bad one." Hume Webster was Hatch's evil British twin: "unscrupulous, inclined to be immoral, a very dangerous spider among foolish flies." Eventually facing trial in criminal court, Webster retreated to his country place and put a bullet through his brain. Together, Hatch and Webster issued a "little pamphlet of gilded glory for the Cattle Ranch & Land Company" to operate in western Kansas, Indian Territory, and Texas. Neither knew anything about cattle; Hatch "was as innocent as a new born babe" in regard to ranching. Even the men who ran the ranches were "more or less novices." And they remained novices during the industry's brief reign. "It was," Clay remembered, "a crude business at the beginning, and it remained so until the end."[71]

The music that pied pipers like Hatch and Webster played was mathematical, and it led investors down the garden path. The math began with calculations of the ability of cattle to turn grass into meat. The numbers promised that if placed on the northern plains a Texas yearling would be ready for market at four years old. The steer would then weigh about 1,000 pounds. And if a longhorn cow was crossed with an improved bull, the offspring—northern range cattle—would reach 1,100 pounds in Montana and Wyoming at two years. Such improved steers brought a higher price.[72]

This was the first set of calculations. The second set tabulated what it cost to run cattle on the range while they fattened for market. Cattlemen put the cost of raising a steer at between $.75 and $1.25 a year, exclusive of the costs of capital. If one knew how long it took to ready a steer for market and how much it cost to keep track of it while it grew, all that was left was to plug in the price of purchasing the yearlings—or the rate of reproduction if an outfit was running its own cows—and the price mature cattle would bring. Subtract from this figure the loss of animals to weather, predation, or accidents, the cost of interest on capital, taxes, and transportation to market, and the result was profit. Figures varied across time and space, but in the 1870s and 1880s the net was always a large profit. When stockmen reported that they could sell a four-year-old Wyoming steer for from $25 to $45, with costs—exclusive of capital, transportation, and losses of animals—at between $3 and $6 a steer, how could they lose?[73]

And it seemed in the early 1880s that cattle companies could not lose. In the years 1879–84 large corporations, many of them Anglo-American, moved into the business. British and Scottish investors alone pumped $34 million worth of capital (declared book value) into the western livestock industry in the United States during the last quarter of the century. In 1883 Wyoming incorporated twenty cattle companies with a capitalization of over $12 million.[74] Anglo-American cattle corporations produced dividends of 15–30 percent between 1881 and 1883.[75]

As with the railroads, the dividends did not necessarily represent money earned. In a kind of Ponzi scheme, new investments were turned into dividends for earlier investors. And, perhaps most significantly, the size of the herds upon which the dividends were calculated bore only a shaky relation to actual cattle. Corporate cattle were hard to count because they were hard to find. As they roamed the range, the herds of various ranchers mixed and needed to be sorted out at roundups. So to estimate their herds, cattle companies created a book count. Book count cattle were just numbers on a ledger, ideally existing in a one-to-one ratio with the animals turning grass into meat. In an age that was perfecting actuarial tables and life insurance policies, there was nothing wrong with making educated guesses on the average survival and reproduction of large numbers of cattle, but optimism and rosy projections are not promising qualities for actuaries.

For the men who made book counts, the West was the Big Rock Candy Mountain, a land of perpetual spring and toothless wolves. They seemed to have taken quite literally the railroads' claims that although range cattle received no care, no supplemental feed, and no shelter, they would survive in greater numbers than the hay-fed and sheltered cattle of settled districts. Real cattle died in much larger numbers than book cattle. They had more accidents and fewer calves. Book count cattle reproduced at a given annual rate, usually 70 percent; their book count progeny flourished and begat more book count calves.[76] Like the character in Gogol's *Dead Souls* who used dead peasants as collateral, western cattle corporations banked both their dead cattle and those never born. The books were immune to the vagaries of western life. As a Cheyenne saloon keeper told a group of disconsolate cattlemen drinking at his bar while a blizzard, certain to take a toll of their herds, raged outside, "Cheer up boys, whatever happens the books won't freeze."[77] The correspondence between the book count and actual cattle became more and more hypothetical as the years went by.

For John Clay it all became a single story that cattle company after cattle company repeated, "one pyramid upon another of reckless mismanagement and extravagance, of criminal neglect, expounding . . . the old adage that 'Fools rush in where angels fear to tread.'"[78] When steers, cows, and calves were counted at the annual roundup, it was easy to dismiss the discrepancies by saying the missing cattle were off somewhere in a coulee and would be found the next year. And if, when four-year-olds were gathered for shipment, there were far fewer of them than the books predicted, then they could be supplemented with three-year-olds or cattle purchased from others, preferably with stock certificates. This created a deficiency for the next year, but that was next year's worry.

As long as the book count stayed up, cattlemen had the collateral to borrow money. These corporations, like the railroads, depended on constant inflows of new capital. Cattlemen bought cattle on credit, and since "normal interest" in the cash-starved West was 10 percent compounded every three or six months in 1883, and since it was usually two years before they saw any return on their investment, capital costs were a sizable expense. The need for loans only increased as cattlemen found it necessary in the mid-1880s to buy land to control water sources and to fence pastures.[79]

A high book count also concealed costs. Cattlemen derived the cost of raising a steer by tabulating expenses, mostly wages and equipment, and dividing them by cattle on their books. But if the denominator—the book count cattle—was a fiction, so was the result, the cost per steer. In theory a high book count should have led cattlemen to worry what their cattle would eat, but since they didn't feed them, and they treated grass and water as free goods, degradation of the grasslands didn't enter the balance sheets. It was as if equipment never depreciated but was as good as new each spring.[80]

These companies were marching toward a disaster that was both financial and environmental. The consequences of grazing vary according to species, aridity, the existing composition of the grasslands, and the number of animals on a given area of land. Generally, heavy grazing does the most damage during years of drought. On the whole rainfall has more impact on the extent of ground cover than on grazing.[81] But cattle, unlike bison, did not range far from water sources and thus tended to hammer the areas around streams, rivers, and seasonal ponds. Significant concentrations of cattle quickly pushed what had been mixed grasslands into short grasses.[82] By the mid-1880s there were more cattle upon the Great Plains than the grasslands could maintain in years of drought and harsh winters.[83] The present "manner of wintering stock," wrote the agent for the Cheyenne and Arapaho Indians, who were leasing lands to cattlemen in the Indian Territory in 1884, "is nothing less than slow starvation, a test of stored flesh and vitality against the hard storms until the grass comes again. The skeleton frames of last winter's dead dot the prairies within view of the agency with sickening frequency." He thought it was "only a question of time when all stock must be provided with feed during the severe winter weather." During the spring roundup slow starvation gave way to what amounted to torture of weakened cattle as cattlemen "work extremely hard, work their horses harder, and nearly kill their cattle to separate their various brands."[84]

The fruits of this manner of doing business matured in the winter of 1884–85 on the southern plains. It drove George Reighard, who "had about $30,000 invested in livestock," out of the cattle business. By Reighard's account "out of one bunch of 1608 head he saved only sixty-six, and only thirty from another lot of 600." He salvaged a carload of hides that he shipped east. Having his business reduced to a carload of hides was a fitting disaster for an old buffalo hunter.[85]

The piling of cattle into the Great Plains has often been described as a tragedy of the commons, but it was nothing of the sort. That the industry was badly organized did not mean that it was not highly organized, structured, and controlled, with all kinds of regulations and claims to privileged appropriation of grass and water. It was virtually impossible to participate effectively in the industry without belonging to the cattlemen's or stock growers' associations that appeared quickly on the northern plains. They not only regulated roundups and the distribution of stray cattle but also protected areas set aside for winter grazing from summer use. The stock growers' association in the Dakotas, organized in part by Theodore Roosevelt, who enjoyed playing cowboy and owned a ranch consisting of five thousand cattle and no land, came into being almost as soon as the range cattle industry did.[86]

Large cattlemen, particularly those from the East and Europe, roman-ticized the industry. Roosevelt later remembered that we "knew toil and hardship and hunger and thirst . . . but we felt the beat of the hardy life in our veins, and ours was the glory of work and the joy of living," but Teddy Roosevelt was a toy cowboy. He was really a visitor on his own ranch, and although he worked the roundup at least once, he did not do it year after year. George Shafer, who grew up on a ranch and later became governor of North Dakota, knew the hardships of the work all too well. He would have none of the romance of rich men. He thought it no wonder that "nearly every cowboy is a . . . physical wreck at the age of thirty-five years."[87] Like the railroads, cattle raising was an industry. Cowboys were workers—poorly paid and often resentful. And like the railroads, which created it, the cattle industry was corrupt, poorly managed, and ill conceived. Looking back on the period, John Clay wrote, "[I]t staggers you to think how we ever got along. It [i.e., the methods of doing business] led to vast amounts of money disappearing as through a sieve."[88]

Money was a wonderful mask for madness; the insanity became apparent only when the money was gone. The general price trend for cattle in Chicago was downward during the long depression of the 1870s, but it rose with the return of prosperity after 1879 and reached a high point in 1882. Prices declined after 1882, fell more rapidly after 1884, and had reached disas-trously low levels by 1886.[89] Range cattle worth $9.35 per hundredweight in 1882 fell to $5.15 in 1886 and $4.60 in 1887. The fall in the price of the lowest grade of steers—grass-fed longhorns among them—was even more precipitous, reaching $1 in the fall of 1886.[90] There was a surplus of cattle.[91]

In 1886 Frank Wilkeson, a prominent journalist, published an article in *Harper's Monthly*—"Cattle-Raising on the Plains"—that was far different from the promotional pieces and romance of the cowboy articles that usu-ally dominated popular journals. When Wilkeson warned of the "cruelties of the business" that were all too obvious when terrible winters struck, as they had on the southern plains in 1884–85, and when he denied that the Great Plains were the country's primary cattle country, he was merely read-ing the census, agricultural reports, and newspapers. In 1880 Illinois, Iowa, Missouri, Kansas, and Nebraska held more than 25 percent of the cattle in the country, and represented 40 percent of the increase since 1870. In 1880, counting cows as well as steers, there were half a million more cattle in Illinois than in Colorado, Wyoming, Montana, New Mexico, Arizona, Utah, Idaho, Nevada, Oregon, and Washington combined. Of the western states, only Texas (and, although Wilkeson did not mention it, California) rivaled the Corn Belt states in cattle numbers.[92] Wilkeson argued that the price of grass-fed cattle in the early 1880s was an artifact of short corn crops in the Midwest and would not last. Shortages of corn "forbade the breeding of swine on a sufficiently extensive scale to keep pace with" the increase in human population and the demand for meat. The limited supply of pork raised the demand for grass-fed beef, but since 1884 good corn crops had cut into the demand for grass-fed cattle and ushered in "an era of low prices." The plains cattle boom was simply an artifact of the destruction of southern cattle during the Civil War, artificially high prices, and unusually mild winters. It would inevitably end, and the open range would give way to hay fields, winter-fed cattle, and smaller ranches.[93]

In hindsight Wilkeson's article was less a prediction than an observation. Cattlemen in Illinois and Iowa had learned that they could not compete with western cattlemen in a race to produce low-quality beef from common stock fed on grass. They could, however, compete if they adopted improved cattle that took on weight more quickly, fed them corn to fatten them, and marketed them at two rather than four years. Cattle fattened at "a younger age [allowed] for a faster turnover of capital." Corn-fed beef brought premium prices. Western cattlemen responded by improving their herds to create better feeders to be sold to Corn Belt farmers not just in Iowa and Illinois but also in Kansas and Nebraska. The shift is reflected in the shipping records on the Union Pacific. In 1883–84 shipments from the grasslands were seasonal, coming in the late summer and fall following the annual roundups. In the first six months of 1884 hardly any cattle were shipped from Wyoming or Colorado. In Kansas and Nebraska, however, farmers shipped cattle the year-round, and in these states large numbers of cattle reached market in the winter and spring. Well before the collapse of the open range, western cattle raising had become the domain of farmers east of the 100th meridian as much as of ranchers to the west.[94] (See Appendix, Charts I and J.)

The long drive came to an end in 1885, but only after helping produce another large increase in estimated cattle numbers in Wyoming (39 percent), and Colorado (20 percent), and Montana (18 percent). Its demise was overdetermined. Both farmers and ranchers with improved stock now had reason to put pressure on Kansas officials and legislators to tighten and enforce the quarantine laws on Texas cattle. When Texas drovers with their usual bluster threatened "to wade [in] blood up to their chins," in order to force passage across the Kansas range of Wilber E. Campbell, who grazed improved shorthorns on his pastures, he summoned other armed ranchers. The Texans went elsewhere. Falling prices made longhorns less and less attractive, and attempts to get federal legislation to establish a national cattle trail failed in large part because cattlemen no longer had a single interest. Congress had become a place for cattle corporations to compete.[95]

Cattle corporations, like the railroads, ran afoul of antimonopoly, but this would not necessarily make railroads their allies. In the 1880s cattlemen moved from the informal rights that were at the basis of the industry to claiming land, often fraudulently, that controlled access to water. They also began to buy the odd-numbered railroad sections. They turned the seeming disadvantage of the checkerboard—which meant that every section bought from the railroad was surrounded by government land—into an advantage by fencing off both and getting two sections for the price of one. They often went further and fenced large tracts of the public domain beyond the checkerboard. The commissioner of the General Land Office reported that in Wyoming the Swan cattle company had illegally run 130 miles of fence and that the Arkansas Cattle Company had illegally fenced a million acres in Colorado. These were among the more egregious cases in a list of those accused of "unlawful inclosure of the public lands" that took two pages of small print to list in the 1885 General Land Office report. And these covered only the cases in court. There were in addition reports of three million acres fenced in Grant and Socorro counties in New Mexico. Ranchers also combined in pools, much like railroad pools, to fence hundreds of thousands of acres in western Kansas. The General Land Office suits brought no judicial relief until 1895.[96]

These land grabs were attempts by a classic nineteenth-century monopoly to claim a public resource for a privileged few. The inevitable backlash brought both government intervention and violence, when corporations terrorized small ranchers in an attempt to control grazing.[97] In Wyoming disputes between big cattle companies and small stockmen, sometimes their ex-employees, led to the Johnson County War of 1892. Large cattlemen accused small ranchers of rustling and brought in gunmen to shoot and hang them. That failed, and the cattlemen and their hired guns had to be rescued by the cavalry. In South Texas, the famous King Ranch enlisted Texas Rangers to dispossess small *tejano* ranchers. They were far more successful.[98] Large cattlemen argued that leasing of the public domain would end such range wars. In Canada, however, leasing gave immense advantages to large cattle corporations and provoked widespread popular hostility.[99]

The summer of 1886 was dry on the northern plains and curtailed the growth of grasses, and the following winter, in John Clay's words, the "[t]hree great streams of ill luck, mismanagement, [and] greed" had met amid the harshest weather living men had ever seen.[100] Summer drought concentrated cattle around a limited number of rivers and watering holes, and they overgrazed all the land within reach. Despite the conditions, cattlemen piled more stock on the ranges. When the blizzards came, the cattle drifted before them and sought shelter in valleys or coulees that became death traps. Newspapers reported snow four to six feet on the level on the sheltered lands and blizzards that succeeded each other so rapidly that they amounted to a two-month storm. Even on the windswept plains, snow piled up to sixteen inches, and it crusted so hard in places that stagecoaches ran on top of it. Cattle, less effective in shoveling snow aside than horses or bison, could not get to the grasses. When they did break through the crust, the hard edges cut them until they bled, leaving trails of red on the whitened plains. Amid temperatures from twenty to forty below, bitter winds, and whiteout conditions, cowboys dared not leave their bunkhouses to force the cattle to move to higher ground, where they had a better chance of finding grass. The plains became a vast meat locker of frozen, emaciated carcasses. For years "you could wander amid the dead brushwood" that bordered the streams. Desperate cattle had "peeled off the bark, as if legions of beavers had been at work."[101] When the snow melted in the spring of 1887 at the end of the "Great Die-Up," the streams belched forth dead cattle.[102]

How many cattle died in the winter of 1886–87 is nearly impossible to determine, in part because the winter had a silver lining for the keepers of corporate books. All the missing book count cattle—those never born or dead in earlier winters or the victims of accidents and predators—could now be blamed on the storms of 1886–87. Men who tried honestly to count the losses found that disaster had struck unevenly. Cows, calves, and steers just brought into the territory fared worse than steers born on the northern plains. Some ranchers suffered losses of 80 or 90 percent, but the most careful assessment for Wyoming put the loss for the territory as a whole at a little above 15 percent. Montana and the Dakotas suffered higher losses.[103] Together the winter of 1886–87, the winter of 1884–85 on the southern plains, later disastrous winters in the Great Basin, and recurring drought in the Southwest brought an end to the open-range cattle industry, but the death was lingering and painful. In some areas it was the big cattlemen who were ruined; in others it was the smaller ranchers who faded away. In Wyoming some companies folded almost immediately; others hung on for several years. The Wyoming Stock Growers Association, which had over 400 members in 1885, had only 183 in 1889. In Wyoming large companies were initially absorbing the smaller ones.[104] This disaster made little difference to the country as a whole. The number of cattle in the United States increased by one-third between 1880 and 1890. The end of the open range and the decline in Great Plains cattle barely mattered. Except in Texas and California, western cattle production was relatively unimportant, although you would never have known this from reading press reports and promotional pieces.[105] Cattlemen expropriated the public domain to produce poor beef and environmental damage.[106]

The collapse of the open-range cattle industry was not a disaster for the railroads; it actually enhanced their transportation of cattle. Cows were born with legs to walk and a specialized stomach to eat grass, but railroads put them on wheels and made them creatures of corn. The early transport of cattle by rail was both crude and cruel. Shippers simply crammed animals into a single open area of a cattle car without water or food. Hungry, thirsty, and half crazed with fright, cattle fell and gored each other and, as the train lurched, they often broke their legs. Cattle cars filled with hurt, terrified, and exhausted animals often disgusted and appalled those who saw them. To feed and water the animals, the trains off-loaded the cattle every twenty-four hours, even though the animals were usually too terrified to eat. In the 1880s, although cattle trains cut some losses by moving at fifteen to eighteen miles an hour, a slightly higher speed than other freight, cattle going from Cheyenne, the great shipping center in Wyoming, directly to slaughter lost an average of one hundred pounds each on the way to Chicago.[107] Weight was money, but not enough money on low-value, low-grade steers to make much difference. Cruelty paid. Even a death rate of about 6 percent on shipped cattle, and far more injured, did not lead to improved conditions. Trainmen dumped dead animals beside the tracks, and shippers were willing to absorb the losses as long as rates remained relatively low. By the 1880s, however, there was an active public movement backed by the threat of legislation to force the railroads to improve conditions. Inventors produced special "palace" livestock cars that kept animals in separate stalls with food and water.[108]

There was a sharp, but only temporary, drop in cattle traffic off the northern Great Plains following the winter of 1886–87. Even this seems to have been confined to the Northern Pacific, which did not run through the Corn Belt.[109] By the 1890s livestock traffic on the Union Pacific and the Fremont, Elkhorn, and Missouri Valley was again on the rise even as cattle numbers in the archetypical rangeland territory of Wyoming steadily declined from 940,000 in 1888 to 800,000 in 1889 and to 700,000 in 1890.[110] Unlike the Northern Pacific, these two roads served both rangeland and Corn Belt regions, and this seems to be the reason for their success at a time when the Northern Pacific faced declining cattle traffic.[111]

Corn Belt roads had more traffic because increasing the trips each animal made more than compensated for declining numbers of rangeland cattle, which moved to market only when they reached maturity.[112] As farmers in the Corn Belt region along and east of the 98th meridian began to specialize in "calf production, the maturing of stockers, and the fattening of feeder cattle," the new system took shape. By the 1890s a steer's tour of the West might have included an original train ride from the Midwest to the Great Plains, then a trip to the Flint Hills of Kansas, which had emerged as a spring and summer pasturing area where western cattle joined local herds to fatten on protein rich bluestem grasses, and finally a train to regional stockyards for redistribution to farms for fattening on grain. The final trip was to Chicago, Omaha, and Kansas City for slaughter or for resale to butchers farther east.[113] (See Appendix, Chart K.)

Like so much in the railroad business, the system seemed quite rational as long as participants did not probe too deeply. In fact, the overbuilt railroads had yielded a rate structure that allowed the lavish expenditure of the stored energy of coal and corn to produce meat on animals that would normally eat grass. The low rates permitted the pervasive cruelty inflicted on these animals as they shuttled across the country. Railroads had managed to turn their own overproduction into a tool for the overproduction and mistreatment of cattle.

III. THE DIVERGING DAKOTAS

The railroads made the cattle industry possible, but railroad corporations never identified their interests with those of cattle corporations. Well before the terrible winters of the 1880s, the railroads were abandoning pastoralism as the preferred future for the grasslands west of the 98th meridian. Ranching could never yield the density of population that the railroads wanted. The products of western farms and the consumption of western farmers would fill their trains.

The easiest product to transport and the easiest to sell on national and international markets was grain, particularly wheat and corn. These were crops that the railroads both loved and loathed. They loved grain because it filled their cars to overflowing. Along with coal, it was their largest source of bulk traffic. They loathed grain because the price they received for carrying it sank as its abundance rose. By the late nineteenth century grain poured out not only from the American West and Midwest but also from Canada, Russia, Australia, Argentina, and India in such abundance that it was not unusual for the harvest to sit in elevators, warehouses, and piles along railroad tracks, where trains were unable or unwilling to move it. In 1887 the amount of grain overwhelmed the capacity of the Canadian Pacific to handle it. Van Horne's policy of elevators rather than warehouses ultimately proved the right one, but in the short run grain simply piled up in mounds along the tracks where there were neither elevators to store it nor enough freight cars to haul it. In the United States surpluses often sat until railroads negotiated within their pools to determine the price at which they would haul the grain.[114]

Wheat can serve as exhibit one in the spatial reorganization of the world in the late nineteenth century. The measure of this reorganization was the price of wheat in Chicago, near the great producing districts, and in Great Britain, the great market for imported wheat. By the mid-1880s these prices had virtually converged.[115] The cost of moving wheat had fallen "from a major charge . . . to insignificance."[116] In moving wheat in the western United States and Canada both water and rail were critical. In California bagged wheat filled ships in San Francisco Bay, while along both Lake Michigan and Lake Superior wheat was loaded onto ships from huge grain elevators, but in both cases railroads carried the wheat to water.

The falling price of railroad transportation enticed farmers to grow wheat even as the long-term price of the grain trended downward. The average price of moving a ton of wheat a mile fell 44 percent between 1867–72 and 1896, and this meant that transportation costs in the 1890s were 56 percent of what they had been twenty-five years earlier, while the average price of wheat was 67 percent of the earlier price. As long as the cost of transporting wheat was falling faster than the price of wheat, the farm gate price—what the farmer received—was enough in most years to keep them in business.[117] But parse these figures more closely and a different picture emerges. Real gains for farmers in the 1870s apparently ceased in the 1880s. And then in the depression of the early and mid-1890s, the price of wheat and corn began to fall faster than freight rates.[118]

There were numerous reasons for the railroads to cut rates, ranging from larger cars, heavier trains, and steel rails, which made the railroads more efficient, to competition, but a major cause was that the high fixed cost of the railroads induced them to take traffic even at a loss.[119] By the late nineteenth century all concerned admitted that American grain was competing in a world market and could be sold abroad "only if it meets the market price." The "conditions of competition are such that only by making a very low freight rate could American wheat be sold at all." The railroads charged wheat what the traffic would bear—that is, a rate that would allow it to find a market abroad. Railroads serving Chicago partially recouped by maintaining higher rates for flour, which had a largely domestic market and did not face similar competition. The Southern Pacific charged relatively low rates for wheat but higher prices for hauling manufactured goods to farmers.[120]

Low railroad rates allowed farmers to dispose of their surplus, but at the same time the rate structure itself encouraged the production of that very surplus and allowed farmers to move farther and farther away from markets. By the mid-1880s Grand Island, just west of the 98th meridian on the unnavigable Platte River in Nebraska, was the leading source of grain shipments on the Union Pacific. Railroad rates encouraged wheat producers to expand both north and south in the Central Valley of California.[121] (See Appendix, Chart L.)

The early 1880s were a golden age for wheat farmers and potential settlers on the northern prairies and Great Plains. These were the years of the Great Dakota Boom stimulated by a temporary upturn in wheat prices, abundant harvests, and rising land values.[122] Between 1878 and 1887 Dakota Territory was, in the words of one booster, "the sole remaining section of paradise in the western world." A booster from Nelson County proclaimed that a "million plows are wanted in the Territory of Dakota." He didn't get a million, but the number of farms in Dakota Territory rose from 17,435 in 1880 to 95,204 in 1890.[123] In what was music to the railroads' ears, some settlers credited this growth to the corporations that had provided more than four thousand miles of lines in Dakota Territory by 1887. By 1889 population had risen to levels justifying not one but two states: North Dakota and South Dakota. Development that supposedly would have taken a century or more without the railroads had taken place over five years.[124]

In the 1880s Dakota was still a single territory, but the two future states were developing along markedly different trajectories. North Dakota had access to two great land grant railroads, the Northern Pacific and the St.

Paul, Minneapolis, and Manitoba, which James J. Hill later made the basis of the Great Northern. The St. Paul, Minneapolis, and Manitoba barely touched North Dakota, but since it largely paralleled its eastern border, it captured much of its Red River Valley traffic. With the exception of a small section of the Chicago and Northwestern, South Dakota had no major railroad receiving land grants within its territory.[125]

North and South Dakota can thus serve as a kind of historical laboratory for comparing two different approaches to railroad construction and their consequences. Subsidized transcontinentals built ahead of demand in what would become North Dakota, while unsubsidized regional roads built to meet demand in South Dakota. The result was two different settlement patterns and traffic patterns.[126]

The most revealing comparison between transcontinental and regional line construction involves lands west of the Red River Valley. The land grant railroads produced particular patterns of settlement: settlers moved along the line of the railroad instead of spreading more evenly across the landscape. In North Dakota the rate of settlement, measured by the issuance of land patents, proceeded roughly twice as fast in counties with rail connections as in those without. The Northern Pacific served as a giant straw sucking people farther west along its line than they otherwise would have gone. In the early 1880s, for example, most settlers in the Great Dakota Boom remained east of the 98th meridian, but in the counties along the Northern Pacific settlers pushed farther west in order to obtain public sections of the checkerboard.[127] The advantages of being near a railway line and obtaining public land prompted settlers to take greater chances with aridity.[128] The combination of cheap or free land with railroad connections was a powerful lure. The public domain without railroad connections settled far more slowly.

South Dakota presented a dramatically different situation. There was only a slight difference in settlement rates between counties with and without railroads. Given few railroad land grants within its boundaries, large amounts of land were available for homesteading in South Dakota. Without railroads, this land should have settled slowly. In fact, the opposite was the case. South Dakota counties settled nearly twice as quickly as those North

Dakota counties with railroads, and three times as quickly as North Dakota counties without railroads. Relatively dense settlement in the 1880s brought the Milwaukee Road and the Chicago and North Western in its wake. These roads then moved slightly ahead of settlers before stopping at the Missouri River. Both were predominantly grain roads, grain comprising 63 percent of the Dakota traffic on the Chicago, Milwaukee, and St. Paul and 44 percent on the Chicago and North Western. By 1887 a relatively compact railroad grid served existing agricultural settlements largely east of the 98th meridian. The railroads' restraint in staying east of the Missouri River was not wholly intentional—the Great Sioux Reservation blocked expansion to the west. (See Appendix, Chart M.)

In North Dakota, American settlement pushed farther west more quickly and created a far less dense agricultural landscape than in South Dakota. In the 1880s track controlled by the Northern Pacific increased from 1,082 to 1,317 miles, but the amount of wheat it hauled, while fluctuating, trended downward. Wheat made up only 28 percent of the total traffic of the Northern Pacific in 1889.[129]

Taken together, the Dakotas seem to offer a compelling argument against land grants in general and the subsidized transcontinentals in particular. Not only did unsubsidized railroads build to meet demand, but they operated more efficiently. Farmers paid less for land, settled the better lands more quickly, and avoided marginal arid lands. The government aided settlers, not railroads, while securing a more efficient railroad network and denser settlement.

IV. RAIN FOLLOWS THE PLOW

Western railroads were creatures of cloudy skies. The correspondence of the Associates of the Central Pacific in the 1870s and into the 1880s was, from November through March, a long and often anxious weather report. West of the Sierras, clear skies meant empty trains. Winter rains produced wheat. On the plains and prairies, spring and summer was when farmers needed rain, and the railroads here, too, watched and measured. And the measurements in the 1870s indicated that somewhere between the 98th meridian and the 100th meridian farmers reached the limits of conventional agriculture. They could push wheat farther west than corn, but, particularly on the central and southern prairies, most farmers initially went no farther west than corn could go.

In 1881 John Wesley Powell became head of the U.S. Geological Survey; he was already famous for exploring the Grand Canyon and, among western boosters, infamous for publishing his *Report on the Lands of the Arid Region of the United States* in 1879. Powell told farmers that they would have to adapt to the aridity of the Great Plains, but railroad officials told them the opposite. They had by the 1880s come to believe that the Great Plains were not permanently arid. They reversed the causality of rainfall and crop production. It was not precipitation that increased crop yields; rather, it was farming that produced rain. Railroad men did not invent the idea that human settlement would change the climate, but they encouraged it and employed those who proclaimed the idea. These were not the vagaries of young men in publicity departments. Charles Francis Adams and Sidney Dillon, both presidents of the Union Pacific, advanced the claim of a changing climate in popular national publications into the 1890s.[130]

"Rain follows the plow" was the promise made by railroad men and boosters, as promoters of settlement and investment were known. F. V. Hayden of the U.S. Geological Survey endorsed the claims, but they were not science. Richard Smith Elliott, who contributed to Hayden's official reports, was the industrial agent for the Kansas Pacific Railroad, and he quite consciously sought to turn official reports into an "advertising machine."[131] The man who gave them the aura of science was Samuel Aughey, a biologist at the University of Nebraska. By breaking up the sod, Aughey explained, cultivation increased absorption of moisture. This turned the soil into a "huge sponge" that slowly put moisture back into the atmosphere through evaporation and through springs, yielding increased rainfall. All the plains needed was more farmers. Aughey admitted in 1880 that the statistics on rainfall west of the 100th meridian did not yet provide evidence of sufficient moisture to grow crops, but he was confident that rainfall "would become even more abundant than it has yet been, especially over the central and western portion of the State."[132]

In the 1880s it appeared that Aughey might be right. There was an unusual amount of rainfall on the plains in the late 1870s and 1880s, but rainfall on the Great Plains was, and is, notoriously variable. Not only do dry months follow wet, but there is considerable variation from year to year, with clusters of wet years and drought. Moving from a string of dry years to a string of wet years made it seem that rainfall was increasing, but this was like believing that a bouncing ball would never fall.[133]

Promoters used the contrast between the widespread drought years in the early 1870s and the ensuing wet years to tell the story of a garden emerging from a desert. Because the wet years accompanied a rush of settlement on the central and northern plains, the settlers could seem to be the agents of climate change.[134]

Increasing rain had a deep ideological appeal for the railroads. By the 1880s the western railroads were under constant attack from antimonopolists, and it was not apparent that building and subsidizing them had been a good idea.[135] In the 1880s few of the railroads' grandiose promises had been fulfilled. California's growth was disappointingly slow.[136] Nevada had begun to earn its reputation as the great "rotten borough," with two U.S. senators and pathetically few constituents. Utah remained Utah. The railroad made it more accessible, but most Americans regarded it as a polygamous embarrassment, a place inhabited by strange and exotic people. And the Central Pacific and the Union Pacific were the most easily justifiable roads. The Northern Pacific, Atchison, Topeka, and Santa Fe, the Atlantic and Pacific, the Kansas Pacific, and the Texas and Pacific seemed utterly extraneous as transcontinentals when they even managed to complete their lines. Oregon and Washington relied largely on water transport and local railroads. Arizona, New Mexico, and western Texas were vast tracts of empty land, cows, and sheep. These herds were in the midst of collapse from drought and overgrazing. Western mines produced silver that no one needed.

The great success of the railroads was the development of a rich agricultural district from the Missouri River west to the 98th meridian, but there was no need to build transcontinentals to develop eastern Kansas, eastern Nebraska, the Dakotas, or Texas east of Dallas. As South Dakota demonstrated, unsubsidized regional roads were quite capable of doing the job. If the railroads by luring farmers west were, however, changing the climate and turning the grasslands into a garden, then the whole enterprise could be redeemed. Railroads could fulfill their critics' fondest hopes: a country chock-full of small producers. They would have served their country well.

Unfortunately rain did not follow the plow. In the late 1880s the Great Dakota Boom shriveled amid sporadic drought, bad crops, and falling prices. There were local droughts in the Dakotas in 1886 and again in 1887 and 1888, and wheat prices fell eleven cents a bushel between 1885 and 1886.[137] Then in 1889 drought struck in earnest on the lands west of the 98th meridian, destroying crops and reducing thousands of farmers to destitution and near-starvation.[138] Farmers lured into western Kansas and Nebraska by wet years retreated east when drought ensued. By the late 1880s and 1890s wheat prices reached new lows, and farmers burned corn they could not afford to send to market. Most western railroads were losing money, and many were unable to meet their fixed costs. Their customers were losing their livelihoods.[139]

Some railroad men blamed all this on the farmers' insistence on sticking with staple grain crops. On the northern prairies and plains, James J. Hill urged farmers to diversify and move away from wheat.[140] Similarly, in California, the Southern Pacific encouraged farmers to turn to fruit.[141] Diversification was good advice, but it followed other very bad railroad advice. The railroads through their own promotions, overbuilding, and rate structures had already created the framework for the agricultural disaster of the late 1880s and 1890s.

The final victims of the Great Dakota Boom were predictably the Indians. The Great Sioux Reservation, which stretched along the Missouri River in South Dakota, had done a great service for South Dakota farmers by keeping them from pushing farther into the arid plains. But taking land from Indians in good times and bad was a program both antimonopolists and railroads could agree on. Senator Henry Dawes, the leading friend of the Indian, ultimately led the charge. Dawes was a stickler for proper procedures and Indian rights, but Indian rights often boiled down to their right to say yes to government demands. In 1889 Congress authorized negotiations to create five smaller reservations out of the Great Sioux Reservation, reducing it by roughly one-half. The government made the Sioux an offer they could not refuse: sell, General Crook, who headed the negotiating team, said, or we will take it anyway. The Sioux sold. They received neither a fair price nor fair treatment.[142]

White settlers, already facing drought and an agricultural depression, did not need the land. They were not advancing; they were retreating. In South Dakota the population between the James River—roughly on the 98th meridian—and the Missouri fell precipitously after 1890, declining 16 percent in twelve of the worst-hit counties. In North Dakota the Northern Pacific by the end of the century considered its remaining lands suitable merely for grazing and disposed of them in immense sales of a million acres or more. Only after 1900 would new agricultural settlement resume, in part because purchasers of Northern Pacific lands, advocating dry farming techniques, were selling them to wheat farmers. This was a policy that the Northern Pacific adopted on its remaining North Dakota lands and in Montana. It would prove no more successful than claims of increased rainfall.[143]

Things were no better in Canada. Despite a number of dry years in the late 1880s, farmers in Manitoba produced more grain by plowing more land. Not only couldn't the Canadian Pacific handle the traffic, but its freight rates also remained higher than in the neighboring United States. If the Canadian Pacific was a test case for natural monopoly, then the theory failed badly.[144] By the late 1880s the railroads' zeal in building track and inducing settlement had produced a situation where, in good years and bad, the main crop was discontent.

Transcontinental railroads were a Gilded Age extravagance that rent holes in the political, social, and environmental fabric of the nation, creating railroads as mismanaged and corrupt as they were long, but this argument does not meet the central contention of their defenders: life for Americans was better because of them. The transcontinentals supposedly yielded more social benefits than Americans paid in social costs.

Economic historians have spent considerable effort in trying to determine whether the transcontinentals required subsidies and, more significantly, whether they delivered social benefits in excess of their costs. Lloyd Mercer, who has looked at this the most closely, has calculated that both the first transcontinentals—the Union Pacific and the Central Pacific—and the last of the nineteenth-century roads, the Great Northern, were not premature, even though investors thought they were. Honestly run—a rather important caveat—they would have made adequate returns on their investments over a twenty-year time frame without a subsidy.[145] I disagree with this assessment of the Central Pacific and the Union Pacific, but my immediate concern is with Mercer's high rates of social return. The devil, as usual, is in the details. His is the classic social benefits calculator with only plus signs and no minus signs. It has no subtracting of the possible social costs of land grants, the endless disputes over taxes and loss of local revenues from taxes, and much more. There is no consideration of environmental costs or losses to Indians. Indian economies might bleed profusely, but they are treated as so many economic blood donors: their losses are counted as benefits to non-Indians.[146]

Because it is so hard to get reliable financial figures on the railroads, land prices and falling transportation costs are used as proxies for social benefits. Land values are presumed to reflect more intensive—and productive—use of land, and this, in turn, is attributed to railroads and cheaper transportation. But rising land prices, as Henry George noticed, were not a simple result of increased productivity. The Central Pacific's land commissioner, W. H. Mills, noted that speculators and higher prices were slowing settlement. Similarly, railroad transportation was definitely an improvement over wagon transportation, but we don't need elaborate models to demonstrate this. The real question is whether railroads could compete with oceangoing and river transport on the Pacific Coast, the only area in the West where water transportation was a viable option. Railroad officials at the end of the century admitted that they still could not meet steamship rates. This is why they paid subsidies to the Pacific Mail to raise rates. That in practice railroads drove up steamship rates for transcontinental traffic seems a problem for seeing them as pluses on the social benefits calculator, but those bent on making them a benefit argue that *hypothetical* steamship rates would have been higher than actual railroad rates if the railroads had not been built. This assumes that steamship lines themselves would not have come into competition. Such attempts to calculate gains from what appears to be loss only demonstrate that what economists count as social benefits might very well on closer examination be social costs of the railroad.[147]

If we measure well-being more directly, simply by income, the transcontinental railroads did not improve conditions for most people in the West. Measured in current dollars, total personal income per capita fell in Arizona, California, Colorado, Idaho, Montana, Nevada, and Wyoming between 1880 and 1900. It rose in Utah and New Mexico, but those two states were still the poorest in the West, with New Mexico virtually Southern in its poverty. It rose also in Oregon and Washington, but only barely. In the tier of agricultural states—the Dakotas, Oklahoma, Nebraska, Kansas, and Texas—we have comparative statistics only for Nebraska, Kansas, and Texas. These states rose in income, but if the measurement had been taken five years earlier in the midst of depression, instead of at the beginning of a long agricultural boom, they, like all the others, would have had much lower numbers. And, in any case, they were creatures of Chicago and St. Louis railroads, not the transcontinentals.

Over much of the West, then, total personal income was falling. There were some predictable reasons for this besides falling agricultural prices and recurrent depressions. Railroads, for example, made migration easier, and more people competing for jobs reduced the original high wage rates in the West. In terms of personal income, the West was still more prosperous than other sections of the country during this period, but it was losing its advantage, and it also had a substantially higher cost of living. The railroads had not created this prosperity in the West; the more the railroads built in the West, the smaller the differences between West and East.

But even this picture is too rosy. Total personal income includes income from both work and property. Segregate out the income from property— largely rents and stocks and bonds owned in the East—and count only the income of farmers, small businessmen, and wageworkers, and we get a decline in per capita income across not only the West but the entire United States between 1880 and 1890. It rises again in the country as a whole by 1900—an artifact of the last years of the century since the depression had hollowed out the 1890s—but these last years did not restore well-being in the West. Over much of the West per capita income from labor in 1900 was less than it had been in 1880.[148]

Over virtually the whole period from 1880 to 1900, things were as the antimonopolists claimed: property was being redistributed upward. Those who worked were receiving smaller and smaller shares. Those who controlled the railroads reaped massive rewards, even if the corporations struggled. Collis P. Huntington died in 1900 with an estate valued at roughly $50 million. In 1900 there were 1,485,053 people in California. Their personal income per capita was roughly $360 a year, less than it had been in 1880.[149] And Huntington's was only a quarter share of the Southern Pacific Railroad fortune. Assuming that the families of the other Associates had done as well, they had collectively accumulated $200 million. Were the Associates and the railroads they controlled worth this?

To focus on income distribution, however, still misses the larger antimonopoly critique. Antimonopolists cared about material well-being, but their main concern was with economic democracy and equity. They wanted an economy that would help produce and protect a republican society, and this economy the western railroads were not delivering.

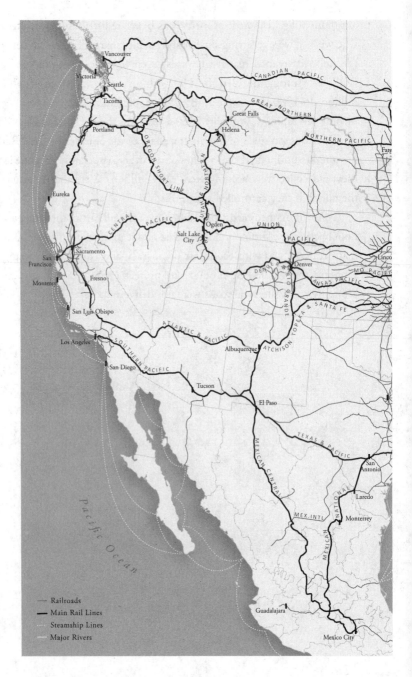

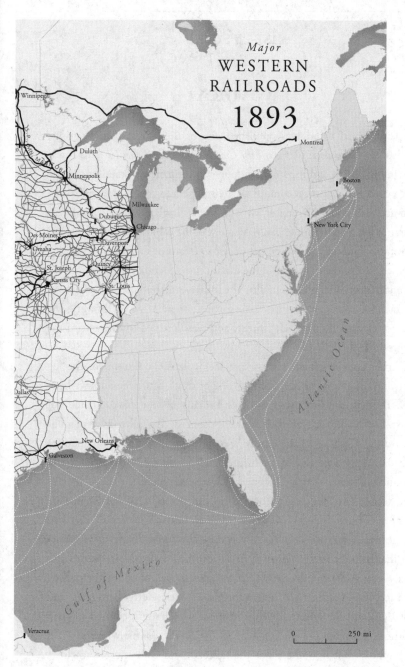

Major
WESTERN
RAILROADS
1893

Toral Patel

MISE EN SCÈNE

———◆———

WOVOKA

In 1868 Currier and Ives published one of their most famous prints, *Across the Continent: Westward the Course of Empire Takes Its Way*. It was explicitly imperial, and it made the imperial mundane and modern. At the print's center is a steam locomotive. The smoke and steam blow off to the right and are about to engulf two mounted Indian warriors, while to the train's left a young American settlement of log cabins yields well-dressed inhabitants who may be passengers about to board or may be travelers disembarking from the train. Far in the distance, the picture's background, are mountains and Indians and buffalo. The Indians and buffalo were in retreat. The track follows the curvature of the earth. It seems to go on forever.[1] The print anticipated the fact. The foreground was destined to overwhelm the background.

Currier and Ives made claims that seem plausible. Except for the log cabins, this could have been Laramie; one of those figures could have been H. K. Thomas. But in Currier and Ives, Indians and the railroad could not coexist. Buffalo and the railroads could not coexist. The railroads were modern, and the West—the great empty West of the print—was a past about to yield to an inevitable and better future. These were the imperial meanings the transcontinentals carried before they were even built.

A decade later the actual construction of the railroad had somewhat altered the claims. Indians had ceased to be an obstacle to empire; they had become merely one of its colorful diversions. *The Pacific Tourist* was a guidebook that helped travelers adjust to palace car life. "From the frequent views of the Great American Desert which the traveler can obtain while passing over this portion of the road, he can form some idea of utter barrenness and desolation, and the great sufferings of those who have attempted to cross it without adequate preparation . . . ," *The Pacific Tourist* wrote of Utah and Nevada.[2] But now there was the railroad, and with it came smelters, and stockyards for shipping cattle.[3] The Indians had been reduced to entries in the guidebook. Past Palisade was the "Shoshone Indian Village." Nearing the Sierras, the guidebooks had informative sections entitled "How the Piutes Bury Their Dead" and "How the Piutes Catch Fish." Indians were picturesque.[4]

In lithographs and railroad magazines alike a division of space fenced off the modern and kept it clear and simple. The modern was where white people were; it was where trains were. White people were inside trains and stations; Indians were outside. The choices were a string of binaries, and they could not be clearer: civilization versus the wild; whites versus Indians; progress versus tradition.

But in Laramie John Richau, the "half-breed" outlaw, had come in to sell mules, and he had talked around the station fire with H. K. Thomas, who found him to be "square." And roughly a decade after *The Pacific Tourist* listed picturesque Paiutes, a party of more than two dozen men rode the trains to see them. There were eleven Lakotas—Kicking Bear, his brother-in-law Short Bull, Good Thunder, Yellow Breast, Flat Iron, Broken Arm, Cloud Horse, Yellow Knife, Elk Horn, Kicks Back, and Mash the Kettle—from Pine Ridge, Cheyenne River, and Rosebud, who in 1890 traveled west by horse in search of a prophet who claimed that God had come to earth to save the Indians from adversity. At Wind River five Shoshones, an Arapaho, and three northern Cheyennes joined them. They went on to Fort Hall in Idaho, where five Bannocks and three Western Shoshones completed the party. At Pocatello they boarded the train.

These Indians in search of Wovoka, the Paiute prophet who promised a West free of white men, rode the Oregon Short Line south and then took the Central Pacific across Nevada. They met Paiutes who had neither vanished nor been reduced to mere tourist attractions along the road. Kicking Bear and the rest were not like many other Indians who rode the trains; they were not allies of the American army coming to fight against other Indians, or prisoners being exiled, or students on their way to schools designed to make them seem less Indian to whites. They were just passengers going about important business of their own.[5] And even as they moved toward Wovoka, other Indians in other places in the West were working on other railroads being built across deserts, plains, and mountains. Pueblos helped build the Southern Pacific; Puyallups helped build the Northern Pacific, which would help dispossess them. Where are the clean lines between the traditional and the modern in all of this?

EPILOGUE

The days they [postwar children] have been born in are not
heroic . . . they are full of fraud, corruption, bargain and
sale. Men are not pushing to the battlefield to die for an idea;
they are pushing into place.[1]

THE GENERATION THAT fought the Civil War, a struggle that called the
entire nation to account, would also build the first transcontinental
railroads, whose accounts would never bear examining. Both were astonishing endeavors in their scale and consequences, but the shadow cast by the
Civil War, with its terrible risks and terrible costs, enveloped everything that
followed. The war provided a standard by which men judged themselves and
others.

The war did not make them better men, and the standard had little to do
with heroism. Charles Francis Adams, whose railroad life would make him
president of the Union Pacific, was an officer at Antietam and Gettysburg,
but his "abiding recollection" of these turning points in the war was "not
of the fierce agony of battle at its height, but the enjoyment of two exceedingly refreshing naps." It was not, Adams wrote, "heroic; but it was, I hold,
essentially war." When the war ended, Adams was a colonel commanding
the Fifth Massachusetts, an African American regiment. Sick with malaria
and addled by opium, Adams left the army after more than three years of
service full of disgust for his last regiment, whose supposed shortcomings he

typically universalized into a racist diatribe: "the negro was wholly unfit for cavalry service, lacking absolutely the essential qualities of alertness, individuality, reliability and self-reliance."[2]

But ironic distance and a sour ending did not lessen Adams's conviction that the war was the central event of his life. Success in anything that followed would not matter as much, and failure would rankle all the more. Adams was thirty when he left the army, and his twentieth-century autobiography devoted 165 of its 215 pages to getting him to that thirtieth year. He had most of his life before him when the war ended, and that life included a period as president of the Union Pacific Railway Company. Although, in his own words, "railroads, and the railroad connection, . . . occupied over twenty years of [his] life," they occupied only 22 pages of his *Autobiography*, and not all of those 22 pages.

Henry Villard, a journalist during the Civil War, later gained control of the Northern Pacific Railroad and pushed that ill-starred line to completion. In his two volume *Memoirs* his narration of the Civil War runs to page 267 of the second volume. Like Adams, he was thirty years old at war's end. But after Appomattox his *Memoirs* switched into the third person, as if he were not fully present for the remainder of his days. It took him a little over 100 pages to narrate the rest of his career. Villard and Adams came to despise each other, but they were similar in the way the skipped over their railroad lives. They slighted the railroads not because they thought them insignificant but because in Adams's case his career in them left him "with a consciousness of failure." Villard felt much the same way: "the catastrophe of the Northern Pacific oppressed him."[3]

Writing retrospectively, Villard and Adams cast the Civil War as the main act of their lives. But the war came when they were young men, and it was, in fact, only a prologue to the long second acts—their railroad lives—that for all their eventfulness and consequence they considered failures. When the United States emerged from the long, dark, bloody tunnel of the Civil War, what opened before these men was a continent about to be defined by railroads. They lived their railroad lives fully, but their large ambitions mocked what they actually achieved.[4]

It is startling how many railroad lives connected to the Civil War ended in failure in the West or Mexico or Canada. General William Rosecrans came to grief promoting Mexican railroads. General John C. Frémont and Samuel Usher, Lincoln's secretary of interior, had western railroad careers that ended in corruption and disappointment. Tom Scott, arguably the most important railroad man of his generation, failed in the West. Jay Cooke sold the bonds that saved the Union, but he went down with the Northern Pacific when that road failed for the first of several times in 1873. Villard went down with the Northern Pacific when he drove it to completion and near-failure in 1883. Both he and the railroad bobbed to the surface only to go down again in 1893. Oakes Ames of the Union Pacific died in disgrace. Those men were not casualties in a great cause; they were businessmen trying to enrich themselves. Much of what they did, they did badly and corruptly, but in doing it they carried the Civil War with them. The Civil War had shaped them and the organizations they managed, and they could never shake the conviction, no matter how inappropriate, that they still served a great national effort. The skills the war had mustered, the ability to conceive and direct large organizations that it inspired, the tenacity in conducting great enterprises that it developed, had yielded, so it seemed to them, only to greed and waste and meaningless competition after the war.

If the railroads were an anticlimax and a disappointment to men who rooted their sense of themselves in the Civil War, they inspired in other men the same claim to a grand national purpose that soldiers had sought on the battlefield. Collis P. Huntington of the Central Pacific and the Southern Pacific railroads never wrote a memoir, but in 1899 he did write a long letter to his banker James Speyer, and earlier still he had provided material for an autobiographical sketch by Charles Nordhoff, a popular writer of the period. These were attempts by Huntington to explain and justify himself and to settle old scores, particularly with his Associate Leland Stanford, whom he regarded as a burden and an embarrassment.

Unlike that of Adams or Villard, Huntington's life boiled down only to railroads, and in the cramped space of these letters and notes he wrote mostly about railroads. He was "satisfied with what [he had] done." His motives had been honest, and his actions had benefited California more than himself. He had excited "the revengeful passions of bad men who have been thwarted in their dishonest schemes." A few hostile newspapers denounced him, but he believed himself thought "well of by the great majority of the citizens of California." He cited as proof of his virtue his victories in litigation, as dubious a proof in nineteenth-century America as it is possible to imagine. But this is not that different an evaluation of a railroad career from those of Villard and Adams. Huntington chose to deny and challenge the same story of insider dealing, manipulation of information, and self-serving lies that Villard and Adams preferred to skip past. All of them recognized that the century did not end in acclaim for the achievement of the transcontinentals and the men who had organized them.[5]

Jay Cooke, perhaps more than any other man, celebrated the glory of Civil War success and felt the pain of railroad failure. Jay Cooke had begun to lay the groundwork for the transcontinental railroads before any of the others had laid a mile of track. In wartime he helped to create modern financial markets that harnessed the small savings of hundreds of thousands of investors and nurtured the links between finance and government. Cooke sold the government bonds that helped win the Civil War. Cooke sold the Northern Pacific bonds that launched a railroad.

Cooke began dictating his memoirs, but he never finished. His business was persuading himself so that he could persuade others, but his claim of a larger success in his ultimate debacle with the Northern Pacific may have been too much for him to swallow. Cooke thought with some reason that his "great financial work during the war" saved the Union; he thought, with less reason, that only his betrayal by jealous, greedy, incompetent, and small-minded men had bankrupted him and the Northern Pacific Railroad. An ardent and devout evangelical Christian, Cooke considered himself but an instrument of a beneficent God. His memoirs are a secular gospel story. Christ-like, he claimed ultimate success in his worldly failures. The Northern Pacific had died only to rise again to make the modern West. Cooke could not "but feel a great satisfaction in having been the instrument in opening & adding so vast and rich a country, so many millions of people, so many churches, schools and colleges, so many wheat fields & mines to our country."[6]

By the twentieth century only James Hill of the men responsible for the transcontinentals was still an active railroad man. The other roads had delivered their disasters in the nineteenth century; the Great Northern saved its disaster for the twentieth. Western North Dakota, eastern Montana, and much of eastern Washington were too arid, too infertile, too distant from markets to sustain the density of settlement and agricultural development that Hill's Great Northern promoted. Over much of the area population had peaked by 1920, and the century since has been one of environmental damage, demographic decline, and slow-motion social decay.

Collis P. Huntington, the last of the original Associates, survived until 1900. His genius had come from building railroads that sometimes went bankrupt but always yielded great fortunes. And when he died, he split that fortune between his wife, Arabella, her son (who was probably also his natural son), and his nephew Henry. Henry divorced his own wife, married Arabella, and made a fortune of his own in real estate developments and street railroads in Los Angeles. He collected the books and art that form the basis of the modern Huntington Library. His estate is the Huntington Gardens, where the library and art collection are housed.

Except for James J. Hill, Charles Francis Adams outlasted all the men who ran the nineteenth-century transcontinentals, and when he died, his funeral in Boston featured, even by New England standards, a strange eulogy. The setting was as proper and Brahmin as 1915 Boston could muster: a public meeting of the Massachusetts State Historical Society held at the First Church in Boston. The Reverend George Angier Gordon gave the invocation and the Reverend Charles Edwards Park the benediction, and Henry Cabot Lodge gave a memorial address that in its printed form ran to sixty pages. The Calvinist core of Puritanism had long since washed away, but the descendants of Puritans still knew how to sit and listen. The deceased—the descendant of two presidents—had left a memoir that clearly irked Henry Cabot Lodge, and although Lodge predictably praised Adams, he also argued with him, criticized him, and patronized him.[7]

These were all dangerous things to do with Charles Francis Adams, but Adams, being dead, was at a certain disadvantage in this argument. Still Lodge by occasionally paraphrasing and quoting Adams's memoir allowed him a say of a sorts. Lodge's criticism sprang from Adams's own criticism: of himself, his New England upbringing, his life work, and the railroads. Lodge did not get far before he became defensive; it was as if the deceased were rising up in one last dyspeptic Adams outburst to flail New England and the entire late nineteenth century. Lodge was not going to stand for it, and that is why the eulogy diverted to trout streams.

Lodge differed with the deceased about who was to blame for Adams's boyhood lack of experience in sports and recreation. Certainly it was not New England. Charles Francis's brother Henry, presumably among the mourners, found himself dragged into the argument, as Lodge criticized him for saying there were no trout streams on Cape Cod. Such a statement was evidence, Lodge thought, of both ignorance and a timidity among the Adamses that barred boyish exploration. Barely into the eulogy Lodge was veering rather crazily into a dissertation on trout fishing in Massachusetts in the 1840s. He righted himself, but then he got cranky at Adams's criticism of Boston Latin School, which launched him into a brief countercriticism of modern education.[8]

Adams was thirty-one years old, a veteran of the Civil War, before Lodge could find him making a decision beyond reproach. "He made a wise if quick choice by turning to the railroad system, to use his own words, 'as the most developing force and largest field of the day.'"[9] Lodge did not let it go at that. Reform, which Adams sponsored, had gone too far. The innocent (meaning railroads and their executives) had suffered with the "mistakes and extreme measures of the present day."[10]

The railroads brought out, Lodge thought, Adams's great fault and strength: his individualism and stubbornness. "When he was brought into relations with larger numbers of colleagues and associates with whom it was necessary to act in furtherance of a common purpose, as in the case of the Union Pacific, we have but to read what he says in this connection of the financial magnates and business men with whom he came in contact in order to realize the difficulties he found in the management of varying opinions and in taking joint action where many men were involved." Lodge did not say what Adams had said; he merely cited it as evidence of a character flaw. And then he embarked on a praise of compromise, politics, public life, and, by implication, Henry Cabot Lodge. For a moment, it was hard to say who was being eulogized.

If the corpse could have spoken, or if Lodge had in this instance quoted the corpse, Adams would have said what he had written.

> . . . *business success—money-getting . . . comes from a rather low instinct. Certainly, so far as my observation goes, it is rarely met with in combination with the finer or more interesting traits of character. I have known, and known tolerably well, a good many "successful" men—"big" financially—men famous during the last half-century; and a less interesting crowd I do not care to encounter. Not one that I have ever known would I care to meet again, either in this world or the next; nor is one of them associated in my mind with the idea of humor, thought or refinement. A set of mere money-getters and traders, they were essentially unattractive and uninteresting.*[11]

The most "developing force and the largest field of the day" had been led and sponsored by the most unattractive and uninteresting men of Adams's and Lodge's generation: here was a paradox of railroads worthy of his brother Henry's *Education*. Adams may have been right. Or he may have been a crank. Or he may have been both a crank and right.

CONCLUSION

❧✺❧

NINETEENTH-CENTURY RAILROADS TRANSFORMED western North America, bringing it into national and world markets with a speed and thoroughness rarely seen in other parts of the globe. The transnational West of Mexico, Canada, and the United States was the region where publicly subsidized corporate enterprises—the transcontinental railroads—reached their zenith; it was also an area where antimonopolism and collective efforts at reform flourished. In describing that transformation, I have admittedly emphasized the United States while slighting western Canada and northern Mexico, because the settlement of large numbers of non-Indians in those places came slightly later than the period covered in this book. They, however, remain part of the larger narrative because they are essential to my point. The transformation of western North America was continental in scale, and the railroads of these three countries formed a single network.

Railroads were the epitome of the modern in the late nineteenth century. Technologically, they were part of the move from muscle—human and animal—and wind power to steam and fossil fuels. They were part of the great wave of wage labor that largely eliminated slavery and indentured workers in North America and cut deeply into the ranks of independent producers. During most of the period between the Civil War and the turn of the twentieth century, the railroads were for all practical purposes synonymous with large corporations in North America. Yet, in terms of their politics, finances, labor relations, and environmental consequences, the transcontinental railroads were not only failures but near-disasters, and in this they encapsulated the paradox of the arrival of the modern world in western North America.

This is not the standard narrative of the evolution of corporations, of American, Canadian, or Mexican expansion, or of the emergence of the modern world in the late nineteenth century. In the standard narrative, capital was firmly in control, and the modern corporation became the template for social and political order. In the Left's version of this narrative, farmers and workers formed the bulwark of antimonopolism and, although brave in their opposition, they were outmatched by industrialists and capitalists who were subsidized by the federal government and supported by federal troops. Their Waterloo in the United States was the 1896 presidential campaign. In the Right's version, capitalism, in the persona of the entrepreneur, forged a glorious future. Both entrepreneurs and their creations were brilliant successes precisely because the new system dealt with failure so ruthlessly. Gilded Age America was an age prone to evolutionary metaphors—survival of the fittest, nature red in tooth and claw—and it never questioned that its dominant figures were, by definition, the fit. Progress was the century's theme. The end result of both versions of the narrative is a modernity forged by the triumph of capital and the corporation.[1]

Nineteenth- and twentieth-century Social Darwinists, who were, strictly speaking, not Darwinists at all, since they confused fitness—the ability of a species to reproduce and replicate itself—with domination and worth, quite seriously thought that the corporations and the men who ran them were superior to those who opposed them. Even much more subtle and sophisticated thinkers could slip easily into this assumption. Joseph Schumpeter imagined nineteenth-century capitalism as a domain of competence, where "in most cases the man who rises first *into* the business class and then *within* it is also an able businessman and he is likely to rise exactly as far as his ability goes—simply because in that schema rising to a position and doing well in it generally is or was one and the same thing."[2]

These are not my guys. My guys were neither particularly competent businessmen nor the Robber Barons of an older literature. The Robber Barons supposedly mastered their world; their corporations were successful and powerful. *Railroaded* is not a kind of Robber Baron redux. The railroad corporations that I have examined here were unsuccessful and powerful. My guys could be ruthless, but their corporations were failures constantly in need of subsidy and rescue. They fascinate me precisely because they do not fit into our usual way of seeing things. And, in part, this book has been a study of how the unsuccessful and the incompetent not only survived but prospered and became powerful.

The Octopus was the dominant metaphor of the corporation well before Frank Norris ever made it the title of his railroad novel, but I have had trouble finding Octopi. Instead, I find quite limited and ordinary men creating new organizations opportunistically, sometimes cleverly and very often quite ineffectually. Transcontinental railroad corporations lacked the brutal competence of Frank Norris's fictional Pacific and South West Railroad, and they never could muster the managerial competence of Alfred Chandler's actual Pennsylvania Railroad. Overbuilt, prone to bankruptcy and receivership, wretchedly managed, politically corrupt, environmentally harmful, and financially wasteful, these corporations nonetheless helped create a world where private success often came from luck, fortunate timing, and state intervention. Profit arose more from financial markets and insider contracts than from successfully selling transportation.

These railroads have led me into a deeper mystery of modernity: how so many powerful and influential people are so ignorant and do so many things so badly and yet the world still goes on. We are confronted with this constantly, yet we often choose to believe that those in high places know what they are doing and that those who achieve great riches are being rewarded for merit. Those paradoxical railroads of *Railroaded* were not the railroads that I expected to find, but having found them, I had to confront the real questions of this book. What were the results of a world dominated by large, inept, but powerful failures whose influence could not be avoided? What were the structural conditions that permitted these corporations to survive and dominate, if not thrive? Seen from within western railroads and Congress, modernity gradually seemed to me the reverse of the homilies of the Gilded Age: it was the triumph of the unfit, whose survival demanded the intervention of the state, which the corporations themselves corrupted.

The Gilded Age that emerged through this lens was a quite complicated amalgam that we have too often reduced to caricature. It was a world where those who controlled corporations could perpetuate gigantic frauds but also a world where reform prospered. In an age supposedly dominated by individualism, the majority of North Americans embraced an ideal of the greater public good and undertook collective measures to achieve it. That reform effort, however, was tragically marred by racial exclusiveness that framed that greater good in terms of white manhood. It was not a world easily reduced to the current platitudes of op-ed columns.

Like any other historical epoch, the late nineteenth century cannot be understood in terms of a dichotomy between a larger capitalist structure that made the men like those at the center of this book inevitable or an idea of human agency that made that structure in too simple a way their creation. Railroads were a remarkable technology, but building so many of them so far ahead of demand and turning them into large systems turned out not to be very good ideas. Asymmetries of information, financial markets that were willing to absorb excessive risk to compensate for declining returns on investment in more developed countries during the "Long Depression," and state subsidies allowed capital to flow into railroads that should not have been built when and where they were. Once main lines were constructed, the trunk lines demanded branch lines to feed them. And because it initially seemed that only competing lines could produce reasonable rates, all kinds of boosters and promoters in small western towns floated bonds and offered subsidies to attract still more railroads.

The result was not only unneeded railroads whose effects were as often bad as beneficial but also corruption of the markets and the government. The men who directed this capital were frequently not themselves capitalists. They were entrepreneurs who borrowed money or collected subsidies. These entrepreneurs did not invent the railroad, but they were inventing corporations, railroad systems, and new forms of competition. Those things yielded both personal wealth and social disasters. The mining, cattle, and wheat busts, the breakup of western Indian reservations and Indian Territory, the surges of population into the arid West with the long depopulation that followed in many areas, the economic collapses triggered by railroad collapses, the environmental deterioration and waste of resources, the corruption of politics—all this and more seems unlikely or impossible without the railroads. The railroads survived those disasters because of another structural change: they thoroughly insinuated themselves into the modern state. Through their lobbies and friendships they could be found in Congress, the legislatures, bureaucracies, and courts. My claim is not that this is the only way that modern corporate capitalism has developed—there are many capitalisms—only that this is how it developed in this section of the world at this time.

Such structural conditions did not make the form of North American railroads inevitable. I am neither an economist nor a political scientist. I am not in search of universal rules. Culture and history matter. European railroads developed quite differently from North American railroads, although both American and European railroads were creatures of a combination of the markets—albeit markets that were themselves politically constituted—and direct politics. It is wrong, however, to reduce the difference between them to a withdrawal of the national state, so significant in European railroads, from North American railroads. The federal role in western railroads in the United States, for example, was not "short lived," nor did Congress leave planning, as Frank Dobbin has put it in his otherwise wonderful book, "to state and local governments in conjunction with private entrepreneurs."[3]

In nineteenth-century western North America, railroads and the modern state were coproductions. The litany of the work that they did together is impressive. The governments of North America lavishly subsidized the corporations, and the corporations assisted in the great state projects of bringing half a continent under the domination of central governments. Not all politicians were corrupt, but many were. They granted public favors to the railroads in exchange for private favors that the railroads gave them. Having helped create private entities that often dwarfed the states, Congress and the courts created ways in which corporations could fail repeatedly and arise again. When railroad workers opposed their employers, the state ultimately stepped in to determine the outcome of the conflict. Usually it helped railroads crush their workers; far more rarely it sided with the workers. When antimonopolist opponents of the railroads captured the legislative branches of the states, and to a lesser degree Congress, the courts often, but not always, intervened to protect the corporations.

But to put matters this way still misses the main point: transcontinental railroad corporations transformed government itself by making the government an arena in which the corporations themselves competed and by making Congress, bureaucracy, and the courts a mechanism for corporate competition. In their cultivation of friends within the government, in their development of the modern lobby, in the "inwardness," as nineteenth-century Americans referred to things different from how they appeared on the surface, of much of the legislation of the period, the corporations underlined how political the economy was—and is. The western railroads needed the state, and needed it badly. Laws and administrative and judicial rulings aided some corporations and hurt others. Congress helped picked winners and losers every time it acted to give or rescind a land grant, investigated a railroad, demanded a sinking fund, changed tax policies, altered policies over the movement of mails and payments for moving troops or government property, granting rights of way through Indian Territory, Indian reservations or military reservations, and so much more. Sometimes Congress acted through existing bureaucracies—the General Land Office, the Indian Office, or the Post Office—and sometimes it acted legislatively, establishing its own investigative committees and passing new laws rather than new rules. Sometimes Congress worked in conjunction with the courts, sometimes against them. The situation was never as simple as a detached state seeking to regulate a private economy. The interlocking of corporate competition and state legislation remain present to this day. Politics still offers a way for corporations to compete.

Knowing that the corporations were political, their opponents confronted them politically, and eventually the western railroads lost much of the power in Congress and legislatures that had made them so formidable. Their lobbies failed them more and more often. By the 1890s the most politically formidable of them—the Southern Pacific—was a caricature of its former self. But the Southern Pacific and its competitors remained transformative failures; they had changed the nature of politics in the United States. One mark of the significance of the change is that the scandals of the

1990s and early twenty-first century seem so resonant with those of the Gilded Age because, with the aid of the state, great corporate failures still produce immense individual rewards. Much has changed, but states and corporations remain intertwined, and structural conditions forged during the Gilded Age have never entirely disappeared. My guys are dead and gone, but their equivalents—and the conditions that allow them to prosper—endure.

Antimonopolists have not fared so well, and this is, in my opinion, both a bad and a good thing. Western workers, farmers, and antimonopolists have suffered from the condescension, although it is often romantic condescension, with which historians often treat failed social movements. They need to be reexamined, warts and all. Antimonopoly is not a model for modern politics. Its deep cultural core depended on an appeal to white manhood, and the evils that have come from such appeals are too well known to tempt any thoughtful person to desire to replicate them. Yet we can learn from antimonopolism without desiring to be nineteenth-century antimonopolists.

Antimonopolism, for all its considerable flaws, can let us step outside of ourselves and our moment to examine ideas and social relations that no longer have a presence but that might appear again. At its heart, antimonopolism was a belief that the economic system of a democracy had itself to be democratic, and that the goal of a republican economy was to produce republican citizens. Antimonopolists also believed that corruption mattered because corruption was the means by which the republic itself could be subverted from its legitimate ends. That they believed these things did not mean they were premodern. As numerous scholars have recently argued, antimonopolists were as modern as their opponents. They did not flee from the state or large-scale organizations or national and international economies. They believed in economic democracy because they were republicans and democrats. They also, and less usefully, believed it because they thought it was part of being a man, a white man. And being a white man turned them against all other shades of men and caused many, but not all, of them rarely to consider women except as the dependents of white men.[4]

The antimonopolists neither totally failed nor totally succeeded; their recognition that the railroads were not a problem that would solve itself was correct. The market did not sort things out, because it could not sort them out. As antimonopolists became more sophisticated, they realized that the issue was not whether politics was going to influence and shape the market but how it was going to do so. The market was always going to be shaped by state interventions, whether obvious or subtle. The issue was whom these interventions would help and whom they would harm. In recognizing this, the antimonopolists were more sophisticated than those academic economists, the marginalists, who were coming to dominate the discipline. The marginalists detested price-fixing but distrusted regulation, and for them American railroads presented a conundrum. They believed fervently in the market and regarded competition as a universal panacea, and yet in the railroad industry it seemed that the only choices were to rely on government to ensure competition—violating their laissez-faire beliefs—or to make an exemption for railroads and regard them as anomalies—natural monopolies. Eventually, they concluded that natural monopoly and ruinous competition were not a permanent condition of the railroad industry. They concluded that excess capacity, such as that which plagued western railroads for thirty years, was just a "short-term" problem. Sooner or later, through careful business planning, managers could correct the problem without either government regulation or collusion. But, as the legal scholar Herbert Hovenkamp has noted, the "'answer' that the overproduction problem existed only for the short run was no answer at all if the short run was thirty years and an industry was in distress the entire time." This was precisely the situation for the transcontinentals.[5]

Ordering the railroads, turning them into a more coherent, less wasteful, and less exploitative system, was the work of twentieth-century reformers who built on the antimonopolist legacy. Some of them had been antimonopolists. The success of regulated competition was a matter of imposing regulation.[6]

The railroads could make even Joseph Schumpeter seem incoherent. He granted them their importance as the great engine of the nineteenth-century economy, and he put them in perpetual crisis. He contended that these crises "set everybody talking about freight wars, cutthroat competition, discrimination, and the evils of unregulated enterprise, to the exclusion of what the thing really meant. As a matter of fact, it paved the way to consolidation, efficient administration, and sound finance, thus ushering in the last step of America's railroadization."[7] But then he appears to reconsider, for the railroads emerge from the depression of the 1890s as an "old" industry, which has a final brief boom and then becomes a declining industry. Railroads seem an industry without a prime, without stability. They are in either crisis or decline. It was like having children whose tantrums disappear only at the moment when they slip into their dotage. Some success.

Celebrated as the conquerors of time, space, and even nature itself, western railroads were always as much a promise as an achievement. They were less an asset that one generation passed on to the next than a debt that the past imposed on the present and future. I mean this quite literally. The seeming durability of the iron, steel, and stone that made up a railroad was, if not an illusion, then largely relative. The wind and the rain, the ice and the snow, the floods and the landslides, the rust, the rot, and the fire that ate away at railroads meant that they had to be constantly repaired and rebuilt or they ceased to function. When nineteenth-century editorialists proclaimed that the fraud, deception, and loss of capital that the railroads entailed ultimately did not matter, because Americans now had the railroad, they did not know what they were talking about. Without constant new investment and labor, the railroads would have been useless. And beyond that, given lower capital costs and improved technology as the nineteenth century wore on, new railroads could have been built at far lower costs and with far less capital than had been required for the older railroads. Those regions east of the 100th meridian and along the Pacific Coast that needed railroads could still have had them without massive subsidies and resulting fraud. Waiting instead of building would for the rest of the West have not necessarily been a bad thing.

The need to invest capital and labor in large amounts to maintain and upgrade what had already been built was one debt owed to the past, but the second one was what Charles Francis Adams in his days as a reformer referred to as a tax on trade. All of the watered stock, money siphoned off into private pockets, waste, and fraud that characterized the building of the railroads created a corporate debt that had to be paid through higher rates and scrimping on service. A shipper in 1885 was still paying for the frauds of the 1860s.

Henry Villard, Leland Stanford, Jay Cooke, Collis P. Huntington, Tom Scott, Jay Gould, and the rest really do matter, but only when placed back in the context of their times. Unlike the dyspeptic Charles Francis Adams, who came to hate them, I have enjoyed the company of these men, flawed as they were. I, admittedly, have had the advantage of dealing with them when they were dead and through the medium of their letters and other documents, but they were usually interesting and sometimes very funny, even if also almost criminally careless, often obtuse, and greedy. I have learned a lot from them. Precisely because they were muddling through, inventing corporate capitalism as they went along and because the dimmer lights among them, such as Leland Stanford, had to have so much explained to them, I have been able to learn things I otherwise would not have known. I owe them much for revealing the "inwardness" of the nineteenth century. They were not necessarily rational actors, but they were quite human actors, who embodied the complexities of social relations as well as competing personal interests that created and worked through larger institutions.

Contingency—the idea that what happens in the world is often a result of the unexpected combination of quite particular circumstances—is the mark of history as a discipline, and, for me at least, the deep common ground of good history is that things did not have to be this way. To say that choices are not limitless, that we always act within constraints imposed by the past, is not the same thing as saying that there were, or are, no choices. A belief in contingency has as its corollary an obligation to imagine alternatives. To imagine a West where railroads were built as demand required is not an exercise in second-guessing. Reformers like Henry George and Charles Francis Adams, in his reform phase, and railroad men like J. M. Forbes advocated such a world. It was a policy that the Chicago roads sometimes, but not always, followed.

A West where railroads were built according to demand is in part a counterfactual West. Only in the eastern half of South Dakota was that largely the case. And, unlike economic historians, most historians have, until relatively recently, been reluctant to engage in counterfactuals on the seemingly incontrovertible grounds that what did not happen is not history. But I have come to think that the opposite is, in fact, true: we need to think about what did not happen in order to think historically. Considering only what happened is ahistorical, because the past once contained larger possibilities, and part of the historian's job is to make those possibilities visible; otherwise all that is left for historians to do is to explain the inevitability of the present. The inevitability of the present violates the contingency of the past, which involves alternative choices and outcomes that could have produced alternative presents. To deny the contingency of the past deprives us of alternative futures, for the present is the future's past. Contingency, in turn, demands hypotheticals about what might have happened. They are fictions, but necessary fictions. It is only by conceiving of alternative worlds that people in the past themselves imagined that we can begin to think historically, to escape the inevitability of the present, and get another perspective on issues that concern us still.

In the late nineteenth-century United States, Canada, and Mexico without the extensive subsidization of a transcontinental railroad network, there might very well have been less waste, less suffering, less environmental degradation, and less catastrophic economic busts in mining, agriculture, and cattle raising. There would have been more time for Indians to adjust to a changing world. The conditions that twentieth-century Indians faced would have been more like those the Navajos faced, with their reservation intact and a functioning economy, rather than those that the Lakotas faced, with their reservations subdivided and allotted and their attempts to adjust thwarted. There would have been less bloodshed and slaughter. There would have been fewer rushes and collapses, fewer booms and busts. Much of the disastrous environmental and social history of the Great Plains might have been avoided. The issue is not whether railroads should have been built. The issue is whether they should have been built when and where they were built. And to those questions the answer seems no. Quite literally, if the country had not built transcontinental railroads, it might not have needed them until much later, when it could have built them more cheaply, more efficiently, and with fewer social and political costs.

APPENDIX

MAP A: DISTRIBUTION OF UNION PACIFIC STOCKHOLDERS BY CITY, 1869

This map reveals the way ownership of the Union Pacific concentrated in New England and New York. However, the map does not represent investment of capital in the road. In fact, many of the largest stockholders had invested little or nothing in the Union Pacific; they had bought stock in the Credit Mobilier. The map, then, is not so much a map of capital invested, much of which came from loans made by the federal government and the rest from bond sales, as it is a map of how the West got a federally financed railroad and the East got the insider networks which controlled it.

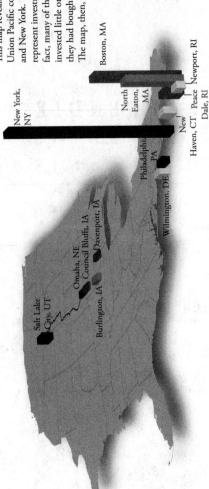

New York, NY

Boston, MA

North Eaton, MA

Newport, RI

New Haven, CT   Peace Dale, RI

Philadelphia, PA

Wilmington, DE

Salt Lake City, UT

Omaha, NE
Council Bluffs, IA   Davenport, IA

Burlington, IA

Toral Patel, Killeen Hanson, Evgenia Shnayder, Richard White—Spatial History Lab, Stanford University

MAP B: KANSAS RAILROADS, 1893

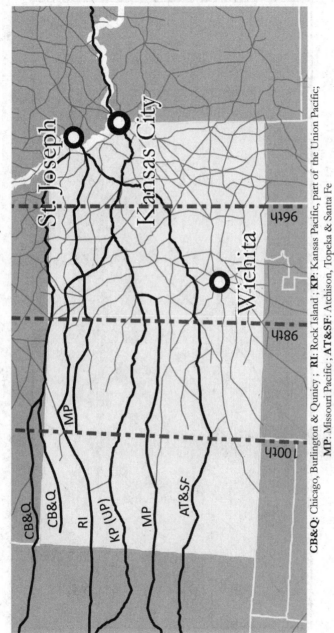

CB&Q: Chicago, Burlington & Quincy ; **RI**: Rock Island ; **KP**: Kansas Pacific, part of the Union Pacific; **MP**: Missouri Pacific ; **AT&SF**: Atchison, Topeka & Santa Fe

Spatial History Lab, Stanford University

MAP C: SOUTHERN PACIFIC AND CENTRAL PACIFIC LAND GRANTS IN THE CENTRAL VALLEY OF CALIFORNIA

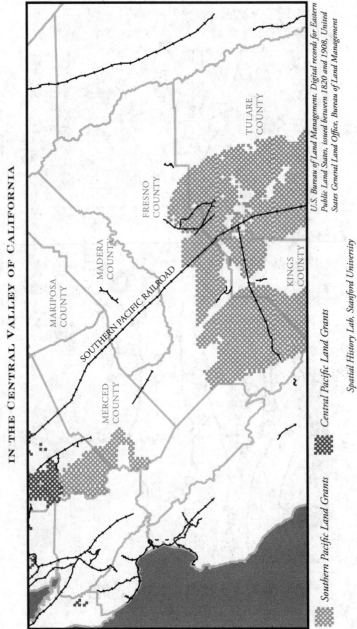

Southern Pacific Land Grants   Central Pacific Land Grants

U.S. Bureau of Land Management. Digital records for Eastern Public Land States, issued between 1820 and 1908, United States General Land Office, Bureau of Land Management

Spatial History Lab, Stanford University

CHART A: PRINCIPAL COMMODITIES AND EASTBOUND THROUGH FREIGHT

Eighteen Commodities as a Proportion of All Eastbound Through
Railroad Traffic from California, 1873–1891

Freight, in Millions of Pounds

800 — 700 — 600 — 500 — 400 — 300 — 200 — 100 — 0

1875   1880   1885   1890

All Eastbound Through Freight

Principal Commodities

Principal commodities include beans, borax, grains, fruit (canned, dried, and green), hides and pelts, hops, leather, lumber, mustard seed, quicksilver, salmon, sugar, tea, wine and brandy, and wool.

Annual Report of the San Francisco Chamber of Commerce, 1882–1893. Spatial History Lab, Stanford University

CHART B: FRUIT AND SUGAR AS PROPORTIONS OF EASTBOUND FREIGHT

Green Fruit, Canned Fruit, Dried Fruit, and Sugar Shipped Eastward by Rail from California,
1873–1892

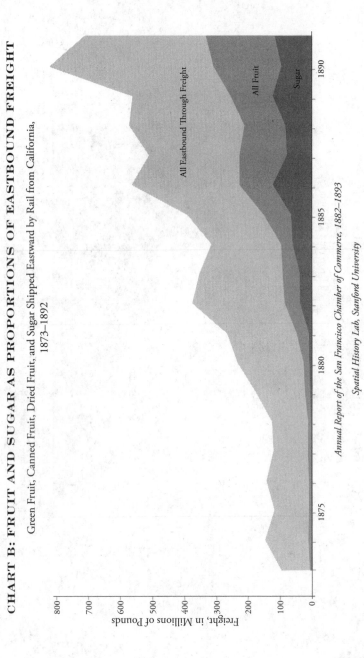

All Eastbound Through Freight

All Fruit

Sugar

Freight, in Millions of Pounds

Annual Report of the San Francisco Chamber of Commerce, 1882–1893

Spatial History Lab, Stanford University

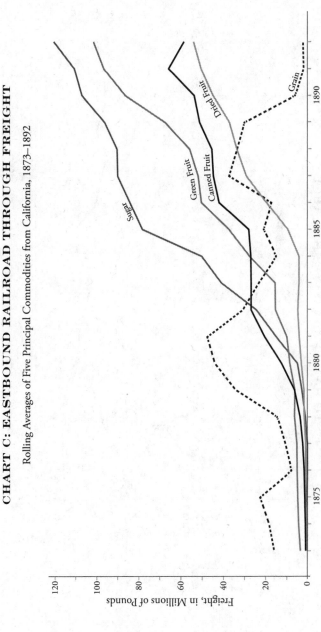

CHART C: EASTBOUND RAILROAD THROUGH FREIGHT

Rolling Averages of Five Principal Commodities from California, 1873–1892

Annual Report of the San Francisco Chamber of Commerce, 1882–1893
Spatial History Lab, Stanford University

CHART D: LOCAL AND THROUGH FREIGHT BY RAIL
TO SAN FRANCISCO, 1875–1891

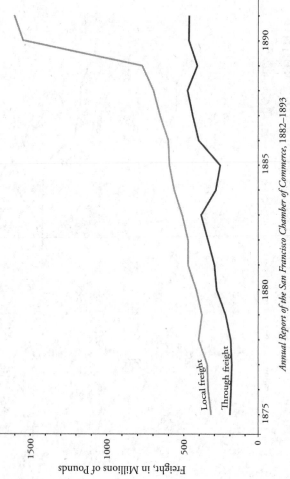

Local freight

Through freight

Freight, in Millions of Pounds

1875   1880   1885   1890

Annual Report of the San Francisco Chamber of Commerce, 1882–1893
Spatial History Lab, Stanford University

CHART E: THROUGH SHIPMENTS TO AND FROM CALIFORNIA BY RAIL, 1873–1891

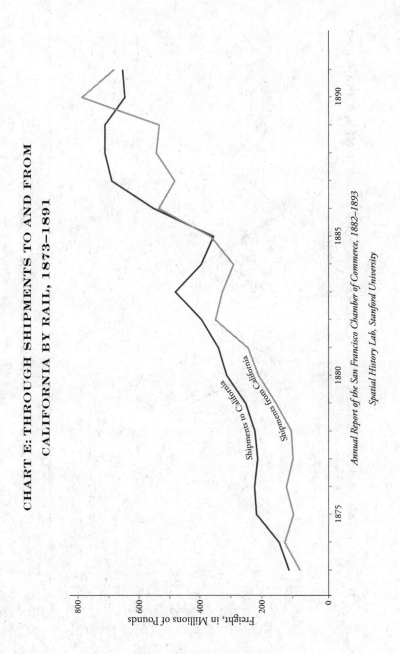

Shipments to California

Shipments from California

Freight, in Millions of Pounds

1875   1880   1885   1890

Annual Report of the San Francisco Chamber of Commerce, 1882–1893

Spatial History Lab, Stanford University

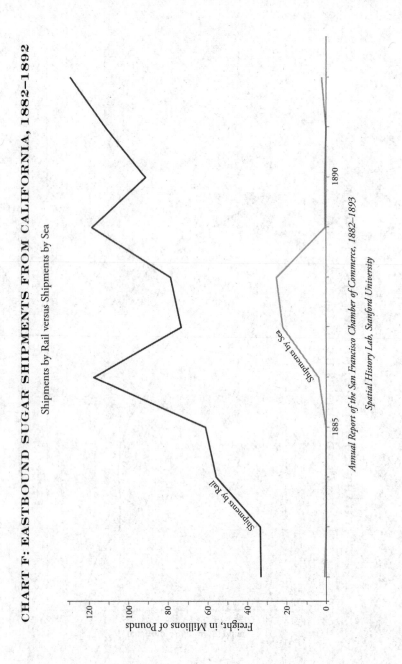

CHART F: EASTBOUND SUGAR SHIPMENTS FROM CALIFORNIA, 1882–1892

Shipments by Rail versus Shipments by Sea

Shipments by Rail

Shipments by Sea

1885

1890

Freight, in Millions of Pounds

120

100

80

60

40

20

0

Annual Report of the San Francisco Chamber of Commerce, 1882–1893

Spatial History Lab, Stanford University

CHART G: EASTBOUND WINE AND BRANDY SHIPMENTS FROM CALIFORNIA

Shipments by Rail versus Shipments by Sea, 1877–1892

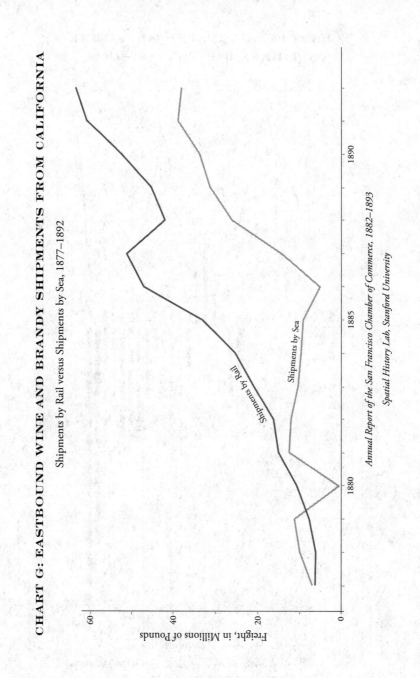

Shipments by Rail

Shipments by Sea

Freight, in Millions of Pounds

1880   1885   1890

Annual Report of the San Francisco Chamber of Commerce, 1882–1893

Spatial History Lab, Stanford University

CHART H: RAIL TRAFFIC ALONG THE
NORTHERN PACIFIC, 1892–1894

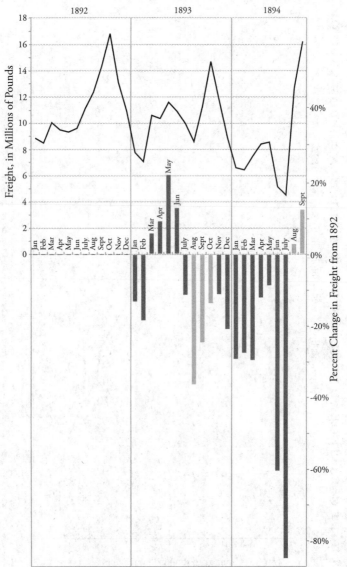

The lighter bars represent harvest months when rail traffic is greater.

*Northern Pacific System Report. Northern Pacific Railway Company Papers,
Settlements Development 1864–1920, Series C, Roll 3*

Spatial History Lab, Stanford University

CHART I: LIVESTOCK SHIPMENTS BY MONTH, 1883

Livestock Shipped out of Nebraska on the Union Pacific in 1883

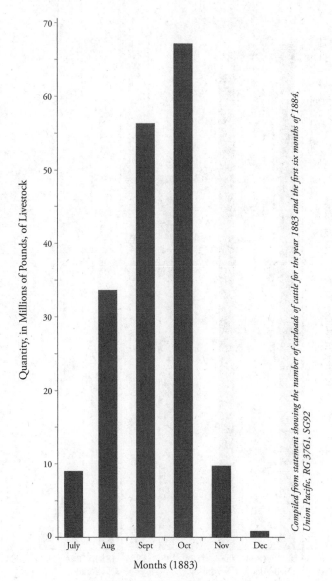

Quantity, in Millions of Pounds, of Livestock

Months (1883)

Compiled from statement showing the number of carloads of cattle for the year 1883 and the first six months of 1884, Union Pacific, RG 3761, SG92

Spatial History Lab, Stanford University

CHART J: LIVESTOCK SHIPMENTS BY STATE, 1883–1884

Livestock Shipped along the Union Pacific in 1883 and 1884

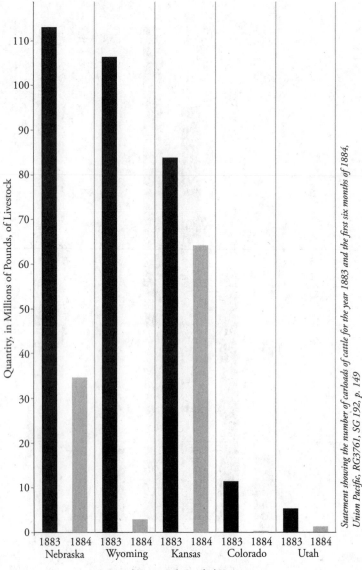

Statement showing the number of carloads of cattle for the year 1883 and the first six months of 1884, Union Pacific, RG3761, SG 192, p. 149

Spatial History Lab, Stanford University

CHART K: CORN AND CATTLE IN THE UNITED STATES, 1890

Density of Cattle compared to Density of Corn

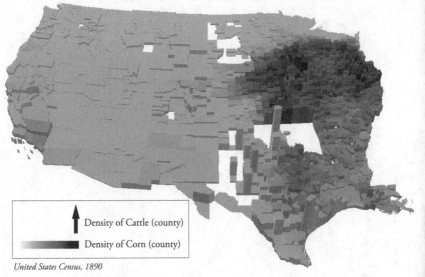

Density of Cattle (county)

Density of Corn (county)

United States Census, 1890

Spatial History Lab, Stanford University

CHART L: GRAIN EXPORTED FROM NEBRASKA, 1883

Quantities of grain, in pounds, being shipped from Nebraska stations
along the Union Pacific Railroad

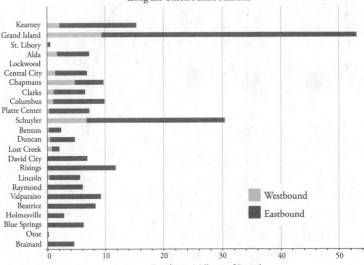

Westbound

Eastbound

Freight, in Millions of Pounds

Freight Auditing Department, Statement showing the number of pounds forwarded from the stations above in 1883

Spatial History Lab, Stanford University

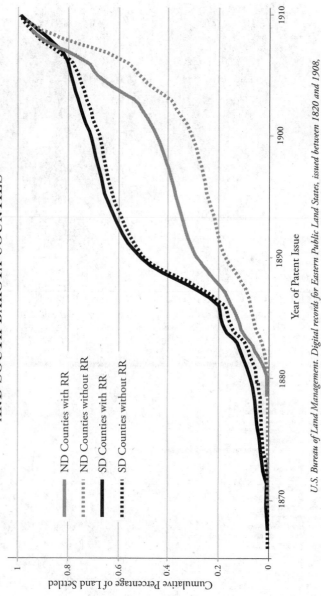

CHART M: LAND SETTLEMENT IN NORTH DAKOTA AND SOUTH DAKOTA COUNTIES

ND Counties with RR
ND Counties without RR
SD Counties with RR
SD Counties without RR

Cumulative Percentage of Land Settled

Year of Patent Issue

U.S. Bureau of Land Management. Digital records for Eastern Public Land States, issued between 1820 and 1908,
United States General Land Office, Bureau of Land Management

Spatial History Lab, Stanford University

NOTES

A much fuller annotated set of endnotes is available on the Spatial History Project website at Stanford University. Many charts referred to in the notes are available in the appendix; the endnotes also refer the reader to visualizations and other materials on the Spatial History website.

GUIDE TO ABBREVIATIONS

CPH is Collis P. Huntington; EVD is Eugene V. Debs; HEH is Henry E. Huntington; LB is letterbook; SG is subgroup; vol. is volume; ser. is series; f. is folder; r. is reel.

Adams Diary: in Adams Papers.

Adams Papers: Charles Francis Adams II; microfilm edition of the Charles Francis Adams II Papers, 1861–1933 (Boston: Massachusetts Historical Society, 1984), 55 reels.

Atlantic & Pacific RR Co., 1870–76: Baker Library, Harvard University.

Barlow Papers: Papers of Samuel L. M. Barlow, 1776–1905, Huntington Library, San Marino, Calif.

Brotherhood of Locomotive Engineers: Brotherhood of Locomotive Engineers, Division 10, Sacramento Railroad Museum.

Canadian Pacific Railway Correspondence: Correspondence Relative to the Canadian Pacific Railway, Presented to Both Houses of Parliament by Command of Her Majesty, March 1874 (London, William Clowes & Sons, 1874).

CB&Q: Burlington Archives, Chicago, Burlington, and Quincy Railroad Company, Newberry Library, Chicago. For a guide, see Elisabeth Coleman Jackson and Carolyn Curtis, eds., *Guide to the Burlington Archives in the Newberry Library, 1851–1901* (Chicago: Newberry Library, 1949).

Chase Papers: The Salmon P. Chase Papers [microform], John Niven, ed., James P. McClure and Patrick Elana, asst. eds. (Frederick, Md.: University Publications of America, 1987), 43 reels.

Colton Case Depositions and Findings: Colton Case. Depositions. In the Superior Court of the State of California, in and for the County of Sonoma. Ellen M. Colton, plaintiff, vs. Leland Stanford et al., defendants, 2 vols. (n.p., 1883–84).

Colton Case Testimony: Colton Case. Testimony (1st–83d day; Nov. 13, 1883–Aug. 1, 1884). In the Superior Court of the State of California, in and for the County of Sonoma . . . Ellen M. Colton, Plaintiff, vs. Leland Stanford et al., Defendants . . . Counsel Appearing . . . 19 vols. (Santa Rosa, Calif.: Sonoma Democrat Print, 1883–84), copy in Stanford University Library.

Cooke Memoir: Unpublished typescript. [Jay Cooke's Memoir.] Baker Library Historical Collections, Harvard Business School.

Cooke Papers: Jay Cooke Papers, Pennsylvania Historical Society, HSP 148, Philadelphia.

Cotton Letters: The Wheat King: The Selected Letters and Papers of A. J. Cotton, 1888–1913 (Winnipeg: Manitoba Record Society, 1985).

CPH Papers: Collis P. Huntington Papers, 1856–1901 (Sanford, N.C.: Microfilming Corporation of America, 1978–79), 115 reels. Series 1: Incoming correspondence, 1856–1904. Series 2: Letterpress copy books, 1868–1901. Series 3: Legal and financial records, 1797–1901. Series 4: Personal papers, 1862–1901.

Crocker Papers: Charles Crocker Papers, Huntington Library, San Marino, Calif.

Dawes Papers: Henry L. Dawes Papers, Manuscript Division, Library of Congress.

Dodge Papers: Grenville M. Dodge Papers, MS 98, State Historical Society of Iowa.

Fahnestock Papers: Harris C. Fahnestock Papers, Baker Library Historical Collections, Harvard Business School.

Fitch Papers: George Kenyon Fitch Papers, 1826–1906, BANC MSS C-B 761, Bancroft Library, University of California, Berkeley.

Foreign Bondholders Cuttings Files: The Newspaper Cuttings Files of the Council of Foreign Bondholders in the Guildhall Library, London, 2nd ser., microform (East Ardsley, Eng.: Microform Academic Publishers, 1993), 18 reels.

Great Northern: Great Northern Railway Co. Papers, part I, 1862–1922, microform, ed. W. Thomas White (Frederick, Md.: University Publications of America, 1986), 25 reels.

HEH Collection: Henry Edwards Huntington Collection, 1794–1970, Huntington Library, San Marino, Calif. These papers were originally organized chronologically and in the midst of this project were reorganized by correspondent. To avoid confusion, I list the letters simply by correspondents and date without the old box numbers.

Hill Papers: James Jerome Hill Papers: letterpress books, 1866–1916, microform (St. Paul, Minn.: James Jerome Hill Reference Library, 1984), 48 reels.

H. K. Thomas Diary: H. K. Thomas Diary, 1870–71, WA MSS 47, Beinecke Library, Yale University.

Hopkins Collection: Timothy Hopkins Transportation Collection, 1826–1942, M0097, Special Collections and University Archives, Stanford University.

Huntington Letters: I have followed the organization in the Huntington Papers for these privately printed volumes, but for clarity I have substituted numbers for the A, B, C, D labels in the microfilmed edition. Vol. 1 is *Huntington Letters to Mark Hopkins, Leland Stanford, Charles Crocker, E. B. Crocker, Charles F. Crocker, and D. D. Cotton* [sic], *from August 20, 1867, to August 5, 1869* (New York, 1892); vol. 2 is *Letters from Mark Hopkins, Leland Stanford, Charles Crocker, Charles F. Crocker, and D. D. Colton to Collis P. Huntington from August 27, 1869, to Dec. 30, 1879* (New York, 1891); vol. 3 is *Huntington Letters to Mark Hopkins, Leland Stanford, Charles Crocker, E. B. Crocker, and Charles F. Crocker, from August 5, 1869, to March 26, 1873* (New York, 1892); vol. 4 is *Huntington Letters to Mark Hopkins, Leland Stanford, Charles Crocker, E. B. Crocker, Charles F. Crocker, and D. D. Colton from April 2, 1873, to March 31, 1876* (New York, 1892–94).

Hyde Papers, William B. Hyde Papers, MS 267, Special Collections, Stanford University.

Ives Papers: Papers of Butler Ives, Hopkins Collection, M 97, Special Collections, Stanford University.

James J. Hill Papers: James J. Hill Papers, Minnesota Historical Society, St. Paul.

Mahl Papers: William Mahl Papers, Manuscript Collections, Center for American History, University of Texas, Austin.

Newspaper Cuttings Files: The Newspaper Cuttings Files of the Council of Foreign Bondholders in the Guildhall Library, London, 1874–93 (microfilm, 266 reels, EP Microform Ltd., 1975).

NP: Northern Pacific Railway Company, Northern Pacific Railway Corporate Records, 1861–1970, Minnesota Historical Society, St. Paul.

NP, GMR, Pullman: Northern Pacific Railway Company, General Manager's Records: Labor, 138.H.8.8 (F), 11A 5 6F, Pullman Boycott Correspondence, Minnesota Historical Society, St. Paul.

NP, LRR, PV: Northern Pacific Railway Company Records, Letters Received, Registered: President and Vice-president, Minnesota Historical Society, St. Paul.

Octopus Speaks: Salvador A. Ramirez, ed., *The Octopus Speaks: The Colton Letters* (Carlsbad, Calif.: Tentacled Press, 1982).

Olney Papers: Richard Olney Papers, Manuscript Division, Library of Congress, 62 microfilm reels.

OTC: Oriental Trading Company Records in Northern Pacific Railway Company, Northern Pacific Railway Company Records, University of Washington Archives.

Pacific Mail Mss.: Pacific Mail Steamship Company Mss., Huntington Library, San Marino, Calif.

Painter Papers: Uriah Hunt Painter Papers, 1855–1936, Historical Society of Pennsylvania, Philadelphia.

Pamphlets, Railroads of Mexico: Pamphlets Pertaining to the Railroads of Mexico, American Philosophical Society, Philadelphia.

PIC Records: Pacific Improvement Company, Records, 1869–1931 (bulk 1883–1927), Archives and Special Collections, Stanford University.

Plumb Papers: Edward L. Plumb Papers, Special Collections, M 149, Stanford University Archives.

Poor, *Manual*: Henry V. Poor, *Manual of the Railroads of the United States . . . 1868–c. 1924*, 57 vols. (title varies) (New York: H. V. & H. W. Poor, 1868–c. 1924).

Powderly Papers: Papers of Terence Vincent Powderly, 1864–1924, and John William Hayes, 1880–1921, microform, The Knights of Labor (Glen Rock, N.J.: Microfilming Corporation of America, 1974), 15 reels.

PRC: Report . . . of the United States Pacific Railway Commission and Testimony Taken by the Commission, 50th Cong., 1st sess. S. Ex. Doc. 51, 10 vols. (Washington, D.C.: GPO, 1887–88).

Pullman Strike: Crim 3059, United States District Court, Northern California, boxes 211–17, 1005A, National Archives and Records Center, San Bruno, Calif.

Ralston Correspondence: W. C. Ralston Correspondence, Special Collections, M0217, Stanford University.

Randall Papers: Samuel J. Randall Papers, Rare Books and Manuscripts Collection, University of Pennsylvania.

Southern Pacific Records: New York Collection, Central Pacific Railroad Vouchers, MS 10, Southern Pacific Railroad, California State Railroad Museum, Sacramento.

Stanford Papers: Leland Stanford Papers, 1872–93, SC033C, Special Collections and University Archives, Stanford University.

UP: Union Pacific Railroad Company, RG3761, Nebraska State Historical Society, Lincoln.

UP, OVP, IC: Union Pacific Railroad, Office of the Vice President, Incoming Correspondence, series 1, subgroup 4, Lincoln: Nebraska State Historical Society.

UP, OVP, OC: Union Pacific Railroad, Office of the Vice President, Outgoing Correspondence, series 1, subgroup 3, Lincoln: Nebraska State Historical Society.

UP, PO, OC: Union Pacific Railroad, Office of the President, subgroup 2, Outgoing Correspondence, microform, Lincoln: Nebraska State Historical Society.

Van Horne LB: Van Horne Letterbook, MG 28 III, National Archives of Canada, Ottawa.

Villard Papers: Henry Villard Papers, Baker Library Historical Collections, Harvard Business School.

White Papers: Stephen Mallory White Papers, M0035, Stanford University Archives.

Wilbur Papers: George Wilbur Family Papers, WA MSS S-1611, Beinecke Library, Yale University.

INTRODUCTION

1 Carlos A. Schwantes and James P. Ronda, *The West the Railroads Made* (Seattle: Univ. of Washington Press, 2008).

2 Charles Francis Adams, "The Era of Change," in Charles F. Adams and Henry Adams, *Chapters of Erie and Other Essays* (Boston: James Osgood, 1871; reprint, New York: Augustus M. Kelley, 1967), 365.

3 Joseph Nimmo Jr., *Railroad Federations and the Relation of the Railroads to Commerce . . .* (Washington, D.C.: GPO, 1885), 8.

4 *Report of the Auditor of Railroad Accounts*, 46th Cong., 2d sess., 1911, H. Ex. Doc. 1, 17–18.

5 The best of these are by Maury Klein; see esp. Klein, *Union Pacific*, 2 vols. (Garden City, N.Y.: Doubleday, 1987).

6 Gerald Berk, a political scientist, has recognized this, as has William Roy, a historical sociologist. Roy, *Socializing Capital: The Rise of the Large Industrial Corporation in America* (Princeton: Princeton Univ. Press, 1997), 95; Berk, *Alternative Tracks: The Constitution of American Industrial Order, 1865–1917* (Baltimore: Johns Hopkins Univ. Press, 1994).

7 Quote, Adams to Moorfield Storey, Feb. 2, 1885, UP, PO, OC, vol. 27, ser. 2, r. 23; for policies during the Civil War, Heather Cox Richardson, *The Greatest Nation of the Earth: Republican Economic Policies during the Civil War* (Cambridge: Harvard Univ. Press, 1997), 170–72, 175, 178–80. See also Dodge to Scott, Jan. 12, 1874, LBs, Texas & Pacific Railroad, box 160, 72–73, 77, Dodge Papers.

8 Most American historians have relegated the study of corporations to the subfield of business history. Business historians have thrived on the neglect of their colleagues and created an impressive body of literature that should be better integrated into the larger narratives of American and Canadian history.

9 Thomas McCraw, *Prophet of Innovation: Joseph Schumpeter and Creative Destruction* (Cambridge: Harvard Univ. Press, 2007), 7, 261.

10 John Joseph Wallis, "Constitutions, Corporations, and Internal Improvements: American States, 1841–1852" (unpublished paper, April 2002), 18–19.

11 Joel Mokyr, *The Gifts of Athena: Historical Origins of the Knowledge Economy* (Princeton: Princeton Univ. Press, 2002), 220.

12 Lance Davis and Douglass North, *Institutional Change and American Economic Growth* (New York: Cambridge Univ. Press, 1971), 140 ff.; Alfred Chandler, ed., *The Railroads: The Nation's First Big Business* (New York: Harcourt, Brace and World, 1965); Alfred Chandler, *The Visible Hand: The Managerial Revolution in American Business* (Cambridge: Harvard Univ. Press, 1977), 1–187. For a critique, see Charles Perrow, *Organizing America: Wealth, Power, and the Origins of Corporate Capitalism* (Princeton: Princeton Univ. Press, 2002), 113–17.

13 Perrow, *Organizing America*, 116–17.

14 Frank Dobbin, *Forging Industrial Policy: The United States, Britain and France in the Railway Age* (New York: Cambridge Univ. Press, 1994), 1–5; Colleen Dunlavy, *Politics and Industrialization: Early Railroads in the United States and Prussia* (Princeton: Princeton Univ. Press, 1994); Perrow, *Organizing America*, 124, 211–12. Charles Perrow, in particular, recognizes that there is never at any given time a single logic at work and that there are always competing interests. Ibid., 212–28. See also Charles Perrow, *Complex Organizations: A Critical Essay*, 3d ed. (New York: Random House, 1986).

15 I would like to thank Woody Powell for this formulation.

16 Although scholars until recently have emphasized the comparative weakness of the American state, the federal government was hardly weak between 1860 and 1876. The classic work here is

Richard Bensel, *Yankee Leviathan: The Origins of Central State Authority in America, 1859–1877* (New York: Cambridge Univ. Press, 1990).

17 James C. Scott, *Seeing like a State: How Certain Schemes to Improve the Human Condition Have Failed* (New Haven: Yale Univ. Press, 1998), 1–3. Jackson Lears, *Rebirth of a Nation: The Making of Modern America, 1877–1920* (New York: Harper, 2009), is a recent and brilliant reinterpretation, but it still embodies much of Wiebe's and Chandler's interpretation.

18 Robert Wiebe, *The Search for Order, 1877–1920* (New York: Hill & Wang, 1967), 181; Chandler, *Visible Hand*, 6–12, 87, 289.

19 Charles Perrow, *Complex Organizations*, 117.

20 I am hardly the first historian to both admire and struggle against Wiebe's artful and capacious narrative, but my technique is a little different in that I focus on the railroad corporation as both modern and disorderly.

21 For a sampling of this literature, see Bensel, *Yankee Leviathan*, for a powerful state at the beginning, not the end, of Wiebe's period. For the modernity of antimonopolism, see Charles Postel, *The Populist Vision* (New York: Oxford Univ. Press, 2007). For newer studies of the evolution of the railroads, see Steven Usselman, *Regulating Railroad Innovation: Business, Technology and Politics in America, 1840–1920* (New York: Cambridge Univ. Press, 2002). For their relation to the state, see Roy, *Socializing Capital*. For information, see Menahem Blondheim, *News over the Wires: The Telegraph and the Flow of Public Information in America, 1844–1897* (Cambridge: Harvard Univ. Press, 1994), and the recent and quite wonderful book by Richard R. John, *Network Nation: Inventing American Telecommunications* (Cambridge: Harvard Univ. Press, 2010).

22 Roy, *Socializing Capital*, 4.

23 David Howard Bain, *Empire Express: Building the First Transcontinental Railroad* (New York: Viking, 1999), 711.

CHAPTER 1: GENESIS

1 "The Railroad Problem in American Politics, August 1, 1874," in Lauren E. Crane, ed., *Newton Booth of California: His Speeches and Addresses* (New York: G. P. Putnam's Sons, 1894), 161; Joseph Schumpeter, *Business Cycles: A Theoretical, Historical, and Statistical Analysis of the Capitalist Process*, 2 vols. (New York: McGraw-Hill, 1939), 1:104.

2 Harold Holzer, *Lincoln at Cooper Union: The Speech That Made Abraham Lincoln President* (New York: Simon & Schuster, 2004), 60–65; James E. Vance Jr., *The North American Railroad: Its Origin, Evolution, and Geography* (Baltimore: Johns Hopkins Univ. Press, 1995), 1–124.

3 William R. Siddall, "Railroad Gauges and Spatial Interaction," *Geographical Review* 59 (Jan. 1969): 29–57.

4 Vance, *North American Railroad*, maps 114–15. George Rogers Taylor and Irene D. Neu, *The American Railroad Network, 1861–1890* (Cambridge: Harvard Univ. Press, 1956), 11–14, 35–41, 53–54.

5 Alfred Chandler, *The Visible Hand: The Managerial Revolution in American Business* (Cambridge: Harvard Univ. Press, 1977), 90–109. T. J. Stiles, *The First Tycoon: The Epic Life of Cornelius Vanderbilt* (New York: Alfred A. Knopf, 2009), 68, 96–97, 167.

6 Samuel Richey Kamm, "The Civil War Career of Thomas A. Scott" (Ph.D. diss., Univ. of Pennsylvania, 1940); Robert C. Angevine, *The Railroad and the State: War, Politics, and Technology in Nineteenth-Century America* (Stanford: Stanford Univ. Press, 2004), 133–34.

7 Kamm, "Civil War Career of Thomas A. Scott," 3–4, 11–18; Douglas E. Bowers, "Logrolling to Corruption: The Development of Lobbying in Pennsylvania, 1815–1861," *Journal of the Early*

Republic 4 (Winter 1983): 469–70; Colleen A. Dunlavy, *Politics and Industrialization: Early Railroads in the United States and Prussia* (Princeton: Princeton Univ. Press, 1994), 80, 138–39; Pamela Laird, *Pull: Networking and Success since Benjamin Franklin* (Cambridge: Harvard Univ. Press, 2006), 18–24, 29–36.

8 Thomas Weber, *The Northern Railroads in the Civil War, 1861–65* (New York: Kings Crown Press, Columbia Univ., 1952) 127–28; Kamm, "Civil War Career of Thomas A. Scott."

9 William Z. Ripley, *Railroads: Rates and Regulation* (New York: Longmans, Green, 1916), 101–3; George H. Miller, *Railroads and Granger Laws* (Madison: Univ. of Wisconsin Press, 1971), 109; "Proceedings of Convention of the General Ticket and Passenger Association, St. Louis, March 9, 1877," *Records of the National General Ticket Agents' Association* (Chicago: J. M. W. Jones, 1878), 465.

10 Kamm, "Civil War Career of Thomas A. Scott," 69–71.

11 Ibid.; Weber, *Northern Railroads*, 128–30.

12 Harry James Brown and Frederick D. Williams, eds., *The Diary of James A. Garfield*, 4 vols. (East Lansing: Michigan State Univ. Press, 1967–81), 2:256, entry of Dec. 7, 1873.

13 Kamm, "Civil War Career of Thomas A. Scott," 122–24, 130–31.

14 Weber, *Northern Railroads*, 130; Maury Klein, *History of the Louisville and Nashville Railroad* (New York: Macmillan, 1972), 41–43.

15 Klein, *History of the Louisville and Nashville Railroad.*

16 Josiah Quincy, *The Railroad System of Massachusetts: An Address Delivered Before the Boston Board of Trade, Nov. 10, 1866* (Boston: Mudge & Son, 1866), esp. 25; Thomas McCraw, *Prophets of Regulation: Charles Francis Adams, Louis D. Brandeis, James M. Landis, Alfred E. Kahn* (Cambridge: Harvard Univ. Press, 1984), 9–10; Charles Francis Adams, "Which Will Quickest Solve the Railroad Question: Force Bills or Public Opinion?" (Address at Oshkosh, Wisc., Sept. 3, 1875), 7–11, in Charles Francis Adams, *Railway Pamphlets*, Stanford Univ. Library; Herbert Hovenkamp, *Enterprise and American Law, 1836–1937* (Cambridge: Harvard Univ. Press, 1991), 139–48.

17 Richard A. Posner, "Natural Monopoly and Its Regulation," *Stanford Law* 21 (Feb. 1969): 570.

18 "Proceedings of Convention of the General Ticket and Passenger Association," 466–67; Quincy, *Railroad System of Massachusetts*, 10.

19 John E. Clark, *Railroads in the Civil War: The Impact of Management on Victory and Defeat* (Baton Rouge: Louisiana State Univ. Press, 2001), 35–38; Weber, *Northern Railroads*, 42–43.

20 Albert Fink, "The Railroad Problem and Its Solution," *Argument before the Committee on Commerce of the U.S. House . . . , Jan. 14, 15, 16, 1880* (New York: Russell Brothers Printers, 1882), 49–51.

21 Albert Fink, *Testimony of Albert Fink before the Select Committee on Interstate Commerce of the United States Senate . . . New York, May 21, 1885* (Washington, D.C.: GPO, 1885), 22.

22 Vance contends regional rather than national integration was determined in part by geographical route ways, in *North American Railroad*, 111–15; George Rogers Taylor and Irene Neu, *The American Railroad Network, 1861–1890* (Cambridge: Harvard Univ. Press, 1956), 53–57, 49–83.

23 Ellis Paxson Oberholtzer, *Jay Cooke: Financier of the Civil War*, 2 vols. (Philadelphia: George W. Jacobs, 1907), 1:51, 56–61, 101–2; capital, Henrietta M. Larson, *Jay Cooke: Private Banker* (Cambridge: Harvard Univ. Press, 1936), 98; David M. Gische, "The New York City Banks and the Development of the National Banking System, 1860–1870," *American Journal of Legal History* 23 (Jan. 1979): 26.

24 Oberholtzer, *Jay Cooke*, 1:131.

25 Ibid., 207–11.

26 Sven Beckert, *The Monied Metropolis: New York City and the Consolidation of the American*

Bourgeoisie (New York: Cambridge Univ. Press, 2001), 121–23; Gische, "New York City Banks," 32–38.

27 Oberholtzer, *Jay Cooke*, 1:212–325, esp. 212–22; Cooke to Chase, Oct. 25, Nov. 12, 1862, r. 23, Chase Papers.

28 Larson, *Jay Cooke*, 119–51, esp. 124–27.

29 Ibid., 96–118; Oberholtzer, *Jay Cooke*, 1:159–65; Beckert, *Monied Metropolis*, 118.

30 Oberholtzer, *Jay Cooke*, 1:133–325, esp. 151, 163–64, 187–88, 193, 229, 231; John Lauritz Larson, *Internal Improvement: National Public Works and the Promise of Popular Government in the Early United States* (Chapel Hill: Univ. of North Carolina Press, 2001), 77; Richard Eugene Sylla: *The American Capital Market, 1846–1914: A Study of the Effects of Public Policy on Economic Development* (New York: Arno Press, 1975), 146–61; Naomi R. Lamoreaux, *Insider Lending: Banks, Personal Connections, and Economic Development in Industrial New England* (New York: Cambridge Univ. Press, 1994), 90–91; John A. James, *Money and Capital Markets in Postbellum America* (Princeton: Princeton Univ. Press, 1978), 74–75; Fisk and Hatch, *Memoranda concerning Government Bonds for the Information of Investors . . .* , 8th ed. (New York, 1881); Larson, *Jay Cooke*, 117.

31 Salmon Chase to J. Cooke, Oct. 25, 1861, J. Cooke to Chase, Oct. 30, 1861, Chase Papers, r. 17.

32 Salmon Chase to J. Cooke, Nov. 21, Dec. 16, 1861, Cooke to Chase, Nov. 5, 1861, r. 18; Chase to J. Cooke, Feb. 2, 7, 9, March 7, 8, 22, 1862, J. Cooke to Chase, Feb. 8, March 10, 22, 1862, Chase Papers, r. 19; Cooke to Chase, June 28, 1862, Cooke Papers; Chase to Cooke, Nov. 13, 1862, Chase Papers, r. 23; Oberholtzer, *Jay Cooke*, 1:207–11, 275.

33 Chase to Cooke, April 29, 1862, Cooke to Chase, April 30, 1862, Chase Papers, r. 20, Cooke to Chase, July 5, 1862, r. 21, Chase Papers.

34 Oberholtzer, *Jay Cooke*, 1:255–63; Chase to Cooke, June 1, 1863, r. 27, Chase Papers.

35 Oberholtzer, *Jay Cooke*, 1:273–75; Cooke to Chase, June 1, 1863, Chase to Cooke, June 2, July 8, 1863, r. 27, Chase Papers.

36 Gische, "New York City Banks," 21–67.

37 Harvey E. Fisk, "Fisk and Hatch, Bankers and Dealers in Government Securities, 1862–1885," *Journal of Economic and Business History* 2 (Aug. 1930): 707–8.

38 Fisk to Alexander Fisk, Sept. 11, 1883, in *Letters of Harvey Fisk*, ed. Harvey Edwin Fisk (New York, 1896).

39 Fisk and Hatch, *Memoranda concerning Government Bonds*.

40 Ibid.

41 Poor, *Manual, 1872–73*, xxxii–xxxiii.

42 Arthur M. Johnson and Barry E. Supple, *Boston Capitalists and Western Railroads; A Study in the Nineteenth-Century Railroad Investment Process* (Cambridge: Harvard Univ. Press, 1967), 197; Maury Klein, *Union Pacific*, vol. 1, *Birth of a Railroad, 1862–1893* (Garden City, N.Y.: Doubleday, 1987), 13–16; David Bain, *Empire Express: Building the First Transcontinental Railroad* (New York: Viking, 1999), 115, 141–43; Robert Fogel, *The Union Pacific: A Case in Premature Enterprise* (Baltimore: Johns Hopkins Univ. Press, 1960), 48.

43 David Lavender, *The Great Persuader: The Biography of Collis P. Huntington* (Niwot: Univ. Press of Colorado, 1998, orig. ed. 1969), 105–7.

44 Ibid., 95, 388.

45 Ibid., 1–10, 94–95.

46 Bain, *Empire Express*, 89–93; Lavender, *Great Persuader*, 95.

47 Bain, *Empire Express*, 91–93; Lavender, *Great Persuader*, 97, 121.

48 Bain, *Empire Express*, 142; *Report of the Commission and of the Minority Commissioner of the*

United States Pacific Railway Commission . . . (Washington, D.C.: GPO, 1887), 71; Lavender, *Great Persuader*, 140.

49 "An Act to aid in the construction of a railroad and telegraph line from the Missouri river to the Pacific ocean, and to secure to the government the use of the same for postal, military, and other purposes," Act of July 1, 1862, *Statutes at Large* 12 (1863): 489; Klein, *Union Pacific*, 22–67; Bain, *Empire Express*, 181–260.

50 Bain, *Empire Express*, 153–56.

51 Klein, *Union Pacific*, 16, 23–24.

52 John L. Larson, *Bonds of Enterprise: John Murray Forbes and Western Development in America's Railway Age,* expanded ed. (Iowa City: Univ. of Iowa Press, 2001), esp. 53–109; Johnson and Supple, *Boston Capitalists*, 197–98; Richard Overton, *Perkins/Budd: Railway Statesmen of the Burlington* (Westport, Conn.: Greenwood Press, 1982), 3.

53 Overton, *Perkins/Budd*, xx.

54 Dunlavy, *Politics and Industrialization,* 45–46, 50, 96; Fogel, *Union Pacific*, 58–60, 97. For growth of markets, see Jonathan B. Baskin, "The Development of Corporate Financial Markets in Britain and the United States, 1600–1914: Overcoming Asymmetric Information," *Business History Review* 62, no. 2 (1988): 210–11; Robert Cootner, "The Role of Railroads in United States Economic Growth," *Journal of Economic History* 23 (Dec. 1963): 477–521, esp. 488.

55 Lavender, *Great Persuader*, 148, 153.

56 Bain, *Empire Express*, 147, 151–56, 201; Lavender, *Great Persuader*, 154.

57 Nathaniel Hawthorne, "Chiefly about War Matters," *Atlantic Monthly*, July 1862, pp. 59–60; http://www.cr.nps.gov/nr/travel/wash/dc36.htm; Bain, *Empire Express*, 178–80; Klein, *Union Pacific*, 32–33; Oberholtzer, *Jay Cooke*, 1:188–89.

58 Klein, *Union Pacific*, 26–33.

59 Hopkins to CPH, Feb. 16, 1864, CPH Papers, ser. 1, r. 1.

60 Klein, *Union Pacific*, 31; *Public Aids to Transportation*, vol. 2, *Aids to Railroads and Related Subjects* (Washington, D.C.: GPO, 1938), table 2, p. 15.

61 Sec. 5, Act of July 1, 1862, *Statutes at Large* 12 (1863): 489. The case was *United States* v. *Union Pacific Railroad Company*, 91 U.S. 72; 23 L. Ed. 224; 1875 U.S. LEXIS 1337; 2 A.F.T.R. (P-H) 2357; 1 Otto 72, Nov. 29, 1875, decided.

62 *Arguments of Horace White* . . . *House Committee on the Pacific Railroad, Union Pacific Railroad Discriminations*, 45th Cong., 2d sess., 1878, 1–3, copy in CB&Q, 63, 1870, 6.8, Pacific Railroad File, no. 29.

63 *Report to the Stockholders of the Union Pacific Railroad, for the Year 1875* (Boston, 1876), 37; "An Act to Authorize the Commissioners of Her Majesty's Treasury to Guarantee the Payment of a Loan . . . 21 July 1873," in *Correspondence respecting the Canadian Pacific Railroad Act So Far As Regards British Columbia* (London: Harrison and Sons, 1875), 98–99.

64 Klein, *Union Pacific*, 31.

65 James C. Scott, *Seeing Like a State: How Certain Schemes to Improve the Human Condition Have Failed* (New Haven: Yale Univ. Press, 1998), 50–52.

66 Henry George, *Our Land and Land Policy*, in *The Complete Works of Henry George* (New York: Doubleday, Page, 1904, orig. ed. 1871), 8:24; Tevis to CPH, Jan. 29, 1878, CPH Papers, ser. 1, r. 14.

67 *Public Aids to Transportation*, vol. 2, table 13; James B. Hedges, *The Federal Railway Land Subsidy Policy of Canada* (Cambridge: Harvard Univ. Press, 1934), 63. See also David M. Ellis, "The Railroads and the Land Office: Administrative Policy and the Land Patent Controversy, 1864–96," *Mississippi Valley Historical Review* 46 (March 1960): 698; David M. Ellis, "The Forfeiture of Railroad Land Grants, 1867–1894," *The Mississippi Valley Historical Review* 33 (1946): 27–60. "Congressional Land Grants for Railroads," Poor, *Manual, 1873–74*, 696–701;

Klein, *Union Pacific*, 514–15; Total Sales of Lands by C.P. R.R. Co., including also the Cal & Oregon R.R. Co. to Jan. 1, 1872, LB, 11:83, box 25, Timothy Hopkins Transportation Collection, 1826–1942, M0097 Special Collections and University Archives, Stanford Univ.

68 *Report of the Auditor of Railroad Accounts*, 46th Cong., 2d sess., 1911, H. Ex. Doc. 1, table 13, 113–15; Leslie E. Decker, *Railroads, Lands, and Politics: The Taxation of the Railroad Land Grants, 1864–1897* (Providence: Brown Univ. Press, 1964), 20–22; Hedges, *Federal Railway Land Subsidy Policy of Canada*, 139.

69 *Public Aids to Transportation*, 2:29, 111.

70 H. Craig Miner and William E. Unrau, *The End of Indian Kansas: A Study of Cultural Revolution, 1854–1871* (Lawrence: Regents Press of Kansas, 1978), 47–48; Paul Wallace Gates, *Fifty Million Acres: Conflicts over Kansas Land Policy, 1854–90* (Ithaca: Cornell Univ. Press, 1954), 137–39; Mark Twain and Charles Dudley Warner, *The Gilded Age: A Tale of To-Day*, 2 vols. (New York: Harper & Brothers, 1915, orig. ed. 1873), 1:198.

71 Decker, *Railroads, Lands, and Politics*, 65–67.

72 Pacific Railway Act (1862), chap. 120; Act of July 2, 1864, *Statutes at Large* 13 (1865): 356; Klein, *Union Pacific*, 16.

73 Lavender, *Great Persuader*, 164; Act of March 3, 1865, *Statutes at Large* 13 (1865): 504.

74 "General Railroad Law of California: An Act to provide for the Incorporation of Railroad Companies, and the management of the affairs thereof, and other matters relating thereto" (approved May 20, 1861; as amended to May 6, 1862). That the company may have sold $100,000 is based on 10 percent down on 10,000 shares. *Annual Report of the Central Pacific Railroad Company of California to the Secretary of State of California of the Year Ending the Thirty first Day of December A.D. 1869*, California State Archives.

75 Lavender, *Great Persuader*, 146–47; Fletcher M. Green, "Origins of the Crédit Mobilier of America," *Mississippi Valley Historical Review* 46 (Sept. 1959): 238–51; Klein, *Union Pacific*, 35; William Z. Ripley, *Railroads: Finance and Organization* (New York: Longmans, Green, 1915), 10–18.

76 *Report of the Commission and of the Minority Commission of the United States Pacific Railway Commission* (Washington, D.C.: GPO, 1887), 69–70; Bain, *Empire Express*, 129; Carman and Mueller, "The Contract and Finance Company and the Central Pacific Railroad," *Mississippi Valley Historical Review* 14 (Dec. 1927): 333; Hopkins to CPH, Feb. 16, 1866, CPH Papers, ser. 1, r. 1. For letting of contract and the shares involved see CPH to Hopkins, May 11, 1866, LB, 1:27, box 20, Hopkins Collection.

77 CPH to HEH, Jan. 5, 1898, HEH 4168, box 62, HEH Collection, 1794–1970; E. B. Crocker to Hopkins, March 29, 1867, LB, 10:7, box 24, Hopkins Collection; Carman and Mueller, "Contract and Finance Company," 333–34; Bain, *Empire Express*, 408, 739; Ripley, *Railroads: Finance and Organization*, 35–36; PRC, 10:71–77, 8:4542, 4548.

78 Bain, *Empire Express*, 207–8, 252–56.

79 Ibid., 206–8.

80 Stanley P. Hirshson, *Grenville M. Dodge: Soldier, Politician, Railroad Pioneer* (Bloomington: Indiana Univ. Press, 1967), 8–9, 69–71; Bain, *Empire Express*, 159.

81 Hirshson, *Grenville M. Dodge*, 50–57, 60, 67, 73, 89.

82 Hopkins to CPH, July 19, 1865, Feb. 16, 1866, CPH Papers, ser. 1, r. 1.

83 Hopkins to CPH, Feb. 15, 1867, E. B. Crocker to CPH, Feb. 12, 25, 1867, Stanford to CPH, Feb. 8, 1867, CPH Papers, ser. 1, r. 1.

84 Crocker to CPH, N.Y., June 16, 1868, box 3, f. 5, Stanford Papers.

85 Lavender, *Great Persuader*, 166.

86 Klein, *Union Pacific*, 67–68; Bain, *Empire Express*, 211; Johnson and Supple, *Boston Capitalists*, 203.

87 "Patterns of Change in Railroad Company Board Members, 1872–1894," Spatial History Project, Stanford Univ.

88 "Distribution of Union Pacific Stockholders by City (1869)," Spatial History Project, Stanford Univ.

89 Johnson and Supple, *Boston Capitalists*, 201–15. Klein, *Union Pacific*, 67–68, 80–83, 108–15, 122–28.

90 Johnson and Supple, *Boston Capitalists*, 209–10; Testimony of Cornelius S. Bushnell, *Report of the Select Committee of the House of Representatives, Appointed under the Resolution of January 6, 1873. To Make Inquiry in Relation to the Affairs of the Union Pacific Railroad Company, the Crédit Mobilier of America and Other Matters . . .* , 42nd Cong., 3d sess., 1873, H. Rept. 78, 40–42.

91 Johnson and Supple, *Boston Capitalists*, 195–215; Maury Klein, *Union Pacific*, 34–44.

92 Klein, *Union Pacific*, 142–43, 156.

93 Sylla, *American Capital Market*, 146–61; Lamoreaux, *Insider Lending*, 90–91; James, *Money and Capital Markets*, 74–75; Fisk and Hatch, *Memoranda concerning Government Bonds*; Larson, *Jay Cooke*, 117.

94 Richard White, "Information, Markets, and Corruption: Transcontinental Railroads in the Gilded Age," *Journal of American History* 90 (June 2003): 19–43; Baskin, "Development of Corporate Financial Markets," 209, 215–18; CPH to Crocker, Jan. 8, 1870, *Huntington Letters*, 3:57; Jeffrey Williamson, "Watersheds and Turning Points: Conjectures on the Long-Term Impact of Civil War Financing," *Journal of Economic History* 34, no. 3 (1974): 651; Hopkins to CPH, July 19, 1865, CPH Papers, ser. 1, r. 1.

95 White, "Information, Markets and Corruption," 19–43; Hopkins to CPH, Nov. 11, 1873, CPH Papers, ser. 1, r. 5, Hopkins to CPH, Dec. 4, 1873, ser. 1, r. 6; Fisk and Hatch to the Holders of Central Pacific Railroad Bonds, Jan. 1, 1874, LB 6:45, L. Von Hoffman and Co. to CPH, Nov. 24, 1873, box 22, Hopkins Collection; *Annual Report of the Board of Directors of the Central Pacific Railroad Co. to the Stockholders for the Year Ending Dec. 31, 1873* (San Francisco, 1874), 7; *New-York Daily Tribune*, March 19, 1877, copy in LB, 9:165, box 24, Hopkins Collection; *Railway Age*, Aug. 24, 1876, p. 204; "An English Opinion," ibid., April 18, 1878, p. 206.

96 Mark Summers, *The Era of Good Stealings* (New York: Oxford Univ. Press, 1993), 50–51; Fogel, *Union Pacific*, 66–73.

97 Summers, *Era of Good Stealings*, 50–51; Fogel, *Union Pacific*, 66–73; John P. Davis, *The Union Pacific Railway: A Study in Railway Politics, History and Economics* (Chicago: S. C. Griggs, 1894), 172–73; *Public Aids to Transportation*, 2:15–16.

98 Fogel, *Union Pacific*, 70–73.

99 *PRC*, 74. For the calculations, see 71–75, table, p. 81. *Public Aid to Transportation*, vol. 2, table 16, p. 132.

100 Heywood Fleisig, "The Central Pacific Railroad and the Railroad Land Grant Controversy," *Journal of Economic History* 35 (Sept. 1975): 555–56; Poor, *Manual*, 564, 682; "The Railroad Problem in American Politics, August 1, 1874," in Crane, ed., *Newton Booth of California*, 161.

101 Poor, *Manual*, 682.

102 Will Bagley, ed., *Scoundrel's Tales: The Samuel Brannan Papers*, vol. 3 of *Kingdom in the West: The Mormons and the American Frontier* (Spokane, Wash.: Arthur Clark, 1999), 264–81, 285–90.

103 Bagley, *Scoundrel's Tales*, 264–81; Lavender, *Great Persuader*, 260–61, 280, 301; *David Stewart, vs. Collis P. Huntington, Depositions of Leland Stanford and Charles Crocker, Taken on the Part of the Defendants* (New York, 1881), 90–125; *David Stewart, vs. Collis P. Huntington, Depositions of David Stewart, E. H. Miller, Jr., Moses G. Cobb, and G. Frank Smith, Taken on the Part of the Plaintiffs* (New York, 1882), 56–59, both bound in *Central Pacific Railroad Pamphlets, 1882–1887*, Stanford Univ. Library; Testimony of Moses G. Cobb, Aug. 11, 1887, *PRC*, 6:3247.

104 Sanderson to CPH, Feb. 4, 1871, LB, 11:59, box 25, Hopkins Collection.
105 Bain, *Empire Express*, 666–69.

A Railroad Life: H. K. Thomas

1 H. K. Thomas Diary, 1870–71, Sept. 23, 29, 1870, Beinecke Library, Yale Univ.
2 Ibid., April 19, 1871.
3 Ibid., May 5, 1871.
4 Ibid., May 3, Aug. 22, 1871.
5 Ibid., June 20, 1871.
6 Ibid., July 17, 1871.
7 Ibid., July 19, 1871.
8 Ibid., Sept. 27, 1870.
9 Ibid., April 12, June 17, 29, 30, Aug. 15, 19, 1871.
10 Ibid., Dec. 10, 1870 (buffalo), March 15, Aug. 22, 1871 (elk).
11 Ibid., Jan. 22, 1871.
12 Ibid., March 12, 1871.
13 Ibid., April 21, 1871.
14 Ibid., April 6, 1871.
15 Ibid., April 7, 11, 1871.
16 Ibid., Oct. 10, 1870.
17 H. K. Thomas Diary, Jan. 27, 1871.
18 Ibid., Dec. 8. 1870, March 8, 9, 1871.
19 Ibid., Dec. 8, 1870.
20 Ibid., March 10, 1871.
21 Ibid., Dec. 17, 1870.
22 Ibid., Jan. 20, 1871.
23 Ibid., Aug. 21, 1871.
24 Ibid., April 28, 1871.
25 David A. Wolff, *Industrializing the Rockies: Growth, Competition, and Turmoil in the Coalfields of Colorado and Wyoming, 1868–1914* (Boulder: Univ. Press of Colorado, 2003), 22.
26 H. K. Thomas Diary, April 4, Sept. 2, 1871.
27 Ibid., Oct. 17, 1870.
28 Ibid., Oct, 26, 27, 1870.
29 Ibid., Jan. 27, 1871.
30 Ibid., May 27, 1871.
31 Ibid., April 25, 1871.
32 Ibid., April 27, 1871.
33 Ibid., Jan. 8, 1871.
34 Ibid., March 11, 1871.
35 Ibid., Sept. 25, 1870.
36 Ibid., Oct. 28, 1870. Thomas recorded the entire trip under this date; he returned Dec. 4, 1870.
37 Ibid., May 7, 1871.
38 Ibid., Dec. 13, 1870.
39 Ibid., Aug. 4, 1871.
40 Ibid., Aug 2, 1871.
41 Ibid., Dec. 24, 25, 26, 1870.
42 Ibid., Feb. 24, 1871, Feb. 26, 1871.
43 Ibid., Jan. 5. 1871.

44 Ibid., Oct. 4, 1870.
45 Ibid., August 17, 1871.
46 Ibid., March 11, 1871.
47 Ibid., Sept. 26, 1870.
48 Ibid., April 12, May 14, 1871.
49 Ibid., March 12, 1871.
50 Ibid., June 28, 1871.
51 Ibid., June 25, 1871.
52 Ibid., Aug. 7, 1871.
53 Ibid., Aug. 8, 28, 1871.
54 Ibid., Sept. 5, 1871.
55 Ibid., Sept. 13, 14, 26, 27, 1871.
56 Ibid., back pages.

CHAPTER 2: ANNUS HORRIBILIS: 1873

1 CPH to Hopkins, Sept. 27, 1873, LB, 5:111, box 22, Hopkins Collection.
2 Towne to CPH, Dec. 5, 1871, CPH Papers, ser. 1, r. 4; Maury Klein, *Union Pacific* (Garden City, N.Y.: Doubleday, 1987), 200–201.
3 Towne to CPH, Dec. 16, 1871, CPH Papers, ser. 1, r. 4.
4 Towne to CPH, Dec. 19, 1871, CPH Papers, ser. 1, r. 4.
5 Cummins to CPH, Dec. 21, 1871, Towne to CPH, Dec. 23, 24, 27, 1872, CPH Papers, ser. 1, r. 4.
6 Klein, *Union Pacific*, 285–86.
7 A. N. Towne to CPH, Jan. 24, 1876, CPH Papers, ser. 1, r. 9; for other bad winters, Towne to CPH, Jan. 26, Feb. 7, 1876, ibid., Towne to CPH, Dec. 18, 1877, ibid., ser. 1, r. 13; Towne to CPH, Jan. 17, 1878, Feb. 26, 1878, ibid., ser. 1, r. 14.
8 Keith L. Bryant, *History of the Atchison, Topeka, and Santa Fe Railway* (New York: Macmillan, 1974), 2–3.
9 Ibid., 84; *The Atlantic & Pacific Railroad Co.: The Route and Its Advantages* . . . (Boston: Printed for the Company, 1870), 5; *The Route for a Railroad to the Pacific Ocean near the Thirty-fifth Parallel of Latitude: Its Resources and Advantages* (Boston: Printed for the Company, 1870), 2–3.
10 *Annual Report of the Directors, Missouri, Kansas, and Texas Railway*, 1872–73 (New York: Missouri, Kansas and Texas Lines, 1873), 24, in *Railway Pamphlets*, vol. 193, Stanford Univ; H. Craig Miner, *The Corporation and the Indian: Tribal Sovereignty and Industrial Civilization in Indian Territory* (Columbia: Univ. of Missouri Press, 1976), 44–46; L. U. Reavis, "The Atlantic and Pacific Railway," *Inland Monthly*, Nov. 1872, p. 568.
11 L. U. Reavis, *An International Railway to the City of Mexico: An Address by L. U. Reavis* (St. Louis: Printed by Woodward, Tiernan & Hale, 1879), in Pamphlets, Railroads of Mexico, vol. 2, no. 10.
12 Ellis P. Oberholtzer, *Jay Cooke: Financier of the Civil War*, 2 vols. (Philadelphia: George W. Jacobs, 1907), 2:295.
13 Poor, *Manual, 1877–78*, viii; Poor, *Manual, 1878*, i.
14 "Tracing Railroad Directors, 1872–1894," and "Patterns of Change in Railroad Company Board Members, 1872–1894," Spatial History Project, Stanford Univ.
15 "Patterns of Change in Railroad Company Board Members, 1872–1894," Spatial History Project, Stanford Univ.
16 Heather Cox Richardson, *The Greatest Nation of the Earth: Republican Economic Policies during*

the Civil War (Cambridge: Harvard Univ. Press, 1997), 170–72, 175, 178–80; Dodge to Scott, Jan. 12, 1874, LBs, Texas & Pacific Railroad, box 160, Dodge Papers; Oberholtzer, *Jay Cooke*, 2:156.

17 Thomas Canfield, Northern Pacific Railroad, *Partial Report to the Board of Directors, May, 1870*, p. 55, Graff 573, Newberry Library, Chicago; Pierre Berton, *The National Dream: The Great Railway, 1871–1881* (Toronto: McClelland and Stewart, 1970), 60–65.

18 Robert Gorsuch, *The Republic of Mexico and Railroads: A Brief Review of Her Past History and Present Condition* (New York: Hosford & Sons, 1881), 9–12; *El General W. S. Rosecrans y el ferrocarril de Tuxpán al Pacifico* (Mexico: José Batiza, 1870), no. 8; *Proyecto de un ferrocarril y telégrafo desde la línea divisoria de México y los Estados-Unidos, partiendo del Presidio del Norte sobre el Rio Grande hasta el mar de Cortés ó golfo de California . . .* (México: F. Diaz de Leon y Santiago White, 1868), no. 7; *Proyecto del ferrocarril internacional sometido al Congreso de la union* (Mexico: Imprenta del Gobierno, 1872), in Pamphlets, Railroads of Mexico, vol. 1, no. 15; *Report of the Secretary of Finance of the United States of Mexico of the 15th of January 1879 . . .* (New York: N. Ponce De Leon, 1880), 51–54; John Mason Hart, *Empire and Revolution: The Americans in Mexico since the Civil War* (Berkeley: Univ. of California Press, 2002), 33–59.

19 David Pletcher, *Rails, Mines, and Progress: Seven American Promoters in Mexico, 1867–1911* (Ithaca: Cornell Univ. Press, 1958), 37, 48; Plumb to George E. Church, Jan. 27, 1872, box 2, f. 20, Plumb Papers; *Copia para el Sov. Ministo de Hacienda de las bases presentadas informalmente al Ministro de Fomento de la República de México, por Don Eduardo Lee Plumb en representacion de la "Compañia de Ferrocarril Ynternacional de Texas". . . Abril de 1872*, box 2, f. 20, Plumb Papers; Hart, *Empire and Revolution*, 31.

20 George Earl Church to Plumb, June 11, 1872, box 2, f. 21, Plumb Papers.

21 Pletcher, *Rails, Mines, and Progress*, 37–49; Hart, *Empire and Revolution*, 10–16, 31–34, 40–41, 37–39, 80.

22 Pletcher, *Rails, Mines, and Progress*, 37–49; Hart, *Empire and Revolution*, 10–16, 31–34.

23 Pletcher, *Rails, Mines, and Progress*, 37–49, 152–54; Robert G. Athearn, *Rebel of the Rockies: A History of the Denver and Rio Grande Western Railroad* (New Haven: Yale Univ. Press, 1962), 5–37; Hart, *Empire and Revolution*, 31–34, 40, 46–49, 52.

24 Pletcher, *Rails, Mines, and Progress*, 37–49; Athearn, *Rebel of the Rockies*, 5–37; quote, Augustus J. Veenendaal Jr., *Slow Train to Paradise: How Dutch Investment Helped Build American Railroads* (Stanford: Stanford Univ. Press, 1996), 65; Hart, *Empire and Revolution*, 31–34.

25 Hart, *Empire and Revolution*, 49–51.

26 Ibid., 52–53.

27 Plumb to Church, July 17, 1872, Church to Plumb, June 11, 1872, Plumb to Wm. Hunter, Aug. 23, 1872, box 2, f. 21, Plumb to Hamilton Fish, Aug. 15, 1873, box 2, f. 23; Plumb quote, Plumb to Horace Porter, Sept. 29, 1871, box 2, f. 19, Plumb Papers; Rose Kingsley, *South by West*, ed. with a preface by the Rev. Charles Kingsley (London: W. Isbister, 1874), 183; Pletcher, *Rails, Mines, and Progress*, 68–71.

28 Pletcher, *Rails, Mines, and Progress*, 41–51.

29 John S. Fisher, *A Builder of the West: The Life of William Jackson Palmer* (Caldwell, Idaho: Caxton Printers, 1939), 210, 217.

30 Kingsley, *South by West*, 183, 225–26, and 207–31 in general.

31 Charles Kingsley, "Preface," *South by West*, viii–ix; Kingsley, *South by West*, 284.

32 Henrietta M. Larson, *Jay Cooke: Private Banker* (Cambridge: Harvard Univ. Press, 1936), 254, 273–95. The Northern Pacific, in part, sold itself to the government as a means to subdue Indians. See Robert G. Angevine, *The Railroad and the State: War, Politics, and Technology in Nineteenth-Century America* (Stanford: Stanford Univ. Press, 2004), 194, 198–99.

33 Larson, *Jay Cooke*, 260, 277.

34 This stock had a par or face value of $41 million and was arbitrarily assigned a value of $600,000. The stock would be issued incrementally as the road was completed. The bonds were a paying investment. See Larson, *Jay Cooke*, 286.

35 Ibid., 287.

36 A. A. den Otter, *The Philosophy of Railways: The Transcontinental Railway Idea in British North America* (Toronto: Univ. of Toronto Press, 1997), 158.

37 John Harnsberger, *Jay Cooke and Minnesota: The Formative Years of the Northern Pacific Railroad, 1868–1873* (New York: Arno Press, 1981), 200–201.

38 Cooke to Gen. George Sargent, Feb. 20, 1870, Northern Pacific, Letters no. 1 (LB), Jan. 19, 1870–Sept. 27, 1871, Private Letters, Jay Cooke, pp. 88–89, Cooke Papers.

39 Larson, *Jay Cooke*, 337–38; den Otter, *Philosophy of Railways*, 168–69; Harnsberger, *Jay Cooke and Minnesota*, 202–5.

40 Larson, *Jay Cooke*, 338; den Otter, *Philosophy of Railways*, 161–62, 170.

41 Cooke to Gen. George Sargent, April 20, 1871, Northern Pacific, Letters no. 1 (LB), Jan. 19, 1870–Sept. 27, 1871, Private Letters, Jay Cooke; tributary, Cooke to Geo. W. Colton, March 26, 1873, LBs, 1873, Cooke Papers.

42 Den Otter, *Philosophy of Railways*, 158.

43 Pierre Berton, *The Impossible Railway* (New York: Knopf, 1972), 8; den Otter, *Philosophy of Railways*, 158.

44 Den Otter, *Philosophy of Railroads*, 170–73.

45 A. W. Currie, *The Grand Trunk Railway of Canada* (Toronto: Univ. of Toronto Press, 1957), 85–137, 299–306; Ann Carlos and Frank Lewis, "The Creative Financing of an Unprofitable Enterprise: The Grand Trunk Railway of Canada, 1853–1881," *Explorations in Economic History* 32 (1995): 273–301; den Otter, *Philosophy of Railways*, 176–78.

46 Den Otter, *Philosophy of Railroads*, 173; enclosure 5, no. 4, Statement by Mr. McMullen with Documents (from the *Montreal Herald*), *Canadian Pacific Railway*, Correspondence, 64.

47 Earl of Dufferin to Earl of Kimberly, Aug. 15, 1873, no. 4. pp. 7, 30. Hincks and Macdonald later tried to cast all this in a very different light. Earl of Dufferin to the Earl of Kimberley, Aug. 15, 1873, pp. 7, 30; Testimony of Sir Francis Hincks, Sept. 4, 1873, "Report of the Royal Commissioners," 94–103, but others associated him with the original goal of soliciting American capital. Testimony of Jan Charles Chapais, Sept. 12, 1873, ibid., 141–42; Testimony of John Macdonald, Sept. 17, 1873, ibid., 171–80, 186; all in *Canadian Pacific Railway Correspondence*; den Otter, *Philosophy of Railroads*, 24, 173–75.

48 Den Otter, *Philosophy of Railroads*, 175.

49 M. John Lubetkin, *Jay Cooke's Gamble: The Northern Pacific Railway, the Sioux, and the Panic of 1873* (Norman: Univ. of Oklahoma Press, 2006), 80–267.

50 Cooke to Windom, July 20, 1871, Northern Pacific, Letters no. 1 (LB), Jan. 19, 1870–Sept. 27, 1871, Cooke Papers.

51 Paul Wallace Gates, *Fifty Million Acres: Conflicts over Kansas Land Policy, 1854–1890* (New York: Atherton Press, 1966), 153–93; H. Craig Miner and William E. Unrau, *The End of Indian Kansas: A Study of Cultural Revolution* (Lawrence: Regents Press of Kansas, 1978), 116–19, quote 116.

52 Miner and Unrau, *End of Indian Kansas*, 27–34.

53 Ibid., 121–32; Gates, *Fifty Million Acres*, 194–229.

54 Francis Paul Prucha, *The Great Father: The United States Government and the American Indians*, 2 vols. (Lincoln: Univ. of Nebraska Press, 1984), 1:527–33.

55 Duane Swanson, "The Northern Pacific Railroad and the Sisseton-Wahpeton Sioux: A Case in Land Acquisition" (M.A. thesis, Univ. of Delaware, 1972), 24, 27, 29, 31, 33–36.

56 Whether Cowen was paid is uncertain, but negotiations moved forward. See ibid., 41, 43–44,

48–54; George Becker and James Smith Jr. to Cooke, Sept. 5, 1872, Jay Cooke to Brother Harry, May 24, 1872; Cooke to Cass, March 17, 1873, Cooke to B. F. Wade, March 22, 1873, Cooke to Maj. Benj. Thompson, March 22, 1873, LBs, all in Cooke Papers.

57 Swanson, "Northern Pacific Railroad," 61–64; Cooke to Professor Carey (?), March 10, 1873, Cooke to Bro. Harry, March 14, 1873, LBs, Cooke Papers.

58 Cooke to Wetmore, St. John's N.B., May 23, 1873, LBs, Cooke Papers.

59 *Argument of Colonel E. C. Boudinot before the Committee on Territories, Jan. 29, 1878* (Alexandria, Va.: G. H. Ramey, 1878), 33.

60 George Ward, Lewiston Mills, to H. L. Dawes, Nov. 28, 1866; Dawes to Ward, Nov. 29, 1866 (two letters), box 37, Crédit Mobilier, Dawes Papers.

61 Oakes Ames, Receipt, Jan. 23, 1868, box 37, Crédit Mobilier, Dawes Papers.

62 Receipt, $195.33, Feb. 10, 1868, Dawes to "My Ever Dear Wife," June 11, 1868, receipt, June 11, 1868, Ames to Dawes, Oct. 30, 1871, box 37, Crédit Mobilier, Dawes Papers.

63 Dawes to Ames, Nov. 19, 1872, box 37, Crédit Mobilier, Dawes Papers; Klein, *Union Pacific*, 291.

64 Ames to Dawes, Oct. 18, 1872, James Garfield to Dawes, March 23, 1873, box 37, Crédit Mobilier, Dawes Papers.

65 Klein, *Union Pacific*, 292–93; J. W. Patterson, *Observations on the Report of the Committee of the Senate of the United States respecting the Crédit Mobilier of America* (Washington, D.C.: McGill & Witherow, 1873), 41–42, copy in box 37, Crédit Mobilier, Dawes Papers; Harry J. Brown and Frederick D. Williams, eds., *The Diary of James A. Garfield*, 4 vols. (East Lansing: Michigan State Univ. Press, 1967), 2:88–89, entry of Sept. 9, 1872.

66 Mark Summers, *The Era of Good Stealings* (New York: Oxford Univ. Press, 1993), 50–54.

67 Klein, *Union Pacific*, 295–96. Jay Cooke took a similar stance. See Cooke to Schuyler Colfax, Feb. 24, 1873, LBs, Cooke Papers; Summers, *Era of Good Stealings*, 51–55.

68 Klein, *Union Pacific*, 302–3; Summers, *Era of Good Stealings*, 50–54.

69 Klein, *Union Pacific*, 291–302; Summers, *Era of Good Stealings*, 231–37.

70 Cooke to A. H. Barney, Feb. 21, 1873, LBs, Northern Pacific; defends land company, Cooke to Edwin Ellis, March 31, 1873, Cooke to Wm. McKnight, May 26, 1873; bond guarantees, Cooke to Fahnestock, March 21, 1873, all in LBs, Cooke Papers; Oberholtzer, *Jay Cooke*, 2:303, 331–32.

71 Fear of Justice Department, Cooke to Brother Harry, July 5, 1873, LBs, Cooke Papers; Union Pacific Railroad in United States Courts, Pacific Railroad file, no. 32: Crédit Mobilier Case, at Hartford, Conn., U.S. Circuit Court, Justice Hunt, etc. (n.p., n.d), 7, 10, 11, 16, copy in CB&Q, B&M (Nebr.), 1870–79, New Lines, 63, 1870, 6.8.

72 Adams to George Miller, April 30, 1886, Memorandum, May 1886; quote, Adams to Hon. A. S. Hewitt, Dec. 10, 1886, all in UP, PO, OC, vol. 37, ser. 2, r. 32.

73 Cooke to Bro. Harry, Feb. 14, 1873, Cooke to Colfax, March 15, 1873, LBs, Cooke Papers.

74 Cooke to Schuyler Colfax, Feb. 27, 24, 1873, LBs, Cooke Papers.

75 Larson, *Jay Cooke*, 351.

76 Jay Cooke to Lorin, Jan. 7, 1873, Cooke to Fahny & Garland, Feb. 1, 1873, Cooke to LDM Sweat, March 1, 1873, Cooke to M. B. Lowry, April 4, 1873, LBs, Cooke Papers; Larson, *Jay Cooke*, 346.

77 Fahnestock to Cooke, Sept. 18, 1869, B.3, f.3-2, Fahnestock Papers.

78 Cooke Memoir, 136, 148.

79 Herman Melville, *The Confidence-Man: His Masquerade* (Evanston: Northwestern Univ. Press, 1984), 75.

80 For attempts to monitor the credibility of stock and bond offerings, see John Bonk to J. L. Worth, Feb. 3, 1876, CPH Papers, ser. 1, r. 9.

81 Richard Bensel, *Yankee Leviathan: The Origins of Central State Authority in America, 1859–1877* (New York: Cambridge Univ. Press, 1990), 243–62; Richard Eugene Sylla, *The American Capital Market, 1846–1914: A Study of the Effects of Public Policy on Economic Development* (New York: Arno Press, 1975), 155–61; Vincent P. Carosso, *Investment Banking in America: A History* (Cambridge: Harvard Univ. Press, 1970), 15–17. For the amounts of bonded debts of railroads, with figures for 1867, including elevated railways, and figures for 1890 excluding them, see U.S. Bureau of the Census, *Historical Statistics of the United States, Colonial Times to 1970*, 2 vols. (Washington, D.C.: GPO, 1975), 2:734, ser. Q, 346–55; Lance E. Davis and Robert E. Gallman, *Evolving Financial Markets and International Capital Flows: Britain, the Americas, and Australia, 1865–1914* (New York: Cambridge Univ. Press, 2001), 5–6, 32, 234, 238, 249–52, 333.

82 Richard White, "Information, Markets, and Corruption: Transcontinental Railroads in the Gilded Age," *Journal of American History* 90 (June 2003): 19–43; Julius Grodinsky, *Transcontinental Railway Strategy, 1869–1893: A Study of Businessmen* (Philadelphia: Univ. of Pennsylvania Press, 1962), 2–4. For European investment in general, see Lance Davis and Robert E. Cull, *International Capital Markets and American Economic Growth, 1820–1914* (New York: Cambridge Univ. Press, 1994), 22–26, for Dutch and Germans and West, 25. For Dutch investment, see Veenendall, *Slow Train to Paradise*; CPH to Stanford, Nov. 16, 1872, LB, 3:37, box 21, Hopkins Collection. David Lavender, *The Great Persuader: The Biography of Collis P. Huntington* (Niwot: Univ. Press of Colorado, 1998), 182; John J. Madden, *British Investment in the United States, 1860–1880* (New York: Garland, 1985), 95–96. For continuing attempts to get information and shape policy, see Edward H. Miller to Speyer & Co., March 21, 1876, ibid., ser. 1, r. 9; Speyer Brothers to Southern Pacific, July 10, 1879, ibid., ser. 2, r. 2, Philip Speyer & Company to CPH, Oct. 31, 1873, LB, 5:163, box 22, Hopkins Collection.

83 CPH to Hopkins, Dec. 19, 1872, LB, 3:177, box 21, Hopkins Collection; Goldsmith and Hart (*sic*) CPH, Oct. 22, 1878, CPH Papers, ser. 1, r. 15.

84 Menaham Blondheim, *News over the Wires: The Telegraph and the Flow of Public Information in America, 1844–1897* (Cambridge: Harvard Univ. Press, 1994), 98–99, 108–9, 191; Richard John, *Network Nation: Inventing American Telecommunications* (Cambridge: Harvard Univ. Press, 2010), 145–46.

85 Blondheim, *News over the Wires*, 129–33, 147–51, 157, 162, 163–68, 174, 98–99; Menaham Blondheim, "Public Sentiment Is Everything: The Union's Public Communications Strategy and the Bogus Proclamation of 1864," *Journal of American History* 89 (Dec. 2002): 6–7, 10, 18–19.

86 CPH to Hopkins, Sept. 15, 1873, LB, 5:59, box 22, Hopkins Collection; Blondheim, *News over the Wires*, 174–77, 183–85, 195.

87 Blondheim, *News over the Wires*, 172, 191.

88 Hopkins to CPH, Nov. 28, 1872, CPH Papers, ser. 1, r. 5; Blondheim, *News over the Wires*, 149, 165, 175; CPH to Hopkins, March 31, 1876, LB, 8:135, box 23, CPH to Stanford, Jan. 30, 1874, LB, 6:121, box 22, Hopkins Collection; CPH to Stanford, Dec. 5, 1870, Jan. 11, 1871 (dated 1870), *Huntington Letters*, 3:219, 235.

89 Adams to Perkins, Sept. 8, 1885, UP, PO, OC, vol. 29, ser. 2, r. 25.

90 CPH to Hopkins, Aug. 25, 1873, LB, 4:162, box 21, Hopkins Collection; Godkin to Villard, June 7, 1893, in William A. Armstrong, ed., *The Gilded Age Letters of E. L. Godkin* (Albany: State Univ. of New York Press, 1974), 446–48; Mahl Memoirs, Huntington J-3, p. 8, box aE461, CPH 1882–1900, Mahl Papers.

91 CPH to Hopkins, Sept. 5, 1873, LB, 5:19, box 22, Hopkins Collection.

92 Harnsberger, *Jay Cooke and Minnesota*, 97–106. For promises to Moorhead and others, see Fahnestock to Cooke, June 22, 1872, June–July 22, 1872, Cooke Papers.

93 Anthony Trollope, *The Way We Live Now* (New York: Random House, 2001).

94 Cooke to Moorhead, July 1, 1871, Northern Pacific, Letters no. 1 (LB), Jan. 19, 1870–Sept. 27, 1871, Private Letters, Jay Cooke, p. 236, Cooke Papers.

95 *Testimony of Wm. Moorhead, Sept. 18, 1874 (2:30 P.M.) in the District Court of the United States, Eastern District of Pennsylvania, In the Matter of . . . Jay Cooke & Co, Bankrupts* (Philadelphia: Allen, Lane & Scotts, 1875), 779, Fahnestock Papers.

96 Larson, *Jay Cooke*, 191–93, 195–97, facing 231; Fahnestock to Cooke, June 8, 1872, Fahnestock to Cooke and Wm. G., Sept. 7, 1872, box 3, f. 3–2, Fahnestock Papers.

97 Robin Winks, *Frederick Billings: A Life* (Berkeley: Univ. of California Press, 1991), 88–89, 193, 195; Harnsberger, *Jay Cooke and Minnesota*, 80–81; Larson, *Jay Cooke*, 258–59, 349, 375, 387; Oberholtzer, *Jay Cooke*, 2:243–45, 23–64. Lubetkin, *Jay Cooke's Gamble*, blames Fahnestock for the bank's fall, but Lubetkin did not use the Cooke Papers, and his evidence, such as it is, seems to have been a rather cryptic comment by Oberholtzer, *Jay Cooke*, 279–82. Cooke Memoir, 138; Fahnestock to Cooke, June 8, 1872, Fahnestock to Cooke and Wm. G., Sept. 7, 1872, box 3, f. 3-2, Fahnestock Papers, Fahnestock to Cooke, June 22, 1872, A. B. Nettleton to Cooke, June 13, 1872, Fahnestock and McCulloch to Cooke, n.d., Sept. 1872, LBs, Cooke Papers.

98 Jay Cooke Jr. to Jay Cooke, Aug. 20, 1872, LBs, Cooke Papers; Red River, Cooke to McCulloch, Sept. 4, 1871, Northern Pacific, Letters no. 1 (LB), Jan. 19, 1870–Sept. 27, 1871, Private Letters, pp. 679–80.

99 Cooke to Lorin, Jan. 7, 1873, Cooke to Cass, Oct. 25, 1872, Cooke Papers; Larson, *Jay Cooke*, 376–77, 392–93, 401, 405; Missouri, Cooke to O. W. Mead, April 1, 1873, LBs, 1873, Cooke Papers; Poor, *Manual, 1873–84*, 393.

100 Fahnestock to Cooke, June 8, 1872, Fahnestock to Cooke and Wm. G., Sept. 7, 1872, box 3, f. 3–2, Fahnestock Papers. For mismanagement, see also Pitt Cooke to Jay Cooke, May 13, 1872, LBs, Cooke Papers.

101 Berton, *Impossible Railway*, 52–55, 77–80, 83, 121; Testimony of John Macdonald, Sept. 17, 1873, "Report of the Royal Commissioners," *Canadian Pacific Railway Correspondence*, 171–73; Americans, J. Gregory Smith to Cooke, March 14, 1872, Cooke Papers; Hugh Allan to "an American gentleman . . . in New York," July 1, 1872, Aug. 7, 1872, 55–57; Earl of Dufferin to Earl of Kimberly, Aug. 15, 1873, no. 4, p. 8; memorandum of Canadian Pacific Railroad Company upon the Statement submitted by the Interoceanic Company to the Govt. of Canada, 34–35; Executive Committee to Provisional President, Interoceanic Railway Company of Canada, Sept. 26, 1872, 43–45; Testimony of Alexander Campbell, April 2, 1873, 158–59, all in *Canadian Pacific Railway Correspondence*; Berton, *Impossible Railway*, 52–55.

102 Cooke to Johnson, Jan. 25, 1873, Cooke to Hon. Wm. Windom, Jan. 24, 1873, LBs, 517 ff., Cooke Papers; Berton, *National Dream*, 88. For quote, see Correspondence between Sir Hugh Allan and his American Partners (from the *Montreal Herald*), Allan to McMullen, Oct. 24, 1872, in Explanatory Statement of Sir Hugh Allan (from the *Montreal Gazette*), encl. 4, no. 4, Earl of Dufferin to Earl of Kimberly, Aug. 15, 1873, 58–64; encl. 5, no. 4, statement by Mr. McMullen with Documents (from the *Montreal Herald*), 67, all in *Canadian Pacific Railway Correspondence*.

103 Cooke to Fahnestock, March 3, 1873, Cooke to McCulloch, March 28, 1873, LBs, 1873, Cooke Papers; Berton, *National Dream*, 86.

104 Cooke to Fahnestock, March 3, 1873, LBs, 1873, Cooke Papers.

105 Earl of Dufferin to Earl of Kimberly, May 3, 1873, no. 1, pp. 1–2 in *Canadian Pacific Railway Correspondence*, den Otter, *Philosophy of Railroads*, 170; Cooke to Hon. L. S. Huntington, Aug. 19, 1871, Northern Pacific, Letters no. 1 (LB), Jan. 19, 1870–Sept. 27, 1871, Private Letters, Cooke Papers.

106 Earl of Dufferin to Earl of Kimberly, May 3, 1873, no. 1, pp. 1–2, in *Canadian Pacific Railway Correspondence*; den Otter, *Philosophy of Railroads*, 170.

107 Opinion in Reference to the Meaning of the 18th Clause of the British North America Act of 1867, encl. 3, no. 1, Earl of Kimberly to Early of Dufferin, June 17, 1873, no. 2, Secretary of State for the Colonies to the Governor General June 30, 1873, no. 3, Earl of Dufferin to Earl of Kimberly, Aug. 15, 1873, no. 4, all in *Canadian Pacific Railway Correspondence*, 4–5, 22–25; Berton, *Impossible Railway*, 64–65.

108 Berton, *National Dream*, 87.

109 Testimony of Daniel Y. McMullen, Sept. 11, 1874, "Report of the Royal Commissioners," 138; Cartier to Allan, July 30, 1872, Extract from Sir H. Allan's Affidavit of July 5, Macdonald to Abbott, Aug. 26, 1872, Cartier to Abbott, Aug. 24, 1872, Allan to undisclosed recipient, Aug. 7, 1872, all in Earl of Dufferin to Earl of Kimberly, Aug. 15, 1873, in *Canadian Pacific Railway Correspondence*, 15–17, 57; Berton, *National Dream*, 87–88.

110 Berton, *National Dream*, 101–3.

111 Testimony of Daniel Y. McMullen (see above, n. 109); encl. no. 3, Correspondence between Sir Hugh Allan and his American Partners (from the *Montreal Herald*), Explanatory Statement of Sir Hugh Allan (from the *Montreal Gazette*), encl. 4, no. 4, Earl of Dufferin to Earl of Kimberly, Aug. 15, 1873, all in *Canadian Pacific Railway Correspondence*, 15–17, 18–29, 57, 58–64.

112 Berton, *National Dream*, 103–4.

113 Ibid., 105–16.

114 Ibid., 115–24; "Report of the Royal Commissioners," in *Canadian Pacific Railway Correspondence*, 15–17, 57, 90–266.

115 Ibid., 124–45; for Cooke, Cooke to Fahnestock, March 3, 1873, Cooke to McCulloch, March 28, 1873, LBs, 1873, Cooke Papers.

116 For Mexico, Pletcher, *Rails, Mines, and Progress*, 34–93.

117 The demand to raise money to pay interest is a constant them in the Huntington/Hopkins correspondence. CPH to Hopkins, May 8, 1872, LB, 2:117, CPH to Hopkins, Aug. 21, 1872, LB, 2:147, box 20, CPH to Hopkins, Dec. 2, 1872, LB, 3:57, box 21, Hopkins Collection; for Northern Pacific, Cooke to Fahnestock, May 26, 1873, LBs, 1873, Cooke Papers; Klein, *Union Pacific*, 250; Bensel, *Yankee Leviathan*, 285–97; Barry Eichengreen, *Globalizing Capital: A History of the International Monetary System* (Princeton: Princeton Univ. Press, 1996), 15–20.

118 *Standard*, Oct. 24, 1874, Foreign Bondholders Cutting Files, r. 219; *National Car Builder*, quoted in *Railway Age*, Oct. 19, 1876, 343; "Capital and Railroad Extension," *Bankers' Magazine and Statistical Register* 10 (Oct. 1876): 279. Lees & Waller to Mills, Ralston, and Bell, Dec. 7, 1872, Lees & Waller to Bell, Dec. 9, 1872, f. 5, Ralston Correspondence.

119 CPH to Charles Crocker, Aug. 21, 1874, *Huntington Letters*, 4:164–65; Hopkins to CPH, Dec. 29, 1872, CPH Papers, ser. 1, r. 5; Naomi Lamoreaux, *Insider Lending: Banks, Personal Connections, and Economic Development in Industrial New England* (New York: Cambridge Univ. Press, 1996), 1–7; John A. James, *Money and Capital Markets in Postbellum America* (Princeton: Princeton Univ. Press, 1978), 56–57; Ira B. Cross, *Financing an Empire: History of Banking in California*, 4 vols. (Chicago: S. J. Clarke, 1927), 1:259–60; Testimony of Horace W. Carpentier, Aug. 11, 1887, *PRC*, 6:3235.

120 CPH to Hopkins, Feb. 7, March 8 (three letters), March 10 (two letters), 11, May 3, 1873; CPH to Stanford, Feb. 19, April 7, 30, 1873, *Huntington Letters*, 3:393–94, 403–9, 4:5–7, 15; CPH to Stanford, Feb. 28, 1873, LB, 3:149, box 21; CPH to Hopkins, March 1 (two letters), 7, 1873, LB, 3:151, 169, 171, box 21; CPH to Hopkins, March 10, 13, 19, 20, 26, 1873, LB, 4:5, 13, 2, 33, 39, box 21, all in Hopkins Collection. For the quoted valuation, Poor, *Manual, 1873–74*, 680–82. They also offered the Southern Pacific for $15 million, but this was deemed "too much." CPH to Stanford, Oct. 1, 1872, *Huntington Letters*, 3:360.

121 Alfred Cohen to CPH, April, 11, 1873, CPH to Hopkins, June 3, 1873, LB, 4:75, 89, box 21, Hopkins Collection.

122 CPH to Stanford, Sept. 27, 1872, *Huntington Letters*, 3:357.

123 Hopkins to CPH, Nov. 23, 29, 1872, CPH Papers, ser. 1, r. 5; *Annual Report of the Board of Directors of the Central Pacific Railroad Company to the Stockholders for the Year Ending Dec. 31, 1872* (Sacramento: Record Book and Job Printing House, 1873), tables 3 and 4, 38–39; *Annual Report of the Board of Directors of the Central Pacific Railroad Company to the Stockholders for the Year Ending Dec. 31, 1873* (San Francisco: H. S. Crocker, 1874).

124 Hopkins to CPH, Oct. 10, 1872, CPH Papers, ser. 1, r. 5.

125 CPH to Hopkins, Jan. 3, 1873, LB, 3:93, box 21, Hopkins Collection.

126 Cohen to Ralston, Jan. 4, 1873, LB, 12:19, Hopkins to Ralston, Jan. 6, 1873, LB, 12:21, Ralston to Hopkins, Jan. 6, 1873, LB, 12:25, Hopkins to Ralston, Jan. 8, 1873, all in box 25, Hopkins Collection.

127 Bensel, *Yankee Leviathan*, 243–48; Oberholtzer, *Jay Cooke*, 2:381–97.

128 CPH to Hopkins, March 10, 1870, LB, 2:96, CPH to Hopkins, March 19, 1873, LB, 4:27, box 21, Hopkins Collection.

129 Cooke to Puleston, Sept. 1, 1871, Northern Pacific, Letters no. 1 (LB), Jan. 19, 1870–Sept. 27, 1871, Private Letters, Cooke Papers.

130 CPH to Hopkins, Feb. 27, 1873, LB, 3:141, box 21, Hopkins Collection.

131 CPH to Hopkins, March 10, 1873, LB, 4:3, March 17, 1873, LB, 4:21, box 21, Hopkins Collection.

132 CPH to Stanford, Feb. 28, 1873, LB, 3:147, box 21, Hopkins Collection.

133 For break with the Crockers, Hopkins to CPH, Oct. 16, 1870, LB, 1:160–61, box 20, CPH to Hopkins, May 2, 1871, LB, 1:177, box 20, Hopkins Collection; CPH to Hopkins, March 17, May 2, 1871, CPH to Stanford, June 6, 1871, *Huntington Letters*, 3:264, 271, 281. For Crocker's return, CPH to Stanford, Oct. 3, 1873, ibid., 3:54; Lavender, *Great Persuader*, 284.

134 Cooke to Wm. Fenney, June 9, 1873, LBs, Cooke Papers.

135 For terms, Cooke to Johnston Bro. & Co, April 10, 1873, LBs, Cooke Papers; Larson, *Jay Cooke*, 401–3, 406.

136 James E. Pollard, ed., *The Journal of Jay Cooke, or the Gibraltar Records, 1865–1905* (Columbus: Ohio State Univ. Press, 1935), 3, 9, 22–23. For a typical day, see May 31, 1872, 249; arrival of news, Sept. 18, 19, 1873, 275–76; U. S. Grant to Borie, Sept. 10, 1873, in John Y. Simon, ed., *The Papers of Ulysses S. Grant*, 31 vols. (Carbondale: Southern Illinois Univ. Press, 1967–2009), 24:211.

137 Timberlake, "Specie Resumption Policy," 38–46; Cooke Memoir, 118; Richardson to U. S. Grant, Sept. 19, 1873, in Simon, ed., *Papers of Grant*, 23:214.

138 Larson, *Jay Cooke*, 408–11.

139 Samuel Rezneck, "Distress, Relief, and Discontent in the United States during the Depression of 1873–78," *Journal of Political Economy* 58, no. 6 (Dec. 1950): 494–512; Sven Beckert, *The Monied Metropolis: New York City and the Consolidation of the American Bourgeoisie, 1850–1896* (Cambridge: Harvard Univ. Press, 2001), 208–9; O. V. Well, "The Depression of 1873–79," *Agricultural History* 11 (July 1937): 237–51; Nicolas Barreyre, "The Politics of Economic Crises: The Case of 1873" (Paper given at SSHA Conference, Nov. 13, 2009); Eric Foner, *Reconstruction: America's Unfinished Revolution, 1863–76* (New York: Harper & Row, 1988), 512–24. For the Panic in perspective, Michael D. Bordo "An Historical Perspective on the Crisis of 2007–2008," Working Paper no. 14569, http://www.nber.org/papers/w14569, National Bureau of Economic Research, Dec. 2008; also Frederic S. Mishkin, "Asymmetric Information and Financial Crises: A Historical Perspective" (1991), Working Paper no. 3400, esp. pp. 14–16, National Bureau of Economic Research.

140 Poor, *Manual, 1878*, i.

141 *London Times*, February 3, 1876, *Hour*, Feb. 4, 1876, *Newspaper Cuttings Files*, vol. 6:88, r. 221; Rezneck, "Distress, Relief, and Discontent," 495.

142 Surrender of Charter, encl. in no. 8, Chamber of Senate, Oct. 23, 1873, *Canadian Pacific Railway Correspondence*, 86.

143 Pletcher, *Rails, Mines, and Progress*, 67–69, 91; W. to Plumb, April 15, 1873, box 2, f. 23; newspapers, Plumb to James Mackie, Oct. 12, 1873, box 2, f. 23, Edward L.; El congreso de la Union . . . Nov. 12, 1873, box 3, f. 25, Plumb to Hurlbert, Nov. 22, 1873, box 3, f. 25; Plumb to P. H. Sheridan, March 31, 1874, box 3, f. 26, all in Plumb Papers. For continued attempts at charters in 1870s, see Hart, *Empire and Revolution*, 106–22.

144 Gould to Dillon, Aug. 21, 1874, enclosed with Dillon to Atkins, Aug. 21, 1874; Dillon to Elisha Atkins, Aug. 21, 25, 26, Sept. 18, 1874, Union Pacific, OVP, IC, n.s. 16000, r. 1. Klein, *Union Pacific*, 312–13, paints a somewhat different picture of this maneuver and does not mention Dillon's actions.

145 All of this is visible in his Sept. and Oct. correspondence, CPH to Hopkins, Sept. 19, 21, 22, 23, 24, 1873, Oct. 29, 1873, LB, 5:81, 87, 91, 95, 99, 159, all in box 22, Hopkins Collection.

146 CPH to Hopkins, Sept. 27, 1873, LB, 5:111, box 22, Hopkins Collection.

147 CPH to Stanford, May 19, 1874, LB, 7:57, box 23, Hopkins Collection. In his testimony to the Pacific Railway Commission, Stanford, either from normal befuddlement or by lying, reversed this and had Fisk and Hatch owing the Central Pacific money, Testimony of Leland Stanford, July 28, 1887, *PRC*, 5:2497.

148 Hopkins to CPH, Nov. 11, 1873, CPH Papers, ser. 1, r. 5, Hopkins to CPH, Dec. 4, 1873, ibid., ser. 1, r. 6; Fisk and Hatch to the Holders of Central Pacific Railroad Bonds, Jan. 1, 1874, LB, 6:45; L. Von Hoffman and Co. to CPH, Dec. 30, 1873, both in box 22, Hopkins Collection; *Annual Report of the Board of Directors of the Central Pacific Railroad Co. to the Stockholders for the Year Ending Dec. 31, 1873*, 7.

149 "Losses in Railway Securities," *Railway Age*, March 22, 1877, p. 802.

150 Quoted in Gerald Berk, *Alternative Tracks: The Constitution of American Industrial Order, 1865–1917* (Baltimore: Johns Hopkins Univ. Press, 1994), 38.

151 "The Truth Needed about Railroads," *Railway Age*, Oct. 19, 1876, p. 372; "American Railroad Credit," ibid., Jan. 10, 1878, p. 20.

152 "Losses in Railway Securities"; *Public Aids to Transportation*, vol. 2, *Aids to Railroads and Related Subjects* (Washington, D.C.: GPO, 1938), 18–19.

A Railroad Life: William Hyde

1 Hyde to Hopkins, Nov. 3, 1871, LB, 2:92–93, box 1, f. 3, Hyde Papers.

2 Ibid.

3 Hyde to Van Nostrand & Co., Dec. 8, 1872, LB, 2:314, box 1, f. 3, Hyde Papers. This is the great theme of Leo Marx, *The Machine in the Garden: Technology and the Pastoral Ideal in America* (New York: Oxford Univ. Press, 1964).

4 Hyde to John Wilson, Auditor, Treasury Department, May 5, 1867, LB, 1:79–83, box 1, f. 1; Hyde to C. D. Morgan, Dec. 10, 1866, LB, 1:61–70, box 1, f. 1, Hyde Papers. Not all of the big four regarded it as a great blunder; as late as 1867 Mark Hopkins was arguing that railroads could never compete with steamships from Sacramento to San Francisco, and Sacramento was the popular terminus. Hopkins to CPH, March 30, 1867, CPH Papers, ser. 1, r. 1.

5 CPH to Hopkins, May 11, 1872, LB, 2:121, box 20, Hopkins Collection.

6 The Hyde material is extensive. See, e.g., Hyde to Bacon, Nov. 26, 1867, Jan. 9, 1868, both in LB, 1:xxx, box 1, f. 2. For expenses, Hyde to (?), July 5, 1868, LB, 1:154–63, box 1, f. 2; Hyde to My dear Doctor, Nov. 24, 1867, LB, 1:101, box 1, f. 2, Hyde Papers.

7 Hyde to Wife, Dec. 8, 1867, LB, box 2, f. 8, Hyde Papers.

8 Hyde to James P. Flint, March 26, 1869, LB, 2:11–16, box 1, f. 3, Hyde Papers. The Central Pacific bought out the Terminal Railroad in April of 1870, Note given for purchase of Terminal RR . . . , April 14, 1871, LB, 12:61, box 25, Hopkins Collection. Quote, Hyde to CPH, Feb. 28, 1871, LB, 2:67–70, box 1, f. 3, Hyde Papers.

9 Hyde to Flint, May 4, 1869, LB, 2:27, box 1, f. 3. Hyde had earlier claimed as a lobbyist that his whole motive was to get the opportunity to build the road. Hyde to Bacon, Jan. 2, 1868, LB, 1:113–15, box 1, f. 2. See also Hyde to CPH, June 22, Aug. 27, Nov. 8, 1872, LB, 2:191–98, 205–9, 308–11, all in box 1, f. 3, Hyde Papers. Hyde was sharing information about his old employer with his new, CPH to Hopkins, Jan. 20, 1870, *Huntington Letters*, 3:63.

10 Hyde to CPH, Nov. 8, 1872, LB, 2:308–11, box 1, f. 3, Hyde Papers.

11 Hyde to Wife, Dec. 21, 1869, LB, box 2, f. 8, Hyde Papers.

12 "Day of election," Hyde to CPH, Aug. 27, 1872, LB, 2:205–9, box 2. Hyde to Wife, Dec. 3, 1869, box 2, f. 8, both in Hyde Papers.

13 Hyde to Wife, Dec. 21, 1869, LB, box 2, f. 8, Hyde Papers.

14 Hyde to Stanford, Sept. 1872, LB, 2:223, box 1, f. 3, Hyde Papers.

15 Hyde to CPH, Oct. 10, 1872, LB, 2:274, box 1, f. 3, Hyde Papers.

16 CPH to Hopkins, Sept. 14, 18, 1872, LB, 2:179, 175–79, both in box 20, Hopkins Collection. Huntington originally proposed a $2 million bribe, but decided $1 million would suffice. He had good judgment in such things.

17 Hopkins to CPH, Dec. 17, 1872, CPH Papers, ser. 1, r. 5; CPH to Hopkins, Dec. 26, 1872, LB, 3:87, box 20, Hopkins Collection.

18 Crocker to CPH, Jan. 29, 1873, *Huntington Letters*, 2:7–8; Storrs to Hopkins, Feb. 5, 1873, LB, 12:29, box 25, Hopkins Collection.

19 CPH to Hopkins March 19, May 8, Aug. 23, 1872, LB, 2:65, 119, 153, all in box 20, Hopkins Collection.

CHAPTER 3: FRIENDS

1 CPH to Hopkins, March 19, 1872, LB, 2:63, box 20, Hopkins Collection.

2 *Union Pacific Employes' Magazine*, Sept. 1886, p. 1; Mark Wahlgren Summers, *Era of Good Stealings* (New York: Oxford Univ. Press, 1993), 109; Conness to Gates, March 13, 1872, CPH Papers, ser. 1, r. 5; Franchot to CPH, Dec. 2, 1873, LB, 6:5, box 22, Hopkins Collection. On constituency I differ from Margaret Thompson's impressive account of Gilded Age lobbying, and the friendship I describe is not the same as what she discusses. Margaret S. Thompson, *The "Spider Web": Congress and Lobbing in the Age of Grant* (Ithaca: Cornell Univ. Press, 1985), 137–39, 157; Glenn C. Altschuler and Stuart Blumin, *Rude Republic: Americans and Their Politics in the Nineteenth Century* (Princeton: Princeton Univ. Press, 2000), 117–18.

3 Texas Pacific, S. 647, Feb. 22, 1871, with House Amendments, 41st Cong., 3d sess.; *Thirty-second Parallel Pacific Railroad, Remarks of CPH . . . before the Committee on Public Lands of the U.S. Senate, Feb. 2, 1884, on House Bill 3933* (New York: John C. Rankin, 1884), 10.

4 C. Vann Woodward, *Reaction and Reunion: The Compromise of 1877 and the End of Reconstruction* (Boston: Little, Brown, 1951), 73–77; for Texas and Pacific and South, see Mark W. Summers, *Railroads, Reconstruction, and the Gospel of Prosperity: Aid under the Radical Republicans, 1865–1877* (Princeton: Princeton Univ. Press, 1984), 168–73; James Arthur Ward, *J. Edgar Thomson: Master of the Pennsylvania* (Westport, Conn.: Greenwood Press, 1980), 205–8; for description of progress, Dodge to Scott, Jan. 12, 1874, LBs, Texas & Pacific Railroad, MS 98, box 160, Dodge Papers; for an older overview, S. G. Reed, *A History of the Texas Railroads and*

of Transportation Conditions under Spain and Mexico and the Republic and the State (Houston: St. Clair, 1941), 364, 556–65. Poor, *Manual, 1876–77*, 344–45.

5 *American Railroad Journal*, Nov. 29, 1873; Julius Grodinsky, *Transcontinental Railway Strategy, 1869–1893: A Study of Businessmen* (Philadelphia: Univ. of Pennsylvania Press, 1962), 17–21.

6 Texas and Pacific Railroad Company Backbone Grant Act, March 3, 1871, 41st. Cong., ch. 122; 16 stat. 573; David Lavender, *The Great Persuader: The Biography of Collis P. Huntington* (Niwot: Univ. Press of Colorado, 1998), 304.

7 CPH to Hopkins, Jan. 10, 1877, LB, 9:123, box 24, Hopkins Collection. For an interpretation and emphasis different from my own, see Grodinsky, *Transcontinental Railway Strategy*, 56–68.

8 Henry Blair to CPH, July 19, 1889, CPH Papers, ser. 1, r. 48.

9 CPH to Crocker, Jan. 8, 1870, *Huntington Letters*, 3:56; CPH to Hopkins, March 16, 1872, LB, 2:51, box 20, Hopkins Collection; CPH to Colton, April 27, 1876, *Octopus Speaks*, 240; Adams to J. M. Thurston, May 10, 1888, UP, PO, OC, vol. 43, ser. 2, r. 38; CPH Papers, to Wm. Mills, Feb. 4, 1893, CPH Papers, vol. 234, ser. 2, r. 33.

10 Wm. Mills to CPH, Dec. 21, 1879, CPH Papers, ser. 1, r. 16; J. A. Slye to CPH, April 10, 1878, ibid., r. 14; John P. Young to Richard T. Colburn, Aug. 9, 1876, ibid., r. 10; CPH to Hopkins, May 8, 1870, March 15, 1876, *Huntington Letters*, 3:149–50, 4:472–73; Mark W. Summers, *The Press Gang: Newspapers and Politics, 1865–68* (Chapel Hill: Univ. of North Carolina Press, 1994), 110, 113; H. Schüler to CPH, Sept. 25, 1877, CPH Papers, ser. 1, r. 13; Richard Franchot to CPH, Jan. 11, 1872, LB, 2:19, box 20, Hopkins Collection; E. P. Howell to CPH, April 24, 1878, and Mary Fields to CPH, April 4, 1878, CPH Papers, ser. 1, r. 14; CPH to Hopkins, March 19, 1872, LB, 2:59, box 20, CPH to Hopkins, Nov. 19, 1875, LB, 8:85, box 23, Hopkins Collection; CPH to Colton, March 18, 1875, *Octopus Speaks*, 88; Crocker to CPH, Jan. 11, 1878, CPH Papers, ser. 1, r. 13; Adams to Isaac Bromley, Dec. 2, 1884, UP, PO, OC, vol. 23, ser. 2, r. 20; Van Horne to Joseph Hickson, Dec. 14, 1886, CPR, Van Horne LB, 19(2), vol. 3. The Southern Pacific kept newspapermen—Hutchins of the *Post* (apparently Stilson Hutchins, founder of the *Washington Post*) and Ayers of the *Kansas City Times*—on the payroll in the late 1880s. Boyd to CPH, Jan. 2, 1889, CPH Papers, ser. 1, r. 47. Also see CPH to Wm. Mills, Feb. 4, 1893, CPH Papers, vol. 234, ser. 2, r. 33.

11 I. Bromley, "The Newspapers and the Company," Aug. 10, 1886, UP, SG2, ser. 1, box 32, f. Bromley-Burness.

12 Ibid.; CPH to Hopkins, May 12, 1876, LB, 9:19, box 24, Hopkins Collection; CPH to Colton, Dec. 8, 1876, *Octopus Speaks*, 325; James Simonton to George Kenyon Fitch, Jan. 21, 1873, box 1, Fitch Papers; Franchot to CPH, Jan. 11, 1872, LB, 2:19, box 20, Hopkins Collection; CPH to Hopkins, March 16, 1876, LB, 8:115, box 23, ibid.; Fitch to Simonton, Dec. 8, 1875, box 1, Fitch Papers; Gould and Western Union, Adams to W. B. Strong, Sept. 19, 1885, UP, PO, OC, vol. 29, ser. 2, r. 25; "Jay Gould and the Associated Press," *Union Pacific Employes' Magazine*, Oct. 1886, pp. 263–64; Maury Klein, *The Life and Legend of Jay Gould* (Baltimore: Johns Hopkins Univ. Press, 1986), 395–96.

13 Grodinsky, *Transcontinental Railway Strategy*, 2–4; CPH to Colton, Oct. 15, 1874, *Octopus Speaks*, 50–51; Crocker to CPH, Sept. 18, 1883, Crocker Papers.

14 John M. Murrin, "Escaping Perfidious Albion: Federalism, Fear of Aristocracy, and the Democratization of Corruption in Postrevolutionary America," in Richard K. Matthews, ed., *Virtue, Corruption, and Self-Interest: Political Values in the Eighteenth Century* (Bethlehem: Lehigh Univ. Press, 1994), 103–15.

15 CPH to Crocker, April 12, 1878, CPH Papers, ser. 2, r. 6.

16 CPH to C. Crocker, May 17, 1871, *Huntington Letters*, 3:275; Crocker to CPH, Jan. 22, 1878, CPH Papers, ser. 1, r. 14.

17 CPH to Stanford, Oct. 25, 1871, *Huntington Letters*, 3:291.

18 Hopkins to CPH, Oct. 10, 1872, CPH Papers, ser. 1, r. 5.

19 Hopkins to CPH, Dec. 8, 1872, CPH Papers, ser. 1, r. 5.

20 Conness to CPH, Nov. 9, 17, 1875, CPH Papers, ser. 1, r. 8.

21 Colton to CPH, Jan. 31, 1878, April 15, 16, 1878, *Octopus Speaks*, 463, 488, 489, 15, n. 18.

22 Pamela Walker Laird, *Pull: Networking and Success since Benjamin Franklin* (Cambridge: Harvard Univ. Press, 2006), esp. 2, 15, 22–23.

23 George T. Clark, *Leland Stanford: War Governor of California, Railroad Builder, and Founder of Stanford University* (Stanford: Stanford Univ. Press, 1931), 290. See also Adams to C. J. Smith, July 6, 1888, UP, PO, OC, vol. 44, ser. 2, r. 39. The most complete, if sometimes hagiographic, biography of Leland Stanford is Norman E. Tutorow: *The Governor: The Life and Legacy of Leland Stanford: A California Colossus*, 2 vols. (Spokane, Wash.: Arthur H. Clark Co., 2004).

24 As a set of rhetorical and cultural conventions, this species of friendship was hardly new. It resembled earlier commercial relationships between Virginia planters and British merchants in the eighteenth century, and political relationships in New York before and after the Civil War. T. H. Breen, *Tobacco Culture: The Mentality of Great Tidewater Planters on the Eve of the Revolution* (Princeton: Princeton Univ. Press, 1985), 84–123; Paula Baker, *The Moral Frameworks of Public Life: Gender, Politics, and the State in Rural New York, 1870–1930* (New York: Oxford Univ. Press, 1991), 31–39.

25 Mitchell to Villard, April 21, 1881, J. H. Mitchell Letters, box 82, Villard Papers; Margaret Kolb Holden, "The Rise and Fall of Oregon Populism: Legal Theory, Political Culture, and Public Policy, 1868–1895" (Ph.D. diss., Univ. of Virginia, 1993), 255–58.

26 Baker, *Moral Frameworks of Public Life*, 27–32.

27 CPH to Crocker, May 17, 1869, *Huntington Letters*, 1:429; W. H. Crain to CPH, March 4, 1891, CPH Papers, ser. 1, r. 49. Crain was a congressman from Texas.

28 Testimony of Leland Stanford, Aug. 10, 1887, *PRC*, 6:3161–200; William Mahl, Memoir, L.E.M. 3, B-15, Mahl Papers.

29 Lavender, *Great Persuader*, 241–42; CPH to Hopkins, Dec. 30 1871, LB, 1:199, box 20, Hopkins Collection.

30 CPH to Hopkins, July 18, 1876, LB, 9:57, box 24, Hopkins Collection; David M. Jordan, *Roscoe Conkling of New York: Voice in the Senate* (Ithaca: Cornell Univ. Press, 1971), 413, 417.

31 Conkling to CPH, Jan. 24, Feb. 1, 1880, CPH Papers, ser. 1, r. 18; CPH to Conkling, Dec. 22, 1880, ibid., ser. 2, r. 12.

32 CPH to Colton, Jan. 14, 1876, *Huntington Letters*, 3:445. *Octopus Speaks*, 286; Lavender, *Great Persuader*, 215, 311.

33 CPH to Hopkins, Feb. 19, 1876, *Huntington Letters*, 4:459.

34 For lobbying, Thompson, *"Spider's Web,"* 53–69.

35 Summers, *Press Gang*, 109.

36 Donald A. Ritchie, *Congress and the Washington Correspondents* (Cambridge: Harvard Univ. Press, 1991), 69.

37 Ellis Paxson Oberholtzer, *Jay Cooke: Financier of the Civil War*, 2 vols. (Philadelphia: G. W. Jacobs, 1907), 2:65.

38 Thompson, *"Spider's Web,"* 167–72, 276–77; George C. Benson, *Political Corruption in America* (Toronto: Lexington Books, 1978), 61; Dodge to Chandler, Dec. 26, 1875, box 160, LBs, Texas & Pacific Railroad, Dodge Papers; Maury Klein, *Union Pacific*, vol. 1, *Birth of a Railroad, 1862–1893* (Garden City, N.Y.: Doubleday, 1987), 374; Legal Expense Voucher of W. E. Chandler, Oct. 31, 1874, Testimony of John P. Usher, *PRC*, 3:1706–7.

39 CPH to Hopkins, June 7, 1870, CPH to Crocker, Dec. 21, 1870, *Huntington Letters* 2:175, 225; Summers, *Press Gang*, 109–10; Adams to Usher, Oct. 13, 1884, UP, PO, OC, vol. 23, ser. 2, r. 19.

40 *Philadelphia Sunday Morning News*, n.d. 1878, enclosure with Frazier to CPH, Nov. 6, 1878, CPH Papers, ser. 1, r. 15.

41 John Covode to U. H. Painter, Dec. 10, 1870, box 2, Painter to Scott, April 9, 1871, box 30, Painter LBs, 1871–76, Painter Papers.

42 Thom. Scott to Painter, Nov. 26, 1873, Painter Papers.

43 Painter to Scott, March 21, 1871, Painter LBs, 1871–76, box 30, Painter Papers.

44 Painter to (?), Jan. 23, 1874, Painter LBs, 1871–76, box 30, Painter Papers.

45 Dodge to Painter, March 31, 1877, Painter to Dodge, April 1, 1877, Dodge to Painter, April 4, 1877, Painter to Dodge, April 5, 1877, GWD to Painter, April 6, 1877, Painter to Dodge, April 8, 1877, Painter to Gould, April 8, 1877, Dodge to Painter, April 13, 1877, box 3, 1874–77, Painter Papers.

46 Stanley P. Hirshson, *Grenville M. Dodge: Soldier, Politician, Railroad Pioneer* (Bloomington: Indiana Univ. Press, 1967); for his relations with Scott, 183–85, 187–88, 190–91; Indian trade, 185–86, 196, 198; Crédit Mobilier, 192–93; lies and exaggerations, 195; Wallace D. Farnham, "Grenville Dodge and the Union Pacific: A Study of Historical Legends," *Journal of American History* 51 (March 1965): 632–50. Farnham questions Dodge's accounts of meetings with Lincoln and his discovery of the route over the Laramie Mountains; Hirshson, *Grenville M. Dodge*, 297, offers a somewhat tepid defense.

47 Hirshson, *Grenville M. Dodge*, 50–57.

48 Boyd to CPH, Jan. 10, 13, 1880, CPH Papers, ser. 1, r. 18; Oberholtzer, *Jay Cooke*, 2:179; Testimony of CPH, *PRC*, 1:24–25.

49 Dodge to Dillon, Aug. 17, 1874, box 179, vol. 382, LBs—G. M. Dodge, 1872–1874, 377, Dodge Papers.

50 CPH to Hopkins, March 15, 1876, LB, 8:111, box 23, Hopkins Collection.

51 The legislative history is very complex, but for a sample of Scott's requests, see H.R. 3869, Dec. 8, 1874, [H. Mis. Doc. 6] 43d Cong., 2d sess.; "A Bill, Dec. 14, 1875," H.R. 25, 44th Cong., 1st sess.; guarantee of interest for only a trunk line, "A Bill, Dec. 7, 1877," H.R. 1919, 45th Cong., 2d sess.; Report (to accompany bill H.R. 3391), Feb. 21, 1878, 45th Cong., 2d sess., H. Rept. 238; "A Bill, Jan. 21, 1878," 45th Cong., 2d sess., H. Rept. 2573; "A Bill, April 17, 1878," 45th Cong., 2d sess., Report no. 619. "A Bill, Dec. 10, 1877," S. 404, 45th Cong., 2d sess.; "Texas & Pacific Railroad, April 17, 1878 . . . ," Report (to accompany Bill H.R. 4398), 45th Cong., 2d sess., H. Rept. 619. "A Bill, May 5–6, 1879," 46th Cong., 1st sess., H.R. 1707; "Texas and Pacific Railroad," 44th Cong., 2d sess., Rept. 139, Pt. 1, 1–8, quote, p. 8.

52 CPH to Colton, Nov. 15, 1877, *Octopus Speaks*, 431.

53 Thompson, *"Spider's Web,"* 50.

54 Flagg to CPH, Dec. 8, 1877, CPH Papers, ser. 1, r. 13; *Octopus Speaks*, 550; S. C. Pomeroy to CPH, May 26, 1876, LB, 9:27, box 24, Hopkins Collection.

55 Painter to Scott, April 20, 1871, Painter LBs, 1871–76, box 30, Painter Papers.

56 *Octopus Speaks*, 548; Lavender, *Great Persuader*, 198, 349. Charles Flanagan was the sergeant at arms for the House and working for the Central Pacific; Flanagan to CPH, June 16, 23, 1879, CPH Papers, ser. 1, r. 17; Adams to Judge Dillon, Jan. 28, 1887, UP, PO, OC, vol. 37, ser. 2, r. 33.

57 Gorham to CPH, Oct. 20, 1875, CPH Papers, ser. 1, r. 6; *Octopus Speaks*, 176, 276. CPH to Colton, Jan. 24, 29, 1876, ibid., 229, 230; Lavender, *Great Persuader*, 260, 311; David J. Rothman, *Politics and Power: The United States Senate, 1869–1901* (Cambridge: Harvard Univ. Press, 1966), 32.

58 Thompson, *"Spider's Web,"* 17.

59 Dodge to Bond, March 1, 1875, box 180, vol. 346, LBs—Calif. Texas Railroad: Letters, 1874–78, 278, Dodge Papers.

60 Dodge to R. Clarkson, Dec. 15, 1874, box 179, vol. 382, LBs—G. M. Dodge, 1872–74, 487–90; Northern Pacific, Dodge to Scott, June 16, 1874, 305, ibid.; Dodge to Bond, July 28, 1875, box 180, vol. 346, LB—Calif. Texas Railroad: Letters, 1874–78, 330; working legislatures, Dodge to Gen. Geo. Manny, Jan. 9, 1875, box 160, LBs, Texas & Pacific Railroad, Letters to heads of departments and employees, May 26, 1874, to May 23, 1876; Dodge to Scott, Jan. 5, 1874, misdated, actually 1875, box 180, vol. 383, LB, Personal & Private Correspondence, 1877–78; Dodge to Throckmorton, Dec. 21, 1875, box 160, LBs, Texas & Pacific Railroad, all in Dodge Papers.

61 The road was chartered as the Texas Pacific in 1871 and reorganized as the Texas and Pacific in 1872, S. 724, 42d Cong., 2d sess., April 25, 1872; Poor, *Manual, 1873–74*, 605; ibid., *1878–79*, 858–59; "Texas and Pacific Railroad," 44th Cong., 2d sess., Rep. 139, pt. 1, 1–8; Dodge to Scott, Jan. 12, 1874, box 160, LBs, Texas & Pacific Railroad, Dodge Papers; CPH to Colton, Jan. 29, 1876, *Huntington Letters*, 4:453. This letter says, "The Texas P. seems to owe almost every one in the whole country." The same letter in *Octopus Speaks*, 230, says "own" instead of "owe."

62 For extent of Pennsylvania system in 1874, Poor, *Manual, 1874–75*, 452–58; for Texas & Pacific, ibid., 597; Poor, *Manual, 1878–79*, 858–59; CPH to Colton, Sept. 23, 1875, *Octopus Speaks*; work, CPH to Colton, 1875, ibid., 196, 201–2; Summers, *Railroads*, 172; Dodge to Bond, March 1, 1875, box 180, vol. 346, LB—Calif. Texas Railroad: Letters, 1874–78, 278, Dodge Papers.

63 Hopkins to CPH, Feb. 4, 1873, CPH Papers, ser. 1, r. 5.

64 CPH to C. Crocker, Feb. 3, 1871, *Huntington Letters*, 3:252–53; Peter H. Argersinger, "New Perspectives on Election Fraud in the Gilded Age," *Political Science Quarterly* 100 (Winter 1985–86): 669–87; Richard Franklin Bensel, *Yankee Leviathan: The Origins of Central State Authority in America, 1859–1877* (New York: Cambridge Univ. Press, 1990), 306–8; Richard Franklin Bensel, *The Political Economy of American Industrialization, 1877–1900* (New York: Cambridge Univ. Press, 2000), 357–60.

65 CPH to Hopkins, March 11, 1872, LB, 2:43, box 20, Hopkins Collection.

66 R. Franchot to CPH, June 12, 1870, LB, 1:143, box 20, Hopkins Collection. For change in politics, see Nicolas Barryere, "Politics of Economic Crises: The Case of 1873" (Paper, SSHA Conference, Nov. 13, 2009).

67 Franchot to CPH, Jan. 9, 1874, LB, 6:71, box 22, Hopkins Collection. See also Tichenor to Dodge, June 17, 1873, W. E. Chandler to Dodge, March 29, 1873, General Correspondence, box 8, Dodge Papers.

68 Franchot to CPH, Feb. 19, 1874, LB, 6:153, box 22, Hopkins Collection.

69 Edward Wislow Martin, *History of the Grange Movement; or, The Farmers War against Monopolies* . . . (Chicago: National Publishing Company, 1874), 6; George H. Miller, *Railroads and the Granger Laws* (Madison: Univ. of Wisconsin Press, 1971).

70 Tamara Venit (Venit-Shelton), "A Squatters' Republic: Land Rights, Reform, and Antimonopoly in California and the Nation, 1850–1920" (Ph.D. diss., Stanford Univ., 2008).

71 Miller, *Railroads and the Granger Laws*, 1–41, 167–68.

72 Henry George, *Progress and Poverty: An Inquiry into the Cause of Industrial Depressions and of Increase of Want with Increase of Wealth: The Remedy* (New York: Robert Schalkenbach Foundation, 1942, orig. ed. 1879), 192.

73 Chester McArthur Destler, "Western Radicalism, 1865–1901: Concepts and Origins," *Mississippi Valley Historical Review* 31 (Dec. 1944): 335–68, esp., 340–41, quote 356. R. Jeffrey Lustig, *Corporate Liberalism: The Origins of Modern American Political Theory, 1890–1920* (Berkeley: Univ. of California Press, 1982), 42–46, is still good on antimonopolism. See, e.g., William Larrabee, *The Railroad Question: A Historical and Practical Treatise on Railroads, and*

Remedies for their Abuses, 10th ed. (Chicago: Schulte Publishing Company, 1898), 317; James F. Hudson, *The Railways and the Republic* (New York: Harper & Brothers, 1886), 287; "Strikes and Strikers," *Union Pacific Employes' Magazine*, Aug. 1886, p. 199. For eastern antimonopoly, Lee Benson, *Merchants, Farmers & Railroads: Railroad Regulation and New York Politics, 1850–1887* (Cambridge: Harvard Univ. Press, 1955).

74 Lustig, *Corporate Liberalism*, 18.

75 Ibid., 43.

76 Crocker to CPH, Oct. 25, 1883, Crocker Papers; Testimony of Edward Rosewater, June 28, 1887, *PRC*, 3:1339–40; William R. Childs, *The Texas Railroad Commission: Understanding Regulation in America to the Mid-twentieth Century* (College Station: Texas A&M Univ. Press, 2005), 61–63.

77 For Booth, Lavender, *Great Persuader*, 311. Rothman, *Politics and Power*, 201, misinterprets Sargent; William Deverell, *Californians and the Railroad, 1850–1910* (Berkeley: Univ. of California Press, 1994), 29–31, 55, 59–60; Ward M. McAfee, "A Constitutional History of Railroad Rate Regulation in California, 1879–1911," *Pacific Historical Review* 27 (Aug. 1968): 267; Curtis Grassman, "Prologue to California Reform: The Democratic Impulse, 1886–1898," ibid., 42 (Nov. 1973): 520–21; Sherrill to CPH, Sept. 6, 1886, CPH Papers, ser. 1, r. 43; Towne to CPH, May 8, 1879, May 17, 1879, ibid., r. 17.

78 *Hassler's Financial Report*, May 19, 1876, *Newspaper Cuttings Files*, American Railways, 1874–93, 7:16–17, r. 221.

79 Crocker to CPH, Oct. 25, 1883, Crocker Papers.

80 CPH to Colton, Nov. 1, 13, 1874, *Huntington Letters*, 4:216, 219.

81 Timothy Gilfoyle, *A Pickpocket's Tale: The Underworld of Nineteenth-Century New York* (New York: Norton, 2006), xv.

82 Scott C. James, *Presidents, Parties, and the State: A Party System Perspective on Democratic Regulatory Choice, 1884–1936* (New York: Cambridge Univ. Press, 2000), 39–40; Testimony of Frederick Heede, July 2, 1887, *PRC*, 3:1499; Testimony of Edward Rosewater, June 28, 1887, *PRC*, 3:1339.

83 CPH to Colton, May 1, 1875, *Huntington Letters*, 4:344; *Octopus Speaks*, 268.

84 *Octopus Speaks*, 281; CPH to Colton, Nov. 11, 1876, ibid., 322; CPH to Colton, Jan. 29, Feb. 26, 1876, *Huntington Letters*, 4:453, 464–65.

85 Boyd to CPH, Nov. 19, 1878, CPH Papers, ser. 1, r. 16.

86 For committee, Boyd to Colburn, April 11, 1879, CPH Papers, ser. 1, r. 17.

87 E. J. Ellis to CPH, Dec. 13, 1879, CPH Papers, ser. 1, r. 18; J. Johnson to CPH, May 28, 1878, ibid.

88 Lavender, *Great Persuader*, 213–22. See also Stanford to CPH, May 1, 1875, SC 33a, box 1, f. 16, Stanford Papers; Testimony of CPH, *PRC*, 1:36.

89 CPH to Crocker, May 17, 1869, *Huntington Letters*, 1:429.

90 CPH to Stanford, May 26, 1869, *Huntington Letters*, 1:433.

91 Jordan, *Conkling*, 104, 420–21; Oliver Ames to E. Atkins, June 11, 1874, UP, OVP, IC; Rothman, *Politics and Power*, 27–30; Charles J. McClain, "From the Huntington Papers: The Huntington-Conkling Connection," *Pacific Historian* 29 (Winter 1985): 31–46; Mark Twain and Charles Dudley Warner, *The Gilded Age: A Tale of To-Day*, 2 vols. (New York: Harper & Brothers, 1915, orig. ed. 1873), 1:242.

92 CPH to Stanford, May 26, 1869, *Huntington Letters*, 1:433, *Octopus Speaks*, 145. For investments for Conkling, CPH to Conkling, Dec. 22, 1880, CPH Papers, ser. 2, r. 12.

93 C. A. Seward to CPH, Dec. 10, 1890, CPH Papers, ser. 1, r. 49.

94 CPH to Hopkins, April 6, 1875, *Huntington Letters*, 4:315.

95 Villard to J. N. Dolph, Nov. 8, 1883, Villard LBs, Private Letters, 40 A, 258, Villard to Dolph, Dec. 4, 1883, Personal Correspondence, LB, 51:454, Villard Papers.

96 Adams to E. P. Alexander, Nov. 24, 1885, UP, PO, OC, vol. 30. David T. Canon and Charles Stewart III, "Committee Hierarchy and Assignments in the U.S. Congress: Testing Theories of Legislative Organization, 1789–1946," Midwest Political Science Association, 2002, web.mit .edu/cstewart/www/papers/mwpsa2002.pdf, tables 1 and 2.

97 "Texas and Pacific Railway, Feb. 27, 1875," 43d Cong., 2d sess., H. Rept. 267; Colton to Crocker, Feb. 24, 1875, *Octopus Speaks*, 82; *Congressional Record*, 43d Cong., 1st sess., Feb. 22, 1875, 1600–1601. For committee power, Thompson, *"Spider's Web,"* 93–96.

98 Woodrow Wilson, *Congressional Government: A Study in American Politics* (Boston: Houghton Mifflin, 1901), 69.

99 Thompson, *"Spider's Web,"* 71–93. In the 1870s the percentage of first-term members ran at or near 50 percent; Nelson W. Polsby, "The Institutionalization of the U.S. House of Representatives," *American Political Science Review* 62 (March 1968): 146; Rothman, *Politics and Power*, 11–42.

100 David T. Canon and Charles Stewart III, "The Evolution of the Committee System in Congress," in Lawrence C. Dodd and Bruce I. Oppenheimer, eds., *Congress Reconsidered*, 7th ed. (Washington, D.C.: CQ Press, 2001), 176; David T. Canon and Charles Stewart III, "Parties and Hierarchies in Senate Committees, 1789–1946," in Bruce I. Oppenheimer, ed., *U.S. Senate Exceptionalism* (Columbus: Ohio State Univ. Press, 2002), 165, 170–71.

101 Albert V. House, "The Speakership Contest of 1875: Democratic Response to Power," *Journal of American History* 52 (Sept. 1965): 252–74; Thompson, *"Spider's Web,"* 177.

102 Dodge to George S. Miller, Omaha, March 30, 1875, box 160, LBs, Texas & Pacific Railroad, 167–68, Dodge Papers.

103 Dodge to Scott, June 16, 1874, Letters to heads of departments and employees, May 26, 1874, to May 23, 1876, box 160, LBs, Texas & Pacific Railroad, Dodge Papers; CPH to Colton, Jan. 29, 1876, *Octopus Speaks*, 230.

104 CPH to Hopkins, March 7, 1870, *Huntington Letters*, 3:93; CPH to Stanford, Feb. 4, 1875, ibid., 4:281. For Grant, see Babcock to CPH, March 24, 1873, CPH Papers, ser. 1, r. 5; Van Horne to Joseph Hicson, Dec. 14, 1886, CPR, no. 19, pt. 2, Van Horne LBs; W. F. Sanders to T. F. Oakes, Jan. 2, 1885, 137 H.4.6 (F), 3A 10F, NP.

105 Klein, *Union Pacific*, 509; CPH to Ingalls, Sept. 28, 1878, CPH Papers, ser. 1, r. 15.

106 Villard to Sen. Mitchell, May 16, 1877, Private Correspondence, LB 16, Villard Papers.

107 W. P. Clough to T. F. Oakes, Feb. 13, 1885, 137 H.4.6 (F), 3A 2 10 F, NP.

108 Adams to CPH, UP, PO, OC, vol. 23, ser. 2, r. 3. Taken together, all, not just political, passes amounted to over $20,000 a week on the Union Pacific in 1884. Adams to S. Dillon, Jan. 15, 1885, ibid., vol. 27, ser. 2, r. 23.

109 Adams to Callaway, March 9, 1887, UP, PO, OC, vol. 39, ser. 1, r. 34; T. F. Oakes to R. Harris, Feb. 2, 1885, 137 H.4.6 (F), 3A 2 10 F, NP; Boyd to CPH, Jan. 31, 1891, Boyd to I. E. Gates, May 11, 1891, CPH Papers, ser. 1, r. 49.

110 Dodge to Isaac Sturgeon, Dec. 16, 1874, box 160, LBs, Texas & Pacific Railroad, Letters to heads of departments and employees, May 26, 1874, to May 23, 1876, 364. For figures and solicitation of Watterson, Dodge to Henry Watterson, Dec. 23, 1874, ibid., 382. To pound, Dodge to Watterson, Jan. 9, 1875, ibid., 390, all in Dodge Papers.

111 Dodge to Scott, Dec. 21, 1875, LB—Calif. Texas Railroad: Letters, 1874–78, box 180, vol. 346, 336, Dodge Papers.

112 CPH to Crocker, May 20, 1881, vol. 28, CPH Papers, ser. 2, r. 6.

113 *Octopus Speaks*, 273; CPH to Colton, Nov. 10, 11, 13, 1875, *Huntington Letters*, 4:404–8; Boyd to Gates, Aug. 29, 1878, CPH Papers, ser. 1, r. 15; Conness to CPH, Nov. 9, 1875, ibid., r. 8;

CPH to Colton, Dec. 22, 1875, Feb. 26, 1876, *Octopus Speaks*, 222, 233, 285–86; CPH to Colton, Dec. 17, 1875, *Huntington Letters*, 4:429; CPH to Stanford, Dec. 1, 1876, ibid., 417, *Octopus Speaks*, 273.

114 "Texas and Pacific Railroad: Memorial of the National Grange, Feb. 20, 1875," 43d Cong., 2d sess., H. Misc. Doc. 89; Hirshon, *Grenville M. Dodge*, 200; "Texas and Pacific Railroad Company: Joint Resolution of the General Assembly of the State of Tennessee," Feb. 15, 1875, 43d Cong., 2d sess., H. Misc. Doc. 79; "Texas and Pacific Railroad, Joint Resolution of the Legislature of South Carolina, Feb. 8, 1875," 43d Cong., 2d sess., H. Misc. Doc. 88; "Resolution of the Legislature of Mississippi . . . , Feb. 27, 1875," 43d Cong., 2d sess., S. Misc. Doc. 117; *Southwestern Pacific Railroad. Address to the People of the United States, Calling a National Convention in Saint Louis, on the 23d of November 1875, to Take Action in Favor of a Southwestern Pacific Railroad, Together with Letters from Leading Citizens upon the Same Subject* (St. Louis: C. E. Ware, 1875); Grodinsky, *Transcontinental Railway Strategy*, 58.

115 Dodge to John Baldwin, Dec. 7, 1874, box 179, vol. 382, LBs—G. M. Dodge, 1872–74, 491–92. Texas and Louisiana, Dodge to Gov. (Throckmorton), Jan. 11, 1874, ibid., 239–41; Dodge to Bond, Feb. 10, 1875, box 180, vol. 346, LBs—Calif. Texas Railroad: Letters, 1874–78, 275–76; Dodge to Bond, March 1, 1875, ibid., 278; Dodge to Scott, Jan. 26, 1875, ibid. Dead for session, Dodge giving up, Dodge to R.E. Montgomery, Feb. 18, 1875, box 160, LBs, Texas & Pacific Railroad, 150; Dodge to George S. Miller, Omaha, March 30, 1875, box 160, LBs, Texas & Pacific Railroad, 167–68, all in Dodge Papers. Southern Pacific opposition, Colton to Crocker, Jan. 11, 1875, CPH to Colton, Feb. 5, 1875, *Octopus Speaks*, 69, 75.

116 House, "Speakership Contest," 252–74; Dodge to Bond, July 28, 1875, box 180, vol. 346, LBs—Calif. Texas Railroad: Letters, 1874–78, 330, Dodge Papers.

117 House, "Speakership Contest," 262–65.

118 Chauncey Black to Randall, May 12, 1877, correspondence, box 34, Randall Papers; House, "Speakership Contest," 260–74; CPH to Hopkins, Dec. 2, 1875, *Huntington Letters*, 4:418; Boyd to CPH, Dec. 25, 1875, CPH Papers, ser. 1, r. 9; Dodge to J. G. Blaine, Dec. 21, 1875, box 160, LBs, Texas & Pacific Railroad, Dodge Papers; Thompson, *"Spider's Web,"* 123, 192–99, 203–4; CPH to Colton, Dec. 22, 1875, *Octopus Speaks*, 222, 283–86.

119 *Octopus Speaks*, 301; CPH to Colton, March 4, 1876, ibid., 234.

120 "Resolution of the Legislature of New York, Feb. 25, 1876," 44th Cong., 1st sess., S. Misc. Doc. 65; T. C. Platt to CPH, Sept. 4, 1876, Boyd to CPH, Feb. 14, 1876, CPH Papers, ser. 1, r. 10; CPH to Colton, Feb. 14, 1876, *Octopus Speaks*, 232, 301.

121 CPH to Colton, March 4, 1876, *Octopus Speaks*, 234; T. C. Platt to CPH, Sept. 4, 1876, CPH Papers, ser. 1, r. 10; CPH to Hopkins, March 3, 1876, *Huntington Letters*, 4:467; Summers, *Railroads*, 172–73; Dodge to Scott, Dec. 21, 1875, box 180, LBs—Calif. Texas Railroad: Letters, 1874–78, Dodge Papers.

122 *Octopus Speaks*, 533; CPH to Hopkins, Dec. 28, 1875, *Huntington Letters*, 4:435; William H. Barnes, *American Government: Biographies of Members of the House of Representatives of the Forty-third Congress*, 3 vols. (New York: Nelson & Phillips, 1874), 2:322; CPH to Adams, May 18, 1886, UP, SG2, ser. 1, box 39, f. 5; "Texas and Pacific Railway, Feb. 27, 1875," 43d Cong., 2d sess., H. Rept. 267; Colton to Crocker, Feb. 24, 1875, *Octopus Speaks*, 82; *Congressional Record*, 43d Cong., 1st sess., Feb. 22, 1875, 1600–601.

123 Dodge to Scott, Jan. 15, 1878 LBs—Calif. Texas Railroad: Letters, 1874–78, box 180, vol. 346, 433–35, Dodge Papers.

124 CPH to Hopkins, July 12, 1876, LB, 9:53, box 24, Hopkins Collection.

125 Dodge to Throckmorton, Dec. 21, 1875, box 160, LBs, Texas & Pacific Railroad, Dodge Papers.

126 Colburn to CPH, Feb. 7, 1876, CPH Papers, ser. 1, r. 9; CPH to Hopkins, March 3, 25, 1876, LB, 8:95, 117, box 23, Hopkins Collection; "liveliest," CPH to Colton, Feb. 14, 1876,

Huntington Letters, 4:457–58; CPH to Colton, Feb. 26, March 4, 1876, *Octopus Speaks*, 233–34; Scott to CPH, July 24, 1876; beach, Scott to CPH, July 26, 1876, both in CPH Papers, ser. 1, r. 10.

127 Klein, *Union Pacific*, 379–81; CPH to Hopkins, Nov. 14, 1876, LB, 9:97, Dec. 2, 1876, LB, 9:99, box 24, Hopkins Collection; *San Francisco Chronicle*, Jan. 2, 1877.

128 CPH to Hopkins, Dec. 14, 1876, LB, 9:107, box 24, Hopkins Collection; CPH to Colton, Nov. 15, Dec. 20, Dec. 25, 1876, *Octopus Speaks*, 323, 327, 328; "Texas and Pacific and Southern Pacific," *Railway Age*, Dec. 28, 1876, p. 570; Klein, *Union Pacific*, 378–84.

129 CPH to Colton, Jan. 29, 1876, *Huntington Letters*, 4:453.

130 "Texas and Pacific," *Railway Age*, Jan. 11, 1877, p. 610; Report, to accompany bill HR 4531, "Texas and Pacific Railroad," 44th Cong., 2d sess., Rept. 130, pt. 1, esp. p. 7; HR 4531 (Rept. 139). In the House of Representatives, Jan. 24, 1877, 44th Cong., 2d sess.; CPH to Hopkins, Jan. 13, 20, 1877 (confidential), LB, 9:127, 133, box 24, Hopkins Collection; CPH to Hopkins, Jan. 2, 1877 (misdated 1876), LB, 9:115, box 24, ibid. *Congressional Record*, 44th Cong., 1st sess., Jan. 24, 1877, 924.

131 CPH to Colton, March 7, May 17, 1877, *Octopus Speaks*, 337, 363.

132 M. of C. from Reading to Randall, May 10, 1877, correspondence, box 34, Jno. W. Polk to Randall, June 16, 1877, correspondence, box 35, Randall Papers.

133 Keating to Randall, Sept. 9, 1877, correspondence, box 38, Randall Papers.

134 Chauncey Black to Randall, May 12, 1877, J. N. Keating to Randall, June 4, 1877, S. J. Sanendweiss(?) to Randall, June 1, 1877, all in correspondence, box 34; Beverly Tucker to Randall, May 2, 1877, W. S. Holman to Randall, Aug. 14, 1877, C. W. Wooley to Randall, May 1, 1877, box 33; I. F. Coyle to Randall, June 22, 1877, box 35; CFB to Randall, Aug. 22, 1877, box 37, all in Randall Papers.

135 N. E. Piollet to Randall, Aug. 3, 1877, correspondence, box 37, Randall Papers; encloses a postcard from D. Aiken to Piollet, Aug. 3, 1877.

136 Crocker to CPH, Oct. 16, 1877, Boyd to CPH, Nov. 29, 1877, CPH Papers, ser. 1, r. 13. Thompson, *"Spider's Web,"* 203, says that the Texas and Pacific failed to get a majority, but Huntington's lobbyists thought otherwise. Boyd to Gates, Dec. 9, 1877, CPH Papers, ser. 1, r. 13.

137 C. Vann Woodward, *Reunion and Reaction: The Compromise of 1877 and the End of Reconstruction* (Boston: Little, Brown, 1951), 65–67.

138 Dodge to Scott, March 28, 1877, box 180, vol. 346, LBs—Calif. Texas Railroad: Letters, 1874–78, 410, Dodge Papers.

139 Woodward, *Reunion and Reaction*, 65–121, 120–29, 132–35, 140–42; Michael Les Benedict, "Southern Democrats in the Crisis of 1876–1877: A Reconsideration of Reunion and Reaction," *Southern History* 46 (Nov. 1980): 489–524; Allan Peskin, "Was There a Compromise of 1877?" *Journal of American History* 60 (June 1973): 63–75. Summers, *Press Gang*, 304; Ari Hoogenboom, *The Presidency of Rutherford B. Hayes* (Lawrence: Univ. Press of Kansas, 1988), 43–50.

140 CPH to Hopkins, March 3, 1876, *Huntington Letters*, 3:467; Summers, *Press Gang*, 109–10; Woodward, *Reunion and Reaction*, 101–21.

141 Bardwell to CPH, May 14, 1878, CPH Papers, ser. 1, r. 14.

142 CPH to Gates, May 1, 1878, CPH Papers, ser. 1, r. 14; Sherill to Gates, May 3, 1878, ibid., r. 17; CPH to Colton, Dec. 5, 1877, *Octopus Speaks*, 439. For Windom's helping the Northern Pacific, see Cooke to Bro. Harry, March 14, 1873, Cooke to Windom, Jan. 24, 1873, LBs, Cooke Papers; Larson, *Jay Cooke*, 344; Buck, *Granger Movement*, 221–23.

143 Flagg to CPH, Nov. 18, 1878, CPH Papers, ser. 1, r. 16.

144 Colburn to Gates, Feb. 6, 1878, Sherrill to Gates, Feb. 10, 1878, CPH Papers, ser. 1, r. 14.

145 Bardwell to CPH, Oct. 18, 30, Dec. 9, 1878, Boyd to Gates, Sept. 13, 1878, CPH Papers, ser. 1, r. 15; Bardwell to CPH, May 15, 1879, ibid., r. 17.

146 CPH to Colton, Jan. 22, 28, Feb. 5, 12, 19, 25, 1878, *Octopus Speaks*, 454, 457–58, 465, 468, 470, 472; Deverell, *Railroad Crossings*, 51–52; Grodinsky, *Transcontinental Railway Strategy*, 60–62; *Report of the California Commissioners of Transportation to the Legislature of the State of California, Dec. 1877* (Sacramento: F. P. Thompson, 1877); CPH to Hopkins, March 21, 1876, LB, 8:119, box 23, Hopkins Collection. For analysis of Scott's involvement, see Railroad Lives section on A. A. Cohen and Towne to CPH, March 7, 1876, CPH Papers, ser. 1, r. 9; Ward M. McAfee, "Local Interests and Railroad Regulation in California during the Granger Decade," *Pacific Historical Review* 37 (Feb. 1968): 51–66.

147 Personal and Confidential, CPH to Colonel Thos A. Scott, May 25, 1877, LB, 9:185, box 24, Hopkins Collection; Thomas Sheridan, *Arizona: A History* (Tucson: Univ. of Arizona Press, 1995), 115–16.

148 Ward to Gates, Aug. 22, 1878, Gates to CPH, Aug. 28, 1878, CPH Papers, ser. 1, r. 15; Frémont to Crocker, Jan. 20, 1879, enclosure with Crocker to CPH, Jan. 27, 1879, ibid., r. 16; Howard Roberts Lamar, *The Far Southwest, 1846–1912: A Territorial History* (New Haven: Yale Univ. Press, 1966), 406–8.

149 Richard Taylor to Samuel Barlow, Feb. 10, 26, 1879, March 1, 1879, box 130, Richard Taylor to Samuel Barlow, March 9, 1879, box 110, Barlow Papers.

150 Boyd to CPH, March 5, 1879, CPH, ser. 1, r. 17; CPH to Colton, Jan. 12, 1878, *Octopus Speaks*, 452; Towne to CPH, March 12, 1879, CPH Papers, ser. 1, r. 17; Rothman, *Politics and Power*, 197.

151 *Report of the Commission and of the Minority Commissioner of the United States Pacific Railway Commission . . .* (Washington, D.C.: GPO, 1887), 84, table 29, showing the gross earnings, operating expenses, and net earnings of the Central Pacific Railroad Company, table 31, Legal Expense Account, *PRC*, 8:4659, 4747; Jordan, *Roscoe Conkling*, 413, 417.

152 CPH to Colton, Dec. 17, 1877, *Octopus Speaks*, 443, 148; CPH to Crocker, Nov. 11, 1874, *Huntington Letters*, 4:213; Testimony of Leland Stanford, Aug. 5, 1884, *PRC*, 5:2949.

153 Leslie Decker, *Railroads, Lands, and Politics* (Providence: Brown Univ. Press, 1964), 52, 60, 86–116; *Report of the Auditor of Railroad Accounts*, 46th Cong., 2d sess., 1911, H. Ex. Doc. 1, 17–18; UP, OVP, OC, G. M. Lane to Adams, Jan. 3, 1885, vol. 5, SG 3, ser. 1, r. 4; railroad objections, Adams to George Hoar, UP, PO, OC, vol. 27, ser. 2, r. 23.

154 Decker, *Railroads, Lands, and Politics*, 54–55; William S. Greever, *Arid Domain: The Santa Fe Railway and Its Western Land Grant* (Stanford: Stanford Univ. Press, 1954), 116; W. H. Mills to Stanford, June 20, 1887, *PRC*, 5:2563–64.

155 E. A. Kincaid, "The Federal Land Grants of the Central Pacific Railroad" (Ph.D. diss., Univ. of California, Berkeley, 1922), chap. 13.

156 Decker, *Railroads, Lands, and Politics*, 70–72.

157 Ibid., 73–86, 97, 113; W. H. Mills to Stanford, June 20, 1887, *PRC*, 5:2563; undated memorandum, c. 1882–83, box 38, f. 277, Villard Papers. The Union Pacific admitted it sold lands without survey to avoid taxes; "Lands sold and not patented," Memorandum, G. M. Lane, Asst. to Pres., UP, OVP, OC, vol. 5, r. 4.

158 CPH to Crocker, Dec. 22, 1881, Jan. 19, 1882, vol. 29, CPH Papers, ser. 2, r. 6; *Thirty-second Parallel Pacific Railroad, Remarks of CPH . . . before the Committee on Public Lands of the U.S. Senate, Feb. 2, 1884, on House Bill 3933* (New York: John C. Rankin, 1884).

159 "Pacific Railroads, April 25, 1876," 44th Cong., 1st sess., H. Rept. 440; *Debate in the United States Senate on the Indebtedness of the Pacific Railroads to the United States Government*, 44th Cong., 2d Sess., 1876–77 (Washington, 1877), copy in "Pacific Railroad in Congress, Sinking Fund," Stanford Univ. Library, quote 173; *The Pacific Railroad: Speeches of Hon. Allen G.*

Thurman of Ohio and Hon. David Davis of Illinois, in the Senate of the United States, March 12, 1878 (Washington, 1878), copy in Pac. R.R. file no. 25, President's Office, CB&Q, 63, 1870, 6.8, CB&Q.

160 *Octopus Speaks*, 387–88; Speeches of Thurman and Davis, 6; Memo unsigned on Pacific Road Debt, Feb. 1877, CB&Q, B&M (Nebr.), 1870–79, New Lines, Miscellaneous, 63, 1870, 6.5–6.7, CB&Q.

161 CPH to Crocker, March 2, 1878, CPH Papers, ser. 2, r. 6; Woolworth to Forbes, June 12, 1878, B&M (Nebr.), 1870–79, New Lines, 63, 1870, 6.9, Kearney Connection, Correspondence 1878, CB&Q.

162 CPH to Crocker, April 12, March 2, 1878, CPH Papers, ser. 2, r. 6.

163 For a more detailed analysis of interpretations of this vote, see discursive footnotes on Spatial History Project website. Rothman, *Politics and Power*, 37–38, 199–200; CPH to Colton, July 26, 1876, *Octopus Speaks*, 257–58; Colton to CPH, Nov. 8, 1877, ibid., 429; CPH to Colton, April 19, 1877 [1878], ibid., 490; Klein, *Union Pacific*, 380–84. The vote is from Poole and Rosenthal, Voteview, no. 45, Roll Call 1878, 4/9/78. With paired votes counted, the vote was 41–30. CPH to Crocker, April 12, 1878, CPH Papers, ser. 2, r. 6; *Congressional Record*, 45th Cong., 2d sess., Senate, Thurman Bill, 15, March 26, April 3–5, 8–9, 1878, 2030, 2226, 2263, 2309, 2331, 2365, 2376, 2383–84.

164 Testimony of CPH, *PRC*, 1:38.

A Railroad Life: Elias C. Boudinot

1 There is a picture of Boudinot in *In Memoria: Elias Cornelius Boudinot* (Chicago: Rand McNally, c. 1890), frontispiece. The best biography of him is James W. Parins, *Elias Cornelius Boudinot: A Life on the Cherokee Border* (Lincoln: Univ. of Nebraska Press, 2006). Parins has done by far the most research and tries, in a limited fashion, to rehabilitate Boudinot by contextualizing him; ibid., 1–2.

2 Dewey Whitsett Hodges, "Colonel E. C. Boudinot and His Influence on Oklahoma History" (M.A. thesis, Univ. of Oklahoma, 1929), 5–8, 18.

3 Boudinot outlined his position in *Speech of Elias Boudinot of the Cherokee Nation, Delivered at Vinita, Indian Territory, August 29, 1874* (St. Louis: Barns & Beynon, 1874); Elias C. Boudinot, *The Memorial of Elias C. Boudinot to the Congress of the United States* (Washington, D.C., 1877); *Speech of Elias C. Boudinot, a Cherokee Indian, Delivered before the House Committee on Territories, Feb. 7, 1872 in Behalf of a Territorial Government for the Indian Territory, in Reply to Wm. P. Ross . . .* (Washington, D.C.: McGill & Witherow, 1872); Parins, *Boudinot*, 85–205.

4 H. Craig Miner, *The Corporation and the Indian: Tribal Sovereignty and Industrial Civilization in Indian Territory, 1865–1907* (Columbia: Univ. of Missouri Press, 1976), 20–29, 42.

5 Ibid., 46. *Speech of Elias C. Boudinot . . . at Vinita,* 1; *Argument of Colonel E. C. Boudinot before the Committee on Territories, Jan. 29, 1878* (Alexandria, Va.: G. H. Ramey & Son, 1878), 1–3; Parins, *Boudinot*, 109–52.

6 Miner, *The Corporation and the Indian*, 46. *Speech of Elias C. Boudinot . . . at Vinita,* 1; *Argument of Colonel E. C. Boudinot before the Committee on Territories,* 1–3.

7 *Speech of Elias C. Boudinot . . . at Vinita,* 1; *Argument of Colonel E. C. Boudinot before the Committee on Territories,* 1–3; Parins, *Boudinot*, 187; Miner, *Corporation and the Indian*, 90.

8 *Speech of Elias C. Boudinot . . . at Vinita,* 13. The details of the Atlantic and Pacific dispute come from "Missouri, Kansas & Texas, received 20 Jan. 1872, from George Denison, containing statement by Frank Bond," Case II, no. 4, register One—378, Records of the Lands and Railroads Division, Department of Interior, RG 48, National Archives. For land grant, *Report,*

Directors of the Missouri, Kansas, & Texas Railway Co, Late Union Pacific Railway Company— Southern Branch, 1872–73 (sic) (New York, 1872), 19.

9 Ibid., Miner, *Corporation and the Indian*, 44–46; *Speech of Elias C. Boudinot . . . at Vinita*, 13.

10 "Speech of Hon. Jacob M. Howard in the Senate of the United States, June 22–23, 1870," Graff 1979, Newberry Library, 7; Howard Lamar, *The Far Southwest, 1846–1912: A Territorial History*, rev. ed. (Albuquerque: Univ. of New Mexico Press, 2000), 392; Miner, *Corporation and the Indian*, 44–46; Tom Chaffin, *Pathfinder: John Charles Frémont and the Course of American Empire* (New York: Hill & Wang, 2002), 490–93; Mark Twain and Charles Dudley Warner, *The Gilded Age: A Tale of To-Day*, 2 vols. (New York: Harper & Brothers, 1915, orig. ed. 1873), 236.

11 Chaffin, *Pathfinder*, 469.

12 Testimony of John C. Frémont, Sept. 23, 1887, *PRC*, 7:3846; David Howard Bain, *Empire Express: Building the First Transcontinental Railroad* (New York: Viking, 1999), 168, 192.

13 "Speech of Hon. Jacob M. Howard in the Senate of the United States, June 22–23, 1870"; "Memphis, El Paso & Pacific Rail Road Co." (Explanation of Wm. Aufermann), *Foreign Bondholders Cutting Files*, r. 219, vol. 2.

14 Mark W. Summers, *Railroads, Reconstruction, and the Gospel of Prosperity: Aid under the Radical Republicans, 1865–1867* (Princeton: Princeton Univ. Press, 1984), 170–71; Jay Cooke to Brother Harry, March 20, 1870, Northern Pacific, Letters no. 1 (LB), Jan. 19, 1870–Sept. 27, 1871, Private Letters, Cooke Papers; "Speech of Hon. Jacob M. Howard," 11.

15 H. Craig Miner, *The St. Louis–San Francisco Transcontinental Railroad: The Thirty-fifth Parallel Project, 1853–1890* (Lawrence: Univ. Press of Kansas, 1972), 43–59; Bain, *Empire Express*, 168, 193.

16 Frank Bond to Andrew Pierce, Aug. 23, 1871, Statement of S. W. See, n.d., in Bond Statement, in "Missouri, Kansas & Texas, received 20 Jan. 1872, from George Denison, containing statement by Frank Bond."

17 R. S. Stevens to A. A. Talmage, Sept. 14, 1872, Statement of O. B. Gunn, n.d., H. H. Harding and James Baker to M. Hilton, Dec. 4, 1871, in "Missouri, Kansas & Texas, received 20 Jan. 1872, from George Denison, containing statement by Frank Bond."

18 Miner, *St. Louis–San Francisco*, 86–87.

19 C. J. Hillyer, *Atlantic and Pacific and Indian Territory* (Washington, D.C.: McGill & Witherow, 1871), 5–6, copy bound with *Atlantic and Pacific R.R.'s Reports*, Stanford Univ. Library.

20 John Benston, "To the American Public," Fort Gibson, I.T., Jan. 12, 1874, Graff 234, Newberry Library.

21 Hodges, "Colonel E. C. Boudinot and His Influence on Oklahoma History"; for lobbying, *Argument of Colonel E. C. Boudinot before the Committee on Territories, Jan. 29, 1878*; for Boudinot, railroads, and attempt to organize the territory, Tom Holm, "Indian Lobbyists: Cherokee Opposition to the Allotment of Tribal Lands," *American Indian Quarterly* 5 (May 1979): 116–18; Parins, *Boudinot*, 216–17.

CHAPTER 4: SPATIAL POLITICS

1 Arthur Mellen Wellington, *The Economic Theory of the Location of Railways* (New York: John Wiley & Sons, 1891), 2.

2 Henri Lefebvre, *The Production of Space* (Cambridge: Blackwell, 1991, orig. ed. 1974), 8–9.

3 Engineering News, *Atlas of Railway Progress, 1888–1889* (New York: Engineering News Publishing Company, 1889).

4 Anthony Trollope, *North America* (New York: Harper & Brothers, 1862), 442.

5 Wolfgang Schivelbusch, *The Railway Journey: The Industrialization of Time and Space in the 19th Century* (Berkeley: Univ. of California Press, 1986).

6 Ives to G. Clark, April 24, 1869, Ives to Brother, Nov. 17, 1867, box 6, f. 3, Ives Papers.

7 Ives to Brother, July 19, 1868, box 6, f. 3, Ives Papers.

8 Ives to G. Clark, April 24, 1869, Ives to Brother, Feb. 27, 1869, box 6, f. 3, Ives Papers.

9 Jno. Valentine to Supts. Union Pacific, Jan. 3, 1872, box 6, f. 3, Ives Papers.

10 Wellington, *Location of Railways*.

11 John Hudson, *Plains Country Towns* (Minneapolis: Univ. of Minnesota Press, 1985), 54–55, 58; Van Horne to E. T. Talbot, *Railway Age*, Nov. 26, 1883, Van Horne LB, no. 3(2):666–84, vol. 1.

12 A. N. Towne to Hopkins, Nov. 13, 1876, Towne to Crocker, Nov. 21, 1876, LB, 12:169, box 25, Hopkins Collection; Hudson, *Plains Country Towns*, 68–69.

13 Walter Vaughan, *The Life and Work of Sir William Van Horne* (New York: Century, 1920), 21.

14 Gerald Friesen, *The Canadian Prairies: A History* (Toronto: Univ. of Toronto Press, 1987), 172; Van Horne to W. Weld, July 27, 1887, Van Horne LB, 22(2):511, vol. 4.

15 Van Horne to Purvis, July 14, 1884, Van Horne LB, 6, vol. 2, 901–10; Van Horne to C. J. Brydges, Feb. 23, 1884, ibid., 4:856, vol. 1. Van Horne to Purvis, Sept. 16, 1885, ibid., 13:455–58, vol. 2; Van Horne to Egan, Jan. 6, 1884, ibid., 4:180–82, vol. 1. Van Horne to C. J. Brydges, July 26, 1883, ibid., 2(2):498, vol. 1; John C. Hudson, "The Grain Elevator: An American Invention," in Frank Gohlke, ed., *Measure of Emptiness* (Baltimore: Johns Hopkins Univ. Press, 1992), 92. The classic account of this transformation of nature into commodity is William Cronon, *Nature's Metropolis: Chicago and the Great West* (New York: Norton, 1991), 97–147.

16 Van Horne to Sykes, April 7, 1885, Van Horne LB, 11:1–2, vol. 2; Van Horne to Purvis, July 14, 1884, ibid., 6:901–10, vol. 2; Van Horne to Editor of the *Manitoba Free Press*, Dec. 24, 1883, ibid., 4:10–26, vol. 1; Van Horne to Stephen, Jan. 14, 1884, ibid., 4:283–92, vol. 1; A. J. Cotton to T. A. Burrows, Feb. 5, 1899, Cotton to Hon. R. P. Roblin, Dec. 29, 1902, *Cotton Letters*, 8, 13, 67; A. J. Cotton, "The Present Elevator System in Our Canadian Northwest" (March 1903), ibid., 71.

17 Cronon, *Nature's Metropolis*, 59.

18 Adams to Callaway, May 22, 1886, UP, PO, OC, vol. 38, ser. 2, r. 33; A. N. Towne to Leland Stanford, July 8, 1887, *PRC*, 5:2545.

19 Wellington, *Location of Railways*, 721.

20 Testimony of John C. Stubbs, Aug. 13, 1887, *PRC*, 6:3365–66; Wellington, *Location of Railways*, 330.

21 Wellington, *Location of Railways*, xii, 1, 2, 6, 7.

22 *The Pacific Tourist: An Illustrated Guide to Pacific R.R., California and Pleasure Resorts across the Continent*, ed. H. T. Williams (New York: Adams & Bishop, 1879), 61, 64.

23 *Railroad Gazetteer* (Central Pacific Railroad), Nov. (1871), no. 27 (25 in pencil), "For Gratuitous Distribution on Railways, Steamers and Stages, Monthly Edition, 1200" (Sacramento: H. S. Crocker & Co., 1871), Graff 923, Newberry Library.

24 Wellington, *Location of Railways*, 1, 2, 6, 7; Adams to G. Dexter, April 28, 1890, UP, PO, OC, vol. 50, ser. 2, r. 45.

25 Wellington, *Location of Railways*, 328–29, 364, 404–5, 50–60, cars, 566.

26 Ibid., 571, quote 576, grades 327, 346–47, 543.

27 Ibid., 659.

28 Ibid., 574, 587–80.

29 Ibid., 719–21.

30 Ibid., 121, 185, 189–90, 193, 206–7, 211, 268.

31 Ibid., 17, 86–87, 395–97.

32 Ibid., 195–97.

33 Schivelbusch, *Railway Journey*, 33–84; *Ocean to Ocean: Pacific Railroad and Adjoining Territories, with Distances and Fares of Travel from American Cities*, by the Author of "Absaraka" (Margaret Irvin Carrington) (Philadelphia: J. B. Lippincott, 1869), 9–10.

34 *Report of the U.S. Senate Select Committee on Interstate Commerce*, 49th Cong., 1st sess. (Washington, D.C.: GPO, 1886), 10.

35 James Scott, *Seeing Like a State: How Certain Schemes to Improve the Human Condition Have Failed* (New Haven: Yale Univ. Press, 1998), 25–33; *Railroad Gazetteer* (Central Pacific Railroad), Nov. 1871, Graff 923, Newberry Library; Cronon, *Nature's Metropolis*, 79.

36 "Freight Rates on Central Pacific and Union Pacific Railroads," *PRC*, 5:2585. The average rates per ton-mile were $5.95 on the Central Pacific and $4.26 on the Union Pacific in 1870; in 1885 the rates were $1.83 and $1.49, respectively.

37 Henry H. Swain, "Comparative Statistics of Railroad Rates," *Publications of the American Statistical Association* 6, no. 43 (Sept. 1898): 116.

38 Ibid., 115–32, quote 132.

39 Robert Higgs, "Railroad Rates and the Populist Uprising," *Agricultural History* 44 (July 1970): 291–98; Mark Aldrich, "A Note on Railroad Rates and the Populist Uprising," ibid. 54 (July 1980): 424–32.

40 Swain, "Comparative Statistics of Railroad Rates," 130–32.

41 Friesen, *Canadian Prairies*, 208–9.

42 William Z. Ripley, *Railroads: Rates and Regulation* (New York: Longmans, Green, 1912), 93–94.

43 John H. White Jr., *The American Railroad Freight Car: From the Wood-Car Era to the Coming of Steel* (Baltimore: Johns Hopkins Univ. Press, 1993), 137, 138.

44 Ibid., 70, 138.

45 Ibid., 122–123, table 1.15.

46 Testimony of John C. Stubbs, Aug. 13, 1887, *PRC*, 6:3362–63; J. C. Stubbs to CPH, July 6, 1883, CPH Papers, ser. 1, r. 33.

47 Van Horne to H. Abbott, Nov. 26, 1886, Van Horne LB, 19(1):370–72, vol. 3; Van Horne to W. Whyte, Nov. 26, 1886, ibid., 19(2):373–76, vol. 3.

48 George Rogers Taylor and Irene D. Neu, *The American Railroad Network, 1861–1890* (Cambridge: Harvard Univ. Press, 1956), 69–76; "Practical Railroading," *Railway Age*, July 5, 1877, p. 1104; "Fast Freight Lines—The Other Side," ibid., Sept. 13, 1877, p. 1308; "The Fast Freight Lines," ibid., July 19, 1877, p. 1144; Adams to Perkins, Dec. 1, 1884, UP, PO, OC, ser. 2, r. 20; Adams to Callaway, Nov. 25, 1884, ibid., vol. 24, ser. 2, r. 21.

49 White, *Freight Car*, 125–31.

50 Ibid., 133–34.

51 Shelton Stromquist, *A Generation of Boomers: The Pattern of Railroad Labor Conflict in Nineteenth-Century America* (Urbana: Univ. of Illinois Press, 1987), 160–63.

52 Van Horne to J. J. Cambie, July 20, 1885, LB, 12:379–80, vol. 2.

53 Pierre Berton, *The Last Spike: The Great Railway, 1881–1885* (Toronto: McClelland and Stewart, 1971), 16–23, quote 19.

54 Pierre Berton, *The Impossible Railway: The Building of the Canadian Pacific* (New York: Knopf, 1972), 252.

55 Berton, *Last Spike*, 23–29, 44, 89.

56 Hudson, *Plains Country Towns*, 48.

57 Ibid., 44–47, 74–78.

58 Richard C. Overton, *Burlington West; A Colonization History of the Burlington Railroad* (Cambridge: Harvard Univ. Press, 1941), 285–89; Robin Winks, *Frederick Billings: A Life* (New

York: Oxford Univ. Press, 1991), 256–59; Carroll Van West, *Capitalism on the Frontier: Billings and the Yellowstone Valley in the Nineteenth Century* (Lincoln: Univ. of Nebraska Press, 1993), 112–84; Adams to C. J. Smith, April 19, 1888, UP, PO, OC, vol. 43, ser. 2, r. 38.

59 Henry George, *Progress and Poverty: An Inquiry into the Cause of Industrial Depressions and of Increase of Want with Increase of Wealth* (New York: Robert Schalkenbach Foundation, 1942), 193; Hudson, *Plains Country Towns*, 48.

60 Adams to G. M. Cumming, Sept. 22, 1888, UP, PO, OC, St. Joseph and Grand Island, vol. 25, r. 21.

61 See Robert Harris to Oakes, March 26, 1886, 137 H.10.10 (F), NP.

62 Frank Leonard, "Diplomatic Forces of the New Railroad: Transcontinental Terminus Entry at Vancouver and Seattle," *Journal of Transport History* 28 (March 2007): 21–58.

63 Lorena Parlee, "Porfirio Díaz, Railroads, and Development in Northern Mexico: A Study of Government Policy toward the Central and *Nacional* Railroads, 1876–1910" (Ph.D. diss., University of California, San Diego, 1981), 168.

64 Norbert MacDonald, *Distant Neighbors: A Comparative History of Seattle and Vancouver* (Lincoln: Univ. of Nebraska Press, 1987), 12–13, 26–33; Leonard, "Diplomatic Forces," 29–31; quote, Van Horne to A. B. Rogers, Dec. 8, 1884, Van Horne LB, 3:91–96, vol. 2; Berton, *Impossible Railway*, 444–46.

65 *Report of the California Board of Commissioners of Transportation to the Legislature of California, December 1877* (Sacramento: F. P. Thompson, 1877), 291–93.

66 *Annual Report of the Board of Directors of the Central Pacific Railroad Company to the Stockholders* (San Francisco: H. S. Crocker, 1878), 4. The president's report on p. 4 values the "farming lands" at $30 million, but the land agent's report on p. 47 makes it clear that the railroad counted the entire land grant of the Central Pacific and the California and Oregon R.R. as farming lands amounting to 11,722,400 acres with a value of $29,306,000. The Southern Pacific valued its real estate, depot grounds "including an undivided half-interest in 60 acres land in Mission Bay" exclusive of its land grant and improvements, at $7,644,636. *Annual Report of the Board of Directors of the Southern Pacific Railroad Company to the Stockholders for the Year Ending December 31, 1877* (San Francisco: H. S. Crocker, 1878), 4.

67 *Eight Annual Report of the Board of Railroad Commissioners for the Year Ending December 1, 1890* [*sic*], *State of Kansas* (Topeka: Kansas Publishing House, 1890), table VII, xlvi–xlvii; Interstate Commerce Commission, *Sixth Annual Report on the Statistics of Railways in the United States for the Year Ending June 30, 1893* (Washington, D.C.: GPO, 1894), 84.

68 The totals, 7,369,447 tons going west and 5,585,332 tons going east, are confusing because the combined figures are far short of the total of 22,824,299, and these lines were predominantly east–west lines, indicating less traffic going north–south. *Sixth Annual Report of the Board of Railroad Commissioners for the Year Ending December 1, 1888* (Topeka, 1888), table III, p. 191. For empties as a gauge of traffic, *Second Annual Report of the Board of Railroad Commissioners of the Territory of Dakota for the Year Ending June 30, 1886* (Grand Forks: Plaindealer Book and Job Rooms, 1886), 207, 231, 271.

69 "Proceedings of Convention of the General Ticket and Passenger Association, St. Louis, March 9, 1877," *Records of the National General Ticket Agents' Association* (Chicago: J. M. W. Jones, 1878), 465; Ripley, *Railroads: Rates and Regulation*, chart, p. 102.

70 See, e.g., A. N. Towne to CPH, Feb. 19, 1875, E. P. Vining to Sidney Dillon, Jan. 29, 1875, enclosed with preceding. See also J. C. Stubbs to Towne, Feb. 13, 1875, all in CPH Papers, ser. 1, r. 7; E. P. Vining to J. C. Stubbs, Feb. 19, 1875, ibid.

71 O. A. Dodge to Villard, Sept. 10, 1883, 137.H.4.2 (F), NP.

72 Gerald Berk, *Alternative Tracks: The Constitution of American Industrial Order, 1865–1917* (Baltimore: Johns Hopkins Univ. Press, 1994), 75–76; William Larrabee, *The Railroad Question,*

10th ed. (Chicago: Schulte Publishing, 1898), 368–69; *Report of the Senate Select Committee on Interstate Commerce*, 49th Cong., 1st sess., Submitted to the Senate, Jan. 18, 1886 (Washington, D.C.: GPO, 1886), 2–3; Testimony of Isaac M. Raymond, Lincoln, Monday, July 4, 1887, *PRC*, 3:1528–29.

73 Adams to S. R. Callaway, UP, PO, OC, Callaway, vol. 30, ser. 2, r. 27.

74 Ripley, *Railroads: Rates and Regulation*, 135–39; Statement of Thomas Sturgis, *Report of the Senate Select Committee on Interstate Commerce*, 49th Cong., 1st sess., Submitted to the Senate, Jan. 18, 1886 (Washington, D.C.: GPO, 1886), appendix, 159–60.

75 Towne to CPH, April 19, 1871, CPH Papers, ser. 1, r. 3; Towne to CPH, Oct. 29, 1877, ibid., r. 13; William Z. Ripley, *Railway Problems* (Boston: Ginn & Company, 1907), 123–44; Gerald D. Berk, *Louis D. Brandeis and the Making of Regulated Competition, 1900–1932* (New York: Cambridge Univ. Press, 2009), 74–78.

76 Berk, *Louis D. Brandeis*, 74–78.

77 C. F. Adams to A. Millar, Aug. 22, 1889, UP, PO, OC, vol. 48, ser. 2, r. 43; C. F. Adams to W. H. Baldwin, Dec. 5, 1889, C. F. Adams to J. B. Haggin, Dec. 5, 1889, ibid., vol. 49, ser. 2, r. 44.

78 William Mahl to Gates, April 12, 1889, CPH Papers, ser. 1, r. 47.

79 Albert Fink, *Cost of Railroad Transportation: Railroad Accounts and Governmental Regulation of Railroad Tariffs* (Louisville: John P. Morton, 1875); Alfred Chandler, *The Visible Hand: The Managerial Revolution in American Business* (Cambridge: Harvard Univ. Press, 1997), 116–20.

80 Albert Fink, *Argument before the Committee on Commerce . . . on the Reagan Bill . . . , Washington, January 14, 15, 16, 1880* (New York: Russell Brothers Printers, 1880), 7; George H. Miller, *Railroads and Granger Laws* (Madison: Univ. of Wisconsin Press, 1971), 140–60.

81 Ripley, *Railroads: Rates and Regulation*, is the classic contemporary account of the making of rates.

82 Ibid., 106–8.

83 Ripley, *Railroads: Rates and Regulation*, 108; Richard A. Posner, "Natural Monopoly and Its Regulation," *Stanford Law Review* 21, no. 3 (Feb. 1969): 570; Joseph Schumpeter et al., "Railway Rate Making: A Discussion," *American Economic Review* 4 (March 1914): 81.

84 Albert Wilbur to George Wilbur, April 25, 1883, box 13, f. 268, Albert Wilbur to George Wilbur, Aug. 29, 1881, box 13, f. 271, Albert Wilbur to George Wilbur, Nov. 17, 1881, box 13, f. 271, Wilbur Papers.

85 *Report of the Board of Commissioners of Transportation to the Legislature of the State of California, Dec. 1877* (Sacramento: F. P. Thompson, 1877), 26, 28, 69; George H. Tinkham, *A History of Stockton from Its Organization to the Present Time . . .* (San Francisco: Wm. Hinton, 1880), 327–29; Michael Magliari, "Populism, Steamboats, and the Octopus: Transportation Rates and Monopoly in California's Wheat Regions, 1890–1896," *Pacific Historical Review* 58 (Nov. 1989): 452–57; David Vaught, *After the Gold Rush: Tarnished Dreams in the Sacramento Valley* (Baltimore: Johns Hopkins Univ. Press, 2007), 152–55.

86 Public Utilities Commission, *Annual Reports*, Central Pacific Railroad Company, California State Archives, Sacramento. As will be discussed later, these rates are in a sense a fiction, since they were not applied evenly to all shippers. Negotiations produced rebates. Still, the rates are analytically useful because they establish the base point for negotiations, and only very large rebates would change the relationship between one place and another, although they certainly altered the competitive relationship of shippers in the same place. For through rates, see "No. 23, Through Freight Tariff Southern Pacific Railroad to Take Effect July 29, 1877 between San Francisco and Stations Named Below." Through rates also were in effect from Stockton, Lathrop, San Jose, and Oakland.

87 No. 7, Central Pacific Railroad, Special Freight Tariff on Grain in Carloads to the General

Markets, Feb. 1, 1876. I am calculating a carload at 10 tons per car, which was the designated weight for a carload on the Central Pacific. Central Pacific Local Freight Tariff (Western & Oregon Divisions), Local Classification. River Rates to San Francisco, untitled document, State Railroad Commission, California State Archives, Sacramento. Albert Wilbur to George Wilbur, Nov. 17, 1881, box 13, f. 271, Wilbur Papers; Magliari, "Populism, Steamboats, and the Octopus," 461.

88　No. 7, Central Pacific Railroad, Special Freight Tariff . . . Feb. 1, 1876; *Report of the Board of Commissioners . . . 1877*, 28, 67, 69. Agents were instructed not to show the tariff book to customers so that they could not compare rates. Southern Pacific R.R., Northern Division, Local Freight Tariff, Jan. 1, 1880, Special Notice, Huntington Library.

89　A visualization created by Peter Shannon, "Seeing Space in Terms of Track Length and Cost of Shipping," illustrates how these freight rates distorted space at the Spatial History Project website, Stanford Univ.

90　Report of Commissioner Foote, *Fourth Annual Report of the Board of Railroad Commissioners of the State of California for the Year ending Dec. 31, 1883* (Sacramento: James J. Ayers, 1884), 142–43.

91　A. N. Towne to CPH, Feb. 19, 1875, E. P. Vining to Sidney Dillon, Jan. 29, 1875, enclosed with preceding. See also J. C. Stubbs to Towne, Feb. 13, 1875, CPH Papers, ser. 1, r. 7; E. P. Vining to J. C. Stubbs, Feb. 19, 1875, ibid.

92　*Third Annual Report of the Board of Railroad Commissioners of the State of California for the Years Ending Dec. 31, 1880–81–82* (Sacramento: J. D. Young, 1882), 79; *Proceedings of the Trans-Continental Association . . .* , *1888*, 148–49, CB&Q, 33, 1890, 7.3–8.1, box 1.

93　Klein, *Union Pacific*, 314.

94　Testimony of Charles Francis Adams, April 29, 1887, *PRC*, 1:110–11; CPH to Hopkins, April 19, 1875, LB, 7:131–32, Hopkins Collection; CPH to Adams, May 18, 1886, UP, SG2, ser. 1, box 39, f. 5; Testimony of J. C. Stubbs, *Report of the Industrial Commission on Transportation . . . Testimony Taken since May 1, 1900*, vol. 9 (Washington, D.C.: GPO, 1901), 763.

95　The Pacific Mail Steamship Company, vols. 42, 44, 45 46, 49, Pacific Mail Mss.

96　*San Francisco Morning Call* in 1892 and then reprinted as *Fettered Commerce: How the Pacific Mail and the Railroads Have Bled San Francisco* (San Francisco: Daily Morning Call Company, 1892), 10–11, 20–21; Klein, *Union Pacific*, 289–90.

97　Klein, *Union Pacific*, 314–17, 387–88; Aims McGuinness, *Path of Empire: Panama and the California Gold Rush* (Ithaca: Cornell Univ. Press, 2008), 5, 54–83.

98　Klein, *Union Pacific*, 289–90; *Chicago Daily Tribune*, Jan. 30, 1880, p. 8, Feb. 1, 1880.

99　Some 6.3 times as much freight moved within California by rail as was shipped outside in 1873; in 1883 4.6 pounds of goods still moved within California for every pound shipped out. *Thirty-Fourth Annual Report of the Chamber of Commerce of San Francisco . . .* (San Francisco: C. A. Murdock, 1884), 41–42, see Chart D in appendix.

100　*Tenth Annual Report of the Board of Railroad Commissioners of the State of California, 1889* (Sacramento: J. D. Young, 1880), 46, table 17.

101　The eighteen items were grains, beans, borax, canned fruit, dried fruit, green fruit, hops, hides/ pelts, lumber, leather, mustard seed, quicksilver, salmon, sugar, tea, wine/brandy, and wool. For shipment of canned goods by clipper ship, Testimony of W. R. Wheeler, *Report of the Industrial Commission on Transportation*, vol. 9, 754. See Charts A, B, and C in appendix.

102　Frank Norris, *The Octopus* (New York: Bantam, 1958), 47.

103　*Chicago Daily Tribune*, Jan. 30, 1880, p. 8; Report of Commissioner Foote, *Fourth Annual Report of the California Board of Railroad Commissioners* (Sacramento, 1883*)* 129, 133.

104　See Charts D and E in appendix.

105　*Fourth Annual Report of the California Board of Railroad Commissioners* (1883), 134.

106 Ibid., 129–33; William Deverell, *Railroad Crossing: Californians and the Railroad, 1850–1910* (Berkeley: Univ. of California Press, 1994), 59–60; Alexander Callow Jr., "San Francisco's Blind Boss," *Pacific Historical Review* 25 (Aug. 1956): 261–71; R. Hal Williams, *The Democratic Party and California Politics, 1880–1896* (Stanford: Stanford Univ. Press, 1973), 24–31.

107 Callow, "San Francisco's Blind Boss," 261–71.

108 Ibid.; Williams, *Democratic Party and California Politics*, 24–31.

109 *County of San Mateo v. Southern Pacific Railroad Company*, 13 Fed. 145 (July 31, 1882); *County of Santa Clara v. Southern Pacific Railroad Company*, 18 Fed. 385 (Sept. 17, 1883).

110 White to Geo. Hayes, Aug. 16, 1889, Correspondence, Outgoing, box 4, Aug. 14, 1889–Jan. 11, 1890, White Papers; Paul Kens, *Justice Stephen Field: Shaping Liberty from the Gold Rush to the Gilded Age* (Lawrence: Univ. Press of Kansas, 1997), 239–43.

111 Williams, *Democratic Party and California Politics*, 31–41.

112 Ward Merner McAfee, "Local Interests and Railroad Regulation in Nineteenth Century California" (Ph.D. diss., Stanford Univ., 1965), 162–68; William A. Bullough, "Hannibal versus the Blind Boss: The 'Junta,' Chris Buckley, and Democratic Reform Politics in San Francisco," *Pacific Historical Review* 46, no. 2 (May 1977): 181–206.

113 Williams, *Democratic Party and California Politics*, 40–46. Williams doesn't believe corruption played a role, but McAfee, "Local Interests and Railroad Regulation," 164–68, presents a very strong case that it did. William Issel and Robert W. Cherny, *San Francisco, 1865–1932: Politics, Power, and Urban Development* (Berkeley: Univ. of California Press, 1986), 130–32.

114 "Railroad Pools: The Atlantic and Pacific and the Transcontinental Association," *Los Angeles Times*, Dec. 12, 1885, p. 1; Klein, *Union Pacific*, 423–74.

115 Klein, *Union Pacific*, 473.

116 Kimball to S. R. Callaway, March 17, 1886, enclosure with Callaway to Adams, March 18, 1886, UP, SG2, ser. 1, box 34, f. 1: Callaway; Kimball to S. R. Callaway, March 22, 1886, enclosure with Callaway to Adams, March 23, 1886, ibid., f. 2: Callaway; Traffic Manager to Editor of *Railway Age*, Jan. 7, 1887, Van Horne LB, 20(1):48–49, vol. 3; Memorandum, c. Oct. 1886, Van Horne LB, 18 (2), vol. 3; Keith L. Bryant, *History of the Atchison, Topeka, and Santa Fe, Railway* (New York: Macmillan, 1974), 97–105; rates, L. S. Anderson to G. M. Lane, June 15, 1886, UP, OVP, OC, vol. 1, r. 1.

117 Adams to Hallgarten & Co., March 1, 1886, UP, PO, OC, vol. 34, ser. 2, r. 29.

118 Adams to Callaway, April 22, 1886, UP, PO, OC, vol. 31, ser. 2, r. 23. Adams occasionally wavered and thought through traffic would improve, Adams to Callaway, Aug. 24, 1886, vol. 32, ser. 2, r. 27.

119 Adams to H. White, Dec. 3, 1885, UP, PO, OC, vol. 30, ser. 2, r. 26; Adams to Callaway, Oct. 10, 1885, ibid., vol. 32, ser. 2, r. 28; Julius Grodinsky, *Transcontinental Railway Strategy, 1869–1893: A Study of Businessmen* (Philadelphia: Univ. of Pennsylvania Press, 1962), 165–66. The percentage for 1886 was 8 percent. Testimony of Oliver Mink, May 24, 1887, *PRC*, 2:624.

120 Van Horne to Sir. John McDonald, Oct. 25, 1885, Van Horne LB, 14:110–12, vol. 2; Van Horne to J. J. Hill, April 21, 1886, ibid., 16:268–70, vol. 3; General Traffic Manager to *Railway Age*, Jan.7, 1887, ibid., 20:48, vol. 3; Van Horne to P. V. Martinsen, Jan. 19, 1887, 19:100, vol. 3.

121 S. R. Callaway to Adams, Oct. 19, 1886, UP, box 35, f. Aug.–Oct. 1886, LB, 53. S. R. Callaway to Adams, Jan. 8, 1887, ibid., box 47, f. 3; Adams to Callaway, March 29, 1886, UP, PO, OC, vol. 33, ser. 2, r. 28; Testimony of Charles Francis Adams, April 29, 1887, *PRC*, 1:112; Partial Memorandum, 1886 Van Horne LB, 18:965–66, vol. 3; General Traffic Manager to *Railway Age*, Jan. 7, 1887, ibid., 20:48, vol. 3.

122 Richard Orsi, *Sunset Limited: The Southern Pacific Railroad and the Development of the American West, 1850–1930* (Berkeley: Univ. of California Press, 2005), 319–22.

123 Pacific Mail Mss., vol. 47, Outward SF, 1886, 233, 237. See Chart F in appendix.

124 Wine and Brandy Shipped out of California Eastbound, *Southern Pacific Annual Report of the Southern Pacific Company . . . , 1890* (n.p., n.d.), 8. See Chart G in appendix.

125 See Chart E in appendix.

126 S. R. Callaway to Adams, Oct. 19, 1886, UP, RG 3761, box 35, f. Aug.–Oct. 1886, LB, 53; S. R. Callaway to Adams, Jan. 8, 1887, ibid., box 47, f. 3; Adams to Callaway, March 29, 1886, UP, PO, OC, vol. 33, ser. 2, r. 28; Testimony of Charles Francis Adams, April 29, 1887, *PRC*, 1:112.

127 *Ninth Annual Report of the Board of Railroad Commissioners of the State of California for the Year Ending Dec. 31, 1888* (Sacramento: J. D. Young, 1889), 38.

128 "Union Pacific Rebates," *New York Times*, July 1, 1887, p. 5; Klein, *Union Pacific*, 385, 592–99.

129 H. F. Scott to CPH, Aug. 12, 1892, CPH, ser. 1, r. 51; Stuart Daggett, *Chapters on the History of the Southern Pacific* (New York: Ronald Press Company, 1922), 293–301; W. H. Mills to CPH, June 7, 1892, CPH Papers, ser. 1, r. 50. San Francisco merchants also gained an advantage over eastern wholesalers by carrying bills for three to twelve months, while eastern wholesalers demanded payment in thirty days. Margaret Kolb Holden, "The Rise and Fall of Oregon Populism: Legal Theory, Political Culture and Public Policy, 1868–95" (Ph.D. diss., Univ. of Virginia, 1993), 231.

130 Address of S. F. Pierson, "Proceedings of the General Ticket and Passenger Agents Association, New York, Sept. 8, 1876," in *Records of the National General Tickets Agents Association* (Chicago: J. M. W. Jones, 1878), 440; Friesen, *Canadian Prairies*, 190–91.

131 James Wilson to Adams, Dec. 16, 23, 1888, UP, RG 3761, box 70, f. 2; Adams to Wilson, Dec. 17, 1888, UP, PO, OC, vol. 45, ser. 2, r. 40.

132 Testimony of William Felker, July 13, 1887, *PRC*, 4:1958; Testimony of Peter Dey, July 1, 1887, *PRC*, 3:1429.

133 Kimball to S. R. Callaway, March 22, 1886, enclosure with Callaway to Adams, March 23, 1886, UP, SG2, ser. 1, box 34, f. 2: Callaway.

134 Fink, *Argument before the Committee of Commerce*, 15–21, in Albert Fink, *Railway Pamphlets*, Stanford Univ. Library; Thomas K. McCraw, *Prophets of Regulation: Charles Francis Adams, Louis D. Brandeis, James M. Landis, Alfred E. Kahn* (Cambridge: Belknap Press of Harvard Univ. Press, 1984), 48–50; Testimony of Charles Francis Adams, July 13, 1888, *PRC*, 4:2003–4.

135 Herbert Hovenkamp, *Enterprise and American Law, 1836–1937* (Cambridge: Harvard Univ. Press, 1991), 214–15.

136 McCraw, *Prophets of Regulation*, 48–49; Charles Francis Adams, *Railroads: Their Origin and Problems* (New York: G. P. Putnam's Sons, 1878), 148–80; Testimony of Charles Francis Adams, April 17, 1887, *PRC*, 1:109. Robert E. Riegel, "Western Railroad Pools," *Mississippi Valley Historical Review* 18 (Dec. 1931): 364–77; Perkins to Forbes, March 17, 1884, 33, 1880, 7.2, CB&Q.

137 Perkins to Forbes, Jan. 29, 1884, 3.2–3.5; Perkins to Forbes, Jan. 4, 1884, 1880, 7.2, both in CB&Q; M. Hughitt to C. F. Adams, Dec. 29, 1888, UP, SG2, ser. 1, box 64, f. 1; Julius Grodinsky, *The Iowa Pool: A Study in Railroad Competition, 1870–84* (Chicago: Univ. of Chicago Press, 1950).

138 Charles Francis Adams, "Which Will Quickest Solve the Railroad Question: Force Bills or Public Opinion?" (Address at Oshkosh, Wisc., Sept. 3, 1875), 9, in Charles Francis Adams, *Railway Pamphlets*, Stanford Univ. Library.

139 Adams to Callaway, Jan. 11, 1887, UP, PO, OC, vol. 39, ser. 2, r. 34; Fred L. Ames to Adams, Oct. 5, 1886, UP, MS 3761, SG2, ser. 1, box 31, f. Adams-Anderson; Testimony of William Felker, July 13, 1887, *PRC*, 4:1958.

140 For early dependence on competition, see Miller, *Railroads and the Granger Laws*, 19, 22.

141 Joseph Nimmo Jr., *Railroad Federations and the Relation of the Railroads to Commerce* . . . (Washington, D.C.: GPO, 1885), 13; Southern Pacific R.R., Northern Division, Local Freight Tariff, January 1, 1880, Special Notice, Huntington Library.

142 Fink, Argument before the Committee of Commerce, 9.

143 Taylor and Neu, *American Railroad Network*, 69–76; "Practical Railroading," *Railway Age*, July 5, 1877, p. 1104. "Fast Freight Lines—The Other Side," ibid., Sept. 13, 1877, p. 1308. "The Fast Freight Lines," ibid., July 19, 1877, p. 1144; E. P. Vining to V. M. Came, March 8, 1884, CB&Q, 1880, 7.2.

144 Testimony of Thomas Kimball, June 22, 1887, *PRC*, 3:1123, 1128. Hovenkamp, *Enterprise and American Law*, 151–52.

145 Testimony of De Witt Woods, July 13, 1887, *PRC*, 4:1964. Testimony of Charles Francis Adams, July 13, 1887, *PRC*, 4:1997.

146 Perkins to Forbes, Sept. 24, 1879, 3 F 3.2–3.3, J. M. Forbes, In-letters, private from C. E. Perkins, CB&Q; A Letter to Hon. S. M. Cullom from Charles E. Perkins, Sept. 21, 1885, 3, P4.12, Chicago, Burlington & Quincy Statement, Charles Francis Adams, May 24, 1887, *PRC*, 2:605–6.

147 Perkins to Larrabee, Oct. 31, 1887, Larrabee to Perkins, Nov. 18, 1887, Perkins to Larrabee, Dec. 2, 1887, all in C. E. Perkins, Out Letters/In Letters 3, P 4.11–P 4.3, CB&Q; Seligman, "Railway Tariffs," 227–28. For Iowa and regulation, see Jeffrey Ostler, *Prairie Populism: The Fate of Agrarian Radicalism in Kansas, Nebraska, and Iowa, 1880–1892* (Lawrence: Univ. Press of Kansas, 1993), 63–68.

148 Maury Klein, "Competition and Regulation: The Railroad Model," *Business History* 64 (Summer 1990): 313–16; Joseph Schumpeter, "Railway Rate Making: Discussion," *American Economic Review* 4 (March 1914): 81–100; Edwin R. A. Seligman, "Railway Tariffs and Interstate Commerce Law," *Political Science Quarterly* 2 (June 1887): 224–30, quote 229; Albert Fink, *Cost of Railroad Transportation: Railroad Accounts and Governmental Regulation of Railroad Tariffs* (Louisville: John Morton, 1875), 75–76; Frank Haigh Dixon, "Recent Railway Legislation in Kansas," *Quarterly Journal of Economics* 13 (April 1899): 336–38; Proceedings of the Conference between Presidents, in Burlington 33, 1880, 7.4–7.6, CB&Q, 52–53.

149 See Berk, *Louis D. Brandeis*, 74–81.

A Railroad Life: Alfred A. Cohen

1 *Central Pacific Railroad Company v. Alfred A. Cohen, Argument of Mr. Cohen, the Defendant, in Person, before the Hon. W. P. Daingerfield, Presiding Judge without a Jury,* Twelfth District Court, City and County of San Francisco (1876), Huntington Library, 67742, p. 49.

2 Ibid., *Statement of the Case*, p. 47, copy in Huntington Library.

3 See, e.g., CPH to Hopkins, Sept. 14, 1872, LB, 2:175; CPH to Hopkins, May 7, 1872, 2:115, both in box 20, Hopkins Collection; *Central Pacific Railroad Company v. Alfred A. Cohen, Statement of the Case* (1876), p. 1, Huntington Library.

4 CPH to Hopkins, May 19, 1871, *Huntington Letters*, 3:276, also CPH to Hopkins, Nov. 2, 1870, ibid., 3:212; CPH to Stanford, Nov. 5, 1870, ibid., 3:214.

5 Hopkins to CPH, Feb. 4, 1873, CPH Papers, ser. 1, r. 5.

6 CPH to Hopkins, Nov. 11, 1873, LB, 5:181, box 22, Hopkins Collection.

7 Cohen to CPH, March 24, 1875, CPH Papers, ser. 1, r. 7; Cohen to CPH, April 27, 1875, ibid., r. 8.

8 D. O. Mills to CPH, Nov. 16, 1875, CPH Papers, ser. 1, r. 8.

9 *Central Pacific Railroad Company v. Alfred A. Cohen* (1876), 2.

10 CPH to Hopkins, March 21, 1876, LB, 8:119, box 23, Hopkins Collection.

11 For complexities of Archer Bill, see Ward M. Mcafee, "Local Interests and Railroad Regulation in California during the Granger Decade," *Pacific Historical Review* 37 (Feb. 1968): 51–66; Towne to CPH, March 7, 1876, CPH Papers, ser. 1, r. 9.

12 CPH to Hopkins, May 15, 1876, LB, 9:23, box 24, Hopkins Collection; A. N. Towne to CPH, March 7, 1876, CPH Papers, ser. 1, r. 9.

13 *Central Pacific Railroad Company* v. *Alfred A. Cohen* (1876), 2–3; CPH to Hopkins, May 12, 1876, LB, 9:19, box 24, Hopkins Collection.

14 CPH to Colton Oct. 26, 1875, *Huntington Letters*, 4:397.

15 *Alfred A. Cohen, Southern Pacific Railroad First Mortgage Bonds: Review of the Statements of Mr. C. P. Huntington, Agent and Attorney* (San Francisco, 1876).

16 CPH to Hopkins, May 12, 1876, LB, 9:19, box 24, Hopkins Collection.

17 CPH to Hopkins, June 10, 1876, LB, 9:39, box 24, Hopkins Collection; *Central Pacific Company* v. *Alfred A. Cohen*, Tuesday, July 18, 1876 ff., vol. 1, Tuesday, July 18, 1876 ff.

18 W. Hoay, Adams Express Company, to CPH, Jan. 13, 1875, CPH Papers, ser. 1, r. 7.

19 *Central Pacific Railroad Company* v. *Alfred A. Cohen, Argument of Mr. Cohen* (1876), p. 49. Cohen was speaking of Crocker's house.

20 A. A. Cohen, *The California King, His Conquests, Crimes, Confederates, Counselors, Courtiers and Vassals: Stanford's Post-Prandial New Years Day Soliloquy* (San Francisco: San Francisco News Company, 1876), 5, copy in Huntington Library.

21 CPH to Hopkins, Jan. 5, 1877 (misdated 1876), Personal, Willard's Hotel, LB, 9:119, box 24, Hopkins Collection.

22 D. Colton to CPH, Sept. 20, 1878, *Octopus Speaks*, 560. Huntington came to regard the attack on Cohen as a colossal mistake. CPH to Hopkins, May 12, 1876, LB, 9:19, box 24, Hopkins Collection.

23 Alfred A. Cohen, *Argument before the Committee on Corporations of the Senate of the State of California, Senate Bill, no. 332, Introduced by Mr. Lindsey* (n.p., n.d.), copy in Huntington Library.

24 A. A. Cohen, *An Address on the Railroad Evil and Its Remedy . . . Saturday, Aug. 2, 1879* (San Francisco: Francis, Valentine & Co., 1879), 12.

25 Cohen to CPH, June 11, 1878, CPH Papers, ser. 1, r. 14.

26 CPH to Crocker, Feb. 4, 17, 1882, CPH Papers, vol. 29, ser. 2, r. 6.

27 Colton to CPH, Feb. 7, March 5, 1878, *Octopus Speaks*, 467, 477.

28 Colton to CPH, March 29, 1879, *Octopus Speaks*, 482.

29 Flagg to CPH, Nov. 15, 1878, CPH Papers, ser. 1, r. 16.

30 Testimony of Alfred Cohen, July 27, 1887, *PRC*, 4:2386, for full testimony, 2381–405.

31 Testimony of Leland Stanford, Aug. 3, 1887, *PRC*, 5:2769, 2774.

32 Testimony of Daniel Strong, Aug. 4, 1887, *PRC*, 5:2864–65, interjections by Cohen and Stanford.

CHAPTER 5: KILKENNY CATS

1 Michael Quinion, World Wide Words, http://www.worldwidewords.org/index.php.

2 Charles Francis Adams, *Charles Francis Adams, 1835–1915: An Autobiography* (Boston: Houghton Mifflin, 1916), 173.

3 Adams to Harris, Nov. 24, 1885, UP, PO, OC, vol. 30, ser. 2, r. 26.

4 Adams, *Charles Francis Adams*, 193.

5 Maury Klein, *Union Pacific*, vol. 1, *Birth of a Railroad, 1862–1893* (Garden City, N.Y.: Doubleday, 1987), 453–57; "Old thief," Edward Chase Kirkland, *Charles Francis Adams Jr., 1835–1915: The Patrician at Bay* (Cambridge: Harvard Univ. Press, 1965), 92.

6 Kirkland, *Charles Francis Adams*, 31.

7 Adams, *Charles Francis Adams*, 172–73, 175.

8 Kirkland, *Charles Francis Adams*, 76–80, 90–91.

9 Klein, *Union Pacific*, 461; Maury Klein, *The Life and Legend of Jay Gould* (Baltimore: Johns Hopkins Univ. Press, 1986), 3.

10 Kirkland, *Charles Francis Adams*, 222; Alfred Chandler Jr., *The Visible Hand: The Managerial Revolution in American Business* (Cambridge: Harvard Univ. Press, 1977), 148–49. Maury Klein, the most prominent historian of American railroads, has written a rehabilitative biography that stresses Gould the manager, organizer, entrepreneur, and builder. Klein, *Jay Gould*, 3–90, 490–97.

11 Adams to Judge (Dillon), Dec. 30, 1887, UP, PO, OC, vol. 42, ser. 2, r. 37.

12 Testimony of Jay Gould, May 19, 1887, *PRC*, 1:588. Testimony of Edward Rosewater, June 28, 1887, *PRC*, 3:1349–51; James F. Hudson, *The Railways and the Republic* (New York: Harper & Brothers, 1886), 276–84.

13 William Z. Ripley, *Railroads: Finance and Organization* (New York: Longmans, Green, 1915), 54–55.

14 Ibid.

15 Testimony of Leland Stanford, July 29, 1887, *PRC*, 5:2527.

16 Richard P. Brief, "The Origin and Evolution of Nineteenth-Century Asset Accounting," *Business History Review* 40 (Spring 1966): 1–23; Klein, *Jay Gould*, 274–75, 306; Albro Martin, "Railroads and the Equity Receivership: An Essay on Institutional Change," *Journal of Economic History* 34 (Sept. 1974): 696–97.

17 Testimony of Jay Gould, May 19, 1887, *PRC*, 1:588. For actual costs, Testimony of James W. Davis, June 21, 1887, *PRC*, 3:1087. The best American bar iron was running between $146 (its peak) a ton in 1865 and $75 in 1870. Pig iron ran between a little under $60 to a little under $40 during this same period. Ties usually ran 25 to 50 cents. Arthur Mellen Wellington, *The Economic Theory of the Location of Railways* (New York: John Wiley & Sons, 1891), 763, 776. In 1868 the Central Pacific calculated 88 tons of iron (at $75 per ton) for rails and superstructure per mile, Testimony, *PRC*, 8:4547.

18 See, e.g., Robert Fogel, *The Union Pacific: A Case in Premature Enterprise* (Baltimore: Johns Hopkins Univ. Press, 1960), 74–76.

19 Charles Francis Adams, "Railroad Inflation," *North American Review* 108 (Jan. 1869): 143–50.

20 Klein, *Union Pacific*, 38–39.

21 Commissioner Anderson, in Testimony of Leland Stanford, July 26, 1887, *PRC*, 5:2630.

22 Poor, *Manual, 1877–78*, 665; Ernest Howard, *Wall Street Fifty Years after Erie: Being a Comparative Account of the Making and Breaking of the Jay Gould Railroad Fortune* (Boston: Stratford Company, 1923), 1–6; Klein, *Jay Gould*, 141, 145, 158.

23 Adams to O. H. Platt, Dec. 11, 1889, UP, PO, OC, vol. 49, ser. 2, r. 48.

24 Julius Grodinsky, *The Iowa Pool: A Study in Railroad Competition, 1870–84* (Chicago: Univ. of Chicago Press, 1950), 70–71; Villard to Grey, April 26, 1875, LB 1, Kansas Pacific Railroad, Villard Papers; Dietrich G. Buss, *Henry Villard: A Study of Transatlantic Investments and Interests, 1879–95* (New York: Arno Press, 1978), 72–79; Testimony of John B. Usher, July 8, 1887, *PRC*, 3:1695.

25 Buss, *Villard*, 69–70.

26 Testimony of Russell Sage, May 12, 1887, *PRC*, 1:346; Testimony of Jay Gould, May 17, 1887, ibid., 1:456.

27 Testimony of Henry Villard, May 14, 1887, *PRC*, 1:428–35, 56. For its overcapitalization, see Report of William Calhoun, Accountant, *PRC*, 9:4891–4919; Henry Villard, *Memoirs of Henry*

Villard, Journalist and Financier, 1835–1900, 2 vols. (Westminster: Archibald and Constable & Co., 1904), 2:280–81.

28 Peter Tufano, "Business Failure, Judicial Intervention and Financial Innovation: Restructuring U.S. Railroads in the Nineteenth Century," *Business History Review* 71 (Spring 1997): 8–19.

29 Southmayd to Holmes, Sept. 5, 1878, Villard Papers, box 3, f. 26; Villard, *Memoirs*, 2:282.

30 Testimony of Russell Sage, May 13, 1887, *PRC*, 1:362–63; Testimony of Henry Villard, May 14, 1887, *PRC*, 1:428–32; Buss, *Villard*, 72–78.

31 Testimony of Henry Villard, May 14, 1887, *PRC*, 1:429; Testimony of Russell Sage, May 12, 1887, *PRC*, 1:344; Testimony of Sidney Dillon, May 5, 1887, *PRC*, 1:198, 200–201; Testimony of James Ham, May 5, 1887, *PRC*, 1:223–24; Villard to Endicott, Jan. 11, 1879, Private Correspondence, LB 32, Villard Papers.

32 Testimony of Jay Gould, May 18, 1887, Abstract of Journal Entries Concerning the Kansas Pacific Pool, Sundries to 4th National Bank, March 7, 1879, *PRC*, 1:497; Villard, *Memoirs*, 2:282–83; Villard to Endicott, April 1, 5, March 7, 1879, Villard Papers, Private Correspondence, 32; Papers; Augustus Veenendaal Jr., *Slow Train to Paradise: How Dutch Investment Helped Build American Railroads* (Stanford: Stanford Univ. Press, 1996), 102; Testimony of Jay Gould, May 17–18, 1887, *PRC*, 1:465.

33 Buss, *Villard*, 72–78; Klein, *Union Pacific*, 318, 397–99.

34 *PRC*, 58–61; Klein, *Union Pacific*, 410.

35 Arthur W. Hoyt, Jan. 13, 1879, "Journals of Travel to Colorado," WA MSS s–1766, Hoyt Papers, Beinecke Library, Yale Univ.

36 Testimony of Jay Gould, May 19, 1887, *PRC*, 1:575, 579–80.

37 Testimony of Russell Sage, May 12, 1887, *PRC*, 1:360. Testimony of Jay Gould, May 18, 1887, Exhibit no. 1, May 18, 1887, *PRC*, 1:492–95; Villard, *Memoirs*, 2:282–83; Testimony of Leonard Smith, July 11, 1887, *PRC*, 4:1722.

38 Testimony of George Arents, May 10, 1887, *PRC*, 1:266–67; Testimony of John H. Haar, May 14, 1887, *PRC*, 1:405–8. Testimony of Albert Rosenbaum, May 6, 1887, *PRC*, 1:246–55; Testimony of Washington E. Connor, May 13, 1887, *PRC*, 1:402; Testimony of John H. Haar, May 14, 1887, *PRC*, 1:407.

39 Testimony of Charles W. Hassler, May 14, 1887, *PRC*, 1:408–18.

40 Testimony of George Arents, May 10, 1887, *PRC*, 1:266–67; Testimony of John H. Haar, May 14, 1887, *PRC*, 1:405–8; Testimony of Albert Rosenbaum, May 6, 1887, *PRC*, 1:246–55; Testimony of Washington E. Connor, May 13, 1887, *PRC*, 1:402; Harrison Hong, José A. Scheinkman, and Wei Xiong, "Asset Float and Speculative Bubbles," *Journal of Finance* 51 (June 2006): 1073–116.

41 Testimony of Jay Gould, May 18, 1887, *PRC*, 1:514–18; Maury Klein, *Union Pacific*, 413–14; Testimony of Russell Sage, May 13, 1887, *PRC*, 1:368–69; Testimony of Frederic Ames, May 20, 1887, *PRC*, 2:666–67.

42 Testimony of Sidney Dillon, *PRC*, 1:210–11; Testimony of Addison Cammack, May 11, 1867, *PRC*, 1:277–81; Testimony of Thomas Eckert, May 11, 1887, *PRC*, 1:283–84; Testimony of Nathaniel Niles, May 12, 1887, *PRC*, 1:334; Testimony of Russell Sage, May 12, 13, 1887, *PRC*, 1:356–57, 370–71, 393–94; Testimony of Jay Gould, May 17, 1887, *PRC*, 1:476–77, 482.

43 Testimony of Jay Gould, May 17–18, 1887, *PRC*, 1:496, 532; Report of William Calhoun, *PRC*, 8:4809; *Report of Pacific Railway Commission*, 56–57, 62, 64; *Report to the Stockholder of the Union Pacific Railway for the Year 1880* (New York, 1881), financial statement, 311.

44 Report of William Calhoun, *PRC*, 8:4809, 4820, 4824–27.

45 Maury Klein defends Gould in *Union Pacific*, 414–17. Brokers doubted that the market could sustain any large public sale of Kansas Pacific stock. Testimony of Oliver Ames, May 31, 1887,

PRC, 2:812–13; Testimony of Jay Gould, May 17, 1887, *PRC*, 1:476; Testimony of Artemas Holmes, May 10, 1887 (recalled), *PRC*, 1:267–76; Testimony of Jay Gould, May 18, 1887, *PRC*, 1:504–5; Testimony of Sidney Dillon, May 5, 1887, *PRC*, 1:207–08; Testimony of James Ham, May 6, 1887, *PRC*, 1:236, 242. Union Pacific officials claimed that they eventually made money off of the securities acquired from Gould, but they sold them only by guaranteeing their interest, see Ham testimony, also Testimony of Amos Calef, May 11, 1887, *PRC*, 1:317. Oliver Ames, Testimony, May 31, 1887, *PRC*, 2:807–12; Report of William Calhoun, *PRC*, 8:4809, 4820, 4824–27.

46 Testimony of Russell Sage, May 13, 1887, *PRC*, 1:383. Testimony of Jay Gould, May 18, 1887, *PRC*, 1:524–28; Testimony of Oliver Ames, May 31, 1887, *PRC*, 2:812. For defense of Gould, see Klein, *Union Pacific*, 412.

47 CPH to Crocker, Nov. 3, 1881, CPH Papers, vol. 29, ser. 2, r. 61; CPH to Crocker, Jan. 7, 1881, ibid., v. 28, ser. 2, r. 6; Klein, *Jay Gould*, 240–42.

48 Adams to George Miller, April 30, 1886, Memorandum, May 1886; quote, Adams to Hon. A. S. Hewitt, Dec. 10, 1886, all in UP, PO, OC, vol. 37, ser. 2, r. 32. The Union Pacific was not quite so helpless. Veenendaal, *Slow Train to Paradise*, 52–53. See, e.g., the Union Pacific's involvement with the Salina, Lincoln, and Western Railway. A. L. Williams to Adams, Dec. 15, 31, 1886, UP, SG2, ser. 1, box 44, f. 5.

49 Klein, *Union Pacific*, 450–51, 454–57; Klein, *Jay Gould*, 331–32; Kirkland, *Charles Francis Adams*, 88–90; Adams to S. R. Callaway, Jan. 18, 1885, UP, PO, OC, vol. 30, ser. 2, r. 27. Adams cast a more positive light on all this in a letter to his lobbyist, Moorfield Storey, intended for use in modifying the Thurman Act; Adams to Storey, Jan. 14, 1887, UP, PO, OC, vol. 37, ser. 2, r. 33. Testimony of Charles Francis Adams, *PRC*, 1:86.

50 Adams to Henry McFarland, Aug. 13, 1885, UP, PO, OC, vol. 29, ser. 2, r. 25. Julius Grodinsky, *Transcontinental Railway Strategy, 1869–93: A Study of Businessmen* (Philadelphia: Univ. of Pennsylvania Press, 1962), 199–202.

51 C. E. Perkins to Hughitt, Dec. 18, 1883, 33 1880 7.2, CB&Q, Adams to Isaac Bromley, Jan. 3, 1884 (misdated 1885), Bromley to Adams, Dec. 14, 19, 1884, UP, RG 3761, box 7, f. 24; Bromley to Adams Jan. 3, 1885, ibid., box 15, f. 24; Colgate Hoyt to Adams, Feb. 27, 1885, ibid., box 19, f. 64.

52 CPH to W. W. Stow, Feb. 8, 1893 (misdated 1894), CPH Papers, vol. 234, ser. 2, r. 33; http:// www.measuringworth.com/uscompare/, calculated for 1878 and 1880.

53 Colton to CPH, May 23, 1877, *Octopus Speaks*, 36.

54 *San Francisco Daily Examiner*, Nov. 14, 1883; *Colton Case Testimony*, 6:2568–69, 2818, 2822, 2872.

55 *Colton Case Testimony*, 8:3555–57.

56 Colton to CPH, Aug. 8, 16, 1877, *Octopus Speaks*, 401, 403; David Lavender, *The Great Persuader: The Biography of Collis P. Huntington* (Nivot: Univ. Press of Colorado, 1998), 300, 308, 328; Testimony of Frank Douty, July 30, 1887, *PRC*, 5:2682–85. The Associates kept virtually all the stock for themselves, although they often put it in other people's names.

57 *Colton Case Testimony*, 3:1002.

58 *Colton Case Testimony*, 3:1011, 1015–16, 1:98–99, 228–33, 6:2632–33.

59 *Colton Case Depositions and Findings*, 1:3–12.

60 *Colton Case Testimony*, 3:1011, 1015–16, 1022–31, 1:98–99, 228–33, 6:2632–33; CPH to Colton, Nov. 16, 1877, *Octopus Speaks*, 432. The sinking funds remained a source of corruption well after the Colton Trial; Charles F. Crocker to CPH, July 26, 1889, CPH Papers, ser.1, r. 48.

61 *Colton Case Testimony*, 3:998–99; *Colton Case Deposition and Findings*, 2:16.

62 W. Milner Roberts to Jay Cooke, Jan. 1, 1872, Cooke Papers; CPH to HEH, Jan. 5, 1898, HEH Collection; *Colton Case Testimony*, 11:5048–59; *San Francisco Call*, May 14, 1884;

quote, Testimony of John Miller, Aug. 4, 1887, *PRC* 5:2888, also 2882–89; N. Green Curtis Testimony, Aug. 8, 1887, *PRC*, 5:3030–31, 3033; James O'B. Gunn Testimony, Aug. 9, 1887, *PRC* 6:3092.

63 William Mahl to Gates, April 12, 1889, CPH Papers, ser. 1, r. 47.

64 French, *Report of the Auditor of Railroad Accounts*, 46th Cong., 2d sess., H. Ex. Doc. 1, 46; Testimony of E. H. Miller Jr., July 28, 1887, *PRC*, 5:2457.

65 Testimony, *PRC*, 6:2946–47.

66 French, *Report of the Auditor of Railroad Accounts*, 46; Testimony of E. H. Miller Jr., July 28, 1887, *PRC*, 5:2457.

67 Poor, *Manual, 1885*, 864–65; ibid., *1894*, 810; Stock Listings, June 20, 1883, *Council of Foreign Bondholders Cuttings Files*, vol. 17, 1st. ser., r. 226; "Central Pacific Railroad," *Money*, May 2, 1883, ibid.

68 Quote, CPH to Crocker, April 5, 1883, CPH Papers, vol. 30:1001, ser. 2, r. 6; CPH to Crocker, Feb. 11, May 3, 1880, CPH Papers, vol. 27, ser. 2, r. 6; CPH to Crocker, Jan. 18, March 1, May 12, May 24, 1881, CPH Papers, vol. 28, ser. 2, r. 6; CPH to Crocker, Dec. 22, 1881, vol. 29, ser. 2, r. 6; J. C. Stubbs to CPH, July 6, 1883, ibid., ser. 1, r. 33; Veenendaal, *Slow Train to Paradise*, 24–25.

69 CPH to Crocker, April 5, 1883, CPH Papers, vol. 30, ser. 2, r. 6.

70 They initially would have preferred to have the Central Pacific simply guarantee Southern Pacific bonds. T. Hopkins to CPH, July 23, 1883, CPH Papers, ser.1, r. 33.

71 Adams to Geo. Edmunds, March 17, 1885, Adams to Colgate Hoyt, March 18, 1885, UP, PO, OC, vol. 28, ser. 2, r. 24; Poor, *Manual, 1885*, 866; ibid., *1886*, xxiii; ibid., *1890*, 1151.

72 Adams to F. L. Ames, April 23, 1885, UP, PO, OC, vol. 28, ser. 2, r. 24; for defense, Testimony of Leland Stanford, Aug. 3, 1887, *PRC*, 5:2818–19.

73 Adams to Geo. Edmunds, March 17, 1885, Adams to Colgate Hoyt, March 18, 1885, UP, PO, OC, vol. 28, ser. 2, r. 24; Poor, *Manual, 1885*, 866; ibid., *1886*, xxiii. From Nov. 1885 to May 1886, the figure was 78 percent of the freight, Callaway to Adams, May 15, 1886, UP, RG 3761, box 34, f. 1. The reaction of the English will be discussed in a later chapter. It can be traced in the Associates correspondence, CPH to Stanford, July 31, 1887, CPH to Gates, July 30, 1887, Speyer Ellissen to CPH, Oct. 1, 1887, Crocker to CPH, Nov. 22, 23, Dec. 2, 8, 14, 21, 23, 1887, Jan. 6, 1888, all in CPH Papers, ser. 1, r. 46. For guarantee, C. F. Crocker to CPH, Oct. 23, 1893, ibid., r. 52.

74 Adams to S. R. Callaway, Dec. 1, 1884, UP, PO, OC, vol. 24, ser. 2, r. 21; Adams to Hoyt, Feb. 4, 1885, UP, PO, OC, vol. 27, ser. 2, r. 23; Adams to Joseph Richardson, Aug. 6, 1885, ibid., vol. 29, ser. 2, r. 25; Arthur M. Johnson and Barry Supple, *Boston Capitalists and Western Railroads: A Study in the Nineteenth-Century Railroad Investment Process* (Cambridge: Harvard Univ. Press, 1967), 273–76; Testimony of Charles Francis Adams, *PRC*, 1:85. For construction, Poor, *Manual, 1886*, ii; ibid., *1880*, v; ibid., *1885*, iii–v, x, xii–xiii. Poor's statistics are often mutually contradictory from table to table, but they are still the best available source for these years. For revival, Adams to Colgate Hoyt, Nov. 5, 1885, UP, PO, OC, vol. 30, ser. 2, r. 26; for Mexico, John Mason Hart, *Empire and Revolution: The Americans in Mexico since the Civil War* (Berkeley: Univ. of California Press, 2002), 121.

75 Daniel Lewis, *Iron Horse Imperialism: The Southern Pacific of Mexico, 1880–1951* (Tucson: Univ. of Arizona Press, 2007), 18–20; John H. Coatsworth, *Growth against Development: The Economic Impact of Railroads in Porfirian Mexico* (DeKalb: Northern Illinois Univ. Press, 1981), 36.

76 Statement of Chicago business to/from and through Denver Colonel during the year 1878, 33 1870 7.42–8.11, CB&Q.

77 Fred Wilbur Powell, *The Railroads of Mexico* (Boston: Stratford Company, 1921), 134.

78 H. Craig Miner, *The St. Louis–San Francisco Transcontinental Railroad; The Thirty-fifth Parallel Project, 1853–1890* (Lawrence: Univ. Press of Kansas 1972), 122; Johnson and Supple, *Boston Capitalists,* 299, Strong quote 304.

79 Adams to Callaway, Sept. 8, 1886, UP, PO, OC, vol. 38, r. 34.

80 Perkins to Forbes, June 30, 1880, J. M. Forbes, In-letters, private from C. E. Perkins, 3 F 3.2–3.3, CB&Q; for Chicago, Grodinsky, *Transcontinental Strategy,* 194–95; CPH to Crocker, Dec. 8, 1881, CPH Papers, vol. 29, ser. 2, r. 6.

81 Adams to Callaway, March 18, 1886, UP, PO, OC, vol. 33, ser. 2, r. 28; for Gould, L. S. Anderson to G. M. Lane, June 22, 1886, UP, OC, vol. 1, L. S. Anderson, r. 1.

82 Adams to E. D. Sawyer, Feb. 13, 1886, UP, PO, OC, vol. 34, ser. 2, r. 29; Adams to CPH, May 17, 1886, ibid., vol. 35, ser. 2, r. 30. The seven routes in 1885 were (1) the UP and CP, (2) ATSF and SP, (3) SP and TP, (4) SP to New Orleans, (5) Burlington, D & RG, and CP, (6) NP, (7) A&P and SP. To these would quickly be added the Canadian Pacific and the Oregon Short Line. By the early 1890s there was also the Great Northern. Exhibit 12, J. C. Stubbs, July 26, 1887, *PRC,* 5:2598; for tonnage, ibid., 2601.

83 Adams to C. F. Morse, April 16, 1885 UP, PO, OC, vol. 28, ser. 2, r. 24; for the Huntington system, Grodinsky, *Transcontinental Railway Strategy,* 163–65; CPH to Crocker, March 14, 1883, CPH Papers, vol. 30: 49–50, ser. 2, r. 6.

84 Adams to F. Ames, April 23, 1885, UP, PO, OC, vol. 28, ser. 2, r. 24; Grodinsky, *Transcontinental Strategy,* 164–65; Adams to G. W. Cushing, July 16, 1889, UP, PO, OC, vol. 48, ser. 2, r. 43; Lavender, *Great Persuader,* 344, 356–58.

85 Testimony of CPH, *PRC,* 1:41.

86 Klein, *Jay Gould,* 250, 258–59, 269–71; note by Timothy Hopkins on letter, Personal and Confidential, CPH to Colonel Thos A. Scott, May 25, 1877, vol. 9: 185, box 24, Hopkins Collection; *Thirty-second Parallel Pacific Railroad, Remarks of C. P. Huntington . . . before the Committee on Public Lands of the U.S. Senate, Feb. 2, 1884, on House Bill 3933* (New York: John C. Rankin Jr., 1884), 14.

87 CPH to Crocker, May 3, 1882, CPH Papers, vol. 29, ser. 2, r. 6.

88 CPH to Stanford, April 5, 1880, CPH Papers, vol. 27, ser. 2, r. 6.

89 The basic outlines of the arrangement of Peirce were broached in 1880; CPH to Stanford, April 5, 1880, CPH Papers, vol. 27, ser. 2, r. 6.

90 Adams to Ames, April 23, April 30, 1885, UP, PO, OC, vol. 28, ser. 2, r. 24; S. G. Reed, *A History of the Texas Railroads* (Houston: St. Clair Publishing Company, 1941), 195–99.

91 Report of Special Committee, The Texas & Pacific Railway Co., Dec. 8, 1885, Powderly Papers, r. 11.

92 Sandra Kuntz Ficker, *Empresa extranjera y mercado interno: El Ferrocarril Central Mexicano, 1880–1907* (México, D.F.: Colegio de México, 1995), 46, 59; Johnson and Supple, *Boston Capitalists,* 292; John S. Fisher, *A Builder of the West: The Life of William Jackson Palmer* (Caldwell, Idaho: Caxton Printers, 1939), 272.

93 Matias Romero, *Geographical and Statistical Notes on Mexico* (New York: G. P. Putnam's Sons, 1898), 196, 214–15; Sandra Kuntz Ficker, "Economic Backwardness and Firm Strategy: An American Railroad Corporation in Nineteenth-Century Mexico," *Hispanic American Historical Review* 80 (May 2004): 279–82, 286–88.

94 The Mexican National was a relatively poorly built narrow-gauge line; *Trade and Commerce of Paso del Norte,* Reports from the Consuls of the United States, vol. 39 (Washington, D.C.: GPO, 1889), 50th Cong., 2d sess., H. Misc. Doc. 141, 754; Fisher, *Builder of the West,* 272–78.

95 Ficker, "Economic Backwardness," 279.

96 Adams to Dillon, June 24, 1895, UP, PO, OC, vol. 29, ser. 2, r. 24.

97 Van Horne to J. H. Pope, May 19, 1884, Van Horne LB, 6:145, vol. 2; John Lorne McDougall, *Canadian Pacific: A Brief History* (Montreal: McGill Univ. Press, 1968), 54–60.

98 Van Horne to Andrew Cleghorne, Sept. 8, 1885, Van Horne LB, 13:223–26, vol. 2.

99 Van Horne to Robert Baird, Jan. 29, 1886, Van Horne to T. Mayne Waly, Feb. 1, 1886, Van Horne LB, 15:133–34.

100 Van Horne to Brown, March 4, 1884, Van Horne LB, 5, Canadian Pacific Railroad, vol. 4.

101 Van Horne to H. Abbott, April 8, 1887, Van Horne LB, 21:2, vol. 4.

102 Adams to Callaway, Nov. 17, 1885, UP, PO, OC, vol. 33, ser. 2, r. 26; A. L. Williams to Adams, Dec. 15, 1886, UP, RG 3761, S62 box 44, f. 5 S1.

103 Adams to John Evans, Aug. 14, 1885, UP, PO, OC, vol. 29, ser. 2, r. 25.

104 Adams to Perkins, Oct. 14, 1885, UP, PO, OC, vol. 30, ser. 2, r. 25.

105 Insanity, Adams to C. E. Perkins, Sept. 28, 1885, UP, PO, OC, vol. 29, ser. 2, r. 25; Adams to Harris, Nov. 24, 1885, ibid., vol. 30, ser. 2, r. 26.

106 Adams to Callaway, Nov. 24, 1884, UP, PO, OC, vol. 24, ser. 2, r. 21.

107 Adams to Callaway, March 18, 1886, UP, PO, OC, vol. 33, ser. 2, r. 28.

108 Adams to Callaway, Nov. 19, 1885, UP, PO, OC, vol. 33, ser. 2, r. 28.

109 Adams to Callaway, March 26, 1885, UP, PO, OC, vol. 33, ser. 2, r. 28.

110 Adams to Perkins, Sept. 19, 1885, UP, PO, OC, vol. 29, ser. 2, r. 25.

111 Adams to Hon. P. B. Plumb, Nov. 9, 1885, UP, PO, OC, vol. 30, ser. 2, r. 26.

112 *Report of the U.S. Congress Senate Select Committee on Interstate Commerce*, 49th Cong., 1st sess. (Washington, D.C.: GPO, 1886), 10; Poor, *Manual, 1892*, xxii. The transcontinental traffic was the most expensive to secure and the least remunerative of all traffic for the Union Pacific. "Freight Department (1885)," P. P. Shelby in "Freight and Passenger Earnings, 1885," UP, unnumbered box, p. 137.

113 Poor, *Manual, 1890*, xv. I have combined the southwestern and northwestern groups in Poor's *Manual* to get all the roads between the Mississippi and the Rockies, again except Louisiana. Hart, *Empire and Revolution*, 122; Ficker, "Economic Backwardness," 270.

114 For Kansas regions, see Scott G. McNall, *The Road to Rebellion: Class Formation and Kansas Populism, 1885–1890* (Chicago: Univ. of Chicago Press, 1988), 70–79. See Map B, appendix, and Spatial History Project website, Stanford Univ.

115 The database of Geospatial and Statistical Data Center, http://fisher.lib.virginia.edu/ allows the mapping of the census data; Univ. of Virginia Library.

116 Adams to Callaway, May 18, 1885, UP, PO, OC, vol. 31, ser. 2, r. 27; Adams to Callaway, Nov. 17, 1885, ibid., vol. 33, ser. 2, r. 26; Adams to Callaway, Aug. 31, 1885, Sept. 7, 1885, ibid., vol. 32, ser. 2, r. 27; Adams to Strong, Sept. 19, 1885, ibid., vol. 29, ser. 2, r. 25; for Missouri Pacific's fear of the Burlington, Adams to Gould, Dec. 16, 1884, ibid., vol. 23, ser. 2, r. 20; Adams to Gould, July 3, 1886, ibid., vol. 29, ser. 2, r. 24; S. R. Callaway to Adams, May 12, 1886, UP, SG2, ser. 1, box 34, f. 3: Callaway.

117 Adams to Perkins, Sept. 25, 1885, UP, PO, OC, vol. 29, ser. 2, r. 25; Calloway to Adams, Jan. 6, 1887, UP, box 57, f. 5.

118 Perkins to Forbes, May 23, 1884, 33, 1880, 7.2, CB&Q; Adams to Perkins, Dec. 30, 1885, UP, PO, OC, vol. 30, ser. 2, r. 26; for Adams's rationales, Adams to Gould, July 3, 1886, ibid., vol. 29, ser. 2, r. 24; Adams to Sidney Dillon, ibid., vol. 28, ser. 2, r. 23.

119 Adams to Callaway, Aug. 31, 1885, UP, PO, OC, vol. 32, ser. 2, r. 25; Adams to Gould, May 10, 1885, ibid., vol. 28, ser. 2, r. 24; Adams to Callaway, Oct. 8, 10, 1885, PO, OC, vol. 32, ser. 2, r. 28; Testimony of Charles Francis Adams, *PRC*, 1:55–56.

120 Adams to Gould, Aug. 14, 1886, UP, PO, OC, vol. 36, ser. 2, r. 31; Poor, *Manual, 1888*, 800; Klein, *Jay Gould*, 343.

121 Adams to A. L. Williams, Feb. 16, 1887, UP, PO, OC, vol. 37, ser. 2, r. 33; W. B. Strong to Adams, March 30, Aug. 13, 1886, UP, SG2, ser. 1, box 44, f. 1.

122 For Atchison, Strong to Adams, June 28, 1886, UP, SG2, ser. 1, box 44, f. 1; Adams to W. Strong, Aug. 16, 1886, UP, PO, OC, vol. 36, ser. 2, r. 31; Missouri Pacific, Adams to Gould, Aug. 23, 1886, ibid.; "Maddest," Adams to J. Blickensderfer, Aug. 30, 1886, ibid.; War into Africa, Adams to A. L. Wallis, Jan. 4, 1887, ibid., vol. 37, ser. 2. r. 32.

123 Adams to F. L. Ames, Sept. 30, 1886, UP, PO, OC, vol. 36, ser. 2, r. 31; Adams to Callaway, Jan. 4, 1887, ibid., vol. 39, ser. 2, r. 34.

124 Adams to Sen. P. B. Plumb, Oct. 10, 1885, UP, PO, OC, vol. 30, ser. 2, r. 25; Adams to Poppleton, Jan. 2, 1885, ibid., vol. 23, ser. 2, r. 20; Adams to S. R. Callaway, Jan. 11, 1887, ibid., vol. 39, ser. 2, r. 34.

125 For practice, A. L. Williams to Adams, Jan. 3, 1887, UP, box 57, f. 3; for rationales for construction, Adams to Callaway, Aug. 31, Sept. 7, 1885, UP, PO, OC, vol. 32, ser. 2, r. 27; Adams to Gould, May 10, 1885, ibid., vol. 28, ser. 2, r. 24; Adams to Callaway, Jan. 7, 1887, ibid., vol. 39, ser. 2, r. 34; Adams to Anderson, April 17, 1888, ibid., vol. 43, ser. 2, r. 38; Adams to Callaway, Oct. 10, 1885, ibid., vol. 32, ser. 2. r. 28.

126 *Engineering News*, July 20, 1889, map no. 16, southwestern states; Adams to A. L. Hopkins, Jan. 14, 1886, UP, PO, OC, vol. 30, ser. 2, r. 26; Adams to J. S. Cameron, March 23, 1888, ibid., vol. 43, ser. 2, r. 38.

127 For continued building, Adams to Callaway, May 15, 1886, UP, PO, OC, vol. 38, ser. 2, r. 33; lease of Central Branch, Adams to Perkins, Oct. 2, 1885, ibid., vol. 29, ser. 2. r. 25; for Shelby, "Freight Department (1885), P. P. Shelby in Freight and Passenger Earnings, 1885," UP, MS 3761, unnumbered box, p. 131; McNall, *Road to Rebellion*, 79; also, O. Gene Clayton, *Kansas Populism: Ideas and Men* (Lawrence: Univ. Press of Kansas, 1969), 29–30.

128 John James Ingalls, *A Collection of the Writings of John James Ingalls: Essays, Addresses, and Orations* (Kansas City, Mo.: Hudson-Kimberly Publishing Co., 1902), 478.

129 Poor, *Manual, 1880*, v.

130 Poor, *Manual, 1892*, xxii.

131 Ibid., xi; Poor, *Manual, 1897*, xvii.

132 Adams to J. M. Wilson, Nov. 5, 1888, UP, PO, OC, vol. 45, ser. 2, r. 40.

133 C. Knick Harley, "Oligopoly Agreement and the Timing of American Railroad Construction," *Journal of Economic History* 42 (Dec. 1982): 798–803, 815–20; Forbes to Dexter, March 6, 1880, B&M (Nebr.), 1870–79, New Lines 63, 1870, 6.9, CB&Q. For an interesting analysis of business decision making and rational narratives, see Naomi R. Lamoreaux, "Reframing the Past: Thoughts about Business Leadership and Decision Making under Uncertainty," *Enterprise and Society* 2 (2001): 632–59.

134 Harley, "American Railroad Construction," 815–20.

135 CPH to Crocker, May 9, 1881, CPH Papers, vol. 28, ser. 2, r. 6.

136 Adams to Perkins, Oct. 14, 1885, UP, PO, OC, vol. 30, ser. 2, r. 25; Memo: re West Bound Canadian Freight Pool, n.d. c. July 1885, Van Horne LB, 12:512–18, vol. 2; Adams to Callaway, Oct. 12, 1885, UP, PO, OC, vol. 32, ser. 2, r. 28.

137 Adams to C. F. Morse, Sept. 8, 1885, Adams to Perkins, Sept. 25, 28, 1885, UP, PO, OC, vol. 29, ser. 2, r. 25.

138 See J. Blickensderfer to Adams, July 9, 1886, UP, SG2, ser. 1, box 32, f. 4; Adams to Perkins, UP, PO, OC, vol. 29, ser. 2, r. 25; Adams to Lane, July 27, 1886, ibid., vol. 36, ser. 2, r. 31; A. L. Williams to Adams, Dec. 15, 1886, UP, SG2, ser. 1, box 44, f. 5. Between 1870 and 1890 municipal subsidies were $16.5 million, half of which came in 1887–88. The state underwrote more than $27 million in bonds. Clayton, *Kansas Populism*, 27–28.

139 Chandler, *Visible Hand*, 170.

140 Adams to J. S. Cameron, May 17, 1888, UP, PO, OC, vol. 43, ser. 2, r. 38.

141 Endicott to Villard, Sept. 27, 1880, Villard Papers; loss, Adams to J. S. Cameron, May 17, 1888, UP, PO, OC, vol. 43, ser. 2, r. 38; Julius Grodinsky, *Jay Gould: His Business Career, 1867–1892* (Philadelphia: Univ. of Pennsylvania Press, 1957), 227–49.

142 For the roads making up the Burlington system, see Poor, *Manual, 1885*, 650.

143 Adams to G. Dodge, Sept. 2, 1886, UP, PO, OC, vol. 36, ser. 2, r. 31.

144 Harley, "American Railroad Construction," 798–803; Adams to G. Callaway, Sept. 12, 1884, UP, PO, OC, vol. 24, ser. 2, r. 20. Adams to Callaway, Dec. 28, 1885, ibid., vol. 33, ser. 2, r. 28; Adams to Storey, Jan. 14, 1887, ibid., vol. 38, ser. 2, r. 33. See also Hughitt to Forbes, Dec. 4, 1881; Perkins to Forbes, Jan. 4, 1884, 33, 1880, 7.21, CB&Q; G. W. Holdrege to Perkins, May 17, 1884, 33, 1880, 7.2, CB&Q; Adams to Callaway, Nov. 10, 1884, UP, PO, OC, vol. 24, ser. 2, r. 27.

145 G. Dodge to Adams, Oct. 27, 1886, UP, SG2, ser. 1, box 38, f. 1.

146 Romero, *Geographical and Statistical Notes on Mexico*, 212.

147 CPH to C. Crocker, June 4, 1881, CPH Papers, vol. 28, ser. 2, r. 6; receipt, stock, April 23, 1883, CPH to John B. Frisbie, Aug. 25, 1881; note of John Frisbie, NY, July 29, 1881, Copy of the agreement celebrated between Messrs. Frisbie and Fernández, Nov. 16, 1881, Agreement between the International Construction Company and the Mexican International Railroad Company, March 17, 1883, all in Mexican International Railroad Company, JL1, box 2–12, ser. 1, PIC Records; Hart, *Empire and Revolution*, 168; Don M. Coerver, "Federal-State Relations during the Porfiriato: The Case of Sonora, 1879–1884," *Americas* 33 (April 1977): 576; CPH to Stanford, Feb. 2, 1881, CPH Papers, vol. 28, ser. 2, r. 6. CPH also put U.S. General James G. Ord on his payroll. Ord had earned the appreciation of Díaz supporters by violating direct order to suppress Díaz's raids across the U.S. border into Mexico during Díaz's revolt; Hart, *Empire and Revolution*, 66–67.

148 The Mexican National Railway (Palmer-Sullivan Concession), 1881 (n.p.) APS Pamphlets Pertaining to Mexican Railroads, vol. 2, no. 15; Hart, *Empire and Revolution*, 119–23; CPH to Crocker, May 20, 25, 1880, May 19, 1881, June 6, 1881, CPH LB, 28, ser. 2, r. 6. For repercussions, see John Coatsworth, "Railroads, Landholding, and Agrarian Protest in the Early Porfiriato," *Hispanic American Historical Review* 54 (Feb. 1974): 48–71; Romero, *Geographical and Statistical Notes*, 196, 214–15; Ficker, "Economic Backwardness," 279–82, 286–88.

149 Robert A. Trennert, "The Southern Pacific of Mexico," *Pacific Historical Review* 35 (Aug. 1966): 265–66.

150 Mexico added some new figures to the mix, such as Albert Kingsley Owen. Hart, *Empire and Revolution*, 107–15; CPH to Crocker, May 9, 1881, CPH Papers, vol. 28, ser. 2, r. 6; David Pletcher, *Rails, Mines, and Progress: Seven American Promoters in Mexico, 1867–1911* (Ithaca: Cornell Univ. Press, 1958), 160–79; Romero, *Geographical and Statistical Notes*, 212; Klein, *Jay Gould*, 274–75, 306; Martin, "Railroads and the Equity Receivership," 696–97; Hart, *Empire and Revolution*, 120–21.

151 Testimony of Artemas Holmes, *PRC*, 1:132 ff., gives an account of Villard as receiver. Also Villard, *Memoirs*, 2:273, 283; Klein, *Jay Gould*, 244–45; Buss, *Villard*, 30–55, 78.

152 Klein, *Jay Gould*, 236; Buss, *Villard*, 43–55, 72–79. The fight with Gould was also international in scope; C. E. Bretherton to Villard, Jan. 10, 1878, Feb. 7, 26, 1879, box 88, f. 641, Villard Papers.

153 Buss, *Villard*, 15–26; Villard, *Memoirs*, 2:270. For a typical Adams reaction to a Villard proposition, see Adams to Endicott, Dec. 18, 1885, no. 33 Summer (*sic*) St. Boston, UP, PO, OC, vol. 30, NS 15986 ser. 2, r. 26.

154 Frederick Billings to Villard, March 14, 1881, box 43, f. 312, Villard Papers. Grodinsky, *Transcontinental Strategy*, 135–41, 203–8; Buss, *Villard*, 56–128; Villard to Bretherton, June 2,

1881, LBs, Private Letters, 40 A, 177–79; Villard to Oakes, Feb. 19, 1881, ibid., 81–86, Villard Papers.

155 Buss, *Villard*, 98.

156 Villard to Col. Gray, Aug. 11, 1881, Villard to Gen. H. Haupt, July 30, 1881, General Manager, NP, both in vol. 719, LBs, 46, Villard Papers; James A. Ward, *That Man Haupt: A Biography of Herman Haupt* (Baton Rouge: Louisiana State Univ. Press, 1973), 219.

157 Villard to Oakes, July 18, 1881, LB, Private Letters, 40 A, 188; Villard to Mr. Norris, July 23, 1881, 198–208, Villard Papers.

158 Perkins to Forbes, Aug. 25, 1881, F 3.2–3.3, CB&Q.

159 Villard to Endicott, Feb. 12, 1881, LBs, Private Letters, 40 A, 69 ff.; Endicott to Villard, Feb. 14, 15, 1882, Jan. 3, 1883, vol. 719, box 84, f. 596, Villard Papers.

160 Villard to Higginson, Nov. 1, 1883, LBs, Private Letters, 40 A, 328–31. For original letter see Villard to Higgenson, Aug. 23, 1883, 296–301, Villard Papers.

161 See, e.g., Villard to Dolph, Oct. 6, 1882, Private Letters, 40 A, 239–42, Villard Papers.

162 Endicott to Villard, Aug. 13, 1883, 1862–1928, Mss. 899e, vol. 719, box 84, Villard Papers; Villard to Oakes, Dec. 16, 1883, Personal Correspondence, LB, 51:477, Villard Papers.

163 *Utica Observer*, Sept. 4, 1883, *New York Tribune*, Oct. 3, 1883, *New York World*, Oct. 13, 1883, Scrapbook Northern Pacific Opening Excursion, Sept.–Oct. 1883, box 52a, Villard Papers.

164 List of German and British guests for 1883 opening, vol. 719, box 32, Villard Papers.

165 Journalists to Villard, Sept. 18, 1883, f. 305, Mss. 8993, vol. 719, 1862–1928, box 42, Villard Papers.

166 German and German American Guests to Villard, Sept. 15, 1883, f. 30, Mss. 8993, vol. 719, 1862–1928, box 42, Villard Papers.

167 Members of Northern Pacific Excursion, Train Four, to Villard, Sept. 12, 1883, Mss. 8993, vol. 719, 1862–1928, box 42, Villard Papers.

168 *Minnesota Tribune*, Sept. 4, 1883, box 51a, Scrapbook of Notices of the Northern Pacific Railroad Excursion, Aug. 29–Sept. 3, 1883, Villard 159, Villard Papers.

169 *Chicago Tribune*, Sept. 2, 1883, *New York Sun*, Sept. 6, 1883, box 51a, Scrapbook of Notices of the Northern Pacific Railroad Excursion, Aug. 29–Sept. 3, 1883, Villard 159, Villard Papers.

170 Northern Pacific R.R. Last Spike Ceremonies, Programme of Exercises, Portland, Oregon, Sept. 10, 11, 1883, Scrapbook Northern Pacific Opening Excursion, Sept.–Oct. 1883, box 52a, Villard Papers.

171 Buss, *Villard*, 138–45; *Chicago Interocean*, Aug. 30, 1883, box 51a, Scrapbook of Notices of the Northern Pacific Railroad Excursion, Aug. 29–Sept. 3, 1883, Villard 159, Villard Papers.

172 Endicott to Villard, May 23, 1883, Mss. 899e, vol. 719, box 84, Villard Papers.

173 Villard to Higginson, Aug. 23, 1883, Private Letters, 40 A, 302; Endicott to Villard, Aug. 24, 1883, Beverly Farm, Mss. 899e, v. 719, box 84, Villard Papers.

174 Villard to Endicott, Aug. 18, 1883, Private Letters, 40 A, 289–95; J. N. Tyndale to Villard, Aug. 30, 1883, Telegram, f. 304, Mss. 8993, vol. 719, 1862–1928, box 42, Villard Papers.

175 Villard to Dolph, Oct. 8, 1883, LBs, Private Letters, 40 A, 311–24; Villard to Endicott, Nov. 7, 1883, Personal Correspondence, LB, 51:400, Villard Papers.

176 Adams to Howard Hinckley, Jan. 31, 1885, Adams to Harris, Feb. 16, 1885, UP, PO, OC, vol. 27, ser. 2, r. 23; Villard, *Memoirs*, 2:316; *Bullionist*, Jan. 12, 1884, *Foreign Bondholders Cuttings Files*, ser. 1, r. 226; Fred. Ames to Adams, April 30, 1885, UP, SG2 S 1 1885, box 14.

177 Villard to Endicott, Nov. 9, 1883, LBs, Private Letters, 40, 332; Villard to Higginson, March 26, 1883, Personal Correspondence, LB 49:225, Villard Papers.

178 Files, 318, 319, 320, Mss. 8993, vol. 719, box 43, Villard Papers.

179 Grodinsky, *Transcontinental Strategy*, 204–8; Buss, *Villard*, 151–68; Villard, *Memoirs*, 2:316; Adams to E. Smith, Nov. 28, 1885, UP, PO, OC, vol. 30, ser. 2, r. 26.

180 *Statement of Mr. Henry Villard to the Stockholders of the Northern Pacific Railroad Company* (New York: John C. Rankin Jr., 1884), 13–14, copy in Mss. 8993, vol. 719, box 61, f. 425, Villard Papers; "Mr. Villard's Defence," *New York Daily Tribune*, Sept. 15, 1884; A. Anderson to Villard, Oct. 10, 1884, Villard to Anderson, Nov. 8, 1884, H. Thielsen to Villard, Dec. 13, 1884, Anderson to Villard, April 16, 1885, box 43, f. 316, Villard Papers.

181 Adams to E. D. Sawyer, Feb. 13, 1886, PO, OC, vol. 34, ser. 2, r. 29.

182 Memorandum, undated, unsigned, box 2, f. 20, Villard Papers.

183 Charles Francis Adams, "Which Will Quickest Solve the Railroad Question: Force Bills or Public Opinion?" (Address at Oshkosh, Wisc., Sept. 3, 1875), 9, in Charles Francis Adams, *Railway Pamphlets*, Stanford Univ. Library; Adams, "The State and the Railroads," 354–55, bound in Adams, *Railway Pamphlets*, Stanford Univ. Library.

184 Martin, "Railroads and the Equity Receivership," 685–709; William Z. Ripley, *Railroads: Finance and Organization* (New York: Longmans, Green, 1915), 402–3; James W. Ely, *Railroads and American Law* (Lawrence: Univ. of Kansas Press, 2001), 177–80; William G. Roy, *Socializing Capital: The Rise of the Large Industrial Corporation in America* (Princeton: Princeton Univ. Press, 1997), 108–9; Gerald Berk, *Alternative Track: The Constitution of American Industrial Order, 1865–1917* (Baltimore: Johns Hopkins Univ. Press, 1994), 47, 51–55, 65, finds a reduction of 27 percent, but lumps the reorganizations before 1893 with those afterwards. Stuart Daggett, *Railroad Reorganization* (Boston, New York: Houghton, Mifflin, 1908), 356–57; Tufano, "Business Failure," 20.

185 Tufano, "Business Failure," 22–26.

186 I. Leo Sharfman, *Railway Regulation: An Analysis of the Underlying Problems in Railway Economics from the Standpoint of Government Regulation* (Chicago: La Salle Extension Univ., 1915), 113. Sharfman was an economist at the Univ. of Michigan.

Mise en Scène: Labor in Nature

1 The literature on this is enormous and starts with Leo Marx's classic, *The Machine in the Garden: Technology and the Pastoral Ideal in America* (New York: Oxford Univ. Press, 1964); John F. Kasson, *Civilizing the Machine: Technology and Republican Values in America, 1776–1900* (1976; reprint, New York: Penguin, 1977), 166, 174; David E. Nye, *American Technological Sublime* (Cambridge: MIT Press, 1994); Thomas Andrews, " 'Made by Toile': Tourism, Labor, and the Construction of the Colorado Landscape, 1858–1917," *Journal of American History* 92 (Dec. 2005): 837–63. For a nuanced view of this literature, see Jeffrey L. Meikle, "Leo Marx's *The Machine in the Garden*," *Technology and Culture* 44 (2003): 147–59. Such pictures were a staple of popular consumption; see, e.g., the Currier and Ives prints *The Great West, American Express Train, Snowbound, Across the Continent*.

2 Henry T. Williams, ed., *Pacific Tourist: Adams and Bishop's Illustrated Trans-continental Guide of Travel, from the Atlantic to the Pacific Ocean: A Complete Traveler's Guide of the Union and Central Pacific Railroads* (New York: Adams & Bishop, 1881), 6–7.

3 *Pacific Tourist*, 172. This kind of rhetoric was common; see "Yellowstone National Park," *Railway Age*, Oct. 23, 1879, p. 511.

4 Van Horne to Harry Abbott, Oct. 7, 1886, LB, 18, vol. 3.

5 For the experience of travel, Wolfgang Schivelbusch, *The Railway Journey: The Industrialization of Time and Space in the 19th Century* (Berkeley: Univ. of California Press, 1986).

6 William Emerson Strong, "Glimpses of Travel in the West with the Lieutenant General of the Army" (Ayer MS 3175), p. 11, Newberry Library.

7 Ibid., 11–15.

8 Much of this discussion is indebted to Meikle, "Leo Marx's *The Machine in the Garden*," 147–59, and John Kasson's *Civilizing the Machine*.

9 Jefferson to Charles Wilson Peale, April 17, 1813, in Robert C. Baron, ed., *The Garden and Farm Books of Thomas Jefferson* (Golden, Colo.: Fulcrum, 1987), 202.

CHAPTER 6: MEN IN OCTOPUS SUITS

1 Quoted in Wm. Mahl, "The Relation That the Accounting Department of Railroads Should Bear to the Stochholders or Owners of the Property," May 27, 1892, p. 3, 2E 462. For similar comments, *London Times*, Aug. 24, 1883, *Foreign Bondholders Clippings Files*, 17:213–14, ser. 1, r. 226.

2 The books and formulations that I have in mind are classics of their literature. Matthew Josephson, *The Robber Barons: The Great American Capitalists, 1861–1901* (New York: Harcourt, Brace, 1934); Frank Norris, *The Octopus: A Story of California* (New York: Bantam Books, 1958, orig. ed. 1901); Joseph Schumpeter, *Capitalism, Socialism, and Democracy*, 3d ed. (New York: Harper & Brothers, 1947); Alfred Chandler, *The Visible Hand: The Managerial Revolution in American Business* (Cambridge: Harvard Univ. Press, 1977).

3 Chandler, *Visible Hand*, 3–12, 79.

4 Ibid., 145–54.

5 Ibid., 120–21, 160.

6 Naomi R. Lamoreaux, Daniel M. G. Raff, and Peter Temin, "Beyond Markets and Hierarchies: Toward a New Synthesis of American Business History," *American Historical Review* 108 (April 2003): 404–33; Naomi R. Lamoreaux, Daniel M. G. Raff, and Peter Temin, "Against Whig History," *Enterprise and Society* 5 (Sept. 2004): 376–87; Timothy Guinnane, Ron Harris, Naomi R. Lamoreaux, and Jean-Laurent Rosenthal, "Putting the Corporation in Its Place," ibid. 8 (2007): 687–729, esp. 688–89; Naomi Lamoreaux and Jean-Leaurent Rosenthal, "Legal Regime and Contractual Flexibility: A Comparison of Businesses' Organizational Choices in France and the United States during the Era of Industrialization," *American Law and Economics Review* 7, no. 1 (2005): 28–61.

7 Guinnane et al., "Putting the Corporation in Its Place," 689, 693–94, 697–98, 704–5, 709.

8 Maury Klein, *The Life and Legend of Jay Gould* (Baltimore: Johns Hopkins Univ. Press, 1986), 93, 146, 195.

9 Norris, *Octopus*, 32–33.

10 Ibid., 386–87.

11 The best account of the management of the Central Pacific and the Southern Pacific is Evelyne Payen-Variéras, "Les cadres salaries du Central Pacific Railroad, 1869–1889," *Revue d'historie moderne et contemporaine* 55 (Oct.–Dec. 2008): 123–59.

12 Norris, *Octopus*, 72.

13 Most of the records of the Canadian Pacific remain closed, and so it may very well also be true of the Canadian Pacific.

14 Chandler, *Visible Hand*, 3–12, 79.

15 Charles Perrow, *Complex Organizations: A Critical Essay*, 3d ed. (New York: Random House, 1986), 34–37.

16 Chandler, *Visible Hand*, 106–7.

17 The best accounts of railroad work and the struggle over it are Shelton Stromquist, *A Generation of Boomers: The Pattern of Railroad Labor Conflict in Nineteenth-Century America* (Urbana: Univ. of Illinois Press, 1987), and Walter Licht, *Working for the Railroad: The Organization of Work in the Nineteenth Century* (Princeton: Princeton Univ. Press, 1983). Memo, Prepared by John B. Nyman, n.d., vol. 6.5, 63, 1870, CB&Q. The organization described below depends on this memo. John H. White Jr., *The American Railroad Freight Car: From the*

Wood-Car Era to the Coming of Steel (Baltimore: Johns Hopkins Univ. Press, 1993), 53, 77. See also *Transportation Rules, Northern Pacific System of Railroads, in Effect Sept. 1, 1883* (St. Paul: Pioneer Press Co., 1883), 6 and passim, pt. 1, ser. B, NS7602, r. 2, Secretary, Printed Materials, NP.

18 Chandler, *Visible Hand*, 87.

19 Pamela Walker Laird, *Pull: Networking and Success since Benjamin Franklin* (Cambridge: Harvard Univ. Press, 2006), 1–50. See, e.g., Chandler, *Visible Hand*, 108; Licht, *Working for the Railroad*, 58–59.

20 Licht, *Working for the Railroad*, 56; Adams to S. R. Callaway, July 30, 1885 UP, PO, OC, v. 31, ser. 2, r. 27.

21 William John Pinkerton, *His Personal Record: Stories of Railroad Life* (Kansas City, Mo.: Pinkerton Publishing Company, 1904), 116–17.

22 Licht, *Working for the Railroad*, 58.

23 Stromquist, *Generation of Boomers*, 50–99, 107, 10, 110; Eric Arnesen, " 'Like Banquo's Ghost, It Will Not Down': The Race Question and the American Railroad Brotherhoods, 1880–1920," *American Historical Review* 99 (Dec. 1994): 1614–15, 1628.

24 *Transportation Rules, Northern Pacific System of Railroads, in Effect Sept. 1, 1883*. The Burlington's early descriptions of duties were even shorter; untitled, "Prepared by John B. Nyman," 63, 1870, 6.5, CB&Q.

25 Adams to Callaway, Aug. 14, 1885, UP, PO, OC, vol. 31, ser. 2, r. 27.

26 Callaway to Adams, March 19, 1886, UP, SG2, ser. 1, box 34, f. 1: Callaway; Adams to S. R. Callaway, May 12, 19, 1886, UP, PO, OC, vol. 38, r. 33, ser. 2. For Santa Fe, James H. Ducker, *Men of the Steel Rails: Workers on the Atchison, Topeka & Santa Fe Railroad, 1869–1900* (Lincoln: Univ. of Nebraska Press, 1983), 107, 113; Licht, *Working for the Railroad*, 262–64; Stromquist, *Generation of Boomers*, 46, 230–34.

27 Pinkerton, *His Personal Record*, 57–59. Railroad workers were mobile, but then so were American workers as a whole; see Stromquist, *Generation of Boomers*, 193–95.

28 Minutes of Meeting between President Adams and the Executive Committee of Knights of Labor, at Albany, Denver, July 14, 1885, UP, RG 2361, box 21, KL. For demands of engineers on the Burlington, see Petition to Robert Harris, c. Dec. 1876, Miscellaneous 33 1880, 8.1–8.16, CB&Q.

29 John H. White, *American Locomotives: An Engineering History, 1830–1880* (Baltimore: Johns Hopkins Univ. Press, 1968), 110, 534.

30 Steven W. Usselman, *Regulating Railroad Innovation: Business, Technology, and Politics in America, 1840–1920* (New York: Cambridge Univ. Press, 2002), 61–75; Payen-Variéras, "Les cadres salaries du Central Pacific Railroad," 147–57; Craig Phelan, *Grand Master Workman: Terence Powderly and the Knights of Labor* (Westport, Conn.: Greenwood Press, 2000), 14. For a description of such a shop on the Union Pacific at North Platte, see No Name to Editor, *Union Pacific Employes' Magazine*, July 1886, p. 188.

31 Adams to S. R. Callaway, Dec. 23, 1885, UP, PO, OC, vol. 33, ser. 2, r. 27; White, *American Locomotive*, 110, 444–45; Klein, *Union Pacific*, vol. 1, *Birth of a Railroad, 1862–1893* (Garden City, N.Y.: Doubleday, 1983), 525–27; Licht, *Working for the Railroad*, 161–63.

32 Usselman, *Regulating Railroad Innovation*, 10–11, 63, 70–76, 99–101.

33 Ibid., 163–87.

34 "Conference between the Management of the Northern Pacific Railroad and the Employees in Its Train Service . . . January 11, 1894," p. 28, 11.A.5.6 F, 138.H.8.8 (F), NP.

35 H. B. Stone to Perkins, Feb. 18, 1888, CBQ 33, 1880, 9.11.

36 White, *American Freight Car*, 6–77.

37 "Conference between the Management of the Northern Pacific Railroad and the Employees

in Its Train Service . . . NP. January 11, 1894," pp. 28, 2, 10, 14, 24, 40–41, 50, 11.A.5.6 F, 138.H.8.8 (F), NP.

38 Ibid., p. 28; Minutes of a Meeting of the Superintendents and Master Mechanics of the CB&Q R.R., held at Chicago, Jan. 10, 1887, Misc. 33 1880, 8.17, CB&Q.

39 Stromquist, *Generation of Boomers*, 119–20.

40 "Conference between the Management of the Northern Pacific Railroad and the Employees in Its Train Service . . . January 11, 1894," p. 28, 11.A.5.6 F, 138.H.8.8 (F), NP.

41 T. F. Oakes to Receiver, Aug. 18, 1893, 11. A.5.6 F, 138. H.8.8 (F), NP; J. Corbin to Adams, Oct. 13, Nov. 18, 23, Dec. 8, Dec. 16, 1886, UP, SG2, ser. 1, box 33, f. 3: Colgate-Cullom.

42 Kimberly to Pearce, Oct. 21, 1893, 11.A.5.6 F, 138.H.8.8 (F), NP; Ducker, *Men of Steel Rails*, 112. Because of arbitraries, it was difficult to compare wages from line to line; Henry Stone to T. J. Potter, June 2, 1880, 33 1880, 3.2 CB&Q.

43 Chandler, *Visible Hand*, 130–32,143, 170; Perrow, *Complex Organizations*.

44 "Railroad Management: A Lecture to Harvard Students by Charles Francis Adams, Jr.," *New York Times*, March 17, 1886, p. 5.

45 Adams to A. Hadley, March 23, 1888, UP, PO, OC, vol. 43, ser. 2, r. 38.

46 Adams to J. K. Choate, Nov. 2, 1885, UP, PO, OC, vol. 30, ser. 2, r. 26.

47 This strain is visible beginning with Robert Wiebe, in *The Search for Order, 1877–1920* (New York: Hill & Wang, 1967), who talked of a "new middle class," and a "revolution in values," which yielded "bureaucratic thought," 111–63, quote 154, through Chandler, *Visible Hand*, 10. Jackson Lears, *Rebirth of a Nation: The Making of Modern America, 1877–1920* (New York: HarperCollins, 2009), 13, 18, 21–22, although keeping aspects of Wiebe, emphasizes manliness and militarism.

48 Deirdre McCloskey, "Bourgeois Virtue and History of P & S," *Journal of Economic History* 58 (June 1998): 300, 304–5, 311–17; Wiebe, *Search for Order*, 147–48; Adams to S. R. Callaway, June 24, 1885, UP, PO, OC, vol. 31, ser. 2, r. 27.

49 Adams to Merriman, Jan. 30, 1885, UP, PO, OC, vol. 27, ser. 2, r. 23; Adams to CPH, Jan. 27, 1886, ibid., vol. 33, ser. 2, r. 29; Adams to Callaway, Dec. 23, 1884, ibid., vol. 24, ser. 2, r. 21.

50 Adams to Poppleton, Feb. 5, 1886, UP, PO, OC, vol. 34, ser. 2 r. 29.

51 Adams to Callaway, Dec. 18, 1884, UP, PO, OC, vol. 24, ser. 2, r. 21. The Oregon Short Line stocks and bonds were offered to stockholders of the Union Pacific; the Union Pacific guaranteed interest on the bonds through a stock guarantee. The road was built on the assumption that the Northern Pacific would not be completed. Testimony of Charles Francis Adams, *PRC*, 1:90–95.

52 Adams to G. M. Dodge, March 26, 1886, UP, PO, OC, vol. 34, ser. 2 r. 29.

53 Charles Francis Adams, *Railroads: Their Origin and Problems* (New York: G. P. Putnam's Sons, 1878), 194.

54 Adams to Callaway, Aug. 24, 1885, UP, PO, OC, vol. 32, ser. 2, r. 27; Perkins to Forbes, May 23, 1884, 33, 1880, 7.2, CB&Q.

55 Adams to Callaway, Nov. 19, 1884, UP, PO, OC, vol. 24, series 2, r. 21; Adams to F. L. Ames, Sept. 30, 1886, ibid., vol. 36, ser. 2, r. 31; Adams to Callaway, Aug. 24, 1885, ibid., vol. 32, ser. 2, r. 27.

56 Adams to Sidney Dillon, Jan. 12, 1886, UP, PO, OC, vol. 30, ser. 2, r. 26.

57 Adams to Callaway, Jan. 20, 1885, UP, PO, OC, vol. 30, ser. 2, r. 27.

58 Adams to Callaway, Jan. 25, 1886, UP, PO, OC, vol. 33, ser. 2, r. 28.

59 Adams to Callaway, March 4, 1886, PO, OC, vol. 33, ser. 2, r. 28.

60 Adams to Callaway, Oct. 10, 1885, UP, PO, OC, vol. 32, ser. 2, r. 28.

61 Initially positive, Adams to Callaway, Oct. 20, 1884, UP, PO, OC, vol. 24, ser. 2, r. 21; negative, Adams to Callaway, Sept. 8, 1885, Adams to Callaway, Sept. 8, 1885, Telegram, President's

Office, ibid., vol. 32, ser. 2, r. 27; conductors stole, Adams to Frank Thomson, July 31, 1885, ibid., vol. 29, ser. 2, r. 25.

62 Adams to Calloway, Oct. 18, 1885, UP, PO, OC, vol. 32, ser. 2, r. 28; Callaway to Adams, Dec. 10, Oct. 12, 1884, UP, SG2, ser. 1, box 7, f. 1; Callaway to Adams, Aug. 19, 1885, Oct. 17, 1885, ibid., box 16, f. 4.

63 Savage to Adams, April 12, 1887, UP, RG 3761, box 56, f. 2.

64 Adams to F. L. Ames, Sept. 30, 1886, UP, PO, OC, vol. 36, ser. 2, r. 31.

65 Adams to J. S. Tebbets, March 9, 1888, UP, PO, OC, vol. 43, ser. 2, r. 38.

66 Adams to F. Gordon Dexter, Sept. 3, 1889, UP, PO, OC, vol. 48, ser. 2, r. 48.

67 Adams to C. S. Mellen, Dec. 30, 1889, UP., PO, OC, vol. 49, ser. 2, r. 44; Klein, *Union Pacific*, 616–20; Adams to G. Dodge, May 1, 9, 1890, UP, PO, OC, vol. 50, ser. 2, r. 45.

68 James A. Ward, *That Man Haupt: A Biography of Herman Haupt* (Baton Rouge: Louisiana State Univ. Press, 1973), 219.

69 Charles Francis Adams, *Charles Francis Adams: 1835–1915, An Autobiography* (Boston: Houghton Mifflin, 1916), 131.

70 Ibid., 147.

71 Ibid., 129; James McPherson, *For Cause and Comrades: Why Men Fought in the Civil War* (New York: Oxford Univ. Press, 1997).

72 Ward, *That Man Haupt*, 166; John Clark, *Railroads in the Civil War: The Impact of Management on Victory and Defeat* (Baton Rouge: Louisiana State Univ. Press, 2001), 147–51, 156, 160; Thomas Weber, *The Northern Railroads in the Civil War, 1861–1865* (New York: King's Crown Press, 1952), 135, 180–83.

73 Gail Bederman, *Manliness and Civilization: A Cultural History of Gender and Race in the United States, 1880–1917* (Chicago: Univ. of Chicago Press, 1995), 10–13. For quote, Adams to Mrs. Mumford, June 15, 1888, UP, PO, OC, vol. 44, ser. 2, r. 39.

74 Bederman, *Manliness and Civilization*, 5–20. Thomas Winter, *Making Men, Making Class* (Chicago: Univ. of Chicago Press, 2002), 1–27, unlike Bederman, sees manhood as remaining dominant over manliness. Winter, ibid., 149–50, also gives a detailed bibliography of this literature on manliness.

75 Adams to Callaway, May 15, 1885, UP, PO, OC, vol. 31, ser. 2, r. 27.

76 Adams to Gould, May 10, 1885, UP, PO, OC, vol. 28, ser. 2, r. 24. See also Adams to Callaway, April 30, 1885, ibid., vol. 31, ser. 2, r. 27; second quote, Adams to William Strong, June 4, 1885, ibid., vol. 28, ser. 2, r. 24. For other examples, Adams to C. E. Perkins, June 7, 1885, ibid.

77 Adams to Callaway, May 18, 1885, UP, PO, OC, vol. 31, ser. 2, r. 27.

78 C. F. Adams to T. M. Cooley, Dec. 27, 1886, UP, PO, OC, vol. 37, ser. 2, r. 32.

79 For T. J. Potter and nervous breakdown, Adams to Callaway, Sept. 13, 14, 1885, UP, PO, OC, vol. 32, ser. 2, r. 27; Adams to Callaway, Oct. 18, 1885; nervous system, Adams to T. J. Potter, April 19, 1887, ibid., vol. 41, ser. 2, r. 36; hopes in Potter, Adams to F. L. Ames, July 5, 1887, ibid., vol. 41, ser. 2, r. 36, and his death, Adams to J. W. Savage, March 17, 1888, ibid., vol. 43, ser. 2, r. 38; needs men to adjust to West, Adams to Coudert, May 1, 1888, ibid.

80 Adams to G. M. Cumming, Dec. 28, 1888, UP, PO, OC, vol. 45, ser. 2, r. 41.

81 C. S. Mellen to Adams, Dec. 24, 1889, UP, box 77, f. 4; Adams to C. S. Mellen, Dec. 26, 1889, UP, PO, OC, vol. 49, ser. 2, r. 44.

82 C. F. Adams to Hugh Riddle, Nov. 8, 1884, Adams to Callaway, Dec. 4, 1884, UP, PO, OC, vol. 24, ser. 2, r. 21.

83 Gail Bederman, *Manliness and Civilization*, 18–19.

84 Adams to Perkins, Nov. 2, 1886, UP, PO, OC, vol. 36, ser. 2, r. 32; Adams to J. Savage, April 11, 1887, ibid., vol. 41, ser. 2, r. 36.

85 Poor, *Manual, 1885*, 778; Adams to John Dillon, June 24, 1885, Adams to McCool, Sept. 8, 1885, UP, PO, OC, vol. 29, ser. 2, r. 25.

86 Adams to James Benedict, Oct. 20, 26, 1885, Adams to Daniel McCool, Oct. 23, 27, 1885, UP, PO, OC, St. Joseph and Grand Island, vol. 25, r. 21; Adams to Perkins, Oct. 24, 1885, ibid., vol. 30, ser. 2, r. 25; Perkins to Adams, Oct. 25, 1886, UP, S62 box 42, f. 1 S1; Adams to Callaway, Nov. 16, 1886, UP, PO, OC, vol. 33, ser. 2, r. 28; Adams to Callaway, July 21, 1886, ibid., vol. 38, ser. 2, r. 33.

87 Adams to Ledyard, July 21, 1885, UP, PO, OC, vol. 29, ser. 2, r. 25; Adams to Benedict, Dec. 4, 1885, ibid., St. Joseph and Grand Island, vol. 25, ser. 2, r. 21.

88 Adams to Benedict, Nov. 28, 1885, UP, PO, OC, St. Joseph and Grand Island, vol. 25, ser. 2, r. 21.

89 Adams to McCool, Nov. 4, 1885, UP, PO, OC, St. Joseph and Grand Island, vol. 25, ser. 2, r. 21.

90 Adams to Callaway, Nov. 10, 1885, UP, PO, OC, ser. 2, r. 28; Adams to Thurston, March 16, ibid., vol. 43, ser. 2, r. 38.

91 Adams to Callaway, April 22, 1887, UP, PO, OC, vol. 39, ser. 2, r. 35.

92 Chandler, *Visible Hand*, 147–48, 159–60.

93 Schumpeter, *Capitalism, Socialism, and Democracy*, 83, 102, 106, 132.

94 Ibid., 74.

95 Ibid., 138.

96 Norris, *Octopus*, 369.

97 CPH to A. N. Towne, Feb. 12, 1880, CPH Papers, ser. 2, r. 12.

98 It is difficult to follow Stanford's activities in the same detail as Huntington's, since his records no longer exist. It was probably Jane Stanford who destroyed them.

99 William Deverell, *Railroad Crossing: Californians and the Railroad, 1850–1910* (Berkeley: Univ. of California Press, 1994), 58–60; *County of San Mateo* v. *Southern Pacific Railroad Company*, 13 Fed. 145 (July 31, 1882); *County of Santa Clara* v. *Southern Pacific Railroad Company*, 18 Fed. 385 (Sept. 17, 1883); White to Geo. Hayes, Aug. 16, 1889, Correspondence, Outgoing, box 4, Aug. 14, 1889–Jan. 11, 1890, White Papers. For Buckley, see earlier and Alexander Callow Jr., "San Francisco's Blind Boss," *Pacific Historical Review* 25 (1956): 261–71; R. Hal Williams, *The Democratic Party and California Politics, 1880–1896* (Stanford: Stanford Univ. Press, 1973), 24–31.

100 Williams, *Democratic Politics*, 103–7; "Stanford Scored," *Los Angeles Times*, Jan. 14, 1891; Edith Dobie, *The Political Career of Stephen Mallory White: A Study of Party Activities under the Convention System* (Stanford: Stanford Univ. Press, 1927), 109.

101 Bruce D. Delmatier et al., eds, *The Rumble of California Politics, 1848–1870* (New York: John Wiley & Sons, 1970), 91–93; Callow, "San Francisco's Blind Boss," 277; Williams, *Democratic Politics*, 103–7; toughest element, Richard Lambert to CPH, Aug. 15, 1890, CPH Papers, ser. 1, r. 48.

102 Mills to CPH, Jan. 5, Jan. 28, 1892, CPH Papers, ser. 1, r. 50; David Lavender, *The Great Persuader: A Biography of Collis P. Huntington* (Niwot: Univ. Press of Colorado, 1998, 1969), 342.

103 CPH to F. Stone, March 3, 1892, CPH Papers, vol. 225, ser. 1, r. 3.

104 Clinton Fisk to Uriel Crocker, Sept. 21, 1876, Andrew Peirce to Uriel Crocker, Oct. 3, 1876, Mss. Vertical File C. 6, Mss. 724, E Steam railroad, F-7-65, Atlantic & Pacific RR Co., 1870–76, Delano Wright G7634. H. Craig Miner, *The St. Louis–San Francisco Transcontinental Railroad: The Thirty-fifth Parallel Project, 1853–1890* (Lawrence: Univ. Press of Kansas, 1972), 130–38; CPH to Crocker, Nov. 3, Dec. 22, 1881, Jan. 31, 1882, stopping A&P at Colorado; CPH to Crocker, Feb. 3, 1882, Seligmans, CPH to Crocker, Feb. 11, 1882, all in CPH Papers vol. 29,

ser. 2, r. 6; Keith L. Bryant, *History of the Atchison, Topeka, and Santa Fe Railway* (New York: Macmillan, 1974), 90–92; Gould accuses Seligmans of betrayal, Gould to J. and W. Seligman, Aug. 1, 1883, CPH Papers, ser. 2, r. 33; for lack of traffic to A&P, Touzalin and Winslow to CPH, Aug. 30, 1883, ibid., ser. 1, r. 33.

105 Nickerson to CPH, Oct. 30, 1883, Crocker to CPH, Nov. 6, 1883, both in CPH Papers, ser. 1, r. 33; Cohen to CPH, Dec. 5, 1883, ibid., r. 34.

106 C. Crocker to CPH, Dec. 5, 1887, CPH Papers, ser. 2, r. 46; for Crocker's urging Stanford to build, Crocker to L. Stanford, Nov. 19, 1886 (copy), ibid., ser. 1, r. 44; the Southern Pacific did some building, C. F. Crocker to CPH, Feb. 10, 1887, ibid., r. 45; diabetes, C. Crocker to CPH, Jan. 1, 1885, ibid., r. 39.

107 C. F. Crocker to CPH, March 16, 1887, CPH Papers, ser. 1, r. 45.

108 Adams to Callaway, Oct. 19, 1886, UP, PO, OC, vol. 38, ser. 2, r. 34; Dillon to Adams, March 13, 1886, UP, SG2, ser. 1, box 37.

109 Adams to S. Dillon, March 18, 1886, Adams to G. Shattuck, March 27, 1886, UP, PO, OC, vol. 34, ser. 2, r. 29. The rate wars did stimulate California traffic; see "California Traffic," W. Wing, April 1, 1886, UP, SG2, ser. 1, box 34, f. 2: Callaway.

110 James Thorpe, *Henry Edwards Huntington: A Biography* (Berkeley: Univ. of California Press, 1994), 69, 306–35.

111 Thorpe, *Henry Edwards Huntington*, 39. "Extract from Our New York Letter," *Union Pacific Employes' Magazine*, April 1887, p. 96. Clifford Edward Clark, *Henry Ward Beecher: Spokesman For a Middle-Class America* (Urbana: Univ. of Illinois Press, 1978); "Praise from Many Lips," *New York Times*, March 14, 1887, p. 8.

112 Lavender, *Great Persuader*, 342–43.

113 In 1880 some 1,640 acres of the Stanford Ranch and its improvements were assessed at $76,475. The cost of the tomb, exclusive of three steel caskets and the transportation of the marble across the country, was $96,700; Real Estate and Improvements, San Francisquito Ranch, box 3, f. 12, and Westmore Morse Granite Company to Caterson and Clark, Nov. 12, 1887, box 3, f. 13, both in Stanford Papers. The assessed ranch in 1880 was smaller than the eventual Stanford campus of over 8,000 acres.

114 Photographs of the Memorial Arch are available at http://collections.stanford.edu/shpc/bin/page?forward=home. For an account and Saint Gaudens's explanation of the iconography, see "The Progress of Civilization in America," *Sandstone and Tile* 8 (Winter 1984): 10–11.

115 Lavender, *Great Persuader*, 344–46. CPH to James Speyer, Dec. 6, 1899, pp. 12–14, CPH Papers, ser. 4, r. 1. Sargent to Stanford, Jan. 11, 1885, box 2, f. 12, Stanford Papers, SC33a.

116 Wm. H. Mills to CPH, July 28, 1893, CPH Papers, ser. 1, r. 52.

117 For Timothy Hopkins, Sidney M. Ehrman, "Timothy Hopkins, 1859–1936," *California Historical Society Quarterly* 15 (March 1936): 97–98; "A Big Sensation Caused," *New York Times*, Aug. 1, 1891; "The Hopkins-Searles Will," ibid., March 6, 1892; on Hopkins, CPH to Gates, March 9, 1889, CPH Papers, ser. 1, r. 47; for Southern Pacific officers and board members, see Poor, *Manual, 1889*, 912; ibid., *1892*, 974.

118 C. Crocker to CPH (Personal), Nov. 22, 1887, CPH, ser. 1, r. 46, for Crocker's irritation with Huntington, C. Crocker to CPH, Dec. 15, 1887, ibid.

119 C. Dunham to Richard Olney, Olney Papers, ct. 17, r. 6.

120 C. F. Crocker to CPH, Jan. 3, 1887, CPH Papers, ser. 1, r. 44; C. F. Crocker to CPH, Feb. 19, 1887, ibid., r. 45; AT&SF, C. F. Crocker to CPH, Feb. 18, March 8, March 14, April 1, 1887, ibid.

121 C. Crocker to CPH, Nov. 5, Dec. 5, 1887, CPH Papers, ser. 1, r. 46; CPH to Towne, Feb. 24, 1887, ibid., ser. 2, r. 27.

122 J. E. Gates to C. Crocker, April 7, 1887, CPH Papers, vol. 101, ser. 2, r. 16. C. F. Crocker to

CPH, April. 27, 1887, ibid., ser. 2, r. 45; for Oregon, C. Crocker to CPH April 11, 1887, ibid., ser. 1, r. 45; for shortages and demands, C. Crocker to CPH, Oct 24, Nov. 5, Nov. 9, Dec. 5, 1887, ibid., ser. 1, r. 46; Towne to C. Crocker, Nov. 21, Dec. 6, 1887, ibid.; C. Crocker to CPH, Jan. 3, 9, 12, 13, 18, March 5, 1888, ibid.; Fred Crocker had hopes for Mexican traffic, C. F. Crocker to CPH, Feb. 1, 1888, ibid.; for Crocker's opposition to further building in Mexico, C. Crocker to CPH, June 29, 1886, ibid., ser. 2, r. 42. The Galveston, Houston, and San Antonio lost over $3 million between March 1, 1885, and June 30, 1889. G. Lansing to C. F. Crocker, Dec. 6, 1889, CPH Papers, ser. 1, r. 48.

123 Last spike, C. Crocker to CPH, Dec. 23, 1887, CPH Papers, ser. 1, r. 46; for deal with Speyer, Crocker to CPH, April 14, 1887, ibid., r. 45; for Oregon, C. Crocker to CPH April 11, 1887, CPH to Gates, July 11, 1887, ibid. (CPH letters from Europe were filed with incoming correspondence); CPH to Gates, July 14, 1887, with enclosed Speyer correspondence, ibid.; for Speyer Brothers, L. Speyer Ellissen, Wm. B. Bonn to CPH, Oct. 11, 1887, ibid., ser. 1, r. 46; C. F. Crocker to CPH, Nov. 22, 1887, ibid. The Associates did take steps to conciliate the stockholders, C. Crocker to CPH, Dec. 2, 1887, ibid.

124 C. Crocker to CPH, Jan. 6, 12, 26, 1888, CPH Papers, ser. 1, r. 46.

125 CPH to Gates, July 12, 1887, CPH Papers, ser. 1, r. 45; CPH to "Friend Stanford," July 13, 1887, ibid.; CPH to Gates, July 30, 1887, ibid.

126 Pierpont Morgan to CPH, Nov. 29, 1887, CPH Papers, ser. 1, r. 46.

127 C. Crocker to CPH, Feb. 3, 1888, CPH Papers, ser. 1, r. 46.

128 C. Crocker to CPH, Jan. 18, 1889, CPH Papers, ser. 1, r. 47.

129 C. F. Crocker to CPH, Jan. 14, Feb. 24, 25, 1888, CPH Papers, ser. 1, r. 46.

130 Problems, C. Crocker to CPH, Dec. 15, 1887, CPH Papers, ser. 1, r. 46. As usual, the Associates worked through interlocking companies, several of which were in trouble; for Southern Development Co., E. Brown to CPH, March 26, 1887, ibid., r. 45; for PIC and SHH&C, W. Brown to CPH, Nov. 25, 1887, ibid., r. 46; C. Crocker to CPH, Aug. 17, 1887, ibid., r. 45; C. Crocker to CPH, April 6, 1887, ibid.; for floating debt, C. Crocker to CPH, Nov. 9, 1887, ibid., r. 46; C. Crocker to CPH, Nov. 22, 1887, ibid. (two letters, same date); for complications of holding companies, C. F. Crocker to CPH, May 29, 1889, ibid., r. 47.

131 T. Stillman to CPH, Aug. 31, 1888, CPH Papers, ser. 1, r. 46.

132 Lavender, *Great Persuader*, 357–58; CPH to Gates, March 4, 1889, CPH Papers, ser. 1, r. 47.

133 Lavender, *Great Persuader*, 359–60.

134 Ibid., 344–46; CPH to James Speyer, Dec. 6, 1899, pp. 12–14, CPH Papers, ser. 4, r. 1. Huntington would, having replaced Stanford, claim that his opposition was only to Stanford's political methods, because Stanford was irrelevant to the railroad: he had "interfered with me so little in the last thirty years." CPH to Mills, Jan. 9, 1892, ibid., ser. 1, r. 50; Mills to CPH, Jan. 28, 1892, ibid.

135 Delmatier et al., *Rumble of California Politics*, 99. Jane Stanford destroyed most of Stanford's papers, but there was left a letter to S. I. Gage praising Stanford. Huntington wrote it when he made his last try to return A. A. Sargent to the Senate and wanted Stanford's help. CPH to S. I. Gage, May 8, 1886, Stanford Papers, SC 33a, box 2, f. 4; for Huntington's suspicions, CPH to S. T. Gage, Nov. 26, 1885, box 24, LB, 9:189, M92, Hopkins Collection; White to J. D. Lynch, Jan. 14, 1887, White to J. W. Hellman, Jan. 14, 1887, White to H. M. Mitchell, Jan. 15, 1887, Correspondence, Outgoing, box 2, Letters from, vol. 1, Dec. 30, 1886, to Jan. 21, 1887, White Papers.

136 CPH to James Speyer, Dec. 6, 1899, CPH Papers, pp. 12–14, ser. 4, r. 1; Frank M. Stone to CPH, May 2, June 1, 1888, ibid., ser. 1, r. 47; Lavender, *Great Persuader*, 360–64; Thorpe, *Henry E. Huntington*, 91–97.

137 For beginning of alliance between Huntington and the managers of the Hopkins interests,

see Stillman to Huntington, Aug. 31, 1888, CPH Papers ser. 1, r. 47; selling off eastern interests, CPH to Gates, March 4, 1889, ibid.; for tensions within Southern Pacific, CPH to Gates, March 6, 8, 1889, ibid.; Lavender, *Great Persuader*, 359; quote, purchase, W. H. Mills to CPH, Feb. 9, 1891, CPH Papers, ser. 1, r. 49 (handwritten notation, W. H. Mills, June 2, 1891); Crocker's position, Woodard to (Gates?), Feb. 14, 1891, ibid.; for Stanford and Farmers' Alliance, John Boyd to CPH, March 5, 1891, ibid.; Mills to CPH, June 2, 1891, ibid.; for Stanford and silver, Stanford to CPH, May 24, 1893, ibid., r. 51; corruption, White to J. W. Hellman, Jan. 14, 1887, White to H. M. Mitchell, Jan. 15, 1887, Correspondence, Outgoing, box 2, Letters from, vol. 1, Dec. 30, 1886, to Jan. 21, 1887, White Papers.

138 Lavender, *Great Persuader*, 359–61.

139 Ibid.; buying votes, J. H. Woodard to CPH, Dec. 1, 1890, CPH Papers, ser. 1, r. 48.

140 J. H. Woodard to CPH, April 10, 1890, CPH Papers, ser. 1, r. 48; for Jayhawker stories, "Jayhawker: A Double-ender: Mr. Stow as a Two-headed Political Manager," *Los Angeles Times*, Aug. 2, 1890, p. 5; "Jayhawker: Manager Stow, His Political Motives and Methods Uncovered," ibid., July 30, 1890, p. 6; "Jayhawker: Markham's Warm Greeting in San Francisco," ibid., April 6, 1890, p. 5; Woodard to CPH, Dec. 1, 1890, CPH Papers, ser. 1, r. 49. Woodard also had worked for the Wabash. Woodard to CPH, May 25, 1890, ibid., r. 48.

141 J. H. Woodard to (Gates?), Feb. 14, 1891, CPH Papers, ser. 1, r. 49.

142 Ibid.

143 W. H. Mills to CPH, June 14, 1892, CPH Papers, ser. 1, r. 50; CPH to Mills, June 21, 1892, ibid., vol. 228, ser. 2, r. 33.

144 J. H. Woodard to (Gates?), Feb. 14, 1891, CPH Papers, ser. 1, r. 49.

145 Ibid.

146 Wm. Mahl to CPH, Oct. 21, 1892, CPH Papers, ser. 1, r. 51; CPH to A. C. Hutchison, April 18, 1892, ibid., vol. 226, ser. 2, r. 33.

147 J. H. Woodard to (Gates?), Feb. 14, 1891, CPH Papers, ser. 1, r. 49; Wm. Mahl to J. Kruttschnitt, Dec. 18, 1895, box 2E460, Mahl Papers.

148 A. C. Hutchinston to CPH, March 3, 8, 1893, CPH Papers, ser. 1, r. 48.

149 Woodard claimed that Huntington ordered him to assure Stanford's friends that their position in the company was in no danger as long they "faithfully discharge the duties of their station"; J. H. Woodard to (Gates?), Feb. 14, 1891, CPH Papers, ser. 1, r. 49; C. F. Crocker to CPH, June 24, 1890, ibid., r. 48; Thorpe, *Henry Huntington*, 95–96; A. C. Basset to Crocker, May 8, 1891, CPH Papers, ser. 1, r. 49. Bassett (the name is spelled two ways) later launched attacks on Huntington, who claimed that a J. M. Bassett was on the railroad payroll when Huntington took over, but no one could tell him what he did and fired him. CPH to President Harrison, Dec. 19, 1892, CPH Papers, vol. 232, ser. 2, r. 33.

150 Mahl to Gates, Oct. 21, 1890, CPH Papers, ser. 1, r. 48.

151 J. H. Woodard to (Gates?), Feb. 14, 1891, CPH Papers, ser. 1, r. 49; J. Stubbs to CPH, Oct. 10, 1892, ibid., r. 51.

152 Mills to CPH, Feb. 4, 1893, CPH Papers, ser. 1, r. 51.

153 CPH to HEH, June 29, 1893, HEH to CPH, Oct. 16, 1893, HEH Collection; William Mahl, "Memoirs," Southern Pacific Co. F3-F-5, Mahl Papers.

154 A. C. Bassett to CPH, May 8, 1891, C. Crocker to CPH, June 30, 1891, W. H. Mills to CPH, July 10, 1891, CPH Papers, ser. 1, r. 49.

155 W. H. Mills to CPH, June 30, 1892, CPH Papers, ser. 1, r. 51.

156 CPH to Mills, Jan. 9, 1892, Jan. 11, 1892, CPH Papers, ser. 1, r. 50.

157 Mahl, "Memoirs," Southern Pacific Co., F-1, Mahl Papers.

158 Ibid.

159 Stuart Daggett, *Chapters on the History of the Southern Pacific* (New York: A. M. Kelley, 1966, orig. ed. 1922), 136–38; Mahl, "Memoirs: P.I. Co.," G1–8, Mahl Papers.

160 C. E. Bretherton to I. E. Requa, May 16, 1894, CPH Papers, ser. 1, r. 53; CPH to Gates, May 8, 1890, ibid., r. 48.

161 Daggett, *Chapters*, 136–38; William Mahl, "Memoirs: P.I. Co.," G1–8, Mahl Papers.

162 C. F. Crocker to CPH, Sept. 3, 1891, CPH ser. 1, r. 50.

163 Mahl, "Memoirs," Southern Pacific Co., F-5, Mahl Papers.

164 S. White to E. B. Pond, Nov. 19, 1890, S. White to H. O. Bradley, Nov. 11, 1890, Correspondence, Outgoing, box 4, Sept. 13, 1890–Jan. 3, 1891, White to J. Irish, Jan. 4, 1892, box 5, White Papers.

165 Mills to CPH, Dec. 25, 30, 1891, Jan. 6, 1892, CPH to Mills, Jan. 12, 1892, CPH Papers, ser. 1, r. 50; Williams, *Democratic Party and California Politics*, 147–52; H. Mills to CPH, Dec. 15, 1891 (two letters), CPH Papers, ser. 1, r. 50.

166 CPH to E. Denison, June 1, 1892, CPH Papers, vol. 227, ser. 2, r. 33.

167 CPH to F. Stone, July 11, 1892, CPH Papers, vol. 228, ser. 2, r. 33.

A Railroad Life: William Mahl

1 I would like to thank Richard Orsi for bringing the Mahl material to my attention. Mahl Memoir, Southern Pacific Co., F 18, Colonel Samuel Gill, SG-23, J. Kruttschnitt to W. Mahl, Dec. 31, 1895, box 2E460, all in Mahl Papers.

2 If Mahl were a novelist, the technique would be what Viktor Shklovsky, father of Russian formalism, named *skaz*, where the narrator describes a scene and delivers a judgment, which utterly misread the scene. *Skaz* creates a reader who knows more than the narrator, but Mahl is not a novelist. Mahl Memoir, CPH 27, B-15, Mahl Papers.

3 Mahl Memoir, Southern Pacific Co., F-7, Mahl Papers.

4 United Syndicate, *New York Tribune*, "William Mahl: Vice-President and Comptroller of the Union Pacific and the Southern Pacific Systems," UT, box 2E465; Mahl Memoir, Albert Fink, AF-11, AF-12, both in Mahl Papers.

5 Mahl Memoir, Colonel Samuel Gill, SG-5, SG-7, Mahl Papers; Poor, *Manual, 1872–73*, 82.

6 Mahl Memoir, SG-3, SG-25–27, Mahl Papers.

7 Wm. Mahl to CPH, May 3, 1883, CPH Papers, ser. 1, r. 32; Mahl Memoir, CPH a–2, a–3, 26, 461, Collis P. Huntington, 1882–1900, Mahl Papers.

8 Mahl Memoir, CPH 26, C-1, CPH 27, B–11, CPH 26, C-13; Mahl to CPH, Oct. 30, 1883, CPH Papers, ser. 1, r. 33.

9 Mahl Memoir, Colonel Samuel Gill, SG-5, SG-6, SG-7 (quote), SG-21, SG-22.

10 Mahl Memoir, CPH 26, C-1, CPH 27, B-11, CPH 26, C-13, Mahl Papers.

11 Mahl Memoir, CPH 32–33, F-5, F-6, Harriman—Southern Pacific S–1, E. H. Harriman, R-1, R-2, R-3, Harriman—Characteristics, W-1, Mahl Papers.

12 Diagram no. 1, Southern Pacific Lines—Pacific System—Tonnage and rates per Ton-mile, 1885–1896, box 2E463, Mahl Papers,; Mahl Memoir, Southern Pacific Co., F-15, CPH, B-11, B-12, Mahl Papers.

13 Wm. Mahl, "The Relation That the Accounting Department of Railroads Should Bear to the Stockholders or Owners of the Property," May 27, 1892, box 2E 462, Mahl Papers.

14 L. M. Clement to Huntington, CPH Papers, ser. 1, r. 33.

15 Mahl, "The Relation That the Accounting Department of Railroads Should Bear to the Stockholders or Owners of the Property."

16 Mahl Memoir, Southern Pacific Co., F-1, Mahl Papers.

17 Mahl Memoir, E. H. Harriman, O-3, O-4, O-5, Mahl Papers.

18 Mahl Memoir, P.I. Co., G-4, G-5, G-6, G-7, Mahl Papers.
19 Mahl Memoir, General Remarks, N-1, Mahl Papers.
20 Mahl Memoir, Southern Pacific Co., F-12, Mahl Papers.
21 Mahl Memoir, Harriman—General O-6, Mahl Papers.
22 J. T. Mahl to William Mahl, Sept. 23, 1895, William Mahl to J. T. Mahl, Jan. 30, 1899, Mahl to Father, Feb. 7, 1899, J. T. Mahl to Father, March 7, 1899, box 2E460, Mahl Papers.
23 Mahl Memoir, Harriman—General, O-6, Mahl Papers.
24 Wallet is in box 2E462, Mahl Papers.

CHAPTER 7: WORKINGMEN

1 Quoted in Kim Voss, *The Making of American Exceptionalism: The Knights of Labor and Class Formation in the Nineteenth Century* (Ithaca: Cornell Univ. Press, 1993), 82; for the loss of this perspective, Charles Perrow, *Complex Organizations: A Critical Essay*, 3d ed. (New York: Random House, 1986), 130–31.
2 Adams to *Nation*, Feb. 2, 1880, *Nation*, Feb. 19, 1880. He enclosed a letter from Touzalin to Adams, Jan. 22, 1880, Perkins to Forbes, March 5, 1880, F 3.2–3.5, CB&Q; Shelton Stromquist, *A Generation of Boomers: The Pattern of Railroad Labor Conflict in Nineteenth-Century America* (Urbana: Univ. of Chicago Press, 1987), 235; W. H. Baldwin to Prof. F. Peabody, July 7, 1886, W. H. Baldwin to Adams, July 10, 28, 1886, UP, OVP, OC, vol. 3, F. H. Baldwin, sb. 3, ser. 1, r. 3.
3 Barbara Miller Solomon, "The Intellectual Background of the Immigration Restriction Movement in New England," *New England Quarterly* 25 (March 1952): 47–59. Thomas Winter, *Making Men, Making Class: The YMCA and Workingmen, 1877–1920* (Chicago: Univ. of Chicago Press, 2002), 3–5, 29–30, 42, 68. *Union Pacific Employes' Magazine*, Jan. 1887, 1–3.
4 Richard C. Overton, *Perkins/Budd: Railway Statesmen of the Burlington* (Westport, Conn.: Greenwood Press, 1982), 5–9, 10, 24, 31–32, 56–57, 60–63; Perkins to Forbes, March 5, 1880, F 3.2–3.5, CB&Q; Donald Le Crone McMurry, *The Great Burlington Strike of 1888: A Case History in Labor Relations* (Cambridge: Harvard Univ. Press, 1956), 264–67; Walter Licht, *Working for the Railroad: The Organization of Work in the Nineteenth Century* (Princeton: Princeton Univ. Press, 1983), 209–10.
5 Overton, *Perkins/Budd*, 6–9, 24, 31–32, 56–57, 60–61; Charles Francis Adams, *Charles Francis Adams, 1835–1915: An Autobiography* (Boston: Houghton Mifflin, 1916), 168–69, 179; for Comte's influence, Gillis J. Harp, *Positivist Republic: Auguste Comte and the Reconstruction of American Liberalism, 1865–1920* (University Park: Pennsylvania State Univ. Press, 1995). See also R. Jeffrey Lustig, *Corporate Liberalism: The Origins of Modern American Political Theory, 1890–1920* (Berkeley: Univ. of California Press, 1982), 100, 83–87, 112.
6 John Stuart Mill, *Auguste Comte and Positivism* (Ann Arbor: Univ. of Michigan Press, 1965), 10–12, 97; "Charles Eliot Perkins," *Business History Review* 31 (Autumn 1957): 97–98.
7 Adams to S. R. Callaway, Aug. 17, 1885, UP, PO, OC, vol. 31, ser. 2, r. 27.
8 Mill, *Auguste Comte*, 24, 38, 77.
9 Ibid., 94, 96.
10 Ibid., 149.
11 Oakes to Carr, Feb. 10, 1878, LB 21a, Villard Papers; Barbara Young Welke, *Recasting American Liberty: Gender, Race, Law, and the Railroad Revolution, 1865–1920* (New York: Cambridge Univ. Press, 2001), 1–42.
12 Oakes to Carr, May 3, Oct. 4, 1877, LB 17a, Villard Papers.
13 Oakes to Carr, Feb. 10, 1878, LB 21a, Villard Papers.

14 Ibid.

15 Martin N. Forney, *The Car-Builder's Dictionary: An Illustrated Vocabulary of Terms Which Designate American Railroad Cars, Their Parts and Attachments* (New York: Railroad Gazette, 1888), 61–63.

16 Yard Master's Mutual Benefit Association to CPH, Oct. 5, 1887, with circular, CPH Papers, ser. 1, r. 46; Mark Aldrich, *Death Rode the Rails: American Railroad Accidents and Safety, 1828–1965* (Baltimore: Johns Hopkins Univ. Press, 2006), 103–4.

17 Steven W. Usselman, *Regulating Railroad Innovation: Business, Technology, and Politics in America, 1840–1920* (New York: Cambridge Univ. Press, 2002), 173, 273; Aldrich, *Death Rode the Rails*, 108.

18 *Transportation Rules, Northern Pacific System of Railroads, in Effect Sept. 1, 1883* (St. Paul: Pioneer Press Co, 1883), 5, 7, 8, also 2, 3, Northern Pacific Railway Company Papers, pt. 1, ser. B, NS7602, r. 2, Secretary, Printed Materials; Aldrich, *Death Rode the Rails*, 82–85, 109–12.

19 John H. White Jr., *The American Railroad Freight Car: From the Wood-Car Era to the Coming of Steel* (Baltimore: Johns Hopkins Univ. Press, 1995), 528–29.

20 Licht, *Working for the Railroad*, 182–83; White, *American Freight Car*, 529; Aldrich, *Death Rode the Rails*, 28; *Transportation Rules, Northern Pacific*, 69.

21 In the early 1870s the Central Pacific sometimes hooked freight cars with fruit, salmon, and silk and, on their return, with oysters onto passenger trains. By then the Union Pacific demanded that all cars on a passenger train be equipped with air brakes. Towne to CPH, Feb. 19, 1873, CPH Papers, ser. 1, r. 5; Usselman, *Regulating Railroad Innovation*, 130–38, 280–85.

22 Usselman, *Regulating Railroad Innovation*, 130–38, 280–85; Aldrich, *Death Rode the Rails*, 114–15; White, *American Freight Car*, 539. By 1891 75 percent to 80 percent of the Northern Pacific freight cars had air brakes; W. S. Mellen to Villard, Feb. 23, 1891, NP, LRR, PV, 137.H.5.8 (F).

23 Mahl to CPH, Jan. 12, 1889, CPH Papers, ser. 1, r. 47; Adams to Rastus Ransom, March 26, 1886, UP, PO, OC, vol. 34, ser. 2, r. 29; White, *American Freight Car*, 541. Fast freight lines also used air brakes; Sam De Bow, California Fast Freight Line in "Freight and Passenger Earnings, 1885," UP, MS 3761, unnumbered box, p. 144.

24 White, *American Freight Car*, 528, 530, 539, 543–45; Aldrich, *Death Rode the Rails*, 114–15; L. S. Anderson to Adams, Feb. 16, 1887, UP, OVP, OC, vol. 2, subgroup 3, ser. 1, r. 2.

25 Henry Cabot Lodge, "A Perilous Business and Its Remedy," *North American Review* 154 (Feb. 1892): 189–95; Seung-Wook Kim, "Accident Risk and Railroad Worker Compensation: An Historical Study, 1880–1945" (Ph.D. diss., Univ. of Georgia, 1988), 4–5, 38, 45, 48–49, 50. The best statistics are in Aldrich, *Death Rode the Rails*, appendixes 1 and 2, 309–40. Charles Francis Adams Jr., *Notes on Railroad Accidents* (New York: G. P. Putnam's Sons, 1879); Steven W. Usselman, "The Lure of Technology and the Appeal of Order: Railroad Safety Regulation in Nineteenth-Century America," *Business and Economic History*, 2d ser., 21 (1992): 292–93, 298; W. S. Mellen to Villard, Feb. 23, 1891, NP, LRR, PV, 137.H.5.8 (F).

26 Usselman, "Lure of Technology," 292–93, 298.

27 Ibid., 290–98.

28 Illegible, Missouri Pacific Railway to Adams, Oct. 19, 1885, UP, RG 2361, box 21, KL; Powderly to Gould, Aug. 29, 1885, Powderly Papers, r. 10.

29 Paul Nagel, "The West That Failed: The Dream of Charles Francis Adams II," *Western Historical Quarterly* 8 (Oct. 1987): 401; Adams Diary, July 14, 1885, Adams Papers, r. 3.

30 Thomas Andrews, *Killing for Coal: America's Deadliest Labor War* (Cambridge: Harvard Univ. Press, 2008); Kathleen A. Brosnan, *Uniting Mountain & Plain: Cities, Law, and Environmental Change along the Front Range* (Albuquerque: Univ. of New Mexico Press, 2002); John P. Enyeart, *The Quest for "Just and Pure Law": Rocky Mountain Workers and American Social Democracy,*

1870–1924 (Stanford: Stanford Univ. Press, 2009), for the Colorado and, to a lesser extent, Wyoming economy and social relations.

31 The best sources on Buchanan are Robert E. Weir, *Knights Unhorsed: Internal Conflict in a Gilded Age Social Movement* (Detroit: Wayne State Univ. Press, 2000), 73–96, Enyeart, *Quest for "Just and Pure Law,"* 25–28, 41–84 passim, and Buchanan's own autobiography, Joseph R. Buchanan, *The Story of a Labor Agitator* (New York: Outlook Company, 1903), stove, 54–55, pistols, 240–41, antimonopoly, 100–102, 254–74, 276–77.

32 Adams to Callaway, Oct. 20, 1884, UP, PO, OC, vol. 24, ser. 2, r. 21; Adams to Callaway, Sept. 26, 1886, ibid., vol. 32, ser. 2, r. 27; Leon Fink, *Workingmen's Democracy: The Knights of Labor and American Politics* (Urbana: Univ. of Illinois Press, 1983), 4.

33 Weir, *Knights Unhorsed*, 76–77. Clark told Buchanan, who believed him, that he had not ordered the cuts, a lie, which was one of the many things that enraged Adams. Buchanan, *Labor Agitator*, 70–77, 82–99; Maury Klein, *Union Pacific*, vol. 1, *Birth of a Railroad, 1862–1893* (Garden City, N.Y.: Doubleday, 1983), 453–54.

34 Weir, *Knights Unhorsed*, 78–79; Buchanan, *Labor Agitator*, 142–46, 154–56, 250–53; Michael J. Cassity, "Modernization and Social Crisis: The Knights of Labor and a Midwest Community," *Journal of American History* 66 (June 1979): 43–48.

35 Adams to Callaway, Oct. 10, 1885, UP, PO, OC, vol. 32, ser. 2, r. 28; Adams to Joseph E. Johnston, July 12, 1885, UP, PO, OC, vol. 29, ser. 2, r. 24.

36 Adams Diary, July 14, 1885, Adams Papers, r. 3; for Adams earlier assessment, Adams to John Dillon, Feb. 10, 1885, UP, PO, OC, vol. 27 ser. 2, r. 23; Minutes of Meeting between President Adams and the Executive Committee of Knights of Labor, at Denver, July 14, 1885, UP, RG 2361, box 21, K.L., and Report of an Interview between Charles F. Adams Jr. . . . and the Executive Committee of the Knights of Labor, UP, RG 2361, KS Div., Labor Disputes; Adams to E. P. Alexander, July 16, 1885, UP, PO, OC, vol. 29, ser. 2, r. 25.

37 Adams to E. P. Alexander, July 16, 1885, UP, PO, OC, vol. 29, ser. 2, r. 25; Alexander to Adams, July 20, 1885, with cover letter, RG 2362, box 20, KS Div., Labor Disputes; Minutes of Meeting between President Adams and the Executive Committee of Knights of Labor, at Denver, July 14, 1885, Report of an Interview between Charles F. Adams Jr. . . . and the Executive Committee of the Knights of Labor, July 14, 1885, UP, RG 2361, box 20, KS Div., Labor Disputes.

38 Stromquist, *Generation of Boomers*, 102, 120–22; A. C. Hutchison to L. Stanford, May 2, 1885, CPH Papers, ser. 1, r. 40, or Schedule No. 1, Schedule of Wages paid Trackmen on the Union Pacific Railway (1886), enclosure with Callaway to Adams, March 10, 1886, UP, SG2, ser. 1, box 34, f. 1: Callaway. Much of this comes through in the columns and letter pages of the *Union Pacific Employes' Magazine*. See EWT to Editor, April 23, 1886, *Union Pacific Employes' Magazine*, June 1886, p. 156; "The Knights of Labor," ibid., July 1886, p. 181; No Name to Editor, n.d. (c. June 1886), ibid., July 1886, pp. 188–89. For work rules and Canada, see ibid., June 1887, p. 133. See also "Powderly at Denver," ibid., June 1887, p. 142.

39 "Charles F. Adams, Jr.," *Union Pacific Employes' Magazine*, April 1887, p. 70.

40 Quote, Adams to Callaway, Sept. 8, 1885, UP, PO, OC, vol. 32, ser. 2, r. 27.

41 Adams to S. R. Callaway, May 12, 1886, UP, PO, OC, vol. 38, ser. 2, r. 33.

42 S. R. Callaway to Adams, Jan. 16, 1885, S. R. Callaway to Thomas Neasham, Sept. 30, 1885, T. Neasham and J. N. Corbin to General Manager, Sept. 26, 1885, UP, SG2, ser. 1, box 21; Winter, *Making Men, Making Class*, 3, and passim. See Adams to E. F. Atkins, March 13, 1890, UP, PO, OC, vol. 50, ser. 2, r. 50; Isabella Black, "American Labour and Chinese Immigration," *Past and Present* 25 (July 1963): 60; Robert Seager II, "Some Denominational Reactions to Chinese Immigration to California, 1856–1892," *Pacific Historical Review* 28 (Feb. 1959): 55–57.

43 I. Bromley to Adams, Sept. 26, 1885, UP, SG2, ser. 1, box 21, p. 11.

44 Callaway to Adams, May 6, 1886 (two telegrams), UP, SG2, ser. 1, box 34, f. 3: Callaway.

45 Enyeart, *Quest for "Just and Pure Law,"* 48–50; Buchanan, *Labor Agitator*, 100–101.

46 Adams to Gen. Joseph E. Johnston, U.S. Railroad Commissioner, July 12, 1886, UP, PO, OC, vol. 29, ser. 2, r. 24; Memorandum, A. J. Poppleton, "In the Matter of the Strikes at Denver, June 9, 1885," enclosure with S. R. Callaway to Adams, June 18, 1885, UP, RG 2361, box 20, KS Div., Labor Disputes—DRG Strike; Adams to John F. Dillon, Feb. 10, 1885, UP, PO, OC, vol. 27, ser. 2, r. 23; Callaway to Adams, Jan. 10, 1885, UP, box 16, f. 5.

47 Cassity, "Modernization and Social Crisis," 43–47; Missouri, Bureau of Labor Statistics and Inspection, *The Official History of the Great Strike of 1886 on the Southwestern Railway System, Compiled by the Bureau of Labor Statistics and Inspection of Missouri* (Jefferson City: Tribune Printing Company, 1887), 25.

48 Voss, *Making of American Exceptionalism*, 82, 83; Craig Phelan, *Grand Master Workman: Terence Powderly and the Knights of Labor* (Westport, Conn.: Greenwood Press, 2000), 118–19; Robert E. Weir, *Beyond Labor's Veil: The Culture of the Knights of Labor* (University Park: Pennsylvania Univ. Press, 1996), 161; Enyeart, *Quest for "Just and Pure Law,"* 41–42, 46–47, 50–54, for workers' gains in West, 55–56. See also Philip R. P. Coelho and James F. Shepherd, "The Impact of Regional Differences in Prices and Wages on Economic Growth: The Unites States in 1890," *Journal of Economic History* 39 (March 1979): 69–85, esp. 72–73, 76–77.

49 Adams to S. R. Callaway, Aug. 2, 1885, R. Blickensderfer, Aug. 15, 1885, UP, PO, OC, vol. 31, ser. 2, r. 27; Adams to S. R. Callaway, Aug. 22, 1885, ibid., vol. 32, ser. 2, r. 27.

50 Fink, *Workingmen's Democracy*, 4–7; Buchanan, *Labor Agitator*, 430.

51 For a brilliant and influential account of the contract theory, see Amy Dru Stanley, *From Bondage to Contract: Wage Labor, Marriage, and the Market in the Age of Slave Emancipation* (New York: Cambridge Univ. Press, 1998). In practice, however, the equivalence between contracts and freedom was never so clear. Kelly Sisson, "Bound for California: Chilean Contract Laborers and *Patrones* in the California Gold Rush, 1848–1852," *Southern California Quarterly* 90 (Fall 2008): 259–302.

52 Gunther Peck, *Reinventing Free Labor: Padrones and Immigrant Workers in the North American West, 1880–1930* (New York: Cambridge Univ. Press, 2000), 65.

53 Ibid., 51–53; Yuji Ichioka, "Japanese Immigrant Labor Contractors and the Northern Pacific and the Great Northern Railroad Companies, 1898–1907," *Labor History* (1980): 326, 330–31, 333, 336–37; Callaway to Neasham, Sept. 22, 1885, Neasham to Callaway, Sept. 26, 1885, both in To the Employes of the Union Pacific Railway Co. from Executive Committee Employees, Sept. 26, 1885, Powderly Papers, r. 10; William F. Chew, *Nameless Builders of the Transcontinental Railway: The Chinese Workers of the Central Pacific Railroad* (Victoria, B.C.: Trafford, 2004), 49–52; Justice to Editor, March 13, 1887, *Union Pacific Employes' Magazine*, April 1887, pp. 94–95.

54 Craig Storti, *The Incident at Bitter Creek: The Story of the Rock Springs Chinese Massacre* (Ames: Iowa State Univ. Press, 1991), 59–66; Isaac H. Bromley, *The Chinese Massacre at Rock Springs, Wyoming Territory, September 2, 1885* (Boston: Franklin Press, Rand, Avery & Co., 1886), 38, 41–45.

55 Peck, *Reinventing Free Labor*, is a superb account of contract labor. For such accusations, see T. V. Powderly, *Thirty Years of Labor, 1859–1889: in which the history of the attempts to form organizations of workingmen for the discussion of political, social and economic questions is traced. The National labor union of 1866, the Industrial brotherhood of 1874, and the order of the Knights of labor of America and the world. The chief and most important principles in the preamble of the Knights of labor discussed and explained, with views of the author on land, labor, and transportation* (Philadelphia, 1890), 212–13, 216. For a description of the system of advancing tickets, see Testimony of F. F. Low, April 11, 1876, Proceedings of the Commission, *Special Committee*

on Chinese Immigration's Report to the California State Senate on Chinese Immigration: Its Social, Moral, and Political Effect (Sacramento: Fr. P. Thompson, 1878), 70–72, 75, 76, 77, 91, 97, 101–2; Chew, *Nameless Builders*, 37–40.

56 Testimony of John C. Stubbs, Aug. 12, 1887, *PRC*, 6:3314–15.

57 For an extension of the anti-Chinese logic to Italians and French Canadians, "Cheap Foreign Labor," *Union Pacific Employes' Magazine*, Feb. 1886, p. 9.

58 The 1880 census put the number of western railroad workers at 36,430, and the western railroads were really only getting started. Their number would increase sevenfold by 1905. *United States Census, 1880, Report of the Agencies of Transportation in the United States . . .* (Washington, D.C.: GPO, 1883), table VI, group VI, p. 277; Stromquist, *Generation of Boomers*, 114.

59 A. Anderson to Villard, Aug. 26, 1881, Telegram, box 38, f. 269, Mss. 8893, vol. 719, Villard Papers.

60 Pierre Berton, *The Impossible Railway: The Building of the Canadian Pacific—A Triumphant Saga of Exploration, Politics, High Finance & Adventure* (New York: Knopf, 1972), 373–77; Tzu-kuei Yen, "Chinese Workers and the First Transcontinental Railroad of the United States of America" (Ph.D. diss., St. John's Univ., 1976), 36; fight immigration restriction, Northern Pacific, Mitchell to Spafford, Jan. 31, 1882, J. H. Mitchell Letters 1882, box 82, f. 579, Villard Papers; Frank Bowden to Villard, Dec. 13, 1881, box 38, Mss. 8893, vol. 719, f. 273, ibid.; Southern Pacific, CPH to Crocker, Jan. 19, Feb. 4, 1882, CPH Papers, ser. 2, r. 6; W. Thomas White, "Race, Ethnicity and Gender in the Railroad Work Force: The Case of the Far Northwest, 1883–1918," *Western Historical Quarterly* 16 (July 1985): 268.

61 Van Horne to Harry Abbott, Sept. 21, 1883, LB, 3(1), vol. 1, Van Horne LB; Van Horne to J. H. Pope, Sept. 10, 1883, LB, 2(2) 1883, ibid.; W. C. Van Horne to J. Egan, June 20, 1883, Van Horne to Editor, *Toronto Globe*, July 16, 1883, both in LB, 2(1), ibid.

62 William John Pinkerton, *His Personal Record: Stories of Railroad Life* (Kansas City: Pinkerton Publishing Company, 1904), 21; Towne to CPH, April 29, 1879, CPH Papers, ser. 1, r. 17.

63 Pinkerton, *His Personal Record*, 24; Testimony of J. H. Strobridge, Palace Hotel, SF, Tuesday Aug. 9, 1887, *PRC*, 6:3107, corrected, 3139–40; Eric Arnesen, " 'Like Banquo's Ghost, It Will Not Down': The Race Question and the American Railroad Brotherhoods, 1880–1920," *American Historical Review* 99 (Dec. 1994): 1607.

64 Testimony of J. H. Strobridge, Aug. 9, 1887, *PRC*, 6:3107, corrected, 3139–40. Chew, *Nameless Builders*, 42–45, says that the maximum number of Chinese workers in the peak month was 5,190.

65 Peck, *Reinventing Free Labor*, 51.

66 Moon-Ho Jung, *Coolies and Cane: Race, Labor, and Sugar in the Age of Emancipation* (Baltimore: Johns Hopkins Univ. Press, 2006), 4–10, 115–16, 121, 138–45.

67 *Connecticut Post*, Oct. 6, 1883, Scrapbook of Notices of the Northern Pacific Railroad Excursion, Aug. 29–Sept. 3, 1883, box 51, 159, Villard Papers.

68 See n. 60, above. See also Testimony of Andrew Onderdonk, Oct. 30, 1884, *Report of the Royal Commission on Chinese Immigration, Report and Evidence* (Ottawa: Printed by Order of the Commission, 1885), 148.

69 John G. Cooke to C. H. Prescott, Feb. 25, 1886, enclosure with Callaway to Adams, March 9, 1886, UP, SG2, ser. 1, box 34, f. 1: Callaway.

70 Adams to Corbin, Dec. 16, 1885, UP, P.O. C.O., LB, 30, ser. 2, r. 26.

71 For "Great Chinee" Company, see P. J. O'Brien to Powderly, Nov. 4, 1885, Powderly Papers, r. 1.

72 Adams to J. W. Corbin and others, Dec. 18, 1885, UP, PO, OC, vol. 30, ser. 2, r. 26; Daniel Lewis, *Iron Horse Imperialism: The Southern Pacific of Mexico, 1880–1951* (Tucson: Univ. of

Arizona Press, 2007), 95; *Report of the Royal Commission on Chinese Immigration*, ix, xi–xxxiii, lxxxi–lxxxiii, lxxxvi–xcv.

73　Alexander Saxton, *The Indispensable Enemy: Labor and the Anti-Chinese Movement in California* (Berkeley: Univ. of California Press, 1971), 116–32, 139, 153–54; Seager, "Some Denominational Reactions," 49–66; Eric W. Fong and William T. Markham, "Anti-Chinese Politics in California in the 1870s: An Intercountry Analysis," *Sociological Perspectives* 45 (2002): 201–6.

74　"An Address to the People of the United States upon the Evils of Chinese Immigration," *Special Committee on Chinese Immigration's Report*, 8–9,10, 17–28, 37, 53.

75　*Special Committee on Chinese Immigration's Report*, 25–27, 29. For examples of selectivity, see Testimony of F. F. Low, April 11, 1876, 69–79, and Testimony of Otis Gibson, April 12, 1876, 90–100, and compare to the "Address" and "Memorial" above. Powderly, *Thirty Years of Labor*, 213.

76　*Special Committee on Chinese Immigration's Report*, 32, 46–56; signed editorial by Henry George, "The Standard," New York, June 80, 1888, quoted in Henry George, *The Life of Henry George*, 2 vols. (Garden City, N.Y.: Doubleday, 1911), http://www.henrygeorge.org/LIFEofHG/LHG2/lhg202.htm. For Chinese women as victims, see Peggy Pascoe, *Relations of Rescue: The Search for Female Moral Authority in the American West, 1874–1939* (New York: Oxford Univ. Press, 1990), 127–45, 157–65.

77　*Report of the Royal Commission on Chinese Immigration*, xcix–cvi, cxxxiii–cxxxiv.

78　Statement of the Committee of D.A. 162, Knights of Labor of California, in Powderly, *Thirty Years of Labor*, 216.

79　Powderly, *Thirty Years of Labor*, 213; Statement of the Committee of D.A. 162, Knights of Labor of California, ibid., 217; Bromley, *Chinese Massacre*, 34.

80　For four books that show how critical issues of gender and race became to politics and social reform in the West, see Neil Foley, *The White Scourge: Mexicans, Blacks, and Poor Whites in Texas Cotton Culture* (Berkeley: Univ. of California Press, 1997); Ian Tyrrell, *True Gardens of the Gods: Californian-Australian Environmental Reform, 1860–1930* (Berkeley: Univ. of California Press,1999); Linda Nash, *Inescapable Ecologies: A History of Environment, Disease, and Knowledge* (Berkeley: Univ. of California Press, 2006); and Nayan Shah, *Contagious Divides: Epidemics and Race in San Francisco's Chinatown* (Berkeley: Univ. of California Press, 2001).

81　A minority among the Knights wanted to include the Chinese; Powderly, *Thirty Years of Labor*, 218. The Chinese, of course, could and did organize against employers. David Montgomery, *The Fall of the House of Labor: The Workplace, the State and American Labor Activism* (Cambridge: Cambridge Univ. Press, 1987), 67, 85; Buchanan, *Labor Agitator*, 276–78.

82　Fink, *Workingmen's Democracy*, 169.

83　Statement of the Committee of D.A. 162, Knights of Labor of California, in Powderly, *Thirty Years of Labor*, 216.

84　F. J. Clark, J. P. Dalton, and A. G. Read, Committee to General Assembly of Knights of Labor, in Powderly, *Thirty Years of Labor*, 216–17; Bromley, *Chinese Massacre*, 38–39; "Statement of Knights of Labor L.A. No. 3,017, Nanaimo, B.C.," *Report of the Royal Commission on Chinese Immigration*, 155–60. Powderly and the Knights' leadership pressed against southern racism but not western racism; Phelan, *Grand Master Workman*, 151–53; Weir, *Beyond Labor's Veil*, 46; Fong and Markham, "Anti-Chinese Politics in California," 205–6, and Eric Fong and William T. Markham, "Immigration, Ethnicity, and Conflict: The California Chinese, 1849–1882," *Sociological Inquiry* 61 (1991): 471–90; Carlos A. Schwantes, "Protest in a Promised Land: Unemployment, Disinheritance, and the Origin of Labor Militancy in the Pacific Northwest, 1885–86," *Western Historical Quarterly* 13 (Oct. 1982): 373–90; Buchanan, *Labor Agitator*, 66; Arnesen, "The Race Question," 1604–6.

85　Thomas Jefferson, *Notes on the State of Virginia* (Baltimore: Pechin, 1800), Early American

Imprints, 166; *Nation*, pp. 68–69, quoted in Leon Litwack, *The American Labor Movement* (Englewood Cliffs, N.J.: Prentice-Hall, 1962); Adams to S. R. Callaway, May 12, 1886, UP, PO, OC, vol. 38, ser. 2, r. 4; Adams to Callaway, Sept. 26, 1885, enclosure with I. Bromley to Adams, Sept. 26, 1885, UP, RG 3761, SG2, ser. 1, box 21, p. 12.

86 Voss, *Making of American Exceptionalism*, 73; Pinkerton, *His Personal Record*, 73. "The 'Knights' and Election," *Union Pacific Employes' Magazine*, Nov. 1886, p. 292.

87 Powderly, *Thirty Years of Labor*, 214–17; Resolutions as Adopted by Joint Committee of 2487 and 3632 (Knights of Labor), Cheyenne, Wyoming, Sept. 13, 1885, Powderly Papers, r. 10; Bromley, *Chinese Massacre*, 74; Weir, *Beyond Labor's Veil*, 37.

88 Jung, *Coolies and Cane*, 136–45.

89 Erika Lee, *At America's Gates: Chinese Immigration during the Exclusion Era, 1882–1943* (Chapel Hill: Univ. of North Carolina Press, 2003), 23–46.

90 CPH to Crocker, Jan. 12, Feb. 4, 1882, CPH Papers, vol. 29, ser. 2, r. 6; quote, CPH to Gates, Oct. 16, 1889, ibid., ser. 1, r. 48. Black, "American Labour and Chinese Immigration," 63; C. Crocker to CPH, Jan. 21, 1882, no. 507, Jan. 27, 1882, no. 517, Crocker Papers, box 1, f. 12.

91 Peck, *Reinventing Free Labor*, 85. Callaway to Adams, Oct. 18, 1885, UP, RG 2361, box 21, Labor Disputes, Oct. 1885.

92 The standard account is Peck, *Reinventing Free Labor*.

93 Agreement, n.d., c. 1898, Great Northern, ser. B, r. 1.

94 Ichioka, "Japanese Immigrant Labor Contractors," 326, 330–31, 333, 336–37; Minnesota, General Superintendent to J. W. Hill, Great Northern Railway, June 12, 1900, Vice President–Operating Division, General Manager Subject File 34-01, OTC, JL 1898–1910, OTC.

95 Milton Turner to CPH, May 8, 1879, CPH, ser. 1, r. 17.

96 Remington to Russell Harding, Aug. 30, 1898, Great Northern, ser. B, r. 1; Harding to J. J. Hill, Sept. 8, 1898, Agreement, n.d., c. 1898, falls to a nickel, Oriental Trading Company to E. L. Brown, Aug. 6, 1908, Great Northern Railway, Vice President–Operating Division, General Manager Subject File 34-01, OTC, JL 1898–1910; A. L. Campbell to P. T. Downs, Jan. 20, 1900, with enclosure, ibid., Direct payment, Gen. Supt. to H. A. Kennedy, Dec. 15, 1901, ibid., all in OTC.

97 Rivalries, C. T. Takahashi to Slade, Aug. 5, 1905, Vice President–Operating Division, General Manager Subject File 34-01, OTC, JL 1898–1910; quote, C. T. Takahashi to Ward, Oct. 10, 1905, ibid., all in OTC.

98 Genl. Supt. to H. A. Kennedy, Dec. 15, 1901, H. A. Kennedy to G. T. Slade, Feb. 6, 1905, Vice President–Operating Division, General Manager Subject File 34-01, OTC, JL 1898–1910; playing railroads against each other, Asst. Genl. Supt. to J. P. O'Brien, April 4, 1902, Kennedy to F. E. Ward, April 6, 14, 1902, ibid., all in OTC.

99 Peck, *Reinventing Free Labor*, 50, 84–114; Phelan, *Grand Master Workman*, 134–37.

100 Bromley to Adams, Oct. 4, 1885, UP, RG 2361, box 21, Labor Disputes, Oct. 1885. Chinese immigrants became, in the words of Mae Ngai, "simultaneously a social reality and a legal impossibility." Mae M. Ngai, *Impossible Subjects: Illegal Aliens and the Making of Modern America* (Princeton: Princeton Univ. Press, 2004), 4.

101 Lewis, *Iron Horse Imperialism*, 94.

102 Bromley to Adams, Oct. 4, 1885, UP, RG 2361, box 21, Labor Disputes, Oct. 1885.

103 D. O. Clark to Bromley, Oct. 28, 1885, UP, RG 2361, box 21, Labor Disputes, Oct. 1885. After the massacre there were 547 Chinese and 85 whites as the company concentrated all of its Chinese employees in Wyoming at Rock Springs for protection. Callaway to Adams, Dec. 3, 1885, UP, RG 2631, Labor Disputes, Nov.–Dec. 1885; Adams to Corbin, Dec. 16, 1885, UP, PO, CO, vol. 30, ser. 2, r. 26. For similar complaints by Central Pacific, C. Crocker to CPH, Feb. 3, 1888, CPH Papers, ser. 1, r. 46.

104 Saxton, *Indispensable Enemy*, 157–97; Cal Ewing to Powderly, Nov. 5, 1885, W. W. Stone to Powderly, Dec. 24, 1885, Powderly Papers, r. 11. Boycotting of Chinese laundries had spread to Wichita by 1886; (?) to Powderly, Jan. 6, 1886, ibid., r. 12.

105 A. Dudley Gardner and Verla R. Flores, *Forgotten Frontier: A History of Wyoming Coal Mining* (Boulder, Colo.: Westview Press, 1989), 19–22; water, Adams to Callaway, April 26, 1886, UP, PO, OC, vol. 33, ser. 2, r. 28.

106 David A. Wolff, *Industrializing the Rockies: Growth, Competition, and Turmoil in the Coalfields of Colorado and Wyoming, 1868–1914* (Boulder: Univ. of Colorado Press, 2003), 5–6, 21–22; Gardner and Flores, *Forgotten Frontier*, 15–16. The best account of western coal mining is Andrews, *Killing for Coal*, 122–56.

107 Wolff, *Industrializing the Rockies*, 33; Gardner and Flores, *Forgotten Frontier*, 26. An exception was the Rocky Mountain Coal and Iron Company, which supplied the Central Pacific.

108 Gould to Silas U. U. Clark, Feb. 29, 1876, HM 62486, Gould to Silas Clark, Aug. 3, 1878, HM 62500, Railroadiana (Western USA), pt. 2, 1869–1901, Huntington Library.

109 "A Plea for Free Labor," in Bromley, *Chinese Massacre*, 90; Storti, *Incident at Bitter Creek*, 59–66; Gardner and Flores, *Forgotten Frontier*, 27–29; Bromley, *Chinese Massacre*, 44–45; D. O. Clark to Bromley, Oct. 28, 1885, UP, RG 2361, box 21, Labor Disputes, Oct. 1885.

110 Gardner and Flores, *Forgotten Frontier*, 27–29, 33–39; Clark to Bromley, Oct. 28, 1885, Orr to Callaway, Oct. 30, 1885, UP, RG 2361, box 21, Labor Disputes, Oct. 1885; Bromley, *Chinese Massacre*, 28–29.

111 I. Bromley to Adams, Sept. 25, 1885, UP, RG 3761, SG2, ser. 1, box 21. See also Bromley to Adams, Oct. 4, 1885, UP, RG 2361, box 21, Labor Disputes, Oct. 1885.

112 Adams to Callaway, July 20, 1886 (two letters), UP, PO, OC, vol. 38, ser. 2, r. 33. Adams publicly testified the next year that the mines were the salvation of the company, but, as with most railroad officials, what he said publicly often differed from what he said privately. Klein, *Union Pacific*, 334; Adams to Callaway, Dec. 4, 1884, UP, PO, OC, vol. 24, ser. 2, r. 21.

113 Adams to Charles Welch, July 14, 1885, UP, PO, OC, vol. 29, ser. 2 r. 24.

114 Buchanan, *Labor Agitator*, 252; "Thomas Neasham," *Union Pacific Employes' Magazine*, Jan. 1887, pp. 4–5.

115 Buchanan, *Labor Agitator*, 100–101, 106; Wolff, *Industrializing the Rockies*, 63–67.

116 For miners and price of coal, Callaway to Adams, Aug. 19, 1885, UP, SG2, ser. 1, box 289, f. UPR Emply Rel.; Testimony of James Maxwell Clark, *PRC*, 4:1825–28, Testimony of Thomas Patterson, *PRC*, 4:1870–72, Testimony of E. A. Slack, *PRC*, 4:2083–85, Testimony of C. W. Riner, *PRC*, 4:2085–88; Testimony of W. H. Root, *PRC*, 4:2112; for defense, Testimony of Robert Rubidge, *PRC*, 4:1925–28; Testimony of Charles Francis Adams, *PRC*, 4:1992–94; hostility to railroad, Adams to Callaway, May 29, 1886, UP, PO, OC, vol. 38, ser. 2, r. 38; mediation, S. R. Callaway to Adams, Jan. 24, 1885, UP, box 16, f. 5; for favored companies, S. R. Callaway to Adams, May 29, 1886, UP, box 34, f. 4.

117 Adams to Callaway, Dec. 4, 18, 1884, UP, PO, OC, vol. 24, NS 15986, ser. 2, r. 21.

118 S. R. Callaway to Adams, Jan. 10, 1885, UP, SG 2, ser. 1, box 17.

119 Wolff, *Industrializing the Rockies*, 88–107; Buchanan, *Labor Agitator*, 106–16; Adams to Callaway, Oct. 10, 1885, UP, PO, OC, vol. 32, ser. 2, r. 28; Adams to Callaway, Aug. 22, 1885, ibid., r. 27.

120 Adams to Gen. F. P. Alexander, Sept. 1, 1885, UP, PO, OC, vol. 29, ser. 2, r. 25.

121 Adams to Powderly, Oct. 28, 1885, UP, PO, OC, vol. 30, ser. 2, r. 26; Wolff, *Industrializing the Rockies*, 97.

122 For a wonderful account of coal mining and its environmental, social, and political ramifications in Colorado, see Andrews, *Killing for Coal*.

123 Daniel Burns, *The Elements of Coal Mining* (London: Edward Arnold, 1917), 97, also 90–105;

Herbert W. Hughes, *A Text-Book of Coal-Mining for the Use of Colliery Managers and Others* (London: Charles Griffin, 1901), 148; Andrews, *Killing for Coal*, 122–56.

124 Neasham quotes, Neasham and J. N. Corbin to General Manager and President of the Union Pacific, Sept. 19, 1885, in Bromley, *Chinese Massacre*, 74.

125 Ibid.; "A Plea for Free Labor," in Bromley, *Chinese Massacre*, 90; quote, Storti, *Incident at Bitter Creek*, 84–85; Thomas Neasham to General Manager, Sept. 19, 1885, Report, Committee of Employes, Thomas Neasham, Chairman, Sept. 19, 1885, enclosed in S. R. Callaway, To the Employes of the Union Pacific Railway Co., Sept. 22, 1886, UP, SG2, ser. 1, box 21; for Knights and manhood, Weir, *Beyond Labor's Veil*, 36 ff. The miners complained bitterly about being compelled to do extra work without pay; Bromley, *Chinese Massacre*, 23, 28–29, 90. For attack on dependency, "Dependency," *Union Pacific Employes' Magazine*, July 1887, pp. 166–67.

126 Callaway to Adams, Sept. 20, 1885 (telegram), UP, RG 2361, box 21, Labor Disputes, Sept. 1885; Storti, *Incident at Bitter Creek*, 108–21. Callaway later reported that only one of the Chinese was shot and killed, but Storti's account clearly indicates otherwise. Callaway to Bromley, Dec. 5, 1885, UP, RG 2361, box 12, Labor Disputes, Nov.–Dec. 1885. Bromley, *Chinese Massacre*, 11, 29, 32–33, 48–50, 55–58. The Chinese names were phonetically rendered. Both men later testified about the incident.

127 Storti, *Incident at Bitter Creek*, 108–21; S. R. Callaway to Adams, Sept. 5, 1885, UP, SG 2, ser. 1, box 17; Bromley, *Chinese Massacre*, 26, 48–53. The Chinese account of the riot is in Memorial of Hon. Huang Sih Chuen, Chinese Consul, Sept. 18, 1885, in Judy Yung, Gordon H. Chang, and Him Mark Lai, eds., *Chinese American Voices: From the Gold Rush to the Present* (Berkeley: Univ. of California Press, 2006), 48–54, original in H. Rept. (1885–86), 49th Cong., 1st sess., no. 2044, pp. 28–32. The Chinese received $150,000 in compensation, p. 48. Adams to Gen. F. P. Alexander, Sept. 1, 1885, Adams to Haskell, Sept. 27, 1885, UP, PO, OC, vol. 29, ser. 2, r. 25; Klein, *Union Pacific*, 467. The details come from Bromley, *Chinese Massacre*, 13, 16, 50–53. Bromley was a government director and an ardent opponent of the Knights. Bromley to Adams, Sept. 23, 1885, UP, RG 2361, box 21, KL. Also see S. R. Callaway to Adams, Sept. 20, 1885, ibid., Labor Disputes, Sept. 1885.

128 For accounts blaming the Union Pacific management, see Bromley, *Chinese Massacre*, 63–69, 87; S. R. Callaway to Adams, Oct. 2, 1885, UP, RG 2361, box 21, Labor Disputes, Oct. 1885.

129 Adams to William Endicott, Sept. 3, 7, 1885, UP, PO, OC, vol. 29, ser. 2, r. 25. Callaway to Adams, Oct. 4, 1885, UP, SG2, ser. 1, box 28, f. UPR Coal Dept.

130 This is compiled from Adams diary entries from Aug. to Dec. 1885; Adams Diary, Adams Papers, r. 3.

131 Bromley, *Chinese Massacre*, 11–21, 78–86. S. R. Callaway to Adams, Oct. 2, 1885, UP, RG 2361, box 21; Bromley to Adams, Oct. 4, 1885, ibid., Labor Disputes, Oct. 1885; Adams to Ayres, Sept. 16, 1885, UP, PO, OC, vol. 29, ser. 2, r. 25; Adams to E. L. Godkin, Sept. 18, 1885, ibid.; Adams to Grover Cleveland, Dec. 1, 1885, ibid., vol. 30, ser. 2, r. 26; Storti, *Incident at Bitter Creek*, 154–56.

132 Charles Francis Adams, "Reflex Light from Africa," *Century Magazine* 72 (1906): 107.

133 For the Knights, see Voss, *Making of American Exceptionalism*, 73.

134 Adams to T. V. Powderly, Oct. 28, 1885, UP, PO, OC, vol. 30, ser. 2, r. 26; Callaway to Adams, Oct. 2, 1885 RG. Powderly to Adams, Oct. 26, 1885, RG 2361, box 21, Labor Disputes, Oct. 1885.

135 Adams to Callaway, Oct. 3, 1885, UP, PO, OC, vol. 31, ser. 2, r. 27.

136 Adams to Powderly, Oct. 28, 1885, UP, PO, OC, vol. 30, ser. 2, r. 26.

137 Adams to Callaway, Oct. 6, 1885, UP, PO, OC, vol. 32, ser. 2, r. 28.

138 Adams to Callaway, Jan. 30, 1886, UP, PO, OC, vol. 33, ser. 2, r. 28.

139 Bromley, *Chinese Massacre*, 69; Storti, *Incident at Bitter Creek*, 139; for Chinese, S. R. Callaway

to Adams, Oct. 23, 1885; boycotts, S. R. Callaway to Adams, Oct. 26, 1885, "Boycott" leaflet, Oct. 17, 1885; Ogden, Utah, enclosure with T. Cahoon to S. I. Smith, Oct. 19, 1885, all in UP, box 21, Labor Disputes, Oct. 1885. For Adams's hope of a general strike, Adams to E. L. Godkin, Sept. 18, 1885, UP, PO, OC, vol. 29, ser. 2, r. 25; Adams to Callaway, Oct. 8, 1885, ibid., vol. 32, ser. 2, r. 28; Adams to Callaway, March 26, 1886, ibid., vol. 33, ser. 2, r. 28; comparative Statement of Tons of Coal Mine (*sic*), enclosure, Callaway to Adams, May 21, 1886, UP, box 34, f. 4.

140　Neasham to Powderly, Nov. 1, 1885, Executive Committee of District Assembly No. 82, K. of L. to Powderly, Oct. 3, 1885; J. N. Corbin to Powderly, Nov. 1, 1885, John Mushett to Powderly, Nov. 2, 1885, Mushett to Powderly with attached affidavit, Nov. 3, 1885, all in Powderly Papers, r. 11; Adams to Callaway, Sept. 22, 1885, Adams to Callaway, Sept. 21, 1885, Telegram, UP, PO, OC, vol. 32, ser. 2, r. 27; threat, Adams to Endicott, Sept. 7, 1885, ibid., vol. 29, ser. 2, r. 25; for end of strikes, Adams to Callaway, Nov. 11, 27, 1885, ibid., vol. 32, ser. 2, r. 28. Some excellent accounts of the Knights still write of them as attempting to "organize all workers, regardless of skill, race, or gender," but make the Chinese an exception. Voss, *Making of American Exceptionalism*, 2, 81, 84; for strikes, Phelan, *Grand Master Workman*, 57–59.

141　Adams to Callaway, Jan. 30, 1886, UP, PO, OC, vol. 33, ser. 2, r. 28.

142　Adams to Callaway, Oct. 18, 1885, UP, PO, OC, vol. 32, ser. 2, r. 28. There were also threats to punish railroad towns such as Laramie that sympathized with workers against the company. John Donnelton to Adams, UP, SG2, ser. 1, box 38.

143　Callaway to Adams, Jan. 15, 1886, UP, box 47, f. 3. Part of dealing with them was having U.S. troops on hand, and as late as 1890 he reacted quickly when the United States made plans to shut down the post at Pilot Butte, near Rock Springs. Adams to R. Proctor, April 2, 5, 1890, UP, PO, OC, vol. 50, ser. 2, r. 45.

144　John Bates Clark, "Possibility of a Scientific Law of Wages," *Publications of the American Economic Association* 4 (March 1889): 39–69; quote in John Bates Clark, "Universal Law of Economic Variation," *Quarterly Journal of Economics* (April 1894): 261.

145　John Bates Clark, "Universal Law of Economic Variation," 261–79, quote 262–63; Clark, "Possibility of a Scientific Law of Wages," 40–41, 69.

146　Here, see Herbert Hovenkamp, *Enterprise and American Law, 1836–1937* (Cambridge: Harvard Univ. Press, 1991), 72–73, and Melvyn Dubofsky, "The Federal Judiciary, Free Labor, and Equal Rights," in Richard Schneirov, Shelton Stromquist, and Nick Salvatore, eds., *The Pullman Strike and the Crisis of the 1890s: Essays on Labor and Politics* (Urbana: Univ. of Illinois Press, 1999), 159–74, which locates the ideological formulations of the judiciary in this larger language of republicanism and free labor.

147　Hovenkamp, *Enterprise and American Law*, 223–25.

148　Clark, "Possibility of a Scientific Law of Wages," 48.

149　"The Helplessness of Labor," *Union Pacific Employes' Magazine*, Sept. 1893, p. 229.

150　Ibid.; Clark, "Possibility of a Scientific Law of Wages," 54–69.

151　Hovenkamp, *Enterprise and American Law*, 191.

A Railroad Life: William Pinkerton

1　William John Pinkerton, *His Personal Record: Stories of Railroad Life* (Kansas City, Mo.: Pinkerton Publishing Company, 1904), 19, 23–25.

2　Ibid., 24.

3　Ibid., 7.

4　For a collection of pictures, see Maury Klein, *Union Pacific*, vol. 1, *Birth of a Railroad, 1862–1893* (Garden City, N.Y.: Doubleday, 1987).

5 Since the Denver and Rio Grande was completed to Leadville in 1880, Pinkerton's trip had to be just prior to this. For roads building to Leadville in 1879, see *Railway Age*, Jan. 9, 1879, p. 13.

6 Pinkerton, *Personal Record*, 52–55.

7 I take the phrase from Paul Johnson, *Sam Patch: The Famous Jumper* (New York: Hill & Wang, 2003), 122. Johnson uses it in a somewhat different sense.

8 Shelton Stromquist, *A Generation of Boomers: The Pattern of Railroad Labor Conflict in Nineteenth-Century America* (Urbana: Univ. of Illinois Press, 1987), 108. Stromquist gives the best account of railroad work. Pinkerton, *Personal Record*, 53, 56–57, 83–89, 100–102, 118–19, 169–72. Walter Licht, *Working for the Railroad: The Organization of Work in the Nineteenth Century* (Princeton: Princeton Univ. Press, 1983), 79–124, 214–43.

9 Pinkerton, *Personal Record*, 12–14, 276–77, and passim. Stromquist, *Generation of Boomers*, 100–41.

10 Pinkerton, *Personal Record*, 104, 246–57; G. L. Lansing to CPH, Dec. 8, 28, 1883, CPH Papers, ser. 1, r. 34; Mark Aldrich, *Death Rode the Rails: American Railroad Accidents and Safety, 1828–1965* (Baltimore: Johns Hopkins Univ. Press, 2006), 164. Aldrich found corporate plans to be minimal and inadequate, but neither union plans nor private insurance covered much of the gap.

11 Pinkerton, *Personal Record*, 61; Aldrich, *Death Rode the Rails*, 173–74; for example of discretionary exam, *Transportation Rules, Northern Pacific System of Railroads, in Effect Sept. 1, 1883* (St. Paul: Pioneer Press Co., 1883), 93–94; Northern Pacific Railway Company Papers, pt. 1, ser. B, NS7602, r. 2, Secretary, Printed Materials.

12 Pinkerton, *Personal Record*, 104–10.

13 *Transportation Rules, Northern Pacific System of Railroads, in Effect Sept. 1, 1883*, 93–95; Northern Pacific Railway Company Papers, pt. 1, ser. B, NS7602, r. 2, Secretary, Printed Materials.

14 Adams to S. R. Callaway, May 12, 1886, UP, PO, OC, vol. 34, ser. 2, r. 33.

15 H. R. Dill to W. H. McCord, March 18, 1895, "Illinois Central Railroad Company, Application for Employment," both are bound in *Railway Pamphlets*, 109, Stanford Univ. Library; Pinkerton, *Personal Record*, 278. A blacklist included union or strike activity, but far and away the most common listing on a Southern Pacific blacklist that survives is drinking; blacklist no. 3, Feb. 1887–91, Ms. 10, Southern Pacific Records.

16 Pinkerton, *Personal Record*, 60–61.

17 Ibid., 188–89; John H. White Jr., *The American Railroad Freight Car: From the Wood-Car Era to the Coming of Steel* (Baltimore: Johns Hopkins Univ. Press, 1993), 530.

18 Wm. Mellen to T. F. Oakes, Nov. 4, 1890, NP, LRR, PV, 137.H.5.6 (F).

19 Pinkerton, *Personal Record*, 24; Testimony of J. H. Strobridge, Aug. 9, 1887, *PRC*, 6:3107, corrected, 3139–40; Eric Arnesen " 'Like Banquo's Ghost, It Will Not Down': The Race Question and the American Railroad Brotherhoods, 1880–1920," *American Historical Review* 99 (Dec. 1994): 1607.

20 Pinkerton, *Personal Record*, 89–90.

21 Ibid., 90–91.

22 Ibid., 93–94.

23 Ibid., 188–89.

24 Ibid., 118–19, 124.

25 Ibid., 124–25.

26 Ibid., 126–27.

27 Ibid., 127–28.

CHAPTER 8: LOOKING BACKWARD

1 Edward Bellamy, *Looking Backward* (New York: New American Library, 1960, orig. ed. 1888), 54.

2 Herbert Hovenkamp, *Enterprise and American Law, 1836–1937* (Cambridge: Harvard Univ. Press, 1991), 270, 273.

3 George H. Miller, *Railroads and the Granger Laws* (Madison: Univ. of Wisconsin Press, 1971), 172–93, esp. 188–89; Hovenkamp, *Enterprise and American Law*, 274.

4 *Report of the Senate Select Committee on Interstate Commerce . . .* 49th Cong., 1st sess., Submitted to the Senate, Jan. 18, 1886 (Washington, D.C.: GPO, 1886), 182, 215–16. For California, see Alfred A. Cohen, *A Letter to the Board of Railroad Commissioners of California on the Policy of Legislative Interference with Railroad Tariffs* (New York: Evening Post Job Printing Office, 1883), Huntington Library 128737, p. 5. See also John Lauritz Larson, *Bonds of Enterprise: John Murray Forbes and Western Development in America's Railway Age*, expanded ed. (Iowa City: Univ. of Iowa Press, 2001), 135–43; for Central Pacific denial, Statement of J. C. Stubbs, July 26, 1887, *PRC*, 5:2574–75; A. N. Towne to CPH, April 18, 1873, CPH Papers, ser. 1, r. 5.

5 James F. Hudson, *The Railways and the Republic* (New York: Harper & Brothers, 1886), 107–24, 135–38; Hovenkamp, *Enterprise and American Law*, 139–48; *Report of the Senate Select Committee* (1886), 41, 175–80.

6 Hudson, *Railways and the Republic*, 9.

7 Ibid., 55; William W. Sharkey, *The Theory of Natural Monopoly* (New York: Cambridge Univ. Press, 1982), 14, 26; Richard A. Posner, "Natural Monopoly and Its Regulation," *Stanford Law Review* 21, no. 3 (Feb. 1969): 570.

8 Posner, "Natural Monopoly and Its Regulation," 548–643; Sharkey, *Theory of Natural Monopoly*, vii–27. Gerald Berk does not see this natural monopoly as describing the mature railroad industry; Berk, *Louis Brandeis and the Making of Regulated Competition, 1900–1932* (New York: Cambridge Univ. Press, 2009), 75–88.

9 Hal R. Varian, Joseph Farrell, and Carl Shapiro, *The Economics of Information Technology: An Introduction* (New York: Cambridge Univ. Press, 2004), 30–33.

10 Thomas McCraw, *Prophets of Regulation: Charles Francis Adams, Louis D. Brandeis, James M. Landis, Alfred E. Kahn* (Cambridge: Harvard Univ. Press, 1984), 9–10; Charles Francis Adams, "Which Will Quickest Solve the Railroad Question: Force Bills or Public Opinion?" (Address at Oshkosh, Wisc., Sept. 3, 1875), 7–11, quote 9, in Adams, *Railway Pamphlets*, Stanford Univ. Library; Hovenkamp, *Enterprise and American Law*, 139–48.

11 Hovenkamp, *Enterprise and American Law*, 274; Sharkey, *Theory of Natural Monopoly*, vii–27.

12 Adams, "Which Will Quickest Solve the Railroad Question," 6–7; Adams to Callaway, Jan. 11, 1879, UP, PO, OC, vol. 39, ser. 2, r. 34; Charles Francis Adams Jr., *Railroads: Their Origin and Problems* (New York: G. P. Putnam's Sons, 1878), 130. For competition as cure, see Hudson, *Railways and the Republic*, 368, but even Hudson recognized the problem of duplicate lines, 415–22. Quote, Adams to E. P. Alexander, July 17, 1886, UP, PO, OC, vol. 35, ser. 2, r. 31.

13 Adams, "Which Will Quickest Solve the Railroad Question," 7–11, quote 9.

14 Ibid., 7–11; McCraw, *Prophets of Regulation*, 9–10; Adams, *Railroads: Their Origin and Problems*, 116–17, quote 130.

15 Arthur T. Hadley, *Railroad Transportation: Its History and Its Laws* (New York: G. P. Putnam's Sons, 1895, orig. ed. 1885), 67–74, quote 69.

16 Ibid., 67–74.

17 Ibid., 70–71.

18 William Z. Ripley, *Railroads: Rates and Regulation* (New York: Longmans, Green, 1912), quote 53–54, 55, 65, 89; Sharkey, *Theory of Natural Monopoly*, 19–22.

19 Berk, *Louis D. Brandeis*, 74–78.

20 Joseph R. Buchanan, *The Story of a Labor Agitator* (New York: Outlook Company, 1903), 430; "Why the Government Should Run the Railroads," *Union Pacific Employes' Magazine*, Oct. 1886, p. 265.

21 W. Kaye Lamb, *History of the Canadian Pacific Railway* (New York: Macmillan, 1977), 155–58.

22 John H. Coatsworth, *Growth against Development: The Economic Impact of Railroads in Porfirian Mexico* (DeKalb: Northern Illinois Univ. Press, 1981), 175.

23 Jeffrey Ostler, *Prairie Populism: The Fate of Agrarian Radicalism in Kansas, Nebraska, and Iowa, 1880–1892* (Lawrence: Univ. Press of Kansas, 1993).

24 The United States did temporarily nationalize railroads during World War I.

25 Charles Postel, *The Populist Vision* (New York: Oxford Univ. Press, 2007), 15.

26 Ibid., 17, 104; Richard J. Orsi, *Sunset Limited: The Southern Pacific Railroad and the Development of the American West, 1850–1930* (Berkeley: Univ. of California Press, 2005), 320–21. Scott G. McNall, *The Road to Rebellion: Class Formation and Kansas Populism, 1865–1900* (Chicago: Univ. of Chicago Press, 1988), 26.

27 Postel, *Populist Vision*, 33.

28 Ibid., 108–11.

29 Ibid., 115.

30 Ibid., 128–30.

31 Ibid., 18–19.

32 Ibid., 148–49; Marion Todd, *Railways of Europe and America* (Boston: Arena Publishing Company, 1893), iii; Thomas Frank, "The Leviathan with Tentacles of Steel: Railroads in the Minds of Kansas Populists," *Western Historical Quarterly* 20 (Feb. 1989): 42–43, 47–48; conservative "developer populists," Peter H. Argersinger, "Populists in Power: Public Policy and Legislative Behavior," *Journal of Interdisciplinary History* 18 (Summer 1987): 101.

33 For range of beliefs, Leon Fink, *Workingmen's Democracy: The Knights of Labor and American Politics* (Urbana: Univ. of Illinois Press, 1983), 7–9.

34 T. V. Powderly, *Thirty Years of Labor, 1859–1889* (Philadelphia, 1890), 84–85. "Servile races" was the term the Knights used.

35 Ibid., 84.

36 Ibid., 174–86.

37 John L. Thomas, *Alternative America: Henry George, Edward Bellamy, Henry Demarest Lloyd, and the Adversary Tradition* (Cambridge: Harvard Univ. Press, Belknap Press, 1983), 117–23; Henry George, *Progress and Poverty: An Inquiry into the Cause of Industrial Depressions and of Increase of Want with Increase of Wealth, The Remedy* (New York: Robert Schalkenbach Foundation, 1942, orig. ed. 1879), 198, 204, 207–13, 271–72, 295–96, 340–41, 352–53.

38 Powderly, *Thirty Years of Labor*, 173–86.

39 Crocker to CPH, July 3, 1890, CPH Papers, ser. 1, r. 48; Testimony of CPH, Testimony of Artemas Holmes, *PRC*, 1:40, 178; Adams to A. B. Stickney, Dec. 6, 1888, UP, PO, OC, vol. 45, ser. 2, r. 40; Perkins to Forbes, Feb. 24, 1881, F 3.2.–3.5, CB&Q; Klein, *Jay Gould*, 232.

40 Donna A. Barnes, *Farmers in Rebellion: The Rise and Fall of the Southern Farmers Alliance and the People's Party in Texas* (Austin: Univ. of Texas Press, 1984), 117–20, 140–44.

41 Ostler, *Prairie Populism*, 2–11, 91–153; C. Crocker to CPH, Nov. 29, 1887, CPH Papers, ser. 1, r. 46; William R. Childs, *The Texas Railroad Commission: Understanding Regulation in America to the Mid-Twentieth Century* (College Station: Texas A&M Univ. Press, 2005); Barnes, *Farmers in Rebellion*, 117–20, 140–44.

42 Ruth Allen, *The Great Southwest Strike*, Univ. of Texas Publication no. 4214, April 8, 1942, 48–49. Irons later told Powderly that he was forced to sign the strike order at the point of a

gun, 56–62. *The Official History of the Great Strike of 1886 on the Southwestern Railway System*, Commissioner of Labor Statistics and Inspection, Missouri, 10–11, 16.

43 Allen, *Great Southwest Strike*, 44–47, 96–97. Hoxie denied these violations, *Official History*, 19; for Knight's accusations, ibid., 51–53.

44 Allen, *Great Southwest Strike*, 49, 71, 82; Michael J. Cassity, "Modernization and Social Crisis: The Knights of Labor and a Midwest Community," *Journal of American History* 66 (June 1979): 53.

45 Allen, *Great Southwest Strike*, 98–99.

46 *Official History*, 13–14; *Correspondence between Officers of the Missouri Pacific Railway Co. and Members of the Knights of Labor of America, etc.*, 19 in *Railway Pamphlets*, vol. 109, Stanford Univ. Library.

47 Jeremy Brecher, *Strike* (Boston: South End Press, 1997), 48; *Official History*, 8, 17–20, 23–24; Cassity, "Modernization," 53; Allen, *Great Southwest Strike*, 100; Maury Klein, *The Life and Legend of Jay Gould* (Baltimore: Johns Hopkins Univ. Press, 1986), 359; *Union Pacific Employes' Magazine*, April 1886, pp. 68, 82. For the Missouri Pacific's presentation of the negotiations between Powderly and Gould, see *Correspondence*, *Railway Pamphlets*, vol. 109.

48 *Union Pacific Employes' Magazine*, Nov. 1886, p. 296.

49 Allen, *Great Southwest Strike*, 50–69; *Official History*, 67–81, 90–101.

50 Allen, *Great Southwest Strike*, 71. *Official History*, 21, puts the strikers at 9,000. At places like Kansas City or Omaha, where the Missouri Pacific and the Union Pacific connected, Union Pacific workers sympathized with the strike but stayed neutral. Callaway to Adams, March 22, 25, 1886, UP, SG2, ser. 1, box 34, f. 2: Callaway.

51 Allen, *Great Southwest Strike*, 71–91; *Official History*, 7, 25, 28–35, 43–55, 57–62; for increase in worker violence, ibid., 81–87, 101–4.

52 Buchanan, *Labor Agitator*, 222–27, 311–12; Michael Biggs, "Strikes as Sequences of Interaction: The American Strike Wave of 1886," *Social Science History* 26 (2002): 585–87, 589, 591–92.

53 Allen, *Great Southwest Strike*, 71–91. Other railroads, while hardly sympathetic to the Knights, were unwilling to go beyond their "contract obligations" to help Gould. Callaway to Adams, March 25, 1886, UP, SG2, ser. 1, box 34, f. 2: Callaway.

54 Cassity, "Modernization," 53–61; James Green, *Death in the Haymarket: A Story of Chicago, the First Labor Movement, and the Bombing That Divided Gilded Age America* (New York: Pantheon, 2006), 150; R. Alton Lee, *Farmers vs. Wage Earners: Organized Labor in Kansas, 1860–1960* (Lincoln: Univ. of Nebraska Press, 2005), 50–53; Nick Salvatore, *Eugene V. Debs: Citizen and Socialist* (Urbana: Univ. of Illinois Press, 1982), 69, 71.

55 Cassity, "Modernization," 56.

56 Lee, *Farmers vs. Wage Earners*, 54–55.

57 Adams to Callaway, March 26, 1886, UP, PO, OC, vol. 33, ser. 2, r. 28.

58 Calvert to Holdrege, April 3, 1886, Holdrege to Potter, April 6, 1886, Potter to Perkins, April 12, 1886, CB&Q, 33 1880 3.1; C. Crocker to CPH, Nov. 29, 1887, CPH Papers, ser. 1, r. 46. For the defeat of the strike, *Official History*, 38; Lee, *Farmers vs. Wage Earners*, 60; Adams to Hanna, Oct. 3, 1888, UP, PO, OC, vol. 33, ser. 2, r. 40; A. L. Hopkins to Adams, March 22, 1886, UP, SG1, ser. 1, box 39, f. 3; G. M. Dodge to Adams, March 26, 1886, UP, SG2, ser. 1, box 38, f. 1. For the report of what appears to be spies, see "3914," enclosure with S. R. Callaway to Adams, Oct. 15, 1885, ibid., box 35, f. Nov. 86, vol. 53.

59 *Official History*, 111–12.

60 "Eight Hours Law," *Union Pacific Employes' Magazine*, April 1886, pp. 86–87.

61 Allen, *Great Southwest Strike*, 123; Green, *Death in the Haymarket*, 145–48, 154–55, 168–71, 174–273; Biggs, "Strikes as Sequences," 605.

62 *Union Pacific Employes' Magazine*, May 1887, p. 115; "Powderly at Denver," ibid., June 1887, p. 138.

63 "Powderly at Denver," 140–42.

64 Ibid., 143–44.

65 Craig Phelan, *Grand Master Workman: Terence Powderly and the Knights of Labor* (Westport, Conn.: Greenwood Press, 2000), 208–10; John P. Enyeart, *The Quest for "Just and Pure Law": Rocky Mountain Workers and American Social Democracy, 1870–1924* (Stanford: Stanford Univ. Press, 2009), 77.

66 "Powderly at Denver," 138; "News," *Union Pacific Employes' Magazine*, June 1887, p. 145; ibid., July 1887, p. 154; ibid., Sept. 1887, p. 251; "The Enemy in the Ranks," ibid., June 1887, pp. 129–31.

67 Robert Weiter, *Knights Unhorsed: Internal Conflict in a Gilded Age Social Movement* (Detroit: Wayne State Univ. Press, 2000), 13, 53–59; for numbers, 186, n. 15.

68 Buchanan, *Labor Agitator*, 305–10; "P.M. Arthur," *Union Pacific Employes' Magazine*, Sept. 1886, pp. 227–28; "Sound Thoughts on That 'Union Meeting,' " ibid., Sept. 1886, pp. 234–35.

69 "Sound Thoughts on That 'Union Meeting,' " ibid., 234–35.

70 Donald LeCrone McMurry, *The Great Burlington Strike of 1888: A Case History in Labor Relations* (Cambridge: Harvard Univ. Press, 1956), 35–36; Buchanan, *Labor Agitator*, 306–10.

71 McMurry, *Great Burlington Strike*, 19–23, 42–45. For 1886 negotiations, see Notes Taken during a Discussion between Mr. Potter and Committee of Engineers with Potter, Copy, March 21, 1886, 33, 1880, 3.1–3.21, CB&Q. For rules, see Burlington and Missouri Railroad in Nebraska, Rules Governing the Pay of Engineers and Firemen, Taking Effect April 1, 1880, 33, 1880, 3.1, CB&Q.

72 JCP to Perkins, Feb. 17, 1888, 33, 1880, 9.11, no. 2, CB&Q.

73 H. B. Stone to Perkins, Feb. 18, 1888, Table . . . What Full Rate Engineers Would Have Received in 1887, n.d., 1888, 33, 1880, 9.11, no. 2, CB&Q; McMurry, *Great Burlington Strike*, 41.

74 G. W. Holdrege to Perkins, Feb. 18, 1888, C. E. Perkins to Stone, Feb. 21, 1888, Perkins to Peasley, Feb. 20, 1888, Perkins to Arthur and Sargent, Feb. 24, 1884, Strike 1888, 33, 1880, 9.11, no. 2, CB&Q; Licht, *Working on the Railroad*, 260–61.

75 The managers in negotiations cherry-picked certain routes to claim that the workers were asking for unjustifiable gains. Stone et al. to S. E. Hoge and J. H. Murphy, Feb. 17, 1888; Table . . . What Full Rate Engineers Would Have Received in 1887; McMurry, *Great Burlington Strike*, 64.

76 Table . . . Miles Run by Full Rate Engineers, n.d., 1888, 33, 1880, 9.11, no. 2, CB&Q. For the CB&Q, passenger engineers the average pay in cents per mile was, main line 3.44, branch 3.26; for freight, main line 4.23, branch 3.9; for B&M passenger, main line 3.17, branch 3.36; for freight, main line 4.27, branch 4.30.

77 Table . . . What Full Rate Engineers Would Have Received in 1887.

78 Stromquist, *Generation of Boomers*, 135; Notes Taken during a Discussion between Mr. Potter and Committee of Engineers, March 20, 1886, also Afternoon Session, March 20, 1886, 33, 1880, 3.1, CB&Q.

79 G. W. Holdrege to Perkins, Feb. 18, 1888, Table . . . What Full Rate Engineers Would Have Received in 1887; McMurry, *Great Burlington Strike*, 39–40. The Chicago and Northwestern had also pursued this policy in the early 1880s. For policy, see G. W. Tilton to H. B. Stone, March 27, 1880, 33, 1880, 8.1–8.16, CB&Q.

80 McMurry, *Great Burlington Strike*, 45–69; won't strike, F. C. Rice to J. D. Besler, Genl. Superintendent, Feb. 20, 1886, Strike, 1888, 33, 1880, 9.11, nos. 1–2, CB&Q.

81 Book of Telegrams, HRS (loose notes, appear to be notes and drafts for CB&Q Official History),

Strike, 1888, 33, 1880, 9.11, nos. 1–2, Platts, July 21, 1888, CB&Q; Salvatore, *Eugene Debs*, 75–76.

82 Stromquist, *Generation of Boomers*, 57; McMurry, *Great Burlington Strike*, 94–100, 278–79; Donald L. McMurry, "Labor Policies of the General Managers' Association of Chicago, 1886–1894," *Journal of Economic History* 13 (Spring 1953): 160–78; Salvatore, *Eugene Debs*, 76.

83 McMurry, *Great Burlington Strike*, 261, 264–68; Donald L. McMurry, "The Legal Ancestry of the Pullman Strike Injunctions," *Industrial and Labor Relations Review* 14 (Jan. 1961): 239–41.

84 McMurry, *Great Burlington Strike*, 257–61; C. D. Dorman to J. L. Lathrop, May 9, 1888, 33, 1880, 3.1, CB&Q.

85 "Killed by a Bomb," *New York Times*, July 6, 1897, p. 1.

86 J. S. Cameron to J. M. Ragsdale, Dec. 12, 1888, UP, SG1, ser. 1, box 60, f. 5.

87 G. M. Lane to I. Bromley, Dec. 30, 1884, UP, OVP, OC, G. M. Lane, vol. 5, sbg. 3, r. 4; Adams to J. Johnston, April 5, 1886, Adams to A. Thurman, March 19, 1886, Memorandum, May 1886, UP, PO, OC, vol. 34, ser. 2, r. 29; Adams to M. Storey, March 1, 1886, ibid.; surprise, Adams to Wilson, Feb. 7, 1887, ibid., vol. 37, ser. 2, r. 33.

88 Adams to J. H. Wilson, Dec. 30, 1886, UP, PO, OC, vol. 37, ser. 2, r. 32. Adams to S. R. Callaway, Dec. 23, 1886, ibid., vol. 39, ser. 2, r. 34.

89 CPH to Adams, Jan. 13, 1887, CPH Papers, ser. 2, r. 27; Adams to E. P. Alexander, Dec. 8, 1885, UP, PO, OC, vol. 30, ser. 2, r. 26; Adams to Moorfield Storey, Jan. 14, 1887, Adams to George Hoar, Feb. 7, 1887, Adams to Wilson, Feb. 8, 1887, Adams to Hoyt, Feb. 25, 1887, all in ibid., vol. 37, ser. 2, r. 33.

90 Adams to Henry Dawes, Feb. 10, 1887, UP, PO, OC, vol. 37, ser. 2, r. 33; CPH to S. A. Penniman, Feb. 4, 1887, CPH Papers, ser. 2, r. 27; C. E. Yost to Callaway, May 19, 1886, UP, box 34, f. 4.

91 Adams to Colgate Hoyt, Jan. 5, 1887 (misdated 1886), UP, PO, OC, vol. 37, ser. 2, r. 35; Adams to O. W. Mink, Feb. 16, 1885, ibid., vol. 27, ser. 2, r. 23; Adams to J. Dillon, March 26, 1886, ibid., vol. 34, ser. 2, r. 29; Adams to W. P. Frye, ibid., vol. 50, ser. 2, r. 45.

92 Adams certainly sought to influence Congress, but he used government directors and only a few agents. Adams to George Hoar, Feb. 9, 1885, Adams to Moorfield Storey, Feb. 9, 1885, UP, PO, OC, vol. 27, ser. 2, r. 23; Adams to Storey, Dec. 1, 1884, ibid., vol. 23, ser. 2, r. 20; Adams to Colgate Hoyt, Feb. 9, 1885, ibid., vol. 27, ser. 2, r. 23; Adams to P. B. Plumb, Aug. 24, 1885; Adams to Ayres, Sept. 2, 1885, ibid., vol. 29, ser. 2, r. 25; Adams to Ayres (n.d., c. Nov. 17, 1885), ibid., vol. 30, ser. 2, r. 26; Adams to A. Thurman, May 6, 1886, ibid., vol. 34, ser. 2, r. 30; no lobby, Adams to Wm. Dickinson, Jan. 30, 1888, ibid., vol. 42, ser. 2, r. 37; Charles Francis Adams, Diary, February 3, 1889, p. 29, Adams Papers, r. 3; Adams to Dodge, March 9, 11, 1887, UP, PO, OC, vol. 41, ser. 2, r. 35; Adams to L. Cassidy, Dec. 5, 1887, Jan. 30, 1888, Adams to Dodge, Dec. 12, 1887, Adams to A. J. Poppleton, Dec. 12, 1887, ibid., vol. 42, ser. 2, r. 37.

93 Adams to Colgate Hoyt, Jan. 5, 1887 (misdated 1886), UP, PO, OC, vol. 37, ser. 2, r. 35.

94 Isaac Bromley, Memorandum, Dec. 10, 1886, UP, SG2, ser. 1, box 32, f. 6: Bromley.

95 Adams to A. L. Williams, Feb. 16, 1887, Adams to Dawes, Feb. 19, 1887, UP, PO, OC, vol. 37, ser. 2, r. 33; Edward Kirkland, *Charles Francis Adams, 1835–1915: The Patrician at Bay* (Cambridge: Harvard Univ. Press, 1965), 109–11; L. S. Anderson to Adams, Oct. 20, 1887, UP, OVP, OC, vol. 2, L. S. Anderson, ser. 1, r. 2.

96 Charles Francis Adams, *Charles Francis Adams, 1835–1915: An Autobiography* (Boston: Houghton Mifflin, 1916), 192.

97 Adams to C. Hoyt, Feb. 8, 1887, UP, PO, OC, vol. 37, ser. 2, r. 33; Adams to E. P. Alexander, Feb. 10, 1887, ibid.; defeat it, Adams to S. Dillon, Feb. 17, 1887, ibid.

 98 Adams to Alexander, Feb. 10, 1887, UP, PO, OC, vol. 37, ser. 2, r. 33; Adams to Hoyt, Feb. 25, 10, 1887, ibid.; Boyd to CPH, Feb. 8, 1887, Feb. 22, 1887, CPH Papers, ser.1, r. 45.

 99 *Congressional Record*, 43rd Cong., 2d sess., Feb. 25, 1887, 2278.

100 Charles Francis Adams, Diary, Feb. 3, 1889, pp. 29–31, Adams Papers, r. 3.

101 Adams to Blake, March 8, 1887, UP, PO, OC, vol. 41, ser. 2, r. 35; Adams to George F. Hoar, Jan. 5, 10, 1887, ibid., vol. 37, ser. 2, r. 32; L. S. Anderson to Lane, June 1, 1886, UP, OVP, OC, vol. 1, r. 1.

102 Adams to Wilson, March 7, 1887, UP, PO, OC, vol. 41, ser. 2, r. 35; Adams to Dodge, March 11, 1887, ibid.

103 Testimony of Charles Crocker, *PRC*, 7:3653, 3655.

104 *PRC*, 5:2452–53.

105 Testimony of Leland Stanford, *PRC*, 5:2519.

106 Stanford testified at the Palace Hotel in San Francisco beginning on July 28, 1887, *PRC*, 5:2461. For the books, Testimony of Daniel Yost, *PRC*, 5:2711–33. For refusal to produce books, Testimony of Frank Douty, Aug. 1, 1887, *PRC*, 5:2724, 2727–28. Vouchers for payments to the Contract and Finance Company and others by the Central Pacific remain, but these give only generic explanations—legal, cash, expenses—for the payments. Southern Pacific, New York Collection, Central Pacific Railroad Vouchers, MS 10, vouchers 1–851.

107 Testimony of Leland Stanford, *PRC*, 5:2769.

108 Ibid., 2769, 2774.

109 Ibid., 2831.

110 Ibid., 2951.

111 Ibid., 2495.

112 Testimony of Leland Stanford and of Charles Crocker Jr., *PRC*, 5:2990–99.

113 David Lavender, *The Great Persuader: The Biography of Collis P. Huntington* (Niwot: Univ. Press of Colorado, 1998), 355. Field had received favors from the Associates, but he later grew more cautious. When Huntington attempted to influence a Supreme Court decision on the Oregon and California Railroad, Field reacted with indignation. Gates to Field, April 3, 1891, Field to Gates, April 4, 1891, Stephen J. Field Papers, BANC 71/34, Bancroft Library.

114 C. Crocker to CPH, Jan. 3, 1888, CPH Papers, ser. 1, r. 46. One of the commissioners, David Littler, made arrangements with the Union Pacific to render assistance to the Union Pacific in Washington once the report was issued. Adams to Dodge, Nov. 30, 1888, UP, PO, OC, vol. 45, ser. 2, r. 40; Lavender, *Great Persuader*, 355.

115 Lavender, *Great Persuader*, 355; T. Stillman to CPH, n.d., c. March 1889, CPH Papers, ser. 1, r. 47; Charles Crocker to CPH, Jan. 25, 1888, ibid., r. 46.

116 Adams to CPH, Oct. 27, 1888, Adams to Villard, Oct. 29, 1888, Adams to Barnum, Oct. 29, 1888, UP, PO, OC, vol. 45, ser. 2, r. 40.

117 Adams Diary, Dec. 23, 1888, Adams Papers, r. 3.

118 I. Bromley, Memorandum on Congress, Aug. 9, 1886, UP, MS 3761, SG2, ser. 1, box 32, f: Bromley-Burness; Adams to William L. Scott, June 14, 1888, Adams to Dodge, July 6, 1888, UP, PO, OC, vol. 44, ser. 2, r. 39; Adams to CPH, Oct. 18, 1888, ibid., vol. 45, ser. 2, r. 40; Adams to Dodge, Dec. 10, 11, 1888, Adams to Oakes, Dec. 14, 1888, Adams to Ayres, Dec. 28, 18, 1888, ibid., r. 41. The Outhwaite bill also suffered from the opposition of Senator Sherman, who was influenced by Colgate Hoyt, who had fallen out with Adams and the Union Pacific. Adams to M. Hanna, Nov. 23, 1888, UP, PO, OC, vol. 45, ser. 2, r. 41. The differences between the Central Pacific and the Union Pacific persisted. Adams to Dodge, March 28, 1890, ibid., vol. 50, ser. 2, r. 45. The Burlington also worked against debt extension; L. S. Anderson to G. M. Lane, June 14, 1886, UP, OVP, OC, vol. 1, L. S. Anderson, r. 1.

119 Charles Francis Adams, Diary, Feb. 3, 1889, pp. 35–36, 40–41, Adams Papers, r. 3.

120 William Elsey Connelley, *The Life of Preston B. Plumb, 1837–91* (Chicago: Browne & Howell Company, 1913), 373; Charles Francis Adams, Diary, Feb. 3, 1889, pp. 31–32, Adams Papers, r. 3.

121 John James Ingalls, *A Collection of the Writings of John James Ingalls: Essays, Addresses, and Orations* (Kansas City, Mo.: Hudson-Kimberly Publishing Co., 1902), 183–98, 341, 393. In nineteenth-century usage "syllabub" meant frothy or insubstantial.

122 Charles Francis Adams, Diary, Feb. 3, 1889, p. 34, Adams Papers r. 3; Connelley, *Life of Plumb*, 309.

123 Connelley, *Life of Plumb*, 287–88; Charles Francis Adams, Diary, Feb. 3, 1889, pp. 32–39. Despite the ICC's making passes illegal, Ingalls continued to solicit them. Ingalls to CPH, March 7, 1891, CPH Papers ser. 1, r. 49. For O. Gene Clanton, *Kansas Populism: Ideas and Men* (Lawrence: Univ. Press of Kansas, 1969), 52–62.

124 Klein, *Union Pacific*, 542–45. Adams despaired of getting the bill passed in 1890; Adams to Dodge, March 28, 1890, UP, PO, OC, vol. 50, ser. 2, r. 45.

125 Ari and Olive Hoogenboom, *A History of the ICC: From Panacea to Palliative* (New York: Norton, 1976), 15–16.

126 Ben H. Proctor, *Not without Honor: The Life of John Reagan* (Austin: Univ. of Texas Press, 1962), 196–98, 218, 255.

127 Crocker to CPH, Jan. 19, 1885, CPH Papers, ser. 1, r. 39.

128 *Congressional Record*, 43rd Cong., 2d sess., Jan. 10, 1887, 490–91.

129 Clipping, *Morning Call*, Jan. 11, 1887, box 4, f. 15, SC 33a, Stanford Papers.

130 Perkins to Forbes, April 28, 1878, 3 F 3.2–3.3, J. M. Forbes, In-letters, private from C. E. Perkins, CB&Q; Proctor, *Not without Honor*, 236; Richard Overton, *Perkins/Budd: Railway Statesmen of the Burlington* (Westport, Conn.: Greenwood Press, 1982), 44–45, 58–59; Charles E. Perkins, Statement, *Report of the U.S. Senate Select Committee on Interstate Commerce*, 49th Cong., 1st sess. (Washington, D.C.: GPO, 1886), 217, 221–22; Boyd to CPH, Jan. 8, 1885, CPH Papers, ser. 1, r. 39. Gabriel Kolko long ago made the point that many railroad men favored federal regulation that would allow them to stabilize the industry. Kolko, *Railroads and Regulation, 1877–1916* (New York: Norton, 1970, orig. ed. 1965), 34–41; Albro Martin, *James J. Hill and the Opening of the Northwest* (Minneapolis: Minnesota Historical Society Press, 1991, orig. ed. 1976), 295.

131 Elizabeth Sanders, *Roots of Reform: Farmers, Workers, and the American State* (Chicago: Univ. of Chicago Press, 1999), 189.

132 Proctor, *Not without Honor*, 218–60; Scott C. James, *Presidents, Parties and the State: A Party System Perspective on Democratic Regulatory Choice, 1884–1936* (New York: Cambridge Univ. Press, 2000), 36–122.

133 Adams to Gould, Dec. 29, 1884, UP, PO, OC, vol. 23, ser. 2, r. 20; *Report of the U.S. Senate Select Committee on Interstate Commerce* (1886), 175.

134 Childs, *Texas Railroad Commission*, 33–34.

135 http://www.civics-online.org/library/formatted/texts/interstate_commerce.html; Sanders, *Roots of Reform*, 187–94.

136 *Travelers Official Railway Guide for the United States and Canada*, 19th year, no. 11 (April 1887): 1½; Gerald G. Eggert, *Richard Olney: Evolution of a Statesman* (University Park: Pennsylvania State Univ. Press, 1974), 26.

137 James, *Presidents, Parties and the State*, 103.

138 Ibid., 115–17; Sanders, *Roots of Reform*, 194; Childs, *Texas Railroad Commission*, 36–40.

139 Adams to J. H. Wilson, Dec. 30, 1886, UP, PO, OC, vol. 37, ser. 2, r. 32; Adams to S. R. Callaway, Dec. 23, 1886, ibid., vol. 39, ser. 2, r. 34.

140 CPH to A. Hutchinson, Jan. 3, 17, 1887, CPH Papers, ser. 2, r. 27; Martin, *James J. Hill*, 295.

141 CPH to A. Hutchison, Feb. 3, 1887, CPH to A. Towne, Feb. 17, 1887, CPH Papers, ser. 2, r. 27.

142 Arthur T. Hadley, "The Workings of the Interstate Commerce Law," *Quarterly Journal of Economics* 2 (Jan. 1888): 162, 170–72.

143 "Hot Shot from a Friend: Charles Francis Adams on Railroad Management," *New York Times*, Dec. 16, 1888, p. 9. For an earlier, similar assessment, see Adams to J. Nimmo, Oct. 26, 1888, UP, PO, OC, vol. 45, ser. 2, r. 40.

144 Adams sent Hadley a copy of the speech, Adams to Hadley, Dec. 26, 1888, UP, PO, OC, vol. 45, ser. 2, r. 41. Hadley and Adams were conferring during 1888. Hadley to Adams, March 11, 1888, UP, SG2, ser. 1, box 62, f. 4.

145 Hadley, "Interstate Commerce Law," 176, 184–87.

146 "Hot Shot," 9; for Gould, Adams Diary, Dec. 23, 1888, Adams Papers, r. 3; for strength, Adams to M. Hughitt, April 29, 1889, UP, PO, OC, vol. 47, ser. 2, r. 42.

147 *Report of the Industrial Commission on Transportation Including Review of Evidence . . . So Far as Taken, May 1, 1900* (Washington, D.C.: GPO, 1900), 4:345.

148 Keith L. Bryant Jr., *History of the Atchison, Topeka, and Santa Fe Railway* (New York: Macmillan, 1974), 148–49.

149 For cooperation, Adams Diary, Jan. 13, 1889, Adams Papers, r. 3; for limits, Adams to G. M. Lane, Aug. 21, 1889, UP, PO, OC, vol. 48, ser. 2, r. 43.

150 See, e.g., Adams to T. F. Oakes, Oct. 5, 1888, UP, PO, OC, vol. 44, ser. 2, r. 40; Adams to F. L. Ames, Oct. 7, 1886, ibid.; Adams to W. S. Grant, Dec. 6, 1888, ibid., vol. 45, ser. 2, r. 40; Adams to J. S. Cameron, Dec. 18, 1888, ibid.

151 Klein, *Union Pacific*, 560–79; Adams to G. M. Lane, April 17, 1889, Adams to R. Harris, April 26, 1889, Adams to R. Grant, May 20, 1889, UP, PO, OC, vol. 47, ser. 2, r. 42. For Harris on dividing territory and cooperation, R. Harris to Billings, July 1, 1887, Harris to T. Potter, July 11, 1887, NP, LB 18, 137.H.11.1 (B).

152 Adams to Gen. W. Swayne, May 15, 1889, UP, PO, OC, vol. 47, ser. 2, r. 42; Fred. Ames to Adams, April 30, 1885, UP, SG2, ser. 1, box 14; Adams to Wilson, April 23, 1889, UP, PO, OC, vol. 47, ser. 2, r. 42; for opposition of O&T, Paul Edes (O&T) to Board of Northern Pacific, Jan. 14, 1886, Henry Villard Papers, Mss 8993, vol. 719, 1862–1928, box 34.

153 Adams to A. H. Holmes, April 9, 1889, Adams to R. Grant, May 20, 1889, UP, PO, OC, vol. 47, ser. 2, r. 42.

154 Adams to Gen. J. Wilson, April 29, 1889, UP, PO, OC, vol. 47, ser. 2, r. 42; Adams to G. M. Lane, Aug. 29, 1889, ibid.; vol. 48, ser. 2, r. 43.

155 Adams to J. W. Midgely, Dec. 8, 1888, UP, PO, OC, vol. 45, ser. 2, r. 41; Adams Diary, Dec. 23, 1888, Jan. 13, 1889, Adams Papers, r. 3; Adams to C. Depew, Jan. 14, 1889, UP, PO, OC, vol. 45, ser. 2, r. 41.

156 Adams Diary, Jan. 13, 1889, Adams Papers, r. 3; *Proceedings of the Conference Between Presidents*, 6–19, 25, 28, 54, 62, 71, 83; Adams to T. M. Cooley, Jan. 14, 1889, UP, PO, OC, vol. 45, NS 15986, ser. 2, r. 41.

157 Adams Diary, Dec. 23, 1888, Adams Papers, r. 3.

158 *Proceedings of the Conference between Presidents*, 55.

159 Ibid., 59.

160 Adams Diary, Dec. 23, 1888, Jan. 13, 1889, Adams Papers, r. 3.

161 *Proceedings of the Conference between Presidents*, 20–21, 25, 36, 49–51.

Mise en Scène: The Death of Johanna Grogan

1 P. Gibbons to CPH, June 9, 1890, CPH Papers, ser. 1, r. 48.

2 The basic details come from W. E. Costello to C. G. Wheeler, June 1, 1890, Aug. 1, 1890, CPH

Papers, ser. 1, r. 48. See also C. L. Cline to A. Manvel, Aug. 4, 1890, illegible, Law Department of AT&SF to J. D. Springer, Aug. 28, 1890, and CPH to Manvel, Sept. 19, 1890, ibid.; also Michael Grogan to CPH, June 7, 1891, ibid., r. 49.

3 CPH to A. Manvel, Aug. 1, 1890, W. E. Costell to C. G. Wheeler, June 1, 1890, CPH Papers, ser. 1, r. 48; CPH to F. H. Welch, Aug. 4, 1890, ibid.

4 See illegible, Law Department of AT&SF to J. D. Springer, Aug. 28, 1890, CPH Papers, ser. 1, r. 48.

5 J. D. Springer to Faulkner, Aug. 29, 1890, CPH Papers, ser. 1, r. 48.

6 CPH to Manvel, Sept. 5, 1890, CPH Papers, ser. 1, r. 48.

7 CPH to Manvel, Sept. 24, 1890, CPH Papers, ser. 1, r. 48; CPH to Manvel, June 19, 1891, Michael Grogan to CPH, June 7, 1891, ibid., r. 49.

CHAPTER 9: COLLAPSE

1 Adams Memorabilia, Journal, Nov. 23, 1890, 152–57, Adams Papers, r. 10.

2 O. Gene Clanton, *Kansas Populism: Ideas and Men* (Lawrence: Univ. of Kansas Press, 1969), 28, 49–62, 73–133.

3 Scott G. McNall, *The Road to Rebellion: Class Formation and Kansas Populism, 1865–1900* (Chicago: Univ. of Chicago Press, 1988), 225–301; for urban vote and workers, 279, 296–310.

4 Charles Postel, *The Populist Vision* (New York: Oxford Univ. Press, 2007). See also Lawrence Goodwyn, *Democratic Promise: The Populist Moment in America* (New York: Oxford Univ. Press, 1976).

5 Clanton, *Kansas Populism*, 28, 49–62, 73–133.

6 Frank Haigh Dixon, "Railroad Control in Nebraska," *Political Science Quarterly* 13 (Dec. 1898): 633, 637; Robert W. Cherny, *Populism, Progressivism, and the Transformation of Nebraska Politics, 1884–1915* (Lincoln: Univ. of Nebraska Press, 1981), 32–33.

7 Cherny, *Populism, Progressivism*, 36–37, 40–43; L. S. Anderson to Adams, Oct. 20, 1887, UP, Assistant to the Pres., OC, vol. 2, L. S. Anderson, ser. 1, r. 2.

8 Cherny, *Populism, Progressivism, and the Transformation of Nebraska Politics*, 44–50.

9 Margaret Kolb Holden, "The Rise and Fall of Oregon Populism: Legal Theory, Political Culture, and Public Policy, 1868–1895" (Ph.D. diss., Univ. of Virginia, 1993), 2–6, 16–17, 19–21, 109–12, 151–52, 175–76, 235–36, 251–55, 406–14, 468, 472, 478–79, 497, 512, 517–27.

10 Howard W. Allen and Erik W. Austin, "From the Populist Era to the New Deal: A Study of Partisan Realignment in Washington State, 1889–1950," *Social Science History* 3 (Winter 1979): 119–21. Elisabeth Clemens, *The People's Lobby: Organizational Innovation and the Rise of Interest Group Politics in the United States, 1890–1925* (Chicago: Univ. of Chicago Press, 1997), 157.

11 John P. Enyeart, *The Quest for "Just and Pure Law": Rocky Mountain Workers and American Social Democracy, 1870–1914* (Stanford: Stanford Univ. Press, 2009), 16–17, 105–6, 109–12.

12 Keith L. Bryant Jr., *History of the Atchison, Topeka, and Santa Fe Railway* (New York: Macmillan, 1974), 93–105, 123–41; Sandra Kuntz Ficker, "Economic Backwardness and Firm Strategy: An American Railroad Corporation in Nineteenth-Century Mexico," *Hispanic American Historical Review* 80 (2000): 270, 282–83.

13 Adams to Dexter, Aug. 20, 1889, Adams to G. M. Lane, Aug. 29, 1889, UP, PO, OC, vol. 48, ser. 2, r. 43.

14 Bryant, *Atchison*, 148–49. Between 1884 and 1888 Atchison stock increased from $60,673,000 to $75,000,000 and bonds from $48,258,000 to $163,694,000.

15 Ibid., 143, 146–47, 150–51.

16 Ibid., 150–51. They, in part, seem to have intervened to stop Jay Gould from taking control. CPH to [Gates], March 14, 1889, cipher telegram, CPH Papers, ser. 1, r. 47.

17 Bryant, *Atchison*, 153–55, 158.

18 Ibid., 143, 156–57; CPH to [Gates], telegram, March 14, 1889, CPH Papers, ser. 1, r. 47; Ari and Olive Hoogenboom, *A History of the ICC: From Panacea to Palliative* (New York: Norton, 1976), 35–36.

19 Albro Martin, *James J. Hill and the Opening of the Northwest* (St. Paul: Minneapolis Historical Society Press, 1991, orig. ed. 1976), 410–11.

20 Bryant, *Atchison*, 143, 156–57; CPH to [Gates], telegram, March 14, 1889, CPH Papers, ser. 1, r. 47; Adams to C. S. Mellen, May 14, 1890, UP, PO, OC, vol. 50, ser. 2, r. 45.

21 Bryant, *Atchison*, 153–55, 158.

22 Alfred Chandler, *The Visible Hand: The Managerial Revolution in American Business* (Cambridge: Harvard Univ. Press, 1977), 109–20.

23 John H. Davis & Co., Monthly Investment Circular—No. 14 (April 1888), copy in NP, LRR, PV, 137.H.5.3 (B); for Southern Pacific, J. Gates, for CPH to W. Porter, Dec. 14, 1882, CPH Papers, vol. 79, ser. 2, r. 13, CPH to C. Crocker, April 5, 1883, CPH Papers, vol. 30, ser. 2, r. 6; George W. Bishop Jr., "Who Was the First American Financial Analyst?" *Financial Analysts Journal* 20 (March–April 1964): 26–28.

24 William Morse Cole, *Accounts: Their Construction and Interpretation, for Business Men and Students of Affairs* (Boston: Houghton Mifflin, 1915, orig. ed., 1908).

25 Ibid., 233.

26 Ibid., 233, 238.

27 Ibid., 233–34, 237–38.

28 Ibid., 229–40; Bryant, *Atchison*, 162–63.

29 Bryant, *Atchison*, 143, 156–57; CPH to [Gates], telegram, March 14, 1889, CPH Papers, ser. 1, r. 47.

30 Adams to G. Lane, UP, PO, OC, vol. 48, ser. 2, r. 43.

31 Engineering News, *Atlas of Railway Progress, 1888–1889* (New York: Engineering News Publishing Company, 1889), 26, 29; Opinion of the Court Upon Motion for an Order of Reference to Take Testimony upon the Petition for Removal of the Receivers, Circuit Court of the United States for the Eastern District of Wisconsin, *The Farmers's Loan & Trust Co.* v. *Northern Pacific Railroad Company, et al.*, Villard Papers, box 61, f. 1893–1894, 719–25.

32 Adams to G. Dodge, Oct. 23, 1889, UP, PO, OC, vol. 48, ser. 2, r. 43; Adams to G. Dodge, Oct. 31, 1889, ibid.; Adams to M. Hughitt, Nov. 9, 1889, ibid., r. 44. For ICRA, see Adams to M. Hughitt, Dec. 2, 1889, ibid.; Adams to Aldace Walker, Dec. 7, 1889, ibid.; Adams to A. Walker, March 19, 1890, ibid., vol. 50 ser. 2, r. 45. Charles F. Crocker of the Southern Pacific thought the Central Pacific should cooperate fully with the Union Pacific and thus become part of this larger system; C. F. Crocker to CPH, July 3, 1890, CPH Papers, ser. 1, r. 48; Maury Klein, *Union Pacific*, vol. 1, *Birth of a Railroad, 1862–1893* (Garden City, N.Y.: Doubleday, 1987), 617.

33 Engineering News, *Atlas of Railway Progress*, 30.

34 Adams to A. Walker, Jan. 18, 1890, UP, PO, OC, vol. 50, ser. 2, r. 45; Klein, *Union Pacific*, 596.

35 Gates to Speyer & Co., Aug. 17, 1880, CPH Papers, ser. 2, r. 12; CPH to Crocker, Jan. 6, 1881, ibid., vol. 77, ser. 2, r. 13.

36 CPH to Crocker, March 14, 30, 1883 CPH Papers, vol. 30, ser. 2, r. 6; CPH to Speyer & Co., Jan. 6, 1881, ibid., vol. 74, ser. 2, r. 13; CPH to Speyer & Co., Jan. 6, 1881, ibid., vol. 13, ser. 2, r. 13; Speyer & Co. to CPH, Dec. 15, 1883, ibid., ser. 1, r. 34; Crocker to CPH, Dec. 20, 1883, no. 269, Crocker Papers.

37 Speyer & Co. to CPH, May 14, 1883, CPH Papers, ser. 1, r. 32.

38 Speyer Brothers to CPH, Sept. 1, 1883, CPH, ser. 1, r. 33.

39 Ibid.

40 CPH to Speyer & Co., Dec. 20, 30, 1882, CPH Papers, vol. 79, ser. 2, r. 13; Speyer & Co. to CPH, Nov. 13, 1882, ibid., ser. 1, r. 34.

41 Gates to Chambers, Jan. 8, 1885, CPH Papers, vol. 92, ser. 2, r. 15. Also Gates to J. T. White, Jan. 31, 1885, Gates to A. N. Towne, July 15, 1885, C. Crocker to CPH, Dec. 10, 1883, no. 260, Crocker Papers.

42 Speyer & Co. to CPH, Feb. 11, 17, 1885, CPH Papers, ser. 1, r. 39.

43 For an account of the Barings in South America, see Philip Ziegler, *The Sixth Great Power: Barings, 1762–1929* (London: Collins, 1988), 229–66.

44 A. G. Ford, "Argentina and the Baring Crisis of 1890," *Oxford Economic Papers*, n.s., 8, no. 2 (June 1956): 127–50, Stable URL, http://www.jstor.org/stable/2661728.

45 Dietrich G. Buss, *Henry Villard: A Study of Transatlantic Investments and Interests, 1870–1895* (New York: Arno Press, 1978), 170–75; Northern Pacific Litigation, Examination of Thomas Oakes, 65, box 61, f. 432, Villard Papers.

46 Ainsworth Reminiscences, Jan. 4, 1882, Mss. 504, Oregon Historical Society.

47 Villard to Oakes, March 1, 1893, box 34, Mss. 8893, vol. 719, f. 231, Villard Papers; Northern Pacific Railroad Company's General Third Mortgage Land Grant Bonds, Issue of $8,000,000 bonds, Dated Dec. 1, 1887, Maturing December 1, 1937, NP, LRR, PV, 137.H.5.3(B); Buss, *Henry Villard*, 175–81; Poor, *Manual, 1889*, 854; ibid., *1890*, 547; Henry Villard to J. C. Spooner and G. P. Miller, May 9, 1895, "Henry Villard and the Northern Pacific," Villard Papers, box 43, f. 315; Remarks by Mr. Colby in nominating Mr. Villard for the Office of the President of the Northern Pacific Railroad Company, Sept. 20 1888, Villard Papers, box 34, Mss. 8893, vol. 719, f. 298.

48 Harris, Notation on bonds, Aug. 1889, NP, President, Letters Sent, LB, vol. 46, 137.H.11.1 (B), 142; Harris to Billings, Aug. 1, 1889, ibid., pp. 90–91. See also Report on Northern Pacific, H. C. Rouse, Receiver, Dec. 4, 1893, NP, 134.F.1.7 (B).

49 Billings to Harris, Aug. 20, 1889, NP, President, Letters Sent, LB, vol. 46, 137.H.11.1 (B), p. 100; Harris to Villard, Sept. 11, 1889, NP, LB 18, 137.H.11.1 (B). For bonds, see Consolidated Mortgage, Northern Pacific Railroad Company to the Farmers' Loan and Trust Company, Dec. 2, 1889, copy in *Northern Pacific Pamphlets*, Stanford Univ. Library.

50 Villard to Board of Directors, March 9, 1891, NP, President, Letters Sent, LB, vol. 46, 137.H.11.1 (B), 356–58.

51 Robin W. Winks, *Frederick Billings: A Life* (Berkeley: Univ. of California Press, 1991), 310–11.

52 Charles W. Calhoun, *Minority Victory: Gilded Age Politics and the Front Porch Campaign of 1888* (Lawrence: Univ. Press of Kansas, 2008), 80–82.

53 Herbert Hovenkamp, *Enterprise and American Law, 1836–1937* (Cambridge: Harvard Univ. Press, 1991), 283, 286–91.

54 R. Jeffrey Lustig, *Corporate Liberalism: The Origins of Modern American Political Theory, 1890–1920* (Berkeley: Univ. of California Press, 1982), 94; I. Leo Sharfman, *Railway Regulation: An Analysis of the Underlying Problems in Railway Economics from the Standpoint of Government Regulation* (Chicago: La Salle Extension Univ., 1915), 59–60; *U.S.* v. *Trans-Missouri Freight Association*, 166 U.S. 290.

55 John J. Binder, "The Sherman Antitrust Act and Railroad Cartels," *Journal of Law and Economics* 31 (Oct. 1988): 443–45. Adams to Storey, May 14, 1890, UP, PO, OC, vol. 50, ser. 2, r. 45; *United States* v. *Trans-Missouri Freight Ass'n*, 166 U.S. 290 (1897), *United States* v. *Trans-Missouri Freight Association*, no. 67, Argued Dec. 8, 9, 1896, Decided March 22, 1897, 166 U.S. 290, Appeal from the Circuit Court of Appeals for the Eighth Circuit, http://supreme.justia.com/us/166/290/case.html.

56 Jeanette Paddock Nichols, "John Sherman: A Study in Inflation," *Mississippi Valley Historical Review* 21 (Sept. 1934): 181–94; Richard H. Timberlake Jr., "Repeal of Silver Monetization in the Late Nineteenth Century," *Journal of Money, Credit and Banking* 10 (Feb. 1978): 27–31.

57 Robert F. Hoxie, "The Silver Debate of 1890," *Journal of Political Economy* 1 (Sept. 1893): 535–87.

58 Adams Memorabilia, Journal, Jan. 1, 1890, 103–4, Adams Papers, r. 10.

59 Ibid., April 27, 1890, 104–5, Adams Papers, r. 10.

60 Adams to Lane, June 11, 1890, UP, PO, OC, vol. 50, ser. 2, r. 45; Adams Memorabilia, Journal, July 4, 1890, 116–18, Adams Papers, r. 10.

61 Adams Memorabilia, Journal, April 27, 1890, July 4, 1890, 106–15, 120, 123, Adams Papers, r. 10.

62 Ibid., July 4, 1890, 123–25, Adams Papers, r. 10; Klein, *Union Pacific*, 618–20.

63 Adams Memorabilia, Journal, July 4, 1890, 125–27, Adams Papers, r. 10.

64 Dodge to Adams, Oct. 1, 1890, Adams Papers, r. 4; Adams Memorabilia, Journal, Nov. 23, 1890, 143, 145–46, ibid., r. 10.

65 Adams Memorabilia, Journal, Nov. 23, 1890, 146–54, Adams Papers, r. 10.

66 Klein, *Union Pacific*, 626–27.

67 Ford, "Argentina and the Baring Crisis," pp. 127–50; Buss, *Villard*, 222–24; Timberlake, "Repeal of Silver Monetization," 30–33; Adams Memorabilia, Journal, Nov. 23, 1890, 152–57, Adams Papers, r. 10; CAV to Marcus, Sept. 20, 1890, Spofford to Villard, Sept. 24, Oct. 14, 21, 1890, Nov. 15, 1890, Spofford to Hoyt, Nov. 7, 1890, LB 84a, Mss 8993, vol. 119, Villard Papers; Colby, Oakes to Villard, Sept. 18, 26, 1890, Hoyt to Villard, Sept. 24, 1896, Nov. 14, 1890, ibid.; Michael Kazin, *A Godly Hero* (New York: Knopf, 2006), 35–38; J. A. Baxter to T. F. Oakes, Aug. 12, 1890, Mullen to Oakes, June 10, 1890, NP, LRR, PV, 137.H.5.5 (B).

68 Adams Memorabilia, Journal, Nov. 23, 1890, 152–57, Adams Papers, r. 10; Ford, "Argentina and the Baring Crisis of 1890," 127–50; Klein, *Union Pacific*, 626–27.

69 Adams to Marvin Hughitt, April 8, 1890, UP, PO, OC, vol. 50, ser. 2, r. 45.

70 Adams Memorabilia, Journal, Nov. 23, 1890, 146–50, Adams Papers, r. 10.

71 Adams to R. S. Grant, Nov. 13, 1890, UP, PO, OC, vol. 51, ser. 2, r. 46. See also Adams Diary, Nov. 12, 18, 19, 1890, Adams Papers, r. 3; Adams Memorabilia, Journal, Nov. 23, 1890, 158, ibid., r. 10.

72 Adams Memorabilia, Journal, Nov. 23, 1890, 160, 163–64, Adams Papers, r. 10.

73 Ibid., 157, 161, Adams Papers, r. 10.

74 Adams Diary, Nov. 22, 26, 1890, Adams Papers, r. 3; Adams Memorabilia, Journal, Nov. 23, 1890, 160–61, ibid., r. 10.

75 Adams Memorabilia, Journal, Nov. 23, 1890, 165–66, Adams Papers, r. 10.

76 Ibid., 166–67, Adams Papers, r. 10; Klein, *Union Pacific*, 631. See Adams Diary, Nov. 19, 20, 22, 26, 1890, Adams Papers, r. 3.

77 Adams Diary, Nov. 22, 26, 1890, Adams Papers, r. 3; Charles Francis Adams, *Charles Francis Adams, 1835–1915: An Autobiography* (Boston: Houghton Mifflin, c. 1916), 198; Klein, *Union Pacific*, 631. Also see Edward Chase Kirkland, *Charles Francis Adams Jr., 1835–1915: The Patrician at Bay* (Cambridge: Harvard Univ. Press, 1965), 124–29. The internal battles continued to the end; see Holcomb to Adams, Nov. 23, 1890, Adams Papers, r. 4.

78 Adams, *Autobiography*, 198.

79 Board Resolution, Special Meeting of the Board of Directors of the Union Pacific Railway Company . . . Nov. 26, 1890, Adams Papers, r. 4.

80 Klein, *Union Pacific*, 643–44.

81 Ford, "Argentina and the Baring Crisis of 1890," 127–50; Buss, *Villard*, 222–24; CAV to Marcus, Sept. 20, Spofford to Villard, Sept. 24, Oct. 14, 21, Nov. 15, 1890, Spofford to Hoyt,

Nov. 7, 1890, LB 84a, Mss. 8993, vol. 119, Villard Papers; Colby, Hoyt, and Oakes to Villard, Sept. 18, 26, 1890, Hoyt to Villard, Sept. 24, Nov. 14, 1890, ibid.; Kazin, *Godly Hero*, 35–38; J. A. Baxter to T. F. Oakes, Aug. 12, 1890, Mullen to Oakes, June 10, 1890, NP, LRR, PV, 137.H.5.5 (B).

82 Oakes to C. T. Barney, Dec. 11, 1890, NP, President, Letters Sent, LB 27, vol. 51, 137.H.11.2 (F).

83 Report of Dr. Siemens of his Investigation of the Condition of the Northern Pacific, Nov. 1893, NP, 134 (F).1.7.B, p. 6.

84 R. Harris to Board of Directors, Nov. 18, 1888, NP, LRR, PV, 137.H.5.3 (B); Wm. Mellen to T. F. Oakes, Oct. 31, 1889, Nov. 2, 1889, NP, ibid., 134.F.1.4 (F); Report of Dr. Siemens of his Investigation of the Condition of the Northern Pacific, Nov. 1893, NP, 134 (F).1.7.B, pp. 7–8.

85 Oakes, Colby, Hoyt to Villard, Oct. 30, 1890, Hoyt to Villard, Nov. 7, 1890, LB 84a, Mss. 8993, vol. 119, Villard Papers; Spofford to Villard, Nov. 14, 1890, April 17, 1891, ibid.; Oakes to Colby, July 27, 1891, NP, President, Letters Sent, LB 28, vol. 52, 137.H.11.2 (F).

86 Villard to Oakes, March 1, 1893, box 34, Mss. 8893, vol. 719, f. 231, Villard Papers; Buss, *Villard*, 175–81; Poor, *Manual, 1889*, 854; ibid., *1890*, 547; Henry Villard to J. C. Spooner and G. P. Miller, May 9, 1895, "Henry Villard and the Northern Pacific," Villard Papers, box 43, f. 315; Remarks by Mr. Colby in nominating Mr. Villard for the Office of the President of the Northern Pacific Railroad Company, Sept. 20, 1888, box 34, Mss. 8893, vol. 719, f. 298, Villard Papers; bonds, Thomas (?) to Robert Harris, July 14, 1888, Deutsche Bank, Berlin, NP, LRR, PV, 137.H.5.3(B); Drexel & Morgan to Robt. Harris, May 16, 1889, ibid., 137.H.5.4 (F); Buss, *Villard*, 180–85; Villard to R. Harris, Aug. 23, 1888, ibid., 137.H.5.3 (B).

87 Oakes to Board of Directors, July 15, 1891, NP, President, Letters Sent, LB 28, vol. 52, 137.H.11.2 (F), 245 ff.; Wm. Mellen to Oakes, July 13, 1891, NP, LRR, PV, 137.H.5.8 (F).

88 Wm Mellen to T. F. Oakes, Oct. 1, 1890, NP, LRR, PV, 137.H.5.6 (F).

89 Villard to Kuhn & Loeb, Sept. 15, 1891, Villard to Speyer & Co., Sept. 15, 1891, NP, Villard to Speyer & Co., Aug. 1, 1892, President, Letters Sent, LB, vol. 46, 137.H.11. 1 (B), 368–69; Spofford to Villard, April 17, 1891, LB 84a, Mss. 8993, vol. 119, Villard Papers.

90 Oakes to J. A. Barker, April 27, 1891, NP, President, Letters Sent, LB 27, vol. 51, 137.H.11.2 (F), 468.

91 J. W. Kendrick to W. H. Knowlton, Aug. 27, 1890, NP, 137.H.5.5 (B); James B. Williams to Oakes, March 10, 1891, NP, LRR, PV, 137.H.5.8 (F), H 2266. For the SLS & E., see Peter J. Lewty, *Across the Columbia Plain: Railroad Expansion in the Interior Northwest, 1885–93* (Pullman: Washington State Univ. Press, 1995), 129–41.

92 Wm. Mellen to Oakes, July 8, 1891, NP, LRR, PV, 137.H.5.8 (F).

93 Oakes to Wright, April 6, 1891, Oakes to Villard April 6, 1891, NP, President, Letters Sent, LB 27, vol. 51, 137.H.11.2 (F); Villard to Oakes, March 9, 1891, LB 84a, Mss. 8993, vol. 119, Villard Papers.

94 Buss, *Villard*, 246–49; Kazin, *Godly Hero*, 35–38; I. E. Gates to CPH, Nov. 5, 1892, CPH Papers, ser. 1, r. 51.

95 J. Nimmo to T. F. Oakes, Oct. 20, 1891, NP, President's Office, Incoming, 137.H.5.9 (B).

96 Joseph Schumpeter, *Business Cycles: A Theoretical, Historical, and Statistical Analysis of the Capitalist Process*, 2 vols. (New York: McGraw-Hill, 1939), 1:341.

97 Kendrick to T. F. Oakes, July 28, 1893, Kendrick to D. F. Dewey, July 28, 1893, UP, LRR, PV, 138.H.6.3 (B).

98 Ibid.; Chart H, Rail Traffic along the Northern Pacific, appendix.

99 "Report of Th. Barth of his investigation of the condition of the Northern Pacific Railroad Company during trip over road Oct. 24th to Nov. 9, 1893," NP, LRR, PV, 137.H.6.8 (F), 10–11.

100 M. V. B. Stacy, to Oakes, July 28, 1890, NP, LRR, PV, 137.H.5.2 (F).

101 Kendrick to Oakes, July 30, 1891, Aug. 10, Sept. 22, 1891, W. L. Darling to Kendrick, Sept. 14, 1891, NP, LRR, PV, 137.H.5.8 (F).

102 Oakes to Mellen, June 30, 1893, NP, President, Letters Sent, 137.H.11.3 (B), LB 34, vol. 58, 341.

103 Ibid.; Oakes to J. W. Cooper, May 10, 1893, NP, President, Letters Sent, LB 34, vol. 58, 137.H.11.3 (B), 341.

104 Oakes to Mellen, April 5, 1892, NP, President, Letters Sent, LB 34, vol. 58, 137.H.11.3 (B), 46 ff.

105 Oakes to Mellen, June 30, 1893, NP, President, Letters Sent, LB 34, vol. 58, 137.H.11.3 (B), 341; Oakes to Hannaford, June 16, 1893, ibid., 137.H.11.3 (B), 252.

106 Mellen to Oakes, Feb. 21, 1893, NP, LRR, PV, 137.H.6.3 (B); Van Horne to Mellen, July 11, 1893, enclosure with Mellen to Oakes, July 15, 1893, ibid., 137.H.6.4 (F).

107 Van Horne to Mellen, July 11, 1893, enclosure with Mellen to Oakes, July 15, 1893, NP, LRR, PV, 137.H.6.4 (F). For a far more positive view of Hill, see the hagiographic biography Martin, *James J. Hill*.

108 Jay Cooke to T. F. Oakes, July 27, 1893, NP, LRR, PV, 138.H.6.3 (B).

109 Report of Dr. Siemens of his Investigation of the Condition of the Northern Pacific, Nov. 1, 1893, NP, 134.F.1.7 (B).

110 Villard to Oakes, March 1, 1893, box 34, Mss. 8893, vol. 719, f. 231, Villard Papers.

111 Buss, *Villard*, 246–49; Kazin, *Godly Hero*, 35–38; I. E. Gates to CPH, Nov. 5, 1892, CPH Papers, ser. 1, r. 51. Leland Stanford was in favor of bimetalism and considered the outflow of gold to Europe a good thing; Stanford to CPH, May 24, 1893, ibid.

112 Report of Dr. Siemens of his Investigation of the condition of the Northern Pacific, Nov. 1893, Northern Pacific Railroad, 1–2, NP, 134.F.1.7 (B).

113 E. L. Godkin to J. Bryce, Nov. 19, 1893, in William M. Armstrong, ed., *The Gilded Age Letters of E. L. Godkin* (Albany: State Univ. of New York Press, 1974), 452.

114 Bryant, *Atchison*, 159–160.

115 Martin, *James J. Hill*, 410–11.

116 Bryant, *Atchison*, 162–63.

117 Klein, *Union Pacific*, 652–58.

118 Richard Olney to George Hadley, Oct. 30, 1893, Richard Olney Papers, ct. 138, r. 49.

119 CPH to A. N. Towne, Feb. 12, 1880, CPH Papers, ser. 2, r. 12.

120 C. F. Crocker to CPH, July 14, 1890, CPH Papers, ser. 1, r. 48. CPH to Mills, March 8, 1892, ibid., vol. 226, ser. 2, r. 33.

121 CPH to Gates, Oct. 25, 1892, CPH Papers, ser. 1, r. 51, unsigned to Wm. Dick, June 11, 1893, CPH Papers, ser. 1, r. 52.

122 C. F. Crocker to CPH, June 9, July 29, 1890, CPH Papers, ser. 1, r. 48.

123 C. F. Crocker to CPH, May 31, 1890, CPH Papers, ser. 1, r. 48.

124 C. F. Crocker to CPH, June 9, 18, July 3, July 12, July 14, 1890, CPH Papers, ser. 1, r. 48; C. F. Crocker to CPH, Nov. 9, 1891, ibid., r. 50; CPH to W. H. Mills, July 6, 1892, ibid., vol. 228, ser. 2, r. 33; CPH to Gates, May 10, 1890, telegram, ibid., ser. 1, r. 48.

125 C. F. Crocker to CPH, June 18, July 12, 1890, CPH Papers, ser. 1, r. 48; C. F. Crocker to CPH, Nov. 9, 1891, ibid., r. 50; CPH to W. H. Mills, July 6, 1892, ibid., vol. 228, ser. 2, r. 33.

126 H. T. Scott to CPH, June 24, 1892, CPH Papers, ser. 1, r. 50.

127 Mills to CPH, Feb. 7, 1893, CPH Papers, ser. 1, r. 51.

128 J. H. Woodard to (?), Feb. 14, 1891, CPH Papers, ser. 1, r. 49.

129 W. H. Mills to CPH, July 12, 1892, CPH Papers, ser. 1, r. 51.

130 W. W. Stow to CPH, June 7, 1892, CPH Papers, ser. 1, r. 50.

131 Ibid.; CPH to Stow, June 1, 1892, ibid., vol. 227, ser. 2, r. 33.

132 W. H. Mills to CPH, June 14, 26, 1892, CPH Papers, ser. 1, r. 50.

133 CPH to Mills, July 27, Aug. 1892, CPH Papers, vol. 228, ser. 2, r. 33.

134 Mills to CPH, Aug. 10, 1892, CPH Papers, ser. 1, r. 51.

135 White to J. D. Lynch, Jan. 14, 1887, White to J. W. Hellman, Jan. 14, 1887, White to H. M. Mitchell, Jan. 15, 1887, Correspondence, Outgoing, box 2, Letters from, vol. 1, Dec. 30, 1886–Jan. 21, 1887, White to Arthur Kearney, June 19, 1890, Correspondence, Outgoing, box 4, Aug. 14, 1889–Jan. 11, 1890, White to Patrick Collins, Aug. 14, 1890, ibid., White Papers.

136 White to Hon. John Swift, Jan. 24, 1891, Correspondence Outgoing, box 4, Jan. 7, 1890–May 10, 1891, White Papers.

137 Figures from Southern Pacific Company, 1885–1911, box 2E460, Mahl Papers.

138 W. G. Curtis to CPH, Sept. 6, 1895, HEH Collection.

139 CPH to J. Kruttschnitt, Aug. 31, 1897, HEH Collection.

140 E. L. Corthell to CPH, Feb. 27, 1893; Simon Stevens to Ignacio Mariscal, April 7, 1893, *The Two Republics*, Aug. 5, 1893, enclosure with Corthell to CPH, Aug. 16, 1893. CPH Papers, ser. 1, r. 51; E. L. Corthell to CPH, Jan. 27, 1894, ibid., r. 52.

141 Speyer & Co. to CPH, Sept. 20, 1892, CPH Papers, ser. 1, r. 51; Tweed to CPH, Sept. 15, Sept. 21, 1892, ibid.; Wm. Barney (J. Speyer Ellisen) to CPH, Nov. 11, 1892, ibid.; CPH to C. Tweed, Oct. 2, 1892, ibid., ser. 2, r. 51.

142 I. E. Gates to CPH, Oct. 13, 1892, CPH Papers, ser. 1, r. 51; CPH to Wm. Bonn, Jan. 20, 1893, ibid., vol. 233, ser. 2, r. 33; Tweed to Speyer & Co. to CPH, Sept. 22, Oct. 5, 1892, ibid., ser. 1, r. 51; Tweed to CPH Sept. 28, 29, 1892, CPH Papers, J. Speyer Ellisen to CPH, Nov. 11, 1892, CPH to W. Salomon, Sept. 29, 1892, CPH to I. E. Gates, Sept. 29, 1892, CPH to C. Tweed, Oct. 2, 1892, Gates to CPH, Oct. 13, 1892, all ibid.

143 W. Barney (Speyer Ellisson) to CPH, Jan. 7, 1893, CPH Papers, ser. 1, r. 51; CPH to Wm. Bonn, Jan. 20, 1893, ibid., vol. 233, ser. 2, r. 33; Gates to CPH, Oct. 19, 1892, ibid., ser. 1, r. 51.

144 Speyer & Company to CPH, May 6, 1893, CPH Papers, ser. 1, r. 51.

145 Extracts from Letter received from L. Speyer Ellissen, May 12, 1893, CPH Papers, ser. 1, r. 51.

146 N. T. Smith to CPH, May 30, June 7, 17, 1893, CPH Papers, ser. 1, r. 52.

147 CPH to HEH, June 13, 1893, HEH Collection.

148 C. F. Crocker to CPH, June 19, 1893, CPH Papers, ser. 1, r. 52.

149 CPH to Speyer & Co., June 20, 1893 (seven separate letters), HEH Collection.

150 C. F. Crocker to CPH, June 19, 1893, CPH Papers, ser.1, r. 52; Salomon to CPH, June 20, June 21, 1893, ibid.

151 Speyer & Co. to CPH, June 14, 1893, CPH Papers, ser. 1, r. 52; Crocker to CPH, June 21, June 22, 1893, ibid.; C. F. Crocker to CPH, c. June 26, 1892, ibid.; J. Speyer to CPH, June 26, 1892, ibid.

152 CPH to T. Hubbard, March 7, 1894, CPH Papers, ser. 1, r. 50; C. F. Crocker to CPH, July 5, 17, 1893, H. Spencer to CPH, Aug. 10, 1893, ibid., r. 52.

153 C. F. Crocker to CPH, Dec. 22, 1893, CPH Papers, ser. 1, r. 52.

154 C. F. Crocker to CPH, June 28, 1892, CPH Papers, ser. 1, r. 52.

155 C. F. Crocker to CPH, June 28, 14, 1892 (letter and telegram), June 19, 30, July 5 (two letters), 1893, CPH to C. F. Crocker, June 16, 1893, all in CPH Papers, ser. 1, r. 52.

156 CPH to C. F. Crocker, July 7, 1893, CPH Papers, ser. 1, r. 52.

157 C. F. Crocker to CPH, June 28, 1893, Crocker to CPH, July 26, 1893, CPH Papers, ser. 1, r. 52.

158 CPH to C. F. Crocker, July 18, 1893, CPH Papers, ser. 1, r. 52.

159 CPH to C. F. Crocker, July 17, 12, 1893, C. F. Crocker to CPH, July 26, 12, 1893, CPH Papers, ser. 1, r. 52; Mahl, "Memoirs: P.I. Co.," G4, Mahl Papers.

160 C. F. Crocker to CPH, July 26, 1893, CPH Papers, ser. 1, r. 52.

161 CPH to C. F. Crocker, July 18, 1893, CPH Papers, ser. 1, r. 52.

162 C. F. Crocker to CPH, July 10, 1893, Speyer & Co. to CPH, July 22, 1893, CPH Papers, ser. 1, r. 52.

163 C. F. Crocker to CPH, Aug. 3, 1893, CPH Papers, ser. 1, r. 52.

164 H. Spencer to CPH, Aug. 23, 1893, CPH Papers, ser. 1, r. 52.

165 T. H. Hubbard to CPH, March 13, 1894, CPH Papers, ser. 1, r. 52.

166 Richard Olney to George Hoadly, May 19, June 19, 1894, Olney to George Hoar, June 8, 1894, Olney Papers, ct. 138, r. 49.

167 C. F. Crocker to CPH, Oct. 5, 1893, CPH to Smith, Oct. 26, 1893, Lloyd and Wood to CPH, Oct. 9, 1893, CPH Papers, ser. 1, r. 52.

168 Mutual Life Insurance Company of New York, Nov. 6, 1893, PIC Records, ser. 1, Business and Legal Papers, JL001, box 6, f. 47.

169 (F. H. Hant?) to CPH, April 4, 1894, CPH Papers, ser. 1, r. 53, also CPH to Speyer & Co., June 20, 1893, HEH Collection.

170 F. Douty to CPH, Sept. 2, 1893, CPH Papers, ser. 1, r. 52; Fair to PIC, Sept. 2, 1893, ibid., r. 51; Speyer & Co. to CPH, Sept. 26, 21, 1893, W. T. Smith to CPH, Aug. 3, 1893, C. F. Crocker to CPH, Aug. 13, 16, 1893, ibid., r. 52.

171 Speyer & Co. to CPH, July 13, 1893, CPH Papers, ser. 1, r. 52.

172 Speyers to CPH, Aug. 27, 1893, CPH Papers, ser. 1, r. 52.

173 CPH to Smith, Sept. 6, 13, 1893, N. T. Smith to CPH, Sept. 7, 1893, Speyer & Co. to CPH, Sept. 15, 1893, CPH Papers, ser. 1, r. 52.

174 Speyer & Co. to CPH, Aug. 23, 1893, CPH Papers, ser. 1, r. 52.

175 Speyer & Co. to CPH, Dec. 6, 1893, CPH Papers, ser. 1, r. 52.

176 C. F. Crocker to CPH, Oct. 23, 1893, CPH Papers, ser. 1, r. 52.

177 C. F. Crocker to CPH, Nov. 6, 1893, CPH Papers, ser. 1, r. 52.

178 Speyer & Co. (Wm. Bonn) to CPH, Jan. 26, 1894, CPH Papers, ser. 1, r. 52; Charles Tweed to CPH, April 2, 1894, HEH Collection.

179 C. E. Bretherton to I. L. Requa, May 16, 1894, CPH Papers, ser. 1, r. 53.

180 Ibid.

181 Speyer & Co. (Wm. Bonn) to CPH, Jan. 26, 1894, C. E. Bretherton to CPH, March 14, 1894, CPH Papers, ser. 1, r. 52.

182 Speyer & Co. (Wm. Bonn) to CPH, Jan. 26, 1894, CPH to T. H. Hubbard, March 8, 1894; Gates to CPH, March 8, 1894, CPH Papers, ser. 1, r. 52.

183 Speyer & Co. (Wm. Bonn) to CPH, Jan. 26, 1894, CPH Papers, ser. 1, r. 52.

184 Speyer Brothers to CPH, March 3, 1894, CPH Papers, ser. 1, r. 52.

185 CPH to Speyer Brothers, March 19, 1894, CPH Papers, ser. 1, r. 52.

186 C. E. Bretherton to CPH, March 14, 1894, CPH Papers, ser. 1, r. 52; C. E. Bretherton to CPH, April. 18, 1894, ibid., r. 53.

187 C. E. Bretherton to CPH, May 13, 1894, I. E. Requa to CPH, May 24, 1894, CPH Papers, ser. 1, r. 53.

188 C. E. Bretherton to I. E. Requa, May 16, 1894, CPH Papers, ser. 1, r. 53.

189 Ibid., CPH to Gates, May 8, 1890, CPH Papers, ser. 1, r. 48.

190 C. E. Bretherton to CPH, May 18, 1894, CPH Papers, ser. 1, r. 53.

191 Gorsuch to CPH, Jan. 27, 31, 1894, Corthell to CPH, Jan. 30, March 4, 1894, CPH to Corthell, March 12, 1894, CPH Papers, ser. 1, r. 52.

192 CPH to Díaz, April 5, 1894, Corthell to CPH, April, 30, 1894, CPH Papers, ser. 1, r. 53.

193 Samuel Killibrew to CPH, June 8, 1894, CPH Papers, ser. 1, r. 53.
194 Gates to CPH, July 8, 1894, T. H. Hubbard to CPH, Feb. 9, 1894, Oakland Bank of Savings to CPH, March 2, 1894, CPH to Hubbard, March 7, 1894, F. H. Davis to CPH, March 16, 1894, CPH Papers, ser. 1, r. 52.
195 Hubbard to CPH, March 6, 1894, CPH to Hubbard, March 6, 1893, March 31, 1894, F. H. Davis to CPH, March 16, 1894, CPH Papers, ser. 1, r. 52; E. Gates to CPH, April 5, 1894, ibid., r. 53.
196 CPH to I. E. Gates, April 10, 1894, CPH Papers, ser. 1, r. 53.
197 CPH to Jane Stanford, May 9, 1894, CPH Papers, ser. 1, r. 53.
198 F. H. Davis to CPH, April 20, 1894, CPH Papers, ser. 1, r. 53; CPH to Davis, April 25, 1894, ibid.; Davis to CPH, May 1, 1894, ibid.; F. H. Davis to CPH, May 3, 1894, ibid.
199 Hubbard to CPH, April 27, 1894, F. H. Davis to CPH, May 1, 1894, CPH Papers, ser. 1, r. 53; other loans, CPH to I. E. Gates, May 7, 1894, ibid.
200 Charles Tweed to CPH, April 2, 1894, HEH Collection.
201 Thos. Hubbard to Speyer & Co., Aug. 27, 1896, CPH, Crocker, and Hubbard to Speyer & Co., Aug. 27, 1896 (two letters), PIC Records, ser.1, Business and Legal Papers, box 6, f. 41; CPH to HEH, Dec. 24, 1897, HEH Collection.
202 CPH to HEH, Dec. 24, 1897, HEH Collection.
203 CPH to HEH, Dec. 2, 1897, HEH Collection.

Mise en Scène: Reading the Newspapers

1 S. White to E. B. Pond, Nov. 19, 1890, S. White to H. O. Bradley, Nov. 11, 1890, Correspondence, Outgoing, box 4, Sept. 13, 1890–Jan. 3, 1891, White to J. Irish, Jan. 4, 1892, box 5, White Papers.
2 Mills to CPH, Dec. 15, 1891, CPH Papers, ser. 1, r. 50.
3 W. H. Mills to CPH, Dec. 15, 1891 (two letters), Crocker quote, Crocker to CPH, Dec. 22, 1891, Mills to CPH, Dec. 19, 1891, CPH Papers, ser. 1, r. 50.
4 W. H. Mills to CPH, Dec. 15, 1891 (two letters), Crocker quote, Crocker to CPH, Dec. 22, 1891, CPH Papers ser. 1, r. 50.
5 W. H. Mills to CPH, Dec. 15, 1891 (two letters), CPH Papers, ser. 1, r. 50.
6 Gray Brechin, *Imperial San Francisco: Urban Power, Earthly Ruin* (Berkeley: Univ. of California Press, 1999), 174–75.
7 Ibid., 176–77.
8 The *Bulletin's* attacks eventually came to worry Huntington, although he didn't think they would do "any harm to our interests." CPH to Mills, Aug. 2, 1892, CPH Papers, vol. 299, ser. 2, r. 33; CPH to (Mills?), n.d., c. Feb. 1892, ibid., vol. 225, ser. 2, r. 33; Frank M. Stone to CPH, Feb. 25, 1892, ibid., ser. 1, r. 50; W. H. Mills to CPH, Feb. 8, 1892, ibid.; CPH to Frank Stone, March 3, 1892, ibid., ser. 2, r. 33; CPH to Mills, May 12, 1892, ibid., vol. 227, ser. 2, r. 33; ambivalence, CPH to Stone, July 11, 1892, ibid., vol. 228, ser. 2, r. 33; CPH to Mills, July 19, 1892, ibid.; CPH to HEH, June 20, 1893, HEH Collection.
9 CPH to HEH, July 7, 1893, HEH Collection.
10 W. H. Mills to CPH, June 14, 1892, CPH Papers, ser. 1, r. 50; W. H. Mills to CPH, July 17, 1892, ibid., r. 51; CPH to Mills, Aug. 2, 1892, ibid., vol. 299, ser. 2, r. 33.
11 W. H. Mills to CPH, June 16, 1892, CPH Papers, ser. 1, r. 50.
12 CPH to Mills, June 20, 23, 1892, CPH Papers, vol. 228, ser. 2, r. 33; W. H. Mills to CPH, June 28, 1892, ibid., ser. 1, r. 50. See also CPH to Mills, July 27, 1892, ibid., vol. 228, ser. 2, r. 33. When Huntington approved the deal is not clear. It was in place by 1894; W. F. Herrin to T. Williams, Sept. 27, 1894, HEH Collection.

13 CPH to Mills, Aug. 16, 1892, CPH Papers, vol. 229, ser. 2, r. 33; W. H. Mills to CPH, June 1892, ibid., ser. 1, r. 50.

14 R. M. Shackelford to CPH, Oct. 13, 1892, E. Curtis to CPH, Nov. 22, 1892, Curtis to CPH, Nov. 29, 1892, CPH Papers, ser. 1, r. 51; R. Hal Williams, *The Democratic Party and California Politics, 1880–1896* (Stanford: Stanford Univ. Press, 1973), 162–73. By Dec. 10, Curtis said it looked as if White would win, Curtis to CPH, Dec. 10, 1892, CPH Papers, ser. 1, r. 51; friend, Curtis to Huntington, Dec. 14, Dec. 16, 1892, ibid.; excellent man, CPH to E. Curtis, Nov. 25, 1892, vol. 232, ser. 2, r. 33; friend, CPH to Wm. Stewart, Dec. 10, 1892, ibid. Stewart had offered to negotiate a deal with White's rival, Foote, who was an old enemy of the Southern Pacific and brother-in-law of Stewart, but who now, according to Stewart, offered to help facilitate a funding bill if elected. Stewart to CPH, Dec. 1, 1892, CPH Papers, ser. 1, r. 51; not friendly, CPH to Mills, Jan. 19, 1893, ibid., vol. 233, ser. 2, r. 33. Stow indicated he could set all the candidates aside and elect a man who could help the railroads. W. Stow to CPH, Dec. 14, 1892, CPH Papers, ser. 1, r. 51; played him for a fool, J. Reddick to CPH, Jan. 17, 1892, ibid., ser. 2, r. 51; on Hearst, Mills to CPH, Feb. 4, 1893, ibid., ser. 1, r. 51. Huntington was a little alarmed by letters White wrote to Democrats to secure the nomination. CPH to R. Carpenter, Jan. 23, 1893, CPH Papers, ser. 2, r. 33, LB, 233; Edith Dobie, "The Political Career of Stephen Mallory White" (Ph.D. diss., Stanford Univ., 1925), 139.

CHAPTER 10: STRIKE

1 Nick Salvatore, *Eugene Debs: Citizen and Socialist* (Urbana: Univ. of Illinois Press, 1882), 83.

2 Ibid., 8–9, 20–21, 60–61; Shelton Stromquist, "The Crisis of 1894 and the Legacies of Producerism," in Richard Schneirov, Shelton Stromquist, and Nick Salvatore, eds., *The Pullman Strike and the Crisis of the 1890s: Essays on Labor and Politics* (Urbana: Univ. of Illinois Press, 1999); Herbert Hovenkamp, *Enterprise and American Law, 1836–1937* (Cambridge: Harvard Univ. Press, 1991), 71–73.

3 Melvyn Dubofsky, "The Federal Judiciary, Free Labor, and Free Rights," in *The Pullman Strike and the Crisis of the 1890s*, 166–67; Thomas Frank, "The Leviathan with Tentacles of Steel: Railroads in the Minds of Kansas Populists," *Western Historical Quarterly* 20 (Feb. 1989): 46.

4 *Union Pacific Employes' Magazine*, Dec. 1893, p. 335.

5 Salvatore, *Debs*, 100.

6 Amy Dru Stanley, *From Bondage to Contract: Wage Labor, Marriage and the Market in the Age of Slave Emancipation* (New York: Cambridge, 1998), 81–82.

7 Salvatore, *Debs*, 90–91; EVD to Clark, Oct. 30, 1892, in J. Robert Constantine, ed., *Letters of Eugene V. Debs, 1874–1912* (Urbana: Univ. of Illinois Press, 1990), 1:27–31.

8 Salvatore, *Debs*, 93; Susan E. Hirsch, "The Search for Unity among Railroad Workers: The Pullman Strike in Perspective," in *The Pullman Strike and the Crisis of the 1890s*, 43–44; Shelton Stromquist, *A Generation of Boomers: The Pattern of Railroad Labor Conflict in Nineteenth-Century America* (Urbana: Univ. of Illinois, 1987), 79–84.

9 Salvatore, *Debs*, 92–98.

10 Hirsch, "Search for Unity among Railroad Workers," 43; Stromquist, "Crisis of 1894 and the Legacies of Producerism," 180; United States Strike Commission, *Report of the Chicago Strike of June–July, 1894* (Washington, D.C.: GPO, 1895, reprint, Clifton, N.J.: Augustus M. Kelley, 1972), 11.

11 Salvatore, *Debs*, 115–17.

12 "American Railway Union," *Union Pacific Employes' Magazine,* July 1893, pp. 178–79; Hirsch, "Search for Unity among Railroad Workers," 43–44.

13 Salvatore, *Debs,* 108–10, 114–18; "About the Union," *Railway Times,* Jan. 1, 1894, p. 1; "The Right Plan," ibid., Jan. 15, 1894, p. 3.

14 Salvatore, *Debs,* 124.

15 Henry James, *Richard Olney and His Public Service* (Boston: Houghton Mifflin, 1923), 8–11, 16.

16 Ibid., 19.

17 Ibid., 19; Gerald G. Eggert, *Richard Olney: Evolution of a Statesman* (University Park: Pennsylvania State Univ. Press, 1974), 40–43.

18 James, *Olney,* 23.

19 Eggert, *Olney,* 14–28.

20 Ibid., 50; John Cook to R. Olney, Jan. 3, 1894, Olney Papers, ct. 13, r. 5.

21 Eggert, *Olney,* 60–61.

22 *San Francisco Chronicle,* May 26, 1894, p. 4, c. 2; in trials after the strike, ARU lawyers would attempt to paint Baldwin as a pro–Southern Pacific marshall; examination of Baldwin, Nov. 15, 1894, box 211, f. 5, NARA case 3059; in the District Court, in the Northern District of California, Dec. 4, 1894, box 211, f. 1, Pullman Strike.

23 Eggert, *Olney,* 53.

24 Almont Lindsey, *The Pullman Strike: The Story of a Unique Experiment and of a Great Labor Upheaval* (Chicago: Univ. of Chicago Press, 1942); for wage reductions, U.S. Strike Commission, *Chicago Strike,* xxxiii.

25 Hovenkamp, *Enterprise and American Law,* 208–11, 218–19; Dubofsky, "Federal Judiciary," 159–75; "The Rights of Labor and the Courts," *Union Pacific Employes' Magazine,* Nov. 1893, pp. 291–96; *Ames et al.* v. *Union Pacific Ry. et al.,* Fed. Rep. 64 (1894); *Toledo, A.A. and N.M. Ry. Co.* v. *Pennyslvania Co. et al.,* Fed. Rep. 54 (1893); *Waterhouse* v. *Comer,* 55 Fed. Rep. 149, 154 (1893); Gerald G. Eggert, *Railroad Labor Disputes: The Beginnings of Federal Strike Policy* (Ann Arbor: Univ. of Michigan Press, 1967), 110–13.

26 Hovenkamp, *Enterprise and American Law,* 234–35.

27 Judge Marshall Harlan quoted in Dubofsky, "Federal Judiciary," 170; *Ames et al.* v. *Union Pacific Ry. et al.,* 14–15.

28 Hovenkamp, *Enterprise and American Law,* 234–35.

29 Quoted in Dubofsky, "Federal Judiciary," 163; *Toledo, A.A. and N.M. Ry. Co.* v. *Pennsylvania Co. et al.,* 739.

30 Hovenkamp, *Enterprise and American Law,* 210–14.

31 See Evgenia Shnayder, "The Rise of the American Railway Union, 1893–94," Spatial History Project, Stanford Univ., http://www.stanford.edu/group/spatialhistory/cgi-bin/site/index.php; Jonathan Garlock, *Guide to the Local Assemblies of the Knights of Labor* (Westport, Conn.: Greenwood Press, 1982), 61, 550.

32 See visualization, "The Rise of the American Railway Union, 1893–94."

33 Stromquist, *Generation of Boomers,* 84–86, first analyzed this data using the ARU newspaper, the *Railway Times*; "The Rise of the American Railway Union, 1893–94," Spatial History Project, Stanford Univ.; Salvatore, *Debs,* 117–18.

34 Quoted in Stromquist, *Generation of Boomers,* 86; U.S. Strike Commission, *Chicago Strike,* xxxiv; "Testimony of George W. Howard," ibid., 12.

35 "The Rise of the American Railway Union, 1893–94." Checking the addresses against the Sanborn Insurance maps of the period indicates that in California, at least, the address was probably the secretary's home address and not a union hall.

36 XXX to Editor, July 27, 1893, *Union Pacific Employes' Magazine,* Aug. 1893, 223–24.

37 Acting General Manager to T. F. Oakes, Aug. 9, 1893; General Manager to T. F. Oakes, Aug. 18, 1893, NP, GMR, Pullman.

38 Kendrick to Oakes, Aug. 18, 1893, NP, GMR, Pullman; Oakes to Ainslie, Aug. 7, 1893; President, Letters Sent, NP, LB 35, vol. 59. 137.H.11.3 (B).

39 General Manager to Oakes, Aug. 18, 1893, NP, GMR, Pullman.

40 Acting General Manager to Oakes, Aug. 9, 1893, NP, GMR, Pullman.

41 J. W. Kendrick to T. F. Oakes, Aug. 28, 1893, J. W. Kendrick, G.M., to T. Oakes, H. Payne, H. House, Receivers, both in Nov. 20, 1893, NP, GMR, Pullman.

42 Mink to E. Atkins, Aug. 1, 1893, UP, SG4, ser. 1, box 1, f. 17; O. Mink to E. Atkins, telegram, Aug. 6, 9, 1893, UP, SG 4, ser. 1, box 1, f. 17.

43 O. Mink to E. Atkins, telegram, Aug. 11, 1893, UP, SG 4, ser. 1, box 1, f. 17.

44 *Union Pacific Employes' Magazine,* Oct. 1893, p. 283.

45 J. J. Hill to A. L. Mohler, Aug. 7, 1893, circular, Aug. 14, 1893, Mohler to Hill, Aug. 18, 1893, Great Northern, pt. 1, 1862–1922, ser. B, Labor, r. 1, Presidential Subject File-1893–95, file 2114 L 22, D82F.

46 One of Your Slaves to J. J. Hill, Aug. 24, 1893, petition, Aug. 31, 1893, Hill to John T. Hall, Sept. 20, 1893; for threat, S.K.O. to Hill, Nov. 16, 1893, all in Great Northern, pt. 1, 1862–1922, ser. B, Labor, r. 1, Presidential Subject File-1893–95, file 2114 L 22, D82F.

47 Kendrick to Oakes, Aug. 28, 1893, NP, GMR, Pullman.

48 General Manager to Dickinson, Nov. 27, 1893, Kendrick to Oakes, Oct. 23, 1893, Kendrick to Hill, Oct. 12, 1893, all in NP, GMR, Pullman.

49 Pearce to Kendrick, Nov. 17, 1893, General Manager to J. T. Odell, Nov. 27, 1893, NP, GMR, Pullman.

50 J. W. Kendrick to T. F. Oakes, Aug. 28, 1893, Kendrick to T. Oakes, H. Payne, and H. House, Dec. 12, 1893, NP, GMR, Pullman, with attachments; see pp. 18–20 for workers' reactions. For rise per train-mile, Kendrick to W. G. Pearce, Oct. 21, 1893, ibid.

51 Kendrick to J. J. Hill, Oct. 12, 1893, General Manager Kendrick to E. Dickinson, Dec. 15, 1893, NP, GMR, Pullman; organization, Kendrick to T. F. Oakes, Oct. 27, 1893, ibid.

52 J. W. Kendrick to T. F. Oakes, Jan. 19, 1894, Conference between the Management of the Northern Pacific Railroad and the Employes in Its Train Service . . . Jan. 11, 1894, Analysis of Discussion of Trainmen's Schedule, n.d., NP, GMR, Pullman.

53 "A Wage Reduction," *Union Pacific Employes' Magazine,* Sept. 1893, pp. 224–27.

54 Ibid.; "The Employes under a Receiver," *Union Pacific Employes' Magazine,* Nov. 1893, pp. 289–91; ibid., Dec. 1893, p. 327; ibid., Jan. 1894, p. 361; Poor, *Manual, 1896,* 919, 948.

55 *Union Pacific Employes' Magazine,* Jan. 1894, pp. 362–63; Sage Brush to Editor, Dec. 24, 1893, ibid., p. 380.

56 Stromquist, *Generation of Boomers,* 87–88.

57 Salvatore, *Debs,* 118–19; William E. Forbath, *Law and the Shaping of the American Labor Movement* (Cambridge: Harvard Univ. Press, 1991), 72–73.

58 "Index to Conferences, March 15–March 29, 1893," UP, SG21, ser. 2, box 14.

59 Pearce to Kendrick, Nov. 17, 1893, NP, GMR, Pullman, Correspondence Re: Schedule Reduction; Eggert, *Railroad Labor Dispute,* 136–51.

60 Representatives of St. Paul Lodge, no. 4; Brotherhood of Railway Carmen, to J. Q. Patee, April 17, 1894, Great Northern, pt. 1, 1862–1922, ser. B, Labor, r. 1, Presidential Subject File-1893–95, file 2114 L 22, D82F.

61 J. C. Nolan et al. to J. J. Hill, Feb. 6, 1894, Great Northern, pt. 1, 1862–1922, ser. B, Labor, r. 1, Presidential Subject File-1893–95, file 2114 L 22, D82F; Salvatore, *Debs,* 119.

62 See Hill's Diaries, Expense Books, and Memoranda Books, 22.D.5.3, 22.D.3.7, James J. Hill Papers.

63 Salvatore, *Debs*, 119–20; Hill (?) to Nolan et al., Feb. 10, 1894, Great Northern, pt. 1, 1862–1922, ser. B, Labor, r. 1, Presidential Subject File-1893–95, file 2114 L 22, D82F, r. 1; E. E. Clark to Brainard, April 15, 1894, pt. 1, 1862–1922, Great Northern, ser. B, Labor, r. 1, President's Subject Files Strike File—American Railway Union, 1893–95, file 2113 L 22, D82F; Kendrick to Oakes, April 13, 1894, NP, GMR, Pullman, Correspondence Re: Schedule Reduction, 1894.

64 R. W. Bryan (*sic*) to C. W. Case, April 12, 1894; James Hogan to C. W. Case, April 13, 1894, R. W. Ryan to J. J. Hill, April 13, 1894; W. T. Riker to R. W. Ryan, n.d., Great Northern, pt. 1, 1862–1922, ser. B, Labor, r. 1, Presidential Subject File-1893–95, file 2114 L 22, D82F; EVD to Frank X. Holl, April 16, 1894, *Letters of Eugene V. Debs*, 1:58; Salvatore, *Debs*, 120; W. Thomas White, "Race, Ethnicity, and Gender in the Railroad Work Force: The Case of the Far Northwest, 1883–1918," *Western Historical Quarterly* 15 (July 1985): 271.

65 EVD to Frank X. Holl, April 16, 1894, *Letters of Eugene V. Debs*, 1:58.

66 Thompson to (?), April 12, 1894; W. C. Broadwater, Mayor to C. W. Case, GM, April 13, 1894, W. H. Norrie, at a mass meeting of the citizens of Crookston, April 21, 1894, Merchants of Butte to J. J. Hill, April 25, 1894, Great Northern, pt. 1, 1862–1922, ser. B, Labor, r. 1, Presidential Subject File-1893–95, file 2114 L 22, D82F.

67 Marcus Daly to Hill, April 18, 1894, Great Northern, pt. 1, 1862–1922, ser. B: Labor, r. 1, President's Subject Files, Strike File—American Railway Union, 1893–95, file 2113 L 22, D82F.

68 J. J. Hill to EVD and S. W. Howard, April 24, 1894, Great Northern, pt. 1, 1862–1922, ser. B, Labor, r. 1, Presidential Subject File-1893–95, file 2114 L 22, D82F; Salvatore, *Debs*, 120.

69 J. J. Hill to EVD and G. W. Howard, April 24, 1894, J. J. Hill to Knute Nelson, April 23, 1894, Great Northern, pt. 1, 1862–1922, ser. B, Labor, r. 1, Presidential Subject File-1893–95, file 2114 L 22, D82F; Schedules and notations, n.d, c. April 1894; C. W. Case and James J. Hill to John C. Curtin, April 15, 1894, ibid.

70 EVD and G. W. Howard to J. J. Hill, April 25, 1894 (two letters), Great Northern, pt. 1, 1862–1922, ser. B, Labor, r. 1, Presidential Subject File-1893–95, file 2114 L 22, D82F; EVD & George W. Howard to J. J. Hill, April 19, 1894, *Letters of Eugene V. Debs*, 1:59.

71 EVD and G. W. Howard to J. J. Hill, April 19, 1894, Hill to EVD and G. W. Howard, April 19, multiple letters on this date, also EVD and G. W. Howard to J. J. Hill, April 23, 1894, Great Northern, pt. 1, 1862–1922, ser. B, Labor, r. 1, Presidential Subject File-1893–95, file 2114 L 22, D82F.

72 EVD and G. W. Howard to J. J. Hill, April 24, 1894, Great Northern, pt. 1, 1862–1922, ser. B, Labor, r. 1, Presidential Subject File-1893–95, file 2114 L 22, D82F.

73 J. J. Hill to C.K. Davis, April 24, 1894, Great Northern, pt. 1, 1862–1922, ser. B, Labor, r. 1, Presidential Subject File-1893–95, file 2114 L 22, D82F.

74 J. J. Hill to Grover Cleveland, April 28, 1894, Great Northern, pt. 1, 1862–1922, ser. B, Labor, r. 1, Presidential Subject File-1893–95, file 2114 L 22, D82F.

75 Eggert, *Olney*, 128–129.

76 Ibid.

77 Eggert, *Railroad Labor Disputes*, 151.

78 There were some arrests for interference with the mails, Hill to Nichols, April 23, 1894, Great Northern, pt. 1, 1862–1922, ser. B, Labor 07, President's Subject Files: Strike File—American Railway Union, 1893–95, File 2113, L 22, D82F, r. 1.

79 Eggert, *Olney*, 129–32.

80 Ibid.

81 J. J. Hill to EVD and G. W. Howard, April 25, 1894, J. J. Hill to W. W. Currier, April 26, 1894 (two letters), J. J. Hill to EVD and G. W. Howard, April 26, 1894; Memorandum, n.d., c. April

26, 1894, W. J. Anderson, to Hill, c. April 22, 1894, Great Northern, pt. 1, 1862–1922, ser. B, Labor, r. 1, Presidential Subject File-1893–95, file 2114 L 22, D82F.

82 J. J. Hill to J.D. Farrell, April 27, 1894, ibid.

83 J. Nolan to (?), April 28, 1894, ibid.

84 Resolution, C. M. Harrington, Chairman, n.d., c. April 27, 1894, C. M. Harrington to J. J. Hill, April 28, 1894, J. J. Hill to C. M. Harrington et al., April 29, 1894, J. J. Hill to C. Pillsbury et al., April 30, 1894, ibid.

85 C. M. Harrington to J. J. Hill, April 28, 1894; J. J. Hill to C. Pillsbury et al., April 30, 1894, ibid.

86 C. Pillsbury to Hill, May 8, 1894, Channing Seabury to C. Pillsbury, May 11, 1894, L. W. Rogers et al., Petition, May 11, 1894, Great Northern, pt. 1, 1862–1922, ser. B, Labor, r. 1, Presidential Subject File-1893–95, file 2114 L 22, D82F.

87 Salvatore, *Debs*, 128–29; Lindsey, *Pullman*, 103–5, 122–26.

88 Salvatore, *Debs*, 128–29.

89 Eggert, *Railroad Labor Disputes*, 156; see also CPH to HEH, June 28, 1894, HEH Collection.

90 Eggert, *Railroad Labor Disputes*, 157.

91 Troy Rondinone, "Guarding the Switch: Cultivating Nationalism during the Pullman Strike," *Journal of the Gilded Age and Progressive Era* 8 (Jan. 2009): 83–108; Richard Slotkin, *Gunfighter Nation: The Myth of the Frontier in Twentieth-Century America* (New York: Atheneum, 1992), 93–101.

92 General Manager to Oakes, June 28, 1894, NP, GMR, Pullman.

93 Olney to B. Storer, July 12, 1894, Olney Papers, ct. 138, r. 49; Telegram, Henry Caldwell to J. H. Mitchell, July 2, 1894, NP, 138.H.8.8 (F).

94 General Manager to C. F. Oakes, June 28, 1894, NP, GMR, Pullman.

95 Ibid., General Manager to All Employees, June 26, 1894, NP, GMR, Pullman.

96 General Manager to C. F. Oakes, June 28, 1894, NP, GMR, Pullman.

97 Ibid.

98 Counsel to Hon. Henry C. Caldwell, June 29, 1894, NP, 138H.8.8 (F); General Manager to C. F. Oakes, June 28, 1894, Finn to Kendrick, June 27, 1894, Kendrick to Kimberly, June 26, 1894, M. C. Kimberly to Kendrick, June 28, 1894, NP, GMR, Pullman.

99 J. D. Finn to Kendrick, June 27, 1894 (two letters), NP, GMR, Pullman.

100 Kimberly to Kendrick, June 28, 1894, (two letters), Kendrick to H. C. Payne, June 28, 1894, General Manager to C. F. Oakes, June 28, 1894, NP, GMR, Pullman.

101 General Manager to C. F. Oakes, June 28, 1894, NP, GMR, Pullman.

102 Missoula, Harrity to John Hickey, June 30, 1894, 3:52 P.M., Beatty to J. H. Mitchell, June 30, 1894, C. J. Wilson to Kendrick, June 29, 1904, NP, GMR, Pullman.

103 Kendrick to Pearson, June 30, 1894, NP, GMR, Pullman.

104 Ibid.

105 Ibid.

106 Kimberly to Kendrick, June 29, 1894, NP, GMR, Pullman.

107 Kendrick to J. H. Mitchell, June 30, 1894, NP, GMR, Pullman.

108 J. H. Mitchell to Ashton and Chapman, June 28, 1894, Telegram, NP, GMR, Pullman.

109 Eggert, *Railway Labor Disputes*, 152–54.

110 General Manager to C. F. Oakes, June 28, 1894, NP, GMR, Pullman.

111 General Manager to S.R. Ainslie, June 28, 1894, NP, GMR, Pullman.

112 G. W. Dickinson to Kendrick, July 3, 1894, NP, GMR, Pullman.

113 W. H. Frances to Kendrick, June 30, 1894, Kendrick to (?), July 5, 1894, NP, GMR, Pullman; W. Thomas White, "Boycott: The Pullman Strike in Montana," *Montana: The Magazine of Western History* 29 (Autumn 1979): 2–13.

114 *San Francisco Chronicle*, May 21, 1894, p. 5.

115 Journal of the Pullman Strike, June 27, 1894, HM 55579, Huntington Library; *Sacramento Record-Union*, June 28, 1894.

116 Journal of the Pullman Strike, June 28, 29, 1894, HM 55579, Huntington Library. HEH to CPH, June 27, 1894, HEH Collection.

117 *San Francisco Chronicle*, June 29, 1894, p. 1.

118 Letter of HEH, *San Francisco Chronicle*, July 3, 1894, p. 1.

119 Telegram, HEH to CPH, July 2, 6, 1894, HEH Collection.

120 CPH to HEH, July 6, 1894, HEH Collection.

121 "Bulletin to Southern Pacific Employes," *Sacramento Record-Union*, June 30, 1894; *San Francisco Chronicle*, June 30, 1894, p. 3.

122 *San Francisco Chronicle*, June 29, 1894, p. 1; Meetings of June 30, printed resolution, July 5, Ms 22, Brotherhood of Locomotive Engineers, div. 10, box 1.

123 *San Francisco Chronicle*, June 30, 1894, p. 3.

124 Ibid., July 2, 1894.

125 Ibid., July 2, 1894, p. 2; ibid., July 3, 1894, p. 2.

126 W. H. Mills to CPH, July 27, 1894, CPH Papers, ser. 1, r. 53. See also William Deverell, *Railroad Crossing: Californians and the Railroad, 1850–1910* (Berkeley: Univ. of California Press, 1994). Mills exaggerated the wage cut.

127 W. H. Mills to CPH, July 27, 1894, CPH Papers, ser. 1, r. 53; CPH to HEH, Aug. 20, 1894, HEH Collection; for arrangement with the *Examiner*, W. F. Herrin to T. T. Williams, Sept. 27, 1894, ibid.

128 J. H. Mitchell Jr. to Hon. J. H. Beatty, June 30, 1894, NP, GMR, Pullman; J. H. Mitchell to Ashton & Chapman, June 28, 1894, ibid.

129 Dickinson to Kendrick, June 30, 1894, NP, GMR, Pullman.

130 J. H. Mitchell Jr. to Hon. J. H. Beatty, June 30, 1894, J. H. Mitchell to Ashton and Chapman, June 28, 1894, NP, GMR, Pullman.

131 Beatty to J. H. Mitchell, June 30, 1894, NP, GMR, Pullman.

132 Kimberly to Kendrick, June 30, 1894, NP, GMR, Pullman; J. McCabe to J. Hickey, June 29, 1894, Kendrick to (?), July 5, 1894, NP, GMR, Pullman.

133 W. O. Chapman to J. H. Mitchell, June 30, 1894, W. E. Cullen to Kendrick, July 3, 1894, NP, GMR, Pullman.

134 "Hanford Resigns; No Impeachment; by Agreement with Congressional Committee Federal Judge Withdraws under Fire," Special to *New York Times*, July 23, 1912, p. 18.

135 Lindsey, *Pullman Strike*, 247.

136 Ibid., 246.

137 *San Francisco Chronicle*, July 3, 1894, p. 1; *San Francisco Examiner*, July 3, 1894, p. 1; Baldwin Cross Examination, Nov. 16, 1894, *U.S.* vs. *Cassidy and Mayne*, case 3059, box 211, vol. 4, f. 6, pp. 312, 325 327, Pullman Strike.

138 Deverell, *Railroad Crossing*, 79–82, 87–88; Charles Tweed to R. Olney, July 23, 1894, July 27, 1894, R. Olney Papers, ct. 17, r. 6; Olney to Tweed, July 24, 1894, ibid.; Olney to G. Denis, Aug. 14, 1894, ibid., ct. 18, r. 6; Petition in Equity, July 1894, R.O. penciled notes as to Southern Pacific bill in equity brought by Denis, Call, etc., July 1894, ibid., ct. 17, r. 6.

139 *San Francisco Chronicle*, June 29, 1894, p. 1.

140 Counsel to Henry C. Caldwell, June 29, 1894, Fargo, Ball & Watson to Kendrick, July 3, 1894, NP, GMR, Pullman.

141 Eggert, *Railroad Labor Disputes*, 158–67; Olney to Hon. Bellamy Storer, July 12, 1894, Olney Papers, ct. 138, r. 49.

142 Eggert, *Railroad Labor Disputes*, 160.

143 Ibid., 159.

144 Ibid., 160–62.

145 Ibid., 163.

146 Ibid.

147 Ibid., 166–69; Donald L. McMurry, "The Legal Ancestry of the Pullman Strike Injunctions," *Industrial and Labor Relations Review* 14 (Jan. 1961): 235–56.

148 Eggert, *Railroad Labor Disputes*, 170.

149 Ibid., 171; Lindsey, *Pullman Strike*, 179–89, 195.

150 Eggert, *Railroad Labor Disputes*, 172–73; U.S. Strike Commission, *Chicago Strike*, xlvi; Lindsey, *Pullman Strike*, 171–75, 203–35.

151 Eggert, *Railroad Labor Disputes*, 174–75; U.S. Strike Commission, *Chicago Strike*, xi, xix; Lindsey, *Pullman Strike*, 218, 203–35, passim.

152 White, "Race, Ethnicity, and Gender," 272.

153 Untitled, undated document, c. July 6, 1894, a transcript presumably by a detective of a conversation between leaders, NP, GMR, Pullman; White, "Pullman Strike in Montana," 10; T. M. Paschal to R. Olney, Aug. 24, 1894, Olney Papers, ct. 18, r. 6.

154 White, "Pullman Strike in Montana," 10–11.

155 *San Francisco Examiner*, July 4, 1894, pp. 2, 4.

156 Southern Pacific Company, Journal of incidents in San Francisco resulting from the American Railway Union Strike, June 27–Aug. 31, p. 20, HM 55579, Huntington Library.

157 A good account is in Deverell, *Railroad Crossing*, 73–75.

158 "The Triumph of Might," *San Francisco Examiner*, July 4, 1894, pp. 1–4; Baldwin Cross Examination, Nov. 16, 1894, *U.S. v. Cassidy and Mayne*, Case 3059, box 211, vol. 4, f. 6, pp. 359, 378, Pullman Strike.

159 This account is from "The Triumph of Might," *San Francisco Examiner*, July 4, 1894, pp. 1–4; for railroad description, HEH to CPH, July 3, 1894, HEH Collection.

160 "Knox Enjoined," *San Francisco Examiner*, July 4, 1894, p. 4.

161 "The Railway War," *San Francisco Chronicle*, June 30, 1894, pp. 1–3.

162 *Sacramento Record-Union*, July 5, 1894, p. 3; *San Francisco Examiner*, July 5, 1894, p. 2.

163 *Sacramento Daily Record-Union*, July 7, 1894, p. 3; *Sacramento Record-Union*, July 9, 1894, p. 1; ibid., July 10, 1894, p. 3.

164 Meetings of July 1, July 12, 1894, Ms 22, Brotherhood of Locomotive Engineers, Division 10, box 1.

165 *Sacramento Record-Union*, July 11, 1894, p. 3, July 12, 1894, p. 3. *San Francisco Examiner*, July 12, 1894.

166 *Sacramento Daily Record-Union*, July 16, 1894, p. 3.

167 *San Francisco Chronicle*, July 3, 1894, p. 2.

168 *San Francisco Examiner*, July 3, 1894, p. 1; *San Francisco Chronicle*, July 3, 1894, p. 1; HEH to CPH, July 3, 1894, HEH Collection.

169 Journal of Pullman Strike, ARU Strike, 1894, HM 55579, July 4–30, Huntington Library.

170 Deverell, *Railroad Crossing*, 79–89. This is an etymology listed by the *Oxford English Dictionary*. For more antimonopolist opposition, Antimonopoly League to Olney, July 11, 1894, Olney Papers, ct. 6, r. 6.

171 Journal of Pullman Strike, ARU Strike, 1894, HM 55579, p. 51.

172 Ibid.

173 Ibid., pp. 52–53.

174 William John Pinkerton, *His Personal Record: Stories of Railroad Life* (Kansas City, Mo.: Pinkerton Publishing Company, 1904), 170–77.

175 Classified Statement, by Divisions, of Number of Men not Re-employed at Close of Strike, July 1894, NP, GMR, Pullman.

176 Foote sometimes appears as H. I. Foote and sometimes as H. S. Foote. Foote had volunteered to lobby for the funding bill in exchange for Huntington's support of his candidacy for U.S. district attorney; Foote to CPH, June 13, 1894, CPH, ser. 1, r. 53; CPH to HEH, Nov. 27 1894, HEH Collection. *U.S.* v. *Cassidy and Mayne*, Case 3059, San Bruno NARA.

177 HEH to CPH, Feb. 25, 1895, HEH Collection.

178 J. A. Fillmore, Manager Pacific System, Circular Letter, June 2, 1896, HEH Collection. There is a surviving Southern Pacific blacklist in the Sacramento Railroad Museum. It dates from before the strike, and drinking and frequenting saloons is the leading cause of blacklisting. Blacklist number 3, Feb. 1887–91, Ms. 10, Southern Pacific Records.

179 Memorandum on Relations between Employers and Labor to J. Kruttschnitt, July 24, 1896, HEH to CPH, Nov. 7, 1895, HEH to CPH, Feb. 4, 1895, M. H. Ward to CPH, Feb. 1, 1895, ibid.; CPH to HEH, Aug. 21, 1895, HEH Collection. Meetings of Aug. 4, Sept. 1, 8, 1894, Brotherhood of Locomotive Engineers, box 1.

180 Eggert, *Railroad Labor Disputes*, 202.

181 R. Hal Williams, *The Democratic Party and California Politics, 1880–1896* (Stanford: Stanford Univ. Press, 1973), 190–205; HEH to CPH, Nov. 24, 1894, HEH Collection; W. H. Mills to CPH, July 28, Aug. 27, 1894, CPH, ser. 1, r. 53.

182 Deverell, *Railroad Crossing*, 96–102; CPH to HEH, Aug. 28, 1894, HEH Collection.

183 CPH to HEH, Aug. 23, 1894, HEH Collection.

184 CPH to HEH, Sept. 5, 1894, HEH Collection.

185 Williams, *Democratic Party*, 219–21; CPH to Mills, Sept. 27, 1894, HEH Collection; "Shall the Government Take the Pacific Railroads," *San Francisco Examiner* petition, copy in Richard Olney Papers, ct. 16, r. 5.

186 CPH to HEH, April 15, 1896, CPH to Wm. Mills, April 16, 1896, CPH to C. F. Crocker, April 29, 1896, HEH Collection.

187 CPH to HEH, May 7, 1896, HEH Collection.

188 Williams, *Democratic Party*, 227; CPH to J. A. Muir, May 12, 1896, W. H. Mills to HEH, May 14, 1896, HEH Collection.

189 HEH to Jas. Agler, Aug. 13, 1895, HEH Collection; Linda Thatcher, *History Blazer*, Nov. 1995, http://historytogo.utah.gov/utah_chapters/statehood_and_the_progressive_era/theshoot ingofarthurbrownexsenatorfromutah.html.

190 Williams, *Democratic Party*, 228–30; Deverell, *Railroad Crossing*, 93–120.

191 Paul Tatout, *Ambrose Bierce: The Devil's Lexicographer* (Norman: Univ. of Oklahoma Press, 1951), 214–18; Daniel Lindley, *Ambrose Bierce Takes on the Railroad: The Journalist as Muckraker and Cynic* (Westport, Conn.: Praeger, 1999), 106–14.

192 CPH to HEH, July 16, 1896, HEH Collection.

193 (W. F. Herrin?) to HEH, Nov. 6, 1896, HEH Collection. H. R. Meyer, "The Settlement with the Pacific Railways," *Quarterly Journal of Economics* 13 (July 1899): 427–44.

Mise en Scène: Following the Detectives

1 CPH to HEH, Nov. 8, 1894, HEH to CPH, Nov. 12, 1894, CPH to W. W. Stow, Dec. 18, 1894, HEH Collection.

2 HEH to T. E. Stillman, April 27, 1895, T. E. Stillman to HEH, May 6, 1895, enclosures with B. A. Worthington to HEH, March 9, 1897, HEH Collection.

3 (John Custin?) to J. A. Fillmore, Oct. 17, 1895, report of operative W.J.F., Oct. 16, 1895, HEH Collection. Most likely, since Henry Huntington knew that Fillmore was using detectives, he

had someone inside Fillmore's office sending him copies of the reports. *San Francisco Call*, June 10, 1895.

CHAPTER 11: CREATIVE DESTRUCTION

1 CPH to F. H. Gassaway, Oct. 22, 1894, HEH Collection.

2 In part these are the changes traced in William Cronon, *Nature's Metropolis: Chicago and the Great West* (New York: Norton, 1991).

3 Richard J. Orsi, *Sunset Limited: The Southern Pacific Railroad and the Development of the American West, 1850–1930* (Berkeley: Univ. of California Press, 2005), 79–81.

4 CPH to Stanford, Dec. 16, 1871, LB, 1:197, box 1, Hopkins Collection; Robert A. Sauder, "The Impact of the Agricultural College Act on Land Alienation in California," *Professional Geographer* 36 (1984): 28–39; Khaled Bloom, "Pioneer Land Speculation in California's San Joaquin Valley," *Agricultural History* 57 (July 1983): 297–307; Paul W. Gates, "Public Land Disposal in California," ibid. 49 (Jan. 1975): 158–78; Stanford to CPH, Sept. 30, 1871, CPH Papers, ser. 1, r. 4. Hopkins to CPH, Nov. 21, 1871, ibid. See Orsi, *Sunset Limited*, 65–74; Map C in appendix, Southern Pacific Land Grants.

5 David Lavender, *The Great Persuader: The Biography of Collis P. Huntington* (Niwot: Univ. Press of Colorado, 1998), 49, 140, 167; David Igler, *Industrial Cowboys: Miller and Lux and the Transformation of the Far West, 1850–1920* (Berkeley: Univ. of California Press, 2001), 101–2, for speculators 65–83; CPH to Hopkins, Feb. 4, 1870, Hopkins Collection, LB, 2:75; Orsi, *Sunset Limited*, 114–15, 116.

6 Walter Alexander McAllister, "A Study in Railroad Land Grant Disposal in California, with Reference to the Western Pacific, the Central Pacific, and the Southern Pacific Railroad Companies" (Ph.D. diss., Univ. of Southern California, 1939), 255–56, 262–63. McLaughlin purchased 78,369 acres in Alameda County, 64,622 acres in Sacramento County, 51,574.55 acres in Stanislaus County, and 133,223 acres in San Joaquin County. Lavender, *Great Persuader,* 186–88.

7 Henry George, *Our Land and Land Policy: The Complete Works of Henry George* (New York: Doubleday, Page, 1904), 47–50, 97; Red River, Hiram Drache, "Bonanza Farming in the Red River Valley," *Papers Read before the Historical and Scientific Society of Manitoba*, ser. 3, no. 24 (Winnipeg, 1967–68), 57–63; Sauder, "Impact of the Agricultural College Act," 28–39.

8 See, e.g., James B. Hedges, "The Colonization Work of the Northern Pacific Railroad," *Mississippi Valley Historical Review* 13 (Dec. 1926): 311–12; David M. Emmons, *Garden in the Grasslands: Boomer Literature of the Central Plains* (Lincoln: Univ. of Nebraska Press, 1971), 25–46.

9 Richard C. Overton, *Burlington West: A Colonization History of the Burlington Railroad* (Cambridge: Harvard Univ. Press, 1941), 455; Philip R. Smith, *Improved Surface Transportation and Nebraska's Population Distribution, 1860–1960* (New York: Arno Press, 1981), 36–41.

10 Overton, *Burlington West*, 388; Stanley N. Murray, "Railroads and the Agricultural Development of the Red River Valley of the North, 1870–1890," *Agricultural History* 31 (Oct. 1957): 57–66.

11 Orsi, *Sunset Limited*, 105, 130–31, 76–84, 148–156. For a sample of promotion literature and its scholarship, Overton, *Burlington West*; Hedges, "Colonization Work"; Maury Klein, *Union Pacific*, vol. 1, *Birth of a Railroad, 1862–1893* (Garden City, N.Y.: Doubleday, 1987), 325–28; Union Pacific Railroad Company, *Guide to the Union Pacific Railroad Lands, 12,000,000 Acres, Best Farming, Grazing and Mineral Lands in America, in the State of Nebraska and Territories of Colorado, Wyoming and Utah . . .*, 5th ed. (Omaha: Land Department, Union Pacific Railroad, 1873 [1872 on title page]).

12 Orsi, *Sunset Limited*, 76–84; Burlington & Missouri Railroad Company, *The Great South Platte Region: B. & M. Railroad Lands* (n.p.: Burlington and Missouri River Railroad Company, 1879).

13 Overton, *Burlington West*, 432.

14 Klein, *Union Pacific*, 325–28; W. H. Mills to CPH, Jan. 31, 1891, CPH Papers, ser. 1, r. 49; Igler, *Industrial Cowboys*, 62–65.

15 Testimony of Leland Stanford, July 28, 1887, *PRC*, 7:2465.

16 Jay Cooke, "Memoir," 145, Baker Library. See also G. Taylor to Northern Pacific, April 30, 1888, NP, LRR, PV, 137.H.5.3 (B).

17 W. H. Mills to CPH, Dec. 22, 1893, CPH Papers, ser. 1, r. 52.

18 Ernst von Hesse-Wartegg, "Across Nebraska by Train in 1877: The Travels of Ernst von Hesse-Wartegg," trans. and ed. by Frederic Trautmann, *Nebraska History* 65 (Fall 1984): 411–15.

19 Hesse-Wartegg, "Across Nebraska by Train," 412–14.

20 See Sidney Dillon, "The West and the Railroads," *North American Review* 152 (April 1891): 443–51.

21 Such questions were asked both by Henry George in *Our Land and Land Policy* and by Charles Francis Adams in "Which Will Quickest Solve the Railroad Question: Force Bills or Public Opinion?" (Address at Oshkosh, Wisc., Sept. 3, 1875), in Charles Francis Adams, *Railway Pamphlets*, vol. 1, Stanford Univ. Library.

22 Joseph A. Schumpeter, *Capitalism, Socialism, and Democracy* (New York: Harper & Brothers, 1947), 63.

23 Ibid., 76.

24 Ibid., 84.

25 Stanley Engerman, "Some Economic Issues relating to Railroad History and the Evaluation of Land Grants," *Journal of Economic History* 32 (June 1972): 443–63. John H. Coatsworth, "Obstacles to Economic Growth in Nineteenth-Century Mexico," *American Historical Review* 38 (Feb. 1978): 99, 100; quote, John Coatsworth, *Growth against Development: The Economic Impact of Railroads in Porfirian Mexico* (DeKalb: Northern Illinois Univ. Press, 1981), 150, also, 153–54, 164–65.

26 Engerman, "Some Economic Issues," 452.

27 Joseph Nimmo, *Report in Regard to the Range and Ranch Cattle Business of the United States* (Washington, D.C.: GPO, 1885), 2. Cronon, *Nature's Metropolis*, 213–24.

28 Nimmo, *Report*, 61.

29 Andrew Isenberg, *The Destruction of the Bison* (New York: Cambridge Univ. Press, 2000); Dan Flores, "Bison Ecology and Bison Diplomacy: The Southern Plains from 1800 to 1850," *Journal of American History* 78 (Sept. 1991): 465–85. William Dobak, "Killing the Canadian Buffalo, 1821–1881," *Western Historical Quarterly* 27 (Spring 1996): 33–52, demonstrates that railroads were not necessarily essential to the eradication of buffalo. M. John Lubetkin, *Jay Cooke's Gamble: The Northern Pacific Railroad, the Sioux, and the Panic of 1873* (Norman: Univ. of Oklahoma Press, 2006), 170; Elliott West, *The Contested Plains: Indians, Goldseekers, and the Rush to Colorado* (Lawrence: Univ. Press of Kansas Press, 1998). For citations on recent literature on bison, see Geoff Cunfer, *On the Great Plains: Agriculture and Environment* (College Station: Texas A&M Univ. Press, 2005), 39–41.

30 I have used Flores, "Bison Ecology," 47, 481, of six million out of an earlier eight million rather than Isenberg, *Destruction of the Bison*, 138, which has the higher number of 15 million following the Civil War. William Temple Hornaday, *The Extermination of the American Bison* (Washington, [D.C.]: Smithsonian Institution Press, 2002, orig. ed. 1889), 504, provides the four million figure. The northern herd was considerably smaller.

31 F. G. Roe, *The North American Buffalo: A Critical Study of the Species in Its Wild State*, 2d ed. (Toronto: Univ. of Toronto Press, 1970), 431.

32 *The Route for a Road to the Pacific Ocean, Near the Thirty-Fifth Parallel of Latitude; Its Resources and Advantages* (Boston, 1870), 5–17.

33 William E. Connelley, *A Standard History of Kansas and Kansans* [rev. ed.], 5 vols. (Chicago: Lewis Publishing Co., 1919), 4:155 (p. 1885), http://skyways.lib.ks.us/genweb/archives/1919ks/r/reighagw.html.

34 Isenberg, *Destruction of Bison*, 131; M. Scott Taylor, "Buffalo Hunt: International Trade and the Virtual Extinction of the North American Bison," Working Paper 12969, National Bureau of Economic Research, March 2007, 9–11, http://www.nber.org/papers/w12969.

35 Isenberg, *Destruction of Bison*, 157, 159; Taylor, "Buffalo Hunt," 46.

36 Richard White, "Animals and Enterprise," in Clyde A. Milner II, Carol A. O'Connor, and Martha A. Sandweiss, eds., *The Oxford History of the American West* (New York: Oxford Univ. Press, 1994), 237.

37 Richard Irving Dodge, *The Plains of North America and Their Inhabitants*, ed. Wayne R. Kime (Newark: Univ. of Delaware Press 1989), 153, 156.

38 Roe, *North American Buffalo*, 442.

39 Ibid., 440–41; Isenberg, *Destruction of Bison*, 136–37; Dodge, *Plains of North America*, 153–56.

40 At 28 pounds per hide, they would have amounted to 24,500 tons of cargo. Given the 10-ton freight cars of the period, this would have yielded the 2,450 carloads. Dodge, *Plains of North America*, 154–55; Isenberg, *Destruction of Bison*, 132–39; for freight car capacity, John H. White Jr., *The American Railroad Freight Car: From the Wood-Car Era to the Coming of Steel* (Baltimore: Johns Hopkins Univ. Press, 1993), 196–98; for weight of hide, Taylor, "Buffalo Hunt," 41; for AT&SF, Poor, *Manual, 1872–73*, 197; ibid., *1874–75*, 641; for meat, Roe, *North American Buffalo*, 432; for an attempt to calculate total kill, ibid., 436–46.

41 Isenberg, *Destruction of Bison*, 140; Hornaday, *Extermination of the American Bison*, 440.

42 H. H. Houston to Saml. Wilkeson, July 1, 1876; H. Towne to G. Stark, July 3, 1876, July 15, 1876, NP, Secretary, Unregistered Letters, Northern Pacific Railway, M459, r. 35.

43 Northern Pacific Railroad, *Report of the President to the Stockholders at the Annual Meeting, Sept. 21, 1882* (New York: E. Wells, Sackett & Rankin, 1882), 68; Northern Pacific Railroad, *Report of the President to the Stockholders at the Annual Meeting, Sept. 20, 1883* (New York: E. Wells, Sackett & Rankin, 1883), 77.

44 Hornaday, *Extermination of the American Bison*, 504, 508, 513. At an average of 28 pounds per hide, this was 8,400,000 pounds or 4,200 tons. Taylor, "Buffalo Hunt," 41; Roe, *North American Buffalo*, 462; White, *Freight Car*, 196–98.

45 Isenberg, *Destruction of the Bison*, 136, 140; Northern Pacific Railroad, *Report . . . 1882*, 68; for freight car capacity, White, *Freight Car*, 196–98; Roe, *North American Buffalo*, 455.

46 Hornaday, *Extermination of the Bison*, 440–41, 513–21.

47 Ernest Staples Osgood, *The Day of the Cattleman* (Chicago: Univ. of Chicago Press, 1959, orig. ed. 1929), 105; James W. Whitaker, *Feedlot Empire: Beef Cattle Feeding in Illinois and Iowa, 1840–1900* (Ames: Iowa State Univ. Press, 1975), 56. The figures for cattle are from the Agricultural Census: Historical Census Publications from the USDA, all located through http://www.agcensus.usda.gov/Publications/Historical_Publications/index.asp. 1860: *Agriculture of the United States in 1860* (Washington, D.C.: GPO, 1864). Table: Recapitulation—1860: Agriculture, p. 184; 1870: *Ninth Census: The Statistics of the Wealth and Industry of the United States*, vol. 3 (Washington, D.C.: GPO, 1872), Productions of Agriculture, Table III—The United States—The Ninth Census—1870, p. 82; 1880: *Report of the Productions of Agriculture . . . Tenth Census (June 1, 1880), . . . General Statistics* (Washington, D.C.: GPO, 1883), Statistics of Agriculture: Table I—Summary for the Ninth Census 1870, p. 12. 1890: *Report on the Statistics of Agriculture in the United States at the Eleventh Census: 1890* (Washington,

D.C.: GPO, 1895), Statistics of Agriculture: General Tables: Summary in States and Territories: Census of 1890, p. 75.

48 David H. Breen, *The Canadian Prairie West and the Ranching Frontier* (Toronto: Univ. of Toronto Press, 1983), 23–24; Herbert O. Brayer, "The Influence of British Capital on the Western Range-Cattle Industry," *Journal of Economic History* 9, supplement: "The Tasks of Economic History" (1949): 87–92.

49 Harvey Levenstein, *Revolution at the Table: The Transformation of the American Diet* (New York: Oxford Univ. Press, 1988), 21–24; Breen, *Canadian Prairie West*, 23–24, 64–69; Whitaker, *Feedlot Empire*, 50–51; Alfred Chandler, "The Beginnings of 'Big Business' in American Industry," *Business History Review* 33 (Spring 1959): 4–8; pork prices, Frank Wilkeson, "Cattle-Raising on the Plains," *Harper's New Monthly Magazine* 72 (April 1886): 793.

50 By cattle, I mean cattle raised for slaughter, not milk cows or oxen.

51 Breen, *Canadian Prairie West*, 23–24; Brayer, "British Capital," 87–92. The two species were *Babesia bigemina* and *Babesia bovis*; *Handbook of Texas Online*, http://www.tsha.utexas.edu/handbook/online/articles/TT/awt1.html. Beef market, Cronon, *Nature's Metropolis*, 218–57; Chandler, "Beginnings of 'Big Business,' " 4–8.

52 Texas fever, *Handbook of Texas Online*; Whitaker, *Feedlot Empire*, 50–62; Statement Prepared by Theodore McMinn, Nimmo, *Report*, 93–94; Statement Prepared by Mr. George B. Loving, ibid., 105; rising prices, Statement Prepared by Theodore McMinn, ibid., 96, 100; Statement Prepared by Mr. D. W. Hinkle, ibid., 111; Appendix 20, Extract from the Annual Report of the Executive Committee and Secretary of the Wyoming Stock Growers' Association for the Year 1885; Texas fever, Nimmo, *Report*, 139–40; for the long drive, David Galenson, "The End of the Chisholm Trail," *Journal of Economic History* 34 (June 1974): 350–64.

53 The classic account of these towns is still Robert Dykstra, *The Cattle Towns* (New York: Knopf, 1968), 38–39, 55, 60–73. Ogallala emerged later as the final terminus of the southern trail. John Clay, *My Life on the Range* (New York: Antiquarian Press, 1961, orig. ed. 1934), 107–8.

54 The number rose to 34,400 in 1875, had more than doubled, to 73,094, by 1877, and then exploded with the return of prosperity, rising to 121,571 in 1881 and 207,574 in 1882, before falling back to 177,651 in 1883. "Eleventh Annual Livestock Report, Kansas City Stock Yards for the Year Ending Dec. 31, 1881," 33, 1880, 1.92, CB&Q; "Twelfth Annual Livestock Report, Kansas City Stock Yards for the Year Ending Dec. 31, 1882," 33, 1870, 8.12, CB&Q; "Thirteenth Annual Livestock Report, Kansas City Stock Yards for the Year Ending Dec. 31, 1883," 33, 1880, 1.72, CB&Q; Appendix 50, Statement by Mr. W. H. Miller, Secretary of the Kansas City Board of Trade, April 17, 1885, Nimmo, *Report*, 189. Only about 25 to 36 percent of the cattle coming into Chicago between 1881 and 1894 were Texan or western, but since "western" included cattle fattened in Kansas and Nebraska, the statistic is hard to interpret. Whitaker, *Feedlot Empire*, 63.

55 David Galenson, "End of the Chisholm Trail," 352–53; Dodge to Bond, Dec. 26, 1875, box 180, vol. 346, Dodge Papers; Osgood, *Day of the Cattleman*, 90.

56 Margaret Walsh, *The Rise of the Midwestern Meat Packing Industry* (Lexington: Univ. Press of Kentucky, 1982), 77.

57 Cecil Kirk Hutson, "Texas Fever in Kansas, 1866–1930," *Agricultural History* 68 (Winter 1994): 74–104; Whitaker, *Feedlot Empire*, 58–60.

58 Clay, *My Life on the Range*, 108–9; Osgood, *Day of the Cattleman*, 86–90; Statement Prepared by Theodore McMinn, Nimmo, *Report*, 96–97; Statement Prepared by Mr. George B. Loving, ibid., 105; David Galenson, "End of the Chisholm Trail," 354–55; trail better than Rail, Appendix 29, Letter Addressed to the Chief of the Bureau of Statistics by Hon. Jas. F. Miller, M.C. of Texas, Feb. 6, 1885, Nimmo, *Report*, 159; for the opposite view, Appendix 31, Statement of Mr. George Olds, General Traffic Manager of the Missouri Pacific Railway System . . . Dec. 24,

1885, ibid., 161; Appendix 33, Statement Furnished by Mr. J. F. Goddard, Traffic Manager of the Atcison (sic) Topeka and Santa Fe Railroad . . . Feb. 21, 1885, ibid., 164. Cattle were also increasing along the line of the Mexican Central, Appendix 22, Letter from the President of the Mexican Central Railway Company in Regard to the Range-Cattle Business in Mexico, April 25, 1885, ibid., 143.

59 Dykstra, *Cattle Towns*, 79.

60 Connelley, *Standard History of Kansas*, 4:155, http://skyways.lib.ks.us/genweb/archives/1919ks/r/reighagw.html.

61 Union Pacific Railroad Company, *Guide to the Union Pacific Railroad Lands*, 7; Dodge to Dillon, Aug. 14, 1874, LBs—G. M. Dodge, 1872–1874, box 179, vol. 382, Dodge Papers; Emmons, *Garden in Grasslands*, 38.

62 Union Pacific Railroad Company, *Guide to the Union Pacific Railroad Lands*, 20.

63 Dodge to Gould, July 11, 1875, box 160, LBs, Texas Pacific Railroad, MS 98, Dodge Papers.

64 White, *Animals and Enterprise*, 257–58; Breen, *Canadian Prairie West*, 25; James S. Brisbin, *The Beef Bonanza; or, How to Get Rich on The Plains, Being a Description of Cattle-growing, Sheep-farming, Horse-raising, and Dairying in the West*, with a foreword by Gilbert C. Fite, new ed. (Norman: Univ. of Oklahoma Press, 1959).

65 Eugene Mather, "The Production and Marketing of Wyoming Beef Cattle," *Economic Geography* 26 (April 1950): 82; *Tenth Census of the United States, 1880*, vol. 3, *Agriculture* (Washington D.C.: GPO, 1883), 141. The Union Pacific reported 3,000 cars of livestock shipped in 1875; *Report to the Stockholders of the Union Pacific Railroad for the Year 1875* (Boston, 1876), 5.

66 Harold E. Briggs, "The Development and Decline of Open Range Ranching in the Northwest," *Mississippi Valley Historical Review* 20 (March 1934): 526. In North Dakota the open-range industry was confined largely to the Little Missouri River country and the Badlands. It flowered between 1883 and 1887. Elwyn B. Robinson, *History of North Dakota* (Lincoln: Univ. of Nebraska Press, 1966), 186–93; Clay, *My Life on the Range*, 88; for the FE&MV, "Our Livestock Traffic," in Freight and Passenger Earnings, 1885, UP, unnumbered box, 149–51, S. W. Powers to P. P. Shelby, Aug. 18, 1885, ibid., box 28, UPRR Freight Dept.

67 J. Orin Oliphant, "The Eastward Movement of Cattle from the Oregon Country," *Agricultural History* 20 (Jan. 1946): 24–38; Osgood, *Day of the Cattleman*, 93. For various estimates of numbers, Statement of E. V. Smalley, Nimmo, *Report*, 76–77. Appendix 2, Statement Prepared by Lorenzo Fagersten, ibid., 85–86, 88, 89; Statement Prepared by Theodore McMinn, ibid., 90–91; Statement Prepared by Mr. George B. Loving, ibid., 106–7; Statement Prepared by Mr. D. W. Hinkle, ibid., 112. As many cattle shipped west as east, Appendix 47, Statement by Major A. W. Edwards of the Daily Argus, Fargo, Dakota, in ibid., 182; Appendix 54, Westward Shipments of Cattle into Northern Ranges by Rail, ibid., 195. The railroads gave lower figures. Northern Pacific Railroad, *Report* . . . *1883*, 77; Briggs, "Development and Decline," 527; for stock coming in from Kansas City by rail, Appendix 50, Statement by Mr. W. H. Miller, Secretary of the Kansas City Board of Trade, April 17, 1885, Nimmo, *Report*, 189; Clay, *My Life on the Range*, 85, 91.

67 Appendix 50, Statement by Mr. W. H. Miller, Secretary of the Kansas City Board of Trade, April 17, 1885, Nimmo, *Report*. 189.

68 Union Pacific, Statement of Livestock Shipments, UP, box 1, 56:192, p. 18; Dillon to Dodge, Aug. 13, 1877, LB: Personal & Private Correspondence, 1877–78, f. 5, box 180, vol. 383, Dodge Papers; Adams to C. T. Morse, Jan. 8, 1885, UP, PO, OC, vol. 27, ser. 2, r. 23; Briggs, "Development and Decline," 526–27. Also see "Our Livestock Traffic" in "Freight and Passenger Earnings," UP, unnumbered box, p. 161. The Kansas Division was the main, but not the only, Union Pacific branch shipping cattle. For animals shipped, Poor, *Manual, 1885*, 754, and *Report to the Stockholders of the Union Pacific Railway for the Year 1879* (New York, 1880), 34.

69 Comparative Statement Cattle Shipments, Feb. 8, 1886, UP, ser. 6, box 192, p. 514; Dykstra, *Cattle Towns*, 76–82, 155–77; Dodge to Bond, June 19, 1875, Council Bluffs, LB—Calif. Texas Railroad: Letters, 1874–78, box 180, vol. 346, Dodge Papers; Cattle Pool in Kansas, May 29, 1876, box 1, f. 4, KPRR Agreements 1876, Villard Papers; Callaway to Adams, Oct. 7, 1884, enclosed with Cullom to Adams, Oct. 7, 1884, UP, SG2, ser. 1, box 7, f. 32.

70 Wilkeson, "Cattle-Raising on the Plains," 788–95.

71 Clay, *My Life on the Range*, 20–25.

72 Statement of E.V. Smalley, Nimmo, *Report*, 74.

73 Ibid., 81–83; Brayer, "British Capital," 94; Briggs, "Development and Decline," 526–27; Osgood, *Day of the Cattleman*, 129.

74 Brayer, "British Capital," 90–92; Breen, *Canadian Prairie West*, 11; Clay, *My Life on the Range*, 91–92, 129–39; Osgood, *Day of the Cattleman*, 97.

75 Brayer, "British Capital," 94.

76 Clay, *My Life on the Range*, 35, 104–5, 158–67, 171, 172, 206; Statement of E. V. Smalley, Nimmo, *Report*, 81–83; Statement Prepared by Theodore McMinn, ibid., 91; Briggs, "Development and Decline," 527–29; Osgood, *Day of the Cattleman*, 103; Wilkeson, "Cattle-Raising on the Plains," 788–95.

77 Clay, *My Life on the Range*, 35, 116.

78 Ibid., 171.

79 Ibid., 129–39, 140.

80 Ibid.

81 Cunfer, *On the Great Plains*, 40–46.

82 J. E. Weaver and F. W. Albertson, *Grasslands of the Great Plains: Their Nature and Use* (Lincoln: Johnsen Publishing Company, 1956), 21–23.

83 Daniel Belgrad, "Power's Larger Meaning: The Johnson County War as Political Violence in an Environmental Context," *Western Historical Quarterly* 33 (Summer 2002): 168, 170.

84 *Report of Agent, Cheyenne and Arapaho Indians*, 48th Cong., 2d sess., 21, S. Ex. Doc. 16. For the whole issue of trespassing on and leasing of Indian lands, see Letter from the Secretary of the Interior, Jan. 3, 1885, 48th Cong., 2d sess., S. Ex. Doc. 17.

85 Connelley, *Standard History of Kansas and Kansans*, 4:155

86 Briggs, "Development and Decline," 523–25. Numerous writers explicitly or implicitly refer to the plains as a tragedy of the commons and then provide evidence for how it was regulated and apportioned. Osgood, *Day of the Cattleman*, 114–24, 130–37, 140, 149–52, 181–88, 190–91; Belgrad, "Johnson County War," 173; Breen, *Canadian Prairie West*, 32–38; Robinson, *History of North Dakota*, 188–90.

87 Robinson, *History of North Dakota*, 189, 190, 193.

88 Clay, *My Life on the Range*, 150.

89 Osgood, *Day of the Cattleman*, 95, 105, 219.

90 Briggs, "Development and Decline," 530; Belgrad, "Johnson County War," 172.

91 Whitaker, *Feedlot Empire*, 50.

92 Wilkeson, "Cattle-Raising on the Plains," 789, 790–92; *Report on the Productions of Agriculture as Returned at the Tenth Census, June 1, 1880* (Washington, D.C.: GPO, 1883), Table VIII, Live Stock and Its Productions, 141; for California, and the relation of the cattle industry to the railroads, see Igler, *Industrial Cowboys*, 52, 58, 148, 153; Whitaker, *Feedlot Empire*, 57, 73–84.

93 Wilkeson, "Cattle-Raising on the Plains," 792–94.

94 Statement Showing the Number of Carloads of Cattle . . . Nov. 18, 1884, UP, Freight Auditors LB, MS 3761, ser. 1, box 1, 56:192; Cecil Kirk Hutson, "Texas Fever in Kansas, 1866–1930," *Agricultural History* 68 (Winter 1994): 74–104; Clay, *My Life on the Range*, 183–84; Whitaker, *Feedlot Empire*, quote 63, 68–69, 123–26. In the appendix, see Chart I, Livestock Shipments by

Month on Union Pacific from Nebraska, 1883; Chart J, Livestock Shipments on Union Pacific System for 1883 and half of 1884.

95 "Our Livestock Traffic," in Freight and Passenger Earnings, 1885, UP, MS 3761, ser. 1, unnumbered box, 149–54; Clay, *My Life on the Range*, 119–21; Galenson, "End of the Chisholm Trail," 350–64; Osgood, *Day of the Cattleman*, 139–40, 169–75, 179–80. There were also quarantine laws north of Kansas; "Rules and Regulations Governing Quarantine and the Admission of Cattle into Wyoming Territory," Aug. 6, 1885, UP, MS 3671, box 2; Hutson, "Texas Fever in Kansas," quote 81.

96 Osgood, *Day of the Cattleman*, 191–93, 204–5, 209–14; *Annual Report of the Commissioner of the General Land Office for the Year, 1885* (Washington, D.C.: GPO, 1886), 318–21; *Report of the Governor of Wyoming to the Secretary of the Interior, 1886* (Washington, D.C.: GPO, 1886), 7–10.

97 Osgood, *Day of the Cattleman*, 209–14.

98 Robinson, *History of North Dakota*, 191. The newest reinterpretation of the Johnson County War is Belgrad, "Johnson County War," 159–77. For South Texas and the King ranch, see Benjamin Heber Johnson, *Revolution in Texas: How a Forgotten Rebellion and Its Bloody Suppression Turned Mexicans into Americans* (New Haven: Yale Univ. Press, 2005), 7–26. Such thefts were usually the appropriation of dogies—orphaned calves—on the range.

99 Breen, *Canadian Prairie West*, 35–64.

100 Clay, *My Life on the Range*, 178.

101 For accounts of the winter, Maurice Frink, *Cow Country Cavalcade* (Denver: Old West Publishing Company, 1954), 57–61; Robinson, *History of North Dakota*, 190; T. A. Larson, "The Winter of 1886–1887 in Wyoming," *Annals of Wyoming* 14 (Jan. 1942): 6–12; Clay, *My Life on the Range*, 176–79, 181.

102 Quoted in Osgood, *Day of the Cattleman*, 221.

103 Frink, *Cow Country Cavalcade*, 58–59; Larson, "Winter of 1886–1887," 10, 13–15; Clay, *My Life on the Range*, 189–90. The losses in Crook, Carbon, and Albany counties in Wyoming were closer to these regions than to the rest of Wyoming. For a good account of Montana, see Clyde A. Milner II and Carol A. O'Connor, *As Big as the West: The Pioneer Life of Granville Stuart* (New York: Oxford Univ. Press, 2009), 260–65.

104 Larson, "Winter of 1886–1887," 17; Clay, *My Life on the Range*, 179, 220–21; W. Turrentine Jackson, "The Wyoming Stock Growers' Association: Its Years of Temporary Decline, 1886–1890," *Agricultural History* 22 (Oct. 1948): 265.

105 *Tenth Census of the United States, 1880*, vol. 3, *Agriculture* (Washington, D.C.: GPO, 1883), 141; *Eleventh Census of the United States, 1890, Statistics of Agriculture* . . . (Washington, D.C.: GPO, 1895), Table D.

106 Charles L. Wood, *The Kansas Beef Industry* (Lawrence: Regents Press of Kansas, 1980), 2. Geoff Cunfer has recently concluded that the ultimate legacy of the range cattle industry was relatively benign. Cunfer, *On the Great Plains*, 38, 50, 51, 54. For an analysis of his arguments and my disagreements, see my expanded discursive footnotes on the Spatial History Project website. See also "Cattle Production in the American West, 1867–1935," "Freight Shipments from Nebraska," "Freight Shipments from Colorado," and "Corn and Cattle Production," which are also on the website.

107 Appendix 49, Information Furnished by Hon. Morton F. Post, Late Delegate in Congress from the Territory of Wyoming, Nimmo, *Report*, 188; The St. Paul, Minneapolis, and Manitoba claimed to have cattle cars average twenty miles per hour. General Manager to J. T. Odell, Sept. 14, 1887, LBs, Manvell, St. P.M.&M., Hill Papers, r. 48.

108 Nimmo, *Report*, 81; White, *American Railroad Freight Car*, 244–65; Whitaker, *Feedlot Empire*, 66–67; Chart K, Corn and Cattle in the United States, in appendix.

109 *Report of the Statistics of Agriculture in the United States at the Eleventh Census 1890* (Washington, D.C.: GPO, 1895), Table 7, 236, Table 9, 274–75, Table 11, 316–17. See also Wood, *Beef Industry*, 10–13; Clay, *My Life on the Range*, 355. If all livestock were cattle (which they clearly were not) and there were two steers per ton, the Northern Pacific at a maximum carried 168,588 cattle in 1885–86 and 165,738 the next year. These figures are, however, far too high, since in 1884 the total number of cattle shipped by the Northern Pacific from Wyoming, Montana, and the Dakotas was supposedly only 76,560 head. Reports to the Dakota Railroad Commission of livestock transported within or through Dakota Territory showed a much more marked decline of 25 percent, from 71,433 tons in 1885–86 to 52,899 in 1886–87. *Report of the Railroad Commissioners of the Territory of Dakota, 1888* (Watertown, SD: Courier-News, 1888), 179–80; *Report of the Railroad Commissioners of the Territory of Dakota, 1889* (Watertown, SD: Courier-News, 1889), 66–67

110 The Union Pacific system, e.g., carried 198,477 tons of cattle in 1886. *Report of the Directors of the Union Pacific Railway Company to the Stockholders for the Year Ending December 31, 1886* (New York, 1887), 132. In 1889, following the collapse of the range cattle industry, the system carried 248,522 tons of cattle. *Report of the Directors of the Union Pacific Railway Company to the Stockholders for the Year Ending December 31, 1889* (New York, 1890), 116. For 1891 the figure was 400,042 tons; for 1892, it was 424,095 tons. *Report of the Directors of the Union Pacific Railway Company to the Stockholders for the Year Ending December 31, 1892* (New York, 1893), 31. It fell off to 393,795 tons in 1893. Ibid., 40. Similarly the total tonnage for animal shipments, 80–90 percent of which were cattle, on the entire length of the roads traveling through Dakota Territory increased from 1,146,466 tons in 1886 to 1,477,740 tons in 1889. *Second Annual Report of the Board of Railroad Commissioners of the Territory of Dakota for the Year Ending June 30, 1886* (Grand Forks: Plaindealer Book and Job Room, 1886), 129–30; *Report of the Railroad Commissioners of the Territory of Dakota, 1889*, 65–66. In Kansas, where the movement of pigs would have formed a larger proportion than in the Dakotas, the tonnage of animals increased from 1,109,459 in 1883 to 3,454,380 in 1891 on the lines traversing Kansas. *First Annual Report of the Board of Railroad Commissioners for the Year Ending December 31, 1883, State of Kansas* (Topeka: Kansas Publishing House, 1884), 40–41; *Ninth Annual Report of the Board of Railroad Commissioners, State of Kansas for the Year Ending December 1, 1891* (Topeka: Edwin H. Snow, 1892), 278–81. In Nebraska, which like Kansas produced pigs as well as cattle, livestock shipments increased on the entire length of the roads passing through the state, from 1,246,809 tons in 1886–87 to 1,491,131 tons in 1888–89. These figures were compiled from the reports of the state railroad commissions in Kansas and the Dakotas and Nebraska. *First Annual Report of the Board of Transportation for the Year Ending June 30, 1887, State of Nebraska* (Lincoln: Journal Company, 1888), 39–40; *Third Annual Report of the Board of Transportation for the Year Ending June 30, 1889, State of Nebraska* (Omaha: Henry Gibson, 1889), 84–87. Even when a state, such as Kansas, had more pigs than cattle, railroad shipments carried a greater tonnage of cattle since normal counts measured two cattle to a ton and ten pigs to a ton.

111 Frink, *Cow Country Cavalcade*, 60–61; Osgood, *Day of the Cattleman*, 222; *Report of Railroad Commissioners . . . 1887*, 82, 233; *Report of Railroad Commissioners . . . 1886*, 208. There were less dramatic fluctuations on the roads east of the Missouri. The Fremont, Elkhorn, and Missouri Valley, which was controlled by the Chicago and North Western, increased its shipments of animals from 93,626 tons for 1885–86 to 159,356 for 1886–87. The traffic in animals fell for the Chicago and Milwaukee from 372,699 tons (5.69 percent of total traffic) to 343,014 (4.67 percent); for the Chicago and North Western it rose from 407,443 (4.78 percent) to 418,098 (4.25 percent); for the St. Paul, Minneapolis, and Manitoba, the least important livestock road, it remained stationary at from 21,126 tons (1.5 percent) to 21,138 (1.2 percent). *Report of*

Railroad Commissioners . . . 1887, 114, 141, 168; *Report of Railroad Commissioners . . . 1886*, 208. In Dakota Territory shipments fell slightly, from 21,700 tons to 21,503 tons, between 1888 and 1889. *Report of the Railroad Commissioners of the Territory of Dakota, 1888*, 179–80; *Report of the Railroad Commissioners of the Territory of Dakota, 1889*, 66–67. A one-year increase following a terrible winter could have reflected the dumping of surviving cattle onto the market, but the continued rise in traffic in the face of declining cattle numbers on the rangelands of Nebraska, Wyoming, and South Dakota is puzzling.

In 1889 Thomas Oakes was not worried that the Chicago and North Western and the Burlington and Missouri would penetrate the region tributary to Miles City. "I do not look upon the movement with any concern, as the cattle business is done at practically cost, and if we lose it all our net revenues will not suffer materially." Oakes to Earl, April 8, 1890, NP, LRR, PV, 137H.5.7 (B) 1890, PN 694.

112 John Clay remembered that by the spring of 1888 there was plenty of water and that reduced cattle numbers meant that "[i]t was a virgin range we had to stock up." Clay, *My Life on the Range*, 92–98, 146. Clay's account of resurrecting the Dickey Cattle Company on the Little Missouri gives some support for an increase in cattle shipments to the West. Although restocking took place, the timing and details in Clay are far from clear; see 192–96, 215; Osgood, *Day of the Cattleman*, 90–92.

113 Wood, *Kansas Beef Industry*, 2, 7, 9–12, 16–17, 19–20, 23–24 70; Whitaker, *Feedlot Empire*, 57–58, quote 63, 99–105, 115, 124–25. This specialization can be seen in a visualization of shipments from Nebraska in 1886, Spatial History Project website, Stanford Univ.

114 C. Knick Harley, "Western Settlement and the Price of Wheat, 1872–1913," *Journal of Economic History* 38 (Dec. 1978): 866; Callaway to Adams, Nov. 29, Dec. 6, 1884, UP, SG2, ser. 1, box 7, f. 33; W. Kaye Lamb, *History of the Canadian Pacific Railway* (New York: Macmillan, 1977), 159–60.

115 Harley, "Western Settlement," 867.

116 Ibid., 866.

117 Ibid., 873, 878.

118 Robert Higgs, "Railroad Rates and the Populist Uprising," *Agricultural History* 44 (July 1970): 291–98; Mark Aldrich, "A Note on Railroad Rates and the Populist Uprising," *Agricultural History* 54 (July 1980): 424–32. Aldrich says rates relative to crop prices fell in the 1870s but rose through the 1880s and mid-1890s.

119 *Report of the Industrial Commission on Transportation including Review of Evidence . . . So Far as Taken, May 1, 1900* (Washington, D.C.: GPO, 1900), 4:41.

120 Ibid.

121 Miller, *Railroads and the Granger Laws*, 95–108. See Chart L: Grain Exported from Nebraska, 1883, in appendix.

122 Gilbert Fite, *The Farmers' Frontier, 1865–1900* (New York: Holt, Rinehart and Winston, 1966), 102.

123 Ibid., 94–97, 100.

124 Ibid., 98–99.

125 *Map of Federal Land-Grant and Bond—Aided Railroads, in Public Aids to Transportation*, vol. 2, *Aids to Railroads and Related Subjects* (Washington, D.C.: GPO, 1938), 43.

126 This comparison excludes the fertile Red River Valley lands along the Minnesota border of North Dakota because they were anomalous in their fertility, the speed of their settlement in the 1870s, and their access to river as well as railroad transportation along the St. Paul and Pacific, which became part of Hill's St. Paul, Minneapolis and Manitoba Railway. Hill claimed his road had carried 20 percent of the spring wheat crop of the entire United States in 1884 and would do better in 1885. For these lines see Albro Martin, *James J. Hill and*

the Opening of the Northwest (Minneapolis: Minnesota Historical Society Press, 1991, orig. ed. 1976), 116–40, 146–63, 177, 190–98; *St. Paul, Minneapolis & Manitoba Ry., Timetable Map* (Buffalo: Matthews, Northrup & Co., 1886); David Rumsey Historical Map Collection, http://www.davidrumsey.com/. For Red River Valley, Stanley N. Murray, "Railroads and the Agricultural Development of the Red River Valley of the North, 1870–1890," *Agricultural History* 31 (Oct. 1957): 57–66.

127 Fite, *Farmers' Frontier*, 104; Report, Population, H. J. Wimsen (?) to T. F. Oakes, Aug. 14, 1882, NP Papers, 1864–1922, ser. C., Settlement & Development, r. 3. By June 30, 1882, growth in the counties along the Northern Pacific had spilled over the 99th meridian and even edged across the 100th. In Barnes County, which was east of the 99th meridian, population tripled in two years, to 4,500, but in Stutsman, which was bifurcated by the 99th meridian, it increased by a multiple of seven to 7,007. Kidder County, whose western boundary edged over the 100th meridian, went from 87 people in 1880 to 2,087 in 1882, and even Burleigh County on the Missouri showed substantial growth. Report, Population, sent to H. Villard, President, Aug. 14, 1882, ser. C, Settlement and Development, NP Papers, 1864–1920, r. 3; Fite, *Farmers' Frontier*, 104.

128 U.S. Land Sales within Limits of the N.P.R.R. Cos. Land Grant for the Year Ending June 30, 1882, ser. C, Settlement and Development, NP Papers, 1864–1920, r. 3. For declining sales, Report, Land Sales, to Henry Villard, Aug. 11, 1882, ibid. See Chart M, Land Settlement in North Dakota and South Dakota Counties, in the appendix, and on Spatial History Project website, Stanford Univ.

129 *Report of the Railroad Commissioners of the Territory of Dakota, 1889*, 67–68.

130 Charles Francis Adams, "The Rainfall on the Plains," Nov. 14, 1887, *Nation*, Nov. 24, 1887, p. 417; Sidney Dillon, "The West and the Railroads," *North American Review* 152 (April 1891): 444–45.

131 Emmons, *Garden in the Grasslands*, 131–33.

132 Ibid., 135–39; Samuel Aughey, *Sketches of the Physical Geography and Geology of Nebraska* (Omaha: Daily Republican Book and Job Office, 1880), 35, 36, 41–47.

133 Cary J. Mock, "Rainfall in the Garden of the United States Great Plains, 1870–79," *Climatic Change* 44 (2000): 191.

134 Mock, "Rainfall in the Garden," 184, 187–88.

135 Engerman, "Some Economic Issues," 458. George himself, while denouncing most subsidies, thought that the subsidies for railroads were justifiable under some circumstances, but he thought cash subsidies were preferable to land. George, *Our Land and Land Policy*, 25–35. For building too quickly, Adams, "Which Will Quickest Solve the Railroad Question," 6.

136 Despite the Civil War, California grew by 47 percent between 1860 and 1870 without the railroad. It grew by 54 percent between 1870 and 1880 with the railroad, reaching 864,694 people. It had grown more slowly and was smaller than Kansas. Calculated from Historical Census Browser, Univ. of Virginia Library, http://fisher.lib.virginia.edu/collections/stats/histcensus/; Orsi, *Sunset Limited*, 130, 193–204, 323–29.

137 Fite, *Farmers' Frontier*, 106–7.

138 Ibid., 108.

139 Ibid., 130.

140 Claire Strom, *Profiting from the Plains: The Great Northern Railway and Corporate Development of the American West* (Seattle: Univ. of Washington Press, 2003), 13–39. Also Cunfer, *On the Great Plains*, 76–80, 82, 85, which finds an increase in diversified farming on the Great Plains after 1900, stabilizing in the 1920s and then slowly declining.

141 Fruit production would not really boom until the twentieth century. Orsi, *Sunset Limited*, 130, 193–204, 323–29.

142 Francis Paul Prucha, *The Great Father: The United States Government and the American Indians*, 2 vols. (Lincoln: Univ. of Nebraska Press, 1984), 2:633–40.

143 Fite, *Farmers' Frontier*, 111; Ross Ralph Cotroneo, *The History of the Northern Pacific Land Grant, 1900–1952* (New York: Arno Press, 1979), 115–42, 162; Francis Paul Prucha, *American Indian Policy in Crisis: Christian Reformers and the Indian, 1865–1900* (Norman: Univ. of Oklahoma Press, 1976), 172–87.

144 Lamb, *History of the Canadian Pacific Railway*, 159–60.

145 As I have argued above, the Central Pacific and the Union Pacific both could make money as regional roads serving San Francisco and Omaha, and through connections Chicago, respectively, but as the subsidies they paid show, they could not make money as a transcontinental. In any case, given the corruption of the books, it is very hard to make any definitive case about either road. Lloyd J. Mercer, *Railroads and Land Grant Policy: A Study in Government Intervention* (New York: Academic Press, 1982), 139–44; Heywood Fleisig, "Central Pacific Railroad and Railroad Land Grant Controversy," *Journal of Economic History* 35 (Sept. 1975): 552–56; Lloyd J. Mercer, "Rates of Return for Land Grant Railroads: The Central Pacific System," *Journal of Economic Histo y* 30 (Sept. 1970): 604, 625.

146 In the case of the Central Pacific, Mercer treated the road as a whole. He does not disaggregate the California portion of the road, which did not need subsidies to be built, from the "transcontinental" part of the road—Nevada and Utah—which probably could not have supported itself. Mercer, *Railroads and Land Grant Policy*, 99–122.

147 Mercer, *Railroads and Land Grant Policy*, 99–118, 227–39.

148 The per capita figure is from Alexander Klein, "Personal Income of U.S. States: Estimates for the Period 1880–1910," Warwick Economic Research Papers, no. 916, Department of Economics, Univ. of Warwick.

149 Ibid. The estimate of Huntington's estate is from James Thorpe, *Henry Edwards Huntington: A Biography* (Berkeley: Univ. of California Press, 1994), 157. For the debt settlement, see Lavender, *Great Persuader*, 374–75.

Mise en Scène: Wovoka

1 Francis F. Palmer, *Across the Continent: Westward the Course of Empire Takes Its Way* [lithograph] (New York: Currier and Ives, 1868).

2 Henry T. Williams, ed., *The Pacific Tourist: Williams' Illustrated Guide to Pacific RR—California and Pleasure Resorts across the Continent* (New York: Henry T. Williams, 1879), 172.

3 Ibid., 173.

4 Ibid., 182, 189.

5 Robert Utley, *The Last Days of the Sioux Nation* (New Haven: Yale Univ. Press, 1963), 62–64.

EPILOGUE

1 *New York Tribune*, May 30, 1878, quoted in David Blight, *Race and Reunion: The Civil War in American Memory* (Cambridge: Harvard Univ. Press, 2001), 95.

2 Charles Francis Adams, *An Autobiography, 1835–1915, with a Memorial Address Delivered November 17, 1915, by Henry Cabot Lodge* (Boston: Houghton Mifflin, 1916), 152, 154, 166, 195; Edward Chase Kirkland, *Charles Francis Adams, 1835–1915: The Patrician at Bay* (Cambridge: Harvard Univ. Press, 1965), 26–27.

3 Adams, *Autobiography*, 195; Henry Villard, *Memoirs of Henry Villard, Journalist and Financier*, 2 vols. (Westminster: Archibald Constable & Co., 1904), 2:365.

4 Scott A. Sandage, *Born Losers: A History of Failure in America* (Cambridge: Harvard Univ. Press, 2005). Sandage writes quite astutely about failure in American life, but he is not concerned with the sense of failure expressed by the very rich and very powerful, such as Villard and Adams.

5 CPH to James Speyer, Dec. 16, 1899, CPH Papers, ser. 4, r. 1; CPH, "Autobiographical Sketch," by Charles Nordhoff, ibid.

6 Jay Cooke, "Memoir," Baker Library, Harvard Business School, 140–43, 145–46, quote 145.

7 Lodge, *Memorial Address*, with Adams, *Autobiography*, ix–lx.

8 Ibid., xix–xxiv.

9 Ibid., xxxiii.

10 Ibid., xxxiv–xxxvi.

11 Adams, *Autobiography*, 190.

CONCLUSION

1 Naomi R. Lamoreaux, *The Great Merger Movement in American Business, 1895–1904* (New York: Cambridge Univ. Press, 1985).

2 Joseph A. Schumpeter, *Capitalism, Socialism, and Democracy*, 3d ed. (New York: Harper & Brothers, 1947), 74.

3 Frank Dobbin, *Forging Industrial Policy: The United States, Britain, and France in the Railway Age* (New York: Cambridge Univ. Press, 1993), 39. I quote Dobbin because he is rightfully so influential and because so much of his analysis is superb.

4 The standard account here is Neil Foley, *The White Scourge: Mexicans, Blacks, and Poor Whites in Texas Cotton Culture* (Berkeley: Univ. of California Press, 1997).

5 Herbert Hovenkamp, *Enterprise and American Law, 1836–37* (Cambridge: Harvard Univ. Press, 1991), 320–21.

6 See Gerald Berk, *Louis D. Brandeis and the Making of Regulated Competition, 1900–1932* (New York: Cambridge Univ. Press, 2009), 1–32.

7 Joseph A. Schumpeter, *Business Cycles: A Theoretical Historical, and Statistical Analysis of the Capitalist Process*, 2 vols. (New York: McGraw-Hill, 1939), 1:340–41.

INDEX

❧〜◖◗〜❧

Page numbers in *italics* refer to charts and maps.
Page numbers beginning with 535 refer to endnotes.